JOHN DE LOREAN

The Maverick Mogul

Hillel Levin

ORBIS PUBLISHING · LONDON

First published in Great Britain by
Orbis Publishing Limited, London 1983

Phototypesetting by Inforum Ltd, Portsmouth
Printed in Great Britain by
Eyre & Spottiswoode Ltd

ISBN   0-85613-561-5

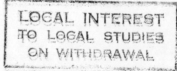

JOHN DE LOREAN

CONTENTS

Acknowledgments   3

Foreword   5

The Shell   7

PART ONE: White Collar Wonder

Dark Secrets   17

A Company Man   27

High Performance   38

Hollywood   47

Falling from the Fourteenth Floor   62

PART TWO: Entrepreneur Extraordinaire

A Very Brilliant Financial Analyst   79

Four Bad Deals   89

100 West Long Lake   118

Silver Beauty   132

Forty-Five Days   149

PART THREE: The Maverick Mogul

GPD   163

Belfast   173

New York   183

Irvine   196

The Ethical Car   206

Out of Control   220

Roy to the Rescue   236

Trapped in a Terrible Tower   249

Aftermath   258

Index   264

ACKNOWLEDGMENTS

Kirk Cheyfitz, the editor of the magazine article I did on De Lorean, remains the guiding force behind this project. In bringing me to Detroit, he restored my faith in the potential of journalism and gave me opportunities that I had never known before in this profession. He continues as my editor at *Metropolitan Detroit*, and I'm proud to call him a friend and teacher.

My thanks also go to the other founders of *Metropolitan Detroit* – Tom Jones, Eric Keller, Jane Rayburn and Jack Felker – who all put up with my repeated absences at a crucial stage in the magazine's development.

As a novice at book writing I'm greatly indebted to my agents, Paula Diamond and Nat Sobel, who have guided and sustained this effort from beginning to end. I'm also grateful for the services of my editor at Orbis, Stephen Adamson, who greatly assisted me in both my British research and preparation of the manuscript.

Other research in the United Kingdom was kindly provided by Paul Webster. The excellent articles of Michael Gillard in the *Observer* helped me with British events. I had further important help from Joan and Robert Griggs.

FOREWORD

I first interviewed John De Lorean on assignment for *New York* magazine in the spring of 1979. Like so many other reporters, I was struck by his charm and intelligence. I was also caught up in his effort, then well under way, to build his own sports car. In preparing a favourable profile, I used no more than our three hours of conversation and his glowing press clips as source information. Before *New York* could run my story, several other De Lorean articles went to print. My editors decided not to be lost in the shuffle and eventually killed my piece.

Two years later, as senior editor of *Monthly Detroit* magazine, I returned to De Lorean in much different circumstances. His first stainless steel, gull-winged cars had already rolled off the assembly line, and I was getting reports from dealers around the country about shoddy product quality. I also received a copy of the prospectus for a new stock offering that significantly reorganized the car company. At just a glance, I could see that the goals he once articulated for the De Lorean Motor Company had drastically changed. What interested me most were other changes in his personal holdings, especially the De Lorean Manufacturing Company. When I hunted up annual reports for this Michigan firm filed with the state's Department of Corporations and Securities, I found a list for other places of business which included Route #1, Salmon, Idaho. From there, I followed a paper trail of lawsuits and court hearings – all leading to an area of De Lorean's past business affairs that had never before been examined by the press.

As I wrote in the magazine, the details that emerged from De Lorean's byzantine empire did not amount to a flattering portrait, but one of 'a man who has reached too far, perhaps jeopardizing all he has already gained'. I gave De Lorean a chance to respond to several disturbing questions about his business conduct raised by my research and he chose to speak with me on the phone. Our tense conversation lasted for ninety minutes. He would call me again, before the magazine went to print, warning me that I was 'doing tremendous injury to the people there in [the] Belfast [Northern Ireland assembly plant]'. It was the last time we spoke. The resulting article, which appeared in December 1981, was some 5,000 words long, but I felt I had only scratched the surface of the De Lorean story.

Other reporters were not as impressed by my findings as I was. Even as De Lorean's car company unravelled around him, the American press was still reluctant to look closely at the legend he had spun. The time would come, almost one year after my article, when De Lorean's record would be scrutinized more carefully, but it took the auto executive's arrest with over $16 million of cocaine to spark the media's interest.

While De Lorean's involvement with narcotics has made him news-worthy, no evidence has surfaced to prove that he had any long-lasting relationship with illegal drugs as either a user or dealer. Instead, his arrest appears to be a jarring coda to a fascinating career – a career which I believe deserves close and thorough examination in its entirety.

John Z. De Lorean remains a sensitive subject with all those who have worked with him. While some people were willing to be interviewed about De Lorean, for a variety of personal reasons, they asked not to be identified by name. I fully appreciate their concerns, and when quoting them, refer to their positions in only generic terms. Many more sources have given me the permission to attribute their quotes directly. I'm deeply grateful to everyone who aided my research.

THE SHELL

Forty-three storeys above Park Avenue, the smoked-glass doors of the
De Lorean Motor Corporation headquarters swung open to an expanse
of white marble floor. An Olympian brown glass reception desk – long
enough for ten secretaries – loomed ahead. No less an industrial light
than the Xerox Corporation had once shone from here. Now it was an
impressive setting for a company that had only just begun manufacturing and which was still far away from turning a profit.

In the autumn of 1981 Robert Henkel became a frequent visitor to
this penthouse suite. 'There was', he says today, 'a tremendous excitement in those offices – not just among the executives. Even down to the
secretaries and maintenance men.'

As executive vice president for the public relations agency of Carl
Byoir & Associates, it was Henkel's job – in the span of a fifteen-minute
promotional film – to transmit that excitement to all the De Lorean
employees, dealers and potential customers who would never ride an
express elevator to the top of the Bankers Trust Building.

He worked mostly with the company's in-house P.R. staff.
Occasionally John Z. De Lorean himself would wander into their
meetings. With a smile and a nod, he would ask what they were up to,
and then sit back, in his light blue Pierre Cardin shirtsleeves, and listen
pensively to their explanations. 'He struck me as a person with natural
curiosity,' Henkel recalls. 'He wanted to know how I did this or that.
He seemed to appreciate the importance of what I was doing. Still, I got
the sense that he was very creative himself.'

It took Henkel but a few months to put the finishing touches on a
proposal for a film entitled, *The De Lorean Dream: A Reality That Works*.
But by the time he submitted the script in December, the dream was
already disintegrating around De Lorean. The public relations project
went no further, and Henkel would not even see payment for his
services.

7

But his still-born proposal remains a fascinating relic of the De Lorean empire – a typewritten inscription for a latter-day Ozymandias. This is the last page of Henkel's film treatment:

> We return now to John De Lorean in his office, standing in front of a worldwide map or some other business graph.
>
> He says something like this: 'Our dream is coming true, and justifying the calculated risk we took. Sure, I'm a risk taker. And the people who drive our De Lorean car are probably risk takers, too. People who dare to lead other people . . . People who live life to its fullest potential . . . People who enjoy the special exhilaration of making things happen . . . People who dream of a better world, and do whatever is needed to transform that dream into reality.'
>
> John De Lorean is next shown sitting inside his car. He ends by saying, 'As hard as I've struggled, I'm one man who can say that my dream has come true. Our difficult efforts have succeeded, life is good, and I'm grateful!'
>
> Then De Lorean closes the car and drives off onto a handsome modern highway with elegant city skyscrapers in the background. Closing music and credits appear over this final radiant scene.

De Lorean's words in the script were his own – pasted together from speeches he delivered over the years – and they ring with the blare of sixties-style pop psychology. Taking risks, daring to lead, making things happen, living life to the fullest: these were the credos of that turbulent, activist decade. De Lorean has kept his sixties sensibilities along with a predilection for long, drooping collars, turtle-neck sweaters and bell-bottom trousers. He has also kept the sixties fascination with dreams. His dreams do not stay cooped up in the bedroom; they tremble on the verge of fulfilment, for one who is bold enough to 'do whatever is needed to transform that dream into reality'. Indeed, proof of what one man can do was to be found in De Lorean's own career – an ascent from working class origins to corporate aerie.

Oddly enough, in the Henkel script as well as the few ads that De Lorean actually completed, the chief executive's personal success was featured more prominently than his stainless steel product. This strategy may have been designed to bestow the car with the glamour of its namesake's wealth and power. But the personal sales appeal worked at another level. De Lorean customers did not just get a car. They also became a part of what De Lorean liked to call his 'personal Horatio Alger dream'.

Undoubtedly, De Lorean would have ended his own story as happily as Henkel closed the film – with himself cast as the modern industrial hero riding his gleaming dream car into the sunset.

But on the night of 19 October 1982, less than one year after Henkel finished his proposal, the eyes of the world were to see John De Lorean in a very different 'radiant scene'; one lit by the icy blue glare of photographers' strobe lights. This time he would not ride off in his own car, but in the back seat of a police car, his hands cuffed behind him.

He was arrested earlier that evening in alleged possession of over $16 million of cocaine. In the first few dispatches to beam out over the news wires, his personality had to take second billing to the Hollywood-style celebrity of the narcotics kingdom itself, with headlines reading, 'Businessman Held In Cocaine Deal'. But if there were some members of the press who were not aware of De Lorean or his car company, the law authorities were quick to provide them with the details. Even the police would reach into De Lorean's dreams and pull out his motive for the drug transaction – a last-ditch, Faustian bid to save his foundering car company.

It was a drama that had been played out for months in packed hotel rooms around the country. The selected audience – federal authorities with videotape cameras – watched behind two-way mirrors. Some of the cast were indeed actors: agents of the F.B.I. and the Drug Enforcement Administration posing as Mafiosi drug dealers. But police charge that other performers, such as pilot William Morgan Hetrick, who smuggled the cocaine and heroin into the country, and his alleged accomplice, Stephen Lee Arrington, were not play-acting. The sting, the authorities say, was staged initially for the benefit of Hetrick and Arrington, and De Lorean was the walk-on who ended up stealing the show. Only moments before his arrest, he held up a packet of dope and crowed, 'This is better than gold. This comes in the nick of time.' He was to bring down the curtain by pouring wine all around and proposing a toast to one of the great moments in his career.

His battery of high-powered defence lawyers were left with the task of proving that the authorities preyed on De Lorean's desperation to save his company and lured him into a deal he would have never attempted on his own.

Such legal strategies may keep a man out of jail, but they do little to salvage his 'good' name. They do nothing to blot out the pictures of a rumpled, downcast De Lorean, slumped in the back seat of the police car. No one understands that better than John De Lorean. His public image was his most finely crafted creation. Ironically, his final attempt to keep up appearances would pull them down forever.

Jail, De Lorean liked to tell reporters, was graduate school for many young men in the tough Detroit neighbourhood where he grew up. He would add, joking, that he was lucky not to have joined them.

De Lorean's own route to incarceration strayed far from the paths of his childhood friends. Along the way to federal prison on Terminal Island – where he stayed two weeks until bail bonds were raised – he passed through the centres of corporate power and high society in America: from the board rooms of General Motors, to Hollywood, Wall Street and Fifth Avenue.

But he would go through another sort of odyssey as well – one of the intellect and soul – that would have greater impact on his life than any stop on his fifty-seven-year itinerary. It started at General Motors when the brilliant young engineer realized that more than mathematical sophistication was necessary to climb the corporate ladder. His concern was then no longer to stop with the gritty mechanics of the automobile, but went further to the overall appearance of the car, and finally how it was marketed to the masses. The public, he discovered, bought the packaging, not the contents.

He rose to be the youngest general manager at Pontiac in the history of the division. With his flair for merchandising he was given the lion's share of the credit for changing the image of what had once been 'the old lady's car'.

In the process, he changed his own image as well. By the end of the sixties, his face had gone through cosmetic surgery. He dieted half his six-foot four-inch frame away and built up the other half with weight training. Even his closest friends were shocked by his obsession with appearance. He filled his home with mirrors and in later years carried a compact to check his face out in the back seats of cars and blot out pale splotches with corn silk. He limited his wardrobe to a few minimum styles and colours which most flattered his figure, and, some say, had many copies of the exact same light blue, high-collared shirt, and dark blue Italian-cut suit.

His efforts at reconstruction went beyond the scalpel, reaching even to his genes and his Eastern European roots. In interviews and his *curriculum vitae* he stopped mentioning his father's Rumanian heritage, or the fact that he spoke Rumanian as a child. For a while, he placed his father's birthplace vaguely in 'middle Europe', and eventually moved it to the Alsace-Lorraine region of France.

Much to the chagrin of his General Motors superiors, he also remodelled his lifestyle. He made more of an effort to spend time on the West Coast, making the nightclub scene with Hollywood celebrities and race car drivers. After he divorced his wife of fifteen years' standing, he dated movie starlets and then took a nineteen-year-old as his second bride. He didn't just marry youth, he incorporated it. Young people, who had long been ignored by Detroit auto-makers, were buying his fast, sleek Pontiacs and turning the division into a power-house. In a time when the media focused on the generation gap, De

Lorean jumped to the other side, becoming a vocal defender of youthful protest and an incisive critic of the establishment, even as he climbed higher into the General Motors stratosphere. Never had the Detroit press corps found a top auto executive so accessible and so controversial. When they pegged him as eventual chief executive material, it was partly wishful thinking.

Yet, his departure from General Motors in 1973 did not dismay De Lorean's admirers. For lesser mortals, it would have been an ignominious development. For De Lorean, it was an act of high moral principle. His initial explanation was to lay the blame on his promotion from general manager at Chevrolet to policy-making vice-president on the vaunted fourteenth floor of GM's headquarters. In his favourite analogy, he had gone from quarterback 'to the guy who owned the stadium', and the cramps from his inactive managerial muscles became unbearable.

But as time went on, the reasons he gave for leaving became more pointed. His most detailed account of the split would emerge with the 1979 publication of *On a Clear Day You Can See General Motors*, a scathing attack on the wisdom and morality of GM's management, which he wrote as a first-person narrative with the considerable aid of long-time Detroit auto reporter Pat Wright. Already embarked on the developmental stages of his own car company, De Lorean had been reluctant to publish the book, fearful that the wrath of GM would snuff out his infant firm. Wright finally printed the book himself, but De Lorean would still garner credit as a courageous critic. Although he did not receive any royalties, the book's place on the best-seller list only added lustre to the De Lorean success story.

He did not need the book to bring him publicity. His supposed gutsy career change and conquest of mid-life crisis was immortalized by Gail Sheehy in *Passages*. Despite his exile from GM, he remained hot copy for business reporters, and always the ideal subject for an interview. He was never too busy for the press. Before an interview was over, he could bring up rock music, mention the latest book from social historian Peter Gay or quote Montaigne. Just as important, he listened. Like a gracious host, he turned encounters with reporters into casual conversations. The results that reached publication were almost reverential. Even his stellar achievements at GM seemed to glow more brightly in retrospect.

The quest to start a new motor company might have been written off, if the seeker had been anyone but De Lorean. However, the press got caught up in his dream to produce the 'ethical car', and closely followed his search for investors. Ultimately, it seemed as though De Lorean had done the impossible. Against all predictions, and his own best expectations, he landed over $90 million in start-up money from the British government. The condition that he build the cars in strife-torn Northern Ireland paled next to the magnitude of the windfall.

Even before one of his stainless-steel, gull-winged cars plopped off the assembly line, he already appeared to be America's corporate, capitalist answer to European royalty. His residential estates, apartments and ranches dotted the country. Their garages were filled with a private fleet of expensive cars. His third wife was an elegant, raven-haired beauty and one of the world's highest-paid professional models. All this, and he still professed social conscience and a desire to be a good corporate citizen.

The image seemed too good to be true.

And it wasn't true.

John De Lorean had not just led a double life. He led a quadruple life. Even as he sealed his deal with the British government and seemed ready to change the face of the automobile industry, the elaborate struts and beams he had propped under his pristine façade were giving way.

Press clips were not the only chronicle of De Lorean during the seventies. Court documents in lawsuits filed across the nation told another story, and they ran alongside the laudatory media accounts like photographic negatives.

Miniature auto race tracks; a break-through engine coolant device; a cattle ranch; an auto dealership; a warehouse of CB radios; movie projectors for salesmen: all belonged to a motley catalogue of soured deals involving De Lorean that ended up in rancorous court battles. In this arena, John De Lorean was not the lone gunfighter up against greedy, corporate giants. Instead, his opponents charged that he was the goliath, trampling their precious dreams underfoot. Moreover, one case suggests that his relationship with a GM supplier might have forced his exit from the corporation.

The records show that De Lorean did pay a heavy price to live his dream, assembling an unwieldy string of incongruous properties that sapped his energy and periodically could have cost him heavily. It was all he could do to hold his byzantine empire together while he canvassed for new partners to support his motor venture.

Looming in all of the lawsuits was a huge, six-foot six-inch former car salesman, named Roy Nesseth. His intimidating presence marks the course of De Lorean's unpublicized business career. Alternately charming and offensive, Nesseth's own record of civil lawsuits runs through the indexes of Los Angeles courthouses like a page torn from a telephone directory.

De Lorean once described Nesseth to one of his auto company executives as 'a mean man who enjoyed being mean'. He told others that Nesseth was a man who could get things done, and he counted on him to extricate the De Lorean name and fortune from investments that went bad. Despite warnings from his associates that Nesseth's bullying – and possibly illegal – tactics did more harm than good, the two men grew only closer over the years.

It was a bond that mystified some De Lorean associates, but, more important, it was a bond that most knew nothing about. In his world of business transactions, the orbits of De Lorean's satellites seldom intersected.

Only one man besides De Lorean is capable of putting the pieces together: his personal lawyer, Thomas Kimmerly. A mild-mannered tax specialist, Kimmerly is the antithesis of Nesseth, preferring to blend into the background instead of taking centre stage. On the board of several of De Lorean's companies and subsidiaries, during the last decade Kimmerly became a close and important business associate.

The car company, like nothing before, tested the power and limitations of De Lorean's illusions. His ability to attract financing, car dealers, and accomplished executives to his unlikely project revealed the stuff that the industry's pioneers were made of. In the process, he whipped up a vortex that pulled the British government and his employees ever deeper even as they lost faith in De Lorean's legendary prowess. The fact that they brought the company as far as they did remains a testament to their own determination.

With the corporate bad boy in charge, there was no committee or superior executive to keep him in check and his expenses skyrocketed. For all the talk of a dream fulfilled, De Lorean's attention wandered off the car and to other projects. Some of his executives wondered whether he was enriching himself at the expense of the British-backed company – much the same accusations he once made against GM top brass. If anything, he seemed intent on repeating the litany of managerial errors he recited in his book. His headlong rush to reap a paper profit – the short-sighted business behaviour he once so roundly condemned – doomed his dream to insolvency.

The wreckage of the De Lorean Motor Company is scattered across continents: from the unpaid bills of a multi-national conglomerate in France to the dashed hopes and dignity of an assembly worker in Belfast, to a small parts supplier in California. But the ultimate victim of his own illusions was John De Lorean.

In the summer of 1982, when all around him saw imminent collapse, he – for the first time – saw a reason to invest personal funds in the dream car. The last evangelist in his own church, he still tried to convince auto dealers and investors that somewhere behind the miasma of mounting debt there had been a stunning success. Even when Kimmerly and Nesseth could not find the impossible solution, De Lorean believed that he could summon a miracle, and took matters in his own hands.

Finally, he would find himself accused of seeking salvation – or so he thought – in a mafia drug dealer. Only then, perhaps, did John De Lorean's illusions start to fade before his own eyes. This was not an investor who cared about an 'ethical car company', or an 'ethical' anything. De Lorean's pitch could be aimed no higher than greed.

In exchange for his piece in a narcotics transaction that could net 60 million dollars, he offered half his stock in De Lorean Motor Company, Inc. In fact, DMC Inc. was something quite different than the De Lorean Motor Company. Formed some time before by Kimmerly, it was abandoned after De Lorean signed the British government deal, and existed as no more than a paper entity – a shell company.

It was one final grand illusion.

PART ONE
White Collar Wonder

Dark Secrets

It took a while, but the phone company finally caught up with John Z. De Lorean. For months, the twenty-three-year-old had plied the city in a battered, green utility truck, offering merchants advertisements in something he called the 'Yellow Pages'. He made enough money on his first calls to even print up a few copies of his 'Yellow Pages' for the advertisers.

The scheme was no news for his close friends at the Lawrence Institute of Technology. The phone company didn't worry him, he laughed. He had just started taking law school at night and had already researched copyright law. Michigan Bell forgot to register 'Yellow Pages' as a trademark. His whole scheme was made in the shade. Of course, Michigan Bell's lawyers were of a different opinion, and they did not want to stop with a civil suit.

The news about the phoney phone books quickly buzzed through Lawrence Tech. The perpetrator wasn't just any member of the 1948 graduating class. If the engineering school had a big man on campus, it was John De Lorean. He wrote a column for the newspaper, sat on the student council, made the honours society and organized the college's first chapter of the American Society of Industrial Engineers. To top it off, he could do the jitterbug with the best of them, and often did, spinning the prettiest girls at the dance. The lanky young man with the unruly shock of hair seemed to have everything else in life at his fingertips. But suddenly, Michigan Bell brought the big bopper down to earth. In the eyes of some classmates a brilliant career hovered on the brink of oblivion even before graduation.

When John De Lorean returned home from college each night, he needed no reminder of how far he had already come in the world and how far he had to go. He still lived with his mother and younger brothers on the east side of Detroit in a narrow wood frame bungalow, crammed between two other small homes. They were just a few streets

17

from the railroad tracks one way, and a few streets from an elevated freeway the other – stuck in a dingy matrix of flat treeless streets crowded with tiny shingled houses. Bars, petrol stations and car body shops dotted the main avenues.

When John was growing up, most of the neighbours were of Eastern European stock: still peasants who sewed postage stamp backyards with vegetable gardens, slaughtered their own pigs, and made their own wine from the vines hanging off the garage. Although they took pride in their small homes, carefully cutting the grass and sweeping up their sidewalks, the working-class neighbourhood never measured up for their children. It was a place to move away from.

John was born to Zachary and Katherine Pribak DeLorean on 6 January 1925, the first of four sons. His father was a tall, dark-browed, brooding man who sweated out a living in the foundries of the Ford Motor Company. Next to last of fourteen children from a farming family that lived just west of Bucharest, he came to America alone as a teenager, working as a ranch hand in Montana, then a steelworker and a cop in Gary, Indiana, before he found factory work in Detroit.

There was evidently no great affection between father and son, as shown by John's later vagueness about Zachary's ethnic origins. In 1974, while on a trip to a car factory in central Rumania, De Lorean actually had the chance to visit Zachary's hometown. He was accompanied by Reo Campian, another Rumanian who grew up on Detroit's east side. 'I couldn't understand it,' Campean recalls. 'Here we were passing by the village where his family was from and he didn't want to see it. I couldn't understand what he was so embarrassed about.'

However, De Lorean was not embarrassed by his father's problems with alcohol or marriage. He is brutally frank in interviews and his recollections to Pat Wright in *On a Clear Day You Can See General Motors*, where he says of his father, 'he was a big man at 6' 1" and 220 pounds and enjoyed a certain amount of physical violence. Not that he was mean, but he got into his share of fights, sometimes after having a few beers with the boys after work.'

While he attributes some of Zachary's garrulousness to his difficulties with the English language, he does not say what his father's native tongue was. Again from the book: 'Part of my dad's inclination toward fisticuffs came from a deep frustration caused by his inability to communicate effectively and thereby capitalize on his mechanical genius. He was uneducated when he came to the U.S. and he couldn't speak English. Though he eventually mastered the language, he always spoke with a trace of an accent.'

John's primary school records report that Rumanian was primarily spoken in the home. He explains further in the book. 'I do know that [my father's] frustration with his inability to verbally get out the things that were inside of him eventually led to a serious drinking problem which resulted in the breakup of our home.'

De Lorean blames Ford for his father's frustration as well. No matter how well Zachary spoke English, he asserts, management would not have taken him seriously. In one interview he says, '[my father] was one of the more intelligent people I've ever met. Among the corporate executives I've known in my lifetime, and I've known a lot of them, I don't know of a single man who was dramatically more intelligent than my father. But the way the world cast its lot, he was destined to be a common labourer all his life . . . He led a frustrated life because he felt he had a contribution to make and the mechanism by which he could make a contribution wasn't available to him. Nobody would listen when you're just a little guy down on a foundry floor.'

In the book, as he did in most interviews, De Lorean graphically recounts his favourite story about the indignities of working for Ford: how company security men broke into his home one morning and ransacked the house in a futile search for stolen tools. He calls the intruders, 'Harry Bennett's goons'. Bennett was a poorly educated tough who rose, as head of Henry Ford's private police force, to become the second most powerful man in the company. Whether or not his men did break into De Lorean's house, two of John's childhood friends recall that it was Bennett who actually hired Zachary for his foundry job to begin with. Evidently the older De Lorean came highly recommended by a local political hack who assured the anti-union Bennett that Zachary was 'a character with a closed mouth'. Certainly his former stint as a policeman in Gary couldn't have hurt. It wasn't unusual for Bennett to hire workers. For a while in the thirties and forties, estimates had one out of three men on the shop floor doing double duty as Bennett spies.

Whatever De Lorean's later reflections on his father's stunted talent, as a child his affections lay with his mother. She too was an immigrant. But she arrived in America from Salzburg as a child and was better adjusted to American life than her husband. The couple often fought, and she would take the children for long periods to join her family in Los Angeles. The De Loreans finally divorced after John left high school, but he continued to live with his mother until he first married at the age of twenty-nine.

In his book, De Lorean calls her 'an incredible woman,' and most who knew her agree. At times she held down two jobs to support her four sons. She worked longest for General Electric as a tool assembler. Active in the local church, she also found time to garden around her house. Neighbours remember her filling trellises with roses.

The constant shuttling back and forth to Los Angeles made it difficult for John to fit in with the kids from the neighbourhood. He tended to hang out with older boys whose fathers worked with Zachary. At one time he earned some money working at a friend's newsstand, although he ended up losing most of the wages to his employer pitching pennies against a curb.

Although most of the parents in the area were hard-working, their American-born children were not as willing to fit into the system as law-abiding cogs. Reo Campian grew up around the corner from the De Loreans. He remembers an adolescence filled with random fights and petty lawlessness. Teams would graduate from stealing the tyres off someone's car to 'breaking and entering someone's house'. 'Some people on my block made a living from stealing,' he says. Today Campian owns a successful engineering firm, but he adds, 'I don't know how I turned out the way I did. A lot of my friends wound up in Jackson [Michigan State Prison].'

The teenagers Campian knew who got into trouble did so on their own. But one contemporary recalls that there were those who had some help from adults. Even after prohibition, the mobs thrived in motor city. The government may have permitted alcohol, but it was loading the drinks with hefty taxes. Canada and cheaper booze lay just a few minutes' cruise over the Detroit River. The smugglers' favourite craft were the pleasure boats they borrowed from the yacht clubs of the city's east side. They even had street kids riding along in the hold to help quickly load the contraband. Children were also used as runners between their night clubs – not the safest job in a time when rival gangs were splattering each over their warehouse bistros.

Despite the romance of crime, most boys looked to a much safer way out of their working-class neighbourhood – the car. In depression area Detroit, cars rumble through a young boy's wildest hopes and fears. Cars were the bitter fruit that sent their fathers home crushed with fatigue from the daily harvest. The cars were also transit to fabulous wealth and power. Henry Ford, the man who choreographed the nightmare of the fathers' working lives, also directed the dreams of the children. He loomed as the prime example of what a little mechanical know-how could reap. No more than a semi-literate farm boy when he first came to Detroit, Ford ended up finding the world's greatest fortune hidden inside an automobile, ready to spill out with the twist of a wrench.

In a rite of manhood born of the twentieth century, adolescent boys clamoured to corner a car and crack open its shiny shell. Underneath lay dark secrets of grease and metal to be fathomed only on endless Saturday afternoons.

John De Lorean was only ten when he grappled with his first car in the tiny wooden garage on the alley behind his house. 'It was an old Model T that my dad bought for us for some insignificant amount,' he remembers. 'We'd take it apart and he'd always have to come out again and put it back together for us.'

Of course, boys did not just take cars apart in the hope of one day becoming only a mechanic in a service station. 'In those days being an engineer was a big deal,' Reo Campian says. 'It was a title and it was a good job. That's the sort of thing kids in the neighbourhood shot for.' From the start John De Lorean too wanted to be an engineer. In interviews and his book he represents himself as poor student in primary school who hung out with juvenile delinquents. 'I know about being a street kid,' he told one reporter. 'I learned about getting in trouble. I thought the whole world grew up like I did.' But De Lorean's neighbours from those days do not think he was as tough a street kid as he says. 'I remember him as being studious,' says one man his age who grew up in the house behind the De Loreans. 'While everybody else was playing baseball, [John] had his books. He wasn't much like the rest of us.'

For a boy who was willing to study, Detroit in the 1930s offered unlimited possibilities. Probably no city in America better demon-strated the opportunities of capitalism and democracy: the public school system meshed perfectly with private industry to offer any good student a secure job after leaving school.

The first rung on the ladder for aspiring engineers was Cass Tech-nical High School. While his elementary years may have suffered from his constant travels to Los Angeles with his mother, De Lorean had to be above average to get into Cass – and getting in was much easier than getting out with a diploma.

Housed in an imposing seven-storey limestone building, Cass offered its predominantly male students practical training in such careers as drafting, mechanical engineering and electronics. But liberal arts educa-tion ran alongside the vocational classes and the standards in those courses were high as well. 'English and maths were especially rough,' Thaddeus Pietrykowski remembers. An engineer today, he entered Cass in the same year as De Lorean. 'I was in one algebra class with twenty-four students and eighteen flunked out. That was pretty typical. They didn't bend over backwards to help you at that school. If you didn't study, you were gone. I believe that in our time only one out of six entering as freshman ever graduated.'

De Lorean primarily made his mark at Cass as a student, and long after he had left the school, his mechanical drawings were still displayed in the hall, they were so neat and meticulous. But his classmates also elected him a class representative and member of the senior council. Among his extracurricular activities were the Radio Club and some-thing called the Star Delta Club, which featured field trips to such places as a radio station transmitter and telephone company switching house.

In the yearbook pictures young John stands surrounded by an ethnic melting pot: children named Ryan, Hrit, Palazzolo, Gotkowski, Soo Hoo and Goldstein. De Lorean was a year younger than most of his graduating class and despite his height, he looks· more immature, although very serious with his dark furrowed brow. His face is soft, with a weak chin, and his head appears disproportionately small on a long neck and gangling body.

College was to be the first of many radical transformations in De Lorean's personality and appearance that divide his life like layers of sediment on sandstone. It is unlikely that he chose the Lawrence Institute of Technology to improve his social skills. Far from being the typical college campus, the school was only one ivy-covered Georgian-style mansion down the street from Chrysler's Highland Park headquarters. Hardly ten years old when De Lorean entered in the autumn of 1941, the school was started by two brothers who felt that even in the midst of the depression the auto industries needed some nearby breeding ground for engineering talent. The brothers' lofty hope was to offer the chance for a degree to all those who wanted one, no matter what their financial status. If they had to work to support a family, they could earn their degree at night. If they were especially bright and able to pass an entrance exam, they could earn a full scholarship for day classes.

But school administrators were wise enough to make Lawrence Tech more than an advanced vocational training centre. Although all the students commuted from home, they could take part in all the typical collegiate trappings – varsity sports, school bands, newspapers and fraternities. 'Whatever impression you might have of engineering schools and students,' says John Fawcett, a professor from De Lorean's era, 'it was actually a very informal, tight-knit place. Most of the teachers were on a first-name basis with the students, and I think the students were pretty close with each other as well.'

With the start of World War II and the spectre of conscription, it was hard even for engineering students to take study all that seriously. In just his freshman year, John De Lorean became the school spokesman for irreverence. He plunged immediately into school activities starting out with the anaemic college band. The group is pictured in a 1942 yearbook wearing Salvation Army style uniforms. De Lorean had picked up the clarinet in high school and had led his own neighbourhood dance band over the summer, and eventually he would push the college ensemble from Sousa to swing.

But first, the freshman became the band's biggest recruiter. He joined the *Lawrence Tech News* and wrote two columns he called, 'Music Makers' and then 'Men of Note'. In one he would ask, 'Where are the jive hounds around this jernt? The LIT band had dwindled from the 31 pieces of Smartie Pshaw's poor man's symphony to the six man size of

Benya Goodman's Sextet (Benny and his five bagels) . . . Gentlemen, Lawrence Tech is a major College that does not have a major dance band. This certainly is not the type of distinction we want. So, let's get out and do something about it!'

The band didn't fare much better, but De Lorean stuck with the bi-weekly paper inaugurating a joke column he called, '5 with D'. He'd later aptly caption the spot as 'a place where old jokes go to die'.

The column was really more a showcase for jive talk than humour. 'Hey, cat,' one party in a story says to another, 'You look shot to the sox.' Or, 'I was talking to a pretty girl and trying to dig up jive for this five minute intermission. I said, "Hurry up Fat Woman, I got a deadline to make." She said, "Tell it to me anyhow." ' The story is followed by De Lorean's offer to give 'a special course to explain my jokes'.

Most of the jokes poked fun at the school administrators and other students, but some were self-deprecating. At first he made the author of each column another variation on De Lorean: H.V. De Loreanborn, Ross De Loreanhollen, and so on. But, more important, he used the newspaper to create another John De Lorean. This version was not Rumanian, but in his words, 'the leering Frenchman'. This John De Lorean was also a hip sophisticate, an insouciant rake and inveterate bar hopper. He leads off one column with: 'What popular, handsome, dashing Tech student got kicked out of 3 jernts last night? What can I do for a bruised eye?' He casts himself as the lead in most of his necking jokes as well: 'I kissed her. She sighed. I said, "Don't mention it, the pressure was all mine." '

His newsprint image may not have been idle boasting. The awkward adolescent had filled out, and his face became longer and leaner. He had the large almond-shaped eyes and dark features of a Hollywood Latin lover. 'He was quite a ladies' man,' remembers one of his college fraternity brothers, M. John DeDona. 'It didn't seem as though he had any problem finding women. But he was very vain about his looks. Whenever he passed a mirror, he glanced over to see himself, or tried to comb down his hair. He was an immaculate dresser, always wearing the most stylish things. I never figured out where he got the money for those clothes.'

The spring semester of 1943 was the last De Lorean spent as a civilian. He signed off for the duration with one more joke: 'In my spare time I've written a book on how to stay out of the army. Those who wish to secure a copy of this infallible book should send 24 cents to . . . Pvt. J. Sachelpants De Lorean at Camp Custard. But, seriously, the best way to stay out of the army is to join the navy . . . s'long JD ERC [Enlisted Reserve Corps].'

The next semester, the enrolment at Lawrence Tech plummeted from 2,000 to 200. De Lorean spent the war on uneventful army duty in the States. He returned for the autumn semester in 1946 and shortly thereafter resumed '5 with D', but the column was to be much more truncated. His costs were being paid under special provision for ex-GIs, but like his fellow demobbed classmates, the twenty-one-year old was anxious to finish college and get out in the working world.

As studying became more frenzied, the social life at the school kept pace. Lawrence Tech's basketball team went big-time, playing colleges from around the nation. Games were held in the Coliseum on the Michigan State Fairgrounds. Afterwards, students adjourned to the nearby Horticultural Buildings for dances that would go on long into the night, often featuring the best of the big bands – Woody Herman, Gene Krupa, Tex Benecke, Stan Kenton. Although he was going to night school as well, De Lorean didn't miss a dance. 'He was the life of the party,' the wife of one classmate remembers. 'I don't think anybody there could jitterbug like he could.'

A fraternity brother says, 'There was something about crowds that turned him on. He always seemed to project himself out front. And he was a fun guy to be around. He liked to laugh and joke. But I don't think he had one best friend. He was one of those sorts who's popular with everyone and not close to anyone in particular.'

The friend remembers De Lorean living up to the reputation he painted for himself in the newspaper column: 'He liked to drink a lot, and he liked to drive his car as fast as he could go. After my brother's wedding, he was pulling out of a long, narrow road and there were some old folks ahead of him going too slowly, so he just bumped up right behind them with his car and started pushing them. Another time I got in his car and as soon as we hit the freeway, he kicked that thing up to what must have been eighty miles an hour. Afterwards he told me he thought he had a blister on his tyre and he was testing to see whether it would blow. That was the last time I ever rode in his car.'

Nothing about De Lorean's social life disrupted his school work. 'He could just thumb through a book a half hour before a test and have the best grades of anyone,' the friend says. Thaddeus Pietrykowski adds, 'He was a genius. It was that simple. He used to say he had a photographic memory and you had to believe it.'

Hurst Wulf, an associate professor at the time, taught De Lorean strength of materials, mechanics and calculus. 'He was one of the best students I had,' Wulf says, 'I can't think of one better. The whole thing seemed to be effortless for him, to come naturally. I liked to schedule tests on Monday, so the boys could study over the weekend, but De Lorean would think nothing of going to Chicago and getting back just in time to get a perfect mark on the exam.'

De Lorean stood out in Humanities courses as well. One of his favourites was world economics, taught by Edwin Graeffe. Almost a

stereotype of the stiff-backed Prussian, Graeffe proudly bore an old
fencing scar raked down the side of his face. Despite his threatening
appearance and the fact his students had recently fought against his
countrymen overseas, Graeffe was among the most respected members
of the faculty. He liked to play devil's advocate and De Lorean enjoyed
battling with him. Having practised law in Europe, Graeffe encouraged
De Lorean to try some legal course at night school, which he did briefly.

But engineering was evidently closer to his heart. Wulf says, 'He
always did like engineering best. And he did get to be pretty good at it.
By his senior year, he figured he could engineer his way out of anything.'

In fact, the only sober break he ever took in his *Tech News* column
was to eulogize the profession. He starts off with a typical wisecrack:
'5 with D: By William De Loreanspeare, "The Immoral Barge." ' But
what follows is evidently, and quite portentously, serious:

> Know you what it is to be an Engineer?
>
> It is to have a dream without being conscious you are dreaming
> lest the dream break; it is to be trapped in a terrible tower of pure
> science . . .
>
> It is to live in a mean, bare prison cell and regard yourself the
> Sovereign of limitless space; it is to turn failure into success, mice
> into men, rags into riches – stone into buildings, steel into bridges,
> for each engineer has a magician in his soul . . .
>
> It is to make the guns roar, the machines hum, the night resound
> with such meaningful glory as sparks fly up from hidden plants
> that nightingales cease song in reverence to listen to the call of
> golden fountains from afar and revel in the promise of moonswept
> silver stars . . .
>
> It is to give deep springs of water to thirsty travelers, to provide
> warmth and shelter for the homeless, to add adventure and allay
> the tedium of lesser men's hours . . .
>
> . . . it is to . . . be perpetuated by the delicacy of illusion of
> distance that too often twilight foretells . . .
>
> It is to be a Conqueror and a coward, a King and a captive, a
> Savior and a slave; it is to be good unto seeming Godlike while
> contrasting evil incarnate; it is to suffer a throne alone in your
> terrible Temple of Science while companions roam the city streets
> make carefree carnival . . .
>
> It is loving and winning only to lose and love again and again, for
> Engineering is a fanciful Goddess clad in fickle fantasy, form fitting
> fortune, and flaming Fool's Gold who recognizes neither disaster
> nor despair . . .
>
> KNOW YOU WHAT IT IS TO BE AN ENGINEER?

De Lorean's purple prose must have struck home with some other students, because he got requests to reprint the column. He would be just as serious in his race for the student council presidency in his final year, with the slogan 'John's Your Man'. In his newspaper solicitation, his backers declare themselves to be, 'the firm supporters of liberal and progressive action . . .' They go on to distinguish their candidate, oddly enough, by his promises: 'You will hear much during this campaign about what the various candidates have done. We prefer to tell you what our candidate will do.'

Ever the visionary, De Lorean promised to cut off 'endless bickering' on the council floor and delegate more responsibility to other officers – actually techniques very similar to the ones he would adopt at GM and in his own car company. Whether they would have worked on the council will never be answered. The election brought out the largest percentage of voters in the college's history, but De Lorean came in second, two hundred votes behind the winner.

Soon after his loss, De Lorean went into competition with a bigger opponent, Michigan Bell. When an outraged customer tipped off the phone company, Michigan Bell lawyers picked up his trail and threatened to take him to court. The incident did not surprise De Lorean's friends. 'It was the sort of stunt only he could have pulled,' DeDona says. 'He always thought big. If we had voted on such things, John would have been voted most likely to succeed and most likely to get into trouble.'

Both professors Wulf and Fawcett remember that the younger faculty members at Lawrence Tech couldn't help but be amused. 'We weren't that much older than he was anyway,' Wulf says. 'We didn't think it was much more than a prank. I really didn't think less of him.'

Rumours circulated among the students that De Lorean was near expulsion or heading for jail. But instead he turned to the admonishment and aid of Doc Graeffe. He returned all the money he had obtained, and in return Graeffe got him off Ma Bell's hook. The whole affair only added some more bite to the appropriately irreverent send-off his editors at the *Tech News* gave him upon his graduation: 'though [De Lorean] has departed to seek his eternal reward, those of us who knew him will draw inspiration from his example. We shall miss his sober countenance and the lofty idealism of his "5 with D" column . . . We shall always remember his sage remark, "Eternal vigilance is the price of dishonesty." '

A Company Man

One day, not long after he was hired by General Motors in 1956, John Z. De Lorean drove to the sprawling campus of the company technical centre to see a special showing of GM's newest models. He arrived to find that he couldn't park near the auditorium. All of those spots were reserved for the top brass in from the headquarters. De Lorean had to settle for a place on the other side of the complex and then run back before they locked the doors. Huffing and puffing, he barely made the start of the show.

De Lorean returned to his office in Pontiac afterwards and told a co-worker about the parking pecking order. He would have been upset if he had missed the show, he said, but he understood why the company did those things. 'It's one more challenge to work harder, so some day I can have a good spot reserved for me.'

Less than ten years after he graduated, the wise-cracking 'D' had lost the edge to his looks and outlook: no more irreverence and no more odes to the joys of late-night drinking. Now he sung the praises of the great corporate system. While other GM engineers had to work for several years before they qualified for the coveted bonus pool, De Lorean garnered this fringe benefit the day he was hired as head of advanced engineering for the Pontiac division. In the process he became one of the youngest executives ever to receive this coveted perk. His age, however, was not to be ascertained by his appearance. He had grown old before his time: his face fleshing out and his eyes sinking beneath dark circles. The shoulders were rounded, and the once trim figure bulged and softened around the middle. A chain-smoker, he no longer had the wind or the time for the clarinet and the jitterbug. Most evenings were reserved instead for homework or a few quiet moments with his wife.

While De Lorean neatly fitted into the lifestyle of the typical GM executive, there was nothing conventional about how he got his job at the megalith. Unlike most of his fellow graduates from Lawrence Tech, he did not head, hat in hand, for the nearest car company. Despite the unprofitable nature of his 'Yellow Pages' business, he was evidently still bitten by the sales bug. In *On a Clear Day You Can See General Motors* he fails to mention his little escapade with the phone company, but does relate a fling as a life insurance salesman – a profession he took up, he says, to overcome shyness (something no one ever accused him of in college). After selling $850,000 worth of insurance (a feat most seasoned salesmen could not have matched in those days), De Lorean claims he tired of the job and started pitching for an auto parts manufacturer.

In later years De Lorean was to express admiration for the selling skills of GM founder William Crapo Durant, who made his first success as a life insurance salesman, and it is unclear whether De Lorean was consciously taking Durant's career as a pattern for his own. It was not unusual for the young men of Detroit to model their careers on his as one of two divergent paths to success.

In 1887, when Henry Ford rode to Detroit on a horse-drawn carriage, he had little more than an idea about mass-producing a cheap motor car for the 'multitudes'. Before he was done, his idea melted down mountains of iron ore, dried up oceans of oil and made America run rivers of asphalt.

In 1908, soon after he turned around the fortunes of the Buick car company, William Durant had the idea to glue together the great auto makers with stock in a holding company he called General Motors. Before the year was out, his idea swirled a blizzard of paper through Wall Street and changed the course of world commerce.

Together, Ford and Durant loom larger than life in the capitalistic pantheon – great men with great talents and great flaws. While Ford was a brilliant engineer, he had very little business sense. Durant's acumen was strictly financial. His salesmanship with car buyers, investors and other auto makers did far more for GM than his mechanical ability.

For the young men of De Lorean's era, the god of ambition wore a face split, like some Hindu deity, between the cold, chiselled features of Ford and the softer, puckish smile of Durant.

Ironically, both men were blinded by the brilliance of their original ideas. Ford relied too much on the Model T, only shifting gears and diversifying in the late twenties to stave off financial ruin. Although Durant's strategy of aggressive agglomeration won out over Ford's monomania, it became his personal undoing. Three times his personal fortune puffed up like a giant, glistening soap bubble only to pop and spatter, leaving slightly oily stains behind. He would die destitute in his hometown of Flint, with a bowling alley and a hamburger joint as his last two ventures.

However, the nature of Durant's demise did not diminish the respect De Lorean had for him. He said in his book, 'The breadth of the General Motors Corporation today is due to the imagination and courageous mind of William Crapo Durant . . . whose expansionary philosophy put substance into the corporation and set a precedent for growth after his departure.'

Throughout his life De Lorean bounced between the two opposite poles magnetized by Ford and Durant. By 1950 he was pulled back again to engineering, and with the help of an uncle who worked at Chrysler, he enrolled in the Chrysler Institute. Like his high school and college, Chrysler Institute was one more boost Detroit offered able young men from working-class backgrounds. The company did not ask for tuition fees. In fact, the students – many of whom came from the best engineering schools in the country – were paid. They spent only a few hours in the classroom each day, and spent the rest of their forty-hour work week in other areas of the company, in a rotating sequence similar to a medical training. After two years the students received a master's degree in Automotive Engineering, and more important, a good shot at a job with Chrysler. In De Lorean's day over 50 per cent of the Institute graduates were still with the company ten years later.

De Lorean was not among them. After working a few months in the tank division, he looked elsewhere. Working for any employer as big as Chrysler was not his style: 'I've always had to see how and what I did integrated with the whole,' he later told one interviewer. 'That was not obvious to me in a large company.'

He turned instead to a much smaller car maker, the Packard Motor Car Company – a company that the financial community did not give long to live. But that possibility made De Lorean's move all the more savvy, as one of his later GM colleagues sees it: 'If John had started out at GM, he would have had to work his way up the ladder. But at Packard, the senior people were already starting to bail out. Before the company folded John had a chance to come away with a good title.'

Packard had other advantages which made it an ideal choice for De Lorean's continuing education. Its small size required the engineering staff to be general practitioners. No one could hide as a specialist on one tiny component of the car as many engineers were required to do at the big companies. Since much of Packard's marketing strategy centred on product innovations, the engineers were also given free rein to experiment as they ranged over the company's limited model line.

But by the time De Lorean applied for work at Packard, the older engineers were starting to lose their influence on product development. After working miracles at Hotpoint, Jim Nance was appointed Packard's president with the mission of pulling the company into the new era of auto manufacturing.

Nance brought along with him a team of bright, young Harvard MBAs with little knowledge of the car industry, but well versed in the latest marketing and finance trends. 'It seemed like all of them wore those pointy dark glasses,' one Packard engineer, Carroll J. Lucia recalls. 'We used to call them the "Whizz Kids".'

For the first time in the company's history Packard engineers had to justify every expenditure, and hard-bitten veterans like Lucia didn't feel equal to the task. 'We figured there was no way we'd out-talk the Whizz Kids. We finally decided that if we didn't have the charisma to impress management, we should hire charisma.'

At that fortuitous moment De Lorean walked into Lucia's office, a tall, presentable young man with no glasses, but an easy smile and impressive, deep-timbred voice. Lucia put him to work on the Ultra-matic transmission – the industry's first automatic transmission and one more of Packard's pioneering innovations.

'When I hired De Lorean, I was afraid about his ability,' Lucia says. 'So I told him, "I'm a little bit old fashioned. I'll start you at six hundred a month. If you're still here after sixty days, you'll get sixty dollars more a month in a raise." Well, he really showed me something in sixty days, and it wasn't long before he was next in line after me in Research and Development.'

The head of the department was Forrest McFarland, an auto industry legend as an engineer. Together Lucia, De Lorean and McFarland worked on the unglamorous, but all-essential guts of the automobile – the transmission and the suspension. Car makers saw a potentially vast market in the woman driver and were convinced that only the gear system stuck in the way. In totally revamping his product line, Packard president Nance pushed hard for a push-button transmission (a system that created insurmountable maintenance problems), and his engineers seemed to have the rest of the industry beaten to the punch.

In 1954, at the age of twenty-nine, with his job secure, De Lorean married Elizabeth Higgins, a pretty blonde pixie from a small town in northern Michigan. They met, ironically enough, while she worked as a representative for the phone company. They had their wedding one autumn afternoon in the Central Methodist Church, a small sanctuary just off Woodward Avenue. For weeks before the event De Lorean had been pestering Lucia about getting his company car. 'I didn't realize what he was so anxious about until I stood there at the ceremony. He wanted to drive off after the wedding in some fancy car. Even in those days he was out to impress people. But wouldn't you know that after the ceremony he drove off in a brand new Cadillac? He was going to Florida for his honeymoon, and it turns out that he offered to deliver the car down there for some Detroit dealer. I don't know how the De Loreans ever got back, but while they were there, he met that ballplayer Ted Williams in a bar and evidently they really hit it off. When John got back to work he was just on cloud nine.'

In *On a Clear Day You Can See General Motors*, De Lorean speaks of the Packard days as among the most rewarding in his career.

'For me [Packard] was the perfect setup. The experience was invaluable. Packard was small enough that an engineer had to do many things – design a part, work with the machinist as he built the first part (I even machined a few myself), help put the part together with the car and then test it. If everything worked out, then I'd go to the guys in production and work with them to make sure the part was built and assembled properly. I was excited by the work, so I put in long hours and learned more in four years with Packard than I would in any similar time since.

De Lorean goes on to relate that he learned a great deal from the shop workers as well:

If you looked at them the wrong way or dealt with them in any manner other than a man-to-man, professional fashion, they would simply reach under their work benches without saying a word, throw their tools into the big box and leave. That was it. Each guy figured, 'What the hell, I don't have to take this from anybody. I'm a pro. I know this business and I am not depending on you or anyone else.'

The craftsmen's self-confidence and independence, he declares, would become the hallmark of his own career. 'From that experience, in part, I developed my own philosophy: That I would work extra hard at whatever I was doing to become so good at it that I would never have to kiss anyone's fanny to keep my job. And I never have and I never will.'

But such claims come as news to his one-time Packard superior Carroll Lucia. 'De Lorean was the biggest brown-noser I ever encountered. It got to the point where the guys who worked with him laughed at it. There was no mistaking what he was doing – it was almost crude. For example, whenever any management big-shot was around, De Lorean always got thirsty, so he'd be at the water fountain just in time to introduce himself.'

Lucia admits that he wasn't too quick himself to notice the naked ambition: 'I was the first guy he felt he had to impress. I could see his potential, but I could also see that this was a guy willing to work twelve and fourteen hours a day on his career. Most of us will work eight hours. De Lorean had bigger things in mind than most of us.

'For a while there, he'd come over to my house damned near every weekend with his wife, Liz. All he wanted to do was talk shop. He always asked about the best way to get noticed by management. There were only ten engineers in the company, but still that didn't mean that the top brass knew each and every one of them. Meanwhile his wife was in the next room telling my wife how John thought I was such a great guy. Of course, my wife never got the idea she was supposed to tell me what Liz said. She'd bring it up a year later.'

The Lucias made the De Loreans godparents for their three children, and Carroll remembers taking John along one afternoon when he was helping his son prepare for the Little League. 'De Lorean got on the mount to pitch to my son and he started throwing knuckleballs like he had pitched all his life. I couldn't hold on to them. It was as though there was nothing too small for him to show off with.'

In time the couples' friendship cooled. 'Eventually I could see what he was doing,' Lucia says. 'And besides, it got to be a bore. We didn't have all that much to talk about, and here I was with three young kids and a new house and a lawn to seed and I didn't have time to sit around all day and socialize with the De Loreans.'

De Lorean found other engineers to visit on a Saturday afternoon, but he continued to take Lucia's advice to heart. Patents, the older engineer told him, were the way to get noticed. 'You have some great inventors who don't have any patents because they're not patent-oriented,' Lucia explains. 'Getting a patent is an art in itself. Of course, all of our patents were assigned to Packard and we didn't get any revenue from them, but as each one came in, the top brass could see your name. Sometimes you had ideas that would never be processed for a patent. Those were usually put in the "B" file. But if you threw a lot of ideas in the "B" file it was another way of gaining visibility.'

Before De Lorean left Packard in 1956 he had twelve patents granted or pending for the corporation and countless other applications languishing in the 'B' file. His patents were not enough to save the company. Nance's expansion plans – especially his merger with Studebaker – inexorably mired Packard in red ink, dooming its Detroit auto production. McFarland became the first key member of the engineering team to leave. Lucia had already been moved to another department, so for a few months De Lorean directed the moribund remnants of Research and Development. But the title didn't hurt. Packard engineers had gained a legendary reputation in the rest of the industry, and the big three moved quickly to snap them up.

Lucia, and Herbert Misch, Packard's chief engineer, prepared to take over at Pontiac, where management had tapped Semon 'Bunkie' Knudsen as new general manager and provided him with *carte blanche* to turn the ailing division around. To their surprise, Knudsen bypassed Misch for the job of chief engineer, turning instead to an Oldsmobile executive, Elliott M. 'Pete' Estes. But Packard was not to be denied representation in the new Pontiac team. Knudsen tapped thirty-three-year old De Lorean as head of the new Advanced Engineering department.

Like his superiors at Packard, De Lorean had also been aggressively searching for a new job. Some of his patents caught the attention of top GM engineers who rushed to recruit him. Today, De Lorean says he was just as inclined to join a small auto parts manufacturer, and he relates his first meeting with Pontiac's outgoing top engineer – 'a nice old guy wearing high-top shoes and a suitcoat stuffed with cigars'. Determined not to work for any 'old ladies' division', De Lorean called Knudsen back to tell him he wouldn't take the job. But Knudsen convinced him to meet Estes, the new chief engineer, before he made up his mind. The two hit it off immediately, and with the assurance that Pontiac was in for an overhaul De Lorean signed on.

In the minds of some car people, Pontiac was riding to extinction bumper to bumper behind Packard. In 1956 the division's clunky product line held only 6 per cent of the market – down from 7.4 per cent in the previous year. 'I left another car company to join Pontiac about the same time John did,' one GM engineer recalls, 'and I remember people telling me I was making a mistake to join Pontiac – that GM was ready to disband the whole division.'

But GM president Harlow H. Curtice gave Pontiac one more chance with Knudsen, the company's resident miracle-worker, at the helm. Knudsen made his first mark at GM during World War II when he increased production in one tank plant by almost 50 per cent. After armistice he turned around the Allison aircraft engine division and then Cleveland Diesel.

With Pontiac he faced his greatest challenge. The heart of the problem, as he saw it, lay in the product's fusty image. Pontiacs were hulking, turtle-like cars, perhaps regarded as dependable but with nothing about the line that provoked any excitement. Market analysts were already reeling with the seismic data of the post-war baby boom, and by the time those infants came of driving age, Knudsen wanted Pontiac to be loaded with youth-oriented cars. 'You can sell a young man's car to an old man,' he would say, 'but you can't sell an old man's car to a young man.'

Robert F. McLean, an engineer with GM's styling section, remembers Knudsen bursting in one day in 1956, shortly after he became Pontiac's general manager. 'There was nothing he could do about the new models or even the next year's models for that matter. But he still wanted to have some imprint on the product to show that there would be a change. In those days, Pontiac had a decoration running along the side that looked like silver railroad tracks. At least he could stop the factories from painting those things on. That horrible Indian-head hood ornament went next.'

Knudsen had more fundamental changes in mind than bonnet orna-
ments. He wanted to revamp the Pontiac from bumper to bumper, and
he assembled the best engineers he could find for the task. To contend
with the hold-overs from prior regimes he created a new division,
Advanced Engineering, circumventing the veterans, while injecting
new blood into product development.

For the new department's chief, moving to Pontiac was a lot like
staying with Packard. De Lorean had still sided with 'the little guy'
against the titans of a larger corporation. The division headquarters in
those days were not much more than a cluster of buildings around the
main assembly plant on the outskirts of the city of Pontiac, some
fifty-five miles from Detroit. While most of the facilities were antiquated, the brick, two-storey engineering building had only been completed a few years before. Upstairs were large open rooms with drafting
tables and blueprints. Below were cubby-holes and shops where union
craftsmen turned the engineers' ideas into substance.

Although GM has since become much more rigidly centralized, back
in the fifties divisions were like duchies in a feudal kingdom. Over the
preceding decades each had created a separate identity and loyalty,
especially among the footsoldiers slogging away in the trenches, and
the general managers often had to claw out their share of the corporate
turf. No one disputed Chevrolet's dominance, although some executives felt the division went too far to maintain it. Cadillac, with its
high-priced, highly profitable products comfortably nestled in a special
niche. The fiercest competition raged between Buick, Oldsmobile and
Pontiac. Somehow the real enemy – Ford and Chrysler – got lost in the
shuffle. The only blows that mattered for GM divisional executives
were delivered against other GM divisions.

Through the years the company's top management debated whether
such internal friction was counter-productive. To dampen the sectarian
feelings, they often transferred general managers from one division to
another, or after a limited tenure kicked them upstairs to corporate
headquarters. But to a great extent the rivalries during De Lorean's era
were the reflection of the rumbustious men who ran the company.
Most of them had battled for their education, their jobs and finally their
positions at GM. There were even occasions when arguments over such
things as fuel efficiency almost brought the top executives to blows.

Bunkie Knudsen was not one to shy away from such arguments, and
gives himself no kudos for diplomacy. 'None of us were easy to work
with,' he says today. 'If we wanted anything we had to fight for it, and
we had some tough battles. But that was part of the act.'

Unlike most of his colleagues at GM, Knudsen had not pulled himself
up from the working class. His father, Bill, had been one of the
industry's pioneers, first as Henry Ford's production chief and later as a

GM president. But in the words of one of his friends, 'However many millions Bunkie may have inherited, he was out to prove he could have earned them on his own.' He had no apologies for his own record at GM, and although he didn't have his father's bulky height, the barrel-chested Knudsen had no trouble filling his shadow. In Bob McLean's thirty-five years at GM, he says, 'Knudsen was the most aggressive executive they ever had. He got up every morning as though he had to show you something.'

Knudsen was able to pass some of that aggressiveness on to his troops at Pontiac, especially the engineers. Their division may have been the runt of the litter, but it was going to be a feisty runt. He had the perfect drill sergeant in chief engineer Estes. Despite his volatile temper, the big, beefy Estes could also be a warm and generous leader, quick with compliments and an arm around the shoulder. Estes often spurred competition among his own staff, assigning one project to two different teams. While some of his subordinates resented those tactics, they still delivered. Pontiac engineers often worked on Saturdays and occasionally stayed until dawn. Bill Collins, who signed on in 1958, does not remember anyone complaining about the hours: 'From an engineer's standpoint the late fifties and early sixties at Pontiac were some of the most exciting years in the history of GM. We seemed to constantly be on the cutting edge of product innovation.'

None of Pontiac's engineers shone as brightly as John De Lorean. In short order he became Knudsen's most potent weapon against the other GM divisions. He continued the work he started on transmissions at Packard, continuing as well to rack up the patents, and his redesign of the body frame became the industry standard. But his boldest stroke was to help Bunkie through a potentially disastrous bout of corporate intransigence.

By the end of the fifties GM's corporate staff was putting pressure on Pontiac to assemble a warmed-over version of the Corvair. The car was the pet project of Chevrolet general manager Ed Cole, a rival and eventual victor against Knudsen in the race for GM's presidency. No one questioned the Corvair's nifty body styling, but some voices in the corporation saw safety problems with the rear engine and suspension – flaws that Ralph Nader would later chronicle in *Unsafe at Any Speed*. Pontiac had been anxious to make an entry into the small car market, but when Knudsen refused to clone the Corvair, corporate management wouldn't give him the funds to manufacture a new creation.

So De Lorean went to work on a pot-luck special – a unique car which would meld components GM already produced. To get a four-cylinder engine he took Pontiac's standard V8 and cut it in half. His biggest challenge came in fitting that engine – mounted in the front of the car – with the underbody of a Corvair. The standard car had a hump down its centre to house the transmission running from the engine to the rear wheels, but with its engine mounted over the rear wheels, the Corvair underbody had no such hump. Instead of having a solid shaft run from the engine to the rear wheels of his hybrid, De Lorean used a narrow, flexible iron rod which could bend beneath the Corvair underbody. The system became known as the rope drive. The resulting hodge-podge car emerged as the 1961 Tempest.

Even De Lorean in *On a Clear Day*, would call the Tempest 'less than successful,' adding, 'There was no mechanical problem, but the car rattled so loudly that it sounded like it was carrying half-a-trunkful of rolling rocks.' After two years Pontiac dropped the rope drive. But back in 1961 the Tempest was De Lorean's greatest achievement. His ingenuity put Pontiac in the small car market at just the right time, and, whatever the problems with noise, the Tempest became the division's best-selling car.

De Lorean no longer had to hang around the water fountain to catch the boss's eye. Knudsen quickly became De Lorean's mentor both inside the company and in the tightly-knit GM social circle in the suburbs of Detroit. 'He was the sort of guy you had to take a liking to,' Knudsen remembers. 'He seemed very enthusiastic about his job and was about the smartest automotive engineer I ever saw in Detroit.'

The young engineer tagged along with Knudsen when he went to corporate meetings in the headquarters, or convened a conference on the first tee of the Bloomfield Hills Country Club. Despite his gruff corporate behaviour, Knudsen was still a man of wealth and refinement capable of introducing De Lorean to art, wine and fancy restaurants. Access to Bunkie's private plane put half the continent at their disposal. 'No person had the influence on my life that Bunkie Knudsen did,' De Lorean told Gail Sheehy. 'It was like exposing a ghetto kid to the finer things of life.'

Among Knudsen's greatest passions was auto racing, and soon after he took over Pontiac he saw a way that the sport could blast Pontiac out of its lethargy. While the rest of the industry shifted to smaller, six-cylinder engines, GM corporate plans left Pontiac languishing last in line for the changeover. If he was going to be stuck with big engines, Bunkie decided they would be the most powerful on the road, and although the car companies had decided in the mid–fifties to limit their support for professional racing, Knudsen wasn't going to let formalities stop him. New engines seemed to go into production only days before the nation's biggest stock car rallies. By 1958 and 1959 with Fireball Roberts at the wheel, Pontiacs started to show their potential on the race track, picking up a handful of Grand National titles. By 1961 Pontiacs were taking the checkered flag in twice as many National Association for Stock Car Auto Racing competitions as any other model.

In many ways the race track became the high-pressure proving ground for the Pontiacs in the showroom. Fuel, engines, aerodynamics: all were shaken out at speeds of over one hundred miles an hour. Some of Knudsen's engineers who had never been to a race track before watched their inventions propel the winner across the finish line. But the expertise did not just go one way. Racing introduced Knudsen to unqualified engineers working in the pits.

Long and lean with sideburns running to the edge of his jaw and a flattened hat that had the brims turned up at the side, Smokey Yunick was the resident mechanical master of the gypsy-like stock car circuit. Although he had no formal engineering background, Yunick was an intuitive genius who squeezed more horsepower out of engines than their Detroit progenitors ever hoped for. He first met Knudsen back in 1958 when the general manager surreptitiously supported the Pontiac racing team. 'He paid me with a personal cheque,' Yunick remembers. Knudsen soon found that Smokey was too valuable to be left at the race track and lured him to Detroit as a high-priced consultant. Walking down the halls of GM's Tech Centre in a zipper jacket and shorts, Yunick was not much impressed by the engineers in their white shirts and ties. He would feel differently about De Lorean. 'Just in talking with him, you could see he had a hell of a mind. He knew the car. Not just one piece of it, but the whole car. Most of the others at GM were pelicans, and you know what a pelican is – something that eats, shits and squawks. In my mind De Lorean was different. He was a hard working son-of-a-bitch.'

High Performance

Woodward Avenue shoots out of the Detroit River and slices a straight twenty-five-mile swath through city and suburb. Like a geometrically drawn aorta, it flowed with the wealth of the auto industry, and pushed deep into the flat Michigan farmland, leaving housing developments, shopping centres, office buildings and factories along the way.

No road was ever more an extension of the cars that travelled it. Whether self-propelled or riding on the back of a flat bed truck, the automobile was the lifeblood of the thoroughfare and all that had sprung up around it.

But by the early sixties a steadily growing phalanx of drivers were not taking the precious four-wheeled commodities so seriously. In the late hours of the night, with Woodward lit up like an endless runway, their cars came hurtling back to Detroit. These were sleek machines that had dropped the bulges and fins of the fifties. Their noses hunkered close to the ground and their haunches were jacked up on thick, over-sized tyres. At every red light, they sought each other out, pairing up on the intersection. Engines snorted and roared. Metal skins trembled as though they were ready to shake to pieces. With the first flash of green, they leaped into the night, leaving only the high-pitched squeal of their tyres and the acrid smell of burning rubber behind.

In time, the very name of the avenue became a verb. For teenagers across the country Woodwarding was the ultimate test of the auto-mobile, and Woodward the ultimate track. The dragsters raced the thickest, straightest stretch of the avenue, from Thirteen Mile Road to Eight Mile Road, through towns named Berkley, Royal Oak and Ferndale – the blue-collar suburbs that were often their homes as well. The machines that had been the hard, gruelling work of the fathers were now the sons' toys – fantastic playthings that could melt all the gas stations, fast-food stands and stores lining Woodward into one multi-coloured blur.

Teenagers weren't the only ones Woodwarding. On some nights a homeward bound Pontiac engineer sidled up to the hot rods, still dressed in his tie and button-down shirt. Even De Lorean and the grey, distinguished general manager, Bunkie Knudsen, took their marks under the stoplights. If the teenagers laughed at the old men behind the wheel, the Pontiac engineers smiled with the confidence that their company cars would leave the hot rods back in their tracks. As one Pontiac engineer puts it, 'We knew the kind of power we had under the hoods.'

But the real race was not between the Pontiac engineer and the teenager. If anything, along with the stock car racer, they were one mind behind the wheel and one hand on the gear shift. All were riding along in the same groove, pushing the car engine as far as it would go.

The sixties were to be a boom time for the car makers and America, and Pontiac's products seemed just the thing for a nation with high octane in its blood. It would 'go' faster and more profitably than any other division at General Motors. By 1960, Pontiac sold 396,000 cars – in volume second only to Chevrolet in GM. The day 'the old ladies' car' passed Oldsmobile for those honours, Knudsen and Estes sent a band marching down the middle of the assembly plant.

In 1962 Knudsen stepped up to the top job at Chevrolet, and Estes took over as Pontiac's general manager. At only thirty-seven years of age De Lorean became chief engineer. During his three years in the job product innovation reached an even more fevered pitch. Although he did not originate all the changes he later took credit for, De Lorean did manage to bring out the best in the men around him.

'There's no doubt that John was a great leader,' Bill Collins says today. Collins took De Lorean's spot in Advanced Engineering and was soon pegged as another De Lorean-style comer in the division:

He worked best with those of us who were the young Turks at Pontiac. We really wanted to impress him. That's what a leader can do, and John had real leadership qualities – at least with us. He had no patience with the older guys. I remember there was one heavy-set engineer nearing retirement, who used to smoke a lot of cigars. John just didn't like the looks of the guy, and one day he went up to him and said, "I don't want to see you anymore. Move your stuff into that corner and stay there." I don't think he got another assignment. He just came in every day and stayed in the corner. At GM, John could get away with burying people like that, and I have to admit, the young engineers thought the whole thing was pretty funny.

In his new job, De Lorean could push even harder for faster cars. The models that won the big races on Saturday were selling out in the showroom on Monday. But hot rodders were taking the big Pontiac engines beyond their limits, literally strangling the machines at sustained high speed. The Pontiac engineers solution was to adopt a simplified version of a professional racing engine using the overhead camshaft. The overhead cam – OHC in hot rod jargon – outstripped anything else on the road.

It seemed only natural to put that new engine in a light-weight, two-passenger fibre-glass body. Bill Collins was the first to suggest it, and De Lorean enthusiastically sold Estes on the idea. They code-named the project XP388 and put young Collins in charge. All work on the car then proceeded with the utmost secrecy. GM had one two-seater sports car, Chevrolet's Corvette, and the Number One division was not likely to countenance any competition. Pontiac managed to produce two running prototypes of the XP388 and then called the top executives to the proving grounds for the unveiling.

Among the guests was Zora Arkus-Duntov, Chevy's staff engineer in charge of high-performance vehicles. For the previous five years the Russian-born engineer had nurtured the development of the Corvette in everything from engine design to body contours. No other man at GM had more vested interest in having Chevrolet maintain its two-seater monopoly. Arkus-Duntov admits that he came to the showing ready to cast a jaundiced eye. 'But I was very favourably impressed,' he says. 'They had a six-cylinder overhead cam engine, and I thought it was quite an achievement. It was very powerful. Otherwise, there were no refinements – no great transmission or suspension. One thing bothered me the most – the style. The car had a very pleasant line – better than the Corvette, and that's what made me very unhappy. Later I talked to Ed Cole [the former Chevrolet chief and newly appointed GM executive vice president], and I said the car may be an empty shell, but it's better looking than Corvette. I don't want such competition.'

The Corvette had special sentimental value for Cole as well, as he had helped the car through infancy as general manager at Chevrolet. Citing poor return on the investment, Cole prevailed upon the other top executives on the Fourteenth Floor to kill the XP388. It was a crushing disappointment for De Lorean, and his first bitter lesson at GM in corporate politics.

But Knudsen and Estes taught De Lorean that there was still plenty of room to manoeuvre round headquarters' dictates. Even if they had to take a new car that came from the corporate cookie cutter, Pontiac could still leave its distinctive stamp on the product. The secret weapon was styling.

The responsibility for much of the outward appearance of GM cars fell to the Styling Section – a separate corporate staff housed under lock and key at the Technical Centre. Starting back in 1927 as the Art and

Colour Section, the department had been formed by then GM president Alfred Sloan to put a little more imagination into automobile design. For the next three decades GM styling was directed by Harley Earl, a Hollywood import who had got his start in the car business by customizing limousines for movie stars. Earl brought a little of the tinsel town with him. The walls of his studio were often covered with pencil and water colour sketches of futuristic vehicles. He also promoted the use of a special, sulphurous-smelling modelling clay, and Italian artisans who had once done decorative plastering in Detroit's skyscrapers would sculpt full-size car bodies to the specifications of styling engineers. Painted and polished, the clay took on the sheen of metal. The wildest, most impractical visions could be moulded into semblance in a single day.

Most of the styling work, however, was not in advanced body design. Primary concerns were dressing up bodies with chrome and interior appointments. Earl created a separate staff for each GM division, and kept each quarantined from the other to calm the paranoia of the general managers. But in many ways, Styling operated as a supplier to the divisions. If one general manager did not like the suggestions of his design staff, the Styling Section was free to pedal them to the other divisions.

As general manager of Pontiac, Knudsen quickly became Styling's best customer. Designers had free rein to change the stodgy looks of his cars, and Knusden was open to suggestions other divisions rejected. In his first, most important styling decision, he allowed a wider space between the tyres. Until then GM had widened the bodies of the car without widening the chassis as well, giving the products an ungainly baby-buggy look. In *On a Clear Day* De Lorean took credit for convincing Knudsen to space out the tyres, but Knudsen and Bob McLean remember the development differently. Working as an engineer in advanced engineering for the Styling Section, McLean had the responsibility of adjusting designs of the old models to fit new body types. He was the first to notice that a wider stance made the car look more stable. Buick rejected the idea as too costly. Pontiac was more receptive. 'As soon as Knudsen saw the drawings he liked the idea, and when he brought Estes in, Pete banged his fist on the table and said, "Damn it, we're going to do it." ' Pontiac's advertising agency would dub the style 'The Wide Track Look', and one of the industry's most successful promotion campaigns was born. It didn't take long, though, before every Detroit car had wide tracks.

While De Lorean was not the originator of the wide track, he was still closely involved with Pontiac's styling. The only sort of input most division executives had in styling was cost. They would listen to Styling's suggestions, and then decide whether a particular model could afford the change. But from his first days at Pontiac, De Lorean made his own modifications in designs, and according to Bob McLean, the Styling Section did not resent the input. 'It was clear that the man had a flair for styling,' he remembers, 'and if anything, most of us at Styling appreciated what he had to say.'

Styling may be De Lorean's most lasting legacy to GM. While he was chief engineer and general manager of Pontiac, the division led the way with such aesthetic innovations as recessed windshield wipers, racing stripes, hidden radio aerials, reinforced bumpers and squared-off headlights. Throughout he championed the cleaner body look, with less chrome ornamentation – a look that weighed less and in turn was more profitable for the company.

In 1962 he learned what just a little tinkering with style could do. He and Estes had pushed to bring out a 'clean look' car they called the Grand Prix. Headquarters refused to let them spend any money on tooling to streamline the new car's roof. Forced to use a standard body, they just removed most of the chrome and added fancier appointments to the interior. The Grand Prix sold out its first run of 40,000.

'John may have been a good engineer,' his friend Smokey Yunick says, 'but he was an even better stylist. He had a natural born talent, and I think the record shows uncanny timing. He knew just when the fender or hood should be shoved one way or another to meet the public's taste. His cars came as close to pleasing the public as any GM ever produced.'

No Pontiac model better reflected De Lorean's savvy for selling cars than the GTO, although again his memory on how this car evolved neglects the important input of others. He has since claimed to be the first engineer at Pontiac to come up with the idea of combining the new light version of the Tempest body with a big engine. Actually, the idea was suggested by Bill Collins, when the two men joined Pete Estes at the proving ground to get an advance look at the new Tempest. He wondered out loud whether the wheel base could be widened to meet NASCAR racing regulations. Only then did they think about trying the car with a bigger engine. By Monday morning, De Lorean had the perfect name for the new creation – GTO: an Italian acronym, already copped by Ferrari and standing for Gran Turismo Omologato, a new international racing classification for high speed cars. In the next few weeks he had put the finishing touches on the body style and suspension.

But the GTO still had a long way to go before GM top brass would permit its entry. By 1963, the corporate staff was beginning to pale on performance cars. Drag racing accidents had begun to mount, and although De Lorean has since claimed that Pontiacs had safer brake and suspension systems, still much of the division's allure was for the teenager who wanted to take his machine beyond the speed limit. When

Pontiac's general manager Estes broached another line of performance cars to management, he heard a resounding 'no'. That rejection, however, was not going to stop him. He called his engineers and told them to go full speed ahead on the GTO. His way around management would be to release the car as a three hundred dollar option for the Le Mans series.

Corporate outrage at Estes' subterfuge subsided with the first sales figures. Quickly outselling the anticipated production run of five thousand, Pontiac ended the model year with over 32,000 GTOs on the road. This wasn't anything like the foreign sports cars and yet it could make most of them eat rubber. A new automotive breed was born which the buffs started calling muscle cars. While the GTOs power was undoubtedly a big selling point, its feline looks didn't hurt either. Two nostrils flared out of the hood, and one headlight was stacked on top of the other on either side of a darkened grille. In its second year GTO's sales climbed to 75,000.

GM management could no longer afford to keep the GTO in the option closet. Finally, during the autumn of 1965 they allowed Pontiac to usher in the first GTO series. The division had a new general manager to oversee the youth-oriented line, and quite suitably, at forty, he was the youngest vice-president in the corporation. By this time, no one familiar with John De Lorean had any worries about his youth. The only questions now concerned how fast he could make it to the presidency of the corporation.

Except for his age, everything else about De Lorean fitted into the standard mould of the ambitious GM executive. Just eleven years after he moved out of the drab working-class neighbourhood of his youth, he had settled into a sprawling English manor house in the woody suburb of Birmingham. A winding cobblestone driveway curved in front of the house and majestic pine trees curled overhead. In local society Elizabeth dutifully played the role expected of a corporate wife. She worked for the Lung Association, raised money for the county college and stuffed envelopes for the Republican Party. In her spare time she restored antique furniture. The day after her husband was appointed general manager she met with the Women's Editor of the *Birmingham Eccentric*, who would describe Elizabeth as 'this sparkling young woman who looks like a little girl'. When asked about her husband's promotion, Mrs De Lorean replied, 'John is only forty and I suppose that's pretty young for this kind of position, but it's his ball to run with. I don't intend to hover. Just be standing by when needed.'

Like most other GM executives, De Lorean had little time for late-night socializing. Most evenings were spent quietly at home with some homework. As for the weekends, as John Quirk, one of his friends from those days, explains, 'Everything revolved around sports.' A manufacturer's representative, Quirk had also achieved success at an early age. In the course of his work and play in the exclusive suburb of Bloomfield Hills he also became close with the top echelon of the auto industry. 'Detroit is very much a sports-oriented town,' he says. 'If you wanted to fit in, you either had to play a good game of golf or convince people that you enjoyed football. There were people with season's tickets to every professional team in the city, because that's the way you bumped into the important people. The socializing then fitted around those events. You had a few drinks after a workout in the gym or a round of golf, or you met everybody at the cafe after the baseball game.'

This social pecking order suited De Lorean well. An excellent golfer, capable of going round in the low seventies, he had no trouble impressing superiors with his athletic ability. 'Quite simply,' Quirk says, 'he was a man's man – the sort of guy you wanted to be around. The charisma was there from the start, and also a driving ambition. You knew he'd make it to the top.'

As general manager of Pontiac, De Lorean soon showed the industry his stuff, uncorking an advertising campaign that would propel the GTO into the sales stratosphere. At the centre of the drive was Jim Wangers, a peripatetic young account executive for D'Arcy McManus, the mammoth agency that had a lock on Pontiac's business. Wangers had been intensely involved with Pontiac's development of high-performance cars ever since he joined the McManus firm in 1958. A hot rodder himself, he went down to the Daytona beach with a super charged Pontiac in 1960 and won the national drag championship. 'De Lorean and I met shortly after I was hired by McManus and we both rose through the ranks together,' Wangers remembers. 'We really had nothing in common. He was in engineering and I was in advertising. But for some reason a bond immediately formed between us, and we both had trust in each other's instincts.'

As he tooled around in his own hot rod, Wangers could see that the muscle cars were more than transportation or even hobbies to their drivers. The GTO was becoming part of an evolving youth culture that emphasized speed and independence. With the right approach, Wangers told GM executives, the car companies could tap into this new market. De Lorean was the first to take him seriously.

'De Lorean understood marketing,' Wangers explains. 'That is so rare for an automotive guy. He made a study of it and I think he discovered he had a penchant for advertising. Unlike so many other guys at GM, he could adapt to new ways of thinking and see the real needs of the consumers.'

With Wangers, De Lorean was ready to embark on some novel approaches to selling cars. While he was still chief engineer, a group called Ronnie and the Daytonas approached Pontiac asking to write an ode to the GTO. The idea appealed to De Lorean and he turned the project over to Wangers who immediately penned the lyrics. The music had the surfing sound of the Beach Boys. The words were just as simple, with a refrain of 'Turn it on, wind it up, blow it out GTO; yeah, yeah, little GTO.'

'Little GTO' sold a million records and helped push the car's sales over 100,000. Picking up on that promotion, Wangers put out GTO T-shirts and licensed GTO 'high performance shoes'. He was even permitted by De Lorean to build a special edition GTO for the 'Monkees' television show.

His print ads featured kids in the song's surf motif, or else just cars poised before a take-off. Clearly, Pontiac had struck a rich vein, and De Lorean tapped it further with the Firebird series.

The free rein De Lorean gave to Wangers typified his management style. If an executive proved himself competent, De Lorean was willing to delegate responsibility to him. Occasionally that meant going around individuals with more seniority than his protégés. 'He singled out just a half dozen guys to run the division,' Wangers remembers. 'One for marketing, sales, engineering, manufacturing and advertising. We all met each morning at 7:30 in his office, and then, over the next half hour we'd make all the important decisions. His attitude with us was, "Tell me about it after it's done." And we'd get the job done, but we also antagonized a lot of people in the process.'

If De Lorean was getting to be less sensitive about those under him, he did not worry either about his superiors. Once more the GM headquarters tried to put the clamps on advertising that emphasized 'high performance'. Too many dragsters were wiping out in Pontiacs. But De Lorean often flouted the policy, putting through ads without running them past the corporate watchdogs first. Although he urged De Lorean to press for the ads, Wangers found himself caught in the middle. Despite his close working relationship with De Lorean, he was still employed by an outside advertising agency, and his bosses were not about to jeopardize their lucrative relationship with GM so De Lorean and Wangers could appeal to the youth market.

Eventually, they relented to the performance strictures. But Wangers still tried to find a subtle way to get his message out to kids while staying inside the restraints. When a TV sketch featuring the line, 'Here comes the Judge,' became the rage, Pontiac named its new series of GTO the Judge. But in staying tuned to his teenage market, Wangers discovered that the GTO driver had his own term of endearment for the car – a goat. From that point of departure, Wangers cooked up his all-time favourite print ad: a proud, teenage owner standing in front of a soaped-up GTO with a bucket and sponge in his hand. Underneath the picture the caption read, 'A boy and his Goat'.

45

Even though the GTO sat stationary in a driveway and no further
copy extolled its hog engine, corporate staff summarily dismissed the
ad. 'I couldn't believe it,' Wangers remembers. 'They told me, "We
can't let you call the car a goat. It demeans the product."

'I immediately wrote a long, angry memo to John. In it I complained
that after all the success we had with the GTO, these old fogies still
didn't understand what it took to sell the car. Of course, I meant for that
memo to be confidential. John did go ahead and ask corporate staff to
reconsider, but he also enclosed my memo with his memo. The next
day my boss called me on the carpet. I came within a hair of losing my
job, and I never had GM's confidence again. Somehow John didn't see
anything wrong with what he had done. When I called to ask him why
he sent on my memo he just laughed and said, "Wangers, if you weren't
making trouble I wouldn't know you were around." '

De Lorean had no reason to fear the wrath of the corporate staff.
Pontiac sales would bulge over 25 per cent during his three-year tenure.
He took the division beyond its muscle image by producing lavishly
appointed luxury versions of the Grand Prix and Bonneville. Later in all
humility, De Lorean would say of the period, 'We were living off the
gullibility of the consumer combined with the fantastic growth of the
American economy . . .'

But top management was not about to tamper with his record of
achievement at Pontiac. The spoiled young executive soon found he
could get away with antics that other general managers dared not try. 'I
was with John once at a Tech Centre meeting,' styling engineer Bob
McLean recalls. 'There were other big shots there too, but all of a
sudden John got up and said to me, "Let's go. This is too goddamn
boring." Together we got in his car, which was some foreign job – a
Mercedes or a Porsche – and he started driving back to Pontiac. He must
have hit 110 miles an hour on the freeway, when some cop pulled us
over. John wasn't worried at all. "You stay here," he told me, "I'll take
care of this." He got out of the car and in a few minutes he came back
and somehow everything was all right. I never asked him what he did.
In those days it seemed natural that John De Lorean could do whatever
he wanted to do.'

Hollywood

When news of John Z. De Lorean's second marriage splashed across the society page on 1 June 1969, the *Detroit Free Press* chose to entitle its account, 'Romantic, Private Wedding'. Nevertheless, the morning paper's anonymous reporter managed to cover this 'private' affair with all the detail of a moon launch.

The 'lush setting', the *Free Press* revealed, was the Bel Air Country Club – a playground for movieland's rich and famous in the Brentwood Hills of Los Angeles. Nearly twenty years before, the Mediterranean-style clubhouse had been the sanctuary for the nuptials of no less than Elizabeth Taylor and Nicky Hilton. But according to the paper, the Saturday evening 'De Lorean ceremony' did not even take a backseat to the likes of Liz and Nicky:

> The ceremony took place at seven in the dining room of the club, where exquisite chandeliers and candles lit the scene. Tall windows were pushed open giving a clear view of the rolling green golf course . . . The white-robed Mitchell Boys choir . . . sang as the wedding party descended the three steps from the lobby into the room.
>
> The bride, daughter of Mr and Mrs Tom Harmon of Brentwood evoked the romantic mood when she appeared, veiled in a cascade of French illusion sprinkled with shimmering aurora borealis beads and white forget-me-nots – an effect she and her sister, Mrs Ricky Nelson, excitedly shared in creating . . .
>
> After the ceremony, the wedding party and their guests left the dining room with its baskets of pink and white flowers and retired to a room called 'The Top of the Tee' for cocktails.
>
> This room, decorated in rust tones with comfortable chairs and small tables . . . overlooks the famous symbol of the Bel Air country club – a 212-yard whitewashed suspension bridge over a ravine, from the tenth tee to the tenth green.

A champagne buffet was laid out in a room off the main dining room . . . There were also seafood appetizers . . . [Served on tables covered with pink cloths] the entree was braised beef stroganoff on rice, with green beans. And of course, for dessert there was the five-tier heart-shaped wedding cake – and ice cream.

Just to make sure nothing happened to the cake, it was moved into the dining room just before the ceremony and screened from the guests until the moment for cutting it arrived. The doves and decorations on the confection were tinted, just faintly, with pink.

The tuxedo–clad Bernie Richard's violinists, favorites of many Los Angeles and Palm Springs social affairs, played for the guests from the balcony.

For the occasion De Lorean did bring a little of Detroit with him. His best man was his old mentor and friend, Bunkie Knudsen. Among the ushers was Pete Estes, his predecessor on the rungs of GM's corporate ladder.

However, the event was far from pristine from the vantage point of certain moralistic matrons in De Lorean's hometown. Only six months before John had divorced Elizabeth, his wife of fifteen years and a tireless helpmate in his corporate and social climbing. The new Mrs De Lorean hovered around nineteen – a fact that evidently caused acute embarrassment for a GM spokesman who unchivalrously added two years to Kelly's age when he first told the press of her engagement to De Lorean.

But for many other middle-aged Michigan males De Lorean fulfilled a double fantasy. At forty-four he had landed a statuesque child bride, and at the same time married into a legend. Only a few years older than the groom, the father-in-law, Tom Harmon, had been the idol of every red-blooded boy from De Lorean's era. During the late thirties 'Michigan's Great Harmon' was a one-man football team for the University of Michigan, kicking, punting and running the school varsity team to victory and breaking almost every ground-gaining record along the way. After starring in a film version of his life, he signed up for new heroics as a World War II fighter pilot. Crashing twice over South America and China, he emerged from jungles only after all hope was lost. At the end of the war he returned to Hollywood and married forties film star Elyse Knox. His celebrity assured him a life of lucrative assignments as a broadcaster and investor. To further cement the Harmons in the pantheon of All-American and All-Hollywood families, Kelly's older sister married Ricky – son of Ozzie and Harriet – Nelson.

The bride looked and acted her age. A college art major who dropped out to try modelling, Kelly told one society writer, 'I don't plan to continue a career. My wish is to have a large, happy home filled with children and animals.' The article has her going on to list 'her loves in the following order: "John, riding, snow and water skiing, music, swimming, poetry, Levis, painting and Rag," a puppy she found at the Los Angeles pound two weeks before the wedding.'

And yet, the middle-aged groom did not appear so ridiculous standing next to the teenager. In the previous decade John De Lorean's aging process took an unusual turn. Gone was the paunchy, jowly executive with the sunken eyes. In his place was a reed-slim fellow who boasted to friends of a thirty-one inch waist. De Lorean had not just captured his youth – he had captured an idealized version of his youth. His weak chin had been replaced by a bold, square jaw. The broad bridge of his nose had become thin and more sculpted. His jet black hair had straightened and it hung fashionably to the top of his collar.

De Lorean had not, however, gone to such rejuvenating lengths to lure a new wife. The transformation had started shortly after he became Pontiac general manager in 1965. Kelly Harmon was only the culmination of a spiritual and physical voyage that eventually had De Lorean adopting Hollywood as his second home.

According to Bunkie Knudsen, De Lorean was not the first GM general manager to be tempted by the West Coast. He explains, 'You start travelling more when you become general manager, because all of a sudden you have to be responsible for things like advertising and the dealer phase of the business. In all that travelling, California has a way of jumping out at you. They start inviting you to studios to see commercials made, or the dealers start taking you on the town. There are a lot of flamboyant people on the West Coast and they really know how to turn your head. Some people can ignore the whole thing. But some others start to find any little excuse to get out there.'

De Lorean could not have had a better guide to the pleasures of California life than his old friend John Quirk. To the surprise of his auto industry buddies, Quirk had sold his firm and moved out to the West Coast to become a novelist. 'John was one of the few people who understood my move,' he says. 'I think there were times when we were both restless with life in Detroit, and we enjoyed the finer things other cities could offer. I remember meeting up with John at Le Club in New York some time around 1966. It was a real jet set dive and we were both pretty impressed with it. I thought the whole thing was fun, but I think John saw public relations advantages to those places. As the years went on he seemed to figure out how to get the best table anywhere we went.'

Quirk quickly became ensconced in California's jet set and he was happy to introduce De Lorean to his new social circle. Together, they were early investors in the San Diego Chargers football team, with De Lorean holding an eight per cent chunk. Barron Hilton was among the largest shareholders and one more cocktail companion for the GM executive.

Quirk also introduced De Lorean to Burt Sugarman, a Beverly Hills native and aspiring TV producer. More than ten years younger than De Lorean and Quirk, Sugarman nevertheless fitted comfortably into their crowd. A college drop-out, he had gone from used car dealer to fancy foreign coupé importer. By twenty-eight, he had made his fortune in Maseratis and Excaliburs, and he was set on new horizons. One successful Sugarman television special and game show followed another, eventually leading to an innovative late night rock show, 'Midnight Special'. Round-faced and snub-nosed, Sugarman had a predilection for dating movie stars of the order of Ann-Margret, and flying them to weekend rendezvous. While he enjoyed playing golf and talking cars with De Lorean and Quirk, he could also show his Detroit friends more frenetic ways to spend their leisure time. They rode dirt bikes in the desert, or during the winter took off in Sugarman's private jet for some skiing on Aspen's slopes.

De Lorean was not the only auto luminary in Sugarman's crowd. Others included Roger Penske and Robert Anderson. Penske had gained national fame first as a professional racing driver and later as leader and namesake for the Penske international racing team – an endeavour that led him to a variety of auto-related businesses. A few years older than De Lorean, Anderson was also an up-by-your-bootstraps product of the Detroit system. From the Chrysler Institute he rose to the top of the Chrysler Corporation. When passed over for the company's presidency, he defected to Rockwell International, helping to make the aerospace conglomerate one of the most powerful and profitable corporations in America.

A *Fortune* magazine profile would call Anderson 'a doer, a man of action'. The description fitted Sugarman and Penske as well. These were not faceless corporate drones waiting for superiors to promote them up the company ladder; they were men who were determining their present and their future. With private jets waiting for them at the nearest airport, they were not about to be tethered by such restrictions as commercial airline schedules when their interests or pleasures called.

Of course, De Lorean had his own access to GM's jets and his own band of subalterns to ferry him around any city he landed in. He once told a reporter that GM executives 'travel like an oil sheik'. And yet De Lorean did not have the unbridled power inside GM that Anderson had in Rockwell. And in the mid-sixties he had none of the name recognition or prestige of Sugarman and Penske.

Whether or not he felt the peer pressure of his California golfing buddies, De Lorean started to chafe more and more against the anonymity GM imposed on its top executives. In 1967 Pontiac ads appeared with De Lorean's face as a backdrop or inset. Tom Adams, chairman of Campbell-Ewald, one of the auto industry's largest advertising agencies, remembers that De Lorean's personal imprint did not sit well with corporate management. 'The corporation eventually quashed that sort of advertising. I don't think they wanted one individual to be too strong a force in any aspect of GM's business. The company's policy has always been that the system is more important than the individual. I know John could make a case for personalized advertising, and I could too. But when you're dealing with an organization that has the level of success that General Motors does, you respect their policies.'

The picture De Lorean used in the ads was over five years old, but he was ready to trade in both the photo and the face. 'After a few years of travelling to Hollywood,' his friend Quirk recalls, 'John acquired a real youth fetish. He had stopped smoking, but then he stopped eating too. He became obsessed with food. It almost became difficult eating with him. At one point his weight dropped from two hundred pounds to one hundred sixty.'

De Lorean's exercise was no longer limited to golf. He got up early enough to run and went to the gym religiously three times a week to do weight-lifting.

But while he could change his body, he couldn't change his face – without some help. The adolescent who was forever combing his hair and frowning at his reflection in the mirror was now a man able to afford the best plastic surgeon in the world. By late 1968 De Lorean had undergone a cosmetic restyling that was obvious to even passing acquaintances. Implants in his chin gave him a jutting jaw. His eye-brows were realigned and the bridge of his nose reshaped. The bags were removed from under his eyes and all the lines pulled back out of his face.

Some of his friends were stunned by the sudden change. 'I barely recognized him at first,' one says. 'He wasn't such a bad looking guy before the surgery. In fact, he was a very striking guy.'

'I remember asking him what happened to his face,' Bunkie Knudsen says. 'He told me he had some trouble with his teeth. I know he told other people the scars on his face were due to an auto accident.'

De Lorean was more specific for *Fortune* writer Rush Loving Jr., claiming he went through the windscreen while test-driving a car in late 1968 at a race track in Lime Rock, Connecticut. The accident had to be covered up, he explained, because GM executives were not supposed to engage in such dangerous pursuits. According to Loving, the man who owns Lime Rock never remembers De Lorean driving there, let alone going through a windscreen.

Back in Birmingham De Lorean's first wife, Elizabeth, was able to document the rumours of plastic surgery with bills the Swiss surgeon continued to send to their address. When she talked about her husband to her friends, she called him Peter Pan, and talked of his fears of growing old.

The bills in the mail, though, were her only clues to her husband's life on the West Coast. The couple had stopped living together, friends say, long before. By March of 1968 she had filed for divorce, citing 'extreme cruelty'.

Harsh recriminations followed. He said she could not cope with his new stature; that she failed to become more sophisticated and could not adjust to his California friends. She spoke bitterly of toiling in high society to further his career. They would not settle until the end of the year. She got the house, his new model Pontiac as well as a GM executive discount on future cars, and $375,000 paid out over fifteen years.

De Lorean did not wait for the divorce to come through before he hit the singles scene. His friend Burt Sugarman had become more of a Hollywood mover and shaker. As a result, Quirk says, 'Burt knew a lot of beautiful young girls. Through him, John and I met some very attractive starlets.'

Detroit gossip columns soon had De Lorean being seen at parties with young actresses and models, including one woman who was the star of a competitor's commercials as 'the Dodge Rebellion Girl'.

'John would fly into Beverly Hills and stay at the Bel Air Hotel,' Quirk recalls. 'At about ten we'd go out and hit the discos – places like the Factory and the Daisy on Rodeo Drive. Those were Hollywood's versions of Le Club with all the beautiful people and some flashing lights and rock music thrown in. We'd walk in and stare at those young girls in the mini-skirts, and many of them would come over and talk to us. We were two yokels from Detroit, but not unattractive and obviously successful, and they seemed to like that. We had a lot of fun.'

De Lorean's record of accomplishment at Pontiac, combined with his 'swinger' image, made him a favourite for the auto industry press corps. *Newsweek* featured him in a September 1968 article titled, 'Flashy Cars – And a Flashy Executive'. One line from the article reads, '[A] willingness to pioneer has earned the darkly handsome, six-foot, four-inch De Lorean a reputation as the auto industry's liveliest new executive model.' *Motor Trend* was to be even more effusive a few months later with a piece called, 'King Mover of Motor City'. If De Lorean had been a Roman emperor, writer Julian G. Schmidt gushes, there would have been no Decline and Fall of the empire:

> Whether lip service is paid to De Lorean under the cloistered ceiling of the GM Building's top floor, is irrelevant. Even if [corporate executives] don't realize it, they love him, if for no other

reason than that he represents exactly what they are not, but must be, in order to deal with the changing market. Sure, they're still the ideal image for final decision-makers . . . stable, impeturbable, stoic. But De Lorean epitomizes the ideal tool to insert into the nitty gritty . . . lots of black hair, six feet, four inches tall, slim, athletic, always with that blue shirt, dark blue tie and incredibly tailored blue-black suit that looks more like someone first built the perfectly proportioned suit, then cast John De Lorean in it. As one of our distaff put it, '. . . one of those men at whom a girl could sit and stare all day, warmly'.

Such glowing prose had some GM executives wondering whether De Lorean wasn't paying a personal press agent. But according to one long-time Detroit auto reporter, it didn't take much for De Lorean to attract reporters. 'The auto industry just didn't produce interesting executives,' explains Pat Wright. Once a reporter for *Business Week*, Wright went on to help De Lorean write his autobiography. 'Every auto executive came out of a mould. When you asked them a question, they all said the same thing, and it was never negative. Most of them had a great fear of reporters and that was engendered by the corporate P.R. departments. They felt their job was to keep the executives away from the press. De Lorean was different. He wasn't afraid of the media. He was very willing to talk, and he always said something quotable.'

Well aware that GM executives felt he pandered to the press, De Lorean often agonized over the pains and pleasures of celebrity in his public statements. In one speech he accepted an award and then proceeded to cogitate on the importance of award-giving. The limelight, De Lorean told his audience, should be an inalienable right of every American: 'It goes without saying that the quests for recognition and acceptance are basic human needs. Even the well-fed man hungers for them. Yet, our society, on the whole, parcels out its attention in extreme ways. It often seems that public recognition comes easiest to those who either accomplish far more than anyone can rightfully expect or those who choose or are unable to meet society's minimum requirements.

Sounding like some Marxist press agent, De Lorean concluded the speech with a vision of utopia as a place 'in which recognition and acceptance comes to each man, woman and child according to his needs'.

As De Lorean became more outspoken, he was careful not to criticize General Motors, but still sounded a distinctly unorthodox note by company standards. He even started to question the traditional Republican affiliation of GM executives – one which he and Elizabeth once shared. 'We in Detroit vote Republican,' he told *Motor Trend*'s Schmidt in 1968. 'They nevertheless seem to be our enemies, and the Democrats our friends. When the Republicans are in power, they threaten GM with the anti-trust suit, but as soon as the Democrats come in, they drop it.' De Lorean did not take sides in the upcoming presidential election, but did tell Schmidt, 'both Nixon and Humphrey are two of the most intelligent candidates we've had for some time, but they don't have any colour'.

Before this interview, De Lorean had already aligned himself with Detroit's much more colourful mayor, Jerry Cavanaugh, an unsuccessful candidate for the U.S. Senate. Despite his Democratic affiliation, as a local power-broker Cavanaugh was not anathema to GM top brass, although none of them would support him with the fervour of De Lorean. But politics aside, the press had also labelled the mayor as a swinger – an affiliation that was more after De Lorean's heart. Car executive and candidate enjoyed being celebrity bar-hoppers as much as political glad-handers.

To help run his Senate campaign, Cavanaugh hired Bill Haddad, a former New York journalist and an old Kennedy hand. JFK had appointed Haddad to be the first associate director of the Peace Corps. A two-fisted liberal, Haddad did not hesitate to tell De Lorean what he thought about GM when the two met at a Cavanaugh fundraiser. 'He listened kind of quietly,' Haddad recalls. 'I remember Jerry kicking me under the table trying to shut me up. But De Lorean ended up inviting me out to lunch at the London Chop House [the city's swankiest restaurant], and agreeing with pretty much every criticism I had.'

Very few men of De Lorean's age and position were ready to entertain such anti-establishment views, but in almost every way – politically, physically, intellectually – his internal time clock turned backwards. Despite his forty-plus years, De Lorean loudly declared his allegiance with the youth of America. He donned Nehru jackets and turtleneck sweaters – a feat comparable to running naked down the halls in a company where even engineers grappling with carburettors wore white shirts and ties.

When Snoopy and the Red Baron were the thing, De Lorean had posters of them in his office and talked of naming a car after the cartoon dog. He kept his car radio tuned to the latest popular music, telling *Newsweek*, 'These rock stations, the things they say, what they discuss, that's what counts. It's the cheapest education you can get.'

When other corporate executives condemned youthful protest, De Lorean argued in front of one civic group, 'We should begin . . . by accepting the turmoil of recent years as a healthy sign of rebellion against the possibility of failure.'

While friends like John Quirk attributed De Lorean's cross-generational posturing to a 'youth fetish', the auto executive offered the media sound economic rationale for his identification with youth. He told

54

Look: 'Since the dawn of mankind, youth has led the way in fashions, and the auto industry is basically a fashion industry. What youth is interested in today becomes tomorrow's products. This small-car thing really has been a youth movement, and we are responding. Today's kids are much smarter than the kids of my day.'

His pronouncements on the wisdom of 'kids' did not stop De Lorean's advancement through General Motors. As long as he continued to produce, his superiors were willing to abide by his idiosyncracies. If anything, a separate standard developed around him. 'The fact that John could walk into work wearing a pair of tennis shoes and an open-neck shirt didn't mean the company was changing,' one engineer says. 'The rest of us knew that they'd never allow us to do the same thing.'

De Lorean's attraction to youth was ultimately certified by his engagement to nineteen-year-old Kelly Harmon in February 1969. The move shook Detroit's snooty suburban society to its core, but it also revealed De Lorean's self-confidence that his personal life was not about to affect his future at GM. Only weeks before he announced his engagement, he was appointed general manager of Chevrolet, the corporation's largest division. News of the promotion reached him on the twelfth tee of the Thunderbird Country club in Palm Springs. His marching orders had him putting down the clubs and returning to Detroit before he finished the game.

Of those three years De Lorean spent at Chevrolet, Smokey Yunick says, 'It was probably the happiest period of John's career. Here he was, still a pretty young cat, and he had one of the biggest jobs in America, with a big salary to go with it. He might have faced problems at Chevy, but you wouldn't have known it. Everything was a kick.'

All by itself, Chevrolet in 1969 was among the ten largest manufacturing companies in the world. The division alone almost sold as many cars as all of Ford. But, in *On a Clear Day You Can See General Motors*, De Lorean depicts Chevy as being a shambles by the time he took the reins: its share of the market falling, its products outdated, and its management half-buried in bureaucracy.

Robert Dewey was Chevrolet's financial co-ordinator for eight assembly plants at the time, and later would be the first financial officer for De Lorean's car company. Dewey does not remember Chevrolet being anywhere as bad as De Lorean claims in the book, but he does say, 'It became a poorly managed division. I don't think that was totally the fault of the general managers who were in before John. The division had been the cash cow for the company, so it was extremely difficult to innovate there. Nobody wanted to change the formula and risk the tremendous income Chevy was bringing into GM.'

That income, as Dewey later explained, permitted a 'proliferation' of management layers inside the division – a situation compounded by De Lorean's predecessor at Chevrolet, Pete Estes. 'Pete was a guy who wanted to make all the decisions. When he arrived at Chevrolet, though, he got buried in detail and nothing seemed to get done. Everyone sat around waiting for Pete to tell them what to do.'

De Lorean's management style, Dewey says, was to contrast sharply with Estes'. 'I think the best thing John did as a manager was to delegate responsibility to other people. That gave him time to lift up his head and look at the big picture. He was very demanding and he expected you to do the best possible job. But he had the leadership qualities to make you believe you were equal to the task. In the finance area where I was involved he introduced the zero budget concept. Instead of the various departments coming to us and asking for increases over last year's budget, they had to justify their whole budget. Obviously it created a lot of work and pressure for me, but I could see how the whole process was saving a lot of money.'

De Lorean tried to upgrade Chevy's product line, but he was forced to execute decisions made years before his arrival. Car development was no longer the focus of his energies as it had been at Pontiac. 'Really his most important product contribution at Chevrolet,' Dewey says, 'was the truck programme. John saw that as an area where we could dramatically increase market share and he barnstormed the idea around the company. He felt that a major stumbling block to increasing sales was the placement of the gas tank. In those days it was behind the driver's seat. He wanted to take it out of the cab and put it under the chassis. Of course there was a cost penalty in doing that, but this was one case where added cost brought back much more with increased sales of trucks.'

For all his leadership qualities, De Lorean became less patient with subordinates – especially engineers. 'John wouldn't mind dressing down some engineer in front of a group of fifty people,' Dewey recalls. 'He seemed to have reached the point where he became contemptuous of engineers, and often the demands he made on them were just unrealistic. For example, during the truck programme, I remember he wanted the tank engineers to channel the fuel in a way that the laws of physics would not allow. John just didn't want to hear that.'

As a student at Lawrence Tech De Lorean had described an engineer 'as trapped in a terrible tower of pure science'. As a General Motor general manager he had broken out of that tower and was ready to let others contend with the prisons of gravity and themodynamics. Marketing, advertising – these were the areas of expertise he now espoused, and they flowed almost naturally with the currents of his career: he had gone from the engineer wrestling with transmissions to the stylist shaping fenders to the advertising man, lifting his product beyond mere substance to the realm of image.

'I really think the day of the chief engineer becoming general manager is about over,' De Lorean told Automotive Industries in 1972. 'The problem that we are looking at in the future is really going to be more in the area of marketing than anything else.'

At Pontiac and Chevrolet De Lorean directed much of his attention to the nuts-and-bolts aspects of marketing. GM, he claimed, wasn't even doing basic consumer research. In *On A Clear Day*, he charges, 'the General Motors marketing effort is guided by men whose training in buyer psychology is no deeper than the Dale Carnegie course they all are required to take, and whose idea of sophisticated sales is having a few drinks with the dealers'.

Despite the drinks, De Lorean discovered, dealers were seldom made to feel they were valued members of the GM team. Most general managers, like De Lorean, rose through the ranks as engineers and had little preparation for interacting with dealers.

The in-bred hostility that has existed between the two is ironic, because in many cases both the dealer and the executive have worked their way out of lower-class neighbourhoods. But the dealer keeps the common touch, as he must, to stay in tune with his customers. And the sort of flamboyance that a dealer needs to sell cars and stay in business is the exact opposite of the reserved, unassuming nature most ambitious executives maintain as they rise through the corporation. As the motor industry has grown, the 'factory' and the franchise have polarized into two warring camps.

Bunkie Knudsen was among the rare general managers who felt he had to keep peace with his dealers, and De Lorean learned dealer relations at his knee. Knudsen spent considerable time criss-crossing the country making calls – with plenty of warning – on Pontiac, and later, Chevrolet dealerships. Often he boned up on names and faces before he blew in for a tour, shocking people he had not seen in years when he asked, by name, after their wives and children.

De Lorean picked up where Knudsen left off. Unlike most other GM executives, De Lorean had tried his hand at sales in his youth, and he found a kindred spirit in the car dealer. In fact, during the course of his business life, he would number more dealers and car salesmen as close friends than motor executives.

Chevy dealers were pleasantly surprised to finally find a general manager on their side. For a time, in the late sixties, George Williams' Los Angeles dealership led the nation in sales. 'Most dealers thought John was great,' Williams says. 'He wasn't a bullshitter. He meant what he said. And he wasn't a corporate man. When we complained about the factory, he'd agree and not come up with excuses. It was like John and us against corporate.'

However, De Lorean's concerns for marketing went beyond his relationship with dealers. He also took an active part in Chevrolet's advertising campaign, and considering the amount of space he devotes to that role in his book, it was clearly a labour of love.

He writes that during his first months at Chevy he became worried by the 'effectiveness and memorability' of the division's television commercials. In concert with Chevy's ad agency, Campbell-Ewald, he says he devised the high-minded 'See the USA in your Chevrolet' campaign that would both sell cars and help restore the consumer's faith in his nation: 'At this time the country was split in the midst of the Vietnam conflict . . . [and] racked with racial conflict. The institutions of the United States including big business, were under fire . . . We wanted to reaffirm our position in the minds of American consumers by building our image around the good aspects of this country and the good aspects of our cars.

'We discussed this approach with the agency, and it developed a campaign around a theme that said, "We live in a great and beautiful country and our car with its instant availability gives you the opportunity to get out and see this beautiful country." If there is one thing that America has, it is fantastic and diverse topography, from the Grand Canyon to Pikes Peak; from the geometrically-shaped wheat fields of the plains states to the sleepy Smoky Mountains of Tennessee . . . We put our cars in these beautiful settings alongside of clean-cut, middle American families with whom just about everybody could identify.'

While De Lorean no doubt meant well with his commercials, much more interesting is the palliative effect he thought they would have on the country; as though 'fantastic and diverse topography' could somehow heal deep social schisms, and not just add a gloss as superficial as the wax shine on a car.

De Lorean gives credit for the ad campaign to the Campbell-Ewald agency and its chairman, Tom Adams. The creative people only got a 'freer hand,' he says, when he stuck out his neck for them with corporate staff. Today, Adams agrees that De Lorean was helpful and had a flair for marketing, 'He was never too busy to attend any meeting that concerned advertising or merchandising. Obviously he loved those things, which is why he always found time for them. He got more involved in the preparation of advertising material than any general manager before or since, but that caused some problems for the agency with the corporate staff. John was too impatient to follow company procedures. He didn't want to wait and give due consideration to the guidelines everyone else had to live by. As he gained more power and authority, he created his own procedures. We were often caught in between his impatience and corporate policy.'

While Adams could see some benefits in De Lorean's close involvement with advertising, he could also see pure ego gratification as well. At one point, the Chevrolet general manager had Campbell-Ewald print up thousands of posters featuring De Lorean and the son he had adopted, Zachary. They were sent for Christmas greetings to dealers and De Lorean's friends around the country.

Although De Lorean's position at Chevy might have presented the world with a picture of domestic bliss, in reality the demanding job was destroying his family. In many ways, friends say, Zachary's adoption had been a desperate attempt to save De Lorean's second marriage. He had tried unsuccessfully throughout both marriages to have children and believed his own infertility was to blame. For all his reputation as a swinger, those closest to De Lorean feel he never wanted anything more than the sort of 'clean-cut middle American' family he put in the Chevy ads. Children were just as important to Kelly Harmon, as she let everybody know in interviews before the wedding. But the two had drifted too far apart by the time Zachary Thomas [the first name for John's father; the middle name for Kelly's] arrived.

Looking back, it would seem that De Lorean tried hard to accommodate his young bride. An avid rider, Kelly shipped her horse to Bloomfield Hills, and the couple joined the local Hunt Club, but the genteel horse owners were soon grumbling about the new members. Kelly favoured jeans over jodhpurs, and her husband, not loathe to show off his weight-lifting, often wandered the grounds shirtless. De Lorean had never been on a horse before he met Kelly, but he cut back on his golf game to learn how to ride, and ended up cracking two ribs in the process when one nag bucked him to the ground.

He did not drag Kelly to cocktail parties or formal dinner parties. As he explained to one reporter, 'Since neither my wife nor I drink, we'd frankly rather take a twilight horseback ride or a late run down the ski slope than go to any party.'

Kelly wanted to extend her love for children, horses and the great outdoors into charity work and turned to a camp for underprivileged youth in Detroit's suburbs. When Kelly suggested opening her own camp, Tom Harmon put De Lorean together with a California real estate agent who ranged the country looking for a suitable site. Strangely enough, they settled on a cattle ranch scooped out of the foothills of the Bitterroot Mountains in the remote reaches of Idaho. De Lorean shelled out close to a million dollars for the property and some adjoining parcels in the fall of 1971. Before the year was out, he and Kelly were looking for another ranch in a mountainous area a few hours out of San Diego.

However much property the De Loreans assembled, they still ended up with less time to share together. When he was climbing up the corporate ladder at Pontiac, De Lorean's first wife, Elizabeth, was willing to put up with his seventy-hour weeks, but Kelly was not so anxious to languish alone in their big Bloomfield Hills house while John toiled at Chevrolet.

When Arthur Hailey's *Wheels* hit the bestseller lists in 1971, Detroit gossips quickly deciphered what they took to be a *roman à clef*. They soon pegged De Lorean as Adam Trenton, the book's hard-charging middle-aged executive whose long hours at the office leave his much younger wife sexually frustrated at home.

De Lorean would later blame the dissolution of his second marriage on the gossips of Detroit's auto society. Kelly, he says in *On a Clear Day*, '[was] never accepted by the tight social circle of GM wives who were much older. While we rarely socialized with GM people, we were frequently thrust together at corporate functions or in the suburban clubs of Detroit, and the reaction to her, while not hostile, was cool and diffident. Kelly's California background and the cool reception she received in the automotive circles made her yearn for more time back home.'

John Quirk does not remember Kelly's reception the same way. The problem, he says, was Kelly and not GM wives. Quirk too had divorced a first wife of many years to marry a much younger woman, who was twenty-one. 'My [second] wife had no trouble adjusting,' he adds, 'and was treated very warmly by the women in the community. Kelly was just one of those young girls who couldn't leave her father's house. She might have seen her father in John when they married, but afterwards there was nothing John could do that would match Tom Harmon in Kelly's eyes.

'Whenever something important came up where John wanted Kelly by his side, she was back in California, watching her brother play quarterback for UCLA or just visiting with her parents.'

In December 1971 De Lorean rented a bungalow on Laguna Beach in California and during the next year Kelly was to stay there more than in Detroit. In August 1972 she asked for an official separation.

At first, De Lorean did not admit, even to friends, that his wife had left him. Later that month *Signature* Magazine prepared a profile on De Lorean, and one steamy day, Chicago photographer Arthur Shay was sent to the subject's Bloomfield Hills home to get a picture of husband and wife.

Already, word had leaked out that De Lorean was about to become a member of the company's top executive staff. It was the sort of promotion, the magazine figured, that would soon make De Lorean the corporation's youngest president ever. But when Shay arrived for the picture session, he did not find an ecstatic *Wunderkind*. Instead, a sullen De Lorean answered the door, wearing only a pair of jeans.

'He must have had eight different types of car sitting in the driveway,' Shay remembered. 'But except for his dogs, I realized that no one else was around. The whole place was deserted. He acted very cordially, but it was clear that he wanted me to get the picture-taking over with.'

Actually Shay had not come just to meet De Lorean, but Kelly as well, for a few shots of the happy couple. He explains, 'I had expected to photograph him with his wife, and he seemed to be very embarrassed that she wasn't there. He didn't tell me they were separated. He just said she was away. The best I could manage was a shot of him sitting under her portrait. He was very easy with the camera, like a show biz person, but there was no way I could make him smile that day. He was pretty down.

'After we were finished he went out in his backyard with golf bag. He seemed eager to get back to work on his golf swing.'

Falling From the Fourteenth Floor

On 28 August 1972, John Z. De Lorean ascended to the Fourteenth Floor of General Motors' world headquarters. Chevrolet's chief *enfant terrible* had been appointed group executive for the car and truck divisions – and by all appearances was headed only for corporate greatness. 'To most GM employees,' he writes in *On A Clear Day*, 'rising to the Fourteenth Floor is the final scene in their Horatio Alger dream. The Mt. Olympus of business. The place where the biggest corporate decisions are made. Getting there assures that you'll be a millionaire.'

Getting there, at the relatively young age of forty-eight, De Lorean argues, gave him 'a better than even–odds chance of one day being [GM] president'. Back in the days following De Lorean's appointment, it is very likely that few in Detroit would have disagreed with his assessment.

But in only seven months, the odds-on president tumbled from the Fourteenth Floor.

His departure from General Motors shocked the industry, and years later the circumstances surrounding his exit still remain murky, although De Lorean has always maintained that he left of his own accord. The press releases of the time say that, but he was given the sort of severance package that usually went to smooth the ruffled feathers of executives the company had jettisoned. Under the condition that he did not defect to another motor company he was given a letter of intent to open a Cadillac franchise in Lighthouse Point, Florida, just north of Miami Beach, and one of the most desirable locations in the country. In time, he readily accepted the media's characterization as the man who 'quit' General Motors'. But all the while, there has been a widespread rumour that as a result of internal investigations De Lorean was fired. There are inconsistencies in both stories, however.

But enough information has been uncovered at least to dispute De Lorean's version of his last days at General Motors. In fact, by his own statements during litigation that occurred years later, De Lorean has revealed that his GM superiors could have found ample justification for dismissing the young vice president. His ability to emerge from the corporation with his reputation unscathed remains one of De Lorean's greatest achievements.

In the light of this, De Lorean's jump to the Fourteenth Floor no longer looks like a promotion, but a kick upstairs and a few steps removed from a boot out the window. When De Lorean's three predecessors as Chevrolet general manager rose to the Fourteenth Floor, they became group vice-presidents. He, however, was consigned to the lower tier of group executives. A subtle ignominy perhaps, but all the more curious considering that Chevrolet was not doing so badly under his leadership.

It is surprising that his sudden yank from Chevrolet was not viewed suspiciously at the time. He had served the division as general manager for only two-and-a-half years. Although sales had plummeted in 1970 and 1971, the drop was due mostly to a strike followed by a recession, and in 1972, when the economy revived, Chevrolet was on the way to a record earnings year. De Lorean had not come near 30 per cent of the market share he boldly predicted he would reach, but he still deserved another few years to hit his goal. Considering the importance of Chevrolet to the entire corporation, headquarters might have been expected to give De Lorean the chance. His predecessor, Pete Estes, had taken the division on a tailspin, and even he got three-and-a-half years before his 'promotion'.

Evidently it was not the division's bottom line that had shortened De Lorean's Chevy tenure. Other factors were involved and they point to the April 1972 issue of the *Gallagher Report*, a weekly newsletter written for marketing, advertising and media executives. One item reads: '*DICK GERSTENBERG TAKES HARD LOOK AT CHEVRO-LET*. New General Motors chairman unhappy with performance of Chevrolet general manager John De Lorean. Too many outside interests. De Lorean part owner of San Diego Chargers pro football team . . . Still under cloud from internal investigation of kickbacks from Chevrolet suppliers . . .'

The blurb infuriated De Lorean and he had his lawyer John Noonan hire a private investigator to find out where the newsletter got the information. His sleuth never did manage to track down the source. But the report touched on more than just idle or malicious gossip.

It was no secret in Detroit that De Lorean had outside interests. They were more extensive than the football team, and more potentially embarrassing for the corporation. Just a few days before he made the *Gallagher Report*, De Lorean became a founding member of the board for Grand Prix of America – the brainwave of his younger brother, Jack.

The idea was to franchise racetracks for miniature Wankel-engine racing cars. The public could pay a per lap fee to race against a time clock. The company leased some land in Troy, Michigan for the pilot racetrack. Coincidentally enough, their landlord was North American Rockwell, the company run by John's old transcontinental golfing buddy, Bob Anderson. More important from GM's point of view, Rockwell's automotive division was a major supplier for Chevrolet and the rest of the car industry.

Another of De Lorean's extracurricular affairs had surfaced the year before when the Securities and Exchange Commission listed him among the directors of Patrick Petroleum Company, an oil and gas exploration firm in Jackson, Michigan. De Lorean first met the company's president, U.E. Patrick, on the auto racing circuit and the two struck up a close working relationship (Patrick was also among the early Grand Prix investors). No one in General Motors was more vocal than De Lorean about the company's need for fuel-efficient vehicles, but his prescience about the on-coming energy shortage was not about to stop him from cashing in on the rest of the business world's short-sightedness. Although De Lorean did not let the oil investments muzzle his calls for small cars, some top GM executives still saw his role with Patrick Petroleum as the height of hypocrisy.

They were further enraged when a newspaper reported that De Lorean sold 1100 shares of GM stock to buy his interest in the oil company. He later explained that the stock had gone towards the purchase of a ranch in Idaho. But his explanation did not sit any better with GM management, who have always worried that one executive's sale of GM stock, if large enough, could touch off a bearish binge on Wall Street.

And yet, just De Lorean's outside investments were not enough to get him fired. Many other GM executives before and after have been heavily involved as directors or investors in other ventures. Far more serious were the allegations of what the *Gallagher Report* called 'kick-backs'.

Ironically, De Lorean touched on the problems of upper management corruption in his book's most controversial chapter, 'How Moral Men Make Immoral Decisions'. One of the tales he tells concerns an auto dealer friend of Ed Cole's who twice got the opportunity to purchase GM real estate and soon after sell the plots for much higher prices (the dealer later unsuccessfully sued De Lorean and co-author Pat Wright for libel). De Lorean does not accuse Cole of reaping any part of that dealer's profits, but elsewhere in the chapter, without naming names, he claims, '. . . there were disturbing activities in upper management in which executives used their positions of power and knowledge to profit *personally* in corporate business. These were by no means widespread and perhaps confined to only a few individuals.'

De Lorean's management style as general manager itself attracted criticism. As Tom Adams explains, 'John had the habit of directly contacting suppliers and bringing them into the fold even before we had the chance to go through departmental procedures. Oft times his selections were right and he managed to pick the people who could best do the job. But even though he was periodically right, it didn't make his arrangements very pleasant or proper when he imposed them on the rest of us.'

One particular deal looms large in De Lorean's legacy at General Motors. In the spring of 1971 De Lorean convened a meeting of his top marketing people at Chevrolet for a special presentation. The guests of honour were two advertising men from Hollywood, Milton Bradley Scott and Peck Prior, who claimed to have a product that would revolutionize the American car dealership. They called it the Mini-Theater. Although the device looked like a television, it actually contained a tiny movie projector and a cartridge of super 8 film capable of running over and over in a continuous loop.

Loaded with films that displayed Chevrolet products, Scott explained, the Mini-Theater would illustrate for any customer all of a car's selling points including those which the salesman couldn't begin to demonstrate or even remember.

The concept was not entirely new, and other technologies like the video cassette recorder seemed more promising than Scott's repeating film cartridge – at least video cassettes could be reused; the film had to be thrown away.

But Scott got the contract with Chevrolet, and according to a *Los Angeles Times* reporter, 'found himself – almost instantly – with more than three million dollars of business'. The Mini-Theater was no GM give-away for Chevrolet dealers. Each month they paid twenty-one dollars for the machine and owned it after two years. They spent an additional $250 each model year for a set of cartridges and $150 for a stand. Some of Chevrolet's 6,500 dealers were not so eager to get into the business, but the factory helped change their mind. 'There was a little arm twisting [by GM],' one California dealer told the *Times*, 'but nobody got hurt – the arm wasn't dislocated.'

Actually, Scott's deal with Chevrolet meant he had all of GM sewn up when the other divisions got into the Mini-Theater act. Many Chevy dealers were also distributors of other GM cars, and the corporation was not so cruel as to foist on them film systems incompatible with the Chevrolet Mini-Theater.

In his arrangement with Chevrolet, Scott was the consummate middleman. His company, United Visuals Corporation, supplied nothing directly to GM. Instead it subcontracted for almost all the services. The projector and cartridge system were the patented products of Technicolor Incorporated. General Motors advertising agencies produced the films. Someone else cut and reproduced the seven-minute reels.

For Scott, the most crucial link in the whole deal was his friendship with John De Lorean. No other connection mattered more. In fact, as both men later testified in court papers, their personal relationship was established long before Scott showed up in Detroit to demonstrate the Mini-Theater.

They first met through De Lorean's film producer friend, Burt Sugarman. An advertising man who once counted the TV-oriented Church of God as his clients, Scott had for some time hovered around West Coast auto circles. At one point, he was a product agent, getting cars on game shows as prizes or in movies as props. For a while he ran his own Chevrolet dealership in Modesto, California. Among his most prized possessions were two Rolls Royces, one of 1920 vintage.

Scott smoothly slipped into De Lorean's jet set crowd. Also tall and athletic (he had been a gymnast in college), Scott could join De Lorean and Rockwell president Bob Anderson for games of golf and tennis.

One of Scott's employees from those days remembers a Christmas party Scott threw in his Beverly Hills penthouse apartment. 'De Lorean showed up, and Scott didn't leave his side for the rest of the evening.

'The only people he ever talked about were De Lorean and Anderson. I felt that he always aspired to that sort of corporate power, and he was ready to do anything to be a part of their lives.'

While suitably flamboyant for Hollywood, if necessary Scott could tone down his image in the company of De Lorean or Anderson. The former employee says, 'What fascinated me about Milt was the way he'd change, like a chameleon, when he had to go to Detroit. He'd take off the gold, and put on a conservative suit and tie. He'd even talk differently to blend into the scene.'

Scott brought some of his own famous friends into De Lorean's circle, including E. Gregory Hookstratten, Hollywood's most powerful celebrity lawyer, whose clients included Elvis Presley, Tom Snyder, Cary Grant and a number of professional athletes, sports broadcasters, coaches and team owners. Hookstratten became one more partner for a good game of golf. Soon after he met De Lorean, Hookstratten represented him in his divorce from Kelly Harmon.

Yet another figure moved on the periphery of this glittering crowd; a man of much lesser accomplishment than the others, but of far greater importance to John De Lorean's career. Roy Sigurd Nesseth's entrée to De Lorean and Scott had been through Burt Sugarman's pharmacist father. Nesseth's greatest stature had been as manager of the Los Angeles dealership, Williams Chevrolet, the nation's best seller.

At six feet and six inches, Nesseth was a man of overbearing size and temperament. He could wash total strangers away with his charm – an ability that made him one of the best car salesmen in southern California. But when his powers of persuasion failed him, he could bully or explode in a fear-inspiring rage. His temper, and what one judge described as 'his fast and loose' way of doing business, had Roy most often finishing his battles in court. As the years passed, all the luminaries who once surrounded De Lorean at Hollywood parties drifted away. Only Nesseth remained. De Lorean's other friends have often wondered about the tie that bound Nesseth and De Lorean together; it was first fastened by Scott and his company, United Visuals Corporation.

All the details concerning United Visuals have only emerged in recent years as Scott has fought with De Lorean and Nesseth for the proceeds of the defunct company. In 1976 Scott sold its assets to Technicolor. Nesseth has sued, claiming he possessed an option – assigned to him by De Lorean – for 49 per cent of United Visual. The suit was still unresolved when De Lorean was arrested by federal agents.

Nesseth once talked of United Visuals with an associate of C.R. Brown, former chief of US operations for the De Lorean Company. The company, he said, provided the 'seed money' for future Nesseth and De Lorean ventures. Most likely, United Visuals also provided the seeds for De Lorean's downfall at General Motors.

Both sides dispute where the idea for the Mini-Theater actually came from. Scott says it was entirely conceived by him and Prior. De Lorean argues in court depositions that Scott and Prior had only thought of using the system to show cartoon clips and National Football League highlights to lure people into the dealership. It was Nesseth, De Lorean claims, who suggested the Mini-Theater be used to actually help sell the cars with demonstration films, and it was Nesseth too, he says, who worked out the two-year lease package offered to dealers.

In any case, De Lorean does not hedge about the importance of his influence in getting Scott the contract with Chevrolet in 1971. While the division's marketing people were interested in the concept, De Lorean testifies, they wanted to go to experienced contractors like the Jam Handy Corporation to implement the project. 'I said, "That's unfair. [Scott] brought the idea in here." ' De Lorean goes on to explain that Scott still had to win a competitive bid, but he adds as well, 'Everybody knew that Scott was a personal friend of mine and that I interceded to protect him . . .

'I think without me, there was no question he had no business at all. I helped him a tremendous amount.'

Of course, while taking the credit for United Visuals' existence, De Lorean denies in his deposition that he had ever been a shareholder or involved in the company's day-to-day operations. Among the original shareholders were Scott, Prior and laywer Hookstratten, who also served as treasurer for the corporation. De Lorean has claimed that Scott promised Nesseth 17½ per cent of the stock, and Nesseth was on the company's payroll for about a year starting in April 1972. 'We never really understood what Roy was doing at United Visuals,' one co-worker remembers. 'Looking back, he could have been De Lorean's man on the scene. He certainly didn't get along very well with Milt.'

Although De Lorean did not directly benefit from United Visuals while he was at General Motors, he was financially involved with Scott in other deals. In yet another lawsuit, involving Grand Prix racing, De Lorean explains that he moved funds in and out of a Scott bank account without Scott's knowledge because they were partners in a business. In court testimony he said, '[Scott and I] owned a joint business and [$65,000 was] taken from my part of the joint business . . . And, of course, at that time [Scott] was an officer of that company.

'It was a company that had a lighting concession in Las Vegas – it was a GE distributor for light bulbs in Vegas. It's a little bit complex, but the whole point was [that the $65,000] was deducted from my share of that business when it was liquidated, so it turned out to be my investment entirely; but at that point in time, the money was borrowed essentially from Scott, but [also] from my portion of the jointly owned business.'

De Lorean went on to describe the company in his testimony: 'We bought a lighting company in Las Vegas that had the concession for the GE light bulbs with the idea that because of all the light bulbs, it was going to be a tremendous success. It turned out it wasn't.'

When De Lorean was asked about his share in the lighting company, he replied, 'It was a partnership,' claiming further that he owned a 50 per cent interest. However, he also admitted that everything connected with the company was in Scott's name.

Scott also mentions a lighting company in his declaration for the United Visuals case. According to him, the Las Vegas firm was liquidated by June 1973 and that Nesseth helped him close it down. De Lorean left GM in April 1973. It is unlikely that he would have participated as a fifty/fifty partner in the lighting company for only the last two months of its existence, and his involvement with Scott's Las Vegas venture must have stretched back into his tenure at General Motors. If it had been discovered by GM executives, as some now say it was, the deal could have been seen as a payoff for the United Visuals contract. Considering the fate of the lighting company, it was not a very good payoff.

De Lorean moved to secure far more lucrative arrangements with Scott after his resignation from GM was announced. Officially, for the next year he was still in GM employment as a consultant as the company gave him a $200,000 salary to serve as president of the National Alliance of Business – a non-profit group supporting employment for the disadvantaged.

In August 1973, Scott says, De Lorean got a loan for $300,000 from United Visuals. The note, however, was in Scott's and not the company's name. In his court declaration, Scott explains, 'Mr De Lorean required that the promissory note be made payable to my order because he did not want there to be any documents indicating that he had any connection with United Visuals Corporation because of his then employment with General Motors Corporation.'

In return for the money, Scott claims, he believed he would get half-interest in the Florida Cadillac dealership De Lorean got as severance from GM. Scott never got a piece of the dealership, nor did he ever get his money back. De Lorean's side of the story is that Scott had to raise much more money for his part of the franchise. When he failed to come up with the more than million dollars needed, De Lorean had to rush elsewhere to find backing – a move he claimed which damaged him. Curiously, Scott has never sued to recover the funds. In his own deposition De Lorean brazenly admits that he still had the $300,000: 'Someday we'll have a lawsuit whether I was damaged by [Scott's] retreating . . . I keep the money in escrow in my Christmas fund when Scott's ready to sue.'

But $300,000 is not all De Lorean got out of Scott after he left GM. In December 1973, Scott gave him an option for 49 per cent of United Visuals. According to the declaration Scott filed in court, De Lorean paid nothing for the option: 'Although the [option] indicates that I received consideration, nothing of any value was transferred to anyone and the recital in the document that I received consideration is completely erroneous. Mr De Lorean dictated the substance of the letter.'

In his testimony, De Lorean denies that he forced the option on Scott. His explanation has it the other way around. After he left GM, De Lorean claims, Scott 'no longer had the great protector in the corporation'. Scott, he says, was afraid GM would then cancel the United Visual contract. 'He pleaded with me to become involved. He wanted me to be chairman. I made a certain number of calls and talked to various people to try to help him along . . . [Finally,] he insisted I accept this option.'

However Scott felt about the option when he gave it to De Lorean, a year later he considered it dead and buried. By this time the two had fallen out over the dealership in Florida and the $300,000 loan. In a final letter asking for his money back, Scott threatened to revoke the option as payment for the note. 'Under any circumstance,' he wrote, 'I will consider the disposition of $300,000 plus interest as full satisfaction of any obligation or understanding relating to your involvement with United Visuals Corporation.'

Scott did not hear any more about the option for over a year until he tried to sell out to Technicolor. De Lorean at first wired Scott to tell him he wanted to exercise the option. De Lorean explains that when Scott refused, 'I really wasn't in the mood to try to take legal recourse . . . I know he treated Roy very badly. Roy had done a lot of work for me in various areas, so I assigned the option to Roy.' As he was to do so often in De Lorean's business career, Nesseth forged into the courtroom to fight De Lorean's battles – a cross between a hired litigious samurai and a kamikaze. De Lorean claimed the two had no 'arrangement' to divvy up the take if Roy did win his lawsuit against Scott.

If back in 1972 GM officials could have foreseen how the United Visuals affair ended up, they probably would have fired De Lorean on the spot. However, at least three different sources confirm that De Lorean's superiors knew enough about United Visuals to get him out of Chevrolet as soon as they could. While the roost on the Fourteenth Floor was a sort of punishment, it was also a second chance. If De Lorean had bided his time, all indiscretions would have been forgiven. He might have had his chance at the presidency, although not to succeed Ed Cole when he retired in 1974. But perhaps after that.

After his 'promotion' to the Fourteenth Floor, De Lorean could no longer hang out with his old crowd and feel like a fellow mover and shaker. Much of the work in his new job was paper shuffling: reading reports and preparing for meetings. In his three decades at GM, Bob McLean remembers some division general managers who turned down the Fourteenth Floor. 'At the top of a division, you're already a chief executive,' he says. 'You have all those departments and assistants under you. You have drivers picking you up in the morning and people escorting you wherever you go. Then suddenly, you go to the Fourteenth Floor and it's culture shock. You just don't get any respect – whatever you do, wherever you go. Some of the executives up there don't even have their own secretaries. They share them with other executives. It's unbelievable, but even as you're on the way to running the company, the GM system first makes you feel like the lowliest functionary.

'De Lorean didn't take long to let everyone know how bored he was with the Fourteenth Floor. At that stage of his life, he just didn't want to sit through meetings.'

In *On a Clear Day* De Lorean offers two rather contradictory reasons for why he left General Motors. One concerns a management cabal out to get him fired. The other involves his growing disenchantment with the company's style and philosophy. But if De Lorean was so disillusioned by GM anyway, what did it matter whether some conspiracy formed to force him out? The group would only do him a favour.

Among his enemies, De Lorean counted Dolly Cole, wife of the president, Ed Cole, and three GM vice-presidents: Oscar A. Lundin, in charge of finance; Anthony G. De Lorenzo, public relations head; and Richard L. Terrell, De Lorean's immediate superior on the Fourteenth Floor. Information about the anti-De Lorean clique in GM, the victim reports, came from his friends who heard Dolly Cole gossip over lunch at the Plaza in New York.

De Lorean never quite understood Dolly Cole's enmity. A beautiful woman much younger than her husband, Dolly married Ed shortly after he divorced his first wife. Her friends say she always resented the acid way De Lorean used to kid Ed, especially about her. The GM executives, De Lorean learned, 'had a personal vendetta against me, and that they were using every means at their disposal to discredit me'.

One of those means, De Lorean charged, was to leak a speech he had prepared for a November 1972 management conference in Greenbrier, North Carolina. While some of his statements touted Ed Cole's fruitless and wasteful pursuit of the Wankel rotary engine, De Lorean also delivered a warning that 'poor quality threatens to destroy us'. He added that 'every defect, each recall, only diminishes the credibility of whatever amount of advertising we do . . . Significantly, there has been a serious and disturbing decline in loyalty among the owners of GM products, especially in head-to-head comparisons with Ford.'

Before he had a chance to deliver the speech, his remarks were reported in the *Detroit News* by veteran reporter Robert Irvin. De Lorean denied having anything to do with the leak, and a short time later, he writes in *On a Clear Day*, another friend at lunch – this time in Detroit – ran across a private investigator who knew GM's operation and who told him that the speech was leaked by a man on the GM public relations staff.

He does not mention that at his own insistence, GM hired a private investigator to track down the leak – the same man De Lorean had once hired to find the source of the *Gallagher Report* rumour. This time the detective's work was far more extensive, but before he had a chance to hand in his report, De Lorean was already on his way out. The investigator never got paid for his effort. Although he never definitely confirmed his theory, the investigator suspected that a GM public relations official close to De Lorean, and not opposed to him, released the speech. As for reporter Irvin, he had worked amicably with De Lorean before the Greenbrier incident, and did a few favourable profiles about him even after he left GM.

Once, back in 1971, De Lorean says, in a moment of disillusion with the auto industry he had asked to resign and was talked out of it. But in 1972, he would ask again, going to Thomas A. Murphy, GM vice-chairman who was heir apparent to the chairmanship after Richard Gerstenberg retired. De Lorean says Murphy told him, 'Jeez, I don't see why you want to leave. Nine chances out of ten, when Cole leaves, you'll be the next president.'

De Lorean was still a rank below Estes and Terrell, who were in fact the favourites for the job. Never before had a GM executive leap-frogged as suddenly or dramatically into the presidency as De Lorean would have had to do according to his report of Murphy's words.

De Lorean says that after Murphy tried to dissuade him he wrote a scathing report 'aimed directly at a lot of corporate people and their actions'. He explains further, 'I figured this memo would demonstrate to management that we could no longer exist together and that it was in their best interests to let me resign on my terms'. Soon after, he says, Murphy told him, 'John, I may have done you a disservice in the past when I said you should stay with the corporation. It is pretty obvious you are unhappy and perhaps you should leave.'

While De Lorean may have written that memo, he has also talked to friends of writing another twenty-page memo directed personally to Murphy. This one too is sharply critical of the company, especially of what De Lorean calls GM's 'lack of social responsibility'. But it is also the sort of memo that De Lorean could have released as an explanation if he were summarily fired, and he once told Bill Haddad that he predated it. A closing sentence reads, 'I assume you will tell me to destroy this memo as you have so many others . . .'

Whatever the real reasons for De Lorean's departure from GM, the criticisms of the corporation that he lays out in the book are still of considerable value. Taken together, they are the best key to the forces that would drive him in his private career.

If one thread runs throughout his indictment, it is the tendency of the GM system to crush dynamic personalities into dull mediocrity. De Lorean well understood why the company could not be swayed by the impulsive actions of one man. As he writes, 'it was Durant's appetite for growth which led to his downfall'. To counter the entrepreneurial boom-and-bust tendencies of one man, a committee system was designed by Alfred P. Sloan, the most influential executive in the company's history. While corporate committees set policy for the entire company, divisions were permitted a certain operational inde-pendence as well. Of this concept De Lorean writes, 'A delicate balance was to be maintained between the freedom of the various operations to manage their businesses, competing internally as well as outside of the company, and the controls necessary to coordinate these operations in the best interests of the corporation's growth and performance.'

Sloan's further division was to divide the corporate committees along financial and operational lines with the chairman holding the purse strings and the president directing operations. 'The imposition of financial controls and the placement of a financial executive so high in the corporation was done not to stultify the flare and creativity of presidents,' De Lorean explains, 'but rather to harness their abilities within the perspective of the money available to build the business and therefore maintain a constantly good return on investment.'

But by the late fifties, De Lorean charges, 'the delicate balance at the top of the world's largest industrial corporation was starting to tip toward the financial side of the business . . .' Creativity, innovation and foresight were to be neglected for 'short-term profit'.

Although De Lorean supports the committee idea in theory, it is the practice that disturbs him most, especially in the conformity it breeds: what he calls team loyalty. He comments constantly on the colourlessness imposed on executive in dress code and behaviour: 'Style and personality in the corporate mold mean simply that a GM executive is a low-profile executive. What is to be most memorable about the corporation today is the letters G and M, and not the people behind the letters. A General Motors man rarely says anything in public that adds the least bit of color or personality to those letters G and M.'

He goes on to lament that the chief executives of other motor companies, like Lee Iacocca, are more familiar faces to the American public than GM officials. While some might see such humility as laudable, De Lorean finds it reprehensible, complaining that 'no one individual is permitted to stand out in the corporation today. When one does, he is rebuked, ordered to disappear into the wallpaper.'

Such executive anonymity, De Lorean argues, breeds public distrust. 'Business in America . . . is impersonal. This is particularly true of large American multi-national corporations. They are viewed by their employees and publics as faceless. They have no personality.' He is just as critical of companies that stonewall the press.

In sum, he proposes an ideal of a company quite different from General Motors – one tied directly to an individual who can provide a face and a personality that people will trust. This is not just executive egomania, De Lorean tells us, it is good business. Of course, Henry Ford tried a personal approach. And so would John De Lorean.

All these arguments justify and reinforce De Lorean's decision to start his own company – some even almost overtly. He decries the fact that in 'major businesses' there are few 'people in management with very substantial holdings of the company stock'. This is unfortunate, he explains, because 'big individual owners of GM, like Sloan or du Pont and others, who owned hundreds of millions of dollars worth of the corporation's stock, had long tenure. Their decisions were biased as much in favor of the long-term growth and health of the company as they were in favor of the short-term profit statement.' This is preferable, he believes, to today's 'short-term and results-oriented' management. Of course, in his litany of big individual owners, De Lorean leaves out Durant, whose concern for pumping up the price of his GM stock almost bankrupted the company.

During one interview De Lorean goes further into the problems of modern management, again anthropomorphizing the corporation. 'I think every institution goes through a cycle. Like a human being. I think the people who built the automobile business were a rough-tough driven bunch of bastards. They used to work an unbelievable amount of hours. They were absolutely an incredible unusual bunch of people. Really the pioneers, the developers, the builders. Once an industry reaches a certain maturity, then that guy winds up being replaced by a sort of keeper – a professional manager.'

Elsewhere in the same interview De Lorean portrays himself as cast in the mould of those pioneers. 'I've always been an accomplishment oriented guy. If I had a job and I believed in it, I'd absolutely leave no stone unturned to accomplish it. That's been my motivation in life: to accomplish . . .'

Much of De Lorean's frustration on the Fourteenth Floor, he writes in *On a Clear Day*, were feelings that he couldn't accomplish anything in his new position. One other executive tells him, 'On the Fourteenth Floor you felt like you'd lost your effectiveness because you couldn't get things done . . . In the divisions you were a doer, and in the corporate management you were an overseer.'

De Lorean paints GM president Ed Cole as one victim of the system: beaten and badgered by the financial men. One senior executive derisively refers to him as 'just the chief engineer'.

It was Cole, De Lorean says, who inspired his departure. He quotes Cole as saying, 'If I was your age, John, I'd get the hell out of here so fast, that you wouldn't believe it. The opportunities in this business are gone. Especially for a guy like you who can get things done. There are a lot of people around here who should stay up here because this is the best they can do. The system protects them. But the opportunities for you are too great.'

With this word of advice from 'a man who had been to the summit', De Lorean says, he made up his mind to resign. Whether or not he quoted Cole correctly, one sentence jumps from his admonition: 'Especially for a guy like you who can get things done.'

Nothing matters more to De Lorean than the image of the 'doer'. And yet, how much had De Lorean really accomplished in comparison with Cole himself? Right or wrong Cole had forged ahead with difficult projects throughout his career at GM. His favourite quote was the one attributed to Hannibal, 'We will either find a way or make one.' Against continuous opposition from other management, stubby, bull-necked Ed Cole made way: first with the Corvette, then with the Corvair, and later his ill-fated $150 million Wankel engine project.

De Lorean had not come close to equalling any of these feats – wrong-headed as they might have been. He was an excellent performer, but in roles written by others. Aside from his unorthodox lifestyle, De Lorean flowed with the system. For all his derogatory statements about Estes as a company man, De Lorean never dared buck corporate commands the way Pete did with the GTO.

Like so many of the men around him, De Lorean was an unalloyed product of the motor industry. Its city had taken him as a boy and provided him with some of the best public education in the nation. Its corporations nurtured him during training and rewarded his performance with six-figure salaries. If anything, General Motors had been a strict but generous parent, and he was to lash out at it like a prodigal son. No doubt there were some bad impulses the company restrained, and some creative energy created by the bonds it did keep around the young executive.

But until April 1973 all of De Lorean's significant accomplishment had taken place in the cocoon of the mothering, smothering corporation – with the support of the best engineering staff, ample capital, and research. If Cole had indeed told De Lorean that he was someone who 'could get things done', how did he know?

De Lorean's true test as a 'doer' would come only after he walked out the doors of General Motors. 'I walked out of an empire,' he told the *Detroit Free Press*. 'Now I've got to show them I knew what was happening all along.'

PART TWO
Entrepreneur Extraordinaire

A Very Brilliant Financial Analyst

Captain Jack's bar and grill, a small building covered with weather-beaten wood shingles, sits on California's Pacific Coast Highway, just across the street from Harpoon Harry's. An aqueduct runs along one side of the restaurant and a canal snakes by the patio in the back. Inside, more weatherbeaten wood makes up the panelling and the exposed beams. Aquariums are sunk into the wall. Varnished masts serve as railings. A wooden effigy of Captain Jack with his pipe and captain's cap stands alongside the ship's wheel, right behind the Hawaiian-shirted manager. The restaurant's speciality is steak.

On some nights, when Roy Nesseth is in town, Captain Jack's can be a little noisier than usual. Living just a few blocks away, Roy is one of the restaurant's most constant customers. A large boisterous man, with a thin, broken nose and rugged Scandinavian good looks, he is the type who can fill a place all on his own. His head practically towers flush up to the low ceiling and his deep voice booms into every corner.

Waiters treat him with the deference due a big tipper, and apparently they don't mind the slaps on the back or all the time he spends bellowing into the payphone that hangs next to the men's room door. Some of the calls are long distance – New York, Idaho, Detroit, even overseas – and occasionally he is just yelling at a foreign operator. As he searches for coins to feed the phone, receipts, crumpled currency and odd scraps of paper come fluttering out of his pockets. With his huge wingspan, he can reach over the bar for change while still holding the receiver with the other hand.

At times, the other customers cannot help but listen to Roy's conversations. He fills the restaurant with talk of loans, and banks, and cars, and racetracks, and cattle, and trucks. Sometimes too, through all the clamour of the busy restaurant, people can also hear Roy talk of John De Lorean.

Never having been shy about working for John De Lorean, Roy has not expected the same loyalty from his employer – and he has not always got it. But whatever De Lorean may say about Roy on any one day in any one courtroom, there is no doubt that the two have been the closest of associates over the last decade. There is no doubt either that the payphone by the lavatory wall became a wayward nerve centre for the debilitated De Lorean empire.

Until autumn 1982 Roy would proudly display a business card from the De Lorean Motor Company. While it identified him as an employee, the caption below did not reveal any title – only 'Office of the Chairman', the chairman being, of course, John De Lorean. The ambiguous job description could not have fitted Nesseth better. Even though Roy carried a salary as high as $180,000 a year, the car company's other top executives never knew exactly what Roy did do for De Lorean or the corporation. But those who first laughed at the former car salesman's blustery behaviour would come to the sober realization that next to general counsel Thomas Kimmerly Roy had more influence over the chairman than anyone else in the company.

The bond between De Lorean and Nesseth mystifies even their closest friends. It is truly an attraction of opposites. Loud and crude, Roy seems incapable of hiding his emotions. Transactions as simple as buying an airline ticket often turn into confrontations. Suave and sophisticated, De Lorean appears to have sublimated all of his feelings behind a forced smile. When angry, his voice gets softer. Silence is his harshest rebuke. Most often he tries to avoid any argument.

Today, car company executives suggest that De Lorean used Nesseth's temper to frighten people. Like someone ready to unleash a junk-yard dog, he often bragged about how mean Roy could be.

However, during his deposition for Roy's suit against Milton Scott, De Lorean's praise for Nesseth's abilities was on a higher order. 'He has an unusual combination of financial acumen,' De Lorean said of Nesseth. 'In fact, I've never met anybody in the world quite like him. In fact, we just closed a deal this last week [of May 1981] where he made, oh, probably a million and a half dollars for me on something that I didn't think I could have made a penny on. He's a very brilliant financial analyst . . . He's not a financial analyst [like] Arthur Andersen [the international accounting and auditing firm]. Somebody like that isn't capable of doing this kind of thing anyhow.'

De Lorean went on to testify how closely intertwined the business affairs of the two men are: 'If he needs one million dollars, I'll lend him one million dollars . . . He pays me back at the market rate interest . . . He brought me a cheque last week for $920,000. He handles a tremendous amount of money for me.'

Yet in courtroom testimony De Lorean and Nesseth have been willing to tailor their relationship to their immediate needs. At times, acting as his legal flak jacket, Nesseth took sole possession of De Lorean interests that went sour, accepting the blame for mismanagement or playing the part of the insubordinate partner. Little more than a year before he praised Nesseth as 'a very brilliant financial analyst', De Lorean was telling a Kansas court that Nesseth was an untrustworthy character beyond his control. De Lorean's lawyer Kimmerly testified in the same trial that he was 'well aware [that Nesseth] was a crook'. In fact, De Lorean went so far as to sue Nesseth in 1975 for a $100,000 debt – so as to take possession of his friend's house later, thereby keeping it out of the hands of other creditors.

By taking the fall to help salvage De Lorean's good name, Roy may have risked his own reputation. But in the minds of lawyers scattered throughout the country Roy has very little reputation left to lose. Almost his entire adult working career can be chronicled in lawsuits. Most are filed in the Los Angeles area court system, but others, are stored in San Diego and several towns in Idaho, and in Phoenix, Wichita and Detroit. The record adds up to a most unflattering *curriculum vitae* with an ever-growing roster of hostile references.

The most serious charge against Nesseth dates back to 1954 when he was closing deals at the Ran Boys used car lot. In two cases Roy was charged with deliberately misleading his customers. He did not lie about the price of the car or the finance charge for the loan. Instead, he confined his deception to the monthly payment – a fact the buyers discovered only on their return home when they took a closer look at the contract and figured out the payments for themselves. Roy was convicted of grand theft and two counts of forgery and released on probation.

While that remains his only criminal conviction, over a score of judgments against Roy in civil suits have followed. Plaintiffs range from two ex-wives (one, a beautician, cited extreme cruelty in her divorce petition), to other car customers, former business partners, banks, ex-friends, travel agents, hotels and other sundry suppliers.

The records seem to show that litigation has become a way of life for Nesseth. According to court records, in 1976 Roy postponed a deposition for an Arizona case so he could be in California, where, on the same day, he had to give testimony to two other suits against him.

Roy's pride and joy is the Huntington Harbour split-level home he shares with his third wife and their three children. Slipped sideways among more imposing houses on a cul-de-sac, the house looks as insular as a Roman villa. The tiny front yard is walled off and even the upper level sun deck is fenced in. Unlike most of his neighbours across the street, Roy has no property on the water, but estate agents conservatively value the house at over $200,000.

Roy's house has been put up for a sheriff's auction to satisfy his debts at least six times, and on each occasion he has come up with the money to redeem his property – once running into the sheriff's office just fifteen minutes before the deadline. Court records show that three of the auctions were initiated by La Jolla lawyer, John H. Thomas.

Thomas has become the resident legal specialist in southern California in suing Nesseth, and his success in collecting on judgments has brought him Nesseth creditors from as far away as Kansas and Florida. While dogging Nesseth through all his professional incarnations from car salesmen to De Lorean executive, Thomas's pursuit has reached Dickensian proportions.

In one suit Thomas describes the Nesseths as modern-day Micawbers, always on the watch for the agents of their creditors: 'I have had to expend hundreds of dollars in fruitless efforts to have them served with various processes, both by peace officers and private process servers. I have had to pay private process servers to "stake out" the Nesseths' residence . . . but Mr Nesseth continually evaded their efforts to serve him . . .'

For obvious reasons Roy does not take kindly to opposing lawyers. He has stalked out of depositions, and during cross-examination in Kansas he bolted off his chair and rushed for the plaintiff's counsel. The first time De Lorean was ever asked about his friend by the press, he made no excuses for his behaviour. 'Roy's a typical automotive guy,' he told one reporter, 'a little too rough and a little too ready.'

But back in the days when Roy Nesseth was making a name for himself among the car dealers of Los Angeles, he was not known for his short temper. Quite the opposite.

'We called him the stroke,' George Williams remembers. Williams, who bears some resemblance to comedian Bob Newhart, occasionally laughs and shakes his head as he reminisces about Roy. He sits in the sort of spare panelled little room in his Chevrolet dealership that Nesseth used when he was hired as manager in 1967. 'The customers just loved the guy. In no time at all Roy could work his way into their confidence. For instance, he'd ask a guy where he was from, and no matter what he answered, Roy had been there. He'd say something like, "You remember that little church with the fence in the square?" and the guy would say, "Yeah, sure." Then they'd go on talking about his little hometown, and Roy had him right in his hand.'

In dealer terminology Roy was not a salesman but a 'closer'. Williams explains, 'A salesman goes out on the floor and lines the guy up. He then quotes a price, and he says my manager will make you a deal. That's when Roy comes into the picture. Sometimes he'll show the guy a different car. I've seen people come in looking for a truck, and Roy ends up making them buy a convertible.'

'When Roy went into a room with a guy, he came out with his

signature on the contract. He was absolutely the best closer I've ever seen. No ifs, ands or buts. One of the advantages he has over the rest of us is the mind he has for maths. He can add figures together faster than most people can with an adding machine. That's a pretty important skill to have when some nervous guy is sitting across from you wondering what his payments will be. Roy would just go down the contract and by the time he got to the bottom, he figured out the payment.'

Although Roy had been convicted of telling customers one thing and putting down another on paper, Williams contends that Roy never used his mathematical feats to trick anyone. In fact, he says, it was a point of honour for Nesseth to make good on any figure he added incorrectly. 'Once Roy and I made a deal to buy the inventory of a Pontiac dealer going out of business. Roy added up all the cars we were buying on the top of a box and came up with an incredibly low figure. The dealer was so desperate, he was ready to take it. But when Roy looked at the box top again, he saw he made a mistake. He went back to the guy and insisted we make up the difference. He was very proud about his mathematical abilities and wasn't going to take anything off of anybody because he made an error. When Roy says the figures equal something, you can believe it.'

His prowess with numbers, Roy told Williams, was developed in his youth, when he worked in his father's wholesale greengrocer's. As he stood waiting to pack up the groceries, he would try and beat the cash register at adding up the bill.

Born in the early 1920s on a farm in the Mid-West, Roy moved to California with his family when his father went into vegetable whole-saling. During a stint in the Air Force, he would later tell friends, he lost all hearing in his left ear and as a result spoke louder than he had to. When Roy got in a car, he drove, so that his good ear was to the passenger.

Roy liked to tell friends that nothing prepared him better for the rough-and-tumble world of the automobile business than the whole-sale produce markets of Los Angeles. The same environment would serve as an incubator for financier Kirk Kerkorian, who also came from a family of grocers. According to Roy, he remained friends with Kerkorian after they both left the food markets, although there is no evidence the two ever did any business together.

Roy became a closer early in his car-selling career. Although his conviction probably prevented him from having his own dealership, it did not stop Roy from working with some of the biggest dealers in southern California. Along the way he got into the newspapers when he and his brother Donald, who was also a car salesman, managed a champion middleweight fighter named Don Jordan. When a dispute arose over who actually owned the fighter, the Nesseth boys took their adversaries to court and eventually won.

The fighter did not do well enough in the ring to get the Nesseths out of the car business. Like so many other times in his life, Roy came close to the big money but not close enough. However, while incapable of investing himself, Nesseth often brought friends together on deals where everyone seemed to make money. Williams regrets that he did not get in on some of those schemes – especially one in Beverly Hills where a bankrupt Toyota dealership was turned into a lucrative Mercedes-Benz franchise.

But Williams did let Roy serve as matchmaker between him and another dealer to start a San Diego Toyota franchise, and in return he loaned Nesseth $25,000 to purchase his own share of the deal. 'Roy has made some good money,' Williams says. 'I know he made some good money with me, but he's also a hell of a spender. It's not that he spends it on any one thing. He's not a drinker. But he's got to do everything first class. He always flew first class and stayed only in the best hotels. Everybody knows him in Vegas. He's the first guy to pick up the tab. It's hard to pay for anything when he's around, and you know he'll leave the biggest tip, too. At least he will if they treat him right. I've been with Roy when he didn't like the service at some restaurant and he grabbed the tablecloth and pulled it out. Dishes, glasses, silverware – they all went flying. Things like that can happen with Roy. You just want to cover your face and pretend you don't know the guy.'

Quite suddenly, in the autumn of 1970, Roy had the chance to enjoy all the power and trappings of great wealth. One of his friend, Ross Gilbert (Roy later set him up in the Beverly Hills Mercedes dealership), introduced him to a lawyer who was trying to find a business manager for one of his clients, a wealthy widow named Hazel Upton.

Hazel Upton originally came from Nebraska, and still speaks with a cornbelt twang. A woman with shining eyes and puckish charm, today she still manages to laugh at the incredible reverses that have shaken her life over the last decade. Of Nesseth she says, 'I've been conned before. I've been conned since. But I've never been conned as bad as I was with Roy. I know it will catch up with him.'

Hazel had been the manager of a small electronics shop when she met her second husband, William E. Upton. He soon got divorced, [?]g most of assets to his first wife, and married Hazel. Together, st[?]ng from scratch they built an empire in the weather-boarding business.

'Bill was a good man with plenty of ability,' she says, 'but he was also an alcoholic. That was hard on him and hard on me.' As their wealth grew, she could not settle back into the role of the idle wealthy wife but had occasionally to take the reins when her husband went on a binge. Still, there were some good times. The Uptons had homes in Palm Springs, in the Virginia Country Club in Long Beach and in Empire

West, one of the smartest blocks of flats in west Los Angeles. They entertained the top executives of Georgia Pacific and Boise Cascade, and nightclubbed with Hollywood celebrities. On quiet weekends they took their hundred-foot yacht south of the border and dined with the Mexican president.

Bill gave up drinking for a few years but then in late 1964, on an extended timber-buying trip in Ecuador, he fell off the wagon. By the time he returned, he was wracked by cancer and beyond help. He died a few days after the New Year. With a trusted lawyer, Hazel sorted out his tangled affairs, and soon she was back in the driving seat, wheeling and dealing in the volatile lumber market. She bought a saw mill in Crescent City, California. She had another plant which was one of the nation's largest manufacturers of bevelled siding and planned on yet another facility to recycle the wood chips and sawdust. She ran a lumber brokerage in Chicago and kept a large office in Beverly Hills. There were other interests in Mexico and Latin America.

An avid Los Angeles Dodgers baseball fan, Hazel became friendly with the players, especially pitcher Don Drysdale. 'I was always crazy about horses and Donnie was also interested in thoroughbred racing. For years he tried to talk me into buying a horse, and finally I gave in. I bought a hundred-acre ranch outside of Anza called Rancho Rojo [red] because it was all built with redwood. I had thirty-two claimers and yearlings. We also bought the 1962 Preakness winner, Greek Money, and put him out to stud. I paid $125,000 to buy him. I then had him syndicated, and we sold all the shares.'

But all the high-pressure interests, Hazel says, proved 'to be taxing on my health'. In 1968 she suffered a massive heart attack. Her doctors ordered her to stay away from the office, and for the next two years she watched helplessly from her convalescence as her business slowly dissipated. When the six-figure debts started to mount, her banks threatened to recall all of her loans and stop further credit.

To make matters even worse, her long-time lawyer and adviser died. She turned to a new adviser to find some way out of her difficulties, who gave her two dismal alternatives: either declare bankruptcy or turn over all her assets to a business manager who might be able to salvage something. Bankruptcy was out of the question for Hazel; her most precious possessions were works of art, crystal and ceramics that she had collected over the years, and she feared that if she ever went into court, the creditors – especially the Internal Revenue Services (IRS) – would seize everything. So her only choice was to find a business manager/partner, and the lawyer introduced her to the man he felt was the perfect candidate.

Hazel remembers the first time she met Roy Nesseth in her lawyer's office. 'I felt confident about Roy. He didn't seem like a fast or shady character. He had a nice wife and family – just like an honest working man.'

Roy assured Hazel that one way or another he could help her find a way out of bankruptcy. All she had to do was trust him. No official agreement between Roy and Hazel was made, no papers signed. 'I guess that makes me look pretty foolish,' Hazel says, 'but I was desperate, and from the point of view of my creditors, this wasn't the straightest thing for me to do. I had liens against everything, and I was in no position to write up any arrangement to divide what I had left.'

Hazel was to retire to her Palm Springs home (she had since sold the house in Long Beach). Roy would make her mortgage payments and split anything he was able to clear above her debts.

At first, the deal seemed to be working well, especially for Roy. He lived the lavish lifestyle Hazel had been accustomed to, using her membership at the Balboa Bay Yacht Club. He also particularly took advantage of the home she had rented in Empire West, one of the smartest apartment blocks in west Los Angeles, and where she had previously entertained the top executives of Georgia Pacific and Boise Cascade. Over 2400 square feet, with two bedrooms, the apartment was decorated with the finest antique furniture; seventeenth- and eighteenth-century oil paintings hung on the walls, porcelain figurines, gold statuary and fine ceramic vases were displayed on table tops and inside book cases, and the kitchen had a complete silver service and Royal Vienna china. It became a popular party spot for Roy's friends, some of the parties being a little louder than Empire West's management would have liked. Two of the most frequent visitors, building employees told Hazel, were John De Lorean and his father-in-law, Tom Harmon.

'Roy told me that the root of my problems had been the horses,' Hazel remembers. 'He said the first thing he did would be to get rid of them.' In fact, Nesseth did not get rid of the horses, and the only departure was Don Drysdale. 'The next thing I know Roy is making the papers as some big horseowner, putting my horses in every race he can under his own name.'

Roy attempted to reorganize Hazel's other properties. He leased the saw mill to another firm, which promptly went bankrupt. He took some of the heavier construction equipment, refinanced it and formed the Pacific International Equipment which also went belly up within a year. Nesseth explained to the Internal Revenue that his bookkeeper had left town, taking the company's records with him, so he could only estimate the loss. The horses too were taking their toll. Feed bills went unpaid and a trainer sued for his share of purses. Eventually Roy was forced to sell off most of the occupants of Nesseth Stables.

Roy's business troubles did not surprise his old dealer buddy,

George Williams. 'Roy never finishes anything. He starts plenty of things, but then his attention starts to wander and he thinks about bigger stakes.'

Only months into her arrangement with Roy, Hazel could see there was trouble. The management at Empire West did not just complain about Roy's parties, but also about unpaid rent. After four instalments Roy had stopped paying her mortgage, and car loans as well. Hazel insisted they meet to discuss the situation. Nesseth told her not to worry, he was very close to a big auto executive named John De Lorean, he said, and De Lorean might invest in the few holdings Hazel had left and save the day.

But Hazel would see no more money from Roy, or from De Lorean, even though he managed to string her along for over a year. 'He always had a story,' Hazel explains, 'a typical car salesman. Something was just about to happen. Or all the problems were my lawyer's fault.'

Roy told the IRS that he paid the lawyer four thousand dollars more for eleven trucks and sundry equipment from Hazel's lumber business. While the price Roy paid for the trucks may seem small, the one thousand dollars he reported paying for all the contents – including all the antiques and paintings – of Hazel's Los Angeles apartment is even more ridiculous.

'By the middle of 1971,' Hazel says, 'I knew I had been taken.' Powerless, she felt, to take Roy to court, she decided instead to take the law into her own hands. 'Let's just say I got Greek Money back. I won't say how, but I did get him back.'

Hazel would sell the horse, and used her last stake from Greek Money to open a bar in Southgate in Los Angeles. Today, she is not as rueful as most people hearing her story would expect her to be, but she does say, 'There were times when I thought about taking a gun to myself or to Roy. Finally to remain sane, I had to pull a shade down over everything that happened and tell myself, "You've got to start over." '

Nesseth's old buddy George Williams had his own bust-up with Roy too, in 1971. 'I had to let him go as manager. He just yells too much and treats the salesmen like dogs. It got to the point where I couldn't hire any help. Nobody wanted to work with him.

'Since Roy's left, we've sued each other back and forth. You always end up in court with that guy.' Roy would get even angrier a few years later when Williams and his partner in San Diego allowed a creditor to buy out Roy's portion of their Toyota dealership.

'I can't say that knowing Roy was a bad experience. If he came in here today, we'd still sit down together and have a laugh. Roy taught me a lot about his business, especially the internals of a new car dealership.

'But the best you can do with Roy is break even. He's not a man to continue doing business with for any period of time. In fact, when he was selling cars, he never stayed anywhere as long as the four years he spent with me. That tells you something.

'But as long as I've known him, he's never bought a car from me. He always wanted me to give up so much it wasn't worth selling the car to him. I can spend all day going around and around with him on a contract, but I can't win. He's too tough. That's his major problem, and it's something I told John De Lorean many times. Roy's just too tough.'

Four Bad Deals

After Roy Nesseth left Williams Chevrolet in 1971 the major source of his income would be John De Lorean, although the official relationship between the two, like Roy's business card, was to remain nebulous. Nesseth was seldom a direct employee of De Lorean, most often making tax returns as a self-employed consultant. But even before the De Lorean Motor Company got off the ground, Roy made a good living off his friend's holdings – in some years with earnings of over $100,000.

Roy started with De Lorean on United Visuals, getting $32,000 from the company in 1972 and half that in 1973. Although his official employer was Milt Scott, Nesseth and De Lorean made no secret about whom Roy was really working for. During the same period he also received consulting fees from Mint Investment. A company run by United Visuals board member, Myles Hymes, Mint had a major stake in a project involving the manufacture of helicopters. In his deposition in the United Visuals case, De Lorean testified that both he and Scott had an interest in Mint, and his share was among the points of contention during his divorce with Kelly Harmon.

Roy never got along well with Milton Scott. Even before United Visuals Scott had hired Nesseth in 1971, he once told the court, 'so [Roy] could take home some money and I tried to get him involved in as many of my activities as possible. He worked in this "trouble-shooter" capacity for a couple of months and then did something that I did not care for and was discharged.' But he put Roy back on the pay-roll little more than a year after his discharge – out of pity, he says; others say at De Lorean's behest.

In his United Visuals deposition De Lorean testified, 'I know [Scott] treated Roy very badly.' But even after Nesseth left United Visuals in the summer of 1973, he got another $20,000 from Scott. He was to scout out locations for the Lighthouse Point dealership that De Lorean got in severance from General Motors, and eventually mind the store once business began. '[Roy] must have been down [to Lighthouse Point] twenty times,' De Lorean says, 'talking to Cadillac zone people.'

The plans for the dealership supposedly went awry when De Lorean sold his franchise to a dealer from Indianapolis who evidently did not need Nesseth for a manager. But over the next five years De Lorean found other ventures where he could use Roy's services. Four in particular stand out as examples of the De Lorean–Nesseth standard operating procedure. As each situation heated up with Roy raging at the centre of the problems, De Lorean retreated from personal involvement, finally contending he was too busy to be either fully aware or concerned about his interests. This diffidence was an interesting pose for a man who so vehemently criticized his former employer's refusal to recognize the full impact of its business on society.

The impact of De Lorean's enterprise on the world of big business was comparatively miniscule, but his business tactics managed to crush the livelihoods and, even worse, the dreams of many 'little' people. Beyond highlighting a streak of unscrupulousness, these deals also raised serious questions about De Lorean's skill as a manager and entrepreneur outside the confines of General Motors – questions that cities, states and nations did not bother to answer before they clamoured to give De Lorean multi-millions of dollars to build his car company.

A Race Track

For once it was Jack Z. De Lorean who had the bright idea.

It probably was not easy growing up in the shadow of his big brother – especially with a name that seemed to be no more than John's nickname. Jack didn't go to Cass Tech; he enrolled instead in the closest public high school. When Jack was drafted into the army, he didn't have John's luck to be assigned to stateside duty. Instead, the army sent him into the thick of the Korean War, an experience that left him physically and emotionally scarred. Eventually he did get an engineering degree and a job at Pontiac, but people laid his hiring to John's influence and not Jack's qualifications.

And yet Jack, not John, was the one to think of Grand Prix of America. The idea was like a cross between an amusement park and a competitive sport. People would get into miniature racing cars and cruise around a track. A large clock would keep note of their speed. They could then match their times with their friends or just go out to beat their own best efforts. They would pay a dollar for every lap they drove, and the track, lit by floodlights, would be open all night long.

When Jack first suggested Grand Prix to his older brother, John was general manager of Chevrolet. He thought it was a brilliant idea, but he did not want to stop with one track. America in the early seventies was going franchise crazy – especially with fast food – and John was convinced that Grand Prix would be a natural franchise operation.

In the spring of 1972 the brothers formed a company, with Jack as president. Documents identified John as just another board member, although he was in fact chairman of the board. Most likely, that title he preferred to keep from his General Motors superiors, who did not usually countenance such active participation in extracurricular affairs. But it was John who found the first investors and raised the seed money for his younger brother's scheme. Some of the early directors were car dealers, and one of those, Norman Weise of Indianapolis, was eventually the buyer of the Lighthouse Point dealership. U.E. Patrick, a wildcat oil developer, was another investor John brought into the fold. Together the board raised $400,000 – enough to buy a few cars and build a pilot track on land they leased from Rockwell International in Troy, Michigan.

Lawyer Thomas Payne remembers driving the few miles from his Bloomfield Hills office to see the track shortly after it opened. 'People were lined up trying to get into there. You couldn't help but feel that this was an idea that could really take off.'

A few of the De Lorean brothers' original backers were pulling back and in the spring of 1973 Payne joined a new team of prominent local backers capable of launching Grand Prix into the national arena. Among these investors were real estate developer Joseph Slavik, engineering contractor Reo Campian and former Detroit Lions football-player and current window manufacturer James Ninowski, Jr. All three were John De Lorean's neighbours in Bloomfield Hills, but they also grew up with him and Jack on the east side of Detroit. They too had climbed out of the tough streets to become successful – and, by the measure of their personal fortunes, far more successful than John. Ninowski played basketball with Jack in high school. Campian was a childhood friend of Charles (Chuck) De Lorean's, the middle brother, and had kept in touch with him. He knew John only on a professional basis from the few times his firm did engineering work for Pontiac, but John was to call Campian himself and ask him to invest in Grand Prix. 'He told me they were in real deep,' Campian recalls, 'and that they needed some more capital to get this thing going. The next day I walked in with a big cheque.'

Together, the new shareholders invested over $1.3 million in Grand Prix of America. But as the crowds around the Troy track continued to grow Jack began to question the strategy of selling franchises. When a group from Malibu, California approached Jack to buy a franchise he turned them down (they later went ahead and started two tracks of their own and sold out for a considerable figure to Warner Communications). His new plan was for Grand Prix to own tracks around the country and forget about the franchises. Real estate developer Slavik helped Jack find possible locations for tracks in other parts of the country. John approached the estate agent who found his Idaho ranch to scout for sites in California.

However, despite all the bold plans, before 1973 was over Grand Prix had already started to run out of steam. 'It seemed like a lot of money was eaten up by overheads,' lawyer Tom Payne remembers, 'especially in legal fees. Some expenses weren't very necessary either, and to be honest, the board members didn't pay that much attention at first. We didn't invest to be managers. Still, by the end of the year we were all wasting a lot of time holding meetings at the Grand Prix office.'

John De Lorean had not been very active in the day-to-day operations of the company. On those few occasions when he did appear, he seemed sullen and distracted. Jack, a much more outgoing personality, was clearly in charge, and some board members felt that was the problem. 'I think everyone liked Jack,' Payne says. 'He's truly a wonderful human being, but they doubted his ability to manage a business.'

As finances grew more desperate, recriminations started to fly. In one heated meeting when John wasn't present, Jack accused his brother of dipping his hand in the till, although the other investors did not believe him and were horrified by the accusation.

But the impact of the sibling squabble on Grand Prix's future would pale next to the Arab oil embargo. 'The fuel crisis came just when we were geared up to start our tracks,' Payne says. 'The timing couldn't have been worse. In fact, it was almost comical. Here we were trying to go national with recreation based on a gas-powered vehicle to be driven at night around a track illuminated by floodlights. All our hopes for any sort of big time success just went up in smoke.'

By 1974, unable ever to make payments on its Troy lease, Grand Prix appeared to be heading for bankruptcy. John had no trouble in putting the blame for the company's travails on Jack's head. (Years later, when a related matter came to court for trial, De Lorean freely testified that Grand Prix failed because of 'my brother's mismanagement'. He went further to say that Jack's 'behaviour wasn't completely rational,' explaining, 'My brother spent a couple of years in a mental institution after the Korean War.') The only way to salvage the operation, De Lorean told the other investors, was to bring in new management on a full-time basis.

'John said he had just the man to get the venture back on track,' Payne remembers. 'He told us, "It's a guy who worked for me in California. He's a real go-getter; a street fighter – he gets things done." And then he introduced us to Roy Nesseth.

'At our first meeting, Roy was his old charming self, and we were all favourably impressed. Besides, other than what Jack told us, we had no reason to believe that John was not an upstanding, competent business-man.'

But there was no way to save Grand Prix. One of the original backers, car dealer Norman Weise pulled out. ('We were surprised when John gave him his money back,' Campian says. Weise had bought De Lorean's Florida Cadillac franchise.) To make matters worse, the De Lorean brothers were at each other's throats. Campian prevailed on Chuck, a successful Cleveland Cadillac dealer, to come down to Detroit and help mediate. While Chuck too had to live in John's shadow – most people in the auto business believed his older brother had got him his franchise – no one denied that Chuck had proved to be a savvy business-man in his own right. Campian believed he, more than John or Jack, could best put the whole venture back on track.

In March 1974, with Chuck as a new investor and Jack off the board, the remaining backers reorganized what assets they had left into a new company they called GPA Systems. This entity would concentrate on selling franchises and get away from track ownership. Roy Nesseth was appointed GPA Systems' first president.

Within days of the reorganization Roy telephoned an urgent message to the investors from a phone booth in California. In the optimistic period before the oil crisis Grand Prix had taken an option on a potential track site in Pomona, California. Now Roy gushed that the plot was too valuable to let slip away. The owner already had an offer over one hundred thousand dollars more than the Grand Prix option price. But they only had two days to exercise the option and make the $65,000 downpayment or the deal was off. Speaking for the other investors, Payne admits, 'We're embarrassed to say that we never did take a look at that property before we made the payment, but Roy couldn't say enough about it. He told us it was a "can't lose proposition – a real touchdown". There were several colleges in the area and he felt the students alone would keep us in business.'

By this time only five of the Detroit investors were still game enough to sink more money into the deal. But they decided to create yet a third entity, Cal Prix, that would do no more than own and operate the Pomona track. Against their better judgement they convinced John De Lorean to join them. Milt Scott, De Lorean told them, would loan him the money to exercise their option before the deadline. (De Lorean later testified that Scott may not have realized that he took the $65,000 from their joint account.) For the first few days of April 1974 the five Detroit investors rushed to wire their share of the downpayment to Roy and De Lorean.

When the dust cleared, Roy reported that he secured the site, but not in the name of Cal Prix. Evidently the seller did not feel obligated to a new entity, so Roy said he was forced to put the property in the name of Grand Prix of America. Just to make sure that a Grand Prix creditor could not swoop down and seize the investment De Lorean took out two deeds of trust on the property worth $100,000. If any claim was made, De Lorean would have first go.

The scenario sounded credible to the investors. In a few months they transferred the deed to Cal Prix and thought nothing more of De Lorean's liens. Nesseth was to supervise construction of the Pomona track for the Cal Prix owners. He would then use it as a model to sell the GPA Systems franchises.

But the Cal Prix investors soon had doubts about Nesseth's business expertise. First of all, the Pomona site was not the showplace he had promised, but an almost industrial setting in the sort of rough neighbourhood that would chase suburban families away. In the eyes of Jim Ninowski, 'There couldn't have been a worse spot in the entire state.'

The Detroit backers had further worries about the way Roy was employing the lean GPA Systems coffers. His contract called for a $25,000 annual salary and $7500 in commissions. But informed estimates had his wages running as high as $64,000 a year, with almost as much in expenses.

To their dismay, John De Lorean did not seem interested in Roy's shenanigans. 'We'd try to reach him on the phone,' Payne says, 'and John would never get back to us.' Jim Ninowski was not about to take De Lorean's brush-off. On one occasion De Lorean's secretary put him on hold for fifteen minutes, and then got back to tell him that De Lorean was tied up and couldn't speak with him that day. Ninowski got into his car and drove to De Lorean's Bloomfield Hills office. When the former football-player reached the secretary's desk, he didn't ask for an appointment, but burst through De Lorean's door. 'He wasn't too happy to see me,' Ninowski recalls, 'and in a few words, I let him know what I thought of him. At one point I said that Roy Nesseth was raping him and the company. I told him that if he continued to associate with Roy and ignored what he was doing, then John De Lorean was as bad as Roy Nesseth. All he said was, "Thanks, I'll look into it." '

The final straw for the Cal Prix investors came when it was time to finance the purchase of new cars for the Pomona track. Each put up a $26,000 letter of credit. Nesseth sent them a telegram confirming that De Lorean had done the same. In fact, he never did. When the rest of the group discovered the deception, Ninowski says, 'We wanted nothing more to do with him.'

But it was not that easy to shake De Lorean. As construction neared completion, Cal Prix's attornies conducted a title search on the Pomona property and found that De Lorean still had liens on the deed. De

Lorean told Payne that his lawyer had merely forgotten to remove the liens and he would see the matter was attended to. But as weeks went by, he claims he could no longer find the documents to make a change.

When Payne suggested a method for cancelling the deeds of trust, De Lorean replied with the demand that he receive $100,000 first. He went on to explain that he deserved repayment for several out-of-pocket expenses.

Payne was furious and let De Lorean know as much. De Lorean told him not to get concerned. He felt there was still some amicable way they could handle this. 'I can remember John saying, "If I'm not entitled to the money then I don't want it." '

De Lorean only asked that Payne meet with his lawyer, Thomas Kimmerly. De Lorean promised that if his lawyer were satisfied with Payne's explanation, he would turn over the deeds of trust.

Payne met with Kimmerly and painstakingly took him through every step of De Lorean's investment in Cal Prix and Grand Prix. An owlish man, with soft facial features, Kimmerly listened impassively and then explained that he was not empowered to make a decision one way or another. Despite De Lorean's promise, he did not have the deeds of trust. However, Nesseth was coming to town and might have brought the deeds along. He asked Payne to return to meet with Roy.

When Payne came back the next day, he did not find the charming Roy of yesteryear. This was a sour, belligerent Nesseth who told him that De Lorean had $100,000 coming. Either he got the cash or he kept the deed. Payne asked to see the expenses to back up De Lorean's claim. 'Roy then said, "I'll testify that you guys gave me the money to buy the property and I kept it. I'll say that John had to come up with the whole $65,000 for the downpayment himself. You don't have any proof that you paid for it. All your cheques were to me and John. There's nothing you can do about that." '

Cal Prix filed suit against De Lorean in 1976, but the matter was not to reach trial until March 1982. Payne travelled to a Los Angeles courtroom to give testimony. Shortly before he left Michigan, the judge called to tell him that De Lorean had offered to remove the deeds of trust for a $40,000 payment. 'I told the judge that we didn't find that an acceptable settlement. We owed him absolutely nothing for those deeds and that was the most we were going to pay.'

De Lorean spent the first morning of the trial under tense cross examination. While claiming to forget most of the details concerning Grand Prix, De Lorean did adamantly maintain that he secured a lien on the deeds to guarantee repayment for certain expenses he had funded. But Payne's lawyer would then contend that those expenses came *after* De Lorean secured the lien – not before. Over the lunch break De Lorean and his lawyer decided not to go any further. He agreed to release the deeds to Cal Prix along with any stock he had left in the company.

Since the settlement, the Cal Prix group had put their track up for sale. At best, they hoped to recoup some of their losses. But almost everyone involved with Grand Prix agrees that the man hurt most by the venture's failure was Jack De Lorean.

One of the earliest officers of Grand Prix remembers hearing from Jack shortly after the whole business went bankrupt. 'Jack gave me a call to say he was going to resurrect Grand Prix – with God's help. It was very strange. Of course there was no way, with or without God, that he'd ever bring back that company. But Grand Prix was probably the one great dream of his life. I guess he couldn't accept the fact that it was dead.'

An Invention

'I'm the best mechanic in the world.' Walter C. Avrea is not a man given to idle boasts. At fifty-eight, with no more than a high school education, he has proved himself to be one of the few natural geniuses of the machine. A handful of automotive inventions, which he patented himself, have made him a millionaire several times over. One such device – his coolant recovery system – is so basic and so significant that it establishes him as one of the most successful independent automotive inventors of the last fifty years. It was exactly the sort of invention that should have let the succeeding years slip by for 'Pete' Avrea in peace and luxury. But after he made it he met John De Lorean and Roy Nesseth, and within months he would be in the fight of his life to wrest back control of his valuable patents.

Nothing ever came easy to Avrea. A tall, lanky balding man, he still speaks with the West Texas drawl of his childhood. As he grew up he had to scrap for a living. He followed his father and then his brother around the south and southwest. His first good job came as an apprentice mechanic for Caterpillar landmovers. During the war he served as a gunner in the Air Force, and when it ended, he went back to fixing Caterpillars in the minefields.

His luckiest break came in Texas, when he met his wife Shirley. A pretty brown-haired woman, originally from Cleveland, she would refine some of the roughness out of Pete, and also give him the ambition to reach for greater things than most of his working buddies expected out of life.

Together they moved to Pico Rivera, California, where Avrea got a job fixing trucks for Navajo Freight Lines. In a year, at the age of twenty-five, Pete was the company's chief mechanic – a job which had its occasional frustrations. 'I was never satisfied with just replacing a part,' Pete remembers. 'I always wanted to find out what caused the failure.' Avrea gave his ideas to truck manufacturers like Peterbilt and Cummings.

'I told him he was crazy,' Shirley says. 'They were getting his ideas for nothing. At least once Pete had to try to get a patent.' The couple took a second mortgage out on their humble $8,000 house. With two children to feed, Shirley was forced to go back to work while Pete stayed at home and fiddled with prototypes in their two-car garage.

His first patent would come with deceptive ease. His idea was to equip trucks with a warning light that would signal wear in the brake lining before the disc tore through and caused major damage. In 1955 the U.S. Patent Office accepted his first application for the Reserve Brake Indicator (over the years he would discover how rare that initial acceptance was), but then Avrea had to find someone to produce and market the invention. He chose an aggressive young manufacturer, who also turned out to be an addicted gambler. When authorities discovered that he had embezzled over one million dollars from his company, he committed suicide. Avrea's invention died along with him.

He persevered and patented a new parking brake for trucks that he called the Anchor Lock. It took three years and untold numbers of trips to Washington before Avrea could patent the device. When he did in 1960, he finally struck gold. From then on he joined the tiny band of inventors who could actually live off their patents.

In 1965, as he tinkered with his wife's Buick, he hit on an idea for an auto part that would dwarf any other mechanical device he ever thought of. Car makers had always had difficulty keeping engines cool. In recent years, power hungry accessories like air conditioners only put more strain on internal combustion. The water-filled radiator was really the last big mechanical breakthrough in engine cooling, but that system was far from perfect. As the coolant circulated through the engine, it did not uniformly quench all surfaces of the engine's chambers, and the rubber hoses funnelling the water from the radiator to the engine often corroded after only a few years of use. As a result, engines overheated and radiators boiled over.

Bubbles, Avrea discovered, were at the heart of the cooling problem. Too much air was getting into the system, creating hot pockets of gas that stopped liquid going to metal surfaces. Oxygen was also the culprit in hose corrosion. Pete's solution was to seal off the entire cooling chain. Instead of permitting the cap to release pressure when steam built up in a hot radiator, which then let air into the system, Avrea put a little plastic reservoir bottle next to the radiator to catch the overflow and he hermetically sealed the cap. The results were dramatic. He did not just reduce corrosion and heat, but without the bubbles the coolant circulated with less vibration, even further diminishing wear and tear on engine parts.

Avrea first filed for his patent in 1967. It took five years before it was finally granted, but then it was reissued shortly thereafter – a medal of honour from the U.S. Patent Office recognizing and further protecting the revolutionary nature of the invention.

Pete didn't need anyone to tell him what he had wrought with his Coolant Recovery System, and he wasn't about to entrust it to some strange and untrustworthy manufacturer. The plastic parts for a coolant kit were so simple that almost anyone could go into business to manufacture them. His older brother Bill had got fed up with his job in Tempe, Arizona, and Pete offered him the chance to start moulding the parts for his invention. Bill set up Saf-Guard Products in 1968. Among his first employees was Pete's son. For sales manager, and eventual president, he turned to Norm Bernier, a former air force colonel who had been a long-time auto buff. Pete moved to Tempe and set up his workshop in their factory.

Orders came in almost immediately. Some were from national chains of motor parts stores; others from the car makers in Detroit – especially Ford and American Motors – which were ready to install Pete's invention as original equipment. One of the largest orders came from Chevrolet in 1971 and 1972, when John De Lorean was still general manager. The division was stuck with the Vega, one of the most poorly designed cars in decades. Within months of the car's introduction Chevy had been deluged with consumer complaints about the aluminium engine overheating. Production was abruptly stopped so Avrea's product could be added on the assembly line. Some kits were even flown in overnight to the Lordstown, Ohio factory.

Within a year Bill Avrea moved out of his two-thousand-square foot plant and leased five times the space. But despite the orders, Pete and his brother quickly discovered that mass-producing relatively inexpensive products was no way to turn a fast profit, even though the president of Saf-Guard Products had estimated that just counting used cars, the potential market for the system worldwide was one billion. It was hard enough to turn out thousands, and the company's production levels seemed nowhere close to paying the bills.

Meanwhile, other manufacturers had stepped in to infringe on Avrea's patent – some being so bold as to advertise their forgeries as coolant recovery systems. Besides depriving the inventor of income, they were also putting out shoddy merchandise which seriously detracted from the patent's reputation. Even some loyal customers, like Ford, became so discouraged when their orders went unfilled that they started producing the kits themselves. Pete had loaned his brother money to help pay for the caps, but now it seemed that their major supplier was also ready to assemble and sell the system as well.

The Avreas started legal action, but they did not have the resources to send out a squad of lawyers after all the infringers. By the spring of 1974 Pete had given up on his brother's ability to market the invention all by himself, and looked instead to sublicense his patent to a large manufacturer. But Norm Bernier gave Pete another idea. He talked of a Detroit motor executive who had just left General Motors – a legend in his own time. All they needed, he told Pete, was to have a man with De Lorean's connections in the motor industry, and Saf–Guard Products would take off into the stratosphere.

In later years De Lorean would claim that he had never heard of Avrea or his inventions until Avrea persistently came knocking at his door. After the inventor's relentless entreaties, De Lorean says, he finally took a look at his cooling system.

But evidence later entered in court showed that the first contact with De Lorean was a letter sent by Saf–Guard president Bernier in the last week of April 1974. De Lorean was, indeed, very interested in Avrea's product. He received the letter on a Tuesday and immediately called the president's home, leaving a message with his answering service. By Friday 3 May, De Lorean was in Pete's workshop.

'Until Norm Bernier told me about him, I had never heard of John De Lorean,' Avrea says today. 'I wasn't the type who followed the auto industry closely.'

But on meeting De Lorean Avrea felt he had found the perfect person to handle his inventions. 'One of the first things John said was, "You know what you're offering me, Pete? You're offering me a twenty-year monopoly on a cooling recovery system. No one in the history of this industry has ever had control of something this important." '

When they walked through Pete's workshop De Lorean continued to pour on the accolades. Avrea's suppliers had difficulty providing him with an air-tight metal radiator cap, so he invented a plastic one comprised of only four pieces – compared to the sixteen in conventional caps. Just the cap, De Lorean told Pete, could make them both a fortune.

Yet De Lorean's compliments did not impress Pete as much as one negative comment. They were both looking at a prototype of another Avrea invention that had a patent pending. 'He told me that the simulator wouldn't work, and he was absolutely right. I didn't want to give away all my secrets in the demonstration model. Right then and there I could see that he really did understand what I was talking about. I went home and told my wife that De Lorean was the smartest man I ever met.'

Before De Lorean left Phoenix, he had Pete write a letter of intent in his Scottsdale hotel room. They would work out the details, but De Lorean agreed to establish a company that would produce and market the coolant recovery system and take legal action against infringers.

Their courtship continued at breakneck speed after De Lorean left, despite two ominous incidents that occurred over the next few weeks. The first concerned De Lorean's choice as president of his new company. He told Avrea that there was a fellow named Roy Nesseth who had done wonderful work for him in California. Nesseth would fly to Phoenix and meet with Avrea and his lawyers to nail down the details of their agreement.

Pete arranged to meet Roy at a Roadway Inn near the Tempe plant for breakfast at 9 a.m. and brought along two lawyers to advise him. Nesseth had not chosen to stay at the motel, but instead had booked into Mountain Shadows, a fancy Scottsdale resort over thirty minutes away. When he showed up for breakfast he was two hours late.

Pete, who admits he has a 'short fuse', was outraged. 'I said, "Mr Nesseth, I've had two lawyers waiting here with me. Do you know what that's costing me?"

'Roy just laughed and said, "I got a gal spread-eagled back at Mountain Shadows. Do you know what that's costing *me*?" '

Pete was not amused. He went to the nearest payphone and called De Lorean and filled him in on Roy's explanation for his tardiness. 'I told De Lorean that if this was the man who would take charge of the company, then there was no way I'd make a deal with him.'

De Lorean apologized profusely and told Roy to take the next plane out of Phoenix. He assured Avrea that he would find someone else for the job, and negotiations continued. But before the end of May, the sky seemed to open up with the sort of manna from Detroit that made everyone forget about Nesseth. General Motors sent Saf-Guard Products an urgent request for 167,000 coolant recovery kits – a purchase worth $750,000.

Avrea now insists that De Lorean knew about the imminent Chevrolet windfall before he flew down to Phoenix to first meet with Pete and sign a letter of intent. De Lorean has replied that the timing of the GM order was merely a coincidence.

Neither the GM order, nor the scene with Nesseth, made Avrea unusually suspicious. Early in June he went to Detroit to sign an agreement with the company De Lorean created to distribute his invention, Saf-Guard Systems. The contract assured Avrea of a royalty equal to 5 per cent of all sales or a minimum of $5,000 a month. He was guaranteed access to Systems' books and a veto over any attempt to license the patent to another company. Avrea went even further and assigned his other patents – including the plastic radiator cap – to Systems under the same arrangements as the coolant recovery kits. De Lorean, however, did not sign a thing. His choice as Saf-Guard Systems president did those honours.

Before the new team could get rolling, Systems had to sign an agreement with the invention's old manufacturer, Bill Avrea's Saf-Guard Products, and negotiations dragged on into the autumn. De Lorean would manage to secure the company's assets for only a promise of royalties a year down the line. In fact, his new company would continue to use Product's bank account, cheques and stationery through its short history.

De Lorean later claimed that he put $100,000 into Saf-Guard Systems to get it off the ground. But the books show that the company was capitalized with no more than the $750,000 purchase order from GM.

Avrea would not have much use for De Lorean's choice as Systems' president. The man seemed bent on commuting to Phoenix from Detroit rather than setting up permanent residence. He showed no commitment to learn the business, and at one point signed a contract to supply the plastic parts of the kit at a price lower than it cost to make them.

Pete was even more concerned by Systems' strategy for dealing with infringers, for De Lorean seemed more inclined to settle than sue. De Lorean later charged that Avrea was too anxious to go to court. Calling him 'eccentric', he said, 'His inventions were like his children. He wanted to tie up too much money going after the companies he felt were infringing on the patent. We had no room left to operate.'

De Lorean would also complain about the minimum royalty he had to pay Pete. However, no one forced him into the contract. Years later, he would admit, 'I woke up and found out I made a very bad deal. When I met Pete he [was] such a big open face, firm handshake type. I fell in love. That was stupid.'

In April 1975 De Lorean sent a telegram to Avrea declaring that it was 'not possible to raise funds or operate Systems'. Instead, he had decided to license out the invention to other manufacturers for $200,000. Of course, Pete refused to accept that option. De Lorean's telegram, his lawyer told him, could be read as defaulting on their agreement, and Avrea could get his patents back to do the licensing himself. Actually, Pete considered breaking up with De Lorean even before the telegram arrived. Contrary to the agreement, he had not received a financial report in months. Also, he had strong suspicions that De Lorean already licensed his patent to another company behind his back – another stipulated reason to cancel their contract.

He replied to De Lorean by sending his own telegram that their agreement was cancelled but De Lorean was not ready to say goodbye. He pleaded with Pete to reconsider, promising to borrow some more money to keep the company afloat. Avrea also insisted that he find another president and De Lorean agreed.

But the situation deteriorated over the summer. In August, De

Lorean told Avrea he had won a settlement from General Motors. Although Chevrolet had been among Saf–Guard's best customers, there had been evidence that GM nevertheless went ahead and produced cooling devices on its own. De Lorean had his dreaded former employer over the proverbial barrel. But for some reason De Lorean did not exact a harsh penalty. In return for past infringements he took only $130,000 and permitted GM to continue infringing on the patents if it chose.

Pete would find no happiness in news of the settlement. The sum was ridiculously low and he let De Lorean know it. There was no way, he said, that he would sign off on that deal. De Lorean convinced him to come up to Detroit and discuss the matter further. 'When we finally got together, I really let him have it,' Avrea recalls. 'I pounded the table and told him what a lousy businessman he was, and everytime I hit the table, he dropped a little lower in his chair. Finally he said, "Pete, you're right."

'I still went ahead and signed that fool settlement. First of all, he promised me that he'd finally fire that president, but then he assured me that GM privately guaranteed him the right to make 50 per cent of all the kits they bought. He told me that he still had friends over at GM who owed him some favours. He claimed that he was the one who got Chevy's general manager his job. I don't know whether any of that's true, but I do know that GM never let us make 50 per cent of the kits they used.'

After he left De Lorean's office that day, Pete would never see another dollar from De Lorean or Saf–Guard Systems. While De Lorean had fired the first president, and replaced him with a former top executive of the Bendix Corporation, there would be little impact on the company. The new president visited Phoenix even less often than his predecessor, and eventually admitted that he was no more than a consultant and had more pressing interests elsewhere.

All at once Pete's worst fears for his inventions were realized. He stopped receiving his monthly royalty cheques. He learned from Systems employees that De Lorean had settled with a major infringer for a royalty of only ten cents a kit. Even worse, the moulds from his plastic radiator cap were missing. When they eventually returned they were damaged. Previously, Avrea had approached the Celanese Corporation, a plastics conglomerate, to consider producing the cap, but De Lorean went even further with the company behind his back, and secured a $200,000 development loan. No one ever found out what happened to that money.

In December 1975 Avrea sent De Lorean another termination notice. At that time, De Lorean would later testify in a deposition, he decided to wash his hands of the entire venture: 'As soon as I saw it was a pain in the ass and a lot of people were trying to nickelshit[me] to death, I said I don't want anything to do with it . . . [There are] all kinds of files and records that will show the harassment and hassle and baloney. It was just too much crap.'

De Lorean claimed he turned all his stock in Saf-Guard Systems over to Roy Nesseth at the end of the month for one dollar. Roy became president and sole stockholder.

Both Nesseth and De Lorean claimed Saf-Guard Systems owed as much as $900,000 to creditors. But Avrea knew of at least $1.5 million that had gone into the company, and he wanted some accounting for what became of those funds. In January, as was his contractual right, he sent his accountant over to the factory to look at the books, but all records had been removed. Nevertheless, some evidence of the firm's fiscal health remained: the phone had been disconnected, rent was long overdue, and creditors's notices were piling up in the mail basket. There wasn't even money left for plastic stock, bringing kit production to a virtual standstill.

Despite the fiscal constraints the company faced, Nesseth did not cut down on his lavish lifestyle. He went to the smartest restaurants in Phoenix and kept his girlfriend in a Scottsdale resort. 'We were getting bills from that hotel for $1800 a week,' one of Systems top executives remembers.

At one point, when Nesseth could not get a local manufacturer to make the plastic reservoir bottles, he shipped the moulds to California. 'He never did get anything out of that,' the executive remembers. 'Roy would often take drastic action and accomplish nothing.'

Nesseth made it clear to his Systems employees that the company was not long for the world. 'He told us he had come to straighten out the mess for John De Lorean and then he'd have to go elsewhere. I remember him telling me, "I wear the black hat." ' Fulfilling that role, Nesseth brought in a locksmith to lock Avrea out of the factory and even his own workshop.

The ultimate Nesseth black hat move would come when one creditor finally forced Saf-Guard Systems to sell the coolant recovery kits in stock to satisfy their debt. A company came to the auction and bid for the entire lot of six thousand kits, but could only truck away half of its purchase that afternoon. When they returned the next morning, Nesseth refused to let them in to pick up the remainder. That night, at nine o'clock, Roy's men tried to sneak off with the kits. Someone tipped off the creditor and the Tempe police were called in to stop the truck.

Avrea had much more trouble catching Nesseth and De Lorean red-handed. He filed suit for breach of contract in February 1976, and it would take two-and-a-half years before the case came to a preliminary hearing. Both Nesseth and De Lorean practised continuous and ingenious delay. They were accomplished subpoena dodgers and writ servers had to chase them across the country before they could catch them. De Lorean kept telling the judge that he was no longer involved in Saf-Guard Systems business and should not have to travel to Phoenix to testify. The judge, eventual Supreme Court justice Sandra Day O'Connor, did not accept his excuse and finally issued a bench warrant.

Avrea remembers De Lorean's first deposition as particularly rancorous. It was given in his lawyer's office. At one point, during a particularly testy cross-examination, Avrea says that De Lorean threatened to knock his lawyer's head off. 'I told John that before he did that, he'd have to deal with me. My lawyer then was a small man who was also ill. I'm not small and I'm not afraid of anybody. That made De Lorean calm down, but before the day was over he said to me, "I'll tie you up in court until your patents run out." '

For a while it looked as though De Lorean could make good his threat. Of all his stalling tactics, the most brilliant was simply not to pay his lawyers. The delays mounted as each legal team withdrew and their successors asked for time to bone up on the case. In just one year De Lorean and Nesseth went through four sets of counsel.

Finally, the suit was set for a hearing on 7 September 1978, the day after Labor Day. Two months before Shirley got a call from De Lorean. He started out sounding cordial, she says, 'But then he started telling me that Pete better settle before this went to court. He told me that if Pete didn't settle, Nesseth would go to the company that was producing another of Pete's inventions and get them to stop payments. Then he said, "And you know, Roy Nesseth can be a very mean man." I then said "Mr De Lorean are you threatening us?" That got him very upset. He said he wasn't doing anything of the kind.'

Pete Avrea went to the hearing, but he never did go to trial. Ill with diabetes and Valley Fever, Avrea had no more stomach for the case. 'I lost four years on the life of my patents, and I had to put De Lorean totally out of my own life.'

He would pay $494,000 to get his patents back. Half the money came out of an escrow fund, the rest De Lorean would collect from the cheap settlements he had made with alleged infringers.

Shirley Avrea says, 'You can't imagine how much it hurt to give De Lorean that money, knowing that he should have paid us. Even today I get tremendously resentful and angry just at the sound of his name.'

But in many ways the Avreas have got the last laugh. When he finally gained control of his patent, Pete pursued his case against one infringer through the courts, and a judge decided that he deserved eleven dollars for every kit sold behind his back. De Lorean had settled with far worse infringers for ten cents a kit. If the judge's penalty had been computed for General Motors' infringement alone, the company would have owed Saf-Guard Systems over $30 million.

In his deposition to Avrea's lawyers, De Lorean declared that the motor industry has 'never made a substantial award to anybody on any patent'. But six weeks after he settled with De Lorean, Avrea got a million-dollar settlement from Ford. And when he won his favourable judgment against the infringer, the car companies and parts suppliers practically fell all over themselves to offer him very substantial awards. Already tens of millions have come Avrea's way and he still expects the biggest settlements or judgments from some large Japanese car-makers.

'If John had been anywhere near a cagey businessman,' Pete says, 'he could have had this and more. I figure, conservatively, he would have made $60 million from Saf-Guard Systems. All it took was a little patience. His problem was that he wanted to go for the quick buck. But look what he gave up in return.'

A Ranch

One day during the summer of 1959 Clark Higley stood in mud up to his ankles and looked out at a flat rocky field covered with sagebrush. It was the most beautiful sight he had ever seen. This piece of scrub, in the town of Rupert, had been Higley's prize in an Idaho homestead lottery. The state had valued the 173 acres at $20,000. But to Clark's wife, Colleen, even that price seemed too high. To get there, the couple had driven for miles through a fierce rainstorm, going over roads that were little more than mud ruts. Now Colleen contemplated leaving Idaho Falls behind to settle on a scrubby patch of ground in the middle of nowhere. 'I stayed in the car,' Colleen says, 'and bawled my head off.'

For a few months, Clark lived alone on his land, in a little 'sheep camp' caravan. He pulled out most of the sagebrush by hand, and then he started building a barn, and finally the house. An aerial picture taken later in that year shows two plain rectangular structures – looking much like the house pieces in the Monopoly board game – surrounded by a sea of flat tilled fields, striated only by a farm track. Less than ten years later, an aerial picture of the spread would look like it came from a different part of the planet. There is a new home and barn in this shot, and a tool shed. Grass grows around the house and a few lawn chairs are scattered in the garden. A boat on a trailer sits alongside the trucks.

Over the years Higley bought more land around his property as it became available, eventually building up over 500 irrigated acres. His big crop was potatoes. 'The idea was to work a piece of land and then take the money from the crops and buy the piece of land next to it. I never wanted to lease someone else's land.'

His two sons became farmers, and together the three men kept expanding their boundaries. Clark made enough money to buy two gift boutiques for Colleen to run in Burley and Rupert, and built another house for themselves in Heyburn on the Snake River. But Higley's fortune was amassed with the backbreaking labour of farming. In 1975, at the age of forty-eight, he wanted to wake up in the mornings to another challenge. 'Every farmer,' he says, 'wants to be a rancher. When you're breeding cattle, there's more prestige. When you're farming, you're a dirt digger.'

With a local estate agent Clark started scouting the state for a cattle ranch. He didn't look long before he found the Pine Creek Ranch in Salmon, almost two hundred miles north of Rupert. Higley is a man with a chiselled, hawk-like visage and his pale blue eyes mist over as he describes the Pine Creek Ranch he saw in 1975. 'It was a gorgeous place,' he says. 'That's why we got in so much trouble trying to own it.'

He also saw the ranch as a way to keep the family together. It was big enough for his two sons and their families and, if the boys came along, Clark felt he could manage Pine Creek without hiring much outside help.

Colleen was not so anxious to leave her stores in southern Idaho and get stranded in Salmon, an area, she says, that made Rupert look cosmopolitan: 'In Salmon you're one hundred and fifty miles from anything.'

The ranch lay in a narrow valley scalloped out between the Bitteroot Mountains on the Montana border to the east, and the smaller Lemhi range to the west. The Lemhi River winds through the valley, swelling and shrinking alongside the two-lane state highway that is the region's main road, and that runs through dense forests and treacherous mountain passes.

The Pine Creek ranch extended for miles on either side of the road, the largest spread in Salmon. It was the sort of place people called a showcase. First hewed out by a reclusive Dane, who drained most of the bog himself, it was sold in 1956 to a friendly cowboy named Emmett Reese. Originally from New York, Mrs Reese was heir to a steel and mining fortune. She had been given up as an old maid when she fell in love with Emmett, one of the hands at a western dude ranch where she was visiting. After their marriage they moved to Salmon. Mrs Reese instantly became the town's leading philanthropist, building the local hospital and financing scholarships to help local children go away to college. Meanwhile, Emmett used his wife's wealth to build one of the best registered Hereford breeding stock in the state. Money was often no object, and at times, Reese would pay the local townspeople to do chores just to have a little company around.

Over the years the Reeses created a storybook image of the perfect Idaho ranch, and local people often brought visitors by for a look on a Sunday afternoon. With a big green roof, the Reeses' house sat on its own little half-acre of grass surrounded by a white wooden fence. On the other sides of a huge circular drive were two smaller white washed homes, a bunk house, brightly painted red bars, storehouses, sheds and haylofts.

By 1971 Emmett had become too old to manage the ranch by himself and Mrs Reese was forced to sell off the property, keeping only a little corner for a retirement home. When autumn came, her lawyers completed the sale, for one million dollars to John De Lorean. It had been a purchase partly inspired by Kelly Harmon, but it was also an investment that made sense as a tax shelter. De Lorean quickly tried to make Pine Creek the GM of ranches. He added to the Reeses' 1600 acres, buying 1000 acres on the other side of the road and four hundred more ten miles south. He then hired a professional manager to run the ranch.

For the first few months of ownership De Lorean played the role of country squire. He paid a few visits with his young wife and they spent weekends riding horses around their massive new range. One picture from that time shows a thin, long-haired De Lorean standing next to his manager and a prize steer. Wearing sneakers with a faded blue denim jacket and trousers, the new rancher does not look the western type, and after his divorce from Kelly, De Lorean's enthusiasm for cattle-breeding began to fade.

'I think I saw John five times in five years,' the manager of the ranch says. But the manager did not stint in keeping up Pine Creek. He was reputed to have a $600,000 credit arrangement at the local bank and he added his own touches, like California-style wooden corrals, to Emmett Reese's model ranch. De Lorean thought about syndicating his herd, but the plans fell through. 'In those years the whole livestock business was in chaos,' the manager explains. 'The ranch just didn't pay its way and the loss was too big for De Lorean to use. He put the place up for sale, but nothing happened.'

In 1975 De Lorean told him to sell off most of the registered herd. To help out he sent the ranch manager a man from California. 'He told me this fellow Roy Nesseth knew about livestock. When Nesseth blew into town. I could see immediately that he knew nothing about it. His only experience had been with race horses, but he seemed to be in charge of John's property.'

Roy claimed that De Lorean had given him a share of the ranch and that he stood to gain much more if he managed to sell it. 'Roy didn't really mix that well with the people in Salmon,' the manager remembers. 'He seemed like the high-powered-salesman type. Quick with the numbers.'

Nesseth apparently had more interest in Idaho than just the Pine Creek Ranch. Along with his brother Don he was opening a Chevrolet dealership in Lewiston. 'Roy wanted me to put the ranch money in a Lewiston bank under his name to show GM he had enough assets to support the franchise. Of course, I would do no such thing without John's approval. But he told me to go ahead. I wrote the cheque for the transfer. I believe that John got the money back as soon as Chevrolet okayed the franchise.' (Three years later Chevrolet would take the franchise away from the Nesseth brothers for 'no longer serving the sales and service needs of customers'.)

Almost everyone living in Salmon would be surprised when Nesseth and De Lorean managed to refinance the ranch with a million-dollar mortgage from the Seattle office of the Metropolitan Life Insurance Company at 10 per cent interest, a mortgage negotiated by the ranch manager. Mortgages of that size weren't often guaranteed by the property alone.

Clark Higley and his estate agent were unfortunate enough to come knocking at Pine Creek's door in November 1975 – just a few months after the mortgage was in place. Suddenly, De Lorean was not as interested in selling the ranch as before.

Higley soon discovered that neither De Lorean nor his manager would do the negotiating. All business affairs regarding Pine Creek were in Roy Nesseth's hands, and at first that suited the Higleys fine.

'Roy can be a real charmer,' Colleen says. 'He keeps telling you how much he loves your family and asks about your grandkids and your folks. We had him over to dinner a few times and he couldn't have been nicer.'

Clark had enough money to swing an outright purchase of the ranch, but Roy talked him out of it. 'He was very persuasive. He told me that there was no way they could redo the Metropolitan mortgage for me, and that it was too valuable to let drop. Instead, he told me I could make the payments in a lease arrangement.'

Higley's estate agent and lawyer tried to talk him out of that course of action, but Roy seemed to have the better arguments. First of all, he told Clark, if they had a lease, then the agent wouldn't have to be paid his commission and there'd be more in the deal for everyone. Nesseth also convinced him that the taxes put on a straight purchase would hurt both buyer and seller.

'Roy was just a mesmerizer,' Clark says today. 'We would sit down and go through all the details and Roy remembered every figure we ever discussed. That impressed me. I thought he had a tremendous mind. He had a way of taking your idea and somehow twisting it to work in his favour.'

In March 1976 they settled on a deal. Higley turned over his house on the river and his potato farm (worth over $800,000 together), $300,000 cash and agreed to make lease payments of $189,000 a year, out of which

De Lorean was to pay the mortgage. In return he got a lease, an option to buy the property, an assignment of the 500 head of cattle and a security agreement on ranch equipment.

Actually, considering what he gave up, Higley received almost nothing. Pointing to the vague nature of the documents Higley signed, his lawyers would later charge that 'none of the . . . written agreements set forth the true intent, purposes and agreement of the parties'. Nesseth, they said, 'so structured the instruments to confuse, misstate, abort and avoid [Higley's] legitimate intent'. Nesseth's lawyer countered that Higley knew very well what he was signing.

Shortly after he moved onto the farm, Clark went over to visit Mrs Reese. Her husband had just died and she didn't have much longer to live herself, but she wanted Higley to watch out for De Lorean. 'She told me her dealings with De Lorean over the ranch had been real tough,' Higley says. 'She believed that if it hadn't been for her New York lawyers, she would have really been taken.'

In his first summer on the ranch Clark realized what kind of deal he had done. When he went to sell the cattle, he discovered that Nesseth still had a mortgage out on the herd. Higley thought that he had bought the cattle free and clear for $300,000.

Enraged, Higley made a frantic call to John De Lorean in New York to let him know that Nesseth had a lien on the cattle. De Lorean agreed to stop off in Boise on his way to the West Coast and meet with Clark. 'He couldn't have been more friendly or sympathetic,' Higley recalls. 'He said, "I don't know what kind of mess Roy's gotten you into, but I'll straighten it out."'

De Lorean promised to pay off the Idaho bank and get the mortgage removed, but until he did Higley was stuck with a herd of cattle and no cash to pay the mounting costs of keeping up a big ranch. 'Now I realize that in that first summer, I should have gotten a recision and backed out of the whole deal,' Clark says. 'In the eyes of the law, I would have had a perfect right.'

But as the second year of the lease ended, Clark had no money left to pay the next instalment, and his credit had run out with his bank. Nesseth offered to secure a loan through his connections, if Higley swapped back the cattle. Clark transferred title to the herd, but Roy never followed through with the loan.

Today, as Colleen Higley listens to her husband rehash the sequence of events, she shakes her head and says, 'What a mess we got ourselves into.'

After two years of hard work, Higley had almost nothing to show for his investment in the Pine Creek Ranch. He had lost his potato farm and $300,000, but no longer had the cattle, and never had title to the equipment (De Lorean and Nesseth still claim they never sold the equipment). To make matters worse, the mortgage holder, Metropolitan, did not receive any of the three lease payments Higley turned over to Nesseth.

On March 1979 Metropolitan Life Insurance started foreclosure proceedings and soon after, when Clark told Roy he wouldn't be getting any more lease payments, Nesseth and De Lorean tried to evict the Higleys.

Clark got another lawyer and fought back in court. Unable to sell off the Pine Creek herd, he used the ranch to graze one thousand head of a friend's cattle. The room and board he charged for the herd helped him eke out a living. Colleen had already sold the boutiques to make ends meet as well.

When summer came around, it looked like a stalemate. While the Higleys held onto the ranch, De Lorean could neither sell it nor pay off the mortgage, his mortgage. But suddenly, a possible compromise cropped up in the person of Utah rancher John Stephenson. Stephenson had looked at Pine Creek even before Higley did, but decided De Lorean's price was too high. However, a portion of his own ranch south of Salt Lake City had been claimed by a Utah power project, and he found himself in a position to reconsider. He and Higley agreed to work together to get control of the ranch. By this time Clark was willing to settle for no more than the 400 acre spread ten miles down the road in Tendoy.

Stephenson and Higley next travelled to a Boise car-dealer friendly with both De Lorean and Nesseth. The dealer had offered to mediate, and if necessary, provide some backing to arrive at an arrangement that would make everyone happy. 'We called up John in New York,' Clark says, 'and I asked him what he wanted to put an end to all this. And he answered, "All I want is $350,000, and for someone to take over the mortgage."

'Well, that was fine with us, and I said, "John, you've got a deal." He then said he just had to make a quick check with his banker and be right back to us. He called back fifteen minutes later to say that the Tendoy ranch was still in Kelly Harmon's name and that he couldn't go through with the deal.

'Of course John was up to his tricks again. We all knew that ranch wasn't in Kelly Harmon's name. He probably called Nesseth and Roy told him to hold out for more money.'

For the next few months Clark felt he was in court more often than he was on the ranch. 'We must have gone to trial sixteen times,' he says. There were some legal victories for the Higleys. They sued De Lorean for ten months of cattle care and feeding, winning a judgment of $100,000. 'We had one deposition session with Roy that lasted from 9 a.m. to four in the afternoon. While our lawyer cross-examined him, he'd get up, cursing and screaming and would leave the room. He must have done that four times.'

But the Higleys could not stave off the foreclosure. Metropolitan seized the property and evicted them in spring 1980. The memory of the day he left Pine Creek behind is still bitter for Clark, 'We had three families and no place to go.'

The Higley's could not collect on their judgment until September and then, by the time the lawyers and the banks were through, only $48,000 was left. For Clark and Colleen, it would be even harder when they returned to Rupert and got a look at their old farm. Roy had changed the name to the Mini-Cassia Ranch, but he had done little else. The fields hadn't been watered. Weeds grew waist deep around the house. Leaning on Clark's reputation in Rupert, Nesseth established credit with merchants around the town. He even took a piece of a short-lived farm equipment dealership nearby. By the time Clark had left Pine Creek, the lawsuits for non-payment against Nesseth had piled up in the Rupert courthouse.

Clark thinks back to all he once had and says, 'It was all reaped out of the ground. No fancy investments. Just back-breaking work. And I thought that was all it would take with Pine Creek. Our friends used to say, "How could you have been so dumb?" '.

Some other people had even worse things to say about Clark. Higley, like most of his neighbours in Idaho, is a Mormon. The more religious types said he had lusted too much after the ranch, or that his problems stemmed from trying to avoid paying the estate agent's commission to begin with. But John Stephenson, standing in the muddy circular drive of what was once the Pine Creek ranch, says, 'I know exactly what happened to him. I did business with Nesseth and De Lorean, and I got beat too.'

After Metropolitan foreclosed, Stephenson still tried to pick up the ranch. Since De Lorean had a year to redeem his property, no one bothered to bid at the sheriff's auction and De Lorean was still free to peddle the ranch. Roy chased Stephenson back down to Utah. 'He was like a flea on a dog. He used to say, "We don't need any attorneys. You know what you want. I know what I want. So we can make a deal." '

But it wouldn't take long before negotiations got heated. 'Roy got to throwing a fit one day in the lawyer's office,' Stephenson remembers. 'He was cussing so badly with ladies around that my son Gordon grabbed him by the coat and took him aside and told him that either he acted like a man and quieted down, or it would be all over for him. Gordon's not the biggest man, but people tend to know you don't mess with Gordon. Roy shut up pretty quickly.'

Stephenson would get trapped when he put his land reclamation settlement from the power company into an escrow account. At last he picked up the entire $1.8 million owed on the mortgage, but Roy got $500,000 more out of him. 'Even with all that they pulled one last stunt. When the contract got written up, they put back the months of penalty on the mortgage that I'd be responsible for. That little one change added another $50,000.'

A week later, during his deposition on the United Visuals case, De Lorean would crow about the Pine Creek land transaction when he addressed Roy's 'very brilliant' financial abilities: 'He made, oh, probably a million and a half dollars for me on something that I didn't think I would have made a penny on'.

Almost a year passed between the time Higley moved off and Stephenson put his own name over the ranch. During the interim Nesseth's manager let the place run down. The houses went unpainted. Fences fell down. Fields went dry. Stephenson hasn't had the money or time yet to make all the repairs and do all the painting necessary. One especially grim winter morning, while he squints off at the clouds breaking over the mountains, he voices doubts whether he can keep up his own hefty interest payments to the bank.

'Once,' Stephenson says, 'Roy came down to my place in Utah and claimed he ran out of cash and didn't have any personal cheques or anything else to get back home with. So I loaned him $300. I never mentioned it again, but everytime I saw him, Roy would tell me he hadn't forgotten about my $300. Finally, six months later, he gave me a cheque for $350, and it bounced. I still have that cheque.'

A Dealership

In the spring of 1976 John De Lorean was not very happy with Roy Nesseth. GPA Systems had gone bankrupt. Saf–Guard was on the verge of failure with Avrea in court and writ servers chasing De Lorean all over the place. Meanwhile, back at the ranch in Idaho, Roy had not paid off the lien on the cattle with Higley's $300,000 and Metropolitan was pursuing De Lorean for a mortgage payment. According to George Williams, De Lorean wondered whether it was a good idea ever to have taken Roy out of the dealership.

'John and I were talking on the phone,' Williams recalls, 'and he said, "George, all that Roy does is cause me grief. You don't know how much trouble he's gotten me into."

'And then he told me that the best thing for Roy was to put him back in a dealership. He said he had found the perfect store for Roy in Wichita and that he was going to give it to him – just to get him away from all the trouble he caused.'

De Lorean had found the dealership while negotiating to buy glass rooftops for sportscars from a manufacturer in Wichita. De Lorean had also come to Wichita to scout out a site to build his sports car on, but it was the glass-maker who told him about a local Cadillac dealer struggling to stay in business. Cadillac dealerships are considered the gold mines of the auto business, and De Lorean quickly sought out the bank financing the franchise. Quite contrary to the stereotype of the conservative banker, Kenneth E. Johnson, chairman of the board of the Kansas State Bank and Trust Company, had a special affinity for freewheeling entrepreneurs. He proudly kept a picture of aviation pioneer Bill Lear on his wall and pointed out to visitors a reference in Lear's biography that mentions Johnson and his memories of a time 'when he talked his own institution into loaning Lear four weeks of payroll' so he could sell a few planes and pay off a short-term note.

Johnson was to be as impressed by De Lorean as he was by Lear. When De Lorean inquired about the faltering Cadillac dealership, Johnson jumped to accommodate the V.I.P. inquiry.

In fact, Dahlinger Pontiac–Cadillac was in no more trouble than most dealerships after the devastating impact of the oil embargo. And Gerald W. Dahlinger was no flaky wheeler dealer, but a responsible young businessman with roots in the community.

If Gerry Dahlinger had a flaw it was an affection for the auto business. The son of a barber, Dahlinger worked his way through college, mostly slogging away at the local refineries. Of those days, he says, 'I never had enough quarters to put back to back.'

One summer he helped out a relative who owned a dealership. It was a job Gerry could see doing himself one day, and when he left college, he tried leasing cars for another dealer. One of his clients had got involved in a fast food franchise, and he convinced Dahlinger to move to Florida and get in on the ground floor. The name of the company was Pizza Hut, and Gerry ended up owning the Florida franchise. When he sold out in 1972, he had turned a $1500 investment into a $500,000 nest egg.

Gerry was ready to come back to Wichita with his bankroll, and he had no doubts what he would do with it. 'My dream had always been to put together a solid deal,' he says, using the auto vernacular for dealership. 'If you stay in business ten years, you become an institution, and when you reach that stage, you have the world by the short hairs.'

He started with a Buick dealership sixty miles out of town, and then bought a failing Pontiac store in Wichita from its ageing owner. He quickly showed GM his skills as a salesman, cutting the losses the prior owners had suffered. Just thirty-eight years old, with a gift for gab and an easy smile, Dahlinger appeared to be heading for a bright future.

Shortly after he took over his second dealership Gerry had the 'sneaking suspicion', that he might be able to 'dual' the store with a Cadillac franchise. When he got that, in August 1975, it was the first time in five years that GM had allowed a dealer to dual their prestige line. To celebrate Gerry had a party in the ballroom of the Hilton.

'I sold twenty-seven Cadillacs before they delivered my first one,' he says, 'but I was undercapitalized from the word go.' Near exhaustion from commuting between dealerships, he sold his Buick store and tried to concentrate on cutting his losses in Wichita. The bank had tried to get him a partner, but after difficult negotiations with Gerry he backed out.

Still, Gerry continued to make progress against his losses, almost tripling his sales volume in three years. 'I had everything I owned in that dealership. And Kenneth Johnson assured me we were going to tough it out. Then one day in late April 1976 he called me to say, "I've got a buyer. The buyer's representative, a guy named Roy Nesseth, is coming to tour the place." '

Nesseth flew into Wichita full of smiles, handshakes and assurances all around that he and De Lorean could pull Dahlinger's dealership into the big time. Johnson turned supervision of the account over to his president, J.V. Lentell. Later in court testimony, Lentell remembered that the first thing Nesseth talked about was 'Mr De Lorean's tenure with General Motors and that one of the benefits of his being interested was the fact that through his friends in General Motors, they could get probably an unlimited amount of Cadillacs which this dealership probably needed more than anything . . . in order to make it go.'

Roy took a quick look and was ready to make a deal. Tom Kimmerly flew in to help him work out the details. Johnson asked Gerry to sign powers of attorney to Kimmerly and transfer his stock. At first he protested, but then, he says, Johnson told him, ' "We'll put this deal together or we'll lock the doors at 5.00." In effect, Johnson had called my loan, and there was no way I'd find the money to pay it off in four hours.'

Dahlinger watched as De Lorean's men took control of the dealership for the debt and a refinanced loan of $200,000. Dahlinger was to get a one-year employment contract for $80,000. But the dealership was still to bear his name, and no official documents would show any trace of De Lorean. Bank president Lentell still secured guarantees from De Lorean, but he asked Kimmerly why De Lorean didn't want his name on the stock. He testified that 'Kimmerly answered me by saying that "I handle it this way because Mr De Lorean and I have our own side deal. We could not permit his name to appear on any records because in addition to his friends, he also had enemies in GM and that would blow the whole deal and his name will never appear in this dealership." '

That answer did not make any sense to Dahlinger. Within days, he asked Cadillac's zone manager to drop by his house and filled him in on the transaction. He promised to keep him informed, but asked that he not move yet and jeopardize his $80,000 employment contract. Besides, Nesseth had promised that once the dealership was 'straightened out'

114

Gerry would have a chance to buy it back.

Roy stayed in Wichita after the papers were signed and asked Gerry to look for a house for him. 'We went to one of the nicest places in town – a home designed by Frank Lloyd Wright, but Roy didn't like it. He said the art inside was worth more than the house, and that he'd probably have to build his own home.'

Roy would be most interested by an abandoned factory. 'He made me stop the car,' Gerry remembers, 'and we got out and walked inside. He was real excited to see there was still some big machinery inside. He had all kinds of ideas of how to get that machinery away from the poor guy who went bankrupt. He then said, "We have to find out who has true title and interest." Whatever that means. He was clearly an expert on bankruptcies.'

Otherwise, Roy was not much impressed by Wichita. 'He let me know it was too small a town for him,' Gerry says. 'Johnson had put him up in the bank's hotel, the Royale, and I met Roy the next day for breakfast. He ordered a fried egg and when the waitress brought it, he told her it was overcooked, and he just tossed it off the plate and onto the floor. That's when I realized what kind of a guy we were dealing with.'

Gerry took the next two weeks off for a holiday. He returned to find that Nesseth had taken over his office and was alternately amusing and terrifying his salesmen. Sometimes he would walk over to one and just push a hundred dollar bill in his hand. At other times, he cursed the air blue, tearing telephones out of the wall, and throwing them across the floor. Roy drew cash freely. No one seemed to be keeping records.

'I was like a blue suede shoe with a bad personality,' Gerry says. 'I wasn't allowed to do anything. I wasn't selling. I just showed up.'

At night Dahlinger would wander through the dealership alone. Like a ghost in a horror movie, he had come back in his old form but without the corporeal substance to affect anything. And yet, most eery of all, his name was still on the door, and as far as everyone but the bank was concerned, he still owned the place.

No one could stop Gerry from reading, and during his late-night haunts Gerry could not help but see that the remnants of the dealership were disappearing. First of all, there was Roy's lavish lifestyle. Dahlinger Pontiac–Cadillac was picking up his American Express and hotel bills which hovered between $5,000 and $6,000 a month. Hundreds of dollars went to clothing stores. One cheque for $566 was written to the Fairmont Hotel in Dallas, where Roy told Gerry he was going to meet a friend for the weekend.

Roy did not scrimp in his salary either, sometimes paying himself $5,000 a week, although not directly. The dealership instead would write the cheque to the bank and it would issue money orders to Roy (better to go unreported with the IRS). Meanwhile, Kimmerly was periodically pulling in thousand-dollar fees and De Lorean was on an annual retainer of $150,000.

There were some large cheques Dahlinger did not understand at all. One, for $10,000, was written to Clark Higley; another, for $5,000, to the Bank of Idaho for the Mini-Cassia Ranch. Roy had the dealership pay $60,000 for two phantom Peterbilt trucks that never appeared in Wichita.

But the greatest recipient of the dealership's payments was Saf-Guard Systems. In just one month Dahlinger Pontiac–Cadillac sent $79,000 to Saf-Guard, and the Phoenix company sent $61,000 back. Along with the cheques, Gerry found frantic notes to Roy from the respective accountants asking for funds to be flown back and forth as soon as possible. One August note from the Saf-Guard bookkeeper mentions two enclosed blank cheques and says: 'I should have at least $15,000 for our needs at Tempe . . . We will have very little coming in in September as August sales were small.'

From some of his notes, the Wichita accountant seems to have found Roy's antics amusing. He writes in the margin of his calendar: 'R.N. gave me two checks he had written, total $1500, to [a clothing store]; said to classify as salesmen's clothes incentives; really were his!!'

But the interstate transfer of funds between the two companies to keep their current accounts afloat – law authorities call it kiting – was definitely illegal and no laughing matter. One other piece of the accountants marginalia anxiously notes that someone had told the bank in Phoenix about the cheques going back and forth between Saf-Guard and Dahlinger.

Gerry spent several nights making meticulous xeroxes of the papers that lay strewn around what was once his desk. Although he had no power, Gerry was still the figurehead president, potentially liable for Nesseth's actions. 'I was walking the tightrope, trying to get my money, but not letting them get away with too much. I'm just sorry I stuck around as long as I did.'

Even written letters to the bank did not seem to sink in. At last, ten months after Nesseth took over, Gerry became convinced that no one would put the brakes on Roy and he walked out. Before he left, however, he let the GM zone manager know that the charade was over. Soon after General Motors moved in to take away the franchise.

The debt for the dealership had soared to $800,000, and the bankers faced the spectre of a total loss. They won a reprieve from GM and found a mutually acceptable dealer to buy the property and franchise from De Lorean, but first they had to consolidate the debt. In a deal worked out with Kimmerly, the bank issued yet another loan and De Lorean got the opportunity to buy the land under the dealership, which he then leased back to the new owner. The remainder of the loan was to be repaid with the sales of the Dahlinger used cars still on the lot. That sum was personally guaranteed by De Lorean.

But as the Kansas state court would later find in its judgment, 'Nesseth proceeded to sell all or a portion of the used cars . . . but with one or two minor exceptions, failed to deposit the proceeds in the [Kansas State Bank].' De Lorean was held liable for the loan. Both Kimmerly and De Lorean defended themselves by distancing themselves from Nesseth. Kimmerly testified 'he was well aware [that Roy] was a crook'.

De Lorean claimed that Roy had gone out of his control. His note, he argued, was solely to 'help' the bank in its time of need. The judge called this argument 'quite unbelievable' and ordered De Lorean to pay $237,124 plus interest – a sum that reached $400,000 by the time De Lorean's last appeal was rejected in the spring of 1982.

Roy wouldn't escape Kansas law either. A doctor who could not get the title to his Cadillac after he fulfilled all his payments sued Nesseth successfully in Wichita for over $130,000 and then pursued the defendant into California, where he finally collected his judgment – with attorney John Thomas's help – in 1982.

As for Dahlinger, he left the state soon after he left his dealership, afraid that his name had been irreparably muddied by the whole affair. 'I had to sell my house, my car, the whole thing,' he remembers ruefully. 'All I had left was furniture and some personal belongings.' He tried to get another start in the Florida fast food business, but that did not work out. His pilot store was coincidentally across the street from a Pizza Hut. 'Six years later,' he says, 'and I'm still busted.'

But in all his dealings with De Lorean, nothing hurts Dahlinger more than the loss of his antique car. Known as the Mercedes-Benz 300SL, it was one of only a few thousand in existence. Gerry had seen it advertised in an Oklahoma City newspaper and picked it up for $6,000. 'The guy could have charged me $35,000.'

It is a car that has developed almost cult status. 'The one thing that makes the 300SL so special,' Gerry says, 'is that it has gull-wing doors. It was the first production model car ever to do that, and the last to do it in any sizable numbers.'

When De Lorean heard Gerry owned such a car, he asked if he could borrow it for a month. He wanted to shoot a commercial with the gull-wing Mercedes to advertise the car he was thinking of making. In December 1976 Gerry had the car shipped to Bloomfield Hills. He flew over as well, just to make sure it arrived in good condition.

He was never to see the car again.

117

100 West Long Lake

On 4 January 1974 Bob McLean became the first employee of the John Z. De Lorean Corporation. For thirty-five years McLean had worked at General Motors, mostly in the design studios and finally as an expert in auto safety. A big man, with a round face and sparkling blue eyes, he laughs as he remembers how De Lorean persuaded him to join his fledgling firm. "John just had a way of working you into his dreams. He talked of us doing great things together – especially about his plan to start his own car company. But he had a few projects that he wanted me to attend to first, so we could get a little seed money."

McLean's initial assignment was to find quarters for the new concern. Previously De Lorean had borrowed office space from Bunkie Knudsen, and McLean merely walked across the street from that location to lease 1800 square feet at 100 West Long Lake Road, a two-storey structure built within the previous year. Propped on stilts, with a grey-slate façade and smoked-glass windows, 100 West Long Lake looked more like a slice of a much larger building. It stood at the hub of professional activity in Bloomfield Hills, America's wealthiest community. Around the corner were the two posh Tudor-style restaurants – the Fox and Hounds and the Kingsley Inn – that were lunchtime favourites for the local elite. The Bloomfield Hills Country Club was just up the street.

"I remember De Lorean brought in some expensive carpeting," says 100 West Long Lake's landlord Jerry Rowin. "But the thing that struck me the most was that he wanted to put up a picture outside his office. Of course, I had no objection to that. It was some kind of contemporary oil painting and it broke up the line in the hall."

The most significant ramification of De Lorean's move to the building would come one morning in the men's room on his floor. It was there that he struck up a conversation for the first time with the lawyer who had the office next door, Thomas Kimmerly. In appearance and manner, the two were as diametrically opposed as possible. Tall and

118

distinctive, with a naturally stentorian voice, De Lorean had no trouble standing out in a crowd, and more than likely wore his favourite office attire: a cotton casual shirt and jeans. On the other hand, short and soft-spoken, Kimmerly tended to blend into the subdued stains of legal suite panelling. He undoubtedly wore his usual dark conservative suit.

Despite their physical disparity, both shared a hunger for greater financial conquests than either one had previously known. Gradually, from their introduction in the toilet, Kimmerly and De Lorean would embark on the most important professional association of their respective careers. As years passed, neither one would be embarrassed to talk about that first meeting or to wonder about what course their lives might have taken, if they had not stopped to talk after they left the urinals.

Kimmerly, one of 100 West Long Lake's first tenants, had moved his three-partner law firm from downtown Detroit to be closer to his retired clients. He also wanted to be closer to his own home as he too approached, in his mid-fifties, gradual retirement from a busy practice. A Certified Public Accountant as well as a lawyer, he had very quietly become the tax counsellor of choice to several wealthy industrialists, and occasionally counsel to corporations as well. Mild-mannered, he had always taken great care to stay out of the limelight. His closest brush with publicity came with an oil exploration venture he had put together with his client and friend, Ray Dahlinger (no relation to Wichita car dealer Gerald Dahlinger), a controversial Detroit businessman who has claimed to be the illegitimate son of Henry Ford. The oil deal eventually fell through, and several prominent Detroit personalities, including one television newscaster, made five-figure losses. It was the last time Kimmerly emerged from advisory shadows.

That is, until he met John De Lorean. In De Lorean, he would find the reason to throw his standard caution to the wind. Kimmerly was later to characterize De Lorean for the *American Lawyer* as "a client of enormous energy and absolute dedication . . . He's head and shoulders above everyone else I've encountered in [the automobile] industry." He started by offering De Lorean tax advice, after De Lorean's longtime accountant died, but in a few years he replaced De Lorean's attorney, John Noonan, who had previously been the auto executive's closest adviser. In time, Kimmerly was to assume positions on the boards of Saf-Guard Systems, Pine Creek Ranch and Dahlinger Pontiac Cadillac. Eventually, the man who had only a few years before contemplated retirement faced the most demanding and potentially risky endeavour of his life as John De Lorean's personal counsel. Throughout, his devotion to De Lorean would be unwavering.

As a calm, steadying grey eminence, Kimmerly countered the more volatile influence of Roy Nesseth. But many deals that emanated from

119

100 West Long Lake involved neither man – especially in the first few years after De Lorean left General Motors.

When De Lorean moved into 100 West Long Lake he was officially working as president of the National Alliance of Businessmen. Although the job was unsalaried, General Motors was donating $200,000 to pay De Lorean. GM chairman Richard Gerstenberg, who then filled the ceremonial NAB chair, had been the one to appoint De Lorean to the one-year presidency. Some in auto industry circles saw the move as an attempt to get De Lorean off the street and away from competitors. It was also a way, some thought, finally to tie De Lorean up with his moralistic rhetoric, as despite his pronouncements about social responsibility, his superiors had often noted sardonically that De Lorean never did find as much time for charity work as his insensitive colleagues.

But according to Fred Wentzel, NAB vice president, De Lorean responded enthusiastically to his non-profit post. Serving mostly as a cheerleader, he travelled the country encouraging local business groups to hire disadvantaged workers. 'Comparing him to other NAB presidents on a scale of one to ten,' Wentzel says, 'I'd give him a seven. John definitely seemed committed to the concept and he spoke with commitment. He wasn't just going through the motions. We have since invited him back to participate in other activities, and he hasn't responded. But to be truthful most past presidents don't respond either.' (In fact, De Lorean's own hiring record at De Lorean Motor Company would be considered dismal by NAB standards. At any one time in the company's history there were less than three blacks at low level positions, and no minorities or women in executive positions.)

Although he kept a townhouse in Washington, De Lorean continued to commute back to Detroit and pursue business ventures on his own. In June 1974, when his presidency of the NAB was up, he told a magazine, 'Now I have to get back into the cold, hard world and earn a living.' But six months earlier he had registered the John Z. De Lorean Corporation with Michigan's Department of Commerce, listing himself as a 'product design and business consultant'.

He had already found that life did indeed go on after GM – if anything the financial world was even warmer and more receptive than before. As a free agent, he rapidly expanded his business interests, especially in New York. He no longer bopped into town just to visit the swinging discos, but also to be seen at the power tables of the 21 Club. In his last year at General Motors he had accepted George Steinbrenner's offer to buy a piece of the New York Yankees baseball team. ('I sat down and drew up a list of men I know to be doers,' Steinbrenner told one reporter when asked how he chose investors.) His investment in the team was relatively small – $50,000 – but it gave him the chance to rub shoulders with the likes of lawyer Thomas W. Evans, oil czar Nelson Bunker Hunt and theatrical producer James Nederlander. Free of GM strictures, he was able to do business with them as well.

He showed his first corporate allegiance in New York to Chris Craft, joining the company's board and eventually becoming a close personal friend of the company's chief executive Herbert Jay Seigel. Among De Lorean's other Manhattan business patrons was William D. Fugazy, a travel and transportation broker whose firm had a number of lucrative contracts with the auto companies. Fugazy provided De Lorean entrée to some of New York's most powerful executives.

A mutual fascination often sprung up between the older business titans and the much younger GM outcast. 'No matter how important John claimed to be,' one of his friends says, 'he was almost mystified by the people who managed to make vast sums of money. He liked nothing more than to talk about how some big deal was pulled off.'

For a while, J. Peter Grace, Jr. was willing to share his big deal magic with the aspiring mogul. In twenty-five years as chief executive of W.R. Grace & Company, Grace had turned his father's shipping and trading concern into a diversified conglomerate with holdings ranging from fertilizer to fast food restaurants. Fugazy introduced Grace to De Lorean and their relationship took off from there. Both were inveterate golfers. Both could discuss their cattle ranch tax shelters. According to Bob McLean, 'Peter Grace was instantly enamoured of John and often asked him along on business trips. He tried to hire him, but John wasn't ready for that. I think John was tremendously intimidated by him. Grace had the reputation as a terribly demanding man. He wanted facts and figures on everything – projections for the next ten years. And he could be ruthless. If the numbers didn't look right, he'd sell a division in an hour. John told me, "A guy like that would just chew me up."

'So John asked instead that he do some consulting work for Grace, and evidently the old man then flipped through his huge array of subsidiaries and found the division he thought would be the right fit. It was called Shasta, and it made recreational vehicles. With that, they decided that John would design a fuel-efficient motor home. John said he told Grace, "In four years you'll be the biggest factor in the recreational vehicle business."'

Grace gave De Lorean a consulting contract that paid him $25,000 a month for 50 per cent of his time and also compensation for two full-time employees. 'I think that consulting fee tended to hurt John more than help him,' McLean says. 'From then on he'd quote that as his monthly retainer and scared a lot of people away.'

A week after the contract with Grace was signed, De Lorean called McLean into his office. 'John told me not to bother with the stipulations of the contract. John always felt contracts were interesting pieces of paper and no more. He said I should go ahead and bill all the people in the office to Grace.'

Many of the other people in the office were working on another project funded by the Allstate Insurance Company. De Lorean had long been the most vocal advocate for the airbag safety device in the auto industry – a cushion installed in the dashboard and steering-wheel that inflated on impact. Allstate chief executive Archie R. Boe held much the same distinction in his own industry and actively sought out De Lorean both to lobby and consult on the airbag. McLean was GM's expert in the safety field and Allstate was willing to back the airbag research he did for De Lorean with a $250,000 investment.

Boe was also taken by De Lorean's talk of producing his own car. With the oil crisis Allstate worried about the fuel-efficient tin boxes that were cruising America's highways and their propensity for fatal accidents. If De Lorean were to design a fuel efficient commuter car that had safety features, Boe told him, Allstate would be willing to underwrite the project. For a payment of $600,000 De Lorean contracted to produce two safety prototypes: one for crash testing and another that Allstate could take on tour around the country. Soon after he boldly predicted to *Ward's Auto World* in June 1974 that he would start manufacturing the mini-car in fifteen months: 'Plans are to start out in the area of 40,000 or 50,000 units and let it go wherever it goes.'

'We never did deliver those cars,' McLean says. 'In fact, nothing even went beyond the paper stage and I was sure that there'd be a lawsuit over it. But somehow the whole thing got smoothed over.' Today, an Allstate spokesman says the company and Mr Boe had no regret over their contract with De Lorean.

Nothing would come of the project for Grace either, although more work had been expended on the motor home than the Allstate commuter car. A De Lorean assistant, who had once been a crack marketing man for General Motors, conducted extensive research on what consumers wanted in motor homes. In what the industry calls clinics, he took people through existing recreational vehicles, closely noting their comments and reactions. 'We had a very clear idea of what people wanted,' McLean says, 'down to the kitchens and bathrooms. We built a styling prototype, which basically shows what the interior of the vehicle will look like.

'We stored the prototype with an industrial designer and one night it caught on fire. It was insured for $100,000, and, although some of us felt it was the property of Grace, John put the insurance money in his pocket.

'In all, Peter Grace must have spent one million dollars on the project, but he just lost patience with John and sold the recreational vehicle division. John couldn't get anyone else interested, and I think he ended

122

up feeling betrayed by Grace.'

De Lorean would engage in even more fruitless discussions with another elder statesman of American business, Armand Hammer. Chief executive of Occidental Petroleum, Hammer had long been capitalism's ambassador to the Soviet sphere of influence. Evidently he approached De Lorean early in 1974 about distributing the Lada – the Russian version of a Fiat subcompact. 'Hammer's office,' McLean remembers, 'was in Los Angeles, not too far away from the Grace recreational vehicle division. Once when we were in town, John had me drop him off. He'd only go up alone to see Hammer, and come back down exhilarated. He was just in awe of the man.'

In June 1975 newspapers carried stories that De Lorean was ready to direct sales of Ladas for the Soviet government import company. But at a time when the American auto industry was in crisis Congress showed no inclination to let thousands of Russian cars into the United States.

Yet the cheap labour costs of Eastern Europe and the desire of the governments to break into American markets continued to appeal to De Lorean, and he did not let the idea drop. At one point he offered to oversee a Rumanian effort to manufacture a Renault subcompact. Even after he started his own company, he considered marketing a Polish-built utility vehicle. While he may have denied his own Eastern European roots, De Lorean could not give up on the region's products.

One of his car company executives believes his motives were not entirely altruistic, 'John used to talk to the newspapers about how cars from Russia would bring international peace, but he'd tell us about the markup he could get on one of those little shitboxes. They don't cost you any more than two thousand dollars a piece, and you can probably get away with selling them here for four thousand.'

Beyond just monetary return De Lorean was also impressed by the reverence communist or industrially backward countries were ready to show western executives. As Armand Hammer had proved, a business-man in that incongruous setting could end up wielding political as well as economic power. Using the imperious 'we', De Lorean told one magazine, 'One thing we plan to do, and that's one reason I went to Rumania recently, is to try to establish a relationship with one of the developing nations, and I would like eventually to win their confidence. I'd like to assume a role as this country's industrial advisor.'

Whatever services De Lorean might have offered a foreign country, some of his employees back home were wondering what he could do for them. Bob McLean lost track of John's proliferating business interests and retreated into a separate division of the De Lorean Corporation that did contract research for the government on auto safety (by 1980 it split away from De Lorean entirely). 'We were probably the only division that made some money for John over a long period of time,'

McLean says. 'Not a lot, but at least we were profitable.' Long before he had put aside his hopes of being a part of De Lorean's new car team. 'John had a way of telling you what a great member of the team you were and then putting you on a shelf. Besides, I could see that it wasn't in his nature to concentrate on any one thing. He got so quickly bored with whatever was at hand, he had to have a thousand other things going.'

In fact, McLean could not even identify all the players without a scorecard, for suddenly there were people in the company whose role he did not have explained to him.

One such was a hulking man named C.W. Smith. Once a Chicago Bears footballer, he had gone on to make a fortune with an engineering firm in Detroit. Although he had some severe reverses, he still had the contacts that interested De Lorean. Some of his deals involved overseas ventures, but few in the office knew what he did. Apparently one of Smith's most productive deals for De Lorean involved a refinery that De Lorean convinced truck magnate James Ryder to buy. After De Lorean had spoken at one of his management meetings on the fuel crisis, Ryder signed him up as a consultant. Ryder says he figured De Lorean to be a 'strong, competent businessman' and that the two considered manufacturing a truck (De Lorean went so far as to incorporate a Ryder–De Lorean subsidiary). However, Ryder adds, 'I decided I didn't want to get into manufacturing.' De Lorean did, however, get him into the oil business when he purchased a Louisiana refinery that C.W. Smith had located. Ryder later sold it to John's fellow Yankee board member, Nelson Bunker Hunt, and De Lorean told friends that he and Smith got a commission from Ryder when he picked up the facility and also when he let it go.

In late morning phone calls and long lunches in dimly lit restaurants Detroit's deal-makers courted John De Lorean. Many of these people did not expect De Lorean to invest personally in their schemes, but were willing to pay him just to be a part – a name on the letterhead or annual report. Inventors and manufacturers trooped into his office showing him new designs or products that only needed his stamp of approval to make a fortune. There could be gains of millions and he didn't even have to lay out a nickel. At most they wanted him to sign those 'interesting pieces of paper' like contracts and letters of credit. By 1976, De Lorean's personal financial statement showed him to be worth over ten million dollars with a varied portfolio of stocks, ranches, business ventures, oil wells and pieces of property development. Banks seldom asked to see anything more.

'De Lorean's name was magic,' Mike Brasch explains. As head of a successful advertising agency, Brasch had the chance both to work for De Lorean on some projects and to be a partner on others. 'The man was like a legend – the sort of person you wanted on your side. First of all, he could galvanize a crowd. He had that sort of FDR charisma that could connect almost individually to everyone in a room, no matter how many people were there. At GM he had the reputation of giving the best presentation of any executive in the company's history. One to one, he was overwhelming. He could turn on the personality and the charm like a light switch, and when he talked to you, it was as though all of his attention was focused on you. He just enveloped you with affection. Soon he'd be telling you how you're an important part of the team or say, "I hear you're doing a great job," and you'd just sit there thinking that you've finally found someone capable of recognizing your talents.'

But once he got involved with De Lorean Brasch found him a difficult partner and an impossible customer. 'John has a nasty habit of not paying his bills. I did a few promotions for some of his business ventures and he owed me $2100. Sometime later, in connection with another deal we were doing together, I was about to turn over a six-figure cheque when I remembered the bill and asked that he pay me back first. He told me he was shocked that I hadn't been paid. This was the first he heard of it, and he assured me that the $2100 would be in the mail that day.

'Of course, I gave him his cheque, but he never sent me my money. Soon after, I went into the hospital for some rather painful surgery. As I lay in bed I couldn't get the whole thing out of my mind. It wasn't the money anymore. It was the principle. For twenty-four hours I kept asking myself how I could have been so foolish as to let him off the hook. When my wife came to pick me up from the hospital, I told her to drive straight to De Lorean's office on 100 West Long Lake. I must have looked like death warmed over, but I barged into his office and told him I wanted my money or I wouldn't leave. Once again, he starts with the crap, saying, "You mean you weren't paid?" and acting all upset. He was going to write me a cheque right on the spot. But then he started to look all over for his cheque-book and he couldn't find it. He was going to call his house and make sure the cheque was delivered to me that day. Believe it or not, I fell for his line again, and left the office. Guess what? No one delivered the cheque that day.'

Once De Lorean called Brasch in to ask his advice about a consignment of Mitsubishi CB radios he had purchased with a sizable bank loan. It was the height of the CB craze and retailers were clamouring for all the radios they could get their hands on. But De Lorean didn't know how best to approach retailers. Brasch put him in touch with importer Larry Yanitz. 'I sold a few thousand with a big retailer,' Yanitz says, 'and once John saw how I did it, he told me he didn't need my services anymore.'

125

But soon after, while Yanitz was on holiday in Florida, he says De Lorean made several frantic calls asking him to help sell off the radios. 'I made a deal with an Oklahoma outfit that was going to pay $30 a radio. I would have gotten five dollars a radio in commission which would have added up to $26,000.'

But De Lorean was not happy with the price. He refused to let the radios out of the warehouse until Yanitz came up with a better offer. In the meantime the Government was making changes to its regulation of CBs. While the merchandise sat in a warehouse, the FCC issued new rules permitting the number of channels per radio to increase from twenty-three to forty. Overnight, De Lorean's stock became practically worthless, and he ended up getting only a few dollars a set. Yanitz later tried, unsuccessfully, to bring suit against De Lorean for his lost commission, but the suit was dismissed.

De Lorean still had to repay the bank for the letter of credit issued against the radios. To come up with the money to cover the loan he sold his share in the San Diego Chargers football team to Barron Hilton. He would later tell a Detroit newspaper that, 'I sold out of [the San Diego Chargers] because I really got very upset when they were fined for that drug thing.' As it turned out, soon after De Lorean left the team, the National Football League received a massive new television contract that practically doubled the value of his stock.

De Lorean stood to bungle even more lucrative deals with another former GM executive, Raymond F. Prussing. Once an overseas salesman for General Motors' Detroit Diesel Allison division, Prussing had the international connections upon which export fortunes are made. In 1975 he became vice president of the John Z. De Lorean Corporation, and through an influential Arab sheik got De Lorean involved with several projects for Saudi Arabia. One was a study for creating a bus system. Another involved shipping auto parts and providing maintenance for Saudi vehicles. Both deals would fall through when the sheik discovered the sort of mark-up De Lorean was taking on the parts.

Their best chance at the proverbial killing came in 1976 when Prussing and De Lorean secured the rights to a diesel engine manufactured by the Japanese auto giant, Isuzu. The De Lorean Diesel Corporation had the licence only to sell the engine for non-automotive purposes, but just the product's agricultural uses still offered them a huge and potentially lucrative market. Although his name was on the letterhead, and he claimed in his financial statements that his interest in the diesel company was worth $500,000, De Lorean had not personally put up the money to buy the licence. Most of the backing came instead from an Oldsmobile dealer in Lansing, Michigan.

Within a year Prussing needed more cash to keep the company afloat, but contrary to repeated assurances De Lorean came up with no further investment. 'Prussing wouldn't take any crap from John,' McLean remembers. 'We got into the office at 100 West Long Lake one day and found that Ray had moved to Livonia [a distant suburb].' In a take-it-or-leave-it proposition, the Oldsmobile dealer gave De Lorean $50,000 for his share in what was now known as Isuzu Diesel North America, Inc. De Lorean took it. Prussing and the dealer would later sell their licence back to Isuzu for several million dollars.

When the split between Prussing and De Lorean hit the newspapers, Prussing told reporters that De Lorean had got out of the project so he could devote more time to building his own car company: 'For John, this new car is the greatest thing in the world. He's so intense on this project it was asking too much of him to expect him in both companies. He had to make a choice on which way he was going to go. Don't go reading anything into this.'

Prussing did not have to worry. The press had not been reading anything negative into De Lorean's career, even though it took him just three years to be associated with the sort of repeated business disasters that might have destroyed the reputation of another man.

His dismal business record had not seriously dented his personal fortune, however. He still had the shares and San Diego property he accumulated at General Motors as well as his share of the Florida dealership he took in severence. But by the mid-seventies every other major enterprise De Lorean undertook was bankrupt, defunct, or defective. This astounding record of entrepreneurial ineptitude was tainted even further by a host of broken contracts and lawsuits which raised serious questions about his honesty and integrity.

And yet, even though several had ended in courtroom feuds that were of a rancorous and controversial nature, none of John De Lorean's misguided business exploits made the news. Journalists continued to write stories about him, but his latest pursuits were tossed off in a few lines at the end of the piece. De Lorean must have learned that if he didn't say too much, the reporter wouldn't bother to check any further. According to De Lorean's 1976 profile in the periodical compilation *Current Biography*, Grand Prix of America was a 'string of miniature race tracks'. In fact, by that time the company had been bankrupt for two years, and even when extant never had more than one track. In the same article he is given further credit for having 'transformed his . . . cattle ranches into year-round camps for underprivileged children', which would have certainly been big news to Clark Higley as he and two other generations of his family struggled to stave off eviction.

Clearly, in the mid-seventies, reporters were not asking the searching questions about John De Lorean. They were still looking for the dirt on General Motors, and the ex-executive was more than willing to give it to them. He had distilled his most cogent criticisms, and they came out in pithy lines and telling anecdotes – more bitterly cynical as time went on. In fact, only months after he left GM De Lorean was already discussing a book project with *Business Week* reporter Pat Wright. By the summer of 1974 they had a contract with Playboy Books for *On a Clear Day You Can See General Motors*. Wright compiled the book mostly using transcripts from lengthy interviews with De Lorean. His other information came from notes, files and memos De Lorean had kept over the years.

In Wright's mind the book was not primarily about John De Lorean. He says, 'I got into this project for one reason: to open up American industry to close examination. General Motors was the prototype of the well-run American business, but anyone who covered the company as a reporter kept asking himself, "How does anything ever get done there?" De Lorean told us that, in fact, it doesn't get done.'

Wright, along with several other veteran motoring writers, found De Lorean's criticisms of the GM system to be valid. His research, he says, was to verify De Lorean's charges. He did not feel, however, that De Lorean himself was worth the same scrutiny. 'I was interested in General Motors' story. I didn't see my mission as doing a biography – authorized or otherwise – of John De Lorean.'

But aside from Wright's work, De Lorean's comments about GM in newspapers and magazines dwelt as much on his own record of accomplishment there as they did on his criticism of the company. And those accomplishments, great as they were, grew even greater in De Lorean's reminiscences.

The only subject who permitted himself to be identified in *Passages*, De Lorean was enshrined by author Gail Sheehy as one of the few 'strivers and superachievers' with the courage to turn his back on the ultimate prize. De Lorean, she writes, 'got religion' and realized that 'big business does not want people with a "broad vision" . . .' Before his departure, she asserts, he was on the brink of the presidency, but 'breathing down the neck of his dream, De Lorean knew at last that it would not be deliverance'.

The fabrication of the De Lorean legend started almost immediately upon his departure with his salary. In just the following few months anyone reading the mass media could have seen his final salary figures jump dramatically, almost as though he had been bestowed a retro-active raise. In the first announcements of his departure in April 1973, *Time* and the *New York Times* put his salary and bonuses at $300,000. Two months later an auto magazine quoted De Lorean's annual pay at '$400,000-plus'. By September *Fortune* was reporting that compensation for De Lorean had been as high as $550,000. One month later, De Lorean told a *New York Times* reporter, 'Even at $650,000 a year, if the job is not satisfying, you do something else.'

As years passed he was portrayed as changing the fortunes of Pontiac single-handed. Some articles failed to mention either Estes or Knudsen. De Lorean also became the sole progenitor of the GTO and the Wide Track look. Reporter Robert Irvin wrote in 1974, 'He brags about his performance at [Pontiac and Chevrolet], although other persons at GM and elsewhere in the auto industry have suggested that he sometimes takes more of the credit than he deserves.'

Reporters, however, did not share the scepticism of those 'other persons'. Some of them would not even bother to check such verifiable boasts as claims to patents. According to *Current Biography* De Lorean 'owns more than two hundred patents, including those for the recessed windshield wipers and the overhead-cam engine'. In fact, De Lorean has been cited by the U.S. Patent Office for a total of fifty-two patents – nothing to sneer at – but nowhere near two hundred. Thirty-one of the patents were for GM, but none for the wipers or the overhead .cam.

Journalists cannot take the entire blame for being sucked into the De Lorean myth. Investors proved just as gullible. There was much about this post-GM De Lorean model – in both his personality and lifestyle – that could blind even the most cynical eye. As his byzantine little empire reeled about him, he could still find time to talk to a reporter and seem as self-assured as ever. Indeed, his memories of pulling the irons out of the fire at GM may have helped bolster his confidence.

Besides, he certainly lived like a successful man. His cars were lined up in the driveways of his homes. When he flew, it was only first class. When he ate at smart restaurants, he was always at the best table. Besides his ranch in Idaho he had another spread nestled in the mountains just two hours northeast of San Diego. He called it Cuesta de la Cammalia, referring in Spanish to the camomile flowers that grew there. The plantation-style entrance was through a gate and up a winding road lined with wooden fences, although the actual home and the two guest houses did not quite live up to this billing. Instead they were unprepossessing ranch-style places – the kind you might expect to see in a middle-class suburb. But sitting alongside the pool, De Lorean could listen to the bees buzz and smell the rich, syrupy smell of the camomile plants growing in terraced gardens nearby, and point to the green hillsides of avocado trees in the distance, or to the lush groves of grapefruit and oranges that rose behind him, and say that all these five hundred acres were his. Later, he would take a visitor out on little motorbikes, to roar up and down the steep tracks that circled his property, or ride down to the country club at the bottom of the mountain, where, of course, he was a member in good standing. After such a tour, it would have been hard for anyone to classify the lord of this manor a failure.

And as befits a man of success in America, there was a beautiful wife back at the hearth. Joe Slavik, one of the Grand Prix investors, remembers going out to Cuesta de la Cammalia with De Lorean. 'I was there to look at the ranch. When we went inside the house, John called out first, "Cristina, are you presentable?" She came out in a bathrobe and I'd never seen anyone so beautiful. She just didn't say hello and go away again. She was very gracious and practically waited on us. I really got to like her.'

De Lorean married Cristina Ferrare just a few weeks after he left General Motors. They met in the office of their mutual divorce lawyer, E. Gregory Hookstratten, and tied the knot five months later. The timing is important here because it deflates De Lorean's reputation as a womanizer. When his divorce with Kelly Harmon became imminent, gossip columnists had him out with Hollywood beauties on the order of Ursula Andress, Candice Bergen and Tina Sinatra. According to a *Detroit Free Press* profile, De Lorean and Roger Penske were "systematically dating and discarding the best-looking girls from New York, Miami and L.A. The two had a gentleman's agreement that De Lorean would get all the girls over five foot eight, Penske all those under." All playboy bravado aside, De Lorean's third swinging singlehood was as short-lived as his second. In December 1972, he reached a divorce settlement with Kelly Harmon. He started dating Cristina Ferrare the next month.

A tall brunette with large almond-shaped eyes, she was two years younger than Kelly Harmon. If anything, De Lorean was proud of their age disparity. When Cristina joined him for one speaking engagement, he started out his remarks by telling the predominantly male audience, "I'm glad, as I see you are, that my wife Cristina could be here with me today. Of course, she had to skip out of school. That's okay, honey, I'll write a note on Monday."

But unlike Kelly Harmon, Cristina Ferrare was no fragile naive schoolgirl. Sophisticated beyond her years, she began modelling at the age of fourteen and eventually rose to the top of her profession, looking out from the covers of the fashion magazines and cosmetic ads. Her father, who had been a butcher in Cleveland, followed her to Hollywood when she tried to break into films. Although she got only a handful of movie roles, her modelling career still supported her family in luxury. While a teenager, she carried on a torrid romance with California computer kingpin, Fletcher Jones, more than twenty years her senior. He died in a plane crash during their affair. She was married briefly, and then in the office of her divorce lawyer, E.G. Hookstratten, met her second husband, John De Lorean.

Having earned a six-figure salary on her own, Cristina had a few lessons to teach her older spouse about the finer things in life. 'John used to complain about Cristina's expensive tastes,' one of the De Lorean

Motor Company executives remembers. 'Evidently she was used to extravagantly expensive things, and he'd say, "Her shopping will break me before the car company will." '

But for all her sophistication, Cristina also had an earthy sense of humour that occasionally shocked some of the more staid auto industry types that surrounded her husband. Often during board meetings she was to send him notes marked 'urgent' with salacious suggestions inside. 'I remember once being out with John and Cristina in New Orleans,' one of the car company executives says. 'We were there for the NADA [National Auto Dealers Association] convention, and the top officers of the company had got together with their wives for dinner. While we were eating, Cristina launched into a story about how John took her skiing shortly after they met and she ended up breaking her leg and getting a cast up to her thigh. She then gave us a graphic description of how they tried to make love around the cast. She thought it was all very funny. My wife and I almost dropped our forks.'

For a while after they married Cristina continued trying to break into acting on the West Coast, especially a role in the long-running television series, 'Charlie's Angels', which coincidentally enough followed the adventures of three beautiful women crime fighters squired about by a smooth talking older man. However, she did not get the part, and reconciled herself to the life of a high-priced model back on the East Coast. With their mutual business interests gravitating to New York, she eventually convinced her husband to move out of his Bloomfield Hills home to buy a two-storey apartment on Fifth Avenue.

Although she kept up her career, Cristina also added a measure of stability and domesticity to her husband's life. John had gained custody of the child he had adopted with Kelly, and Cristina raised Zachary from the age of eighteen months as though he were her own son. Soon after their marriage, a reporter from the *Detroit Free Press*, Paul Hendrickson, visited the De Lorean household and left the world an enduring picture of the harmonious, prosperous family: 'At home, on three-and-a-half rolling acres in Bloomfield Hills, set off by white fences and a fleet of cars in the driveway [John De Lorean seems] a warm, happy man, surrounded by three romping dogs, a wife who playfully cuffs and pokes at him and is yet incredibly mature, a baby who mugs for pictures better than Carol Channing. When there is soft snow falling and symphonic music coming from another room, it can all kill you softly. You couldn't care less how many Picassos are on the wall.'

Silver Beauty

'John started out with an image of the car in his head,' Bill Collins says. 'He'd say it was a hazy view of the car sitting in a field somewhere with the gull-wing doors open.'

Bill Collins was the man John De Lorean chose to bring his hazy image to life. Just six months after De Lorean left General Motors Collins followed. For the next five years he would learn both the exhilaration and disappointment of making another man's dream come true.

Although De Lorean had reportedly promised GM to stay out of the car business for a few years in exchange for the Florida dealership and his deferred bonus payments, his ultimate career objectives were almost immediately clear to anyone who knew him. 'It was always the sports car,' Bob McLean says. 'From the moment John De Lorean left GM, he was determined to build his own sports car.'

De Lorean always had been something of a sports car fanatic, happier tooling around in a Maserati than a Cadillac. But his reasons for wanting to manufacture sports cars on his own were more practical than aesthetic. 'He had to start out with a limited production car that had a big price tag,' McLean explains. There was no way De Lorean could immediately produce the hundreds of thousands of moderately priced cars that are meat to Detroit's big three. Tens of thousands were far more manageable for the novice manufacturer, and, if expensive enough, could also be more profitable.

Ironically, De Lorean fashioned his independent auto-making ways after a General Motors example. Since 1953 Corvette had been an almost self-contained little corner shop inside the giant supermarket of the Chevrolet division. Officially, the two-seater sports car was part of the Chevy line, but its appeal was not for the middle-class family, like the rest of the division's products. It was the only American product which legitimately met the performance standards of a sports car, and it attracted the same wealthy young men who shelled out big bucks for the foreign coupés.

When De Lorean took over as Chevrolet general manager, he was taken aback to see how profitable the sports car was, especially considering how little the company was putting into the product. The car had undergone minimal styling and engineering changes since its inception, and was still assembled in an antiquated World War I vintage factory in St Louis.

The Corvette did suffer to some extent from the lack of innovation. In typical GM fashion, headquarters had been reluctant to approve any wholesale changes in the car as long as it continued to make money. In the late sixties Corvette's pre-eminent engineer, Zora Arkus-Duntov, tried to buck the status quo. For two decades he had monitored the car's slow development, and believing the time had come for an abrupt change of course, he designed a new version that shifted the engine closer to the centre of the car. The advantages of placing a car's power plant just behind the driver were manifold: the driver had a better field of vision; the car had a lower – hence safer – centre of gravity, and no need for convoluted exhaust and steering systems.

But when Arkus-Duntov made his radical redesign sketches, some Corvette purists, including De Lorean, found the change too much to take. 'At one point while I was working on the design,' the engineer remembers, 'De Lorean came to look at the clay styling model and he didn't like some of the vents I was putting into the body, so he'd say, "What is this? It looks like a hole to piss in." '

Arkus-Duntov believes De Lorean helped kill his first attempt at pushing the car through, but he prevailed on his old friend and mentor Ed Cole to save the project. Cole was mired in his own hundred-million-dollar mission to convert General Motors to Wankel rotary engines (ultimately, a fruitless effort), and he saw the Corvette as a prime candidate to lead the way. Arkus-Duntov had his mid-ship sports car restored, but he reluctantly went back to the drawing board to accommodate the Wankel. Again, De Lorean was initially antagonistic. 'I told him at one product meeting that with the Wankel the car doesn't have the power it should. But then De Lorean started yelling at me, trying to embarrass me in front of everyone else. He said, "You're supposed to be such a genius, so why don't you invent something to make the engine more powerful?"

'That made me very mad. I ran out of the room and got in my car and drove back to the technical centre. But by the time I got there, I figured out how to get more performance from the engine. My idea would make De Lorean turn around one hundred eighty degrees on the mid-ship Corvette. He became my biggest supporter next to Cole.'

But Cole and De Lorean were not enough to convince the rest of

GM's top brass, and one more innovative project bit the dust. It did not, however, lose De Lorean's wholehearted support. Shortly after he left General Motors he managed to buy the designs for the mid-engine Corvette, much to the surprise of their creator. 'One day, late in 1973, I went over to see De Lorean when he was occupying Knudsen's office. Then he first told me he wanted to produce the mid-ship Corvette on his own, and he asked me if I wanted to be chief engineer. I declined. I decided to stay with Chevrolet until I retired in one more year. And I knew that after that, my contract wouldn't let me work full-time for a possible GM competitor.' A few months later De Lorean invited Arkus-Duntov to his home for dinner and made one more stab, but the engineer was not to be lured away.

De Lorean continued to court the Wankel as well. At one point he had an option to buy thirty thousand Wankels a year from one company, and when that firm went under he tried to make the same agreement with Mazda, Japan's foremost Wankel evangelists. But while the rotary engine was cheap to build and easy to maintain, it had an inordinate thirst for petrol. Arkus-Duntov estimates that his mid-engine Corvette might have got six miles to the gallon – an unacceptable ratio in the wake of the fuel crisis.

Bob McLean was to shift De Lorean's attention away from his prospective car's engine and closer to the skin. At first De Lorean had envisaged using the standard sports car shell made of fibreglass. Although lighter, cheaper to produce, and more aesthetically pleasing than steel, fibreglass also required safety measures that made a car a little heavier and more complicated than engineers would have liked. With a tendency to disintegrate on impact, a fibreglass body required a steel skeleton and backbone underneath to protect the passenger and keep the shell in place. McLean would tell De Lorean of a friend who had found an amazing alternative to fibreglass – a new plastic material that was stronger than steel and almost half the weight. The process was called Elastic Reservoir Moulding (ERM), and its ingredients were as simple to confect as the chemical equivalent of a toasted cheese sandwich. Epoxy resin – quite standard stuff found in glues and coatings – was placed between two sheets of open-celled foam. A fibreglass mat or cloth would then go on either side of the sandwich and all would be pressed together. The glue squooshed right through the foam, creating a new super-hard substance between the outer sheets.

There were other resin and foam combination plastics on the market, but they required expensive and time-consuming methods of moulding. Like a good pair of trousers, the ERM seemed to need no more than a quick press.

'De Lorean hopped on a plane to go and take a look at it,' McLean recalls, 'and he came back very enthusiastic. The next thing I knew, he and his patent lawyers were travelling all over trying to license the rights to ERM.'

De Lorean found that a unique three-way patent linked Shell, Dow and Freeman Chemical Corporation. Much smaller than either Dow or Shell, the Winconsin-based Freeman had the lock on the all-important fabricating process, and De Lorean turned to them first. Once he had secured from Freeman exclusive rights to ERM in all ground transportation, Shell and Dow fell into line. While he paid a total of $100,000 to gain the licence, his contract put further payments into the future and guaranteed that certain amounts would be spent each year on research.

De Lorean saw ERM as the lynchpin of a new innovative vehicle. First and foremost its minimal weight would require a smaller engine to tug it around and produce better fuel efficiency than any other sports car. Its strength meant that the fuel savings could be had without sacrificing safety. Also an ERM car would be easier and cheaper to make than a steel one. A few plastic moulds could take the place of all the tools, equipment and extra manpower necessary to machine metal. De Lorean sold both the safety and fuel efficiency aspects of ERM to Grace and Allstate, making ERM development an integral part of those never-to-be-finished projects.

While De Lorean may have abandoned the Allstate safety prototype, he did not lose faith in the market potential for a safe car. Passenger protection, he felt, would significantly contribute to a sport car's appeal. The ERM process went a long way in providing structural strength, and he also wanted to make airbags standard equipment, along with bumpers that could withstand impacts of 10 mph without any damage (the industry standard was 3 mph). The major car companies had always downplayed safety features, fearful of associating danger with driving in any way. But De Lorean saw safety – especially in the Nader era of consumer consciousness – as an important selling point.

ERM did have one major drawback, which was that it couldn't be painted. But De Lorean would turn that factor into one of the car's most striking features. Forced to cover the plastic with a thin metal coat, he decided to go with the most durable material available – stainless steel. Back in 1936 the stainless steel company Allegheny Ludlum had fitted a Ford in a demonstration with a stainless steel body, and the car still looked like new. Stainless steel was armour that would never rust, and also never need paint. As a result, the car would come in only one colour, but that made it easier for repair shops to stock De Lorean panels. 'You can have the car in any colour,' De Lorean joked, modifying Henry Ford's observations on the Model T. 'As long as it's stainless.'

Stainless steel gave the car a futuristic look, especially as it was combined with another radical feature – gull-wing doors. Nothing about the De Lorean car was to make a greater impression than its entry hatch. Gull-wings had first been used by Mercedes Benz after World War II to cut down on the wind resistance in their racing cars. But the German company put the doors in only one production series, the 1956 Mercedes 300SL – the car that Gerry Dahlinger had owned. Despite their distinctive appearance, they proved too much of a headache to engineer and maintain, and Mercedes did not waste another production run to work out the wrinkles.

De Lorean would not be the first entrepreneur to think of reviving the gull wing. Nor was he the first to see the financial advantages of producing a two-seater sports car with an accent on safety features. In August 1974 Malcolm Bricklin, a thirty-five-year-old entrepreneur who had made a fortune first in convenience hardware and then as a Suburu importer, began producing his own two-seater gull-winged-safety car in two New Brunswick plants. Much of his start-up capital came from the federal and local Canadian governments in a bid to bring down the province's chronic unemployment, but little more than a year and three thousand recall-ridden cars later the company crashed to a halt.

It was exactly the sort of still birth that could have discouraged De Lorean's own efforts at conception. And it was only the latest in a junkyard full of attempts by new companies to break into the American market during the preceding fifty years, including Kaiser-Frazer and the Tucker. Walter Chrysler, back in 1924, was the last to make a go of it. But De Lorean had an answer for anyone who raised the Bricklin spectre before him. As he explained to *Motor Trend*, 'I don't think that since Walter Chrysler . . . you've really had anybody who's been professional about it, from the standpoint of having a background in the business . . . Walter Chrysler was general manager of Buick when he decided to go off and start his own motor company. He really knew the business, and he hired some of the finest technical people of the day. . . I think that we have, and are assembling an extremely competent and professional organization of people who have been quite successful in their own end of the business . . .'

Whatever De Lorean thought about the stodginess of the American automobile industry, he realized that nothing would add more credibility to his own company than seasoned executives from Detroit's big three. While part of his hiring strategy was directed at impressing investors, he also looked for the sort of 'doers' who could force projects through to fruition – at least in the context of a big corporation.

De Lorean recruited the first key member of his team in October 1974 when he hired Bill Collins away from General Motors. One of Pontiac's engineering stars, Collins had followed in many of De Lorean's footsteps as head of the division's advanced engineering and later as assistant chief engineer. They worked together on the GTO, Tempest, and most important, Pontiac's ill-fated two-seat sports car. When GM's corporate staff decided to make their entire line of cars smaller, they pooled the best engineering talent from all the divisions and put Collins in charge. To some GM oldtimers, Collins was the latest, although more subdued, model of John De Lorean. A tall, angular man, with a prominent forehead and, in those days, a carefully trimmed moustache, Collins also stood out from the rest of the pack. Renowned for the meticulous care he showed every project, he was pegged as another bright young engineer with a very bright future.

But Collins was to have less stomach for corporate politics than De Lorean, and shortly after De Lorean left the company he let an engineering headhunter know that his scalp was available for other endeavours. Quite unexpectedly he got a call from one of the references he listed on his *curriculum vitae*. 'As usual, John was calling from an airport somewhere,' Collins remembers. 'He wanted me to be president of Grand Prix of America. I told him I had no interest in that sort of a job. That was entertainment, not engineering. But he kept after me about helping him build his own car.'

De Lorean's marketing man had already worked up a presentation featuring a De Lorean Safety Vehicle. 'I remember,' Collins says, 'that it had gull-wing doors, advanced safety features and an engine somewhere in the back.'

At first Collins tried to talk De Lorean out of the gull wing, but eventually he agreed that the door did add something to the car's sex appeal and also had practical benefits. 'If a two-door car is low to the ground, the door has to be very wide to get comfortably inside it. That made it difficult getting out of a car in tight parking spaces. With the gull wing, you could park within fourteen inches of a wall and still get out of the car.'

Collins had important design work to do even before he knew what the car was going to look like. The basic concept of any vehicle must start with the driver's seat, or more specifically, the anatomical seat of the driver: what designers delicately call the Depressed 'A' Point. De Lorean and Collins, both around six feet three inches in height, obviously had a taller driver in mind and since they wanted to end up with a sports car, they envisaged the Depressed 'A' Point riding as low to the ground as possible. With that information, the roof, steering wheel, dashboard and gear shift were positioned. Eventually all the interior appointments were arrayed in a little sit-down cage known as a seating buck.

To arrive at the outward appearance of the car, Collins, De Lorean and Ray Prussing went in 1974 to the mecca of sports car styling –

Turin. Much as Milan is to clothing fashions, Turin is to the latest in car body fashions, whose new styles are decked out each November in the Turin Motor Show. Collins and De Lorean passed by the biggest names at the show, like Sergio Pininfarina and Giuseppe Bertone, and took their closest look at a relatively new arrival on the scene, Giorgetto Giugiaro. 'Far and away, Giugiaro's was the look we wanted,' Collins says. 'It was the cleanest and most contemporary.'

Some might have even called Giugiaro fancifully futuristic. Although his most widely known design was to be the Volkswagen Rabbit, in those days Giugiaro was concentrating on low, wide metallic wedges that he incorporated into model lines for Maserati and Alfa Romeo. In 1970 he completed a prototype for Porsche, called the 914/6 Tapiro, and it became his model for the De Lorean car. It too had gull-wing doors, but he would not use hidden headlights with the De Lorean, coming up instead with a wide, but thin snout that could take exposed headlights and a heavy-duty bumper.

In February 1975 Giugiaro came to Detroit to finalize contracts with De Lorean and get the specifications from Collins's riding buck. In the summer he finished his full-size wood and plastic mock-up. Collins was amazed that Giugiaro's services added up to a total cost of only $65,000, payable when the car went into production.

For most of 1975 Collins conducted research and development on the sports car through the charity of Allstate, W.R. Grace, a seat belt company in Canada and the French auto giant, Renault, which had De Lorean conduct clinics on Le Car, its new entry into the American small-car market. Collins would be listed as a participant in several of these projects, even though he worked mostly on the sports car.

By the end of the year the car was far enough along for De Lorean to go out on the hustings and start attracting backers. On October 1975 the De Lorean Motor Company filed with the state of Michigan to become a registered company. As Bill Collins became the guiding genius of the De Lorean car, Tom Kimmerly became the guiding genius of the corporation. Starting a new car company was nothing new for the lawyer, as he had been peripherally involved with two prior unsuccessful attempts: Tucker and Kaiser-Frazer. But De Lorean did not see that experience as a dangerous omen. He relied on Kimmerly's counsel to structure a complex web of wholly owned subsidiaries and the transactions that took place between them. Earlier Kimmerly had formed the Composite Technology Corporation, which had the sole task of getting ERM ready in time for the car's production. Shortly afterwards he added yet another layer to the top of De Lorean's cake by creating Cristina, a Nevada corporation, which held all the stock in the John Z. De Lorean Corporation, which in turn held De Lorean's share of the stock in the motor company. While the two latter firms had to comply with the unusually stringent reporting requirements of Michigan, Cristina needed to file little more than a list of the officers to satisfy Nevada law.

For the company's first funding vehicle Kimmerly devised the De Lorean Sports Car Partnership. Limited partnerships of this kind were seldom used sources of financing for fledgling companies, but they offered several advantages to both investors and investment. If the funding were directed at research and development, the IRS offered generous tax shelters for the partners. That was enough to keep the investors very silent and let management maintain control. The Sports Car Partnership offered thirty-five units at $100,000 a piece, and in return, the partners got the chance down the line to convert their unit into a healthy slice of De Lorean Motor Company stock. With the $3.5 million the partnership put up, De Lorean expected to finish the development of a prototype and a dealer network that would eventually sell the cars when they came off the assembly line.

Kimmerly got the prestigious New York firm of Webster, Sheffield to give the limited partnership offering a legal stamp of approval. But that would not be enough to sell the idea to sceptical investors, and De Lorean quickly found that his wealthy friends were not so eager to jump on his car company bandwagon. It was one thing to say nice things about him at dinner parties, but another actually to put $100,000 on the line. In the case of old buddies Roger Penske and Bob Anderson, neither wanted to do anything to jeopardize their valuable connections with Detroit's motor industry and General Motors in particular.

De Lorean was forced to hit the road and appeal to strangers. But along the way, in Houston's prestigious Petroleum Club, he stumbled across someone who offered to make the fundraising ordeal more painless. After he had finished appealing to a group of oil executives, De Lorean was approached by a former Ford executive who had moved down to the sunbelt and gone into the risk capital business. His partner was Tom J. Fatjo, Jr., a young man in his early thirties who was already a Wall Street sensation. Just a few years before he had bought out a Houston construction company, and fuelled by share floats, built the nation's largest private garbage collection company, Browning-Ferris Industries. Now, he was ready to pass his wondrous Wall Street formula on to other growth companies.

De Lorean and Fatjo hit it off as soon as they were introduced. The Texan soon followed him back to Detroit and 100 West Long Lake where they quickly struck up a deal. De Lorean promised to pay Fatjo's firm a $250,000 annual retainer and 10 per cent of all the stock they sold in a future offering. De Lorean had yet to hire a comptroller, and Fatjo helped him work up a credible business plan he could show investors.

Feeding on each others' optimism, De Lorean and Fatjo looked ahead to a future Wall Street offering. Preliminary talks started with the Texan's underwriter of choice, E.F. Hutton. The limited partnership was all but forgotten. Units sold at a snail's pace, and hardly one third were gone by the end of the summer.

What transpired next between the two is a matter of dispute. Fatjo was to end up in court with De Lorean, like so many of the others who did business with the auto executive. Unhappy with the partnership's progress, De Lorean refused to pay Fatjo's fees, claiming that they were only meant as commission for any units Fatjo helped place. By September, De Lorean testified in his deposition, Fatjo became 'convinced that we were not going to make the grade . . . and completely lost interest'.

Fatjo countered that he was owed payment just for working up De Lorean's business plan. He claimed he never promised to sell units, only make a few contacts. (For a while Fatjo and his partners were officers in the partnership, which allowed them to sell units directly. One unit he did work on was bought by a New York Cadillac dealer who also wangled the exclusive franchise for two of the city's boroughs – an arrangement De Lorean sales people later regretted.)

According to Fatjo's testimony, when they decided to part De Lorean admitted he owed him $150,000 for services. Later, Fatjo said, he settled for one-and-a-half units of the partnership instead. De Lorean was to have sent him a cheque for his services and he was to return it in exchange for a share of the Sports Car Partnership. Fatjo returned the cheque, but he never got his units and later sued in Dallas court (De Lorean eventually settled).

In several interviews, De Lorean freely admitted that he was ill-prepared for the world of high finance and the vagaries of fundraising. 'When you work for General Motors,' he told *Business Week*, 'and you want to build a new foundry in Tonawanda, New York, and you need $600 million, you fill out a form and send it away. You might get a phone call or two, or you might not. Then within a few months this document comes back with one hundred signatures on it which says go spend the $600 million. Unfortunately, that was all I knew about raising money.'

In real life, he found, coralling investors was a much more laborious process, and something he preferred to leave to others. Fortunately for the car company, vice president C.R. Brown was more than willing to slog through the carpeted trenches of hotel conference rooms. During his stormy tenure with the De Lorean Motor Company, Brown continually pulled the irons out of the fire, and he, probably more than anyone else, salvaged the limited partnership.

The De Lorean Motor Company was not Brown's first start-up. Back in 1971 he took command of the North American operations of the Japanese auto-manufacturer, Mazda, and within two years brought the company from no standing in the market to fourth place among all importers. He is not shy about commenting on the magnitude of his own feat, and claims that it eclipsed anything De Lorean had accomplished at General Motors. 'My position at Mazda could be more taxing and significant tnan that of any general manager at General Motors,' Brown explains. Japanese executives would visit him regularly to query him on the state of Mazda in America, and he had to be thoroughly prepared with answers to questions on all aspects of the business – financial, administrative and legal.

The first time he met De Lorean, Brown says, he found him, 'congenial, articulate and enthusiastic,' but he adds pointedly, 'I wasn't awestruck by the man. John didn't know as much as I did about putting together a company. It was the idea that impressed me.'

De Lorean, he says, approached him twice when he ran Mazda's American operations: first, to offer consultation on fuel economy, and later to ask Brown to hire Jim Wangers – one-time father of the GTO ad campaign. Brown did not take him up on either request.

But when De Lorean came back a third time in August 1975 Brown had already left Mazda in the wake of controversy, helped dispose of a bankrupt electronics company, and was thinking about opening his own Chrysler dealership in Garden Grove, California. Brown flew to Detroit and met De Lorean in the office at 100 West Long Lake. 'The idea of starting a new car company from the ground up did not terrify me,' he says. 'I felt I had come pretty close to that with Mazda. I've always felt that if you had competent management and enough capitalization, it's possible to break into the American market with an entirely new product.'

When Brown agreed finally to work with De Lorean it was initially as a consultant and his pay was to be accumulated until the company could afford to reimburse him. Brown took the flyer, working on and off for De Lorean throughout the first half of the year. 'One month I didn't think John was going to make it,' he says, 'and I went ahead and opened up the dealership.'

Born of evangelistic stock, Brown could turn a business goal into something of the order of a religious mission. His fervour was not one of exhilaration, but deep and troubling responsibility, and it seemed to weigh in the lines of his broad, fleshy face, and the deliberate pattern of his speech. His gravity was perfectly suited to selling shares in an investment that some more sceptical souls might find flighty.

Brown took De Lorean's rudimentary presentation and tried to give it some polish. He hired a former promotions man from his Mazda days to put together an audio visual slide show, and he choreographed a programme that had him as the master of ceremonies and De Lorean as the star act.

Hamilton Gregg, a New York broker in 1976, was one of those in the audience during a team De Lorean performance. 'Somebody had told me about De Lorean and suggested I go hear him talk about his plans for a car company,' he remembers. 'His little meeting was at one of the hotels – somewhere like the Waldorf – and to my surprise I found it to be quite impressive. They had slides with enlarged drawings of the car and a film about their patented plastic process. Bill Collins explained the car's engineering principles, and then Brown spoke about building the dealer network. I most remember some very convincing statistics on the potential for a sports car in the American market. De Lorean made a big deal about how GM was making so much profit on the Corvette without really trying. Seventy million, he said, which was peanuts for them, but a good thing for a smaller producer.'

Of course, De Lorean did not talk to his audiences about his own entrepreneurial experiences after he left General Motors. He concentrated instead on his achievements while he was with the company. Ironically, for all the fault he found with GM, his experience there was his greatest mark of distinction. Gregg for one saw his vaunted corporate record as De Lorean's greatest attribute, 'In my mind, John's background at General Motors was exactly what set him apart from failures like Bricklin. Until he left, he was expected to be president one day – at least that's the story I heard. I did some independent checking of my own. I called up a few dealers I knew, and they said he was the real thing. If anything, they felt he took their side against the company. They told me he had also been a demon on service and used to stress that service could build driver loyalty. Evidently most general managers only stressed sales.

'Obviously, the Sports Car Partnership was a risky venture, but I found a few very wealthy people who were interested. These were people in the 70 to 80 per cent tax bracket anyway, so they didn't stand to lose much. One of them was once the head of a major corporation. He was a guy with tons of money, and he told me this wasn't his first investment in a new car company. Evidently way back when, he had helped finance a man named Olds who started a car company that eventually became Oldsmobile.'

With Gregg's help, the units sold a little faster. Ten went to dealers, who got franchises in the bargain, including John's younger brother, Chuck. The biggest share, four and three-quarters, were held by a group of executives at the brokerage house of Merrill Lynch Pierce Fenner & Smith. Although the firm considered making the offering, officers finally decided it was wiser for them to invest as private individuals and they formed their own partnership, M.L. Associates, to buy the De Lorean units. The rest of the shares were scattered among the usual mix of investors: wealthy widows, a Texas oil man, and a couple of corporate executives. In a relative rush, the remaining two thirds of the sports car partnership sold between September and November 1976.

One of the last partners was a California motor dealer invited in by Brown. De Lorean and Brown had assembled several South-Western dealers for the presentation in a Las Vegas hotel. 'Besides the dealers,' Brown says, 'there were two other men who I didn't know. After the meeting my friend, who had been already to purchase a unit, came up and pointed out one of the men and asked, "Is that Roy Nesseth?" I had never met Nesseth so I couldn't answer, but my friend said, "If Nesseth is involved with De Lorean then I don't want anything to do with this. Nesseth has a deplorable reputation."

'Immediately I pulled John aside to ask about Nesseth. John was very smooth. He went over to the dealer and told him not to worry. He said Nesseth was just an old friend who had stopped by to see the presentation. At one point he said, "I give you my assurance Roy has nothing to do with the car company." '

Almost as soon as the limited partnership funds were raised, they were spent. Collins finished the first running prototype in October and immediately got started on the second. Throughout the following year of 1977 there'd be a constant scramble for money to keep the company afloat while executives travelled around the world seeking a site for the car's eventual assembly and asking governments to provide tens of millions for the privilege.

One young employee of this nervous era remembers both the excitement and the anxiety at 100 West Long Lake. 'At times, it seemed as though we were some colossally important corporation that just happened to be run by a few people. The phone would ring from city and state governments all over America trying to get our car. Eventually we just couldn't take any more calls from the chambers of commerce. We were talking about raising ninety million dollars and breaking new ground with research partnerships. And on top of that Collins was working on this futuristic car that would be the best and the safest thing on the road. Everything at De Lorean was the biggest and the best and the newest.

'But we were also stuck in this cramped little office wondering whether or not we could make next week's payroll.'

The precarious budget balancing was handled by another De Lorean recruit from General Motors, Robert M. Dewey. For twenty-six years, Dewey had been keeping financial tabs on various aspects of Chevrolet operations. As De Lorean's chief financial officer he would prove invaluable in preparing the very speculative business plans for the car company. He would also become, in short order, one of the De Lorean plant site ambassadors. 'For all the troubles of those first years,' Dewey says, 'it was still a hell of an experience, and a hell of an ego trip. I knew what we were doing was a monumental task, but I thought that if anybody could do it, John De Lorean could.'

In the midst of all the turmoil, De Lorean himself was not often around. In 1977 he and Cristina had set up their household in a duplex apartment overlooking Fifth Avenue and Central Park. A tiny office at the Chris Craft headquarters down the street became his principal place of business. On his brief visits to Detroit, he stayed at a condominium owned by Roger Penske (although that arrangement and their friendship fell apart in a dispute over lease payments).

When De Lorean did appear at 100 West Long Lake, the junior staff member says, the troops clamoured for his attention. Different camps were beginning to form. In one was Kimmerly, in another Collins and Dewey, and then the third: the motley, and to him, mysterious band of deal-makers that included C.W. Smith. 'Everyone,' he said, 'was jealous of John's attention and affection.'

The immediate goal was to find some money to replace the diminishing partnership dollars. Wall Street experts had advised De Lorean and Kimmerly that they were unlikely to push through a public share offer. But Brown suggested they try a more limited issue, directed solely at car-dealers. For $25,000 they would get a block of shares as well as a franchise to sell the car. His plan was a radical departure from motor industry history, and although each dealer would in fact have a tiny piece of the entire pie, he had an interest beyond the number of cars on his floor to see the De Lorean Motor Company do well. Perhaps of even greater symbolic importance, he was not just a pawn of this car company, but a part of it.

Kimmerly would shoulder the burden of preparing the share registration, and he quickly found that any share issue, even a limited one, is at best a time-consuming obstacle course. Besides passing muster before the Securities and Exchange Commission (SEC) in Washington, the offer also needed the approval of state agencies. The process was to drag on throughout the year.

Six states – Louisiana, New Mexico, South Dakota, Texas, California and Wiconsin – would not approve the shares without modifications. The sceptical state commissioners wondered whether the dealers were really getting their money's worth from the investment. If De Lorean sold every share to the maximum number of four hundred dealers, the issue could bring in ten million dollars. But after having contributed over two thirds of the cash equity, the dealers would be left with only 13 per cent of the shares. John De Lorean, in the corporate identity of the John Z. De Lorean Corporation, would control 65.6 per cent.

On the books De Lorean was shown as paying absolutely nothing for his share of the company, although he claimed a $3.5 million value on all the developmental work for the prototype and ERM before the registration of the car company (developmental work actually subsidized by Grace and Allstate). But even if De Lorean's contribution was computed at $3.5 million, he would have still ended up paying only 35 cents a share for his holding. The dealers, meanwhile, were asked to pay 5 dollars a share.

California demanded that De Lorean first donate some of his shares back into the company, which he did, and eventually Texas made him sign an agreement not to sell out his equity for a number of years.

The U.S. Securities and Exchange Commission was to be no easier on the De Lorean offering than the states. Each month new hoops were held up for the company to jump through.

In the rush to get off the mark, De Lorean executives almost committed a fatal error. When the SEC examiner asked how many dealers would be necessary to have a viable company, Brown came up with the round number of 150. Unknowingly, he had erected the hurdle, and the company would soon be forced to jump over it. Finally in August 1977, the SEC approved the offering, but it was set to expire on 31 October. In only four months, the De Lorean Motor Company had to sign up the 150 dealers or go into extinction before a car rolled off the assembly line.

To make matters worse, the company ran out of money just before the big share push. Help came from an unexpected source, whom SEC registrations first identified as John W. Carson. He was more widely known as the host of the popular TV chat-show 'Tonight', Johnny Carson. For $500,000 he received 250,000 shares and 'the right on terms and compensation to be negotiated, to be a public spokesman for the Company in connection with the sale of the Company product'. In other words, if the pay was high enough, he wanted the right to make commercials for the car – a right De Lorean would have gladly surrendered to Carson (although that sort of advertising never did come to pass).

The social connection with the entertainer came through Cristina. But it was not Carson himself who was involved in protracted negotiations over the share purchase, but his business manager and lawyer: the 'Bombastic Henry Bushkin' he jokes about in his monologues. Bushkin would later be named Carson's designee on the motor company board.

Compared with the Johnny Carson deal, the share sale to the dealers was to be a tedious and disappointing affair. The company could not cash a cheque until the minimum number of dealers had invested. Other SEC restrictions kept muzzles on Brown and his staff. There could be no talk of pizzazz – only the cautious objectives and risks laid out in the prospectus. Their one big attraction was Collins's first prototype. Although the engineer still had some work to do on it, Brown appropriated it for the road show.

'I conducted almost all the dealer meetings,' Brown says. 'We would invite from ten to seventy-five dealers at a time. Each state had different requirements about who could make a presentation. In some you had to be an officer or a registered broker just to talk about the deal. I tried to stick as close as I could to the prospectus.'

Brown remembers De Lorean attending about one out of five of the presentations, but he says, De Lorean wouldn't help much because he 'invariably exaggerated', putting them in jeopardy with the SEC, and moreover alienating some of the conservative dealers. 'They're not stupid. In fact, they're very astute businessmen,' he says, 'and yet, John could make the wildest claims. He'd talk about how many barrels of fuel we saved by not painting cars. None of us had any idea how he got those figures. In those days he also kept telling people he'd have a twenty-five year warranty on the body. At that point, we had no idea what our warranty programme was going to be, but we could be sure it wasn't twenty-five years.

'He went on about the more irrelevant things. When it looked like we'd build the car in an air force base in Puerto Rico, one of his favourite pitches was how we'd fly the cars into the country. He'd say, "Can you imagine the impact of all those silver beauties with the gull wings open lined up on the runway?" '

Brown would be most astounded by De Lorean's claims that he had sunk four million dollars of his own money into the company. 'First of all I knew that wasn't true, but secondly, there was no way the dealer could see any evidence of John's four million dollar investment in the prospectus. All those statements could do was confuse them.'

After presentations Brown had four field representatives who followed up with the audience. William A. Morgan, who worked with Brown at Mazda, was one of the first representatives he hired. Morgan's memories of De Lorean's performance are a bit more positive: 'I thought John was great with a group and really held their attention. I think he was even better socializing with them afterwards. He had a very amiable way about him that made people think he was the type of person who would listen to them.'

Morgan soon learned the intensity of feelings for De Lorean among GM dealers. 'There was no grey area,' he says. 'They either thought he walked on water or they hated his guts. A lot didn't like his lifestyle, or what they thought his lifestyle was. But I found that as a group, Pontiac dealers had the most respect for him.'

Whatever dealers thought of De Lorean, Morgan still had an uphill battle selling them shares. 'Dealers aren't the most flamboyant investors in the world,' he explains. 'They go for safe investments like real estate, not something nebulous like stock. We really had to concentrate on the hard business aspects of getting a franchise – how the car would increase their traffic in the showroom, and how they stood to make some good money on the markup.'

By early September, eight weeks before the deadline, Brown had signed up 110 dealers. 'I thought we were doing very well. I had just four guys with me. One of them signed forty-eight dealers. But during that month we had a very big meeting scheduled for Chicago which John attended. I could see he was very nervous that we weren't going to make the deadline. He told me, "I don't care what this takes. I don't give a shit if we have to pay someone, but I want this to get done."

'I told him it was getting done, but then he told me that he wanted Roy Nesseth to come in. "Roy has guys who can get it done." I told him that unless they were experienced, they wouldn't help. John said I could teach them what they're supposed to know.'

Soon after Roy appeared with ten other men and they set up shop near Brown's Garden Grove dealership with a bank of phones. While so-called boiler room tactics are fine with selling stationery, they are specifically prohibited by the SEC.

'I spent two weeks going over the programme with them line by line. They were supposed to wait for dealer meetings,' Brown says, 'and then do follow-up after the dealers heard a proper presentation. But they didn't wait. They went out and tried on their own.'

A couple flew into Bill Morgan's East Coast territory. While he gave them a few dealers to check back with, he soon found that they were making other calls as well. 'At one point, they called every dealer on Long Island, Philadelphia and some of the top people in New England. Later when I got back to some of those dealers, they were still mad. They'd made a point of telling me that they'd already been hit by "De Lorean's boiler room".'

Both Brown and Morgan maintain that Roy's crew picked up no more than a handful of dealers, which did not matter much anyway since they came in at eight dealers over the minimum.

But De Lorean was to hold a different opinion of Roy's efforts. In later years when a reporter asked about his relationship with Nesseth, De Lorean quickly replied, 'Back in 1977, Roy saved DMC [De Lorean Motor Company]. It's as simple as that. I never forget the people who help me.'

De Lorean went on, without any reservation, to describe Roy's boiler room methods. 'Roy dropped everything. He immediately set up operations, bringing in people to help and totally disregarding everything else in his life.'

His reward for Roy was to be a salaried position with the company, starting at $75,000. 'That whole story about Roy saving the company,' Morgan says, 'was just a way John had of rubbing C.R.'s nose in the dirt.'

No matter who saved the company, it was not saved by much. The stock offering yielded another $3.4 million – not enough to finance much further development. Major hopes for big funding rested with the government entity that most wanted a De Lorean assembly plant.

But out of the blue, an alternative in the private sector suddenly emerged – right in the midst of the rush to meet the SEC deadline. One of De Lorean's friends in Detroit had approached financier and Diners Club founder Alfred Bloomingdale about investing in the De Lorean Motor Company, but he found that Bloomingdale had a better idea. Along with senior partners of Lehman Brothers and other Wall Street power brokers, Bloomingdale had secured options on a sizeable chunk of shares in the foundering American Motors Corporation. AMC chairman Roy Chapin was about to be forced into retirement, and the company's president was slated to take his place. An opening then remained for AMC's chief operating officer. The mere announcement of De Lorean's appointment as president, Bloomingdale figured, would have made the AMC stock soar, and mean even more exponential gains for his options.

De Lorean eagerly entered into frenzied negotiations. For two weeks a top AMC officer visited 100 West Long Lake to brief the putative president on the company's shaky finances. 'They were ready to let De Lorean build his sports car – do anything he wanted,' explains the go-between. 'The major interest of the Bloomingdale group was the stock. John would have gotten some of that action too – maybe several million from the whole deal. But John had never negotiated this sort of a deal before with someone on the level of a Bloomingdale. With people like that, their word is their bond. Once you agree verbally on a contract, whether it's signed or not, you live up to it. But John always tried to squeeze that extra bit, and this time he squeezed the wrong guys. The morning when the board was ready to vote on his financial package, John got in touch with one of the Lehman Brothers partners and told him he wanted the deal doubled. That was the end of negotiations with John De Lorean.

'Bloomingdale called me at home that night, and he didn't sound very upset. I remember he said, "I'm delighted we had a chance to find out what he's like before we hired him."

'A little later John called me. "Hell," he said, "I was just trying them on for size. Why don't you call Bloomingdale and tell him I was just kidding."

'I told him I was sorry, but it was too late. These people don't listen to apologies.'

Forty-Five Days

On the last Friday morning of July 1978 the Manhattan conference room of Stroock, Stroock and Levan was packed with lawyers and government officials. After a year of hard-fought negotiations the De Lorean Motor Company finally seemed resigned to signing an agreement to build its factory on an abandoned air force base sixty-five miles north-west of San Juan in Puerto Rico. Assembled for the occasion were representatives of the island's governor and business development agencies, their legal counsel from Stroock, Stroock and Levan, United States officials from the Federal Farmers Home Administration and the federal Economic Development Administration. Only one person was missing – an officer of the De Lorean Motor Company. Only a lawyer representing De Lorean had shown up, and he seemed genuinely shocked to find himself alone on the other side of the table. As the rest of the room started to fume, he grabbed the nearest phone and frantically tried to find out what was happening, but in vain. He would not hear a word from De Lorean all day.

A few blocks away in New York's Hilton hotel Bob Dewey sat anxiously in his room and listened to his phone ring. For two days he had alternately stalled and cajoled Puerto Rico's disparate forces. He knew full well that across the Atlantic Ocean another team of De Lorean officials was frantically moving to close a deal with the British government that would put the assembly plant in Belfast. It was the ultimate squeeze play conducted over international phone lines, although one party doing the squeeze – Puerto Rico – would not know anyone else was in the game until it was finished.

The De Lorean people had hoped the British deal would be signed earlier in the week, but on Thursday both sides were still thrashing out the details. On Friday morning, as he dressed in his hotel room, Dewey was all but ready to walk down the street and sign an agreement with Puerto Rico, but De Lorean called before he left. 'They were close to

149

signing with the British,' Dewey says, 'and John told me to stay in my room.'

They arranged to talk again at noon, and agreed to meet at a nearby hamburger joint for a quick bite. The British were offering more than the $90 million the car company's executives estimated they would need to start production. Never had De Lorean's dream of manufacturing his own car seemed so close, but when he joined Dewey at the luncheonette, he did not look like a happy man. 'John was extremely nervous, and it seemed to me that he was more worried that the deal was going to go through. I think he realized he had what he asked for. He would finally be forced to show the world what he could do. The shopping days were over.'

Before Collins had finished designing the car, De Lorean had started looking for a factory to build it in. While there was some doubt about the market for new luxury sports cars, there was no doubt about the market for motor assembly plants. Governments all over the world clamoured for new industry – for the jobs created on the site, and the employment spill-over to the myriad smaller firms that spring up around a large factory. Even the giants of the industry, like Ford and General Motors, who often complained about government regulations, were more than happy to have governments intervene in financing new facilities, and during the seventies they began pitting state versus state and nation versus nation to see which could come up with the sweetest package of incentives to lure an expanding conglomerate. Bricklin proved that governments could be just as receptive to speculative new ventures as well.

From the start, De Lorean did not feel constrained to limit his sights to the borders of the United States. Among his first contacts was an entrepreneurial Jesuit priest with connections with the King of Spain, Juan Carlos. De Lorean's one-time diesel partner, Ray Prussing, put him in touch with the priest, and they initially discussed a plan to sell Spanish castings to American industry. In the course of several trips to Spain in 1975 and 1976 De Lorean was shown an old abandoned Ford factory. 'Right off the bat, John had an offer from the Spanish government that was over $100 million,' says one man involved as an intermediary in the deal. 'But the Spanish government wanted a lot more control than John was willing to give up, and they also wanted to push a few partners on him who had some sort of family ties.'

De Lorean's search did not neglect territory closer to home, either. When he worked with Tom Fatjo, he seriously considered another old Ford plant in Fort Worth. He looked at potential sites in Wichita and one in Marysville, Ohio where Honda eventually built its first U.S. plant. There were several meetings on a site in Allentown with Pennsylvania governor, Milton Schapp, and midnight telephone calls,

De Lorean told one magazine, from the Alabama governor, George Wallace.

However, the most serious and realistic offer came from the Commonwealth of Puerto Rico. No other political entity had previously offered either the financing or the tax advantages that were available in the commonwealth. The initial contact with the Puerto Rico Economic Development Administration had been made by the investment banking firm of First Boston Corporation and aides from the governor's office were closely involved throughout the negotiations.

The Puerto Ricans were ready to come up with two thirds of the $90 million needed, primarily through a mixture of loans guaranteed by federal and local authorities. Forty million dollars worth were to be backed by the Federal Farmers Home Administration (since some of the site was on agricultural property) and the Economic Development Administration. Puerto Rican agencies and banks provided $20 million more in low interest loans, half of which would be converted into shares. The commonwealth was ready to throw in an additional 3 million if certain employment levels were met and 90 per cent tax reduction for fifteen years.

On 4 April 1977 De Lorean signed an agreement with Puerto Rico. The island promised to keep its offer open until May, and in turn De Lorean gave assurances that he would not look elsewhere. But the car company still had a long way to travel before it could even qualify for the deal. American bureaucrats insisted that De Lorean first raise the extra $30 million of privately backed capital. On top of that, they wanted to see orders for 40,000 cars.

The car company executives had hoped to raise 10 million from their dealer offering (as it turned out, an over-optimistic assessment), and if indeed, 400 dealers participated, each could easily average ten orders. But raising $20 million on top of that was a different and much taller order.

Again, Kimmerly thought about a limited partnership, but he needed more help to bring off one of this unprecedented size. On the advice of another De Lorean lawyer, Eric Javitz (son of New York senator Jacob Javitz), he turned to the investment banking firm of Oppenheimer & Company, one of New York's most innovative speculative capitalists. Several of the senior Oppenheimer executives got involved as both planners and participants in the mammoth undertaking. The eventual package priced over 130 units at $150,000 a piece.

There was no way De Lorean was going to meet the first deadline. But the Puerto Ricans willingly pushed it back seven more times over the next year as the dealer share sale continued to bog down in red tape. They even permitted De Lorean to entertain offers from other locations. Their accommodation, however, did not make the company's executives feel any fonder of Puerto Rico. Concerned about language barriers and the island's work ethic from the start, they eventually found enough tangible reasons to relegate the deal's status from 'most likely' to 'last resort'.

Their principal criticism lay with the site itself, a one-time military installation called the Ramey Air Base. Isolated from major roads, the location depended on either the airstrip or a small nearby port for heavy transportation. 'When I was at the site during one negotiation,' Dewey says, 'they had a brownout [an intentional small-scale blackout]. It lasted about four hours. I found out later there were brownouts a couple of times a month out there. Do you have any idea what that would do to assembly line production?'

Other details of the original agreement also became unravelled. The government was not sure it had proper deeds to the plot where the factory would be. Originally the land had been confiscated from local peasants to make way for the air force base, and government officials feared that the relatives of those refugees might return with documented claims to the site. Some officials involved in the early negotiations left the government, and their replacements were talking about a tax on each mechanical drawing.

The federal government's willingness to guarantee $40 million of loans for the De Lorean project did not go unnoticed by states and cities who felt themselves just as deserving of his plant. Early in 1978, after a four-month study of its own, Detroit offered De Lorean a $50 million financial package, most of it loans from federal urban development grants.

Shortly after the city made the offer, *Detroit Free Press* reporters Kirk Cheyfitz and Allan Sloan discovered the trouble De Lorean had selling shares to dealers. In a lengthy phone interview De Lorean explained that some of his plans had gone awry when he put his faith in a wealthy Arab financier who was ready to underwrite the costs of the entire project. According to De Lorean the sheikh backed out rather than identify himself as federal securities laws required. 'Back in the sixties, any moron with any idea could raise capital,' De Lorean told the reporters. 'Now, it's impossible.' If he did manage to raise the money he needed, De Lorean exclaimed, 'it will be the most incredible accomplishment of the last hundred years'.

Detroit officials were not dismayed by De Lorean's problems in raising private funds. 'We had our own peculiar reasons for backing the project,' then city planner Anthony P. DeVito says, 'and I don't think they would have applied to any other city. We saw De Lorean as an opportunity to build a new assembly plant on a prime piece of real estate. Even if he went under, we knew that in Detroit we could find an occupant for the most modern auto assembly plant in the world. I don't think Puerto Rico had that option building something out in the middle of nowhere.'

DeVito's prime concern was whether the big three motor companies would tolerate a competitor, tiny as it may be, cropping up in their backyard. 'We wanted to be absolutely sure that nobody in General Motors wanted to sandbag the whole thing. Quite to my surprise, the auto executives we sounded out really didn't care. In fact, with all the talk of anti-trust suits against GM, I think they would have welcomed the evidence that someone else can compete. I was somewhat new in town, and personally I couldn't gauge whether or not they were hostile. It just seemed to me that most of the corporate executives were not much for direct entrepreneurial action themselves and had no real envy of De Lorean, or even understanding why he was going to all this trouble. My feeling was they didn't much care what happened to his venture.'

DeVito says he did not feel the need to check into De Lorean's personal background. 'All we were concerned about was the viability of the car company, and our consultants, who were some of the top people in the industry, felt it could work.'

Although he had a few meetings with De Lorean, DeVito says most of their negotiations were conducted over the phone. 'I could see that people like Dewey were not in a position to make the decisions. He seemed to have as much trouble reaching John as I did. Still, we must have spoken over twenty times. I had one conversation with [De Lorean] when he was in his San Diego ranch that must have gone on over four hours.'

Bob Dewey was having problems reaching De Lorean at that time, and often wondered whether De Lorean really wanted to settle on a site for the factory. 'At times, I thought John didn't want to go anywhere. It seemed he was always afraid something better would walk in the door.'

Dewey did not see the Detroit deal as any better than Puerto Rico. 'In essence, they kept telling us that we could still get the car on the market if we downsized the plant and tooling. In that case all we needed was 45 million in outside financing, which coincidentally enough was the figure they were offering.'

Other offers competitive with Puerto Rico appeared from another island state, the Republic of Ireland. Again, an intermediary made the first contact for the car company. In this case, the go-between was the Canadian branch of a Swiss investment bank, Wood Gundy Limited. Having already invested in Bricklin, Wood Gundy should have been reluctant to get burned a second time, but director G. Edmund King had tried to get De Lorean to help on other projects, and afterwards was impressed enough by De Lorean to take another risk on his car. Wood Gundy invested $500,000 in a deal similar to Johnny Carson's, and offered to provide introductions to Irish officials.

By now De Lorean's negotiating team had changed considerably from the time he first dealt with Puerto Rico. Among the new members was legal counsel Alan Cohen, a senior partner at the New York law firm of Paul, Weiss, Rifkind, Wharton and Garrison and a specialist in corporate negotiations. The other addition was square-jawed and taciturn Walter P. Strycker, a former top financial officer at IBM and Pittsburgh's Wheelabrator Frye who met De Lorean through their mutual friend at Rockwell, Bob Anderson.

Together Strycker and Cohen made a formidable combination. Both had played games of corporate poker with antes that could have buried casinos in chips. Both could operate behind curtains of icy calm. Unfortunately, their leader was not capable of the same reserve, and his impromptu comments made some negotiations difficult.

Strycker tells of a typical De Lorean outburst during a crucial meeting with Irish officials. 'John had a habit of pontificating. He'd say things that really were not relevant to the proposals on the table. One statement he made continually was how he saw the company eventually becoming an adjunct of Ford or Chrysler, manufacturing a separate line of luxury sedans and sports cars.

'Now you have to realize Ireland had been hurt by multi-nationals like Ford and Chrysler, which at the first sign of economic recession in America closed their Irish plants. Before we went into the meeting, I told John that the last thing these people wanted to hear was that we wanted to sell out to a big multi-national. But at a key point in our negotiations, when we get to the future of the company, John says, "We'll then be in a position to negotiate for acquisition with Chrysler or Ford."

'I think there were sixteen people in the room on their side, and in unison their mouths dropped and their faces went white. They then asked to be excused and went out to caucus. When they came back, they wanted no more negotiating. They just said, "Here are our terms." '

They included government control over the company for seven years, and the use of a huge, antiquated facility in Limerick. These were unacceptable. Strycker says, 'We told them we can't live with that sort of a deal. We all but resigned ourselves to either Puerto Rico or Detroit.'

But the Wood Gundy representatives travelling with the De Lorean negotiating team felt that there were further possibilities in the emerald isle. Northern Ireland was competing furiously with the Republic for international industrial development, and it was suggested they should at least compare notes with the authorities there.

Thirty days later they were in Belfast talking to the Northern Ireland Development Agency (NIDA). 'That day John was in one of his sulking moods,' Strycker remembers. 'He wasn't happy with the meeting and after a half hour, he just got up to leave. So it was up to me and Al Cohen to explain the project and the status of the Puerto Rico deal and the Oppenheimer partnership. Then we all hammered out the basis for financing.

'They made it clear we had to locate in Belfast, and that the worse the area, the more financing they'd give us. But there wasn't one person who said you have to hire somebody, or use someone else as a supplier. They were truly interested in creating jobs, and the social and economic impact of a major manufacturing facility. We were to be the momentum project that could get things going for them. They said, "We have the people, labour and money. You have the project, management and market. We're willing to let you make a profit on our investment, so we can have the opportunity to do this with another manufacturer again." '

When Cohen and Strycker mentioned the funding they would need, they did not see the usual shocked expressions – only nodding heads. They signed an agreement in principle before they left Belfast. 'When Cohen called to tell John about the Belfast offer,' Dewey says, 'John wanted to know whether it was real. He told me, "There was no way it could be better. It was too good to be true." '

Nevertheless, some obstacles remained to the deal. British tax laws blocked any government financing from going directly to a foreign company. The only way to circumvent that barrier was to create a British subsidiary in which NIDA had a controlling interest.

NIDA officials followed Cohen and Strycker back to New York for a longer meeting with De Lorean. They expected their ideas about a British subsidiary to be, at best, politely rebuffed. But they would find a 'comfortable and urbane' De Lorean who seemed more content to chat about the political situation in Northern Ireland than discuss the details of a plan. 'To our surprise,' one of the NIDA officials remembers, 'he was happy to agree with everything we suggested. He had no problems with a subsidiary, or controls, or our demands for representatives on both the boards of the subsidiary and the car company in the States.'

As the magnanimous magnitude of the NIDA offer began to emerge on paper, the agency demands looked less important to De Lorean executives. Besides the equity investment of NIDA, the company was also offered grants and loans from Northern Ireland's Department of Commerce. 'John got the best deal I've ever seen,' Strycker says. The total package was worth $97 million, of which almost one third was an outright grant. An additional $20 million of loans could be converted to grants if employment goals were met. Another $32.5 million came in NIDA equity. A further $12.3 million was loaned on the factory.

'Almost all of the Puerto Rico deal was a leveraged loan,' Strycker explains, 'but in Belfast the only debt was the mortgage on half the factory, and that didn't start to bear interest until production started. So for next to nothing, you end up with a brand new facility, tooling, training, equipment, working capital and money for marketing, research and development. On top of that, John got one of the strongest partners you can get in venture capital – a government. Obviously it was fully capable of keeping him alive and helping him develop his business plan.'

From that first meeting in New York negotiations proceeded with NIDA and British officials in a white heat. The following weekend De Lorean was back in Belfast with a business plan. When there, he met Don Concannon, Minister of State responsible for trade and industry in Northern Ireland. A big, burly man from a rough mining constituency, Concannon escorted De Lorean around Belfast, showing him training centres and the boggy field between Catholic and Protestant enclaves where De Lorean's plant would be located.

'I think he had a bit of conscience about the area,' Concannon says, 'and wanted to do some good. At one point some information about his project leaked out in the press, and the letters started to pour into my office – people begging for jobs and not even asking about the wage rate, and he found that impressive.'

Concannon remembers that De Lorean's biggest reservation about Belfast was the security. 'I told him the one thing terrorists didn't do was bomb their own people out of work. He also got a chance to talk to political, religious, and community leaders in this area. They were able to rid him of the complex that there's a bomb on every corner.'

If anything, Concannon explains, the factory would have bolstered security. 'Creating new jobs was part and parcel of our security policy. We felt that if the young people getting out of school had an opportunity for a job, they wouldn't be hanging about to make trouble. My job was to scour the world looking for what we called feeder industries, that would not just provide job opportunities on their own, but create other jobs for the suppliers that would feed the factories.'

In the fifties the government had used economic development to quell political unrest in Northern Ireland. A renewal of violence in the late sixties, combined with the worldwide fuel crisis in the early seventies, stopped whatever industrial growth had occurred and started the country sliding backwards. But the programme was to be revived again with even more vigour as part of the overall carrot-and-stick policy of Roy Mason. Appointed Secretary of State for Northern Ireland in 1976, Mason threw himself at the job with the same ferocious tenacity he brought to other high-level Cabinet positions. He showed no quarter to the IRA, whom he would only call terrorists, and pursued the controversial campaign to intern suspected members under emergency powers. His political views also swung to the right and while his militaristic moves in Northern Ireland raised the hackles on some members of his own party, they found bi-partisan support among the leaders of the Conservative Opposition. In his three decades in Parliament, this one-time miner had gained financial acumen that was respected by fellow members and ministers and he was as anxious to establish industrial stability in Northern Ireland as he was to stamp out the IRA. Together with his junior minister, Don Concannon, he made progress in attracting foreign companies, but the going was slow. As he later wrote in *The Times*, 'De Lorean happened at a time when no private enterprise would have entered west Belfast without government intervention, government cash, and had bold decisions not been taken by ministers.'

Accused of rushing the De Lorean project through without an adequate study of its feasibility, Mason replies in *The Times* piece that at least fifteen government departments took part in the decision. He writes that they raised questions about the cost and trade implications of the project, and also wondered whether the plant might be better suited for Wales or Scotland. But he finally got the deal through with the support of all of them. There was further surprising acquiescence in Parliament, the most vocal critic being a member of Mason's own party. The Secretary of State had enough respect among the Opposition to hear only isolated complaints about the cost of the De Lorean plan and the economic wisdom of government economic involvement with a private business.

Less attention was given to De Lorean's own background. Concannon explains that he quickly dismissed the stories about De Lorean's flamboyant lifestyle: 'What we did was checking on what he'd done for General Motors. Here was some investment that was going to provide a lot of jobs . . . and of course what we were more considerate of was his capabilities of doing that job. We have a lot of flamboyant people in the House of Commons. That's not to say they can't do their job . . . What we were looking for was a fellow who could get things cracking in Northern Ireland and help us out with our policy of jobs and security.'

When pressed, Concannon admits he did search further into the reasons why De Lorean left GM. At the time, he was concluding an agreement with General Motors to build a seat belt plant in Belfast, and he had contact with a few of the company's high-level executives. 'Basically [I] was looking for somebody to do the dirty on him at GM, but no one did. The only comments I heard were if one man in the world could get a green field into a plant that would start production, it was De Lorean. Besides, if anything were wrong with him, then why had Puerto Rico and Detroit all but signed him up?'

However, one lower-level official in Concannon's department remembers that a few people were, in fact, willing to 'do the dirty' on De Lorean. 'We knew about that race track he ran with his brother and the dealership in Kansas. But we didn't take those things very seriously. American businessmen always end up in court over one thing or another. I don't think it's unusual for an entrepreneur to have a few companies go bankrupt when he's starting up.'

A Master Agreement was signed in just forty-five days after NIDA officials first saw De Lorean in New York. Throughout that time, De Lorean kept up negotiations on another front, for while one squad in Belfast rushed to adjust the business plan to the different demands of an Irish site, Bob Dewey continued bargaining with Puerto Rico – not just to put pressure on the British, but also to keep their investment banker Oppenheimer & Company happy. The investment firm had already sold $20 million worth of units in a research partnership, but their solicitation was based on building a plant in Puerto Rico. If De Lorean did opt for Northern Ireland, the research partners could rescind their investments, and the Oppenheimer executives did not relish that prospect. 'They told John to stop screwing around,' Dewey says, 'and settle down in Puerto Rico.'

The final agreement with NIDA would come as a crashing anti-climax. De Lorean signed the document quietly at Al Cohen's office. No one bothered to break the news to the Puerto Rico contingents of lawyers still waiting for a De Lorean representative to appear.

'We never did celebrate the signing,' Dewey says. 'I think each of us had different feelings about it.' Mentally and physically exhausted, Dewey just wanted to take the next flight back to Detroit. De Lorean was on the verge of his self-proclaimed 'most incredible accomplishment of the last hundred years', but when Dewey stopped by his Chris Craft office to say goodbye, he found the miracle worker petrified by the prospect of an imminent meeting. 'John had decided to see Howard Phillips from Oppenheimer to tell him we had signed the British deal, and he wanted me to be there with him. John hated confrontations. I told John I wanted to go home and I had a five o'clock plane to catch. But he was like a little kid. He didn't want me to go and leave him alone to face Phillips. He kept saying, "You can't let me down like this."

'I told him that if he wanted company when Phillips came, he should call Al Cohen. Then I left.'

De Lorean did not bother to meet any of the representatives of Puerto Rico. On the following Monday the commonwealth still could not believe the car company had actually backed out. An angry Governor Carlos Romero Barcelo told the *New York Times*, 'Today, I tried personally to get in touch with Mr De Lorean and he has evaded my calls. This demonstrates without doubt his bad faith to everyone.'

Officials in Washington were just as angry. The director of the business development office for the Economic Development Administration never had a company turn down loan guarantees as large as the ones he offered De Lorean. 'This does not sit too well with us,' he told the *New York Times*. 'We put a lot of time and money into this.'

If both the federal government and the Commonwealth of Puerto Rico were taken for a ride, the feat was all the more amazing considering the scanty resources of the man at the wheel and the highly speculative nature of his enterprise. The eventual $97 million De Lorean culled from NIDA with the help of an unrequited Puerto Rico added up to the greatest triumph of his business career. However, his success was also a dangerous lesson in how sometimes image can suffice without substance.

Despite the largesse of the British government, De Lorean's executives could see that a long haul still lay before them in taking a car company literally from the ground up and starting production a year and a half later, as the stock prospectus promised. Concannon and the rest of Northern Ireland's authorities were confident in De Lorean's ability to do this, as they saw him as 'a fellow who could get things cracking'. But as far as De Lorean was concerned, things were already cracked with the British deal.

In a *Business Week* interview after the signing he indicated that the NIDA agreement was the crest of the hill, not the bottom. In four years, his car company had raised barely $5 million. In a span of forty-five days, the coffers swelled twenty-fold. 'The hardest part is pretty well behind me now,' he told the magazine. 'I think our chances of making it are 95 per cent. That's nearly double what they were a year ago.'

PART THREE
The Maverick Mogul

GPD

On the morning of 18 October 1978 a junior executive in the 100 West Long Lake office of the De Lorean Motor Company received a summons from his chief executive. He took the next plane to New York City and just before noon was standing by John De Lorean's desk at the Madison Avenue headquarters of the Chris Craft Corporation.

De Lorean had not brought him to Manhattan to discuss the revised business plan or help with the company's impending move to its new Park Avenue office. Instead, he asked the executive to do no more than spend the day running an errand. The first leg of his mission would be a taxi ride downtown to the Wall Street branch of the Chemical Bank – no small feat in New York's lunchtime traffic. He would then search out a bank officer and draw a cheque on the account of the De Lorean Research Limited Partnership. Made out to a company called GPD Services, the cheque would be for $12.5 million.

After matter-of-factly issuing his instructions, De Lorean returned to his papers, but his courier left the office in a daze. Within an hour he would be holding more money in his hands than most people would see in several lifetimes. 'I don't care how honest you are,' he says of the incident today, 'but for that one moment you wonder whether you could get away with having the cheque made out to cash and taking the next plane to Rio.'

He also wondered about De Lorean's purpose for the funds. After De Lorean made his decision to build the assembly plant in Northern Ireland, Oppenheimer & Company had not been enthusiastic about going through with the research partnership. They consented, but the investors could drop out if they chose, and several did. Finally, after taking its 10 per cent commission, Oppenheimer deposited what was left – $16.8 million – in the partnership account. Now just one month later, almost 75 per cent of the assets were going to GPD Services, a firm he had never heard of before.

163

After getting the cheque drawn, the executive returned to Chris Craft again for De Lorean to sign it, and then went back to the bank for the appropriate officer to countersign. He finally handed over the endorsed cheque to De Lorean that afternoon in his Fifth Avenue apartment. De Lorean folded the bank draft as though it were no more than a scrap of paper and slipped it into his wallet.

'It was a cool fall day,' the executive remembers, 'but that night, when I got home and took off my jacket, I saw that under my arms my shirt was stained with huge rings of perspiration. I looked like I had run a race.'

GPD Services remains the most ominous mystery of the De Lorean Motor Company. More like a ghost enterprise than a shell company, it has an address in a post office box in Geneva, Switzerland. The only employee of the firm ever identified has been a woman whom De Lorean referred to as a Mrs Juhan. She does indeed exist, but she refuses to speak about GPD or John De Lorean. Just a few weeks before De Lorean drew the cheque from the research partnership, GPD was first registered, in Panama and its Panama City lawyers are just as silent as Mrs Juhan. Within a year, two De Lorean Motor Company subsidiaries paid GPD $17.76 million. No trace of that money has yet been found.

For De Lorean executives, GPD became the most unsettling aspect of their company's affairs. When vice-president Bill Haddad first looked into the company so that he could respond to questions from British reporters, he found that in Belfast, 'GPD is a "hush-hush" subject'. Like an unhinged silencer, GPD dragged along throughout the brief, tumultuous ride of the De Lorean Motor Company, first shooting off sparks, then scraping louder and louder until it came clattering to the ground.

The most suspicious aspect of GPD Services is the failure of De Lorean Securities Exchange Commission files to mention it by name after 1979. From then on, the firm is called an 'independent contractor' and no more.

According to that first and last reference in the 1979 De Lorean Motor Company share offering, GPD was to assist the company in 'completion of product design development'. Although Collins had already made two prototypes, there was still a great deal of design work to do. In effect, his work to that point could be likened to a film script. The property still had to go into production. Someone had to cast suppliers, design the set for the factory, choreograph the assembly, and most important, build the props – tooling – needed to fabricate the various parts of the car. Very few companies in the world are capable of performing this transitional service, and even Detroit car companies have trouble doing it on their own. De Lorean claimed that he had searched desperately for such help on both sides of the Atlantic. The leader in the field, Porsche, asked too high a price and too long a lead time.

His salvation, he says, came when he was 'suddenly contacted' by GPD in the early autumn of 1978. According to De Lorean, besides providing its own engineers, GPD also subcontracted Lotus Cars Limited, along with its celebrated founder, Colin Chapman, to supervise the development.

Exactly how De Lorean and Lotus decided to join forces is a matter of dispute. De Lorean has said that GPD was the matchmaker. But there is plenty of evidence that De Lorean was known to Chapman and Lotus before GPD. First of all, Chapman had a long-standing relationship with Chris Craft – where De Lorean was on the board – to make boat hulls out of the plastic process he patented. Furthermore, early in the summer of 1978 De Lorean had contacted Chapman's engineering director, A.C. Rudd, about a job in the engineering squad he was going to assemble. Rudd turned down the offer, but according to several Lotus executives then asked De Lorean to consider subcontracting the Lotus staff.

During all of De Lorean's deliberations with Lotus, no one ever saw a trace of GPD. 'All I knew was that in September 1978, Chapman and [Lotus's managing director, Michael J.] Kimberly spent a day in the car while it was in Phoenix,' Bill Collins says. 'That was the beginning of their involvement with the company. They were then supposed to issue a report suggesting the best way to get the car into production. I never met anyone from GPD, and I never heard that anyone else from the De Lorean Motor Company met anyone from GPD.'

The relationship between Chapman and De Lorean lies at the heart of the GPD enigma. Once again, De Lorean had found a doer, and in this case, a certified winner as well. An aircraft engineer by training, Chapman started building racing cars in the garage behind his house in the late forties. Over the next two decades he revolutionized the car-racing sport, single-handedly creating the Formula One/Grand Prix event we know today. He was the first to incorporate aircraft techniques to harden aluminium and reduce the weight of the coffin-like car body he called the Monococque. Later he mastered the use of plastic for structural material and learned to harness the force of air rushing under a race car to increase its speed and control around curves. As a result of his constant innovations, Team Lotus captured the lion's share of victories on the world racing circuit during the sixties and early seventies.

'He can be a prima donna sometimes,' De Lorean once said of Chapman, 'but he really is a genius. He's just one little guy and he beats these racing teams that literally have governments backing them.'

In 1957 Chapman brought out his first touring car for the public. This limited-edition luxury vehicle would not enjoy anything like the success in the showroom that his racing vehicles had on the track, but when Chapman took his company public in 1968, he became a millionaire overnight.

In the mid-sixties Chapman moved out of London and settled among the flat farming fields of Hethel, some fifteen miles of winding, treacherous roads west of Norwich. Ironically, the car-maker chose this relatively isolated area so he could take over an abandoned RAF facility and have a private airport for his fleet of planes. His home and corporate headquarters were the nearby Ketteringham Hall, a rambling castle-like mansion that once served as a boys' school. 'I think John was instantly enamoured with Colin [Chapman] as soon as he saw the setup he had in Norwich,' Bill Collins says. 'Maybe he was the type of guy John always wanted to be.'

A short, debonair man with a precisely trimmed moustache, the balding Chapman was usually seen with a jaunty cap or porkpie hat. He had a distant manner which some considered to be almost regal, others just arrogant. 'Chapman always looked down on the rest of us in racing,' says Smokey Yunick, a veteran of the American stock car circuit. 'You couldn't talk to the man. He always knew it all.'

Chapman did not treat Bill Collins any better than he treated the racing engineers. Lotus's appropriation of the DMC–12 came as an abrupt shock to the man who had created it from the seating buck up. Already housed in Coventry, Collins was preparing to assemble his own team of engineers to do the production engineering. He thought his years at General Motors prepared him well for the task of guiding a new car into production, and he believed he could recruit similarly suited sorts from the car companies of Europe. But with Chapman suddenly on the scene, Collins was denied the chance to deliver his own baby. De Lorean assured Collins that he would be able to consult with Lotus and direct the company's progress, but Collins found that he wasn't wanted.

Colin Spooner, the Lotus engineer put in charge of the De Lorean project, sympathized with Collins's predicament. 'I don't think De Lorean ever bothered to define a specific role for Bill,' he says. 'John always tended to let things like that sort themselves out.'

Collins sorted himself out of England and back to the States. He had devoted almost four years of his life to De Lorean's dream and made it his dream as well. His immersion in the project nearly wrecked his twenty-year marriage. He worked alone on designs when everyone told him the car would never get off his drawing board. He spent nights and weekends in the workshops helping mechanics assemble the prototypes. Now, when the impossible project was finally on the verge of fruition, De Lorean considered him expendable. 'I was pretty much stranded in England with people I had convinced to go out there,' Collins recalls, 'and we found ourselves with nothing to do. John just wouldn't intervene with Chapman.

'I think I made the mistake of trusting John. He always said he was interested in people. But he never was – even in those people who did the most for him. My wife saw that from the start. Unfortunately, it took me a little longer.'

Several motor industry experts questioned whether the Lotus staff was equipped to help De Lorean with a production vehicle. While he planned on eventually turning out 30,000 cars a year, Lotus had never produced much over a thousand annually. Its procedures were considered more hand-tooled than assembly line.

But Chapman did have one important qualification that set him apart from any other motor company. He too used a plastic moulding system for the body panels of his car, in a process he variously called vacuum resin injection moulding (VRIM) or vacuum assisted resin injection (VARI). The plastic was one of Chapman's greatest achievements. 'It was Colin Chapman's inspiration that brought us VARI,' says Colin Spooner. 'In two short years we went from the impossible to a fully developed process that could produce the quality of mouldings necessary for a car.'

Like De Lorean's ERM plastic, VARI produces a hard, light substance, but it required tools that injected heated resin into a mould – a far more expensive and time-consuming process than the one De Lorean had licensed. VARI, however, had been tested for years in Lotus cars, and it seemed adaptable to mass production. De Lorean did not have the same confidence with ERM, and VARI was a convenient alternative if De Lorean's subsidiary, Composite Technology Corporation, were unable to develop ERM in time.

Considering that De Lorean did have good reason to use Lotus, one question remains: why was so much money directed through a middleman? Chapman cannot say as he died of a heart attack shortly after De Lorean's arrest.

There was, in fact, no reason for any third party to intervene, and all the evidence suggests that none did. When the executive who drew the cheque from Chemical Bank asked De Lorean what the $12.5 million was for, 'De Lorean said that he was negotiating with Lotus and their subsidiary GPD. He told me, "We need them and this will be the carrot. It's earnest money." '

The then chief financial officer Walt Strycker says, 'I was excluded from the deal. At the time, I was told that John and Tom Kimmerly were going over to Switzerland to negotiate the acquisition of Lotus, which was in precarious financial condition. I was also told that a few NIDA officials would be there as well.'

Almost three weeks after De Lorean drew the cheque (and three weeks of lost interest to the research partnership account), he and a lawyer took the draft to a hotel in Geneva where they met Chapman, one of his aides, and the elusive Mrs Juhan. The result of their session was a sloppily prepared contract, which spelled out two areas of responsibility for GPD: vehicle engineering to be conducted with the research partnership payment of $12.5 million, and development of Chapman's VARI process to adapt it to the DMC–12 – that task was underwritten with a $5.15 million fee paid for by the new British–backed subsidiary, De Lorean Motor Cars Limited. At that time it was decided that the partnership's initial payment be reduced to $8.5 million. De Lorean wired the $4 million back to New York. But two months later it all went back again to GPD.

Even after the payments were made, no one mentioned GPD to Strycker. 'John told me they couldn't make a deal to acquire Lotus, that Chapman wouldn't sell. Instead, he demanded two payments – one for licensing the VARI process, and then another for product engineering.'

Consisting of ten pages, the GPD contract was apparently typed on two different typewriters, and copies that were released to other car company executives look to be authentic. They show the signatures of De Lorean and Mrs Juhan on the bottom of each page. All blank spaces are crossed out to prevent any addenda from appearing after the signing.

The contract provided that Lotus would be paid any costs above the $17.65 million. While Lotus records admit receiving over $24 million directly from De Lorean Motor Cars Limited, there is no mention of any payment from GPD and no trace of the $17.65 million. The sum of the two payments comes to over $41 million – a price for the car's development even higher than the one requested by Porsche. But the concerns about GPD go beyond just cost, because the question remains whether any of the GPD funds went towards the car's development, and no record has been found to show that they ever did.

De Lorean has not just tied GPD to Chapman in private comments to his executives but in a few public statements as well. In a statement he issued to the press about GPD he wrote, 'GPD has the rights to and markets the patents and technology for the VARI process by which we produce our car body.'

In fact, De Lorean was prohibited from contracting with GPD, Lotus or anyone else for the rights to a developed process. The whole tax write–off for the research partnership required funds go to legitimate research and development of untested processes. Licences requiring no further development are not included in that category. The same tax benefit existed for the British subsidiary as well. However, the GPD contract specifically gives away its rights to Lotus's plastic process under a section which reads, '[De Lorean Motor Cars] Limited will be entitled to the royalty free use of all patents, shop rights and know-how related to Vacuum Resin Injection Moulding solely for use in the De Lorean Sports car the subject of this contract and other De Lorean automotive products.'

Chapman strongly objected to the suggestion that he had anything to do with GPD. He raged to the *Sunday Telegraph* in his only public comment about GPD, 'De Lorean wanted the deal done like that – ask him why GPD got the contract and then subcontracted to us.'

Of course, Chapman did not add that he had other dealings with GPD Services, or that Marie-Denise Juhan had been associated with Lotus before. However, the meaning of the initials, as deciphered by the *Sunday Times* Insight team, suggests otherwise. At one point, De Lorean had declared that the three letters stood for General Product Development, but actually they were Grand Prix Drivers. Chapman, who was reputed to have a maze of offshore companies to evade the stiff British income tax, reportedly used GPD as a conduit of prize money to his Formula One racers.

The very wording of the GPD contract indicates that someone British had a strong hand in its preparation. Anglicized spelling is used throughout the text.

What happened to the GPD money concerned senior members of the De Lorean staff, especially Strycker. 'When we finally heard about GPD,' Strycker says, 'some of us thought about the possibility that John and Chapman put their hands on that money. But just as quickly, we dismissed the idea. Here John had the opportunity to make hundreds of millions with the car company. Why should he risk that before the thing had even gotten off the ground? It would be such a goddamn stupid thing to do, we just couldn't believe that John would have done it.'

De Lorean categorically denies that there was anything wrong with the GPD contract. As he pointed out in his press release on the subject: 'The contract with GPD was submitted to, approved by and is on file with The Bank of England (Exchange Control), The Department of Commerce, and The Northern Ireland Development Agency. Each of the agencies reviewed, approved and consented to the arrangement before any payment was made. The only benefit I or anyone else in our Company has received from this contract is a truly outstanding auto-mobile design delivered in less than half the normal time at a fraction of the normal cost.'

But De Lorean's own behaviour after the GPD payments draws more suspicion to his participation in the deal than anyone else's accusa-tions. Suddenly, during spring 1979, he was on the lookout for what he would later call 'an income-producing investment'.

It was a time when the De Lorean Motor Company had reached a critical juncture, so the chief executive's search for new investments seems all the more unusual. Never did his young company need his energies and resources more: the car had to be prodded through Lotus, the factory had to be built, scores of top executives hired and the dealer network finished. In the early days of General Motors William Durant went on his own buying spree, but he did the buying for the corporation, and then only picked up companies that would complement the existing GM divisions. After he lost control of General Motors for the second time, in the early 1920s, he started the Durant Motor Company. It was another boom and bust effort, but this time Durant's fatal flaw was spending only part of his time on the car company and dissipating the rest on unrelated matters – especially playing the stock market. De Lorean, familiar as he was with Durant's career, did not seem to learn any lessons from it.

Among the outside interests he pursued was the First Bank and Trust of Palm Beach County, but his efforts would be frustrated by an amazing coincidence. The bank's owner had turned to Wichita lawyer Paul Kitch for advice on the sale. 'He called to tell me that this Washington bank expert claimed to be representing a very wealthy individual named De Lorean,' Kitch remembered. 'He told him De Lorean wanted to buy a bank in Florida, any bank in Florida. He was prepared to make an offer, and all my client had to do was name a price and deliver the stock.'

But upon hearing De Lorean's name, Kitch warned his client to beware. As counsel for the Kansas State Bank and Trust Company, the lawyer was still in the process of suing De Lorean in connection with the Dahlinger Cadillac dealership. It was one of the rare occasions when the auto magnate's bungled entrepreneurial past came back to haunt him. Kitch says, 'I told my client that this guy De Lorean was a crook, and I offered to be there at their first meeting. He called back De Lorean's lawyer to tell him that their appointment would have to be rescheduled so I could be there. I guess all De Lorean had to do was hear my name. He never showed up for the meeting.' To buy the bank, Kitch estimates, De Lorean would have had to make an offer of $15 million.

Undismayed by the one bad experience, De Lorean took his search for an investment from the Florida beaches to the mountains north of Salt Lake City, in Logan, Utah. There, in a little compound of grey aluminium buildings he found a company that manufactured off-track utilities vehicles. It was owned by the Pennsylvania chemical conglomerate, Thiokol. De Lorean had been familiar with the parent company back in his GM days when they supplied windscreen sealants and the chemical inflating components of air bags. Years later, one of the company's retired executives let him know that the company was divesting subsidiaries unrelated to chemicals. The Logan division had long been such an aberration. It was formed first as a favour to nearby Utah State professors who patented a huge tank tread that would not get stuck in snow. The company's best-selling vehicles groomed the top of ski slopes, and although Logan dominated the domestic market – 'a little GM', De Lorean called it – the division turned only a million dollar profit on $16 million of sales.

Because the bulk of Thiokol's contracts are defence-related, the company is able to veil much of its financial activity. The year it sold the Logan division it lumped the proceeds in with other divestitures. But some Logan employees have seen De Lorean's purchase package and they put its total at $13.4 million. It included $7.5 million in cash, a $1.25 million note to Thiokol and a land swap, done for tax purposes, involving 450 acres of De Lorean's San Diego avocado groves valued at $4.65 million. Beyond that expense De Lorean also brought in another $7.5 million line of credit from the Continental Bank of Illinois to supply operating capital.

To facilitate these moves, the title of the John Z. De Lorean Corporation was changed to the De Lorean Manufacturing Corporation – providing a new name for the Logan division, but also a DMC acronym that could be confused with the De Lorean Motor Company. In just 1979, the year of the purchase, company records would show the assets for Manufacturing jumping from $616,464 to $15.8 million.

When asked about his purchase of the Logan firm, De Lorean explained to reporters that it was financed solely with the land swap. But those close enough to know otherwise wonder where he got the $7.5 million cash and the collateral for the $7.5 million credit line.

Coincidentally, the same executive who first drew the $12.5 million cheque for GPD would take a call from the Continental Bank of Illinois one day in the New York headquarters shortly after De Lorean purchased the Logan division. He was the only financial officer available during lunch hour. The bank called to confirm that the necessary funds had been transferred from the Swiss bank account. Without knowing what the message meant, he passed it on to Walt Strycker. Since he had first suggested De Lorean go to the Continental Bank to finance a loan for Logan, Strycker was well aware what the call referred to. His suspicions were further aroused a few months later, he says, when he and De Lorean were discussing interest rates on export loans. 'John said we should try to do it through a Swiss bank. Then he said he had just gotten a loan from a Swiss bank.'

Continental Bank officials had told Strycker that they were ready to loan De Lorean more money for the purchase of Logan, but that he had given the business to another bank – a 'foreign source'. It was hard for

Strycker not to start putting two and two together. GPD had been a Swiss transaction. Shortly afterwards De Lorean had bought Logan and secured credit for the acquisition with the help of a foreign bank. Then his assistant got the call confirming the wire of funds from a Swiss bank. 'When you looked at that chain of events,' Strycker says, 'you didn't have to be overly suspicious to realize that something was very wrong.'

Belfast

'It was fantastic. It was unbelievable.'

Billy Parker sits in the narrow wood booth of a Belfast pub and remembers the first time he heard about the new car factory. At twenty-six, he is a thin, pale man with the long, straggly beard of an Old Testament prophet. He has already been married ten years and has three children.

In the beginning, he did not see how talk of De Lorean's deal would do anything to help him. Getting a paying job had never been easy, and even harder after the Troubles, when his opportunities to paint and do maintenance work were restricted to impoverished Catholic housing projects. 'There was massive publicity,' Billy Parker says, 'all about this American businessman and his movie star wife and a strange new car. You really couldn't believe it.'

Northern Ireland had not seen any new industrial development since civil strife erupted in 1971, and before that most new plants ended up in Protestant areas anyway. But most amazingly, this plant was supposed to go up in the industrial town of Dunmurry, in a marshy field that was a no man's land between the Twinbrook Catholic housing project and a Protestant neighbourhood.

There were still sceptics, even when the political dignitaries and local priests joined De Lorean executives for the sod-turning on 2 October 1978. A few of these doubting sorts gathered by the police cordons guarding the festivities and shouted, 'Yankees go home.'

But then the trucks and bulldozers came, and the first few hundred men from the area were hired to clear the field, reroute the little muddy streams that passed through it, and fill the swamps with stones. A railway embankment screened out the construction from the Protestant side, but in one spot, near a high-rise block of flats, the locals wore a footpath up a little knoll. There among the saplings, they watched steel canopies rise up out of the ground, and then, patch by patch, get

173

covered over with a metal skin. These were not your typical factory buildings pocked with grimy windows or studded with smokestacks but some new industrial creatures: long, rectangular and sleek with neat grey bricks on the foundation, a darker grey corrugated metal above and gleaming furrowed aluminium roofs.

From this Protestant vantage point the new landmark stood in stark contrast to its surroundings. Two shabby housing projects spilled down the hills behind it, and to the other side, just as depressing, were the grimy and mostly abandoned shops and factories of the Dunmurry Industrial Estate, which was built in the fifties and was now the wasted vestige of another era's attack on high unemployment in Northern Ireland.

Belfast's ship-building industry – responsible for the *Titanic* – was in decline. The linen industry, another mainstay of the economy, seemed just as doomed as that notorious ship, as the world turned to man-made fibres and the low-cost competition from the Orient.

By the fifties Northern Ireland had become an enclave of unemployment unequalled in the western world. The government's solution was to build – right in the midst of the jobless – spanking new 'advance factories' and then scour the globe looking for some itinerant multi-national corporation to fill them.

Going after the man-made hair of the dog that bit them, Irish development officials concentrated on the synthetic fibre conglomerates and managed to lure some of the biggest, including Courtaulds, Monsanto, Dupont and ICI. From 1950 to 1970 over three hundred new plants opened up in Northern Ireland, and of the total 170,000 employed in the country, over 70,000 worked in the new industries. But the so-called 'footloose' industrialists who were so anxious to move in had little compunction about moving out either. When their tax concessions ended or recession hit their home markets, they started to look for greener and cheaper pastures outside Ireland. Sectarian strife further complicated matters. Often, the composition of a factory work-force fell in line with the surrounding neighbourhood – a development that ended up helping Protestants more than Catholics. The conglomerates, however, did not like being caught in the middle. During the seventies one out of three manufacturing jobs in Northern Ireland would be lost.

The waves of both economic and social devastation washed over the Catholic neighbourhoods behind the De Lorean plant. The Dunmurry estate which had once employed three thousand only had three hundred workers by the time De Lorean set up shop. With unemployment estimated by some local officials at 80 per cent the area was a hotbed of IRA activism. A huge cement block building with narrow windows and a ten-foot high steel slat fence serves as the local primary school. Up a barren asphalt road the older homes are known as Cherry Hill. Next to them is a new project called Twinbrook, built to catch the overflow of Catholics fleeing the eastern sections of Belfast. The houses are drab one-colour affairs, built in step-up clusters of three, and hastily scattered over the hills. Back gardens are a maze of fences and clothes-lines. Political graffiti are painted on the walls. From the Catholic side there was a more direct view of the factory site, but it was over a boggy dump, littered with tree stumps, garbage and the occasional hull of a burned-out car. Two rings of barbed wire separated the plant from the housing complex. The Protestants and Catholics would each have their own entrance.

For first-time visitors to Belfast the signs of the deep national division are hard to ignore, starting with the stringent baggage checks at the airport. 'I can remember my first visit to the Conway Hotel across the street from the plant site,' one De Lorean employee says. 'I came in directly from the airport, and looking out the taxi at night, I wondered what all the fuss was about. We went by some very nicely kept up Georgian style homes and then came to the hotel entrance. It's up a winding, tree-lined driveway – like a little version of San Simeon [William Randolph Hearst's home in California]. On the way you pass a garden house with a pool and fountain. Then the taxi stops and you're in front of a hotel that's surrounded with barbed wire eight feet high and enough floodlights to light up a ball park. After you get out of the cab, you go through a little trailer where they frisk you and look through all your luggage. Just so you remember that you're a guest, there's a big sign over the entrance that says, "Welcome." When I checked in, I asked why they went to all these lengths for the security. Then they told me that this was the *new* Conway Hotel. The *old* Conway was blown to pieces ten years ago.'

No one would be more concerned about security than the car com-pany's namesake. During the entire life of his plant in Belfast, De Lorean never stayed in the city's hotels more than a handful of times. He preferred to spend the night in the Connaught or the Savoy in London and shuttle on the plane. At one point he put Bill Haddad in charge of security, and throughout their discussions on protecting the facility and executives from terrorist attack De Lorean constantly brought up his desire to find a ground-length bullet-proof leather trench coat. He had heard that Henry Kissinger had had such a protective armour and he kept after Haddad to do the same for him. Haddad's security expert quickly got in touch with Kissinger and discovered that the raincoat ended up being so heavy he never bothered to wear it. Bill passed the information on to De Lorean, thinking that was the end of the matter, but soon after, when he sent a memo suggesting that they 'work out the long overdue local security system (office, homes, procedures, etc.)', De Lorean returned the memo with a note scrawled on the bottom:

'OK – where's my raincoat?'

When De Lorean got his raincoat, he did not take too many opportunities to wear it. In the early days the top job in Belfast – managing director of De Lorean Motor Cars Limited – became the key spot in the company. To fill it De Lorean turned to a man who knew how to cope with unusual locales. For years, Charles K. Bennington had been building and operating overseas installations for the Chrysler Corporation. England, France, Germany, Italy, Turkey, South Africa: all were stops along his career path. Originally from Detroit, he had come to appear more stateless than American. The clipped cadence of his speech almost sounded British. He kept his hair brushed back and his beard Van Dyked with the tips of the moustache twirled. He preferred a leather jacket and a turtle neck to a suit and tie.

Starting out with just six people, Bennington proceeded to move heaven and earth to build the plant on schedule. He had faced tougher jobs before, and, in countries like Turkey, more primitive conditions, but Belfast still posed its own problems. Among these, the site proved to be far more marshy than anyone expected, and besides covering up a brook and diverting it outside the property, Bennington also had to bring in half a million tons of stone before the ground was stable enough to build on.

Despite the difficulties, as 1980 approached Bennington had the plant going up according to plan. Once again, De Lorean had found a take-charge guy, and he was willing to give him free rein. Two months before Bennington came on board De Lorean had hired a management consultant to draw up a critical path 'the step-by-step time-line' for getting the factory finished. Bennington did not bother even to glance at his work. 'He didn't need a manual to tell him how to build a factory,' DMC Limited's treasurer Ken Gorf says. 'Chuck knew intuitively. He had done it before and he had the guts to make those hundreds of decisions that must be made each day on a project of that sort. Of course, a couple of calls might have been bad, but you cause more damage by delay. He was an energetic, enthusiastic pioneer, and a man capable of working extremely long hours.'

But he was also a difficult man to work with and another British executive explains, 'Chuck didn't want to know what other people thought. In many ways he was a loner, who didn't share the load and he kept taking an increasing amount of pressure from De Lorean. There was a daily barrage of phone calls and memos, and Chuck tried to handle them all. He was living in a very intense way and it started to show.'

Other De Lorean employees, especially those from the sales organization in California, were not as enamoured of Bennington's abilities. In early 1980 they needed information for parts catalogues and service manuals to prepare for the car's arrival in the States, but they had trouble getting Chuck's attention. One emissary cooled his heels in the Conway for two days before Bennington found time to see him.

'To me,' one of the California executives says, 'he was like the Bob Fosse character in the movie *All That Jazz*. He even looked like the guy. He was working and playing his way into a heart attack, and nobody else but God could butt in.'

Other Bennington detractors pointed to his extravagance, especially in remodelling a home on the factory compound that was meant to be the guest house and residence for the managing director. Over £20,000 was spent on the bathrooms, part of which went for gold-plated taps from Harrods – a move which De Lorean later characterized for the press as 'stupid, dumb and indiscreet'.

But Bennington's harshest critics were those who didn't work with him. While his colleagues in Belfast found him reclusive and occasionally arrogant, they respected his energy, and looking back, most doubt whether the plant could have got up as fast as it did without him.

The big delay did not come in getting the plant up, but getting the car out of Lotus. Here Bennington could not be solely to blame. Chapman wasn't content to just work from Collins's prototype. Instead, he practically redesigned the car from the ground up. He was partly encouraged by De Lorean. Ten months after Lotus took charge, De Lorean sent the car back to body stylist Giugiaro for a few 'minor' alterations to keep his original design up to date. Chapman and De Lorean liked to refer to the changes he made as 'tweaking' the car. But for some others in the car company, the change was more like a splat than a tweak, which ignored many of the parameters Bill Collins and De Lorean first set for it. The car moved even lower to the ground, and the interior became much more cramped. While there was more than enough headroom for the shorter Chapman De Lorean was to find his own car a much tighter fit than he ever intended.

Whatever anyone's view of the changes, they were keeping the company off the timetable. Pilot production was to have started in May 1980, but in October Lotus still had the car and several design decisions still had to be made – from the suspension to the car windows. More important, time-consuming tests needed to be done on the few prototypes in existence to determine whether the car could meet U.S. safety and exhaust emission standards.

One of Bennington's solutions to get the project back on track was the creation of an Engineering Policy Review Committee – in essence an excuse for a group of De Lorean executives to visit the Chapman domain in Norwich periodically and politely pass on their sense of urgency. Bennington would tell his aides, 'It's like massaging the belly of a pregnant woman. You know the baby's there. All you can do is ease it along until it comes out.'

But he found himself interposed between two jealous and anxious fathers – De Lorean and Chapman. Neither one was ready to confront the other, but that did not prevent them from venting their frustrations on subordinates. The difficulty of Bennington's situation was illustrated all too clearly on film when De Lorean permitted film makers D.A. Pennebaker and Chris Hegedus to do a documentary on the company's early stages, which was eventually shown in the United States with the title, *Start-Up*. In one scene De Lorean is squired through the old aircraft hangars where Lotus is making the car. Later, he is shown finishing up a leisurely lunch with Lotus executives at Ketteringham Hall. They sit on French provincial chairs at a long table covered with a sumptuous spread of fruit and cheese. Light streams through the window. De Lorean is not talking about the delays that have mired his car at Lotus; instead he gossips about Ford's troubles with the Pinto fuel tank – 'a stupid design issue', he says, his voice dripping with disdain.

But the next day, at a board meeting for De Lorean Motor Cars Limited, he speaks with similar loathing about Lotus – again for the camera. 'We've got to get out of Lotus now,' he tells Bennington. 'What are you going to do to get us out of there?'

Unhappy with Bennington's answers, De Lorean continues to ask other needling questions about fees from the engine-maker, Renault, and methods to convert the cars to right-hand driving. Nothing is being done fast enough for De Lorean. The camera sees a man who has aged decades since his departure from GM. He has let his hair go grey – at the suggestion of investment counsellors – appearing more distinguished. The lines are returning to his face, especially around the mouth. His contact lenses are no longer enough, and here he is seen wearing a pair of half-lens reading glasses, which he pulls off and tosses on the reports in front of him. He repeatedly tells Bennington, 'This is asinine.' The camera cuts to the Belfast managing director nervously chain-smoking cigarettes.

In just the few minutes of the October 1980 board meeting that Pennebaker and Hegedus got on film, it seems as though something is very seriously wrong with this infant company – even before cars are rolling off the line. Amazingly, the chairman of the board ends the meeting by an admission that even when the sports car is in production sales in America won't be enough to keep DMC afloat. New markets and another product must be developed first. 'You cannot support this kind of overhead with one car,' he tells the board, 'and we've known that for a long time. We really have got to keep this moving. No matter where we've got to steal the money to do it. This is not a matter of something extra. This is a matter of pure survival.'

Of course, De Lorean didn't really consider stealing. But with the

British government behind him, he found that he could go to the Exchequer's well once too often. His relationship could not have been better with the Labour Party ministers he first dealt with, and Don Concannon agrees, 'At first, what was going on was a partnership between us and De Lorean. Both sides wanted to make it work and we were more than willing to cooperate. As far as we could see, he was delivering everything we asked for in getting the plant up.'

If anything, the relationship got a little too clubby for some bureaucrats when De Lorean tried to hire NIDA executive Shaun Harte. More than anyone else in his agency, Harte had spearheaded the negotiations with the car company. He was later NIDA's designated watchdog on both the boards of the De Lorean Motor Company and De Lorean Motor Cars Limited. The offer to chuck his government job for five times the salary was a strong enticement indeed, and it most concerned his immediate superior, NIDA chairman Ronald Henderson. 'At first Ronnie refused to let John hire Shaun,' Walt Strycker says. 'But the whole job offer just put everyone in a bad position. Shaun was left fuming at Henderson and obviously not happy about staying with NIDA . . . Eventually Ronnie had to let him go to us and the whole thing just left a bad taste in everyone's mouth.'

But not necessarily for Concannon, who found such exchanges to be expected and even palatable. He explains, 'That's what usually happens in Northern Ireland. Once these international companies start coming into Northern Ireland, they look for good local people, and the very fact is, the best people they can find are the ones who helped them get a good foothold there. I find this to be part and parcel of the process. It didn't worry me at all. In fact, it was very helpful that I knew somebody was in there who had Northern Ireland at heart. I was only concerned because I lost some good men.'

Accommodating sorts like Concannon and Roy Mason, however, were not to be around much longer. When the Conservatives won the General Election of May 1979 De Lorean found himself dealing with a Cabinet which eschewed government involvement in any private sector business – especially on the scale of the De Lorean deal. It was a state of affairs that John De Lorean later commiserated about with his Labour mentors. 'If you talk to De Lorean,' Concannon says, 'he sees [the change of governments] as the turning-point of the project. Before that point, he was working with a lot of ministers who only wanted to see him succeed. Then suddenly overnight they disappeared and he gets a set of ministers who couldn't care less whether it succeeds. In fact, in their basic philosophy, they don't want it to succeed.'

However, when offered Concannon's assessment how conditions for the company changed when the Conservatives came to power, DMC Limited's one-time treasurer Ken Gorf disagrees: 'That's a lot of crap.

We had as much support from the Tories as we did from the Labour party. And it lasted until the Tories said enough is enough. I should know, because I negotiated a lot of the extra loans we did get from the Thatcher government, and they were substantial. The fact is, the day-to-day contacts in the Northern Ireland Department of Commerce did not change. They continued to be helpful. We did end up with a new chief executive at NIDA, Tony Hopkins, but he wasn't hostile. He just wouldn't give John everything he wanted. He tried to get the best deal for NIDA, as he should have done.'

De Lorean first went to Hopkins in the summer of 1980 when development costs with Lotus were skyrocketing and he could see that it would still be months before the company could market the car. There were several loopholes in the contract that could have permitted De Lorean to ask for more support. One stated that the Northern Ireland Department of Commerce should 'be prepared to consider' the needs for money in such cases as inflation, construction delays or fluctuations in the exchange rates between dollars and pounds. 'We figured we were entitled to over $47 million in grants,' Gorf says. 'Hopkins was not ready to give it to us and it looked like we'd have to go through some hard bargaining to get what we wanted.'

De Lorean ended up going over Hopkins's head to the new Secretary of State for Northern Ireland, Humphrey Atkins. Leaving NIDA and Department of Commercial officials in the waiting room, the minister and De Lorean went into a closed-door meeting. They emerged with an agreement to loan the car company some $33 million. The British press played it as a coup for De Lorean, but the other car company executives were astounded that he was willing to settle for so little and a loan to boot. 'The last thing we needed was a loan at high interest rates,' one of the Belfast executives recalls. 'Here we were all expecting a grant. Instead, we got a millstone with no benefits.'

To make matters worse, in return, De Lorean let the government strike out the inflation and exchange rate adjustments that were in the original deal, preventing him from going back for additional funding again.

Over the next few months, De Lorean would realize how little he did get from Atkins. In one scheme, he saw a way he could force the government to turn over all of their equity in the project by 'rattling the sabre' and threatening legal action. If Americans controlled all of the stock, De Lorean hoped, the car company would look more appetizing when he went to Wall Street. In a September memo to Haddad and Kimmerly, he wrote, 'Obviously this is an idealized scenario fraught with potential pitfalls and problems, but one we must pursue aggressively.'

But his British executives in Belfast did not think such hard-nosed tactics would pay off. 'We were trying to convince John that he had to start being more diplomatic,' one says. 'When Thatcher first came into office, I warned him that he needed some Conservative contacts, and he didn't listen. After the summer I thought he started to see the importance of politics. We set up several meetings for John with committees of Parliament, and we tried to arrange a few informal gatherings too. John can really shine in those situations, and I felt it wouldn't take much to put some of his backbench critics at ease. But he never kept the appointments. For some reason he just didn't want to do the diplomatic thing. He believed the politicians couldn't let him go down and lose all those jobs in Belfast. Looking back, I wonder whether he was scared of the questions they might have asked him, in particular about the Lotus cost overruns and the payments to GPD.'

After he left General Motors, De Lorean never expected to answer to any higher authority, but suddenly with his own corporation, he found himself in the hotseat again, and some of these governmental overseers were far more demanding than the committees on the Fourteenth Floor. His reaction was to be as rebellious and insouciant as in any tantrum he ever threw at GM. In December he dashed off a telex to NIDA's Tony Hopkins designed to pressurize him. Forgetting his agreement with Atkins over the summer, De Lorean claimed he still deserved $28 million of 'inflation adjustment'. He further demanded that he get the $19 million the government was ready to give him during the original negotiations, when it looked like the Oppenheimer limited partnership wouldn't go through.

Summing up his bill of fare in the telex, De Lorean bluntly charged, 'You owe us $20 million. If you give it to us we have enough money to finish the job in proper fashion.' Earlier De Lorean had promised to raise further capital by going to the American stock market, but here he explained, 'Unfortunately, it is not possible to raise external financing unless the government financing is complete – no one will put $10 million into a company that is $50 million short of having enough funds to complete the job. We now have a legal opinion from our U.K. counsel indicating that, as DMC and DMCL directors, we are verging on fraud to continue to place purchase orders [with American car buyers] for which we have no identifiable means of payment.'

As he would do many times in the future, De Lorean closed his missive with the spectre of laying off his Irish workers. 'It is squarely up to NIDA. If you cannot or will not provide the balance of the funding you owe us, we plan to shut down our operations on both sides of the Atlantic immediately. We cannot incur obligations without means of payment. If you have decided to shut us down for whatever reason, let us do it in a manner that will allow us to salvage the expenditure to date and eventually repay the government. To do this we need a coordinated, planned effort.'

De Lorean would not get twopence of further grants out of the government. However, he did get Northern Ireland Department of Commerce guarantees on over $40 million more of bank loans from Barclays' and New York's Citibank, which in time, turned out to be as good – or as bad – as a grant. But De Lorean's Christmas telex set the tone for his future strained relations with the Conservative government and NIDA officials.

His upper hand would be Belfast workers like Billy Parker, who continued to flow through the factory gates, unaware of the apocalyptic warnings to the government that continued to issue from New York headquarters. At first Parker never expected the plant to be built. When he lined up behind the hundreds of others who applied for work, he never expected to be hired. But the morning came when he and thirty other men walked into the brand new factory building for their first day of work. It was unlike any factory they had ever seen, with scrubbed white linoleum floors and freshly painted steel girders. And there on the floor right in front of them was the sleek, silver car they would be building. 'I had never seen it before that time,' Parker says. 'We all just stood and looked at it, our mouths hanging open. We would have sworn the car was real. The body looked just like stainless steel. But when we touched it, we found out it was wood.'

It was fantastic. It was unbelievable.

New York

Walter P. Strycker was a hard man to stare down. John De Lorean could see that the first time he met him. With Bob Anderson's help he convinced Strycker to help him raise money for his car company and then push through negotiations for a plant site. After Bob Dewey left in August 1978, De Lorean prevailed on him to become the next chief financial officer. Strycker was just the sort of tough-minded comptroller that wary bank officers and investors wanted to see. In the 1979 SEC filing he was listed as a vital cog in the De Lorean wheel, 'the loss of whose services could have an adverse effect on the Company'.

But before the year was out De Lorean found himself sitting on the other side of Strycker's piercing eyes and he did not appreciate the view. 'John doesn't like confrontations,' Stryker says. 'He tries to avoid them. Rather than shout you down, he excludes you from the important decisions.'

It was not the first time De Lorean had to face down his chief financial officer. Disputes with Dewey led to his early departure from the company. De Lorean later attributed Dewey's resignation to his unhappiness with the selection of Belfast, but Dewey says, 'I made up my mind early in 1978 that I'd leave. It was just more proper to wait until the financing was in place. I realized that John and I couldn't work together. There were too many tiffs over the way he was spending the money.'

Dewey now says that if he had read *On a Clear Day You Can See General Motors* first, he would never have got involved with De Lorean. 'Financial guys like me come out as the villains in that book simply because we look at the bottom line. I think the major accusation is that GM paid too much attention to the bottom line, but where else do you look? I never realized how much he resented us until I read his book. In many ways the comptroller is the corporation's conscience. In some situations that isn't a pleasant role to play.'

183

For months before he left Dewey battled with De Lorean and general counsel Kimmerly over expenses he felt were unwarranted. 'Tom would start off my day calling with crazy invoices for services and supplies which had no connection to the car.'

The arguments increased when a decision was made to move the corporate headquarters to Park Avenue. At first Dewey objected to the costs of living in Manhattan, advising that a Detroit location, closer to consulting engineers, might be more useful. But De Lorean insisted that he needed to be near New York financiers to raise further capital. He also managed to secure the penthouse of the Bankers Trust building on a sub-lease from Xerox at a bargain basement price by Manhattan standards.

But as part of the move, De Lorean charged the company $40,000 for the old furniture in his 100 West Long Lake office which never did find its way to New York. Although he had been living in his Fifth Avenue flat with Cristina and their two children for two years, De Lorean also took $78,100 as removal expenses for moving from Detroit – what the company decorously called a Locale Adjustment.

When Dewey objected, De Lorean told him he did not want to argue over 'petty bullshit'. The comptroller says he replied, 'When you only have $100,000 in the till, one dollar looks like a lot, especially when you're talking about other people's money. Investors want to see a start-up be as bare bones as possible.'

Dewey continues, 'It got to the point where John said, "Do it my way or else." His name was on the door, but I had fiduciary responsibility too. I could see that as the dollars got bigger, this sort of thing would get worse. I felt I owed it to the other people to ease out quietly. When John wanted some help over the next few years, I'd come back on a consulting basis.'

Ken Gorf, the treasurer of the Belfast subsidiary company, watched incredulously as the costs of the headquarters office mounted. 'At their peak, New York had over thirty people and an annual budget of $8 million. Before we could transfer funds overseas, we needed approval from NIDA and the Department of Commerce, but at best they gave the invoices a cursory glance.'

One good chunk of the expenses went in salaries. Although De Lorean did not take a salary, his private company was getting over $300,000 in consulting fees. Kimmerly ended up with both a $108,000 salary and a $180,000 retainer for his law firm. Brimming with six-figure contracts, the entire executive payroll including fringe benefits was well over $2 million a year.

Beyond the high salaries and expenses, Gorf and other sceptical DMC Ltd observers wondered what the executives in New York were doing. 'Fundamentally,' Gorf says, 'I saw headquarters contributing

184

very little to the sports car project.'

Strycker had the same impression from inside the beehive, and unlike his predecessor, he was not ready to back out quietly. In December 1979 he turned over his criticism to both the Audit Committee on the board and the company's certified auditors, Arthur Andersen & Company. The Audit Committee was comprised of Johnny Carson lawyer Henry Bushkin, Wood Gundy director G. Edmund King and NIDA representative (soon to be DMC Ltd employee) Shaun Harte. They chose to defer to the decisions of the auditors. Arthur Anderson dismissed the bulk of his complaints, asking for only a few minor alterations from De Lorean. When Strycker brought up the Swiss loan transactions concerning GPD and the purchase of the Logan division, the auditor replied that the approval of the British government was sufficient certification for the transaction. Shortly afterwards Strycker resigned his position as chief financial officer. 'With John,' he says, 'you end up playing the policeman and I didn't want to do that anymore.'

At the time the De Lorean Motor Company account was being handled out of Arthur Andersen's Detroit office, under the supervision of managing partner Richard Measelle. Measelle has refused comments on any specific parts of his audit, but two years after he looked into Strycker's criticisms, Maeselle did volunteer for one reporter his high regard for John De Lorean. 'I think the world of him. He's one of the greatest individuals this city has ever produced, and my association with him has been one of the best professional experiences of my career.'

Strycker's main worries concerned De Lorean's expenses. 'He had a high burn rate,' Strycker says. 'Obviously with his wife's taste and his homes all over the country, he was tied to an expensive lifestyle, but a lot of his travelling and socializing was done on his company expense account. There were some quarterly reporting periods where he was going as high as $28,000. Everything he did was first-class. Only the best suites in any hotel he stayed in. No restaurant was too expensive and the stockholders picked up the tab. When you questioned John on this, he said you were nickel-shitting him. He felt he was entitled to a certain extravagance.'

In California the company purchased a $53,000 Mercedes which C.R. Brown delivered to Cristina at her favourite San Diego health farm with a ribbon wrapped around it. Another company car, a Mazda RX7, was being driven around by her younger brother – De Lorean later explained that these cars were 'evaluation vehicles' to compare with the sports car and the future luxury car. Top executives in New York got credit cards to Tiffany's and the 21 Club. De Lorean regularly dined at the exclusive 'Boardroom' club in his building.

The royal lifestyle included a company-paid entourage. Strycker reported that two young men who worked as chauffeurs and servants for the De Loreans were on the company payroll. The comptroller liked to remind other executives that similar expenses caused serious SEC inquests for Gulf & Western chairman Charles Bluhdorn (De Lorean later reimbursed the company for their payment).

The chief courtier was someone not on the payroll, but a paid consultant on interior decoration, named Maur Dubin. For some of the auto executives he was an incongruous and irritating presence. Eastern regional sales manager, Bill Morgan says, 'I remember when Dubin first came tripping into the office with his full-length mink coat. I said to John, "Who is this guy?" and John said, "I think he likes you." '

As time went on, Morgan says, the little man became a more noticeable nuisance. 'He had some sort of antique business. I know because the company would lease vans that Maur and his friends would use to haul furniture and *objets d'art* around.'

Occasionally those vans were found wrecked or impounded. Morgan spent a day bailing one vehicle out of the police pound after it had been involved in a hit-and-run accident. 'Once Maur called one of my dealers and started to blister his office manager. He had taken one of the dealer's vans and then claimed it had been registered improperly and impounded. The dealer called me up and told me he didn't need this guy's lip. I called Dubin and told him that either he'd leave my dealers alone or I'd come over there and throw his ass down the forty-three storeys of the Bankers Trust Building.'

Strycker had his own run-ins with Dubin. He estimated that over $40,000 in company funds had been spent on works of art for the office – so much that paintings lay stacked against the walls in hallways for months.

Both Strycker and Dewey were to glimpse the different worlds of John De Lorean in the ledger books. People they did not know were collecting consultancy fees.

'Sometimes I felt we were all stuck in the middle of a play,' Dewey says. 'Only one actor knew who was going to come onto the stage next, and that was John.'

Strycker felt he never got a satisfactory answer from De Lorean about the precise role that Nesseth played in the car company, but De Lorean told Measelle that Roy was the marketing 'back-up' for C.R. Brown. Brown, however, vehemently denied working with Nesseth when accountants from the firm of Arthur Andersen called to confirm that information.

What concerned Strycker most was the staff time and money spent on projects he called 'crazy tangents' – none of which had much to do with getting the sports car into production. The NIDA agreement specifically prohibited the De Lorean Car Company and De Lorean

Motor Cars Limited from either 'acquir[ing] any other company or enter[ing] into any joint venture except with each other'. But within months of his deal with the British government, De Lorean contemplated building on his British-borrowed assets to buy the ailing Chrysler Corporation. 'I told him that Chrysler had just shut the doors in the U.K. leaving a billion-dollar debt behind,' Strycker says. 'There was no way the British government would support buying the parent company. But John kept working on the idea. At least $300,000 worth of salaries and legal fees went into preparing an offer. He actually made a presentation for Iacocca, who probably got a big kick out of the whole thing. John never heard from him again.'

Even before De Lorean had turned out his own car, he envisaged using his dealer network to distribute other sports cars. He engaged in protracted negotiations with Alfa Romeo and Citroën. He even offered a deal to Lotus, although Chapman wasn't enthusiastic about the idea. And, to the amazement of the executives, De Lorean continued to pursue his fascination with cheaply built Eastern European vehicles. Two weeks after he closed his deal with the British, he flew off to Russia to discuss once more distributing Ladas. He also contemplated manufacturing an Eastern European utility vehicle, currently used by the French military, to be called the DMC–44, and he had his special projects director in California assemble a few promotional films featuring the bizarre little flatbed truck.

Roy suggested that he consider going into the 'replicar' business – selling kits to assemble vintage cars. The company went so far as to borrow a Bugatti for preliminary studies. Moreover, as early as 1979, with his car still in developmental stages, De Lorean was talking to Mattel and other toy makers about producing pint-sized replicas of his own car.

Then there were the inventions: a gas sniffer capable of searching out deposits of natural gas in the desert floor (this deal fell apart when a private investigator discovered that the inventor had established a distinguished record as a con artist on the West Coast); De Lorean took an option on a three-cylinder engine that his old friend Smokey Yunick developed; and he tried to raise venture capital for a group of engineers working on a Stirling (external combustion) engine in San Diego. For the latter project he enlisted the aid of former Secretary of the Treasury, William Simon, who today laughs off the failed engine effort as a 'non-starter'.

Still the list doesn't end. De Lorean tried his hand at leasing and non-mechanical endeavours such as boat chartering and shipping. 'John had the ability to recognize a good opportunity,' Strycker concludes, 'but he didn't know how to make it happen.'

Strycker could not make out where official company business ended and De Lorean's private affairs began. At least three top executives, he believed, were working practically full-time on extracurricular activity. He saw the De Lorean Manufacturing Company as the most flagrant example of violating the stockholder's trust. 'It was a definite conflict of interest. I told John he and every executive involved with Manufacturing should keep meticulous records of the time they spent working on it, and that John should then reimburse the car company for their time. Then I got a letter from Kimmerly telling me that 100 per cent of his time was devoted to the car company, and that he did no legal work on Logan.' But corporate records showed Kimmerly as both treasurer and vice president of Manufacturing, and Strycker found it unlikely that he played a passive role on a three-member board.

Furthermore, an outside law firm, Paul, Weiss, Rifkind, did all the legal work on the acquisition. While it is not known whether the law firm billed Manufacturing as well, Strycker found that during the last half of 1979 Paul, Weiss, Rifkind was charging the car company as much as $35,000 a quarter for its services.

Shortly after Strycker resigned De Lorean began implying to other executives that he had been fired at the request of the British. In fact, NIDA officials made no such demand. One month after Strycker's departure they echoed his concerns about the extent of De Lorean's outside interests. In June they again emphasized that the company shouldn't be working on any project other than the sports car. Claiming that all the non-car activities had never cost more than $277,978, De Lorean nevertheless promised to stop. However, all evidence suggests that his special projects continued at an even more fevered pitch.

When Ernest 'Gus' Davis first met John De Lorean at New York headquarters in December 1980, he thought he was applying for a job in the car company. A former production executive for Harley-Davison he felt he could fit in well with a small manufacturer like De Lorean. 'But De Lorean told me he didn't have a position open in the car company. He said he was having troubles in Logan and that things had to be straightened out there.' Other car company executives ate lunch with Davis and filled him in on the troubles at Manufacturing.

After investigating the problems in Logan and writing a report recommending diversification and expansion, Davis was hired to run the shop – or so he thought – with a mandate to build the business. Instead, he watched helplessly as money was drained from the operation to banks in Michigan and New York. 'John or one of the car company financial officers would call and have me wire the money. It would go out in $400,000 shots. On top of that De Lorean was taking a salary of $200,000. In barely a year, he bled $3 million from the assets.' Further complicating matters for Davis were sporadic visits by Roy Nesseth – a man, De Lorean said, who knew a great deal about marketing. Roy was paid by Manufacturing on a consultant's fee basis that brought him as much as $100,000 in 1980.

Manufacturing and the car company sometimes pursued the same objectives. Davis remembers being called in to help evaluate the ill-fated DMC–44, and at one point car company executives prepared a prospectus for Manufacturing that would have offered a research and development partnership for the vehicle. Both the car and the snow-grooming machine wore the same DMC emblem, and at trade shows the stainless steel car was often driven in for promotion to pair incongruously with its hulking cousin.

De Lorean, however, rarely made personal appearances with the off-track vehicle or at Manufacturing's plant in Logan. Most of the executives in his New York office were not aware what was going on in Utah or its connection with the car company. But another of the headquarters' non-car ventures was much more visible and controversial inside the company, and at its helm was the equally visible and controversial Bill Haddad.

At first officers like C.R. Brown could not understand why Haddad was on board. Aged fifty-two, he had spent much of his life fighting the good fight for causes that were a bit too liberal for most auto executives' blood. A Kennedy political operative, Haddad was the first associate director of the Peace Corps. He later served in the office of Economic Opportunity, lost a race for the congressional seat on Manhattan's west side and was an outspoken member of the New York City Board of Education during Mayor John Lindsay's decentralization campaign. As an investigative reporter for the *New York Herald Tribune* he railed against the price-fixing policies of the international pharmaceutical conglomerates and spearheaded a campaign to promote the prescription of cheaper generic drugs. Later, as an aide to the speaker of the New York State assembly, he continued his crusade against big corporations, sponsoring inquests into utilities, oil and pharmaceutical companies.

Haddad had recruited De Lorean's aid for some of his causes, and he believed De Lorean was sincere when he talked about corporate responsibility to society. For Haddad, De Lorean's attempt to build his own car was one more fight pitting the little guy against the big bad guys. 'I didn't go to work with John for the money,' he says. 'I believed his talk about the ethical car, and I wanted to help him show big business it was possible to make a good product and a good profit without ripping off the consumer.'

Trying to dissuade De Lorean from hiring Haddad, Brown had someone peruse his voluminous file of New York clippings. The resulting report characterized him as 'left-wing,' 'racially divisive' and 'anti-business'. Brown later concluded that De Lorean expected Ted

Kennedy to be the next president and he hired Haddad to have an 'in' to the White House.

But Haddad quickly showed his detractors the valuable role he could play in public relations. His gregarious nature and his own experience as a reporter helped him win over a sceptical press. While De Lorean had downplayed his animosity for the GM system, for fear the company would discourage its dealers from signing on, Haddad showed him how such conflict could redound to his value. When Pat Wright finally went ahead and published *On a Clear Day*, De Lorean refused to endorse the book, calling Wright's version of his interviews too severe, but that didn't stop Haddad from copiously xeroxing the newspaper articles that followed publication. While there wasn't much juice to an article about another entrepreneur trying to make a quick buck, it was much easier for a reporter to get wrapped up in a story about a maverick fighting back against an entrenched, self-serving industry. For all the press attention De Lorean generated on his own, it surged noticeably when Haddad started to beat the hustings.

But Haddad was not content to remain the company spokesman. He spurred De Lorean to pursue yet another venture – manufacturing buses. Strycker still laughs at the prospect. 'It was ridiculous. What did Haddad, or De Lorean for that matter, know about buses?' But for some time De Lorean had seen the American bus industry as ripe for competition. General Motors held a virtual monopoly in the market with minimal competition from Grumman. When the federal Department of Transportation put out bids for a product they called Transbus, which could accommodate the handicapped and also achieve certain fuel efficiency, American companies declined the offer. Then Haddad and De Lorean tried to step into the breach with a German import that came closer to meeting the DOT's standards. Once again, in the fall of 1979, De Lorean started talking to cities about a prospective plant site – this time for bus manufacturing.

This improbable venture would end when an improbable banker backed out. An impoverished section of Miami had been selected as the site for the factory, and according to Haddad, *Star Wars* director George Lucas, looking to invest in a good cause, was ready to put in $5 million of seed money. But the deal unravelled during dinner with Lucas's lawyer and the president of his film company. 'Out of nowhere, John started talking about them putting the money into the car company, instead of the bus. It just came out of the blue and you could see them shift gears. It made the whole bus deal look like some sort of scam to lure car investors. That was the last we heard from them and that's probably the point where I started to go sour on John.'

Throughout his tenure at the car company Haddad clashed with Tom Kimmerly, as did the other top executives. No one spent more time with De Lorean than his trusted lawyer. Besides the raft of personal affairs, he was conducting probably the major enterprise of the New York office, preparation of a public share float for the car company. 'We must have had a prospectus for every day of the week,' one of the executives who worked with Kimmerly remembers. 'As conditions in the market changed we were constantly updating and changing our registrations with the SEC. I often wondered about all the business we were giving the company that printed up our prospectuses.'

Working up a stock offering for Wall Street, and the resultant reorganization of the company, proved to be a much more complicated affair than a limited sale to car dealers. At times over thirty lawyers would be jammed into a room, and small quiet Tom Kimmerly, the tax lawyer from Detroit, would be in charge.

Strycker saw Tom Kimmerly's role in management grow with the company. 'Until the company was funded by the British, he stayed in the background. But afterwards he surfaced as the general counsel and then started showing up on the pay-roll. From what I knew of the personal deals he had with John, his motive was to buffer him from documentation as the corporate officer and secretary.'

According to some executives Kimmerly was reluctant to sit on the board and become an officer of the car company, doing so in March 1979 only at De Lorean's insistence. While his influence was felt in almost every area of the company – from marketing and financing to production – he still seemed content to remain behind the scenes. 'We called him the corporate snake,' Brown says. 'If we had a disagreement with Tom and we came to New York to argue our side, as soon as we left John's office we'd see him slither back to John so he could get in the last word.'

At times, Kimmerly's executive assistants created more friction in the office than he did. Virtually separated from his wife and child in Detroit, Kimmerly was a close companion to the two middle-aged women who served successively as his administrative assistants. 'At first, when we moved into New York,' Strycker says, 'this one woman wasn't even on the pay-roll of the company. She was paid through his law firm. But one week while I'm out of the office, she tried to fire my secretary. I didn't appreciate someone who didn't even work for the company firing my employee – especially while I was out of the office. I called this woman up to find out what the story was, and she told me to talk to Tom. Well, I told Tom to take his so-and-so secretary and send her the hell back to Detroit.'

But whatever companionship Kimmerly may have found with his secretaries or any other members of the staff, all relationships paled next to his monastic devotion to John De Lorean and the company. His work day often reached into the late hours of the night and weekends. He walked back to his small one-bedroom apartment on Central Park South from the office, stopping by Harry's Bar in the Waldorf Astoria on rare occasions first for a beer, but usually going straight back to bed. There is no evidence that his mentor tried to introduce him to New York's night life or that Kimmerly would have taken him up if he had. At most, the two could be seen having lunch at the 21 Club. 'When John came into a crowded room,' one executive says, 'Tom would almost visibly start to recede. He just didn't step back or into the corner. He became less noticeable – like a snowman melting away in the light of the sun with a little smile on his face.'

Bill Morgan says, 'Kimmerly impressed me as a guy with an inordinate admiration for John. He just got extremely defensive about the least little comment you made about John. I remember having dinner with him and Dick Brown one night. Brown is a very religious guy and he was wondering what De Lorean was doing getting married three times. You could see that comment really upset Tom. He got very huffy and said, "Why are you so interested?" '

Haddad found his own disputes with Kimmerly were not necessarily rooted in business disagreements. 'I think he was jealous of John's attention. If some new person came on the scene and John showed interest in him, Tom would be there behind his back trying to cut the guy down.'

For young executives new to the New York office, the De Lorean Motor Company headquarters were a classic anomaly. On one hand, they seemed to glow with the possibilities of a thriving company. In 1980 total employment went over 1,000 and continued to grow by the hundreds each month. Mailbags were overflowing with expectant car buyers seeking more information about the car or requesting the name of the nearest dealer where they could order one. Telexes went off like buzzsaws with messages from Belfast and California. Almost everyday members of the press trooped in with tape recorders or cameras in hand.

And yet, on the other hand, behind the façade of bustling prosperity, the warren of offices on the penthouse floor seethed with corporate intrigue. Serious questions remained about the state of the car's development and whether there was enough financing to keep the company afloat until it came off the assembly line. To make matters worse, the corporate staff seemed riven into factions. There was first the Strycker camp and then the Haddad camp. All were at odds with Kimmerly and the group of young lawyers and accountants surrounding him. Secretaries were scouts and spies. Memos to John reporting who said what were the most potent weapons.

'When I first came into the company,' one executive says, 'I figured it would be as rigidly regimented as GM. That's where De Lorean cut his teeth and I thought he'd duplicate their system inside his own company.

But it was exactly the opposite. There was practically no direction or there was too much direction coming at you from all sides. I expected De Lorean to provide that leadership. Instead he'd wander into your office in his shirtsleeves, very friendly, but no help at all. He'd nod and say, "How are you doing?" or "What are you up to?" and sit there and listen. At most he'd tell you some anecdote that had nothing to do with the matter at hand.'

From what his executives could see, De Lorean was toiling away at the centre of the cyclone he created, but he seemed to be as buffeted by the winds as everyone else. His mornings could start as early as six o'clock, and much of the rest of the day could be spent on the phone or hunched over his desk. 'He wrote constantly,' his one-time executive assistant Marian Gibson says. 'Every little thought that came into his head he had to put down in a memo. Some were about the car company, others were about people. Some seemed to be just stray ideas. I suppose that was what they taught him at General Motors, but we had a typist going full time just typing up all his notes. There were times when he'd just disappear for a few hours in the middle of the day without warning anyone and sneak over to the New York Athletic Club and lift weights.'

His employees rarely got a glimpse of his social life. Occasionally the papers and gossip columns made mention of John and Cristina at some benefit ball, and he talked of the dinner parties with Herb and Ann Siegel, or the chief executive of Norton Simon, David Mahoney and his wife Hilly. They also dined sometimes with nearby neighbours on Fifth Avenue in the television business.

On rare occasions the two worlds would mingle. Some employees remember a Christmas party with several of the New York celebrity friends in attendance. Maur Dubin was at the door acting as manager and Cristina was in the kitchen doing most of the cooking. But the one-time swinger would complain to his older executives that Cristina wanted to do too much partying. He preferred spending quiet evenings at home with her and the children. At least once, he took Zachary with him on a trip to Belfast, but he never tried to be away from the family for an extended period of time.

Despite his earlier fears of infertility he was capable of having a child and his wife gave birth to a daughter, Kathryn, in 1978. He was especially enchanted by her and as she grew older, would look more like her father than her mother. During one interview with a reporter, the nurse stopped by with the two-year old and left her with De Lorean. He propped her on his lap behind his desk and continued talking to the reporter, unmindful as she grabbed the nearest pen and scribbled over every exposed piece of paper in sight.

A few years later one New York businessman explained why he first got involved with De Lorean. 'My father was driving down Fifth

Avenue early one morning and he saw John walking his daughter to nursery school. I figured that with all the concerns of his company, if he could still find time to walk his kid to school he had to be all right.'

There were some nights when De Lorean brought his workday world home with him. One executive remembers following the boss home for dinner. The lift of their block of flats brought them right up to the foyer of their home. A winding marble staircase led up to the bedrooms and the two sleeping children. While Cristina prepared dinner, De Lorean took the visitors on tour, showing them the seventeenth- and eighteenth-century pictures hanging on the wall. Most of the furniture was French provincial. Expensive-looking antique clocks and vases sat on the mantels and tables. 'I was more impressed by the wallpaper behind the dining room table,' the executive says. 'There was some pastoral scene hand-painted on the paper. You don't see something like that very often.' At times De Lorean's conversation could wander to contemporary subjects and on this night he discussed the wisdom of legalizing marijuana.

At one point in the evening De Lorean walked over to the living room window and drew open the blinds. A picture post-card scene of Central Park in the evening spread out before them, complete with the horse-drawn carriages cantering along by lantern light. 'Isn't this spectacular?' he asked.

But in just another year he was negotiating to buy an even more spectacular sight in Bedminster, New Jersey. This twenty-five room home sat in the middle of 430 acres and was valued at $3.5 million. De Lorean claimed to have swung this deal with the proceeds of the Pine Creek Ranch Roy unloaded in Idaho. Deeds show the official title-holder to be a syndicate headed by Tee-Kay International, Tom Kimmerly's private corporation.

These were all the trappings of American capitalist royalty, from the estates to the international company. The boy from the grimy Eastern European neighbourhood had become a name, and as an added fillip to his manufactured persona, he even changed his name. During the mid-seventies, as graphic designers fooled with letterheads and emblems, they continued to have difficulties with the unlikely surname of DeLorean. De Lorean willingly consented to a space between the 'De' and the 'Lorean,' further emphasizing his bogus claims to French origins.

After his car moved close to production, he discouraged the use of anything as anonymous as the DMC–12 on the name plate, opting instead for simply calling the car a 'De Lorean', and using a contemporary, rounded calligraphy designed by the car's stylist, Giugiaro.

The personal identification of the car was pushed further. Advertisements followed stamping the product with the personality of its maker.

Cutty Sark Scotch started a campaign with De Lorean's face super-imposed on a frontal view of his silver beauty with the doors opened. The legend above the ad read, 'One out of every 100 new businesses succeeds. Here's to those who take the odds.' The copy repeats the mythos of De Lorean 'on the way to the presidency of General Motors when he quit to build his own car company'. (Here forty-four patents with GM are cited – again, the actual number was thirty-one). The hook is that Cutty is 'the Scotch with a following of leaders'. (C.R. Brown scoffs: 'Imagine a safety car being advertised with a bottle of Scotch.') Supplier Goodyear Tires started another campaign featuring De Lorean standing against a car in some empty field.

And yet, the regal serenity that peered from the still photographs did not come through in life. Documentary maker D.A. Pennebaker was to find De Lorean an uneasy subject for his motion picture camera. Over the years anxiety started to creep through the look of superior calm. He seemed to be constantly adjusting his head on his long slender neck, cricking it backward and side to side. His flaring, curved eyebrows no longer arched for emphasis at the end of a sentence, but seemed to rise and fall of their own accord. He could press on a forced smile, but the sparkle and focus would go out of his eyes.

'He was so tight,' Pennebaker says, 'he twitched.'

Irvine

C.R. Brown would rather not be called by his first name, Cecil. Instead he prefers his initials, his middle name, Richard, or just Dick. But he does not shy away from talking about his namesake, Uncle Cecil Brown, who died on an evangelical mission to the jungle when he was attacked and eaten by a band of cannibals.

It is a fitting piece of spiritual history. Throughout his career Brown has worked with the intensity and urgency of a man who any minute expects the savages to be at the door. At times, he has heard them knocking before anyone else, and just as often they have barged in.

Raised in Detroit of middle-class origins, he, like De Lorean, cut his teeth at the Chrysler Institute, but was directed towards the marketing side of the business. Over the years, he became a troubleshooter for the company's dealer network, and when he took over as assistant regional manager for San Francisco, he moved sales in his region from last place to first in just four years. Frustrated with Chrysler's slow promotion rate, he jumped to American Motors as president of the Canadian division. His move was to coincide with a catastrophic down-turn in the company's fortunes and he watched for a year as AMC racked up unprecedented losses. Then a chance encounter with a Bank of America official in 1970 had him meeting a team of executives from Mazda who were looking to expand sales in America. Brown says he intended to do no more than give the group some advice as a favour to his friend at the bank, but after one session the Japanese hired Brown as their general manager for Mazda Motors of America.

Today, one former Mazda executive says that the Japanese only intended Brown to be a West Coast regional manager, but if this was their intention, then he soon annexed the rest of the country under his authority. Some auto industry analysts labelled his marketing strategy for America as fatuous. Franchises only went to dealerships which carried Mazda and nothing else. But in a matter of two years under

Brown, the number of Mazda dealers went from thirty-one to 412.

Brown's idiosyncrasies made him a difficult man to work for. His employees soon learned of his propensity for late hours, and few could keep up with it. 'Brown would fly into our regional office for dinner meetings,' one former Mazda executive remembers. 'There'd be a long dinner, and then for a couple of hours, we'd have to listen to C.R. hold forth over a glass of wine on the state of the auto industry. At about one in the morning the meetings would start. Brown would be grilling guys into the dawn hours while they were practically falling asleep in their chairs.'

Many found his temper fearsome, and even worse when they attempted to argue back. 'There was just something in him,' another former employee says, 'that made him want to kick you one more time after he already made his point.'

In contrast to his ferocity with co-workers Brown maintained a deep religious devotion. He had a soft spot for a man with a wholesome family, and often overlooked faults in those breadwinners that he would have picked apart in more rootless sorts. Many believed his moralistic attitudes were best expressed in his own home. Married over twenty years, he raised his three daughters and a son in a private estate in Long Beach. His daughters went to the state college at the bottom of the hill.

Brown's last days at Mazda were to be steeped in controversy. During autumn 1973, just in time for the oil crisis, the Environmental Protection Administration released mileage figures showing that the little Mazda cars with their rotary engines got only ten miles to the gallon. Convinced that the test had been conducted improperly, Brown engaged in a heated debate with the EPA officials, only further publicizing the disastrous information. Meanwhile over 100,000 1974 Mazdas sat in the docks. Reportedly, the last car of that shipment was not sold until 1981. Brown says he left the company of his own accord, and he takes credit for some of Mazda's current popular product line, which he encouraged back in the early seventies.

Despite his difficult working habits, when Brown joined De Lorean he was able to recruit several of the men who worked with him at Mazda. As one explains, 'For all the crap Dick dished out, he was at least a man of his word and exactly the sort of driven son-of-a-bitch who could make something as crazy as the De Lorean Motor Company work.'

Brown was not overly impressed by De Lorean, but 'I took it for granted that he knew what he was talking about. I had great respect for the executives around him like Bill Collins and Bob Dewey. We felt we had the horsepower to get the job done. We just wanted John to be what he said he was, and since we were representing him, we wanted him to play it straight.'

But quite early in the game, Brown discovered that De Lorean did not always play things straight. He recoiled at De Lorean's tendency to exaggerate at dealer meetings. He was more distressed when De Lorean permitted Roy Nesseth's minions to sell the stock with boiler room tactics. 'John used to tell me that my problem was trying to be purer than the driven snow,' Brown recalls. 'He'd say, "Real successful people have had to cut corners and manipulate. That's the way things get done." '

But if De Lorean had turned out to be a less savoury person than Brown would have preferred, the question remains why he stayed on. 'I was hooked,' he admits. 'At a certain point I got too many of my friends involved as investors, dealers and employees. I couldn't let them down and just back out.'

If anything, Brown dived in deeper. A few times in the course of his tenure, when it looked like the company could not pay his California office staff, he dipped into his own bank account to tide things over. During the first week of August 1978 both men were in Hollywood, Northern Ireland to sign the NIDA agreement. Only a few days before, De Lorean's putative plant manager had quit, disgusted with De Lorean's high-handed treatment of an architectural firm that had contributed over $300,000 of services in preliminary design work on the factory. After the ceremony was completed, De Lorean took Brown into a corner. 'He put his arm around my shoulder and told me he had no one around who knew about launching the company. He asked if I could stick around in Belfast and help set up the procedures to get the plant going.'

For the next few months Brown would spend most of his time in Dunmurry. He made the rounds of the Belfast public relations circuit in De Lorean's place, visiting schools and business groups. Coincidentally, he discovered he had a long lost uncle living nearby – not a bad development when he was trying to win the local community's acceptance. He brought in a Californian building contractor to start initial ground clearance, and turned to the brother of a next-door neighbour in Long Beach who had once handled personnel for Chrysler Europe to help recruit European executives. This man suggested Chuck Bennington; they employed him and built the rest of the team around him.

From the moment he started working for De Lorean Brown expected to be appointed president of the company. In the early developmental days De Lorean talked about moving the headquarters to southern California some day, so that he could be close to the market where he would sell most of his cars. But later he made it clear to Brown that his headquarters would remain in New York and that he expected his president to reside there as well. Brown refused to move to the East, but he still held out hope that De Lorean would come to his senses and relocate the headquarters to the West Coast.

'In the spring of 1979, after things had been set up in Belfast,' Brown says, 'I came back to California and the employees had organized a lunch where I was presented with a plaque that one of them had drawn up. It was a very nice affair. Afterwards, as we were leaving the restaurant, they told me that John had sent something he wanted me to have. I went outside and there was a new Mercedes 450SEL. When I called John, he said, "I know you'll be upset hearing this, but I'm bringing in Gene Cafiero as president. I didn't want you to be upset." I told him I appreciated the thought, and I guess it was a nice gesture. John was capable of nice gestures.'

Like so many other De Lorean operating officers, Eugene A. Cafiero had come from Chrysler, but both more auspiciously than the others and less so. In 1975, at the age of only forty-nine, he became the corporation's president and chief operating officer. But during his tenure Chrysler reeled towards bankruptcy, and, whether or not he deserved it, he got all the approbation of the skipper on the *Titanic*.

From De Lorean's point of view, Cafiero had nevertheless been chief executive of a major American car manufacturer. It was the sort of distinction he never had, and it was the sort of distinction that investors might appreciate on Wall Street. Brown, however, strongly advised against hiring him, a fact he did not try to hide from Cafiero. 'We first met in Turin on a trip to Giugiaro,' Brown says. 'He was there with Chuck Bennington and John. Later in the hotel I told him that I didn't recommend him to John. When he asked me why, I explained that I had been a Chrysler dealer during two of the three years of his tenure and that both the product and the production quality had suffered dramatically in that period. He then went into a two hour dissertation on why that wasn't his fault.'

A week later Brown tried to make amends with a letter telling Cafiero, 'Just in case there was any doubt resulting from our brief conversations last week, I want you to know that you can depend on our support and best wishes for success in your new role.' But his initial conversation set the tone for their relationship, and he found that his new superior could be just as caustic. Adding insult to injury, Cafiero started with a salary that topped out at $375,000 a year, compared to Brown's $155,000. To make up for the bonus provisions he lost from Chrysler, Cafiero was also given a payment of $164,800.

De Lorean's announcement of Cafiero's hiring would be as interesting as the appointment. To some extent it reflected the qualms employees were having about De Lorean's ability as an entrepreneur. The piece in the company's newsletter began: 'Not all successful executives in large corporations can adjust their talents to beginning a new company, and so, in our search for innovative executives, we needed those with a full range of automotive experiences and skills, necessary not only to build a new car, but also a new corporation. Gene Cafiero is one of those talented professionals. During our meetings, I found that Gene's impressive background was not a barrier to that entrepreneurial quality we needed to direct our automotive operations.'

Despite these encomiums Cafiero was never willing to contend continually with the palace intrigue. When De Lorean insisted he take control of the factory in Belfast, Cafeiro recoiled and looked instead for someone to replace Bennington. In his first year he issued a handful of memos, the lengthiest concerning paid holidays. 'See this memo,' Brown would tell his California executives. 'It cost about $375,000.'

For his part Brown needed no prompting to get involved in the company – as far as De Lorean and Kimmerly were concerned, too involved. When an Arthur Andersen official called to check out De Lorean's story that Roy Nesseth was working for the company, Brown strongly denied it. Another of the auditor's questions dealt with the vintage gull-wing Mercedes Roy had taken from Gerry Dahlinger. According to the books DMC bought it from Nesseth for $20,000 – a transaction that Brown queried. He was keeping it in storage and had learned it would cost $40,000 to restore. Brown also confirmed that he delivered the Mercedes to Cristina and that he picked up the Mazda sports car from her brother's house.

This brought him a curt memo from John De Lorean a few weeks later. 'Roy Nesseth is a consultant to me,' he wrote. 'I talk to him virtually every day on various DMC projects and concepts. I find his advice invaluable. As you know, he saved our company when it was obvious we were going to miss our 150 dealer target.' De Lorean went on to praise Roy's ideas about the Bugatti replicar and a Canadian distributor (a scheme that came to nothing). 'Again,' he added, 'since you and he don't get along, I keep you apart.' De Lorean then denied that he ever told Arthur Andersen's Measelle that Nesseth was Brown's 'back-up'.

The biggest confrontation between Brown and De Lorean was to come during the cash crunch of the summer. The delay in the car's production had been difficult for Brown to handle. His restive body of dealers was starting to wonder whether their money had been thrown down the drain. But Brown was also nervous about the overheads in the New York office. The original business plan had never envisaged so many people working out of headquarters and earning so much. Further complicating matters, the British government commissioned a report from the auditing firm of McKinsey and Company, which raised questions about the costs of the New York office – predicting the U.S. operation would be $2.5 million over budget in 1980 – and suggested that De Lorean was never going to meet his sales projections.

Brown helped De Lorean prepare his reply and offered his own experience at Mazda as an example of how sober market estimates could be exceeded. But Brown was not ready to cooperate in a bizarre bail-out plan De Lorean and Kimmerly concocted in the middle of July. They presented a motion to the board that permitted the company to borrow $600,000 from De Lorean's private firm, the De Lorean Manufacturing Company. The loan was underwritten by virtually all the assets of the car company.

When the motion reached Brown's desk in Irvine, he was shocked. 'The way John was spending money in New York,' he says, 'I figured that $600,000 wouldn't last thirty days. John confirmed that.'

The motion was signed by De Lorean, Gene Cafiero, Johnny Carson's lawyer Henry Bushkin and Wood Gundy director Edmund King. Brown decided to take it up with the latter three: 'I called Gene and told him that we had fiduciary responsibilty as board members to protect the minority stockholders. This resolution would give away the company for $600,000.'

Then Brown called Bushkin and King. A member of the audit committee, Bushkin himself was becoming far more involved with the company and John De Lorean than he had ever intended when he first advised Johnny Carson to invest. He performed legal work for De Lorean in California and tried to finance some of his private deals by using his influence at a bank in which he and Carson had an interest. In return, De Lorean at one point had Brown and his employees search for a suitable car dealership in the Los Angeles area that Carson and Bushkin could buy. The car company also got entangled in the production of an auto theft alarm system with an unlikely inventor who also composed music for Carson's *Tonight* show. NIDA set up a partnership with several Irish businessmen who would handle the manufacturing from Belfast. The products were made and shipped, but none ever arrived in working order. Throughout its short life De Lorean and Brown were on the company's board and Bushkin was chairman.

But despite Bushkin's other contacts with De Lorean, Brown felt the lawyer remained one of the few independent and influential powers on the De Lorean Motor Company board. When the lawyer was alerted to the motion, he was grateful for Brown's vigilance. 'Bushkin told me, "Thank God somebody in this company is thinking. I was in a hurry when I signed this, and I didn't read it closely first." '

The next morning, a Thursday, De Lorean called Brown in a rage. He started out by saying that he deserved $46 million from the British and just needed time to collect it. He couldn't understand why Brown wouldn't sign the resolution and he went on to accuse him of running down Bennington to the British. Brown shot back that the only person who was denigrating the executives in the company was De Lorean himself. 'After we got through all that, John said, "Come into New York Monday and let's talk. You really haven't participated in the management of the company." '

Later in the morning he'd hear from Kimmerly as well. 'Bushkin had called and scared the daylights out of him. Evidently he said that if the 84 per cent stock holder doesn't have enough confidence to loan the company $600,000 without tying up all the assets, then that worries everybody.'

When Brown arrived in New York on Monday, he learned that a board meeting had been called for Thursday. De Lorean asked Brown and Dewey to work on a survival plan that would get them through without any more money from the British. The next day, Brown would first hear that De Lorean was to reconstitute the board and leave him off. De Lorean had given him no hint of doing anything like that when they met earlier in the day. Brown would also hear from Cafiero that NIDA was furious about the upheaval.

On Wednesday, at a management meeting, Brown and Dewey presented their proposal for halving expenses in the New York office. Brown was interrupted by De Lorean. 'John just took our proposal and tossed it aside. He stated he had called a meeting with NIDA for next week – of course I knew they called him – and at that meeting he would tell them that they owed us $46 million. "Either they come up with the the money," he said, "or they could stuff it."

'From there he went into a diatribe, calling the British "cowards" and "dumb fucks". He said, 'A $2.5 million shortfall for the U.S. is peanuts. I'm not going to be nickeled and dimed by those bastards. I'm not going to run a nickel-shit company. We're going to keep California, Detroit and New York at their present spending levels and continue to do all the things we think are necessary, and if they don't like it, I'll close it down next Friday."

'He finished by saying, "Our car is a $30,000 car and there is no way we can proceed without the diversified programmes." Then he left the room.'

The next day a calmer John De Lorean walked into the office Brown was using in New York and perched himself on the arm of a chair. He had talked with Hopkins and NIDA was willing to advance some money to tide them over for another month. He added again that he was serious about shutting down the company if he did not get the rest of the money they owed him.

But then, Brown says, De Lorean abruptly changed gear. 'He told me he knew how some of the things the board was doing bothered my conscience. He said he wanted me to keep a clear conscience and not to worry as much as I did, so he dropped me from the board. I told him that action was all too indicative of his character. He couldn't bear having anyone disagree with him, so he had to stack the board his way.

'John just nodded and said, "That right. It's my company and I'm going to do what I want to do – when you get your own company, you can do the same." '

Brown shot back that De Lorean's problems came from 'listening to the scum of the earth, then making your business decisions based on a premise of bad information, including rumours, lies and innuendo'.

Brown did not have to specify who he meant as scum of the earth, and De Lorean didn't ask. Instead he told Brown that he hoped they could try and start a new relationship with 'a clean slate'.

Among those De Lorean 'stacked' on the board was his own wife, Cristina. SEC files subsequently identified her as 'self-employed in the advertising and entertainment fields since 1965'. The description neglected to add that in 1965 the board director was fourteen years old.

Disconsolate, C.R. returned to California, thinking his days at the company were numbered. 'Dick never hid the fact that he believed De Lorean had no moral fibre,' one executive says. 'He just didn't hold it against John. He held it against everyone in the New York office. The crazy thing was that we worked for the De Lorean Motor Company, but if we said a complimentary thing about De Lorean himself, we were in the doghouse with Dick.'

But in the few weeks following his return from New York Brown would again work his way back in the good graces of De Lorean by supplying a vital piece of the distribution network. Brown had already put De Lorean in touch with the shipping company he had used with Mazda, Pasha International. At De Lorean's request Pasha studied the feasibility of flying the cars over from Northern Ireland, but eventually settled on a system of ocean freight. Loading cars with gull wings on and off a ship and then truck carriers was no easy process, but Pasha proved to be sophisticated enough to overcome the obstacles.

Once cars were brought to the ports, the car company needed to pay its manufacturing subsidiary, Pasha and the various hauliers who transported the car to the dealer. This sort of financing is known as a 'bridge financing'; it was crucial to the survival of the company, but as the first delivery of cars loomed only months away, De Lorean still had no arrangements for it. 'Kimmerly kept telling me he was going to take care of it,' Brown says. 'He went to Chemical, Continental and Citibank and was turned down by all of them. I could see in the summer of 1980 that the cars were only months away from delivery, so I asked to try on my own. I know Kimmerly was laughing up his sleeve, and never expecting me to do it. I went first to the Japanese bank that Mazda used. Then I went to Bank of America.'

In October Brown secured a $31.2 million loan agreement from Bank of America for the cars and an additional $2.3 million for parts.

'Tom called me up to say he didn't know how I did it.'

During this same period Brown was engaged in building his own De Lorean Headquarters West in a 50,000 square foot warehouse building in Irvine, California. It was, he says, a bargain that rented for only $14,250 a month – compared to the $80,000 a month New York was paying for its offices – he still spared no expense in decking out his domain. He had the cement block building carefully painted in a two-tone grey and black to match the corporate colours, and when he didn't like the look of carpeting he had bought for the first floor, he had it torn up and replaced for another $5,000.

Office decoration for Brown was no small matter. He thought nothing of walking into an executive's office, straightening the pictures on the wall and sometimes replacing them. Over $70,000 was spent on office furniture. Some $8000 on Brown's office alone, including a $2000 desk and $600 chair. The walnut conference table, measuring ten feet by four feet, was bought for $2550. There wasn't a metal desk or piece of composition board in the place. De Lorean's office, next to the conference room, had only one narrow vertical window. It overlooked the end of a little visitor's car park on the side of the building, so Brown had that piece of asphalt torn out and replaced with grass and some landscaping. When he did not like the landscaper's choice of bushes, he had those torn out and replaced as well.

Kimmerly reprimanded Brown for what he regarded as lavish expenditures. 'Our auditors', Kimmerly told Brown, 'feel that someone is building their own rec room out there.'

'Are you serious?' Brown says he replied. 'Do you mean using the funds personally?'

When Kimmerly answered, 'Yes', Brown asked that they come out and conduct an audit.

But the squabbles over office furniture were quickly forgotten when the first cars started to roll off the assembly line. 'Suddenly John and Tom saw how much they needed Dick Brown,' one New York executive says. 'If he couldn't sell their car, they were in big trouble.'

When Brown saw the first pilot vehicle, however, he had his doubts. 'It was flown in and delivered in a truck,' one of Brown's assistants remembers. 'It was partially disassembled, and we were like little kids at a Christmas tree, putting it together as fast as possible to see what had hatched. Unfortunately, the car looked nicer disassembled. There were poor body fits. The trim was falling apart. Water leaks all over – through the roof and window. It scared the crap out of Dick.'

Brown dashed off a memo with fifty suggestions for improvement to Belfast touching on everything from the number-plate holder (the designer had forgotten to include one on the car) to wiring that dragged too close to the ground. However, when he wrote to dealers announcing the arrival of the first pilot car, he enclosed a copy of a decidedly different Belfast memo: 'We have spent the last three days in rather intensive evaluation from the standpoint of technical features, appearance, appointments and on-the-road handling characteristics . . . My personal feeling as well as the feeling of all people at DMC–California is that: "It's a Winner!" '

The Ethical Car

Few American automobile buyers have ever had the chance to receive a thank-you letter from the name that appears on the car. But such was the added distinction of owning a De Lorean. The car-maker's message read as follows:

> I am pleased to learn that you have purchased a De Lorean automobile. I wanted to write you myself because the purchase of a revolutionary new product, particularly one as significant as a car, is an act of faith, perhaps even courage, qualities very much at the heart of forming and developing the De Lorean Motor Company.
>
> It has now been several years since we undertook to bring another kind of automobile into being. The goal was to design and build a car that would be as safe as possible, reliable, comfortable, handle and perform well, be enormous fun to drive and unmistakably elegant in appearance. We wanted people to be able to buy a car which they truly liked and then keep it year after year, much as one does one's home.
>
> If, as you come to know your car better, you want to comment on how well we have achieved our goals, or how we might even improve, I do hope you will do so. You can be sure that we are concerned about the attitudes and experiences of our owners and your comments will be valued.
>
> Warmest personal regards,
> John Z. De Lorean, Chairman

Some De Lorean owners who had come to know their cars better did send in their comments. But, they did not all come with the warmest of personal regards. Stuart Perlen, an industrialist from Long Island City, New York wrote:

> I am proud to be the owner of a De Lorean automobile. However,

due primarily to your poor quality control, I am embarrassed to be the owner of a De Lorean.

The car is a show piece and is always on display. When it doesn't start due to a short in the inertia switch, I am embarrassed. When the headlights don't turn off, I am embarrassed. When the signal lights don't work, I am endangered. When the fuel gauge doesn't work, I get stuck. And when the roof leaks, I get wet. I could enumerate many other problems. I should also state that my [Ford] Mustang was delivered with fewer defects.

Some of the letters of complaint were incredibly forgiving. A lawyer from the Chicago area reported that he 'noticed a number of small problems', and lists a few:

1. Side window sticks in the up position.
2. Fuel pump is excessively noisy.
3. Dye from the optional floor mats comes off and stains clothing, shoes and skin.
4. Interior body fit of the door is not excellent.
5. Owner's manual does not state the type of light bulbs to use (several were burned out on delivery).
6. The radio is terrible – especially in the FM Stereo position.
With the exception of the above I have found the car to be great.

Other correspondents were not as accommodating. Laguna Beach developer Paul F. Murray wrote:

I have had my De Lorean for three and one-half months. During this time it has been in the shop for repairs a total of six weeks. It was towed in three times . . .

The problem is that on five occasions I have been unable to start the car in the morning and keep it going. It starts and remains at 1000 rpm. When you depress the gas it doesn't go any faster and when you release the clutch it jerks forward and kills. At the same time a loud humming noise comes from under the gear shift lever . . .

A second problem is the driver's window. Three times I have put it down and the glass has fallen out. [The dealership] cannot get a replacement part. They glued the window in and told me not to use it . . .

The car is of no use to me because I cannot be sure when it will run. If you cannot fix this automobile in five days, my attorney has been instructed to file a class action lawsuit to recover the money I paid for the car as well as the inconvenience I've been through. Enclosed is a copy of a $90 towing bill . . .

One of the De Lorean executives who had to field complaints like these quickly came to a sorry conclusion: 'You get warranty claims on all cars. Car companies average three or four claims for each car produced in the course of a year. But the De Lorean was pulling three or four claims per car per *month*.'

The quality-control problems were apparent to Brown from the first pilot vehicle he saw. His fears were heightened further when Belfast air-freighted more cars for the February 1981 Los Angeles National Auto Dealers Convention. When a pilot car arrived in Detroit Jeffrey C. Synor, Mid-West technical manager, was sent to the airport to release the doors, which had jammed shut, immobilizing it on its wooded pallet. Moreover, 'you had to be careful how you opened the hood. I used to say it was a British car with body by Wilkinson Sword.'

Belfast was meanwhile making over five hundred cars ready for shipment in the next two months, but De Lorean had not been concentrating on assembly problems. Brown immediately waved the red flag. In New York the major fear had been that the engine wouldn't pass exhaust emission tests, and a plan was put forward to ship the first batch of cars to Canada where pollution standards were lower. The move sounded very similar to an incident De Lorean relates in *On a Clear Day* when a strike left GM with 400 year-old Camaros and Firebirds that didn't meet Environmental Protection Administration guidelines. 'At one of the GM [board] meetings,' he writes, 'somebody suggested that we sell the cars in Canada where the safety and pollution laws were less stringent.

'So we set out to peddle these cars in Canada. The only trouble was that some public-spirited guy at the Norwood plant leaked the plan to the Canadian press which jumped all over "giant General Motors" for trying to sell in Canada cars which were too dirty and unsafe for the United States. At a time when Canadian nationalistic spirit was rising and "ugly American" ownership of Canadian industry was under attack, the decision to try to sell these Camaros and Firebirds in Canada was the worst thing we could have done.'

But it was not a bad enough experience to teach De Lorean a lesson: instead, it gave him ideas. This time, however, a 'public-spirited guy' wasn't needed to blow the whistle. Other executives realized that it would take so long to pass Canadian import requirements anyway that nothing could be gained by unloading the cars there.

Brown's alarm signals turned everyone's attention away from the engine towards the rest of the car, and De Lorean put Cafiero on the spot to stop the problems at the gate. Back in October 1980 C.K. Bennington had been yanked from his post as managing director of the Belfast plant and brought back to New York. In his place Cafiero hired the retired chief executive of Chrysler and Chrysler International, Donald H. Lander. A benign, balding man with an easy smile, Lander was to be one of the few people in the entire company who would win praise from all factions, but he came in only two months before production started. On April Fools' Day De Lorean flew in to see whether any progress had been made on the condition of the cars, and went back home apparently satisfied after test-driving a few. He sent Cafiero to make the final inspection before the cars left. On 14 April the president telexed back to New York and California: 'Inspected this a.m. 216 okay cars at Stormont dock and additional okay units at plant. Quality and appearance level much improved since my last visit. In my opinion these units with U.S. prepping are satisfactory for shipment to U.S. dealers.'

However, that assurance was not enough for an anxious Brown. The boat arrived in the middle of May. 'Fortunately,' Brown says, 'the press stayed just long enough to see the first cars come out. Of the 250 on board we had to roll out 150.'

De Lorean and Cafiero flew to Long Beach to see what he was complaining about. One executive remembers, 'Cafiero looked at the cars and said, "These are perfect. Better than Cadillac." We all just stood there and tried not to laugh.'

De Lorean dashed off his own urgent telex to Belfast with two columns. One was headed 'Must be corrected before any sales', and included:

1. Door seal, poor quality, falls off getting out of car; must be replaced and mechanically fastened in customer contact area.
2. Radio interference must be corrected . . .
3. Shim out rear wheel to avoid tire interference.
4. How do you enter locked car with dead battery?

De Lorean also had problems with the key fitting into the door lock, the way the doors shut and the way the stainless steel stained even before the cars hit the road. Among the items that did not need immediate correction he referred to the poor visibility out the rear window and wrote, 'Car does not park. Is this legal?'

'I think the poor state of the cars became a moment of triumph for Dick,' one of his executives says. 'He had given everyone warning and it was clear the cars couldn't be sold in that condition. De Lorean gave him carte blanche to do anything that had to be done to get those cars to the dealers.'

Brown used his mandate to create what some executives called his own little kingdom – Quality Assurance Centers (QACs). He set up three processing points in Santa Ana, California, Troy, Michigan and Bridgewater, New Jersey. Brown told the press that the QACs only performed dealer preparation, no more than the Japanese imports did –

shine the body and tighten any little bolt that came loose in transit. In fact, Brown was reassembling the cars.

The big push started with the very first boatload of cars. One executive remembers, 'Brown called in every district manager and technical expert he had. At that point we did all the processing in Irvine. We were working twenty hours a day. Some people fell asleep under the cars. For dinner Dick would spend two or three hundred dollars on pizza and chicken. While we were eating, he'd come down out of his office and give us pep talks. Here we were – big-time auto executives stuffing our faces with Colonel Sanders and up to our shoulders in grease.'

One of the staff mimeographed a cartoon drawing entitled, 'Be a POG for De Lorean!' It defined a 'Pog' as someone who worked like a dog and looked like a pig. Qualifications included: 'A PhD in automotive technology with heavy emphasis on finance, education and accounting. Your own metric hand tools helpful but not essential.'

Brown alternately badgered and cajoled the troops, at times telling those who left that they could not come back. A few wondered whether he was striving for unattainable perfection. 'We spent more time on the body than anything else,' Jeff Synor says. The plastic bumper material – fascias – on the front and rear of the car were not often flush with the rest of the car. 'We could work two days readjusting the other panels of the car so the fascias would fit. Then they'd sit out on the lot and expand in the sun and we'd have to do it all over again to pass muster with C.R. He used to take a little metal gauge to the edge and if he could slip it behind the fascia it wasn't good enough.'

However much Brown frustrated his staff, they all knew he was putting more hours in than anyone. During the days he was on the phone to his dealers, trying to assure them that the cars were on the way. At night he sat at his desk, working on memos, or pacing the halls railing against the idiots in New York and Belfast. For his workers he became as fearsome and tortured as Ahab, but some wondered whether the 'great white whale' he was out to harpoon was none other than the man with the name on the door.

Forced to get cars to the dealers as fast as possible before financing ran out, Brown spared no expense in bringing in the necessary parts to finish off the cars. Orders went out in frantic and often wasteful fashion. According to Synor 'C.R.'s favourite expression was: "I don't care what it costs, just get the job done." We Federal Expressed everything – from tyres to slips of paper.'

One of his hastier decisions was to replace the hidden radio aerial embedded in the windscreen with an inexpensive, non-collapsible whip type. 'The problem with the hidden antenna was the wire they were using,' Synor explains. 'It was more suited to defrosting the windshield than picking up radio signals. Rather than try another wire which might preserve the original concept, Brown insisted on installing an external aerial. He hated the whole idea because hidden antennas were the De Lorean trademark at GM.'

But Brown's alternative meant drilling a hole through the stainless-steel panel just above the front tyre. When De Lorean later offered car owners a more discreet powered aerial, the panels with the holes had to be replaced at a cost of $200 apiece.

What distressed staff most about Brown's fixes was his unwillingness to refer to his trained engineers. He was more likely to ask the hourly Mexican mechanics for advice while his executives fumed nearby. The whole problem was that Brown was making mechanical decisions and he wasn't an engineer.

However, Brown was the only man in the company who was making decisions, and that was a vital role to fill when the company faced intense pressure to deliver cars as fast as possible. There would be no more nagging memos from Kimmerly or De Lorean during those launch months. In fact, one of the dealers most chagrined at not receiving cars was DMC Ltd's partner Chuck De Lorean. Finding no special influence with his brother, he threatened – for at least a few weeks – to revoke his franchise.

By August Brown had still not met his goal of getting out at least one car to every dealer. Only ten cars were leaving the QACs a day. Eventually he geared up his QAC kingdom to include almost 250 hourly workers in all three locations. 'When we started out,' Brown says, 'we spent an average of 150 man hours per car. Eventually it got down to sixty-eight hours. Finally ten. When you added up all the expenses, we spent between $1500 and $2000 in additional labour on each car.'

Ideally, the QACs should have withered away after the first few bugs were shaken out of the production process, and Brown continually sent expeditions over to the Belfast plant to track down where the errors were coming from. His envoys found one of the most modern and sensible assembly lines in Europe. The initial work on doors and the body were done on lines, and the parts were carried by overhead carriers. They were later married with the chassis and put on a robotic moving platform – first pioneered by the Swedish car-maker Volvo – which followed wire tracks embedded in the floor. If a car presented problems, the platform could be taken off the line and pushed to the side.

However, no matter how good the system was, it took men to run it. In the critical days when production was first gearing up to speed, IRA conflict heated up again during the hunger strikes of 1981. Bobby Sands, one of those who died, had lived just behind the De Lorean factory in Twinbrook. The strikes after his death prompted the first serious absenteeism at the plant. When the army marched in to quell the violence that followed Sands' funeral, they used the De Lorean grounds as a short cut – a move that made the plant site a target of two firebombs. One touched off a fire in a small prefabricated building where engineering drawings were kept. The company later claimed $10 million of damage – a claim which a sceptical government has yet to settle.

Apart from the effects of the strike, the civilian strife that rolled around the plant did not, however, find its way inside. Brown's staff encountered willing workers who reported early and seemed truly dedicated to putting out a good product. The problem was that many were still adjusting to their first industrial jobs. Some had never even held a screwdriver before, let alone worked on an assembly line, and very few had cars. 'I was watching one guy putting in water seals around the door,' a California executive says, 'and he was having trouble making it all fit at once, so he was cutting it into pieces, and fitting one little piece at a time. He just had no idea what the seal was for and how it worked.'

However, one of the Irish shop stewards, Malachy Higgins, says the workers were well aware of the defects. 'These people came in from California to watch us, and we weren't supposed to know who they were. I think they were worried about insulting us. But we knew who they were, and we knew there were troubles with the car. But we were told to let those things go and not slow up the line.'

DMC Ltd's managing director, Don Lander, liked to tell the visiting delegations that every new car programme had to cope with first-run gremlins. He had seen several in just as much trouble when he ran Chrysler in Europe and Canada. Adjustments to the line, he warned, could only be made gradually. Eventually, he said, all the knots would be straightened out.

But until they were the company had to support the onerous cost of Brown's Quality Assurance Centers, and cars still went out with serious defects. The car's most prominent feature – the gull-wing door – was most prone to failure. Its two latches were on either side of the door (instead of on the bottom, as Collins originally designed), and occasionally both didn't engage at once, which ended up jamming the mechanism and making it difficult to pull open the door. A double lock system – built in for convenience – kept both doors locked when one was jammed. In a notorious incident a spectator at a Cleveland motor show was trapped in a car for over an hour until he was prized out. During the interim, the event's sponsor notified Brown that a De Lorean car had taken a hostage. He was ready to send Synor to the rescue on the next available plane.

Part of the door problem would be solved by one of Brown's home-made solutions – a metal guide over each latch. But until the moulds for the guides were made in Belfast, he had an elderly Irvine machinist make them out of metal. Each week, the man showed up with the latest batch in a paper bag, taking $40 cash for every set.

Cold weather created other problems with the door. Moisture gathered in the seal on snowy nights, freezing the perimeter of the gull-wing shut. One employee manning the complaint lines says, 'I remember getting a call from a guy in a phone booth on some miserable Sunday afternoon in Chicago. He had just come out of the stadium after watching a Chicago Bears football game and couldn't get his door open.'

The car's incompatibility with cold would be proven in laboratory tests but they were not conducted until the car had been on the road for seven months. In extreme cold the windscreen did not defrost and the struts in the door jammed. At intervals the door stuck shut or it did not shut at all. From his regional headquarters in Michigan, Jeff Synor discovered that moisture gathered within the throttle cable and froze overnight. 'People got up the next morning and when they opened the throttle it stuck there. I know of one incident where a woman rode up on a kerb and into a gas station parking lot. It's a miracle no one was hurt.' The solution was a rubber boot at the end of the throttle cable. But it took, Synor believes, an unconscionably long time before California recognized the urgency of the problem.

Winter weather was also unkind to the striking stainless steel coat. Salt on icy roads left lingering white spots. In warmer climates cars could be tattooed with finger and handprints. De Lorean executives recommended a variety of waxes to keep the cars clean, but most owners found it was not long before their silver beauty looked like the smudgy toy of some giant four-year-old.

Even the car's most public owner and investor, Johnny Carson, would fall victim to the gremlins. Brown took care to deliver his car personally, but on the comedian's maiden voyage down to the drugstore the battery failed in front of an appreciative crowd.

'Some of that initial word-of-mouth on the car was disastrous,' Brown sums up. 'I don't think you can calculate the damage it does, but you know it's considerable.'

Brown tried to make up for the difficulties by replying promptly to complaints. His executives took turns manning a complaint line during evenings and weekends. 'I don't think any company was ever more eager to please,' Synor says. But in many cases, the help was after the fact.

No one was more aware of the product quality backlash than John De Lorean. In his own understated way he offered Brown a solution – buy back the first 5000 cars off the assembly line, giving the customers the option of getting a new model De Lorean instead. It was the sort of grandstand move, De Lorean told Brown, that could turn them from bumbling idiots to heroes. Brown convinced him to put aside his generosity, as the move would show up as a $115 million liability on the company's books.

Certainly, De Lorean did not deserve all the blame for production problems that showed up in his car, but he was responsible for the bulk of the car's drawbacks. Somehow his personal dream car did not merit his attention – when it was most needed – either to details or overall concepts.

When he was general manager of Chevrolet, De Lorean was saddled with the disastrous Vega. It was a car, he says, designed by committee, and it missed all of its announced objectives by a mile. In *On a Clear Day*, the chapter on the Vega opens with a press conference conducted by GM chairman James M. Roche. De Lorean recounts his over-optimistic assessments of the price and characteristics of the car and its ability to compete with the cheap imports. He writes:

> A study of the conception and gestation of the Vega reveals not a lesson in scientific marketing and development, but rather a classic case of management ineptitude . . .
>
> When Roche announced the car, his information came from statistical abstractions. Not one prototype had been built or tested. There was no model to point to because the car existed only in financial statistics and blueprints derived from a consensus of the existing sub-compact cars, all of them foreign and some of them built by GM overseas. The engineering blueprints were costed out by the central financial staff in conjunction with the Chevrolet finance staff. Their work was to be proven shoddy and haphazard. All of this information provided a weight and price class for the car that became the foundation for the chairman's startling small car announcement. Shortly thereafter, the first prototype was delivered from the central staff to Chevrolet . . . Already the small, svelte American answer to foreign car craftsmanship was putting on weight – twenty pounds in understructure to hold the front end intact. Thus began a fattening process of the 'less-than-2,000-pound' mini-car that would take it to ponderous proportions in weight and price compared to the original car described at the opening of the new GM building in New York City . . . To be a viable product on the road, the Vega was going to arrive on the market heavier and costlier than the company's target because it was already close to 200 pounds heavier than planned.

De Lorean ends the discourse on the Vega by adding, 'I hope the Vega lesson was learned well by GM management and that the knowledge gleaned from this lesson is applied in the development of future products . . .'

It was another lesson De Lorean chose not to learn. If anything, he took GM's shoddy product forecasts to a higher degree. His goal was not to fight off imports, but, as he told reporters, to make an 'ethical car' that was durable, fuel-efficient and safe. Like Roche with the Vega, De Lorean made wild claims about his car from no more than 'statistical abstractions'. But when his prototype came out of the blocks, he continued to make the wild claims. As late as January 1979 he told *Newsweek* that the car would get 32 miles per gallon on the highway and it would accelerate from 0 to 60 miles per hour in under eight seconds. These performance goals he keyed to a prospective curb weight of 2200 pounds. 'In theory,' he told the magazine, 'you could drive it for twenty or twenty-five years, and nothing should happen to it. It's not designed for early obsolescence.' De Lorean put the price at $15,000. In other magazines he said that the price would come within $1500 of the Corvette's $19,000.

But like the Vega, his baby would be overweight when it came off the production line. Not just by two hundred pounds. The De Lorean weighed over 900 pounds more than the early projections, according to the motor magazines that tested it. The surge from 0 to 60 miles per hour, *Road & Track* discovered, did not take eight seconds, but a lumbering 10.5 seconds – faster than a Cadillac, but nothing like a real sports car. As far as durability was concerned, De Lorean's statements about a ten-year, 100,000 mile guarantee came crashing to the ground. The company offered the standard one year, 12,000 mile protection. His Goodyear tyres were recommended for eight to ten thousand miles – not the 100,000 he projected. Finally, the price came out close to $26,000 – $7000 over the comparable Corvette.

If the car approached any of De Lorean's promises, it was in the area of safety. Tests done for the National Highway Traffic Safety Administration found the car to be safer than most, but the tests were conducted with airbags – another feature De Lorean touted which never showed up in the final product. Gone too were bumpers capable of withstanding ten miles an hour of impact. When Giugiaro's redesign lowered the car, the field of vision became much worse. Beams on either side of the windscreen grew wider and the view through the louvre-covered rear window became next to impossible. As the test driver for *Road & Track* wrote, 'Looking straight back through the louvres is somewhat like being far-sighted. You can see things off in the distance fairly well but up-close vision is limited, so parking can be a challenge.'

On one level, De Lorean's unsupported hype for his car was a foolish mistake – especially when he had the experience of the Vega fallout under his belt. And yet, maybe De Lorean sincerely felt he could meet his own extravagant claims – or at least inspire someone else to meet

215

them. One of his senior executives says, 'I spent more time with John chasing coloured balloons than doing anything else. He believed anything you imagined was possible, and he gloried in the idea that somehow he could make it work. But he let other people come up with the somehow.'

The real 'doer' was better off clawing to the top of the big corporation. As De Lorean discovered, the price for being on his own was constant compromise, and with a limited production vehicle, he was at the mercy of component makers. His original desire for a mid-engine car had to give way to a rear-engine design when Renault became the only supplier willing to accommodate him. On his own, he was incapable of producing air bags and no company was then making enough of the safety devices for a production car. Cost exigencies also helped choose his tyres and several other important parts. As president of GM, De Lorean could have produced his own air bags or ordered a new mid-engine model for the Corvette, but the political compromises of the corporate board room paled in comparison with the practical compromises a smaller businessman made every day.

And yet, the tragedy of De Lorean's car is not the compromises that were forced on him, but the compromise that he did not have to make. While De Lorean may have portrayed himself as a maverick and rebel, as a business leader he was much more the conformist taking the least path of resistance. No move demonstrated that more than his arrangement with Lotus.

'The De Lorean car never had a father,' the original designer Bill Collins says. 'It was a bastardized Lotus.'

Although De Lorean officials vehemently denied the charge, it was apparent to the most novice auto buff. Except for the doors and the stainless steel, the car had much the look of the Lotus Esprit. Pennebaker's documentary caught Colin Chapman admitting as much to a reporter at the Geneva motor show. 'As you see,' he says, 'the chassis has a very Lotus-like design but this is what we understand and what we believe works well. It's very nice to see John De Lorean productionizing it and producing it in such large volumes.'

Statements like that were part of Collins' whole argument for not turning over the project to Chapman. 'He wasn't going to make the car we wanted,' Collins says. 'He was going to use the process, the design and the materials that he was the most familiar with. He also wasn't going to make a product that was any better than the one he was selling.'

While Collins' statements could be dismissed by some as sour grapes, they are supported by his successor as De Lorean's chief engineer, Michael Loasby. Having worked in a similar capacity for sports car maker Aston-Martin, Loasby was part of the British school of car-makers, yet he is in total agreement with Collins. 'Chapman tore Bill Collins's baby apart. They came up with a totally different car, and I don't believe the change was at all justified.'

Colin Spooner, who headed the Lotus team, admits that his group was at odds with the car's three most basic design concepts: the gull-wing doors, the rear engine and the stainless steel. 'But John wanted us to adhere to those requirements,' he says. 'Evidently he felt they were important from a marketing standpoint. But we didn't see how they worked from a functional standpoint. The doors were complex and heavy, and the stainless steel was redundant. The Lotus VARI plastic can be painted. That's what we do with our cars. We didn't need a second skin. It only added further weight to the car.'

Adding even more weight was the steel backbone required to hold the Lotus plastic underbody together. In keeping with his promise not to use any metal parts that would corrode (although the car did use standard fasteners, which tend to rust before anything else), De Lorean demanded that the backbone be dipped in a protective epoxy, which had the same effect as dolloping a comb in molasses. The molten material collected in every recess. 'We couldn't get the coating thin enough,' Spooner says, 'so it added more weight just in the areas where you didn't need it.'

De Lorean executives still argue that the ERM plastic process was not given enough of a chance. 'From the moment John signed with Lotus he gave up on ERM,' one says. 'You can see that just looking at the budgets for Composite Technology, the subsidiary that was doing the research on ERM.'

They had only continued research on ERM for possible use on other cars and some minor parts of the car, including the licence-plate holder and engine panel, were made of ERM. The major problem in using the material was to create a press so large that it could mould a big enough section of the car. 'If you broke the underbody into too many pieces,' Spooner says, 'it would offer no protection in a crash. We felt you needed as few pieces as possible and that they had to be continuous.'

Of course, there could be an acceptable, although charitable, view of De Lorean's relationship with Lotus. Perhaps the time element in meeting deadlines – set by his prospectus and British agreement – left him no choice but to opt for Chapman's proven engineering squad and plastic process. Even so, there was no excuse for not getting involved in some of the critical design decisions Chapman made.

No part of the De Lorean was so susceptible to damage as the front-end suspension. In essence, Lotus had put the torso of a weight-lifter on arthritic and spindly legs. Chapman also refused to permit adjustable caster and camber on the wheel. Spooner explains, 'His genius was in simplicity and economy of design. The idea of an adjustable

217

suspension was alien to our principles. You build in adjustments and someone is likely to put it out of adjustment.'

Such principles were fine for hand-tooled cars, but as Loasby argues, 'In production cars you never can duplicate the dimensions that finely. You normally design in adjustment so you can cope with that imperfection.'

The suspension eventually prompted three recalls when the De Lorean hit the road. Company engineers admitted that the fixing was merely a sticking plaster; the real wound needed attention on the drawing board.

'John did not want to argue with Chapman on issues like suspension,' Loasby says. 'He just didn't have time for the details of the project. But attention to detail is everything. I had understood that De Lorean made his reputation at General Motors as a man who paid attention to detail. But I suspect he had been away from the shop too long.'

When De Lorean did get into the picture, it was with suggestions that seemed more like distractions than help. 'He came in one day,' Loasby says, 'to say we should hook into the cooling system and make a little icebox for a six-pack of beer behind the driver's seat. Or another time he told us to work on a sixty watt radio speaker that could be detached and hung outside the car for picnics.'

Only months from production, electrical components had not been chosen, nor details as significant as the car windows designed. American engineers would later be shocked to see that De Lorean permitted Lucas electrical supplies in his car – long the laughing stock of the auto industry, but still the preference of chauvinistic British engineers. The most serious blunder would be using a weak British alternator that burned the battery out when more than a few accessories were going at once. Brochures were printed up showing a window that slid manually to the side, but eventually it was redesigned to resemble a letterbox – which added to the claustrophobic atmosphere of the car – and it was operated electrically.

'We'd get these visitors from De Lorean like Brown,' one Lotus engineer says, 'and he'd be full of suggestions. Everybody came with a suggestion, but nobody took any authority to sort those suggestions out – it was a case of too many cooks spoiling the broth. The first thing you usually design for a car is the wiring. But with De Lorean, we put it in last and had to go around everything that was already in place.'

Eventually, to force the car out of Lotus, Cafiero brought in four retired production engineers from Ford, a move that rubbed Chapman up the wrong way.

But as the car rushed pell mell to production, important elements of the process went uncompleted. No complete parts list or shop manual was then available. The factory was in the position of an orchestra playing a symphony from a recording and not a score. 'It may sound incredible,' Loasby says, 'but up to that time we did not have specifications for all the parts and tools for the car; some parts didn't even have drawings. The first cars off the production line were not built to a specification.'

Loasby had expected to oversee that work, but De Lorean was not willing to create an engineering staff. 'I joined on the premise of ultimately taking over the engineering from Lotus, but now I realize John had no inclination to create an engineering department. Instead, he chose to abdicate total responsibility for engineering. I'm not entirely clear why. As an engineer himself, I would have thought he'd be sensitive to the fact that the car still needed continued design work after it got out of Lotus. An engineering group should have been established in Belfast long before.'

Loasby has his suspicions why De Lorean could not justify the expense of more engineers. 'His problem was that he already paid $18 million to this mysterious Swiss company for his engineering work. If this company was doing its work, an in-house engineering staff would be redundant. I'm afraid that when you look at the whole thing, the letters GPD loom very large.'

Out of Control

Everyone else had gone home for the night. Only Marian Gibson remained. Alone in a suite of De Lorean Motor Company offices, a shopping bag in one hand, she methodically flipped through the memos and documents piled on desks and spread out on filing cabinets. After a quick look she dropped them into the bag. Then she turned out the lights and left.

It had not been an easy summer for Marian Gibson. For two years she had devoted her life to the De Lorean Motor Company and its chairman, and suddenly in June she was being told by some young executive that she was no longer 'a perfect fit' and might have to be phased out of the company.

An apple-cheeked woman with short blonde hair, she was born some forty years before in London, and had been living in the USA since 1960. She got her interview for the job as De Lorean's administrative assistant in September 1979, shortly after he moved into his Park Avenue headquarters. Struck by her British accent and efficient manner, De Lorean had her come to work the next day. He had been especially fond of his capable secretary in his 100 West Long Lake office, but he was unable to persuade her to move, and as a result he would let Gibson take charge of his daily regimen. She scheduled his appointments, typed up his confidential memos and helped balance his personal bank account.

In the process Marian Gibson got a glimpse of the varied and disparate pieces of De Lorean's life. There would be urgent calls to Roy Nesseth, which meant picking through a score of different phone numbers and ringing anywhere from a steak house in Huntington Harbour to Logan or Boise before she could find him. She reminded De Lorean when Cristina wanted him home for a certain party and commiserated when he complained about his wife's social calendar. At other times she chatted with interior decorator Maur Dubin and his retinue of young male assistants as they sat waiting for De Lorean to get off the phone.

In October 1980 she got a rise and a promotion to the title of deputy administrator, becoming office manager and supervising the secretaries and ordering supplies. But in the course of the year, she found herself caught in the office intrigue. Both she and Kimmerly shared the same maid, and, according to Tom, Marian told the maid that she did not have to empty his cat's litter box. From this point of contention, Marian says, a feud would escalate and be taken to extremes by Kimmerly's obstreperous personal assistant. In June, Gibson was demoted from her job as office manager, and offically became secretary to Bill Haddad, but it was clear she was not wanted. In the ultimate act of secretarial degradation, she says, they had her fill in during lunchtime for the young woman at the switchboard – the lowest spot in the office pecking order. 'They wanted to humiliate me,' she says. 'I worked too hard too long to deserve that treatment.'

She found a sympathetic ear with Haddad, who was also on the outs with the inner circle. But his fight didn't start over cat litter. In July Kimmerly and his legal minions had registered a share float with the SEC. If successful, it would bring in over $22 million. But the issue did more than raise money; it also significantly restructured the entire organization, creating a new entity, the De Lorean Motors Holding Company, which would exchange stock on a one-for-one basis for De Lorean Company shares. The initial offering price was to be twelve dollars a share. By virtue of his control of 83 per cent of DMC, De Lorean stood to collect 9.95 million shares in the deal – worth on paper $120 million.

Executives did not come out as well in the plan. Although they had options on 1.79 million De Lorean Motor Company shares, they would not be allowed to exchange those options for Holding Company stock and a chance at a $22 million killing. In Wall Street parlance they weren't taken 'upstairs'. Kimmerly and De Lorean weakly explained that there were tax implications that had to be considered first, but most of the executives – especially those in the New York office – did not accept the explanation.

Haddad says that long before the options became an issue he had been disillusioned with De Lorean's behaviour with potential bus company investors. He was also repelled by De Lorean's attempts to bully the British government. At times he discussed the company's heavy-handed tactics with Marian Gibson, and he mentioned the battles with NIDA during the fall of 1980 when De Lorean was first trying to get more grants out of the agency and then opting for more equity. With the new share float NIDA would get only 3.6 per cent of the holding company and shares worth just $8.4 million – not much of a deal considering that the government had already poured close to $147 million of grants, loans and bank guarantees into the company.

Haddad's talk, Gibson says, sent the Union Jack up the flagpole. De Lorean wasn't just doing her in – he was going after her homeland too. Marian still felt an allegiance to the U.K. and visited often. 'The whole thing had me in quite an emotional state,' she says. 'Sometimes out of nowhere, I'd start crying. But I felt that if any good was to come out of my job at De Lorean, it would be to stop that stock issue.'

She had already planned a trip back to Britain in mid-September, but the voyage was now going to be more than a vacation and she assembled her brief for the prosecution. 'I don't even know all that I picked up,' she says of the papers she gathered in late-night forays. A few, she adds, came from 'disgruntled employees', whom she won't name.

Fate chose an unlikely repository for Marian Gibson's revelations. Through the advice of a friend she contacted Nicholas Raymond Winterton, MP for Macclesfield. Until he met Gibson at the Chelsea home of their mutual friend, Winterton had spent an otherwise sedate and obscure tenure on the Conservative backbench. All that would change. Marian let loose a welling tide of accusation against her former employer, touching on everything from De Lorean's original investment and NIDA equity to fancy bathrooms in Belfast. Winterton understood little of what he heard, but as he told *The Times* later, he believed his informant 'was genuinely concerned about the interests of the country and the long-term prospects of the people who worked for De Lorean'.

The MP asked for some documentation to support her charges and six days later Gibson appeared at his office door with two file folders stuffed with letters, documents and memos. 'Nicholas is really a very nice guy,' Marian says, 'and I told him I was sorry for putting a bombshell on his doorstep, but he replied, "Look, if you lift the rock and maggots are under it, you've got to sweep them out."'

Although Winterton found the files a little too long and too obtuse for his eyes, he still put in an urgent message to 10 Downing Street for a personal appointment with Margaret Thatcher. But the prime minister – not known to be a fan of De Lorean or his project – had just left for Australia and a meeting of Commonwealth officials.

Meanwhile Marian Gibson returned to New York, expecting the transatlantic news wires to start chattering with stories of the De Lorean inquest as soon as she reached the airport. But no word came, and one of Marian's first assignments on returning to work was to retype the prospectus for the stock offering. 'They were telling me it was coming out any day.'

Gibson put in a frantic call to England, and her friend, after talking to

Winterton, told her nothing could be done until the PM came back from Australia. 'I could see nobody was going to move,' she says, 'and I had to do something on my own. I had to call in the press.' Before the evening was over she phoned London freelance journalist John Lisners. 'I told him I had a great story that could make him a lot of money.'

For three days the reporter stayed in Marian's apartment rummaging through documents, and saw enough to burn up the cables back to Fleet Street trying to sell his story. His best deal came from *The News of the World*, which satisfied Marian as she wanted the widest coverage she could get. She only asked that her lawyer look at the story first.

She says Lisners did not pay her that courtesy. Early on Saturday, 3 October, after wiring the story to London for the next day's paper, Lisners called De Lorean to ask his reaction to Marian's charges. 'Later in the morning,' Marian says, 'Maur Dubin delivered a letter to my apartment building. It went something like, "Dear Marian, what are you doing?" He wrote that John wanted to see me, and then he ended it saying that Jonathan sent his regards. Jonathan was one of his young friends, and we used to enjoy chatting when he was up at the office.'

Later in the day one of the De Lorean Motor Company lawyers was in the lobby of the flats. 'He told me again that John wanted to see me. I asked him to go away.'

However, the story was not to run in *The News of the World*. According to British press reports, it was killed at the last minute by the publisher, Rupert Murdoch, who, as the proprietor of the *New York Post*, was a Manhattan neighbour of De Lorean's. Reportedly he found Lisners's submission, with liberal references to Dubin and his gay crowd, even too scabrous for his Sunday paper. Reports also say that he gave De Lorean warning of what was in the works, suggesting that the material was libellous.

After his interview with De Lorean Lisners met Marian again and played her part of the tape. 'Just hearing the voice made me very fearful. There's something very penetrating and deep about his voice that's beyond description. As I heard that tape in the cab, I decided I had to get away. I left on the next flight to England.'

Marian had warned Winterton that a news story was coming, and he in turn tried to warn the prime minister. This time he told her personal secretary why he had tried to reach her, and a message was sent to Australia. The prime minister asked that the Attorney-General take a look into the matter.

Fleet Street was still looking sceptically at Lisners's story, but when the papers called Winterton he confirmed that an investigation had begun. He later told *The Times*, 'I regret it has become public.'

The day after her arrival in London Marian was a sudden tabloid celebrity. Without warning her first, Lisners had placed her story in that

Tuesday's *Daily Mirror*, which chose to run solely with Winterton's reports of an inquest and excerpts from a Bill Haddad memo dated December 1980 which read:

> I continue to be concerned about our efforts to set up a scenario under which the British relinquish their share of equity in the program. . . I am also worried about what a Parliamentary inquiry will uncover about our expenditures on both sides of the ocean. There are the 'official' complaints which can be sensationalized even though the accountants, SEC, et al., will give a clean bill of health. The [former chief financial officer Walt] Strycker picture is a highly personal one of John Z. De Lorean milking the company for his private profit. Some of the discredited Strycker charges can be succulent journalist morsels for the Fleet Street crowd never overly concerned about separating accusation from fact. As you know, I am also troubled by some of the actions regarding the house [by the assembly plant in Dunmurry] and some of the expenditures appear to have been 'fuzzed' (like a £10,000 expenditure [actually £2,000] at Harrod's [for] gold faucets [taps]). I recently learned, for example, that we have hidden some of the capital expenses of the house in expenses for the project. In short, the books were altered. Silly, because the house can be justified. . .
> Why wasn't JZD there [in Belfast] to oversee everything? Was he, as Strycker charges, pursuing other interests?

Claiming that they were doing no more than pursuing 'routine' inquiries, Scotland Yard, under the Solicitor-General's orders, flew to New York on the Wednesday to interview Haddad. The car company's first response had been that the memo was a forgery, and that Marian had been no more than a typist. A press release further averred, 'The company's affairs are a matter of public record and have always been open to the fullest examination and scrutiny to the satisfaction of the government.' But Haddad confirmed his authorship and that he was engaged in a contract dispute with De Lorean. Haddad says De Lorean asked him the next day to fly with him to Jacksonville, Florida. On the way, he says, De Lorean offered to settle the contract differences if Bill forgot about the memo. 'He wanted me to hole up in a motel in Atlanta and hide from Scotland Yard.' But Haddad went ahead and saw the Yard in his lawyer's office on Friday. Haddad was to leave within the month. It was an acrimonious parting. At the turn of the year he charged that De Lorean had opened his mail in the office and tried to break into his apartment, and De Lorean replied that Haddad had engineered a press campaign to destroy his company. There would be no settlement of this rift. Haddad sued for $18 million in damages, claiming breach of contract, slander and fraud. De Lorean countersued for $30 million.

Back in England, Marian decided to hide on her own. She first stayed in a hotel under an assumed name, but then took off for the Midlands and the cottage of an elderly aunt. To her surprise, she was starting to feel like something of a criminal herself. 'At one point I was in a taxi,' she says, 'and without letting on who I was, I asked the cabbie what he thought about the De Lorean affair. He said, "I think that secretary is wrong. She shouldn't have gone removing documents that way. It's a messy business." I think a lot of people felt that way, although they didn't seem happy with De Lorean either. Like the cabbie said later, "If they gave us ten quid a piece instead of giving it all to him, we'd be better off." '

De Lorean decided to take on the 'furor' in person. Looking natty in a double-breasted blazer, grey slacks, a turtle-neck sweater and sun-glasses, he arrived at Heathrow on the Friday night after the *Mirror* piece appeared. He told reporters, 'I still can't understand how a troubled, nervous old typist and an MP who was never known for his intellectual clarity can cause so much trouble.'

De Lorean continued to attack Gibson and Winterton in interviews he granted from his luxurious suite at the Savoy Hotel. He also started to imply that some larger conspiracy was at foot. 'There is quite clearly much more to this than we have heard so far.'

But the rest of the press had started to ask questions beyond those raised in Haddad's memo. Some of those articles did no more than dredge up facts that were public when De Lorean made his deal. Winterton expressed surprise to the BBC that De Lorean had put so little money into the venture, and the *Sunday Times* Insight team, taking its first close look at published SEC documents, realized that if the car company did succeed, De Lorean was permitted to buy back British shares before the government could make a killing on its original investment.

Neither of these topics should have come as revelations. Far more explosive stuff was in a *Sunday Telegraph* story by reporter Stella Shamoon. One month before she had looked at Lotus's involvement with De Lorean and mentioned the dreaded acronym 'GPD'. In the first sentence of another article two days after his arrival in London she asked, 'Why should a Panama-registered partnership based at "PO Box 33, 1211 Geneva, Switzerland" have received on behalf of Colin Chapman's Group Lotus some $18 million from the state-aided De Lorean sports car concern in Belfast?'

Armed with a written statement, De Lorean flew to Belfast on Monday ready to respond to the allegations. 'We didn't want John to shoot from the hip on this,' one of his British Belfast executives says.

'We told him to first meet with the city editors of papers and give them a chance to see that he wasn't a charlatan. But he really believed he knew best how to handle the press. He wanted to do it the American way and come on like a big whale. He called a press conference at 4.00 and then moved it up to 2.00. He asked whether it would be feasible for him to hold it outside, so he could burst through the crowd of reporters in a car and get out to read his statement.

'He ended up doing it in normal fashion, but he was very tense and aggressive. He hadn't allowed us to read it first, and evidently it had been prepared by his lawyer. It was reported quite fully on television and the papers. But at that hour there weren't too many heavyweight journalists in attendance.'

De Lorean offered a point-by-point refutation of what he called 'charges that have virtually destroyed our company'. In the case of his comments on GPD, his prepared text cited the company as a licensing agent for the VARI plastic, contradicting both his own previous comments and remarks Lotus had made to the press.

But before De Lorean responded to the charges against him, he made his own accusations:

I must say that I find it very hard to believe that a troubled, unstable typist, an unemployed writer and a solitary MP could have damaged our company so severely. I must make note of the fact that no one bothered with us until the past few months when it began to look like De Lorean Motor Cars might succeed . . .

I have a strong feeling that the loud public alleging of these spurious and fictitious charges, each of which could have been easily answered to Mr Winterton and his associates by our auditors or the government accountants without damage to the company and without destroying jobs in Northern Ireland, is part of a wider conspiracy. I'm a car-maker. Wiser heads than mine will have to seek out the motives of those who would destroy us and with us Ulster's proudest achievement.

I think all right-thinking people will share my view that the circulation of these lies in circumstances where they destroy a fledgling business and deprive three thousand people of their employment is totally reprehensible.

There is a conspiracy to bring down the De Lorean Motor Company. The allegations that have been made could have been made for political or economic reasons.

A foreign country may have been involved in the plot to destroy Ulster's proudest achievement. I dare not name the country I have in mind.

226

It is unlikely that a group of minor people of limited ability could have created the problem alone. Why did it all happen when we started looking like we were going to make the grade?

I don't know whether a competitor in the car industry could have been responsible. That's certainly a distinct possibility.

The company will be filing libel writs against the most serious perpetrators of this terrible crime against the company.

Early on 3 October, rumours reached me that an unemployed writer, Mr John Lisners, and Marian Gibson, a former typist at De Loran's New York office, were negotiating to sell a story to the *News of the World* [whose] reporters contacted our public relations department, but eventually . . . decided against publishing the story for fear of libel since they were not able to confirm its allegations.

De Lorean's executives listened to the rambling diatribe in stunned silence. To their surprise, the press were not much more vocal. One of the British staff says, 'The reporters were permitted questions at the end; almost nothing was said. I don't know whether they all sat there in awe or ignorance.'

De Lorean followed through on his threat and slapped Gibson, Lisners, Winterton, the *Mirror* and both the BBC and ITV with libel writs. His lawyer was the formidable Lord Goodman, and the move had a more than chilling effect. For the next few critical months it froze solid all further close examination of De Lorean in the press, with the exception of *Private Eye*.

For its part, the British government did all it could to put a lid on the commotion. The day of the press conference, the Attorney-General and the Director of Public Prosecutions announced, 'no evidence has emerged to support any of the allegations of criminal conduct on the part of Mr De Lorean or the company . . . [We] are agreed that there aren't any grounds for continuing the police investigation.'

From her country cottage hide-away Marian Gibson saw a cover-up. 'When the police came to interview me, I could tell they weren't interested at all in what I had to say.'

One government official agrees that Her Majesty's legal legions were not eager to turn too much up. 'I think the greatest argument De Lorean had for quelling all this talk of allegations and investigations was that float. The feeling of everyone involved – pro and con – was let him go to Wall Street and suck the fool Americans into his bloody project, and God's speed. If he were capable of raising wads of dollars and got rich to boot, that was fine. Just as long as he got off our dole.'

Among the few politicians jumping publicly to De Lorean's defence was Roy Mason. In a *Times* centre-page column he proclaimed that the car company had already met the five-year goal of employment and that the 'breakthrough' product was in heavy demand in the States. The heading for the column was 'De Lorean is a winner, damn it!'

And for a few brief moments in the early autumn of 1981 it looked as if De Lorean *was* a winner and that his stock issue would be a hit on Wall Street. At last cars had got to the dealerships, and from Anchorage, Alaska to Portland, Maine local newspapers were treating the arrival of the eye-catching wedge like the visit of an extra-terrestrial. A few greedy dealers took the lid off the suggested retail price of $27,000 and were getting as much as $35,000. One of the Texas limited partner/dealers was offering a $5,000 premium for every De Lorean his fellow dealers would rustle up. In October, monthly sales shot to a high of 710, more than the previous two months combined.

But the warm glow coming off the De Lorean Motor Company was only the first sign of the flames convulsing it from within. Even if the company continued to sell 710 cars a month, production in Belfast was going at twice that rate. 'In July,' one of Belfast's British executives says, 'John came to Belfast to tell us that production had to be up to 80 cars a day [a rate of 20,000 a year] by the autumn season. It was a decision he made against the recommendations of the entire team here and a decision he made in the teeth of adverse political conditions. But John had the power to make those decisions.'

As for Brown, this observer remembers him backing De Lorean's stand. 'He told us he could sell every car we could make.'

The move to press production to those limits was probably the single most disastrous decision De Lorean made. Absolutely no marketing data he received supported the increase. It was exactly the sort of wishful thinking he excoriated GM superiors for in *On a Clear Day*. He wrote, 'Where modern industry prepares an overall marketing strategy which scientifically ascertains customer needs, designs products to bring the need, the product and the consumer together, GM relied on little more than rah-rah sales pitches and hard-sell techniques.'

De Lorean purchased the best marketing expertise in the automotive industry, J.D. Powers & Associates, and then chose to ignore their advice. Back in 1980 Powers's volume projections showed the company at best selling over 20,000 cars a year if each were priced below $18,000. Over $21,000, cars would sell at a mean of 16,000 a year. But those figures dropped dramatically after the price went above $24,000. Then the company could hope for only 10,000 a year. At $28,000 – under 4,000.

The introductory price for the De Lorean cars, with taxes and delivery charges, was dangerously close to $28,000. Both Brown and De Lorean hoped to make up some of the slack with exports, but that was years away. De Lorean wanted the best of both worlds – high price and high production. In September he wrote to Brown, 'In our planning and analysis, it is important to realize that we are tooled to produce efficiently in the 25,000 unit to 30,000 unit range. At 11,500 units we become a relatively expensive manufacturer . . . join[ing] the Lotus and Renault Alpine camp – again we can't win. This financial analysis also demonstrates the urgency of bringing our sedan on stream. We probably cannot sustain this volume beyond two years. If we don't have a sedan by then, we will have to reduce our overhead by 50 per cent in both the UK and the US.'

In fact, De Lorean had no evidence he could 'sustain this volume' for one year, let alone two. Ken Gorf remembers the process he used to delude himself. 'He had Powers do a study a second time and found that we might be able to sell 16,000 cars if the price was close to $20,000. So John took that figure and said, "You have to factor in the glamour quotient associated with my name. That should bring it up to 20,000 at least. So then he raised the price of the car to $26,000 and told everyone he had hard figures from J.D. Powers to say he could sell at least 25,000 cars.'

Nothing made that projection more foolish than the trend lines Brown had charted. The bar for the hoped-for volume of the De Lorean stuck out next to the actual sales figures of similarly priced sports cars like a skyscraper in a field of anthills.

To some extent, executives explain, De Lorean was committed to the higher production. Long-term contracts with suppliers like engine-maker Renault called for certain numbers of orders, and those suppliers were not interested in figures of less than 20,000. He was also committed to employment targets to convert the Department of Commerce loans into grants. However, he was already overshooting those targets. 'I'm afraid any business says slow and steady wins the race,' one Belfast executive laments. 'Our figures showed that this was a viable company with half the production. If the extravagance had been cut out of New York, we could have broken even just making 6,000 cars a year. But that wasn't fast enough for John. First he had to build his paper empire in the stock market. A creditable success was not enough for him. He wanted to be an overnight sensation.'

But in early autumn De Lorean even started talking about outstripping the 20,000 unit ceiling. At a business forum lunch on 28 October, while Brown sat in attendance barely believing his ears, De Lorean jubilantly rattled off his production goals. 'We have 3000 highly motivated employees [in Belfast] who are producing 80 cars per day. The consumer and dealer reception has been spectacular. In fact, on the basis of public reaction, we have raised our production targets up to 30,000 for 1982. In thirty years in the business, it's the first time people have told me our price is too low – and we're sold out through the end of 1982.'

Back in Belfast two of those motivated workers could already tell that the bubble had burst. 'In October new workers were just pouring through the doors,' Malachy Higgins says. For him, the new recruits on the trim line meant extra money, as, rather than create a training force, the company paid experienced workers like Higgins to help another worker adjust to the job. 'A day after you were hired you were on the assembly line.'

More crews also trooped into the powdery mist of the Body Press Building where shop steward Billy Parker moulded the VARI plastic underbodies. 'It was amazing. The work was just piling up. We had enough moulds for 100 cars. We had nowhere to put it all. They didn't tell us, but we could see all around us that their cars weren't selling in the States. It was a cruel thing to see all these people coming on to work and knowing that they'd all be laid off in a month or two.'

The wisdom of market reports would come crashing home to Brown in November. Car sales dropped to 578 for the month, and winter was setting in – traditionally the slowest time for sports cars. He remembers, 'The month of December started with a sudden influx of notices from dealers to hold shipments until further notice.'

Meanwhile, in the middle of the month, De Lorean made a rare trip to Belfast for a meeting with the new Secretary of State for Northern Ireland. James Prior was the 'wet' on Margaret Thatcher's Cabinet. Booted out as employment minister for not cracking down on the unions, he publicly proclaimed that the last job he wanted was Secretary of State for Northern Ireland. That said, he took the post – at least going in equally despised by both Catholics and Protestants. After the initial *faux pas*, he showed himself to be more activist than any of his predecessors in Thatcher's Cabinet. In many ways a maverick in his own party, Prior might have been the one Conservative best able to get on with De Lorean.

They were to first meet at the Dunmurry plant early in the day, and De Lorean would lead the royal tour. Stout and ruddy, with an unruly mane of white hair, Prior trudged through the snow to arrive on time. Hours would go by before De Lorean showed up. His tardiness did not necessarily set the stage for the asking of favours, but De Lorean went ahead and tried. First he asked for £4 million, which was rejected, and then for an extension on repayment for £10 million of loans that were coming due at the end of the month. That request was granted. 'When he asked for the loan renewal,' a Belfast executive says, 'John went overboard telling Prior how good things were going to be next year. He told him sales were over projections and that new shifts would start soon. He just needed time to renegotiate his bridge loan with Bank of America and put the stock on Wall Street. Prior looked pleasantly surprised by the news. I have to say that some of us couldn't believe the news either. We instituted a new bonus plan for the workers if they met production goals. But only days after John left, a very gloomy Dick Brown showed up. It hadn't been more than a few months before when he was telling us he could sell every car we made. But now he said, he couldn't even handle the cars we were producing. The bottom fell out of the market.'

Brown went into urgent meetings with managing director Don Lander. Brown would be 'shocked' to hear they added another shift. 'I thought we had only one choice and that was to cut back on sales and credit line immediately, and I convinced Lander as well. We then placed a call to John in New York over the speaker phone. When we told him the plan, he was his typical vulgar self. He said, "That's bullshit. You cut production now and all you do is blow the [share] offering." '

But the float was already in serious trouble. The sole underwriter Bache Halsey Stuart, Inc. (then, the bargain basement of brokerage firms) was getting leery as each week passed. The offer was cut in half to $12 million and the warning was added that 'investment in the units involves a high degree of risk and should be considered only by those who can afford a total loss of their investment'. While the prospectus estimated that capital projects would cost $41 million, it admitted that the company 'currently hasn't any funds available, or commitments from outside sources, for any portion of such $41 million'.

A bitter winter, a lousy car market, a soft stock market: all seemed to strike together with the force of one sudden knock-out blow. Executives were already bailing out. Cafiero resigned, claiming he had been cheated out of his share options by the new offer. Anxious to hush up any acrimony, De Lorean settled for a million dollars before his former president even filed suit. The third chief financial officer would also quietly take his leave.

Despite the bad press, De Lorean still tried to muster another nationwide dog and pony show to sell his amputated share float. He and the executives met with brokers and potential investors in some seven cities complete with another slide show and closing remarks from the chairman. De Lorean, Brown says, was as enthusiastic as ever, but also as hyperbolic. Although Brown felt they were well received, when they returned from the whirlwind tour their broker announced that the issue was being pulled from the market. In the newsletter *New Issues* the publisher called De Lorean 'a classic case of go public or go broke'.

The executives agreed. Ken Gorf says, 'Everything was riding on the stock offering. When it didn't go through, we all knew it was over.'

Failure loomed everywhere. Only 259 cars would sell in January. While some De Lorean spokesmen claimed that over 5000 cars had been sold, in fact, over 5000 had been shipped to dealers, and only 3300 were actually sold. Over 1800 cars languished in showrooms or the lots out back. No matter how the company fudged the figures, the stark reality of the poor sales was there to see in the car advertisements of most major newspapers as panic-stricken dealers offered the car at fire-sale prices.

Meanwhile the bills started to pile up – from niggling to gargantuan. Dealers forced to service the cars on a practically monthly basis were sending in warranty claims. 'We never did get a computer service to process warranties,' one California executive says. 'So at first we made neat little stacks on a counter about fifteen feet long. It was like a little garden. You'd walk by each day and watch it grow, until it got to the point where there was no more order, just one mound of paper.'

For a few weeks Brown optimistically anticipated new orders from the better-selling dealers. As soon as cars were shipped, he could tap their credit lines. But now they only accepted cars reluctantly and asked for no more.

Over $18 million was owed to the Bank of America and over $22 million to the British government for the last months, but some Bank of America financing was still available for parts, and overnight a team prepared an order for virtually every part in the Belfast plant. De Lorean sent Roy Nesseth over to expedite what was to be the last boatload of stainless steel cars bound for California. Brown says, 'I heard him tell Roy to get every car out of that plant and on a boat.'

For his part, Brown had the ignominious task of calling back the company cars given out to V.I.P.s and investors like Sammy Davis, Jr., who had one of the $150,000 De Lorean Research Limited Partnership units. 'Davis didn't want to give the car back,' one of the Irvine executives remembers. 'We had a hell of a time tracking both him and the car down. I guess he was under the impression the car was his as part of the bargain for the investment. C.R. had to get on the phone with his secretary and threaten to send out a tow truck before we could get them to cooperate.'

Yet, even as car sales in the States slowed to a standstill De Lorean was careful not to fire the 2600 workers in Belfast. They were the last bit of leverage he had. The plant went on a three-day working week instead, and a few hundred of the least senior employees received notices that they might be laid off.

As before, as always, the last hope lay with the British government. With the Bank of America unlikely to extend the bridge financing De Lorean turned instead to the British government's Export Credit Guarantee Department, and asked for a $65 million credit. Once again, there was the problem of a government agency directly funding an American company, but over the autumn Kimmerly had restructured the company to overcome that obstacle. The Irvine operations had been cloistered into a separate subsidiary called De Lorean Motor Cars of America, with Brown as president. If the British gave the go-ahead, it could be reallocated again as a marketing division of the Belfast factory.

But the British were not about to give the go-ahead. De Lorean later said the government reneged on its agreement. However, government officials say the export agency was never very enthusiastic about the idea. The plan could have only been hammered through by a cabinet minister, but James Prior was not in the mood to argue with bureaucrats for the sake of John De Lorean. 'Why should he have stuck his neck out for this caricatured American?' one of De Lorean's British executives says. 'Just remember, only four weeks earlier – before the Christmas break – De Lorean had promised that the production would go up, that the stock issue would go forward, that cars would start selling again. Well, then Prior comes back from holiday and he sees the plant's working week reduced, the stock dead and car sales worse than ever.'

De Lorean made it clear to the press that the Belfast jobs hinged on the export credit, but this time the government would not give in. In a brief meeting on 28 January Prior told De Lorean that there'd be no $65 million. But that wasn't his only bad news. He had also called in the London branch of the accounting firm Coopers & Lybrand to conduct a major review of the government's relationship with the car company. The inquest would be under the supervision of the estimable one-time Lord Mayor of London, Sir Kenneth Cork.

The mere mention of Cork's name struck terror in the hearts of businessmen everywhere. As a government-appointed receiver he had disposed of an imposing roster of industrial bankrupts that included Rolls Razor, Fire Auto and Marine, Vehicle and General. Cork greatly resented his sobriquet 'the undertaker'; as he told reporters, his reorganizations often helped save companies, not just embalm them. But at sixty-nine, age had played a cruel trick on him, hunching his bald head forwards, and his stooped shoulders combined with his thick glasses and weak chin made him very much the human caricature of a buzzard.

At five o'clock, the morning after the British government refused the export aid Don Lander called in the shop stewards for an urgent meeting. 'He told us that he had some bad news,' Billy Parker remembers. 'He said there was a slump in car sales – that America suffered its worst winter in thirty years. Then he said that within the week they'd let over 1100 men go. We thought they were bluffing to force the government's hand. Under our employment act, they were supposed to have a ninety-day consultation before they made anyone redundant.'

Reporters trekking to Belfast nevertheless found the workers sympathetic to De Lorean's plight, and more upset with the government. The *Daily Express* headed an article, 'Why De Lorean is Still a Hero', and quoted one laid–off employee saying, 'If the government came up with more money it would be seen as an important gesture to the Catholic people. Fair play to John De Lorean. He made a lot of money, but he has given a lot of people jobs.'

De Lorean, however, was not ready to give Belfast fair play. The day after Prior turned down the export aid he returned to New York and in an interview with *The Times* dispassionately blamed Belfast for most of his problems. 'We had a terrible time producing a management team because Englishmen would not work there. We grossly underestimated the magnitude of the problems.' De Lorean went on to cite 140 fire bomb incidents and added that his executives were constantly the targets of snipers. 'Trying to keep a management team together under those circumstances, especially of people who are good enough to work anywhere, is difficult.'

'Of course those statements about Belfast were unmitigated bullshit,' one of the Belfast executives claims. 'He implies that he had to settle for a team of incompetents. But we weren't the ones who decided to increase production and increase it even when the inventories were bulging. The statements about the firebombings are just evil. We had the one incident during the hunger strike but that was because the blasted army tramped onto our property. The fire did destroy that hut where we had some drawings, and it did cause some damage – not the $10 million John claimed, and nothing we lost was responsible for putting us in trouble. As far as snipings went – there was one stray bullet in a water tank. Period.'

As all came crashing down around him, De Lorean appeared confident, even serene. Among his visitors in early February was one of his major service suppliers. 'My contract was running out,' he says, 'and I was passing through New York, so I went in to see what John wanted to do. I knew termination would have a devastating impact on his business.

'The secretary met me in the lobby and showed me to John's office. From what I could see, the place looked pretty deserted. I guess he had let most of the people go. But there was John sitting in his office acting like nothing had happened – just as pleasant as always.

'He had quite a view up there and when I sat down, he stared out through the windows and started telling me how his little boy had just been robbed. Someone on the street grabbed his watch. "It was just a Timex," he said, "but what are we going to do about the crime in America?"

'From there he just took off. I didn't say a thing. I just sat there listening. He was going on about our government, and then he was talking about the Russians. He said, "Let Russia have Europe. They already have most of it. Just as long as we get Central America and

South America. We'll give Asia to the Japanese. They can handle that.''

'I couldn't believe it. Here his whole business was disintegrating to ashes and he was solving the problems of the world. This went on for forty-five minutes. Finally I looked at my watch and told him I was sorry to interrupt, but I had to catch a plane soon, so we should start talking about my contract.

'It was like I had thrown cold water on him. He looked down at his desk and started shuffling through his papers. He said, "I don't know about that. Talk to the lawyers. They know what's going on there. They'll handle it."

'Then he stood up and looked at his watch and said, "I've really got to be going." '

Roy to the Rescue

By March 1982, like one of its defective cars with the throttle stuck open, the De Lorean Motor Company was careening down a canyon road – lurching across lanes, bumping off guard rails, barely making the curves – and at the wheel was Roy Nesseth. No longer did Roy have to lurk in corners or hide behind vague titles. Now, he was out front. Big, bad Roy. Charming, 'buddy-buddy' Roy. Screaming, fist-pounding Roy. Finally he had control of John Z. De Lorean's dream, as it hurtled to destruction, and nobody but John was going to say anything about it.

In just one twenty-four hour period Roy would send out armed guards on two coasts to flout the authority of a bank agreement and set in motion forces that would jeopardize another $18 million deal and definitely kill off a potential $100 million investor. By the time the smoke cleared, Roy had fired the company's two most senior executives and negotiated settlement on a $278,000 debt with an exchange of worthless shares. Just another day for Nesseth. As one executive who worked with Roy explains, 'Roy is the kind of guy who likes to show he's doing something by taking a sheet of paper, tearing it into little pieces and throwing it into the air. He only forgets that somebody has to come back and pick up the pieces.'

Back in early February De Lorean was ready to forget the car company and wave goodbye. Once the export aid was refused and Prior called in Sir Kenneth Cork no one had any doubt that the plant was going into receivership. John De Lorean had not left General Motors to have some fusty old receiver looking over his shoulder and questioning every move.

'From their first meeting,' a Belfast executive says, 'Cork and De Lorean hated each other. It was a classic case of "this nation isn't big enough for the both of us" – two egos that would never be reconciled. John would start in about how the British government wasn't giving him a chance and Sir Kenneth would talk about extravagant overheads.

Each was out to cut the other down.'

Court records show that early in the month Kimmerly called in Detroit's best bankruptcy lawyer, Lawrence C. Snider, to discuss a Chapter XI bankruptcy – a reorganization designed to stave off liquidation. But if he contemplated a quick exit, De Lorean was not ready to leave without a consolation prize. On 9 February he proceeded to buy from the car company a few assets, like office furniture and works of art, at bargain prices. He also took over the mortgage on the old Bridgewater car dealership building that had been a QAC. The property was on the way to De Lorean's Bedminster home and he had strongly recommended the site when regional director Bill Morgan was looking for a good location. 'As far as the company was concerned,' he says, 'it was out of the way. But the place was in a prime development corridor and John said, "It's a hell of deal. If we don't buy it, I'll buy it for my own account." Then he said he knew he was buying a facility and moving in the cars was a tough job. He said if I needed help, Roy was available to help with the details.'

Without any request from Morgan, Roy was on the scene, screaming at movers, sending through orders and giving Morgan more aggravation than help. Despite his genial manner, the barrel-chested Morgan was not ready to tolerate Roy's antics. 'The man just wreaks havoc wherever he goes. I had enough of it. I told him either he left the building or I'd throw him out.' Roy meekly took the nearest exit, Morgan said, later complaining to De Lorean about the regional manager's inclination to violence.

But De Lorean let Roy go ahead and handle the details of the property transaction. The landowner was in serious financial straits, and in the midst of negotiation Roy turned to the bank with a lien on the property and found a better deal. It was just one more bank which, without knowing better, wanted John De Lorean's business. 'The guy went belly-up,' one California executive says, 'and Roy just couldn't stop crowing about how he screwed the guy.'

The mortgage for the property came to only $900,000 – but when De Lorean became personal owner, the car company entered into a very sweet deal with its chairman by pre-paying two years' worth of rent, which came to $200,000.

As De Lorean expected, the British government placed the Belfast factory in receivership on 19 February. While Cork said he felt the company could be made viable with an additional capital infusion, the rest of his report was kept secret. But like so many previous British efforts to set De Lorean's house in order the investigation was too little too late. One of De Lorean's British executives was critical of Cork: 'He was too tough and too easy at the wrong times. How could he have assessed the viability of the car company in just a two-week study? If he had really been intent on saving it, he would have booted De Lorean out in February.'

If the company needed more capital, Prior made it clear that the British government was not to be the source. As he told the press, 'I had to reiterate to Mr De Lorean that there was no question of further public money.'

It was a moment, Fleet Street thought, of utter humiliation for De Lorean, but to their surprise the development left him ebullient. As he prepared to board the Concorde to fly home he told reporters, 'I am delighted by the outcome.' Implying that he was the only candidate to buy the plant anyway, De Lorean explained that receivership 'ensures the continuity of production, sales and service for the De Lorean car'. He then told reporters that he was to put in $5 million of his own money and in return the government would write off $70 million of investment.

When told of De Lorean's jubilant assessment of receivership, Prior replied, 'That is what I might describe as a piece of De Loreanism. When someone buys the restructured company he will still be responsible for these debts on which the government will have first charge.'

But later the government did admit that they had signed an agreement to write off $70 million in loans after De Lorean put up $5 million first. But their generosity was not due to any renewed faith in De Lorean. Instead, out of the blue, an investor appeared who really was capable of saving the day. When De Lorean first approached the government with the offer, they had reason to be sceptical, as De Lorean had been constantly promising for a year that some new Arab sheik or international company was just around the corner eager to invest millions. But Alan H. Blair was no figment of De Lorean's imagination.

An international businessman ensconced in Beverly Hills, Blair had built a fortune many times over in European manufacturing and pharmaceuticals. He was introduced to the car company by a friend who was a client of DMC board member, Robert Benjamin, and Blair instantly envisaged a way he and four partners could save the De Lorean car and use the factory more efficiently. 'We didn't think there was the market for the sports car that De Lorean saw,' Blair says. 'We had in mind adding another vehicle. Many countries these days are looking for a cheap, utility truck and we felt we could swing that in Belfast. We obtained about $100 million in private capital. $40 million would have gone to clear up the situation with the British government.'

Blair adds that if he had taken charge, he would have radically restructured the company. 'The underlying principle was that if De Lorean was there, it would be primarily to contribute his name – whatever underlying value that may have been. But he certainly would have nothing to do with management. That was a condition we set forth among ourselves, and John seemed amenable. He simply was not a businessman himself. I could see that right off the bat. Of course things are different in General Motors – you have accountants and financial people giving you help, watching your spending. I think it was like being in the military and then trying to do something alone. He couldn't operate on his own.'

Blair had only one condition. He wanted the British government to write off the $70 million dollars of loan guarantees and credit. De Lorean set off to London to get an answer from Prior on the day receivership was announced. Those around De Lorean remember him being unusually jubilant when he left. 'I don't think he expected Prior to go along with it,' one says. 'And that meant he'd have the perfect excuse to wash his hands of the whole thing. It would be clear that even with a legitimate backer, the British didn't want to make it work. He felt he could then leave with his conscience clear and reputation intact.'

But when Blair first met Prior, he found the government was not about to scuttle his deal. 'Prior,' he says, 'is the best man in the cabinet. Although he has the dirtiest job, he's unfailingly pleasant and low-key. He can still be a very tough man to deal with. It's hard to get a yes out of him. But he did have a chance to check me out first, and knowing of my arrangement, they were ready to cancel the $70 million of credit.

'They had yet to see De Lorean, and I went over to Claridge's where he was staying to brief him. I told him I was quite happy to say that they were forgiving [writing off] the $70 million in loans. But then he turned to me and said, "I want to put $5 million of my own money into the project."

'I couldn't believe my ears. I told him not to mention that. Just let Prior say his piece, say thank you and get out of there. He sort of looked away from me and didn't answer.'

'De Lorean then left, and soon after I received a phone call from Prior. I remember him saying, "I can't work with the man. I just can't work with him." '

Prior then told Blair that De Lorean's first words when they met were that he wanted to invest $5 million of his own money into the company. 'After that,' Blair says, 'what could he have said, but fine, we'll forgive $70 million when you deposit $5 million. And both Prior and I knew he'd never put up that money. I was just livid. When De Lorean came back I asked him, "Why did you do it?"

'Then he said, "You don't think I'd take all that money from the British government without putting up my own money, do you? I don't want their charity."

'I told him that now he had no choice but to put up his own money. He said all he had to do was to go back to Citibank. Of course, he never did put up that money.'

De Lorean returned to New York on Saturday, 20 February, and upon his arrival met Kimmerly to tell him about putting his own money into the company. He was ready to sell his Fifth Avenue flat to raise it. Stunned, Kimmerly called one of his young executives and asked, 'Do you think John is losing his judgment? Why would he want to put his own money into the company now?'

Tom turned to his occasional uneasy ally, Roy, to talk De Lorean out of this spate of generosity. Roy's strongest ally in the struggle was De Lorean's wife, Cristina, who, according to John, did not want any of their personal assets involved with the car and especially not her precious flat.

Yet, while Roy and Tom were against investment, they were also against declaring bankruptcy. According to New York executives, after the British put the factory into receivership, bankruptcy lawyer Snider strongly recommended De Lorean declare Chapter XI for his side of the operations. One of the inner circle remembers, 'Roy started yelling, "What the hell do you think a bankruptcy lawyer is going to advise? It's his business to have people go into Chapter XI." Tom's argument was that if they went into reorganization, all the assets would be gone. He and John weren't about to stick around to handle what was left.'

And there were still two thousand tempting stainless steel assets left, with a street value over $40 million. But there were debts of over $43 million, and at least $22.5 million were claimed by the receiver in Belfast. The plant never got paid for over 1500 cars that went out. De Lorean countercharged that he was owed $22 million by the plant for product quality repairs. Warranty claims were another $1.1 million chunk of the car company's debt, along with $1.7 million from various suppliers. But the most worrisome liability was the $18 million owed to the Bank of America. Despite the crucial role the bank's bridge financing had played in the company's existence, De Lorean had always left direct contacts to Dick Brown, who had succeeded in getting the bank to extend the loan, but now De Lorean decided to handle matters himself.

On 23 February, just ten days before the deadline, De Lorean flew into Los Angeles with Nesseth, Kimmerly and Snider. They first met Alan Blair in his Beverly Hills mansion for a strategy session, and then it was on to the Bank of America. De Lorean talked there of restructuring his car company much as Germany's BMW did when it went bankrupt. He had learned his lesson, he told the bankers, and he was scaling down his production goals.

But the bankers sat in glacial silence. They had gone as far with the De Lorean Motor Company as they were willing to go. A seething Nesseth later said that Dick Brown was behind their cool reaction.

Although he was putting on a brave front for reporters, Brown was waiting for the other shoe to drop. For five years he had staved off the influence of Roy, but in the last few weeks Nesseth had moved into De Lorean's office by the conference room and set up shop. Even with Brown's plush carpets, the halls rang with his curses.

Nesseth had also brought in four friends in another mission to save the company. In this case 'the henchmen' – as De Lorean employees called them – were renegotiating with creditors. Roy Nesseth, the best car deal closer in southern California, had finally graduated to closing out entire companies. His men would get a creditor on the phone, and then Roy would lock him up on a deal for so many cents on the dollar. Before he left Roy's office, a hapless supplier had signed an agreement promising not to sue if Nesseth met the terms of the contract. To some De Lorean staff members the whole arrangement did not appear to be on the level, and accusations have been made that violence was threatened, but no supplier has said that this was the case. However, one staff accountant would be reprimanded when she took contracts with big spaces in the middle of a page and filled them in to make sure nothing was added after the supplier signed.

At times, Roy didn't stop with just cents on the dollar. He also tried to push some of John De Lorean's personal shares on the biggest creditors. His biggest share drop came with the company that had finally provided the car with a successful radio system. The vice president of finance for the Louisville company, Audio Systems, Inc., accepted 25,000 shares of Motor Company stock in partial payment. Roy offered the shares even though he was not registered to do so and even though he knew they were worthless as anything more than a novelty souvenir.

Brown had to bite his tongue and watch Roy's antics in silence. He kept in touch with Bill Morgan on the East Coast over the phone and the two became aware of designs on the 2000 cars left in their care. Any day the bank was ready to slap a lien on the entire stock. But De Lorean and his crew appeared to have their own plans for the vehicles. 'One day in the middle of February,' Morgan says, 'I got a call from John asking me to find 450 of the latest models that hadn't been sold yet and get them out of sight. I told him that you just couldn't put that many cars in somebody's basement. You needed a few hundred thousand square feet. He just let it drop, but I left that conversation tucked away in my memory.'

Occasionally at weekends Morgan would have a couple of cars driven the few miles to De Lorean's Bedminster estate so he and some visitors could 'evaluate' them. But near the end of February, when he sent to have two picked up, he was told that De Lorean had already attended to the cars. They were going to be shipped out to Ross Gilbert

241

in Beverly Hills, the man Roy set up in a Mercedes dealership. For Brown, the cars meant some $34,000 of badly needed income to meet the week's payroll, but when he had someone go out to pick up the payment from Gilbert, he returned with a cheque for only $4000. When Brown called to ask what happened to the balance, he says Gilbert replied, 'You owe me for warranties.'

In fact, the car company owed every dealer for warranties, but industry practice does not permit dealers to take those costs off vehicle purchase prices. Gilbert was not going to bother talking about it any further. Brown then tried to ask Nesseth to intervene, but he found that Roy was well aware of the transaction. Brown says, 'He told me, "You take care of your friends like Bank of America, so I can take care of my friends too." '

But the Gilbert transaction would only be the beginning. On 3 March, the day before the bank officially went into default, the telex snarled disturbing messages about the company's health. They'd already had to lay off sixty-seven of the 117 people working in the sales organization. Brown had been cutting back steadily for weeks. He created a tight-knit crew over the years – sometimes most united in its irritation with him – but that was something he understood and even fostered. After all the months of pep talks, all the cajoling and badgering, he found it tough to announce that the efforts were all over. On the same day he learned that the health insurance for all employees had been allowed to lapse.

Before 3 March was over another telex would come through from board member Benjamin. 'He wanted me to come to New York and talk to him. The day was so hectic, I ended up missing my plane. Now I realize it was part of the scheme. They wanted me out of the city.'

But Brown had yet to hear the bad news. This time it wasn't the teletype machine, but a phone call from De Lorean himself. Brown knew the ultimate showdown was coming, and he knew that when it came, it would never be face-to-face but on the phone. 'John started in about the Coopers & Lybrand report from England. He said, "You criticized my management." I told him I didn't criticize anybody personally. I criticized the structure of the company. Then John said, "I don't see how you could take someone's money and then criticize him behind his back. I think we should separate."

'I said, "It's not your money." I told him I'd send him a letter.'

But while Brown sat on a powder keg in Irvine, Morgan was up to his neck in strange requests. Nesseth was holed up in New York and calling every few hours. 'Roy told me he wanted to get fourteen cars outside the gate so John could make payroll that week.' The cars had actually been ordered the day before, but anticipating default the bank refused to let them go. Pasha International, the importing company, also served as the bank's agent and had a man on the premises in both California and New Jersey to watch over the cars.

Morgan called to ask Brown's advice and Brown told him the cars belonged to the bank, and that under no circumstances should they be let off the property. But that night Morgan received an urgent call from the Pasha guard at the QAC. Five armed men had shown up claiming to be from De Lorean and demanding the cars. Spearheading the take-over was the nervous young office manager from De Lorean's New York headquarters. Morgan called the QAC and asked him: 'Do you know what you're getting into?' With that the take-over ended, although the office manager told Pasha's guard that from now on two De Lorean guards would be posted at the door.

In minutes Morgan's phone rang again. At the other end was Nesseth, the Patton of the De Lorean invasion. Moments before he had called to congratulate his troops, only to find them in full retreat. Now he wanted to know what Morgan had said. Roy yelled, "What the fuck are you doing?" I told him the cars belonged to the bank and then he said, "Who's your allegiance to – the bank or De Lorean? If it's the bank, then go work for the bank because you're fired." '

The next morning, Morgan called to see whether he had actually been fired, and he talked to one of the De Lorean lawyers who promised to put a call through. But in the end it was Roy who got back to him to say that both he and Brown were fired.

That night Nesseth's men returned. This time there was a Pasha regional supervisor, Earl Hanson, on the site. Hanson later testified that the De Lorean guards did not let him use the telephone. They told him instead that Pasha's contract had been terminated by De Lorean and he should leave the premises. Hanson sent his man out to a payphone to call the police and then went to telecopy the notice of default from the Bank of America, but the armed guards wouldn't let him use that equipment either. When the police arrived, the only documentation they saw was the deed De Lorean held to the property. This time, it was Hanson who was forced to retreat, but he kept his assistant posted in the parking lot. That night, the scout watched in his darkened car while fifteen of the De Loreans were driven out of the warehouse and onto their namesake's property.

It was Brown who originally got George Pasha involved with the De Lorean Motor Company – a fact that caused Brown some acute embarrassment when Pasha called to give him the sordid details of the Bridgewater takeover. Brown promised he wouldn't let the same thing happen in Santa Ana. First he called his people in the warehouse and warned them to be ready, then he called the police. By the time Brown arrived at the scene, the police had already barred four armed men from access to the QAC. Inside, there was a call waiting from Roy Nesseth on the phone. He was at his favourite New York hangout, the Peacock Room of the Waldorf Astoria Hotel. As Brown and his warehouse supervisor listened, Nesseth screamed, 'If you want to stay alive and if you want your family to stay healthy, you'll cooperate.'

Brown says he then asked if that was a threat. Nesseth replied, 'You can call it whatever you want, but you know that I can back it up.'

Kimmerly was also with Nesseth at the restaurant, Brown says. 'He took the phone from Nesseth and he said, "What are you doing there? You have no business there. You didn't have to be notified."'

'Then I asked, "Does that mean I'm terminated?"'

'And Kimmerly answered, "Yes. You're terminated."'

'I hung up the phone and I went home.'

Brown was wakened at six o'clock the next morning by De Lorean. 'He asked me where my letter of resignation was, and I told him my attorneys were handling it. He said, "Fuck that. I don't want to deal with attorneys. I want it done quick." But I told him, after six years I couldn't just walk away from the company. Besides, my situation had changed. Kimmerly had told me I was fired. Then I asked John, 'Don't you know what happened at the QAC?"'

'He said it was all just one big misunderstanding.'

For Roy, Brown's exit was a cause for celebration. Now, he had the run of the Irvine office and he had eliminated his arch enemy from the corporation. But Brown's loss would have an immediate and devastating impact on the company by permanently alienating Alan Blair – the one investor who could have saved the plant. 'While I was sitting there one day with Nesseth and De Lorean,' Blair says, 'they were talking about getting rid of Brown. The whole thing almost sounded as though they intended some sort of physical threat. Nesseth said something like, "I'll knock his head off."'

'From what *I* saw, Brown was very good. He had done all the work with the sales organization. I respected his credibility and his past history. But there was just a terrible personality clash with De Lorean; I suppose to the point where De Lorean was ready to cut off his nose to spite his face.

'Now I didn't think highly of Nesseth at all. In fact, in all my experience in the business world, I had never met anyone like him. There seemed to be a relationship between him and De Lorean that I just couldn't fathom. Unfortunately, he just had a tremendous influence over De Lorean, and that really didn't penetrate until I read about Brown's dismissal.'

The warehouse escapade had other ramifications as well, which De Lorean discovered as soon as the United States court for the southern district of New York went into session on Tuesday, 9 March. The Bank of America immediately brought suit to stop sales of all De Lorean cars

244

in the United States and the judge, the Honorable Charles L. Brieant, was ready and willing to cooperate. When De Lorean's attorney explained his client's company was in financial difficulty the judge shot back, 'You don't work yourself out of the financial difficulty by sending people in with force and arms . . . If the allegation be proved at the hearing that somebody came with guns in the 1980s, we don't allow that. I am very doubtful we would have allowed that in the 1880s . . .'

De Lorean's lawyer was not in a very good position to respond. He had been retained only one hour before (and was just beginning to run up a $47,000 bill, which would never be paid).

After indicating that the seizure was considered a criminal act under most state laws, the judge restrained the sale of all De Loreans and demanded the return of the missing cars, adding, 'Please understand: if the order is not complied with, somebody is going to jail – fast.'

De Lorean returned the cars, but for Nesseth the restraining order had been a blessing in disguise. Roy had just not spent the night of 4 March ordering guards into warehouses, he also sat and watched John De Lorean sign away virtually every car in the putative possession of the De Lorean Motor Company. It was a deal Roy never wanted to see him make, and it was a deal De Lorean regretted as soon as he signed it, but it was also a deal Tom Kimmerly told him he had to sign.

'When these two little Jewish guys showed up from Ohio and said they'd buy the entire inventory,' one De Lorean executive says, 'Kimmerly and Roy were laughing themselves silly. They never really expected them to come up with much money. Whatever it was, they thought it would be like taking candy from a baby. Roy started off treating them like a couple of Joes in to buy one of his used cars – first slap them on the back, swap a few stories about Columbus, and then hit them hard and leave them ragged.'

But anyone familiar with liquidation in America could not take Sol Shenk or Jerome Schottenstein lightly. From a personal bankruptcy in the auto parts business, Sol Shenk had built an empire on the detritus of other men's broken dreams. Bricklin, Fiat Lancias, Diamond Reo trucks: Shenk's Consolidated International was the garage in the sky for the failed oddities of the American road. He specialized in more prosaic and profitable buy-outs of such things as appliances and auto parts. A good part of his inventory appeared to be crammed into every available corner of his cluttered one-storey headquarters. Posted prominently on his panelled wall is an autographed version of De Lorean's Goodyear Ad with the inscription: 'To Florence and Sol Shenk with my best wishes, John De Lorean.'

A crusty man of advanced years with a bald head and thick oversized glasses, Shenk likes to get quickly to the point. There are deals to be made and time can't be wasted on long answers. 'Our business,' he explains, 'is buying excess inventory. Buying – not selling. When I read that De Lorean had two thousand cars sitting around and the Bank of America was screaming for money I gave him a call. He was desperate to stave off the creditors. My primary concern was buying the cars.'

On most big deals Shenk's partner is Jerome Schottenstein, whose cagey acquisition of failing clothing stores has made him one of America's largest clothing retailers. Together they went down to New York during the last week of February, and after days of solid negotiation signed a letter of intent. 'Nesseth was originally doing the negotiations with us for De Lorean,' Schottenstein says. 'And it was very tedious. He's a very excitable person and I tried to stay cool. Every so often he'd get up and bring De Lorean in. Usually when people do deals with us, they're anxious to finish. De Lorean seemed to be dragging his feet.'

Shenk says, 'De Lorean was acting the part of a bigtime executive. You could see him in the office next door reading the magazine. I think he was pretty down. He told us he was prepared to step out, but he wanted to save face. He said he personally had a lot of money, so it wasn't a matter of him being forced to hang on.'

After a week of negotiating, a mind-bending agreement emerged. De Lorean's bankruptcy lawyers would later call it a giant hock, but Shenk and Schottenstein would be careful to structure it solely as a purchase. If De Lorean went bankrupt, they did not want to share the cars with creditors.

The easiest part of the deal to understand is the $14,887,500 Consolidated put down for the 1191 cars in the Santa Ana QAC. Much more difficult was the option De Lorean had to buy them back and maintain the exclusive rights to sell the car through his dealer network. First of all, he had to buy at least 400 cars each three months. His purchase price per car would be $13,500 (Consolidated bought them for $12,500 apiece). On top of that, he'd have to pay Consolidated interest on the total price of all the unsold cars and meet certain other payments at ninety-day intervals.

'Whenever we dealt with De Lorean and his people,' Schottenstein says, 'it would be very boring. Hours would drag by. Sometimes we felt we had to read his mind. I thought that because he had an engineering background, he was never really much of a businessman. He needed people around him to conduct business – although he still wanted to be a part of it.

'When we finally finished writing the contract, he kept us waiting even longer.' Schottenstein had no idea that warehouses were being stormed on both sides of the country. 'I just sat around drinking coffee. John would call me in and ask for a change, and then he wouldn't sign it. Nesseth said he had to go to a quiet place and read the contract to himself. The whole office was empty. I really didn't understand what he meant by quiet.

'After an hour I walked in to see how Roy was doing. We're talking about a forty-page agreement and he's on page four. I come back an hour later. He's back to page three. It was ridiculous. I just took the contracts into John's office and spread them out on his couch. I told him he could either sign them or I was going home. After he signed, I yelled through the door at Roy that the contracts were signed. He never said a word.'

Roy Nesseth had finally got beaten by someone tougher than he was and he didn't like it. Although he had done most of the negotiating, he blamed Kimmerly for letting De Lorean sign the deal. Beyond the conditions of the repurchase, the contract also called for a bulk sale announcement to all of De Lorean's creditors. It was a risky proposition. Some creditors – especially the British government – might fear that all the company's assets would be dissolved in the transaction and try to force an involuntary bankruptcy.

Rather than go ahead with the bulk sale announcements as they promised, De Lorean's brains trust let the bank's restraining order languish while they hunted up other sources of money. Consolidated soon got the picture and tried to intervene, since its deal with De Lorean could solve the Bank of America's problems. 'Roy tried to chase me out of the court during one of the Bank of America hearings,' a Consolidated lawyer says. 'He kept telling me I didn't belong there.'

Meanwhile, De Lorean was actively pursuing other deals. One was with Budget Rent A Car. The company's chief executive, Morris Belzberg, had dealt with De Lorean back in the days when he ran Chevrolet. 'I thought he was a remarkable person,' Belzberg says. 'Our deal went through two phases – the first would have us purchase one thousand cars. Those would be repurchased between four and six months later. Evidently he would take the dollars from our purchase to satisfy his loan requirements with Bank of America. But this deal fell through when my lawyers felt we could be involved in some sort of litigation if the company did go into bankruptcy. They felt we wouldn't end up with proper title to the cars and they were afraid receivers could then step in and take the cars back.

'The next deal involved a lease. They'd get so many millions for that. Each car would have a few months' lease and then they'd be turned back. But by then I got a call from Schottenstein. He had evidently read about the deal in the press, and he said, "If you want to lease cars, lease them from me."

'I called Nesseth and he said, "Don't worry. I'll handle him. His deal is not a deal. We'll go ahead with our deal." But by then we decided we couldn't go ahead. We were concerned by our exposure, and when we called several dealers, they told us, "We're not being paid for warranty." That meant we ran the risk that if something went wrong with one of our cars, dealers wouldn't service them.

'Little by little we were also concerned by Mr Nesseth's behaviour. He would make statements that wouldn't bear up later, especially regarding the Bank of America. They told us they'd have nothing more to do with Nesseth and that if I did, I should proceed with caution. He really didn't accept no for an answer. At one point I was in San Francisco for a meeting with our parent company, Transamerica, and I became ill with a bleeding ulcer. While I lay in the hospital, Nesseth kept calling me. I was really in no condition to get into arguments with him, and somehow he didn't understand that.'

Nesseth and De Lorean were very blunt with Belzberg about their unwillingness to go ahead with the Consolidated deal, and Schottenstein could see they were reluctant suitors. He says, 'They seemed to have a fear of completion. Sometimes details arose which De Lorean wasn't familiar with and then seemed reluctant to get.'

Meanwhile Roy was becoming more of a nuisance. 'He kept giving me a distorted picture of what each party involved was saying,' Schottenstein explains. 'So I arranged for representatives from the bank, Budget and the receiver to meet at De Lorean's office. Roy tried to put us each in a separate office and wouldn't let us talk to each other. When I saw what was happening, I started knocking on the doors and telling them to come out. Roy yelled back, "You can't come in here."

'The whole thing was so amateurish it was almost funny. We all finally got together in the lobby to find out what the real story was. I don't know what the relationship was between Nesseth and De Lorean, but from my point of view it wasn't doing John or the company any good.'

At last in April, with no other source of funds and the bank threatening to take in all the cars and auction them off, De Lorean went ahead with the Consolidated deal. To the surprise of executives and bankruptcy lawyers, the British government did not force an involuntary bankruptcy. Instead, the receivers made arrangements with Shenk and Schottenstein to purchase some of their excess stock.

But in the minds of the remaining few executives at the top of the company the bulk sale was as good as a bankruptcy. 'The night they shipped out all their titles to Consolidated,' one insider says, 'they were dead in the water.'

Trapped in a Terrible Tower

During the last spring and summer of his car company's life, John De Lorean was spending an increasing amount of time at his Pauma Valley ranch. Often he came alone and for days conducted his business by phone out on the flagstone patio by the pool.

The four houses and fifty acres had been on the block since 1979 when he sold the avocado groves. Cristina never did like the place, and told visitors she was worried about snakes in the grass. She did not like being out in the middle of nowhere.

But as his life grew more complex and difficult, John appeared to love the solitude even more. He could no longer look out at the neighbouring hills and say they were his. Still, as he lay sunning himself by the pool, there must have been some serenity in wealth. He could look down from the piece of mountain side he still had left, or watch his three Mexican hands move easily through their tasks, their little dogs chasing after them.

Back in college, when he wrote, 'Know you what it is to be an Engineer?' he answered, 'It is to be trapped in a terrible tower of pure science.' Evidently he liked that image, because he practically repeated it further in the piece, writing, 'It is to suffer a throne alone in your terrible Temple of Science . . .'

In the middle of 1982, De Lorean was trapped in another sort of tower, and if he still sat on a throne, he did suffer its burdens alone. The way he reached these heights had nothing to do with 'pure science'. In fact, as he discovered long before, a mastery of physics or engineering was not enough to attain affluence in America. If he had remained just an engineer, the corporate laws of gravity would have kept him back at Pontiac, poring over the drafting board during the day and going home to quiet evenings with his pretty blonde suburban wife.

Real success lay in the hazy fields of finance and public relations, but the greater the gains, the more ignominious the losses. The college

249

student once felt he could design his way out of any engineering problem. The business tycoon would find his predicaments far more complicated and far more intractable.

Never before had John De Lorean's name been so publicly associated with failure. In all the other deals that went bad, like Saf-Guard and Grand Prix, he had been insulated from disrepute. But the car company was different. His greatest accomplishment had been to bring his dream to world attention. Now the spotlight wouldn't go away.

In the past, when the fortunes of his little companies turned sour, he could turn to Roy and Tom. But it became clear that neither one was capable of the big solution that would save the De Lorean Motor Company. Roy had not delivered his Boise dealer friend as the Canadian distributor and that dashed hopes for at least $750,000.

As for Kimmerly, he had not produced on the stock issue, nor had he got the best possible deal from Consolidated. On 12 March Kimmerly resigned from the board, along with Henry Bushkin and G. Edmund King. Kimmerly later explained the move by saying that his new status would enable him to represent De Lorean in lawsuits if the need arose, although trial law would have been an unusual new tack for the tax counsel so late in his career.

'The tougher the Consolidated deal looked,' one of the financial executives says, 'the more John and Roy held it against Tom. During the spring De Lorean froze Tom out of the key decisions in the company.'

As of 3 March, against the advice of all of his lawyers, De Lorean started issuing all company disbursements on his own bank accounts. A new multi-million dollar credit facility at Citibank helped him swing the bigger payments. The move was touched off when Gene Cafiero's lawyers served a writ on the bank accounts of the car company to recover the $180,000 that remained in his contract settlement.

For the skeleton crew that stayed on in California the company entered a strange limbo period. Most of the senior staff left with Brown. The two key replacements would be Steven Allred as the new chief financial officer for the sales division and Bruce McWilliams, the vice president in charge of advertising. Both had tangled with C.R. in the past, although both would later admit that their perspective would change once they arrived in California.

Previously associated with American marketing for Mercedes and British Leyland, McWilliams was a gentle and genteel man who could offer De Lorean a welcome diversion from the troubles of the day with erudite talk about international motoring. He had joined the company in 1981 and helped secure the supplier ads like Cutty Sark and Goodyear. Subsequently he got into disputes with Brown over the miniscule advertising budget, but he now believes that De Lorean was the entire cause of their feud. 'John likes to pit people against each other,' he says. 'He was telling each of us different things.'

McWilliams had no inkling of the chaos that was to follow in the wake of Brown's departure. 'My total preoccupation was in keeping the place afloat – nothing more complicated than that. I arrived to find a bare-bones staff completely demoralized. They spent their days milling around. Some of them were bringing suit to collect their pay. They'd be offended if I lifted up the phone and ask why we couldn't spend the long distance phone costs on them.

'As far as bills were concerned, we owed everybody. Creditors were storming the place. These guys would come in, sit in the lobby and refuse to leave until they got paid.

'There was one cliffhanger after another. Every week was a cliffhanger as to whether we'd get pay-roll from John, and then it was a matter of finding cheque cashing companies that would handle his personal cheques so people didn't have to wait two weeks for them to clear.

'Then there was the cliffhanger whether we'd sell enough cars to make the Consolidated quota. We'd be on the phone from early in the morning to late at night pushing it through.'

McWilliams tried to get his head high enough above water to envisage some rudimentary sales campaign. In one of his first moves he had De Lorean send out a flyer marked, 'Urgent and Important To All Dealers'. Claiming that the purchase of just six cars apiece could 'save the [company's marketing] program', the telegram asked for 'total commitment now by the entire dealer organization'. It ended, 'Please call or cable what you can do. God bless you all.'

One other staff member remembers: 'When John saw the copy of that telegram, he said, "This has got to be the end." '

'We sent telegrams to 345 dealers,' McWilliams says. 'Out of all those dealers only one Mid-West dealer responded. He wrote back, "No thanks." '

Early in May, McWilliams did manage to pull off a more beneficial effort gathering forty dealers from the south-western region for a meeting. 'Our California dealers were just desperate to know whether the company would survive. John was absolutely incensed that I tried to organize this meeting. He said he wasn't going to come. He accused me of panicking. I answered, "You must come, John. These people idolize you." I think he truly was terrified of being heckled.'

'Our regional directors were convinced he wouldn't show. He was late, but he turned out to be an enormous success. I think he more than assured the dealers about the company. Of course, John didn't tell the truth. He claimed the twin-turbo engine would be ready by the next year, and there was no way that would happen. When they asked about a shop manual, he said it was coming from the printer.

'But he was so well received, he came up later to thank me for forcing him into doing it.'

However, by June, McWilliams was gone, the principal reason being Nesseth. 'I never really knew about Roy until I moved to Irvine,' he says. 'All John told me about Roy was that he'd do the dirty work. He said, "Some people are mean from time to time, or mean in some way or other, but that Roy Nesseth was a mean man who enjoyed being mean."'

'We had no idea what sorts of laws the men he brought in were breaking. We knew two were ranchers, one was a distributor for some sort of Amway or Mary Kay company and the other a nebulous realtor.'

When Roy swept in, pandemonium followed. He was making deals over the phone to sell off cars; he was shouting threats to suppliers; he was constantly arguing with practically everyone in the office. There were still a few lawsuits trailing after Roy, and at times, when the staff got too sick of his bellowing voice, one or the other would call the sheriff to let him know that Roy was back in town.

Life for Roy had never been more hectic. 'Roy lived on airplanes,' Gus Davis says. 'The man didn't think anything of booking three or four different flights in different directions and not deciding where he was going to go until he got to the airport.'

Davis had to deal with Roy's peripatetic habits when he worked with him at the De Lorean Manufacturing Company in Logan, Utah. 'One day we were discussing a contract with a firm in Geneva, and without any warning, Roy just went and took the next flight to Geneva. The next thing we know, he's demanding to speak to the chief executive of our distributor there, who just happened to be out of the office that day. I don't think John was too happy with that trip.'

What disturbed McWilliams and Allred the most was the way Roy's son Jeff had the run of the premises. 'It got to the point where my salesmen didn't have company cars while four were sitting in the Nesseth family driveway,' McWilliams says. 'One day Jeff brought his De Lorean into the shop to be fixed and Allred wouldn't let him take it out. I think Allred at least asked that one of the other cars be returned in its place. Well, we are in the midst of a board meeting when all of a sudden young Nesseth barges in and screams he wants his car. I told him to leave the premises and if I saw him hanging around again I'd call the police. I called John about it, but he really didn't care less. The next thing I know, Roy corners me to say he'd separate my head from my shoulders.'

Those threats, combined with the fact that he had not been paid in almost a month, sent McWilliams back home to the East Coast. De Lorean was not in a position to crack down on Nesseth. He was keeping the company afloat between his deals with suppliers and his new methods of finance. The major hitch with the Consolidated contract was that Shenk required cash before he delivered a title. But the car company couldn't get cash from the dealer until it delivered the car. Roy's solution was to use his dealer friends for the bridge financing. They'd advance him $13,500 to get the title from Consolidated, and once he got the money from the dealer, he gave some of the profit back to his financier. Contractually, Consolidated required that the cars not be sold for any less than $17,500. But to meet the three months' sales quotas, Roy was often letting cars go for much less – and in some special circumstances for hardly any more than his cost. Among those recipients was Chuck De Lorean and one of Roy's dealer/bankers who did so well selling the De Loreans that he considered buying the company. However, word of the special discounts reached some of the companies original limited partner/dealers, and a group of five paid a visit to see for themselves. The invoices they saw confirmed their suspicions. A few suspended their orders before they left and promised not to buy another car.

With all of Roy's fudging, the company was hitting the Consolidated sales quotas, but not meeting the other payments due. To make the first contractual ninety-day tab in July, De Lorean dug into his own pocket and came up with $300,000.

By now California comptroller Allred had left along with McWilliams. An accountant from Belfast was brought in to take his place but soon after, Irvine lost the woman who handled accounts receivables. She was unceremoniously marched out of the building when she continued to prevent the 'henchmen' from filling in additional figures in their settlements with suppliers.

No amount of budget-stretching by Roy was going to save the company. De Lorean had to find a major investor, not only to start production in Belfast, but also to help wrest the existing inventory away from Consolidated.

After Blair dropped out of the picture, the closest De Lorean came to another angel was New York City property dealer, Peter Kalikow. Back in his college days, Kalikow was bitten with the auto bug and for a few years he tried producing a line of hand-tooled cars in Italy. He returned to the more concrete world of his family's construction business in Manhattan and helped make it one of the city's most successful developers. A mutual friend introduced Kalikow to De Lorean, and it took the builder only a few weeks in April to come up with a plan. Kalikow says he was ready to sink $35 million into the project, and he admits, 'I never drove the car or even sat in it. From what I've read and seen, I thought there was nothing wrong with it that wouldn't be too monumental to solve. My dealing with De Lorean was straight forward. I wanted him to remain involved with dealers and marketing, but I felt he couldn't handle production – that was the company's primary problem. We spent about five weeks preparing a plan. I wanted the British government involved, because I wasn't ready to pour money into their factory. They built it. They put it in a lousy location – why did I have to be responsible for capitalizing it?'

Sir Kenneth Cork sent his assistant, Paul Shewell, to talk further with Kalikow, but he didn't find the developer in a mood to haggle over his offer. 'I'm not a lawyer,' Kalikow says. 'When I say ten, I don't mean eight.' Realizing that the British would put no more money into the assembly plant, Kalikow ended all negotiations.

Following Kalikow's withdrawal, every few weeks De Lorean heralded the approach of another new backer or group of backers. There were investors from the Far East, and investors from the Middle East. There were investors comprised of car dealers on the West Coast, and other dealers who might invest from the Mid-West. One potential backer was from Cleveland and rumoured to be allied with Chuck De Lorean, although soon after his name appeared in the press his phone was disconnected and all trace of his company vanished. De Lorean identified another solitary sugar daddy as a California insurance man 'worth $60 million'.

De Lorean's plethora of promising prospects should have tried the patience of the British officials, but a Commonwealth island other than Ireland was attracting the government's attention. After Argentina invaded the Falklands, the De Lorean Motor Company faded entirely from the limelight. Besides, in one day, Her Majesty's armed forces were spending as much as the nation's entire $150 million investment in the stainless steel car.

Both the distraction and the new financial perspective of the Falklands War offered De Lorean some breathing space, but no real chance for a major investor emerged. Instead he had the time to engage in another sort of deal, which – to his great misfortune – he would eventually consummate.

The genesis of this deal, De Lorean says, went back four years earlier to Pauma Valley, when his son Zachary started playing with an older boy who lived down the road. The playmate's father, James Hoffman, was never very specific about how he made his living. Instead, he told his wealthy neighbours vague tales about dangerous escapades in South America. At that time, De Lorean says, his contact with Hoffman was limited to a brief chat on his drive after their sons had come back from an outing.

They would not meet face to face again until 11 July 1982. By then, unbeknownst to De Lorean, Hoffman had agreed with federal authorities to be a confidential informant in narcotics investigations. Hoffman's version of his subsequent meetings with his one-time neighbour would be part of the eventual indictment for drug trafficking issued against De Lorean by the federal grand jury for the central district of California. Before his trial, the defendant chose the *Rolling Stone* magazine as the forum for his side of the story.

It was Hoffman who called him, according to De Lorean's interview, and offered to help raise some money to save the car company. Both men agree they first met to discuss the deal in the stuccoed bar of the Newport Beach Marriott Hotel, only a few miles down the road from De Lorean's Irvine office. Hoffman, De Lorean says, claimed he could come up with $15 million in return for a $1.8 commission. Narcotics crept into their conversation, but De Lorean contends that Hoffman was talking about what he might do with his commission. Still, his talk did not scare De Lorean away. He continued to follow Hoffman around the country to meetings with the broker's other 'investors'.

Their negotiations picked up pace in early September. The two got together again in the plush L'Enfant Plaza Hotel in Washington, D.C. Then, De Lorean says, Hoffman first insisted that the funds be deposited in an escrow bank account so he could collect commission without the knowledge of the investors he corralled. During this exchange, De Lorean tells *Rolling Stone*, he first became frightened about Hoffman's connections and decided to make believe he had a few tough guys in his corner as well. Only months before, De Lorean had complained to British reporters that the IRA terrorists were partly responsible for the demise of his car company. Now he informed Hoffman that the Irish Republican Army were on his side in his search for funds.

Four days later, De Lorean again met Hoffman in San Carlos, California, just a few miles south of San Francisco. There, he was introduced to a man he thought was an officer at the Eureka Federal Savings and Loan Association. Banker James Benedict was, in fact, FBI Agent Benedict Tisa, who was performing in one of the federal government's best-kept sting operations. Eureka was an authentic bank, and the chairman of the board, Kenneth Kidwell (his real name), had been gutsy enough to let federal agents use his operation to lure big-time drug dealers in search of laundries for their cash collections.

Two weeks later, De Lorean was in another hotel, the Bel Air Sands of Los Angeles, meeting strangers at Hoffman's behest. This time, the guest of honour was Morgan Hetrick, who did not hide the fact that he had made his fortune as a narcotics smuggler. De Lorean later described him as 'an old, fatherly schoolteacher type', although Hetrick is in fact seven years younger than De Lorean. Coincidentally, he had once known Cristina and had developed a crush on her, when he was the pilot for her old flame, Fletcher Jones. The two had often talked as

Hetrick flew her to and from the computer magnate. Shortly after Jones' death, Hetrick tried to date the boss's girlfriend, which didn't sit well with Cristina. According to De Lorean, 'she got pissed [off] that the guy would be so callous and insensitive'. Still, De Lorean gave his wife a chance to renew her acquaintance with the pilot when he invited her out to dinner with his new associates, including 'Benedict' and Hetrick, at the ritzy Beverly Hills restaurant, La Scala. Despite the millions of dollars he had amassed, Hetrick rarely wore anything but a tattered, soiled jumpsuit. His money was spent in other places, and often, as on this night, he had a teenage prostitute in tow. It's difficult to imagine how De Lorean explained the motley dinner companions to Cristina.

De Lorean had one more important hotel meeting, in L.A.'s Westin Bonaventure, before Hetrick left to make his Columbia pick-up. This time, De Lorean was introduced to a Drug Enforcement Agency man who openly acknowledged that he was a drug distributor with mafia connections. By now, De Lorean had backed away from putting any cash into the transaction. Claiming he no longer had the $1.8 million of commission for Hoffman, he offered shares instead. They were from De Lorean Motor Cars, Inc., an umbrella company formed to circumvent creditors if De Lorean ever managed to start manufacturing again. When he turned it over to the purported mafioso, it was hardly worth the paper it was printed on.

Of course, federal prosecutors and De Lorean have two different interpretations of his role in the Hoffman deal. The authorities say he willingly conspired eventually to bring 220 pounds of cocaine into the country and share in the $60 million of proceeds. Although the stock was worthless, they still charge De Lorean had made a deal with the banker to exchange it for $1.8 million and his $15 million share (Hetrick managed to smuggle sixty pounds of cocaine back to Los Angeles).

De Lorean maintains he never intended to take an active role in a drug deal – only to find an investor for his company. When he discovered the nature of Hoffman's investors and tried to back out, he says, Hoffman threatened the lives of his children.

Whoever may be telling the truth, one point is certain: during the course of his association with Hoffman and the undercover agents, De Lorean acted alone.

An important deadline, one set by the British government, was facing De Lorean. Only a few weeks before, De Lorean had signed an agreement with the receivers giving him control of the plant if he could come up with just $10 million by 18 October. But the day came and went and no money appeared in the company bank account. Although other deadlines had come and gone in the past, this deadline Secretary of State Prior declared as the final, final deadline. (De Lorean has since charged that American officials warned the British government that the auto executive's arrest was imminent, so that ministers would not be embarrassed if he did indeed raise money in time to secure the factory. However, this theory has one major flaw – why would the narcotics officials jeopardize their sting by removing the honey that they thought was attracting the renegade bee?)

Clearly, De Lorean entertained some hope of getting back his factory when late in the afternoon of 19 October, he walked into the Sheraton La Reina Hotel near the Los Angeles International Airport. Just one day before, Morgan Hetrick had gone to Room 501 to pick up his pay for the cocaine haul and was arrested before the night was over. Unaware of Hetrick's bust, De Lorean followed his footsteps into Room 501. When he was shown the smuggler's handiwork, packed in a suitcase, he appeared jubilant. Grabbing a bag of coke, he issued forth with the words that a hundred newspaper headlines would memorialize: 'This is as good as gold,' and it came 'in the nick of time'.

Videotape cameras then show him passing around the wine glasses and offering a toast. He was in fact frightened, he told *Rolling Stone*, but still happy: 'What I was toasting was starting up the factory again'.

What he was toasting was a Lazarus-like climb back from the grave, and an amazing new addition to the De Lorean legend. The last two years of product quality flaws, court cases, poor sales and British receivers would be forgotten. Once again, John De Lorean had pulled off the miracle when all around expected him to fail.

Moments later the police told him he was under arrest.

At first there would be stunned silence. But when the agents closed his wrists in handcuffs, he said, 'You have the wrong man.'

Aftermath

For John Z. De Lorean, one dream has been fulfilled. His name will surely take its place alongside the auto industry pioneers of the twentieth century. But contrary to his plans, any historical prominence he receives will be tied to the grand scale of his failure – not his success. Before law enforcement officials slammed his business career to a halt, his rush for glory touched the lives of thousands and cost the British government, investors and suppliers over $250 million.

Not everyone associated with De Lorean can be called a casualty. Engineers at General Motors still speak fondly of his inspirational leadership – although few want to be quoted. Young executives who worked at the De Lorean Motor Company are obviously more cynical about De Lorean's abilities, but are still grateful for what they call a 'once in a lifetime' opportunity to help start up a car company. Fittingly, those who profited most from De Lorean's dream car were the dealers. Company executives know of no dealer who did not at least recover his $25,000 stake before De Lorean's arrest. Most did far better – especially those who didn't stick with the price on the label in those heady days when the cars first appeared in America. While most dealers were stuck with unpaid warranty claims, they found the service charges more than offset by the added showroom traffic the stainless steel curiosities generated.

But when all the ledger sheets of John De Lorean's various ventures are totalled in both human and economic terms, the losses far outweigh the gains. The losers range from De Lorean's own brother, Jack, to J. Peter Grace; Clark Higley and Gerry Dahlinger to cabinet ministers of two British governments. The most visible and most pathetic victims of De Lorean's shattered schemes are the 2600 Irish workers at his plant and the thousands more employed by local suppliers. Some, like shop steward Malachy Higgins, gave up precious jobs to get on board. Others, like shop steward Billy Parker, never knew steady employment. For the majority, the pay-cheques lasted no more than a few months in 1981 – deceptively long enough to finance deposits on homes and the few luxury items they never expected to see in their own living rooms.

However, despite the disparaging comments De Lorean later made about Belfast, factory workers do not blame him for the company's demise. They point instead at the Conservative government of Margaret Thatcher. But whatever the Tories' philosophy, De Lorean's extravagance and heavy-handed bargaining tactics provided the perfect argument against future government subsidies of private enterprise.

Among the unsuccessful bidders for the Belfast factory in the summer of 1982 was a group of British suppliers who planned resuming a limited production of the TR7 – a sports car discontinued by British Leyland. Technically a proven product, the little car had established enough of a market in the US – annual sales of 8000 – to support the scaled-down operation of the assembly plant with a tidy profit thrown in. The group still needed subsidies of ten million dollars, but after De Lorean, the government was no more likely to condone aid to a sports car company than it was to purchase the Brooklyn Bridge.

For the men who ran the De Lorean Motor Company, no other aspect of John De Lorean's debacle is more disturbing than the bad name he's given independent motor manufacturers. In spite of De Lorean, they say, they proved that a revolutionary new product could roll off the assembly line and be marketed in America. In their minds, just a few right calls from the man at the top could have made the whole project viable.

For these executives, De Lorean's involvement with cocaine is the most bitter of denouements. Sharing the blame for the car company's demise was bad enough. But then, one morning in October 1982, they woke up to find their reputations hazarded even further by unwitting association with De Lorean and his scandalous funding ploy. In their eyes, De Lorean represents more than a symbol of avarice or incompetence and it takes an evangelist's son like C.R. Brown to verbalize their loathing. 'When I look at John,' he says, 'I can see the devil.'

For anyone taking a more dispassionate look at John De Lorean and the course of his career, it is difficult not to see him as one more victim of his unrealized dreams. It would be wrong to write him off as no more than a con man. There's little evidence to suggest that De Lorean ever entered deals solely to bilk people, corporations or governments. Nothing would have pleased him more if the sundry ventures he started had truly blossomed to the benefit of everyone involved. That success alone may have been his greatest reward. The unethical practices most often stemmed from his attempts to sort out the chaotic consequences of his managerial incompetence.

If anything, the media taught De Lorean that a good front was all that was needed to cover a variety of sins. Speaking for other car company executives, C.R. Brown says, 'We wanted John to be what he said he was,' and evidently reporters were of the same persuasion. Rarely did they look for the substance that lay behind the bold rhetoric. The maverick auto engineer was too compelling a character to be deflated with investigative journalism.

For De Lorean, the impressive stack of press clippings were a potent weapon. No other entrepreneur in business history used publicity as well in amassing his seed capital, and he found that investors were as unlikely to look behind his image as reporters. In the skewed double standards of his finance, De Lorean underwent only the most cursory check into his background before he was loaned hundreds of millions of dollars. Ironically, if there had been anything small-time about De Lorean, the banks and the British government might have persevered in turning up the business failures and court cases that followed his resignation from General Motors. But there was nothing small-time about De Lorean. The ability of his car company to spring forth fully capitalized remains an unparalleled feat. Still, it was never big enough for De Lorean. The chief executive pushed his factory into higher gear, even when sales in the United States dictated against increased production: one more hype to help sell his $20 million share float.

His executives claim that the company could have survived without the share issue if De Lorean had lowered his sights and been satisfied with just turning out a few thousand cars a year. Unfortunately, such practical thinking would never have got De Lorean off the ground. In today's world of manufacturing, the costs of a plant and equipment make it virtually impossible to build up an assembly line product gradually. Only an artist working on a grand scale could have realized the production of a newly designed car. Only a canvas of the largest dimensions could have swept up the executives, suppliers and investors needed to finish the picture.

De Lorean as much as anyone else became a prisoner of his own outsized vision. Eventually no one became more deluded and daunted by De Lorean's favourable and uninformed press than De Lorean himself. A Wizard of Oz, he scrambled behind the curtain to maintain his credibility, turning the levers over to more dynamic types like Roy Nesseth with no concern about the methods they used to keep his reputation and investment intact.

But finally, De Lorean was left alone in his shrouded booth. If he had been just a con man, he would not have offered to invest $5 million before he would accept Prior's offer to restructure the debt on the Belfast factory, and he would not have bothered to use his own bank account to keep the car company afloat when all around him saw it sinking. 'How could you tell him it was all over,' one advisor explains, 'he had pulled off so many miracles before?'

De Lorean remained the last believer in John De Lorean's ability to work miracles, and pride, above all else, dictated his desperate attempts to save his company. Eventually, there were no more hopes for a quick killing in the stock market or another windfall from a gullible investor, but De Lorean was out to salvage his reputation as the ethical business man who could survive in the savage world of finance, and in his effort to preserve the image, he was ready to destroy the substance. By getting involved with Hoffman and the federal agents he thought were mafiosi, De Lorean was not playing the part of the devil but was knowingly dealing with the devil.

Once again, no words on De Lorean's activity are more damning than his own. He admits to *Rolling Stone* reporter Aaron Latham that when he decided to deal with Eureka Bank, he believed it might have been controlled by Mafia interests. Where, Latham asked, did De Lorean think the bank money came from? His answer: 'It could be organized crime. It could be drugs. It could be anything. But as long as it came to us through a recognized financial institution, I really didn't give a shit. To be very candid.'

It could be anything . . .

In just those few words, the whole De Lorean façade collapses. If it could have been anything, why did he not compromise himself and stay at General Motors? Why did he create the 'corporate citizen' if he were ready to resort to anything to keep it alive?

There are no firm answers. The questions ring only with the hollow-ness of De Lorean's pretensions. Ironically, in claiming that law enforcement authorities went to illegal ends to entrap him, De Lorean points to his own exalted reputation as the cause for their malevolent designs. He explains to Latham that he was the lure to hook drug smuggler Hetrick. 'Until they used me and my name, they couldn't get Hetrick to go ahead and get into a transaction.' Later he speculates that GM was behind the set-up or even the IRA via influential American friends. He concludes his speculation by adding, 'I'm a fifty-eight-year-old guy who knows nothing but how to build automobiles. I'm not that important a guy. I don't understand.'

De Lorean surely does understand, and his importance came crashing home to him after his arrest. The glamour he so carefully cultivated made him prime meat for the media. In twenty-four hours he learned how quickly his crystalline reputation could shatter. Periodicals that had been circumspect about his car company were suddenly recycling the grist of the few negative stories ever done about him. Industry executives who once had only kinds words or silence about De Lorean were coming out with derogatory anecdotes.

Fame was no longer something that got him the best table at '21', it also brought international shame and degradation. On the front pages of newspapers the world over were pictures of a haggard De Lorean in his open-necked shirt. All the careful cosmetic conditioning fell away. From some angles, the loose flesh on his neck betrayed his age, but for those who knew him especially well, the awkward way he held his head was at the same time reminiscent of the shy, homely adolescent of so many years before.

Worse than the newspaper photos were the TV transmissions that followed. One clip, a day after his arrest, showed De Lorean getting on board a transport bus in a blue prison jumpsuit, manacles on his hands and legs. In England, Colin Chapman, estranged from De Lorean for over a year, saw the scene and cried.

If John De Lorean had not become so important – if he had remained just a guy who knew nothing but how to build automobiles – he wouldn't have been brought to the public pillory. But then again, he probably wouldn't have found himself dealing with narcotics agents.

Perhaps such thoughts cross John De Lorean's mind as he awaits the eventual verdict on his narcotics indictment. As the years have passed, he has become even more tied to his wife and children. His unwillingness to be away from home for long, his car company executives say, jeopardized his business. Now, as he faces what could be a life sentence, his attempts to save his business have jeopardized his family.

Shortly after his arrest, De Lorean was seen clutching a Bible on his way to and from the courthouse. A few months before his trial was set to begin, he and Cristina were reported to have taken their vows as born-again Christians. Such behaviour, sceptics might say, was no more than posturing – this time to impress a jury. Indeed, a Detroit television reporter learned that De Lorean had written to the director of a suburban camp for disadvantaged children, asking him to send a letter about the motor executive's past service to the charity. The request only backfired when the camp director publicly replied that the real benefactor had been De Lorean's second wife, Kelly Harmon, and not De Lorean.

But De Lorean's turn to religion cannot be dismissed as a charade. Close friends say he occasionally went to church before his arrest. Often prayer gave him solace during his most difficult business and personal trials. Probably no words in the Bible would have more significance to a contrite De Lorean than the admonition from the Preacher in Ecclesiastes, 'Vanity of vanities; all is vanity.'

Nevertheless, it's hard for the world to imagine John De Lorean closeted in his house poring over a Bible. Once it saw another John De Lorean. This image was his greatest creation; greater than any car he engineered at General Motors or the car he had engineered after he left.

It was the image of a handsome man of deep moral conviction and great talent building his own car only as he knew how to build it.

We return now to John De Lorean in his office, standing in front of a world-wide map or some other business graph.

He says something like this: 'Our dream is coming true, and justifying the calculated risk we took. Sure, I'm a risk taker. And the people who drive our De Lorean car are probably risk takers, too. People who dare to lead other people . . . People who live life to its fullest potential . . . People who enjoy the special exhilaration of making things happen . . . People who dream of a better world, and do whatever is needed to transform that dream into reality.'

John De Lorean is next shown sitting inside his car. He ends by saying, 'As hard as I've struggled, I'm one man who can say that my dream has come true. Our difficult efforts have succeeded, life is good and I'm grateful!'

Then De Lorean closes the car and drives off onto a handsome modern high-way with elegant city skyscrapers in the background. Closing music and credits appear over this final radiant scene.

INDEX

Adams, Tom 51, 58, 65
Alfa Romeo 138, 187
Allegheny Ludlum 135
Allison aircraft engines 33
Allred, Stephen 250, 252, 253
Allstate Insurance Company
    122, 135, 138, 145
America, Bank of 196, 203, 230,
    232, 240, 242, 243, 246, 247
American Express 115
American Lawyer 119
American Motors 98, 148, 196
Amway 252
Andersen, Arthur 80, 185, 186,
    200
Anderson, Robert 50, 64, 66,
    139, 154, 183
Andress, Ursula 130
Ann-Margaret 50
Arkus-Duntov, Zora 40, 133,
    134
Arrington, Stephen Lee 9
Aston-Martin 216
Atkins, Humphrey 180, 181
Audio Systems Inc. 241
Automotives Industries 57
Avrea, Bill 98, 99
Avrea, Shirley 96–104
Avrea, Walter C. 'Pete' 96–105,
    112

Bache Halsey Inc. 231
Bank of England 169
Barcelo, Carlos Romero 158
Bankers' Trust Building 186
Barclay's Bank 182
Bedminster 194, 237, 241
Belfast 13, 149, 154, 155, 156,
    157, 158, 173–82, 192, 198,
    199, 200, 202, 204, 208, 209,

210, 211, 212, 219, 222, 225,
    228, 229, 230, 232, 233, 234,
    236, 237, 240, 253, 259, 260
Bell 17
Belzberg, Morris 247, 248
Bendix Corporation 102
Benedict, James 255, 256
Benjamin, Robert 238, 242
Bennett, Harry 19
Bennington, Charles K. 176,
    177, 178, 198, 199, 200, 201,
    208
Bergen, Candice 130
Bertone, Giuseppe 138
Beverly Hills 50, 52, 66, 84, 85,
    238, 240, 242, 256
Bitteroot Mountains 59, 106
Blair, Alan H. 238, 239, 240, 244,
    253
Bloomfield Hills 44, 60, 91, 94,
    117, 118, 131
Bloomingdale, Alfred 148
Bludhorn, Charles 186
Board Room Club 185
Boe, Archie R. 122
Boise 109, 110, 220, 250
BMC 238
Brasch, Mike 124, 125
Bricklin, Malcolm 136, 142, 150,
    153, 245
Bridgewater 209, 237, 243
Brient, Charles L. 245
British Government, the 12, 13,
    149, 179, 182, 187, 200, 232,
    233, 236, 237, 238, 239, 248,
    254, 256, 257, 258, 260
British Leyland 250, 259
Brown, C. R. 140, 141, 142, 143,
    145, 146, 147, 185, 186, 189,
    191, 195, 196, 197, 198, 199,

200, 201, 202, 203, 204,
    209, 210, 211, 212, 213,
    218, 228, 229, 230, 232,
    250, 251, 259, 260
Browning-Ferris Industries
Budget Rent A Car 247
Bugatti 187, 200
Buick Car Company 28, 3‹
Buick cars 97, 113, 114, 1³
Bushkin, Henry 145, 185,
    207, 250
Business Week 53, 128, 140,
Byoir, Carl, and Associate

Cadillac 30, 34, 90, 93, 114,
    132, 140, 209, 215
Cafiero, Eugene 199, 200,
    202, 208, 209, 218, 231,
Cal Prix 93–6
Camaro 208
Campbell-Ewald 51, 58, 5‹
Campian, Reo 18, 20, 91,
Canadian government 136
Carnegie, Dale 57
Carson, John V. 'Johnny'
    153, 185, 201, 213
Cass Technical High Schoc
    90
Caterpillar land movers 9‹
Cavanaugh, Jerry 54
CB radios 125, 126
Celanese Corporation 102
Channing, Carol 131
Chapin, Roy 148
Chapman, Colin 165, 166,
    169, 177, 178, 216, 217,
    225, 262
Charlie's Angels 131
Chemical Bank 163, 167,
Chevrolet 11, 34, 39, 40, 5‹

63, 64, 65, 70, 91, 98, 100, 102, 107, 108, 129, 132, 133, 134, 143, 214, 247

heyfitz, Kirk 152

hicago 24, 85, 213

hicago Bears 124, 213

hris Craft Corporation 121, 144, 158, 163, 164, 165

hrysler 22, 34, 50, 141, 154, 176, 187, 196, 198, 199, 209, 212

hrysler, Walter 136

hrysler Institute 29, 50, 196

hrysler International 208

itroën 187

leveland 93, 130, 212, 254

leveland Diesel 33

ohen, Alan 154, 155, 158

ole, Dolly 71

ole, Edward N. 35, 40, 62, 64, 70, 71, 72, 74, 133

ollins, Bill 35, 39, 40, 42, 132, 136, 137, 138, 143, 144, 145, 150, 164, 165, 166, 177, 197, 212, 216, 217

olumbia 256

ommerce, Department of (Northern Ireland) 180, 182, 184, 229

omposite Technology Corporation 138, 167, 217

oncannon, Don 156, 157, 159, 179

onservative Party 157, 180, 181, 222

onsolidated International 245–8, 250, 251, 253

ontinental Bank of Illinois 171, 203

oopers and Lybrand 233, 242

ork, Sir Kenneth 233, 236, 237, 254

orvair 35, 75

orvette 40, 75, 132, 134, 142, 215, 216

uesta de la Cammalia 129, 130

urrent Biography 127, 129

urtice, Harlow H. 33

ahlinger, Gerald 113–17, 136, 200, 258

ahlinger, Ray 119

ahlinger Pontiac-Cadillac 113–17, 119, 170

aily Express 233

aily Mirror 224, 225, 227

avis, Edward 'Gus' 188, 252

avis, Sammy, Jr. 232

De Lorean, Charles 'Chuck' 91, 93, 142, 211, 254

De Lorean, Jack 63, 64, 90, 258

De Lorean, Kathryn 193

De Lorean, Kathryn Pribak 18, 19

De Lorean, Zachary 18, 19, 131, 193, 254

De Lorean, Zachary Thomas 59

De Lorean Corporation, John Z. 120, 123, 126, 138, 144

De Lorean Dream: A Reality that Works, The 7, 263

De Lorean Manufacturing Corporation 171, 188, 201, 252

De Lorean Motor Cars Inc. 256

De Lorean Motor Cars Ltd 163, 176, 178, 179, 181, 184, 187, 200, 205, 211, 212, 226

De Lorean Motor Cars of America 233

De Lorean Motor Company 7, 12, 13, 14, 67, 80, 89, 120, 130, 138, 140, 144, 145, 148, 149, 163, 164, 165, 170, 179, 185, 186, 192, 197, 201, 203, 220, 221, 223, 228, 236, 240, 241, 243, 245, 250, 254, 258, 259

Democratic Party 53, 54

Detroit Free Press 47, 130, 131, 153

Detroit Lions 91

Detroit News 71

DeVito, R. Anthony 152, 153

Dewey, Robert M. 55, 56, 143, 144, 149, 153, 158, 183, 184, 186, 197, 202

DMC-12 168, 178, 194

DMC-44 187, 189

Drysdale, Don 85, 86

Du Pont 73, 174

Dubin, Maur 186, 193, 220, 223

Dunmurry 173, 174, 198, 224, 230

Durant, William Crapo 28–9, 72, 74, 170

Durant Motor Company 170

Earl, Harley 41

Economic Development Administration 149, 151, 158

Elastic Reservoir Moulding (ERM) 134, 135, 145, 167, 217

Environmental Protection Administration 197, 208

Estes, Elliot M. 'Pete' 32, 35, 39, 40, 42, 43, 48, 56, 63, 72, 75, 129

Eureka Federal Savings 255, 261

Evans, Thomas W. 121

Excalibur 50

Export Credit Guarantee Department 232

Fatjo, Thomas J., Jr. 139, 140, 150

Fawcett, John 22, 26

FBI 9, 255

FCC 126

Federal Farmers' Home Administration 149, 151

Ferrare, Cristina (Mrs John De Lorean) 130–31, 138, 144, 145, 184, 185, 193, 194, 203, 220, 249, 255, 256, 262

Fiat 123

Fiat Lancia 245

Fifth Avenue 10, 131, 144, 164, 184, 193, 240

Fire Auto and Marine 233

Firebird 208

First Bank and Trust of Palm Beach County 170

First Boston Corporation 151

Florida 82, 117, 126, 127, 170, 224

Ford Henry 19, 20, 28, 29, 34, 73, 119, 135

Ford Model T 20, 28, 135

Ford Motor Company 18, 19, 34, 55, 71, 98, 105, 135, 150, 154, 178, 218

Fortune 50, 51, 128

Freeman Chemical Corporation 135

Frye, Wheelabrator 154

Fugazy, William D. 121

Gallacher Report 63, 64, 71

Gay, Peter 11

General Electric 19, 68

General Motors 10, 11, 18, 34, 35, 36, 37, 39, 40–44, 50, 51, 52, 53, 55, 56, 57, 60, 62, 64–73, 90, 91, 100, 102, 104, 107, 108, 113, 114, 116, 118–22, 125, 127, 128–33, 136, 137, 139, 140, 142, 143, 146, 150, 157, 166, 170, 178, 181, 183, 190, 192, 193, 195, 208, 211, 214, 216, 218, 236, 239, 258, 260, 261, 263

General Motors, On a Clear Day

You Can See 11, 18, 28, 31, 36, 41, 55, 57, 60, 71, 74, 128, 183, 190, 208, 214, 228
Georgia Pacific 85
Gerstenberg, Richard C. 62, 63, 72, 120
Gibson, Marian 193, 220–27
Gilbert, Ross 241, 242
Giugiaro, Giorgetto 138, 177, 194, 199, 215
Goodman, Lord 227
Goodyear Tires 195, 250
Gorf, Ken 176, 179, 180, 184, 229
GPA Systems 93, 94, 112
GPD Services 163–72, 181, 185, 219, 225, 226
Grace, J. Peter, Jr. 121, 122, 123, 135, 258
Grace, W.R., and Company 121, 138, 145
Graeffe, Edwin, 25, 26
Grand Canyon 58
Grand Prix of America 90–96, 250
Grant, Cary 66
Gregg, Hamilton 142
Grumman 190
GTO 75
Gulf and Western 186

Haddad, Bill 54, 72, 164, 175, 180, 189, 190, 192, 221, 222, 224, 225
Hammer, Armand 123
Hanson, Earl 243
Harley-Davison 188
Harmon, Kelly 47, 48, 49, 55, 59, 61, 66, 89, 107, 110, 130, 262
Harmon, Tom 47, 48, 59, 60, 86
Harmon, Mrs Tom 47
Harte, Shaun 179, 185
Hegedus, Christopher 178
Henderson, Ronald 179
Hendrickson, Paul 131
Henkel, Robert 7–9
Hethel 166
Hetrick, William Morgan 9, 255, 256, 257, 262
Higgins, Elizabeth 30, 31, 43, 48, 51, 52, 59
Higgins, Malachy 212, 230, 258
Higley, Clark 105–11, 116, 127, 258
Higley, Colleen 105–11
Hilton, Barron 49, 126
Hilton, Nicky 47
Hoffman, James 254, 255, 256, 261

Hollywood (Northern Ireland) 198
Hollywood (USA) 10, 41–61, 66, 130
Honda 150
Hookstratten, E. Gregory 66, 68, 130
Hopkins, Tony 180, 181, 203
House of Commons 157
Houston 115, 139
Houston Petroleum Club 139
Humphrey, Hubert 54
Hunt, Nelson Bunker 121, 124
Hulton, E. F. 140
Hymes, Myles 89

Iacocca, Lee 73, 187
IBM 154
ICI 174
Idaho, Bank of 116
Indianapolis 90, 91
Industrial Engineers, the American Society of 17
Internal Revenue Service 85, 86, 87, 116, 139
Ireland, Northern 154–9, 173–82, 226, 230, 254
Ireland, Republic of 153, 154
Irish Republican Army (IRA) 156, 157, 174, 211, 255, 261
Irvin, Robert 71
Irvine 204, 210, 212, 232, 242, 244, 252, 253, 255
Izuzu 126, 127
Izuzu Diesel North America 127

Javitz, Eric 151
Javitz, Jacob 151
Johnson, Kenneth E. 113, 114, 115
Jones, Fletcher 130, 255, 256
Jordan, Don 83
Juan Carlos, King 150
Juhan, Marie-Denise 164, 168, 169

Kaiser-Frazer 136, 138
Kalikow, Peter 253, 254
Kansas State Bank and Trust Company 113, 117, 170
Kansas State Court 117
Kay, Mary 252
Kennedy, Edward 190
Kennedy, J. F. 54, 189
Kenton, Stan 24
Kerkorian, Kirk 83
Ketteringham Hall 166, 178
Kidwell, Kenneth 255

Kimberly, Michael J. 165
Kimmerly, Thomas 13, 80, 8 95, 114, 116, 117, 118, 11⁹ 138, 139, 144, 151, 167, 18 184, 188, 190, 192, 194, 2(201, 202, 203, 204, 211, 2² 232, 237, 240, 244, 245, 2⁴ 250
King, G. Edmund 153, 185, 2(250
Kissinger, Henry 175
Kitch, Paul 170
Knox, Elyse 48
Knudsen, Semon 'Bunkie' 32– 39, 40, 41, 48, 49, 57, 118, 12⁹ 134
Korean War 90, 92
Krupa, Gene 24

La Jolla 82
Labour Party 179, 180
Lada 123, 187
Lander, Donald H. 208, 209, 21 231, 233
Latham, Aaron 261
Lawrence Institute of Technology 17–26, 56
Lear, Bill 113
Lehman Brothers 148
Lentell, J. V. 114
Lighthouse Point dealership 8 91
Lindsay, John 189
Lisners, John 223, 227
Loasby, Michael 216, 218, 21
Look 55
Los Angeles Auto Dealers' Convention 208
Los Angeles Dodgers 85
Lotus Cars Limited 165, 166, 167, 168, 170, 177, 178, 18 187, 217, 218, 225, 226
Loving, Rush 51
Lucas 218
Lucas, George 190
Lucia, Carroll J. 30, 31, 32
Lundin, Oscar A.

Macclesfield 222
McFarland, Forrest 30, 32
McKinsey and Company 200
McLean, Robert F. 33, 35, 41, 4⁶ 70, 118, 119, 121, 122, 123, 124, 127, 132, 134
McManus, D'Arcy 44
McWilliams, Bruce 250, 251, 252, 253
Madison Avenue 163

266

ia 261
iosi 9, 261
serati 50, 132, 138
son, Roy 156, 157, 179, 228
ttel 187
zda 134, 141, 146, 196, 197,
02, 203
zda RX7 185, 200
aselle, Richard 185, 186, 200
rcedes-Benz 46, 84, 136, 185,
42, 250
rcedes 300SL 117, 136, 300
rcedes 450OSEL 199, 200
rrill Lynch Pierce Fenner and
mith 142
tropolitan Life Insurance
Company 108, 110, 111,
12
chigan 30, 38, 48, 64, 91, 95,
26, 138, 139, 188, 209, 213
chigan Bell 26
chigan Department of
Commerce 120
ni-Cassia Ranch 111, 116
ni-Theater 65, 67
nt Investment 89
sch, Herbert 32
tsubishi 125
, Associates 142
nsanto 114
rgan, William A. 146, 147,
85, 192, 237, 241, 243
tor Trend 52, 53, 136
rdoch, Rupert 223
rphy, Thomas A. 62, 72
rray, Paul F. 207
stang 207

der, Ralph 35, 135
nce, Jim 29, 30, 32
rcotics 14
tional Alliance of
Businessmen 120
tional Highway Traffic
Safety Administration 215
vajo Freight Lines 96
derlander, James 121
lson, Harriet 48
lson, Ozzie 48
lson, Ricky 48
lson, Mrs Ricky 47
sseth, Donald 83, 107
sseth, Jeff 252
sseth, Roy Sigurd 12, 13,
66-7, 68, 70, 79-90, 92-5, 96,
100-104, 107-12, 114-17,
119, 143, 147, 186, 188, 189,
198, 200, 220, 232, 236, 237,

240-45, 247, 248, 250, 252,
253, 260
New York Board of Education
189
New York Citibank 182, 203,
239, 250
New York Herald Tribune 189
New York Post 223
New York Times 128, 158, 159
News of the World 223, 227
NFL 67, 126
Ninowski, James, Jr. 91, 94
Nixon, Richard 54
Noonan, John 63, 119
North American Rockwell 64
Northern Ireland Development
Administation (NIDA) 154,
155, 156, 158, 159, 167, 169,
179, 180, 181, 182, 184, 185,
186, 188, 198, 201, 202, 221,
222

Occidental Petroleum 123
O'Connor, Sandra Day 104
Olds 142
Oldsmobile 32, 34, 39, 126, 127,
142
Oppenheimer and Company
151, 155, 158, 163, 181

Pacific International Equipment
86
Packard 29-34
Park Avenue 7, 163, 184, 220
Parker, Billy 172, 182, 230, 258
Pasha International 203, 242, 243
Passages 11, 128
Patrick, U. E. 64, 91
Patrick Petroleum Company 64
Paul, Weiss, Rifkind, Wharton
and Garrison 154, 188
Payne, Thomas 91, 92, 93, 95
Peace Corps 54, 189
Pennebaker, D.A., 178, 195,
216
Penske, Roger 50, 130, 139, 144
Perlen, Stuart 206
Peterbilt 97, 116
Pico Rivera 96
Pietrykowski, Thaddeus 21, 24
Pine Creek Ranch 106-12, 119,
194
Pininfarina, Sergio 138
Pontiac 10, 27, 32, 33-55, 57, 59,
83, 90, 91, 113, 129, 137, 146,
249
Porsche 46, 138, 165, 168
Porsche 914/6 Tapiro 138

Powers, J. D., and Associates
228, 229
Prior, James 230, 233, 234, 236,
238, 256, 260
Prior, Peck 65, 67, 68, 239
Private Eye 227
Prussing, Raymond F. 126, 127,
137, 150
Puerto Rico 146, 149-59

Quality Assurance Centres
209-12, 237, 243, 244, 246
Quirk, John 43, 44, 49, 50, 51, 52,
54, 60

Reese, Emmett 106, 107, 109
Reese, Mrs Emmett 106, 107,
109
Renault 123, 138, 178, 216, 229
Renault Alpine 229
Republican Party, the 53, 54
Road and Track 215
Roberts, Fireball 36
Rocke, James M. 214, 215
Rockwell International 50, 66,
91, 154
Rolling Stone 255, 257, 261
Rowan, Jerry 118
Rudd, A. C. 165
Rumania 18, 123
Rupert 105, 106, 111
Ryder, James 124

Saf-Guard Products 98-105, 112
Saf-Guard Systems 100-105,
112, 116, 119, 250
San Diego 81, 84, 87, 127, 129,
153, 171, 185, 187
San Diego Chargers 49, 59, 63,
126
Schapp, Milton 150
Schmidt, Julacn G. 52, 53
Schottenstein 245, 246, 247, 248
Scotland Yard 224
Scott, Milton Bradley 65, 66, 67,
68, 69, 70, 80, 89, 93
Scottsdale 99, 100, 103
Securities and Exchange
Commission 144, 145, 183,
186, 191, 203, 221, 224, 225
Seigel, Herbert Jay 121
Shamoon, Stella 225
Shasta 121
Shay, Arthur 60, 61
Sheehy, Gail 11, 36, 128
Shell 135
Shenk, Don 245, 246, 248, 253
Shenk, Florence 245

Shewell, Paul 254
Siegel, Ann 193
Siegel, Herb 193
Signature 60
Simon, Norton 193
Simon, William 187
Sinatra, Tina 130
Slavik, Joseph 91, 92, 130
Sloan, Alfred P. 41, 72, 73
Sloan, Allan 152
Smith, C. W. 124, 144
Snider, Lawrence C. 237, 240
Snyder, Tom 66
Spooner, Colin 166, 167,
    217Start-up 178
Steinbrenner, George 120
Stephenson, Gordon 111
Stephenson, John 110, 111, 112
Strook Strook and Levan 149
Stryker, Walter P. 154, 155, 167,
    168, 169, 171, 172, 179, 183,
    185, 186, 187, 188, 191, 192,
    224
Studebaker 32
Suburu 136
Sugarman, Burt 50, 52, 66
Sunday Telegraph 169, 225
Sunday Times 169, 225
Synor, Jeffrey C. 208, 210, 211,
    212, 213

Taylor, Elizabeth 47
Team Lotus 165
Technicolor Inc. 66, 67, 70
Tee-Kay International 194
Terrell, Richard L. 71, 72

Thatcher, Margaret 180, 181,
    222, 230, 259
Thiokol 170, 171
Thomas, John H. 82, 117
Time 128
Times, The 157, 222, 223, 228,
    234
Tisa, Benedict 255
Tonawanda 140
Tonight 145, 201
Toyota 84, 87
TR7 159
Transamerica 248
Transbus 190
Transportation, Department of
    (US) 190
Trenton, Adam 60
Troy 64, 91, 92, 209
Tucker 136, 138
Turin Motor Show 138
Twinbrook housing project
    173, 174, 211

United States Congress 123
United States Patent Office 97,
    98, 129
United Visuals Corporation 65,
    67, 68, 69, 70, 89, 112
Unsafe at Any Speed 35
Upton, Hazel 84, 85, 86, 87
Upton, William E. 84, 85

Vacuum Assisted Resin
    Injection (VARI) 167, 168,
    226, 230
Vacuum Resin Injection

Moulding (VRIM) 169
Vega 98, 214
Volkswagen Rabbit 138
Volvo 211

Wallace, George 151
Wangers, Jim 44, 45, 46, 1
Wankel engine 64, 71, 75,
    134
Ward's Auto World 122
Warner Communications 9
Webster, Sheffield 139
Weise, Norman 91, 93
Wentzel, Fred 120
Wheels 60
Wichita 81, 112, 113, 114,
    116, 117, 150, 170
Williams, Robert 57, 66, 82,
    84, 86, 87, 89, 112
Williams, Ted 31
Winterton, Nicholas Rayme
    222, 223, 224, 225, 226, 2
Wood Gundy Ltd 153, 154, 1
    201
Woodward Avenue 38, 39
Wright, Frank Lloyd 115
Wright, Pat 11, 18, 53, 64, 1
    190
Wulf, Hurst 24, 26

Xerox Corporation 7, 184

Yanitz, Larry 125, 126
Yunick, Smokey 37, 42, 55, 1
    187

268

THE BOLT SUPREMACY

Also by Richard Moore

In Search of Robert Millar
Heroes, Villains and Velodromes
Slaying the Badger
Sky's the Limit
The Dirtiest Race in History
Étape

THE BOLT
SUPREMACY

Inside Jamaica's Sprint Factory

RICHARD MOORE

YELLOW JERSEY PRESS
LONDON

1 3 5 7 9 10 8 6 4 2

Yellow Jersey Press, an imprint of Vintage,
20 Vauxhall Bridge Road,
London SW1V 2SA

Yellow Jersey Press is part of the Penguin Random House group of companies
whose addresses can be found at global.penguinrandomhouse.com

 Penguin
Random House
UK

First published by Yellow Jersey Press in 2015

www.vintage-books.co.uk

A CIP catalogue record for this book is
available from the British Library

ISBN 9780224092302

Printed and bound by Clays Ltd, St Ives plc

For Virginie

LIST OF ILLUSTRATIONS

Page

ix   Men's 100m final, London Olympics 2012 (Getty Images)

14   Bolt with lightning at the 2013 IAAF World Championships,
            Moscow (Getty Images)

23   UTech Classic, 2014 (Robin Moore)

38   Usain Bolt's first running track

58   UTech Classic, 2014 (Robin Moore)

78   Javon Francis, UTech Classic, 2014 (Robin Moore)

86   Dennis Johnson, 2014 (Robin Moore)

108   Statue of Herb McKenley, Jamaica (Robin Moore)

119   Stephen Francis with Asafa Powell (Getty Images)

143   Usain Bolt practises starting while coach Glen Mills watches on
            (Rex Features)

155   Dr Hans-Wilhelm Müller-Wohlfahrt (Offside)

168   Shelly-Ann Fraser-Pryce in front of her family home, 2008 (Getty
            Images)

183   Usain Bolt winning the men's 100m Olympic final, Beijing, 2008
            (Getty Images)

205   Yohan Blake, 2014 (Getty Images)

216   Victor Conte (PA Images)

236   Paul Wright, 2014 (Robin Moore)

257   UTech Classic, 2014 (Robin Moore)

263   Usain Bolt is disqualified from men's 100m final for a false start at
            the 2011 IAAF World Championship, Daegu (Rex Features)

267   Shelly-Ann Fraser-Pryce with her mother in front of her family
            home, 2008 (Getty Images)

297   UTech Classic, 2014 (Robin Moore)

308   Zharnel Hughes, 2014 (Robin Moore)

CONTENTS

Prologue 1

1. A Force Five Hurricane 7
2. The Wellspring 18
3. Bolt's Own Country 35
4. The Brotherhood 57
5. Donkey Man 72
6. The Architect 85
7. Cuban Swimming Pool Crisis 106
8. Shifting the Paradigm 117
9. Jets and Sharks 133
10. Healing Hans 153
11. Real As It Gets 167
12. Shock and Awe 178
13. The Beast 200
14. Threads 210
15. The Tester 233
16. Genes and Yams 245
17. The G of the Bang 260
18. After the Hurricane 284
19. The In-Between 302

Acknowledgements 318

In Jamaica little is done without a touch of embellishment or some panache. Jamaicans walk with style, drive cars with style, and play with style. It is not so much scoring a goal or hitting a boundary that is important, but the way that it is done. People leaving church will admit openly that they did not understand what the preacher said, 'but he sound good'.

Mervyn C. Alleyne, *Roots of Jamaican Culture*

PROLOGUE

Even the simplest assessment of the circumstances surrounding the explosive success of Jamaican sprinting sets off alarms . . . What are the odds that a tiny island country suddenly dominates global competition . . . just because?
Dan Bernstein, CBS Chicago

London, 5 August 2012, 9.45 p.m.
The eight men are called to the blocks. Each goes down slowly and methodically. They dig their feet in and delicately place their hands in the corners of the lane. A plastic bottle lands behind them, thrown by a man in the crowd, but it goes unheard. They wait and 80,000 people in London's Olympic stadium hush. An echoey, tense kind of silence.

They are called to 'set'. They hold this position for two seconds. The gun goes and an electric charge runs through the crowd.

I am sitting thirty rows from the front, level with the finish line, experiencing the paradox of the 100 metres: simultaneously the quickest and the longest nine-point-something seconds. Trying not to blink, aware that it will all be over quickly, but concentrating so hard that the seconds seem to stretch. The dots gradually enlarge and emerge as a line of sprinters, one of them, when he is unfurled, a full head taller than the others: Usain Bolt.

1

Justin Gatlin is quickest out of the blocks, Yohan Blake, Bolt's clubmate and the world champion, a fraction slower, then Tyson Gay in the next lane along. Asafa Powell, the third Jamaican, reacts almost as quickly as Gatlin, and Ryan Bailey is also up. Bolt is sixth, though he is 'still with the crowd', as he puts it later; still in contact with the five in front.

They are approaching now, growing larger. Bolt draws level with Gatlin at fifty metres. Gay is still marginally ahead; Powell is fading, so is Bailey. Now Bolt and Blake lead, but it's still close. They reach seventy metres, and Bolt surges, as though engaging a new gear. It is an extraordinary spectacle, Bolt in full flight, and it makes the outcome inevitable. Blake dips for second, Gatlin takes bronze.

It is different to Beijing, four years earlier, when the twenty-one-year-old Bolt produced a performance seared into the imagination, one that left an imprint like only a few other moments in sport, when incredible talent combined with soaring ambition and absolute fearlessness. How many compare? Having galloped into an out-rageous lead against the fastest men in the world, Bolt was able to look left, look right, thump his chest, spread his arms, then visibly relax and spend the final ten metres coasting and celebrating. It was as decisive and seemingly effortless as Diego Maradona's mazy run against England in 1986, Mike Tyson's ninety-second demolition of Michael Spinks in 1988, or, in the same year, Ben Johnson's 9.79-second destruction of Carl Lewis in the Olympic 100 metres final.

In an event measured by fractions of fractions of seconds, Bolt did something in Beijing that should not have been possible. It looked like he was playing a different game, or that he belonged to a different species. And it was all so graceful. 'He's beautiful to watch,' said Renaldo Nehemiah, the former 110 metres hurdles world record holder. 'His stride, I mean, it's poetry in motion. He's not like a beast running. He's like a gazelle.'

In London four years later there is no showboating, apart from a small gesture by Bolt's standards: a finger to his lips, 'Sssshhhh.' 'I almost did what I did in Beijing, I almost did it,' he chuckles later. 'But I thought, Nah, I'll just run through the finish.' He wins in 9.63 seconds, a new Olympic record.

In a low-ceilinged, brightly lit room deep in the bowels of London's Olympic stadium, somewhere below the main stand, Usain Bolt shuffles into the press conference, this one after the 200 metres, which he has also won. First he requests a drum roll. 'I'm now a legend,' he says. 'I am the greatest athlete to live. To all the people who doubted me, who thought I would lose here, you can stop talking now. I am a living legend.' Then he explodes with laughter.

Who, now, does he regard as his peers in the sporting world: Muhammad Ali, Michael Jordan, Pele? Beyond sport, has he superseded Bob Marley as the greatest Jamaican in history?

'Ali was the greatest in his sport, Jordan the greatest in his, and I am the greatest in mine, so I guess I am at that level,' Bolt replies. 'I am in the same category as Michael Johnson too. Bob Marley? I'm just carrying on his duty. We have the same goal, to make Jamaica a country that is loved around the world.'

Twenty minutes later, about to leave, he asks once again for the reporters' attention. There is a glint in his eye and a smile on his face. 'I have one more thing to say. I am now a living legend. Bask in my glory. If I don't see that in the paper and on TV in all your countries I will never give an interview again. Tell everyone to follow me on Twitter.'

It wasn't just Bolt. It was Shelly-Ann Fraser-Pryce, Yohan Blake, Warren Weir. It was Asafa Powell, Veronica Campbell-Brown, Nesta Carter, Sherone Simpson. Seven gold medals from the eight sprint events in London: Jamaica, a tiny island, had come close to complete domination for a second Olympic Games in succession. Twenty of the fastest twenty-five men's 100 metres in history had now been run by Jamaicans. It was, depending on where you stood, incredibly impressive, or deeply suspicious.

Like many – such as Carl Lewis, the nine-time Olympic gold medallist, or Dan Bernstein, the CBS columnist, who wrote 'Anyone wasting words extolling the greatness of Usain Bolt should know better' – I was, if not suspicious, then certainly sceptical. Bernstein was right: if we didn't know better than to assume that the Olympic 100 metres champion was clean, then we hadn't learned anything from Ben Johnson, Marion Jones, Justin Gatlin and countless others, nor from the asterisks, denoting drugs cheats, that rain down like confetti on the all-time fastest list.

I had another reason for being preoccupied by this question during the London Games. I had gone there straight from the Tour de France – there were only four days in between. A toxic atmosphere engulfed the Tour. It had been noxious for years as the full extent of institutional doping became apparent, but in 2012 it was especially bad. Bradley Wiggins led for most of the race and was asked daily whether he was cheating. The questions were fuelled by justified, historical suspicion (not necessarily of Wiggins, but of the event) and sustained by the simmering rage of social media. One day Wiggins exploded when asked about his cyber critics: 'I say they're just fucking wankers, I cannot be doing with people like that. It's easy for them to sit under a pseudonym on Twitter and write that sort of shit, rather than get off their arses in their own lives and apply themselves and work hard at something and achieve something.'

The questions were legitimate, but they led us all – journalists, fans, athletes – into an endless downward spiral. This was not journalism: it was journalists responding to and genuflecting before the echo chamber of social media. It made no distinction between facts and conjecture, opinion and evidence.

Going from the Tour de France to the London Olympic Games was like stepping from a sewer into a golden meadow. The sun shone, a sweet scent filled the air, and the tweets emanated from birds rather than trolls. London itself was transformed. People smiled. Conversations were started on the Tube. Policemen posed for pictures mimicking Bolt's victory pose, which some call 'the Lightning Bolt' but Bolt himself calls 'To Di World', inspired by a Jamaican dancehall move.

There was no cynicism, no angst, no hand-wringing. Only innocence and joy. In Bolt's press conference, he was not asked if he was a cheat. He was asked: 'Are you a legend now, Usain?'

It was intoxicating, almost impossible not to be swept along on this tide of goodwill. It was also unsettling: superficial and fake. I loved it, and hated it. Which is also how I feel about the doping question. Conflicted. Because for all that the atmosphere at the Tour was poisonous and corrosive, the question itself fascinates me. It encompasses lying, cheating, subterfuge, deceit, mystery – all the things that make crime fiction so compelling. It goes to the very heart of elite sport: to what lengths will people go? It also goes to the heart of the experience of watching and enjoying sport: should we – can we – believe what we are seeing?

It is *the* question. Yet at the Tour I became weary of it, partly because journalism should be about trying to find things out, not asking the same thing every day; but also because I believed Bradley Wiggins was clean. I had followed him closely for over a decade. I knew the people around him. I was convinced he was no Lance Armstrong, against whom there had been strong evidence from the start, whereas really the only 'evidence' against Wiggins was the fact that he was winning an event with a dubious history.

When I heard the cynical view that Olympic gold medals and Tour de France victories were impossible without drugs, I passionately disagreed. As an objective journalist I shouldn't have cared, but as a human being I felt the treatment of Wiggins – the things asserted by people who I knew had no idea – was unfair. Yet I didn't know, and my only 'evidence' was anecdotal. I couldn't know unless I lived with him. I couldn't know unless I *was* him. And this was what was so unsettling.

With Bolt, I knew less. But because I knew less, I seemed more inclined to agree with the Lewises and the Bernsteins and assume the worst. Ironically, the greater the distance, the easier it seems to be to form a strong opinion. The closer you get, the more aware you become of contradiction and nuance; the more your certainty begins to crumble while ambiguity flourishes. Which seems a good reason not to remain at a distance, with your hazy view and lazy opinions, but to at least try and get up close to find out what you can.

That is what I resolved to do in the days after the London Games. The broader question that inspired this book was not: is Bolt clean? That is too loaded. Rather, I wanted to find out why he is so good. The two questions might be related. But equally, they might not be. In a way, my question was: how can we be certain of our heroes? Can we dare to hope?

In trying to find out, I found myself drawn more to the culture that produced Bolt than to Bolt himself. Because he is not a one-off; far from it.

1

A FORCE FIVE HURRICANE

I ain't doing no interviews.
Glen Mills

Moscow, August 2013

It's the eve of the world athletics championships in Moscow, and the Jamaican team is holding an open training session. They are gathered in clumps on a warm-up track that is semi-hidden amid trees and statues in the grounds of the Luzhniki Stadium, a grey, hulking Communist-era structure about to stage its final international event before it is rebuilt for the 2018 football World Cup – only the outer walls and the Lenin statue will remain.

No doubt this feels a very long way from home for the Jamaicans warming up in front of us, working in little groups, practising starts, stretching in the warm Moscow sunshine or having their muscles kneaded on massage tables.

The post-Olympic year can feel low-key: a bit after-the-Lord-Mayor's-Show. Few athletes are at their best. When he appeared at the Golden Gala in Rome in June – and suffered a rare defeat to Justin Gatlin – Usain Bolt admitted that it is a struggle for the mind and also the body, 'because Olympic year is when most athletes push themselves to the limit'.

But the difficulties faced by the Jamaican athletes in 2013 have gone well beyond the usual post-Games hangover. It's an Olympic hangover all right – a hangover of Olympic proportions. It began days after the Golden Gala with the news that Veronica Campbell-Brown, the three-times Olympic gold medallist, had tested positive for a diuretic. A month later, the news was even more shocking: five failed drugs tests at the Jamaican national championships, including two more of the country's biggest stars, Asafa Powell and Sherone Simpson.

It appeared to be nothing less than a cull. And confirmation of the doubts that had swirled around the Jamaicans. In response, some prominent Jamaican athletes seemed to adopt a siege mentality. In Monaco, before the Diamond League meeting in late July, Shelly-Ann Fraser-Pryce, the double Olympic 100 metres champion, took part in a bizarre press conference.

Fraser-Pryce had travelled there straight from Lignano, the northern Italian town where she had been training with Powell and Simpson, both clubmates. Their hotel had been raided by Italian police and products seized from Powell and Simpson's rooms. It wasn't clear yet whether they contained any banned substances – nor, indeed, whether Powell and Simpson were guilty of a doping offence. But as she sat down beside Carmelita Jeter, the American who had finished second to her at the London Olympics, the usually exuberant Fraser-Pryce displayed the body language of a crime suspect.

'No questions will be answered on the doping cases,' said the translator, opening the conference. 'This was a remark they asked us. Questions only on the competition tomorrow and the world championships.'

The second question came from Simon Hart of the *Telegraph*. 'If we're not allowed to ask about doping, can I ask Shelly-Ann what the atmosphere is like among the athletes at Lignano who haven't tested positive?'

'There will be no answers on that,' the translator cut in. 'They don't want to answer on that. Not today. Sorry.'

'Why?' chorused the journalists. Jeter picked up the microphone, said, 'Thank you,' and walked out. Fraser-Pryce looked unsure what to do, then followed. The press conference had lasted two minutes thirty-one seconds.

Even stranger was an incident I witnessed weeks later at the Diamond League meeting in Brussels, after Fraser-Pryce won the 100 metres. 'Shelly-Ann, have you been drug-tested in Brussels?' asked John Leicester of the Associated Press.

'No, I haven't been drug-tested here in Belgium,' Fraser-Pryce said testily. 'Do you want to drug-test me?'

'No, I don't want to drug-test you,' said Leicester, 'that's not my job. How many times have you been drug-tested this year, do you know?'

'Well, I'll count all those pink papers that I have, and I'll definitely try and send them to you, but many times, more than eighteen times for the year.'

'More than eighteen, or eight?' Leicester persisted.

'More than eighteen, OK?'

'Well I'll take you up on your offer,' said Leicester.

'Certainly, you can leave your email address and fax number with my manager at the back.'

Afterwards, in the corridor outside the room, Leicester spoke to Fraser-Pryce's manager, Adrian Laidlaw. 'The good thing about this conversation is I'll now make sure that she never makes a statement like that again,' he told Leicester.

In Moscow three weeks later, I am watching Fraser-Pryce, the five-foot-zero 'Pocket Rocket', practise her starts, exploding out of the blocks, sprinting thirty metres, then slowing and walking languidly back to the start, hands on hips, the sun reflecting off the pink streaks in her hair.

Bolt is here too. With his workout finished, his sluggish movement suits the muggy, oppressive heat of Moscow in August. He heads to the massage table, set up between the track and the small rickety stand, and lies down, propping himself up on his elbows so he can talk (which makes him unusual: most athletes don headphones the second they stop training). Bolt's masseur, serious and stern-faced, tackles his legs with vigour: first calves, then hamstrings, stopping regularly to apply more baby oil to his hands. He rolls up Bolt's knee-length shorts until he is kneading his buttocks. Gradually Bolt surrenders to it, resting his head on the table while the masseur goes on kneading, thumbs probing.

Nearby is Bolt's walrus-like coach, Glen Mills, who achieves the near impossible by showing even less urgency than Bolt. He plays a game with the dozen or so journalists clustered at the front of the small stand, sitting close enough to be able to hear them calling his name, far enough away that he can pretend he doesn't. The Jamaican assistant team manager, Dave Myrie, is dispatched to ask Mills for an interview. He wanders towards him, then returns shaking his head. 'You know Glen by now.'

Muzak wafts across the track from tinny speakers on top of the single-storey pavilion on the back straight: 'She Loves You' and 'My Way' are staples. Now, over the strains of Queen's 'I Want to Break Free', the seated Mills half turns, and says, 'I ain't doing no interviews.'

Bolt eases himself off the massage table and puts on his oversized headphones, then his rucksack, which hangs low and loose on his back. He ambles towards the track centre, stumbling theatrically over a parking cone on the way. Mills, sitting nearby, doesn't flinch. He doesn't seem to notice.

Only when Bolt is gone do you begin to take in the other Jamaican athletes going through their warm-up drills. 'No talent, all guts' reads the slogan on one T-shirt, but the talent here would grace any national team. Yet it is deprived of three of its biggest stars: Powell, Campbell-Brown and Simpson (a fourth, Yohan Blake, is missing through injury). 'They will be well missed,' lamented the veteran coach, Fitz Coleman, when the team gathered in Kingston before flying to Moscow. 'As far I'm concerned, they are still a part of our team.'

In light of Mills's reticence, Michael Clarke, the head coach in Moscow, steps forward. Clarke wears a black Puma cap, dark Ray-Bans, a yellow Puma T-shirt, and a thick gold chain around his neck. The interview gets off to an awkward start when a Russian reporter, clutching black-and-white photocopied pictures of Bolt and Fraser-Pryce (to help her identify the athletes, she explains), asks, 'Who's that man in blue?' Clarke turns to look. 'That's Coach Mills.'

Clarke says that the team is aiming for more medals than the nine they won last time. 'Any black horses?' asks the same Russian reporter. Some of us stare in embarrassment at the ground, but Clarke is unruffled. 'Well, I think this year's going to be a change of the guard,' he says. 'We have a very young team; I think the average age is around twenty-one, twenty-two. And we should have some young persons vying for some medals. As for specifics, I can't tell you right now who they are.'

'Has morale been affected by the recent controversies?' Clarke is asked.

'From what I have seen thus far, coming from a cross section of athletes, there doesn't seem to be any negative impact on the present situation as it concerns the drugs situation,' says Clarke.

Has he spoken to the squad as a whole? 'Not on that issue.'

What about the recent claims that the Jamaicans are years behind in drug-testing? 'I don't think we are behind. I think we are slowly keeping pace with what's expected.'

As he's speaking, Dennis Gordon, the team's media liaison officer, appears at Clarke's shoulder and leans in. 'Answer no questions about doping,' says Gordon.

'What?' says Clarke.

'Answer no questions about doping.'

'Ah,' says Clarke, looking back up, 'I've just been instructed by our media liaison person not to take any questions about doping.'

A change of tack. Bolt – how is he? 'Usain is one of those unique individuals with a very capable personality – very affable, very genial, very funny. I think everyone gravitates towards his charisma. He's fine.'

Back to the main point, in a roundabout way. Why are the Jamaicans so fast? Clarke gives it some thought. 'In recent years, academic research has been done to explain somewhat, or to give some understanding as to why we are as good as we have been. I think part of it is genes and some have postulated about yam and some are saying it's because of the system we have in place.

'We have various competitions from the infant level to the primary school to the secondary school to the clubs, tertiary, even community track and field. And most organisations have what you call sports day and primarily the sports day consists of running events – or egg-and-spoon races. That basically comes from our English background. It's the system that's in place and it's highly competitive. The athletes at the 1948 and 1952 Olympics have given us a platform to build on.'

It is Clarke's first time as head coach to the senior national team, but he feels no pressure. 'Expectations, yes, but there is no pressure.' The spirit in the squad, he adds, is 'very high, very good. And calm. It's like a volcano waiting to erupt.'

Warren Weir saunters over to speak to some journalists. The baby-faced Olympic bronze medallist, a clubmate of Bolt, says he wants to put a smile back on people's faces. 'Yeah, it's always good to give people good news after the bashing our sport has gotten. People want to see people running clean, people running fast and clean, and it's always good to let them know there are clean ones out there.'

So when we see so many Jamaicans run so fast, we can believe in them? 'Yes!' Weir splutters. 'Yes, you can still believe that there are good athletes out there: I myself can testify to that. I'm one of the clean ones. So there are actually good ones out there. We can't bash all for some.'

Team morale is unaffected, he says. 'It hasn't shifted us. We are rallying together; whether bad news or good news we always look on the positive side of life. We don't let the bad news hold us down or make us underperform.'

That much appears to be true. In Moscow, the Jamaicans simply pick up where they left off in London. On day two, Bolt reaches the 100 metres final along with three of his countrymen: Nesta Carter, Kemar Bailey-Cole and Nickel Ashmeade. It's a dark Moscow night and the rain is lashing down as the runners are introduced, Bolt with his hands on his hips, his head tilted back as though meditating. When the TV camera pans from Justin Gatlin to him, he begins an elaborate routine of pretending to open and put up an umbrella. The rain falls harder than ever and Bolt stands under his imaginary umbrella wearing a fake-bemused expression.

Gatlin gets away quickly, bull-like, head down, low. 'The rain made it slick under the fingers,' he says later, 'but I got out the blocks. Reacted well. Drove about forty-five metres, then felt Bolt next to me.' As he feels Bolt's presence, Gatlin makes the fatal mistake of reacting. 'You know, I gotta remember in my head that I'm not six-five. I'm only six-one. When you get someone who's six-five, you try to match the stride length; I shoulda just kept attacking the ground.'

Although Gatlin beat Bolt in Rome, the script at a major championship is by now familiar, and when Bolt draws level, there can be only one outcome. He pulls clear, wins in 9.77 seconds, while Gatlin hangs on, dipping too early ('We call it the phantom finish line – you see the person in front of you dip and you dip as well') for second. Carter wins what seems like a separate race for bronze. Lightning illuminates the sky as Bolt crosses the line, and Bob Marley's 'Three Little Birds' fills the Moscow air:

> *Don't worry 'bout a thing,*
> *'Cause every little thing gonna be alright . . .*

In the mixed zone, inside the stadium, where athletes are shepherded through pens and reporters hang over barriers catching their words

on recorders, there is a stir when Bolt finally appears after his lap of honour. There is always a stir when Bolt appears. He shuffles through the pen in his socks, while Ricky Simms, the Irishman who is his agent, follows holding his Puma spikes in one hand.

Bolt starts to speak in his deep baritone. He explains that he would have liked to go faster, closer to his world record of 9.58, but a niggle after the semi-final put paid to that. Still, it looked quite easy. 'I never look at it as easy,' he says. 'I work hard. I push myself through a lot of pain.'

According to some, Bolt came to Moscow to 'save' the sport after a year of terrible headlines, most of them about athletes from his country. His face crumples into a smile, and he giggles, as though the question is ridiculous: he is only one man. 'For me, I think I go out there . . . I'm just doing my part by running fast, letting the world know you can do it clean.'

*

Twenty-four hours after the men's 100 metres, Fraser-Pryce, despite 'pain in my left butt-cheek', appears for the women's final. Apart from the pink ponytail ('Fuchsia,' she clarifies later. 'It makes me pretty . . . prettier'), she doesn't go out of her way to attract attention, not like Bolt. She quietly and intensely focuses on what she has to do, oblivious to the crowd and the other runners, narrowing her eyes, squinting down the track.

Her start is explosive – much better than it was in London twelve months earlier – and she surges in the second 50 metres for a convincing win, over two-tenths of a second clear of Murielle Ahouré of the Ivory Coast, with Jeter third. Her time, 10.71 seconds, is just one-hundredth outside the championship record. Afterwards, Fraser-Pryce says that she'll celebrate 'with some ice on my gluteus maximus'. She has been working hard all year on her 200 metres, and has her eyes on a first sprint double in a major championship.

She reaches the final of the longer event and starts in lane four, with Allyson Felix of the US, the reigning world and Olympic 200 metres champion, in lane three. There's the explosive start again, and Felix is straining to stay in contact on the bend – straining too hard – when she pulls up and collapses to the track clutching her hamstring. It's a second gold for Fraser-Pryce. Twenty-four hours later, Bolt does the same, winning ahead of Weir.

The Jamaican men and women win the 4x100 metres too. And after the men's relay there's an exchange with Bolt inside the stadium that reveals another side of his personality. As he waited for the baton, with Gatlin in the lane inside but moving to the outside of his lane, the two almost collided. In the confusion, the US, slightly ahead on the final bend, messed up the transition. They handed the advantage to Jamaica – to Bolt – for the final leg. Gatlin was furious, claiming afterwards that without the mistake, the US would have won.

'They couldn't have said that,' says Bolt when told what Gatlin said. Shaking his head, affecting a casual pose as he leans against the fence in the mixed zone, he continues: 'They couldn't have said that, they couldn't have said that.' He tries to make a joke of it, but the sparkle is missing from his eyes, which have turned dark. He is angry – affronted. 'They were like two metres in front of me. I've been in a worse position running from my blocks and won. I wasn't worried at all about the US beating us. We had a great team.'

If not two metres, then how much would the Americans have needed to beat the Jamaicans? 'Probably they would have had to have ten metres to win that race,' says Bolt. We laugh. He isn't smiling.

Beijing, Berlin, Daegu, London and Moscow merely continue Jamaica's extraordinary domination of the sprint events at the major championships. Yet the mood in Moscow is very different to London. I can feel it, it's in the air. There's the scepticism of the outside world, the defensiveness of the Jamaicans. It's all very reminiscent of the Tour de France. The Olympics feel a long time ago.

On the day after the world championships comes another bombshell. 'An inside look at Jamaican track's drug-testing woes' reads the headline in *Sports Illustrated*. The article is by Renée Anne Shirley, the former executive director of the Jamaica Anti-Doping Commission (JADCO), and in it she describes the positive tests for Powell, Simpson and Campbell-Brown as equivalent to 'a force five hurricane crossing directly over the island'. A table accompanying the article shows how little drug-testing JADCO did in the six months before the London Games.

On the eve of my first visit to Jamaica, I met Shirley at an anti-doping conference in London, where she was speaking. Her participation in the conference had been in doubt – she had problems getting a visa, which she believed was connected to her article. She explained that if the positive tests unleashed a 'force five hurricane', her revelations unleashed another one. 'I've been called a Judas, a traitor, that I've committed treason, that my passport should be taken away,' she said. Then she described 'the lonely road of the whistleblower': 'I expected a lot of it, I have weathered a lot of it, but it amazes me the things said about me . . . pressure has been put on my family. I have been blacklisted. I don't get invitations to anything, I don't get Christmas cards. The other issue is personal safety. I've relocated, I've taken precautions. I have to be careful.'

This all sounded ominous. Then Shirley, who lasted eight months at JADCO before leaving, said something else that interested me. 'As a proud Jamaican, all I wanted to do was be able to defend the Jamaicans as best I could.' Instead, when people like Carl Lewis asked questions, or when Shirley herself raised her concerns about the effectiveness of anti-doping, they were attacked.

'Every time something comes up, it's "This person is against Jamaica,"' said Shirley. 'But to come out and say, "The rest of the world is against us," it does not answer the question.'

There were lots of questions. And only really one place to try and find the answers.

2

THE WELLSPRING

Jamaican youth continue to excel in track and field because the poorest child from the deepest rural hinterland of Jamaica and the most depressed urban ghetto can get a chance to compete.
Betty Ann Blaine, *Jamaica Observer*

Kingston, March 2014

Outside the stadium it is like a large music festival or major sports event. Stalls and street vendors line Arthur Wint Drive, selling food and drink, flags and memorabilia in team colours.

In the stifling heat, women sit beneath umbrellas and beside large coolboxes filled with drinks, and men materialise alongside me as I walk from the car park to the arena, hustling and hassling – 'higgling', they call it. 'Cold drink, man?' 'Mi have ticket – you want ticket?'

It's Tuesday, day one of Champs, Jamaica's boys' and girls' inter-schools championships. A schools athletics meeting like no other. Security is tight. At the gate, there's a long queue, at the end of which uniformed men and women check tickets and bags and even peel labels off non-sanctioned soft drinks. My bottle of Pepsi is confiscated while a guard pulls at the sticker. 'Why are you doing that?' I ask.

'Advertising,' he says.

'But Pepsi is one of the sponsors.'

'Oh . . .' His colleague nods confirmation. He hands the bottle back.

Inside the grounds of the National Stadium, more security guards carry walkie-talkies or wear earpieces. The stadium, opened in 1962, the year that Jamaica gained its independence, is a low-slung sand-coloured bowl that sits in a relatively affluent New Kingston neighbourhood. The Blue Mountains are on one side, the rump of the city – the ghettos and slums and garrisons – sprawling and shimmering all the way down to the sea on the other.

It's hard to believe, as I negotiate the throngs of people, and listen to the thrum of anticipation, that this is a schools championship. But Champs is the only show in town. The newspapers are full of it: front, back and letters pages. The radio stations are dominated by discussion of the young athletes – some of them already household names – who will star over the five days. There are public service announcements advising spectators to lock up and register their guns with the police. There is live TV coverage.

The man in charge of it all, the meet director, is none other than Usain Bolt's coach, Glen Mills. He is also one of the first people I spot when I enter the main stand and sit on the bench seat. He wears a pale blue T-shirt, loose-fitting jeans and trainers, and greets people with a shy, toothless smile (he is missing his front two upper teeth), but generally doesn't stop to talk, moving slowly up the stand. Mills doesn't look relaxed, he looks catatonic. Finally he reaches the top of the steps and the last row of seats and sits down heavily. I have been told that he will not be speaking to journalists during Champs (or at any other time).

Picking up a programme, I read the mind-blowing statistic that at the current time, every global male 100 metres champion, in every age group, is Jamaican: Olympic, world, Commonwealth, Youth Olympic, world junior and world youth. But on the very next page is something that jars with the celebratory, self-congratulatory tone. It says that from 2015 it has been propsed that drug-testing will be introduced at Champs, testing kids from ten years old upwards. 'It is such a pity that the hard work and natural talent of our young athletes are now being scrutinised with suspicion,' says the article, before going on to question whether drug-testing children is to ensure fairness, to protect 'Brand Jamaica', or to 'appease international critics'.

'Hey, you a coach?' an American voice asks to my left. We are sitting in the half-empty main stand before things hot up and the stadium fills later in the week.

He is unmistakably an American sports coach: neatly pressed polo shirt, college logo, knee-length shorts, baseball cap, sunglasses. He introduces himself as Keith Barnier, head track and field coach at Abilene Christian University (ACU) in Texas. He has come to Champs early, he tells me, to get a head start on the other US college coaches. Most arrive for the final day, the climax to the meeting, and then, Barnier says, 'get the hell back out as soon as possible'.

'They think Kingston is dangerous,' he explains. 'They say, "What the hell do you do there for five days?" But my wife is Jamaican, and I know you gotta be in the club of Jamaican people. You take care of them, they take care of you. Trust is everything here.'

Barnier clicks his tongue in appreciation as he watches Christopher Taylor, a fourteen-year-old from Calabar, win a 400 metres heat in 48.72 seconds. 'Forty-eight for a fourteen-year-old!' he laughs, as though the idea were preposterous (which it would be anywhere other than here). Taylor is small, wiry and smooth as silk. The crowd becomes excited to the point of hysteria as he glides down the home straight and lunges for the line.

Barnier says he's here mainly to study athletes in their final year, with a view to recruiting them for ACU. 'I look at the green bananas,' he says. 'But what I need are yellow ones.

'These guys are like soldiers,' he continues. 'And this, Champs, it prepares them for war. There's nothing like this anywhere else in the world. This is a freak show.' He means this in the nicest way. 'I'm serious. These kids are running for a better life and they are not messing around. The coaches are not messing around. And they are good coaches.' What makes them good coaches? 'They give a shit.'

Barnier knows most of the coaches and knows how they operate, explaining that they might initially send him a less talented youngster. 'They'll toss you a bone. It might not be their best athlete, but if you do well for them they'll send you a better one. That's what I mean about trust. When you make a promise to the Jamaicans, you gotta keep it. Americans say things they don't mean. My wife catches me for that.'

I meet Barnier the next day, and the day after, and the day after. He spends long hours at the stadium, but increasingly away from the main arena, in the stand by the side of the warm-up track; 'hustlin'', as he puts it. 'This is the boiler room,' he tells me, having sneaked me into what is technically a no-go area for journalists. 'This is where it all happens – not out there on the track.' Here, backstage, are coaches watching groups of athletes going through their paces; other athletes on tables, masseurs kneading their muscles, physiotherapists attending to injuries; and a lot of slow, languid movement. The athletes are different but the scene is identical to Moscow before the world championships, which tells its own story: the professionalism is striking (I don't remember sports masseurs and physios at my school).

Barnier picks his moments to approach the coaches – 'not just before a race' – at one point returning and holding up his wrist, where there used to be a watch. 'Traded it for an athlete,' he says. A joke. I think. But he does say that one coach offered his best athlete if Barnier could get his own son a basketball scholarship. In terms of what he is actually offering the athletes, Barnier says: 'I'm handing out $46,000 scholarships.'

At one time this would have been the holy grail. A scholarship to a US college was something every Jamaican athlete coveted – it was the whole point of excelling at athletics; it offered a ticket out of Jamaica to a better life. But there seemed to be a sporting cost attached: lots of promising young Jamaican athletes went to the States and were never heard of again. These days, a 'bone' might be all a US college gets. Some of the best Jamaicans are staying at home.

Barnier is familiar with the stories, and also the criticism that at US colleges Jamaican athletes are over-raced and burned out, or transferred to other sports that demand speed – perhaps basketball, or American football. In terms of popularity (and money), track and field lags a long way behind these sports in the US. (One theory is that if Usain Bolt had gone to an American college, he would have come under pressure to become a basketball player instead of a sprinter.) Change came in the early 2000s. Lots of young Jamaican athletes still go to the US on athletics scholarships, but they no longer have to. The best ones – Bolt, Yohan Blake, Asafa Powell, Shelly-Ann Fraser-Pryce, Warren Weir, Nesta Carter, Kemar Bailey-Cole – have opted instead to stay at home and train under Glen Mills or the other guru, Stephen Francis. Powell was the trend-setter. Or the trend-reverser.

It has made it harder for Barnier and his colleagues. But not impossible. 'What I'm selling,' he says, 'what I tell 'em, is: "I will not run you into the ground. I will help you run faster. I will let you run for your country if selected. And you'll get a great education in a beautiful school."'

A scholarship to a US college is still enormously appealing to lots of young Jamaicans. Some of them approach Barnier at the warm-up track. One very shy boy, who was hovering for a long time before plucking up the courage to approach me, eventually comes up and asks, 'Are you a coach, sir?' He looks crushed when I tell him I'm a journalist. He is a decathlete who missed out on selection for his school, Kingston College, in his main event but still harbours hopes of earning a scholarship based on his athletic ability.

The concept of recruitment is not new to a lot of them. 'All these kids, the good ones, are recruited by their high schools,' Barnier tells me. 'They understand that track and field can be their way out. And they're really easy to coach. They're not afraid of hard work. If you

get a bunch of 'em on your team, you're laughing. I would take any five of these guys tomorrow.'

What exactly is he looking for – how does he spot talent? Barnier laughs. 'I mean, the talent ID part is easy as hell. Look at these guys jogging. They jog faster than my guys run. Beautiful.

'If you give them shoes, and a track to run on, they're very grateful, they can't stop thanking you. The American kids are not like that. But a lot of these kids we're seein' here are not getting three square meals a day. Half of them have seen knife fights, they've seen someone get shot. Hope is so important.'

That is what he is really selling, says Barnier: hope.

On the final day of Champs, towards the end of the closing session, I sit on the baking concrete oval that ribbons around the athletics track. It's a cycling track whose disrepair testifies to its lack of use; now it acts as a buffer between the bleachers and the infield. All around me the National Stadium is rammed: there are 30,000 people, and they have been here since 4 p.m., five hours before the end of the meeting, when the gates were closed.

The bleachers are bouncing. Spectators are arranged in blocks of colour: yellow and red in one section; green and black in another;

purple and white; red; pale blue. Each block jumps and sways to its own rhythm; each has its own band. 'The melodies of school songs swirled and clashed in the air,' said Colin Channer, the Jamaican writer, describing the atmosphere at Champs. 'Drumbeats from different corners organised themselves into a bangarang . . . The stands were a stand-in for Jamaica, a nation of passionate, noisy, tribal people. We Jamaicans are most at ease in disorder.'

The atmosphere in the stadium is raucous. Despite the warnings of fights and concealed weapons, it feels friendly, more a carnival than a riot, but with the fervour of a big football match. Yet compared to most British football matches, it is positively benign. There are whole families: men, women, children and lots of babies clutched to mothers' breasts. The vuvuzelas supply a constant high-pitched hum, like a billion mosquitoes, a sound that mirrors that state of intensity. Perhaps there is a parallel here with another Jamaican cultural phenomenon: music. 'I don't know what it is about Jamaican music, but creatively it just seems to take place at a higher amperage,' wrote the American essayist John Jeremiah Sullivan. 'It may be an island effect. Isolation does seem to breed these intensities sometimes.'

The flags around the top of the fifty-two-year-old stadium now lie flat against their poles; earlier they blew furiously. Darkness is closing in quickly, and the Blue Mountains, illuminated during the day by blinding sunshine, are now ominous dark shadows that twinkle with the lights from the homes of the people who live there. They include some of the athletes so many of the schoolkids aspire to emulate – Bolt, Blake and Powell all have large houses in the hills above Kingston. Beverly Hills, where Bolt lives, is the most prominent area, with the best views of Kingston, the ocean and the National Stadium.

In the bleachers and main stand there is frenzied chaos. But in the track centre there is perfect order. It is as though the island's two biggest influences – Africa and Great Britain – are represented by this juxtaposition: the colour and vibrancy of Africa in the stands, the restraint and authority of colonial Britain in the centre.

Records have been broken all week at Champs. Twenty-one will fall in total, but not all records are equal. The schoolboy feats of Bolt and Blake loom over this meeting like the Blue Mountains over Kingston. Zharnel Hughes destroys Blake's 100 metres record, set in 2007, running 10.12. Hughes is eighteen, from Anguilla (though his mother is Jamaican); he lives in Kingston and trains with Glen Mills's group. He is in Bolt's mould: tall at six-three, and like Bolt, he devours opponents over the final forty metres. Like Bolt, too, he is a product of the IAAF high-performance training centre in Kingston, where he has been since he was sixteen, training most days with Bolt and Blake. 'When I just got here and saw these guys,' he tells me after his record run, shaking his head. 'Bolt, man! I couldn't believe I had the chance to run with those guys.'

Blake was teasing Hughes before Champs. 'Big man, you can't beat my record, you can't beat my record. The closest you're going to come is 10.27.' Blake's record was 10.21. In the event, Hughes slices almost a tenth of a second from it. But the next day he pulls out of the 200 metres, feeling a twinge in his hamstring and deciding not to take any chances. He comes anyway to support his school, Kingston College, and says he isn't disappointed to miss out on the chance of the sprint double. 'No, man, every setback sets you up for a major comeback.'

It is difficult to keep track of all the outstanding performances. People are talking excitedly about young Christopher Taylor, the 400 metres phenomenon. 'I call him a freak,' smiles his coach at Calabar, Michael Clarke. 'He's small. I ask him, "Chris, how you generate so much power?" He's on the quiet side, but he's quietly aggressive.'

Then there's Jaheel Hyde. He has something about him beyond the fact that he sets a new national junior record in the 400 metres hurdles. He also wins the 110 metres hurdles. Recovering in his 'pen' afterwards, he carries himself with quiet, steely confidence; as self-contained as Usain Bolt is exuberant. His father, Lenworth Hyde, was one of Jamaica's greatest footballers, and Jaheel is said to be equally talented with a football – he was in the national under-17 squad – as he is on a track. To his father's disappointment, he has opted for athletics. Only in Jamaica would that be a rational rather than an eccentric choice.

Before the 200 metres comes the 400 metres final for the Class 1 boys. This is perhaps the most eagerly anticipated event on the programme because it features an athlete who is already a household name in Jamaica.

Six months earlier, Javon 'Donkey Man' Francis was selected for the senior world championships in Moscow. He was eighteen. But in a surprise move, Clarke, the Jamaican head coach, who also happened to be Francis's coach at Calabar, didn't just select him for the final of the 4x400 metres relay – he put him on the anchor leg.

On the night, in the old grey Luzhniki Stadium, Francis appeared unfazed as the Americans raced into a big lead. Behind them a small pack emerged: Russia, Great Britain, Belgium and finally Jamaica. With the Russians in contention for a medal, the atmosphere was as lively as it got in a city that seemed quite ambivalent about hosting the world athletics championships. Coming up to the final lap, and Francis's first appearance on the big stage, the runners jostled, stepping on each others' toes. The tall, slightly gangly Donkey Man bounced up and down as though the track was red hot, and urged his teammate on: 'Come on, come on,' he seemed to be gesturing with his hand. Then he settled into a semi-crouch, as though about to dive off a cliff, and waited still and poised, arms outstretched.

Francis took the baton with Jamaica lagging in fifth, slightly detached from the other medal contenders. He followed the others round the bend and then, on the back straight, attacked. He looked to be sprinting flat out as he passed the British runner, and then the Belgian. And then he overtook the Russian too. Jamaicans at home could only watch through the cracks in their fingers. What was Javon doing? The 400 was the most unforgiving distance: he'd die in the home straight, surely. He had hopelessly misjudged his run.

LaShawn Merritt of the USA was clear for gold. Francis had got the Jamaicans up to second. The Russian came back on the final bend, drawing level on the home straight. Now Francis would fade and die, and slip out of the medals. But incredibly, he surged again, and held on for second. His split was 44 seconds dead.

It would be an exaggeration to say that the world sat up and took notice of this extraordinary performance. But Jamaica noticed, and hailed the Donkey Man. It wasn't so much the time, though that was impressive; it was the way he attacked athletes older, more experienced and more respected; it was the aggression and the belief that flowed through him as he took off down the back straight, not merely to try and win a medal, but gunning for Merritt. The way that when the Russian came back, Francis didn't settle for bronze, but kicked again.

The reporters waiting in the mixed zone were unprepared, however, for Donkey Man's arrival. He entered this enclosed, claustrophobic part of the stadium – it felt like an underground car park – with the movement and swagger of a boxer. He danced towards a television reporter and took the microphone before speaking directly to the camera: 'A super donkey just did it!' he said, giggling, then turned serious. 'I listen to what coach say. To run my own race. Go out there. Last night me and him have a good discussion. Told him I wanted to get a medal to show my mum and dad. Now I got a medal to go home with.'

Francis was gap-toothed and goofy. For all his swagger, he had a sweet innocence about him. When his older teammates took their turn with the microphone – each one speaking shyly and uncertainly – he danced excitedly in the background and spoke over them in his thick Jamaican accent, lurching frequently into patois. Finally he grabbed the microphone again: 'I'm happy happy happy. I go home with a medal to show I am a future champion . . . I feel great about myself.'

'A super donkey just did it!'

Now, back in Kingston, all eyes are on the super donkey, this latest golden child of Jamaican athletics. Francis grew up in an impoverished settlement, Bull Bay, nine miles up the coast from Kingston. When he was recruited to Calabar, he left his parents' modest home to move in with a guardian in the city. Despite his background, he is smartly and expensively attired: new Puma-branded green-and-black Calabar High School vest, shorts and spikes, tracksuit and rucksack.

The Calabar principal, Albert Corcho, is among the 30,000 spectators at the National Stadium as the boys' Class 1 400 metres finalists line up. Corcho recalls what Francis told him on the eve of Champs: 'Sir, I am going to break Usain Bolt's record. I am going for the record.' Bolt's record, set in 2003, stands at 45.35.

The gun goes for the start and Francis attacks. Here is the fearless athlete we saw in Moscow. Here, too, is an explanation for his coolness in Moscow, his ability to execute his race despite the atmosphere and sense of occasion. Because make no mistake, the world championships was nothing compared to Champs. Bolt has always said it: that if you can cope with Champs, you can cope with anything (he also suggested that it's why Asafa Powell has always frozen on the big stage – not enough experience of Champs: his school didn't always qualify).

From lane four Francis sprints around the first bend, hunting down the other runners then passing as though oblivious to them. By the second bend he is the clear leader. But he is not really racing the others; he is racing Bolt. Again there is that fear, or expectation, that he will run out of oxygen, his legs turning to jelly, running through mud up the home straight. Again it doesn't happen. Francis keeps attacking down the home straight, all the way to the line, over ten metres ahead of his nearest rival. He crosses the line with his arms stretched wide and his mouth open in a roar as the clock stops at 44.96.

The stadium erupts. The green-and-black block, housing· the Calabar fans, bounces violently, as though it might burst open and spill on to the track. Donkey Man ignores the rest of the stadium and points to them, then drops to the ground and, mimicking the vanquished Bolt, starts doing press-ups. He manages three, then rests on his haunches, throwing his head back and stretching his arms out again, like Jesus. He gets back up but now seems to be in a daze. He mimics Bolt again with his 'To Di World' gesture, finishing it off with what looks like a salute, but he is staggering now, as though drunk. His time is readjusted to 45.00: a 0.35-second beating of Bolt's record.

And then Donkey Man collapses. He has been lurching around, trying to take it all in, while also milking it for all it is worth, when suddenly it overwhelms him. He crumples to the track. A stretcher appears. (Over the course of the five days, I count fifteen young athletes being carried out of the stadium on stretchers. When I ask one of the medics about this, I am told it has been a long season, with meetings every weekend, and that this is Champs: an injury is not going to stop an athlete competing.)

Francis is helped on to the stretcher. He lies there for no more than a few moments, blinking and recovering his composure, his chest heaving, before pushing the stretcher-bearers away and bounding back up. Maybe he has remembered that in two hours he has the 200 metres final. And that in 2003, Bolt, having set the 400 metres record that Francis has just broken, was back on the track three hours later to set a new record for the 200 metres.

'Ladies and gentlemen, please, we ask you to be quiet for the start of this event. Sssshhhhh.' The decibels drop a little, the low hum interrupted by a few isolated vuvuzelas. Then, from a distance, the far corner of the track, comes a clean, rasping sound: *poch*.

The boys' 200 metres starts and the vuvuzelas recommence, along with the brass bands and drums. Coming out of the bend, Javon Francis pulls up injured. It's a race too far for him. Jevaughn Minzie of Bog Walk, second to Zharnel Hughes in the 100, wins in 20.49, missing Bolt's record.

By 9 p.m., with Kingston now in total darkness and Champs winding down, sixty policemen have moved in to line the perimeter of the stands. They stand ten metres apart facing the crowd. The army appears for the closing ceremony as the schools re-emerge for the trophy presentations and fireworks. Calabar are declared boys' winners; Edwin Allen High School, from the farming community of Frankfield – in the dead centre of the island – win the girls' competition.

The fireworks are still going off as I join the thousands streaming out of the stadium, many of them heading to the after-parties. These are permitted again following a police ban that lasted several years. 'Promoters promise violence-free events' reads the headline in that morning's *Star* newspaper. The twenty-one Champs records will be on people's minds and in tomorrow's papers, but they also raise questions. If there is a doping problem in Jamaica – as the recent positive tests seem to indicate – does it also exist at schools level? While most celebrate the records, others wonder and some doubt.

Although the atmosphere at Champs was exuberant, an air of suspicion had descended on Jamaican athletics. It explained the pledge to begin drug-testing at schools level, as well as the defensiveness I encountered in some when I raised the topic. 'I'm not going there,' said Donald Quarrie, one of Jamaica's sprinting greats, when I asked him about drug-testing at Champs. Others professed surprise and confusion. Mark Ricketts, a friendly economist and former journalist who now lives in California, prowled the stands at Champs, hawking his book, *Jamaican Gold*, about the rise of the island's athletes. Ricketts said that the recent positive tests for Asafa Powell and Veronica Campbell-Brown 'baffles everyone's mind. But because they're kind of over the hill, people look at it and say, "Were they desperate, or did they make an innocent mistake?"'

My American coaching friend, Keith Barnier, didn't know what to make of it. 'You know the dirty coaches because they use all these long words you don't understand. They know what drugs do what.' Barnier looked thoughtful. 'Y'know, I kinda like it when people say my guys are on steroids. Means they're fast.'

Some Jamaicans were angry, but it seemed to me that many were less annoyed with the athletes who'd tested positive than with people like Renée Anne Shirley who asked awkward questions, or who claimed the cases pointed to a darker truth. Listening to the radio one evening mid-Champs, while driving back to my lodgings in Stony Hill, on the outskirts of Kingston, I heard the presenters grilling Anna Legnani, the IAAF's deputy director of communications. The main presenter seemed less interested in hearing what Legnani might have to say than in mounting a shrill defence: 'Bring in WADA [World Anti-Doping Agency] and the IOC!' he implored. 'Bring in the top officials and let them see what happens at this unique event in the western hemisphere! There's a difference between a doping violation and a culture of doping, and I know there isn't a culture of doping.

'It's good that Anna is here,' continued the presenter, well-spoken, with the perfect diction of well-educated Jamaicans. 'Let her see where it all starts, let her see that there isn't a culture of doping here. This, Anna, is the nursery for Jamaica's track and field.'

It seemed as though he was about to invite her to speak . . . but no, he carried on: 'There will be doping violations – we hope it doesn't happen – but this is where it begins. Your thoughts on what you're seeing, Anna; how long are you going to be here, by the way?'

'I'm leaving on Monday,' replied Legnani.

'When you are here on Saturday [the final day], you will see what we're talking about. You haven't seen anything yet. Your thoughts on what you're seeing, Anna. Have you seen anything like this in the world?'

'Erm, no. I mean the level and the depth of some of the performances we've seen—'

The co-presenter pitched in: 'Are high school kids drug-tested at meets like this in Europe and the States?'

'We don't have high school meets like this,' said Legnani. 'School sports are kind of disappearing in Europe, which is a shame. But it's such a reservoir of talent you have—'

'Are you saying that high school meets in Europe do not rise to this level, and wouldn't merit testing?'

'They are not at this level.'

'Why should we in Jamaica test when the rest of the world is not testing?'

'Um, well, that's a good point—'

'I don't see why we should be guinea pigs for the rest of the world.'

This was followed by a long, awkward silence, with shuffling and muffled talking; perhaps Legnani was gesturing that she had had enough of being grilled. Finally the main presenter spoke again: 'Yes, I . . . I want to move from that because I think we've exhausted that . . . And Anna, I know she's a good jumper, but she's going through the hoops, and she's not going to answer that, so we're flogging a dead horse.'

The radio presenters were right about one thing: there is nothing like Champs. It is surely the world's biggest schools athletics meeting, and perhaps also the oldest. 'For over a century it hasn't missed a beat,' I was told by the former prime minister, P. J. Patterson.

Over the five days of the meeting, I spoke to coaches, athletes, journalists and seasoned observers. Where had the Jamaican athletics' success started? I asked. Who or what was responsible? Lots said Champs. Nobody said Usain Bolt. Donald Quarrie, the Olympic 200 metres gold medallist in 1976, said that if there was one person who deserved more credit than anybody else, it was Herb McKenley, the hero of the Helsinki Olympics. 'Every Jamaican athlete has a bit of Herb in them,' said Quarrie (an accidental double entendre in the land of the 'holy herb'). Mike Fennell, president of the Jamaica Olympic Association, agreed: 'Herb was first. He used to seek opportunities for the youngsters. He was a fantastic individual.' Even Bolt, when asked in 2014 who his Olympic hero was, didn't hesitate: 'Herb McKenley.'

There were other names, some from further back: Gerald Claude (G. C.) Foster, who sailed in a banana boat to the London Olympics in 1908 only to be told he couldn't compete. These days, the G. C. Foster College is where the island's athletics coaches are all trained. Other names: Norman Manley, the father of independence, a schoolboy champion who held the Champs 100 yards record for forty-four years; Jamaica's first Olympic champion, Arthur Wint; George Rhoden; Don Quarrie; Bert Cameron; Asafa Powell. Not forgetting the women: Merlene Ottey; Grace Jackson; Juliet Cuthbert; Deon Hemmings; Cynthia Thompson, the 100 metres sprinter, the first Jamaican woman to reach an Olympics final and the first to break an Olympic record at the 1948 London Olympics.

And the coaches, Glen Mills and Stephen Francis, who oversaw the two leading Jamaican clubs – MVP and Racers. 'You have a lot of brilliant people in Jamaica,' Mark Ricketts told me. 'Mills and Francis are brilliant people. Francis is very well read and intelligent: a genius.' I had spotted Francis – who coached Powell, Shelly-Ann Fraser-Pryce and others – at Champs, sitting watching in the main stand, wearing a wide-brimmed hat. He was even bigger than Mills, and more serious and intimidating-looking.

'Mills is withdrawn,' Ricketts continued. 'He's so quiet, unassuming. You see him sitting up there.' He pointed to Mills in his favourite seat, high in the stands. 'He wanted to be an athlete and recognised he wasn't going to be an athlete, so he has studied everything. Like a surgeon. Like a neurosurgeon. Like a brilliant scientist. He has done everything to be the best sprint coach in the world.'

In Jamaica I wanted to meet as many of the key people as possible, though I ended up travelling to the Caribbean more in hope than expectation. I realised, having tried to set up some interviews, that this is not how they operate in Jamaica. A typical conversation would go like this:

'When did you say you get here?'

'Next week.'

'Call me next week, man.'

That was fine. Until a phone call on a Monday, attempting to arrange a meeting for later in the week, would go like this:

'What day?'

'Wednesday.'

'Call me Wednesday, man.'

There was a certain thrill, a sense of exhilaration, to this. I had much to do, lots of people to see in Kingston. But my first stop after Champs was the countryside. I was heading to the other side of the island, to rural Trelawny, home to the Maroons, the tribe of people who escaped slavery and survived on their wits, strength and endurance in the lush, mountainous and harsh interior. And also home to Usain Bolt.

3

BOLT'S OWN COUNTRY

William Knibb knew, long before Jamaica at large was aware,
the special talent it had in its hands.
Letter to the *Jamaica Observer*, 2 April 2014

I stop the car, wind down the window and say: 'Mr Bolt's house?'

The routine is repeated five times. Each time an arm extends, a finger points, instructions are offered. The first time it is a woman emerging from a shop that I think might be Wellesley Bolt's general store, not realising that there are identical stores – huts opening on to the road – every few hundred yards. The second is a Rastafarian youth sitting on a tree stump. The third and fourth are workers who have stopped for a break. Then there's a man walking along the road holding a machete. 'It in Coxheath,' he says.

Coxheath is out the other side of Sherwood Content, just before the bumpy road peters out altogether. When I arrive at the Bolt family residence, I realise that stopping and asking was unnecessary. You can't miss it. It's the only house enclosed by a large and recently added wall, with an iron gate, and, on the roof, an enormous satellite dish.

The gate is open, and at the end of the small path, the front door to the house is ajar, the sound wafting out that of a football match on television.

As soon as I appear at the gate, Mr Wellesley Bolt materialises, filling the doorway. He steps out to the porch, waves me forward, extends his hand and invites me to sit on one of the two chairs. He is wearing a baseball cap, and a T-shirt with a picture of his son on it. 'Bolt', it says.

Wellesley says that neighbours regularly drop by to watch games beamed in from England. As for Usain, he lives in Kingston and returns home when training allows. Given how hard he trains, that isn't often, says his father. We sit down, the door remains open, and it's possible to make out the outline of a man on the sofa. Is it . . . ?

The thirty-minute drive to Sherwood Content from Falmouth, the coastal town where Bolt attended secondary school, plunges you deep into lush forest. Initially you follow a river on one of the sinuous, heavily potholed roads that dominate the interior, and which make driving so treacherous. (That, and the driving habits of some locals. Another hazard is that they drive on the left in Jamaica, except on blind corners. 'Undertakers love careless overtakers' reads one billboard.)

From the air, much of the island looks uninhabitable. Apart from its pale, sandy fringes it seems to be mainly thick green tropical forest on triangular mounds that resemble moguls on a ski run (for giants). The forest is at its densest in the north-west, in and around Trelawny. This is Cockpit Country, where, most famously, the Maroons camped out. A popular if unproven theory is that the people of Trelawny are endowed with the toughest, strongest and, evidently, the fastest genes of all Jamaicans due to the fact that so many of their ancestors survived in such hostile terrain.

It seems to be borne out by the number of athletes who come from here. As well as Bolt, there is Warren Weir, Steve Mullings, Veronica Campbell-Brown, Omar Brown, Voletta Wallace, Lerone Clarke, Inez

Turner and Debbie-Ann Parris, with Merlene Ottey and Yohan Blake from the neighbouring parish. Together they come from an area with a population of 74,000. That's the size of Carlisle. It's the same number of people as live in a *square kilometre* of Manhattan Island.

When you get to Sherwood Content, it would be impossible to be unaware that it is home to Usain Bolt. A large white triangular sign has a hand-drawn cartoon of Bolt doing his famous pose. And beneath the picture, the message:

Welcome to Sherwood Content
Home of the World's Fastest Man
Usain Bolt
World record: 9.58 in (100m) 19.19 in (200m)

As you drive through the village, there's another big white board, with another almost passable likeness of Bolt, same pose. 'Welcome to Usain Bolt Apparel Gift Shop' this one reads. This is the home of his Aunt Lilly, whose Bolt-themed gift shop opened a few months before my visit.

Just before you reach the scattered houses that make up Sherwood Content, home to a community of 1,500 people, you pass Waldensia Primary School, a collection of colourful buildings with corrugated tin roofs perched on a grassy hill. And on a small clearing before the slope begins to rise, seven parallel lines are scorched into the grass: Bolt's first six-lane running track. Not an oval – there isn't space – but a straight, no longer than fifty metres.

Sherwood Content seems like a sleepy place where, ironically, given that its fame now rests on being home to the fastest man in history, nothing happens very quickly. One house might have a satellite dish that wouldn't look out of place at NASA headquarters, but the water still comes from the local river rather than through pipes and is stored in large drums in people's gardens. The Bolt association has brought new sports facilities (a multi-purpose court, branded with Digicel, the

phone company and Bolt's long-time sponsor), but there is still no mains water, despite Bolt himself highlighting the issue, Red Stripe donating £100,000, and pipes being laid: they've been arguing for it for more than forty years. According to local legend, it worked for one week only – the week that followed Bolt's world records at the 2009 world championships in Berlin.

Wellesley Bolt is tall. Not as tall as his son. 'I'm six-three,' he says. 'My father was tall. I am not sure how tall was my father, but taller than I am. So was the mother's father.' He frequently refers to his wife,

Jennifer, as 'the mother', and to his son simply as 'Bolt'. It's a Saturday, so Jennifer is at church. She's a Seventh-day Adventist.

You don't imagine that Wellesley has changed with his son's success. The Bolts still live in the same house, doing the same things, and Wellesley seems as laid-back as the youth I passed sitting on the tree stump. But life is different in some ways. 'Well, financially, yes, it has changed,' he says. 'Because it was difficult when he was going to school. I was working in the coffee industry, then I was made redundant and so I travel abroad, do some work, come back to put him to school.

'But things has changed. The house wasn't this big.' He flashes a grin and leans back to take it in – it's a large house, perhaps not the biggest in the village, where there are several old Victorian houses, but it's no mansion. Bolt's neighbours are, according to Wellesley, relaxed about having such a famous, and wealthy, family in their midst. There's the wall around the property. But the gate is wide open.

Wellesley was the victim of crime on one occasion, in Falmouth in June 2013, when thieves broke into his Toyota pickup and stole $4,000. But he seems perfectly happy to welcome a stranger if not quite into his home, then at least on to his porch. (Aunt Lilly, who I visit later, is more circumspect. Initially, as she opens up her gift shop for the potential customer, she is friendly and chatty, but she becomes guarded on learning the visitor is a journalist. When I ask if she travels to watch her nephew run, she replies: 'I stay home and keep the journalists away.')

'We have the dish,' Wellesley continues, gesturing towards the roof as the football commentary drifts out to the porch (Chelsea vs Stoke City). 'And I have two vehicle. A motorbike. So, you know. A lot of changes.'

When his son attended Waldensia Primary School, Wellesley went and watched him compete at sports day. 'Ricardo Geddes, he's the only person who beat him at school,' he recalls. 'And he cry, he cry when Ricardo beat him. I said to him, "Don't worry, man, you'll get him the next time round." And he put that in his head and Ricardo never beat him again.'

Wellesley continues: 'I would go and watch the kids, and think, Hey, he's winning almost all the races. Probably this guy may have some talent. Time goes by, and at twelve, I realised he was doing well at track. He was awarded a track scholarship to William Knibb' – the high school in Falmouth. Was it a big decision to send his son away? 'Well, he has to go somewhere. He has to travel from here to somewhere: William Knibb or Clark's Town or Wakefield. But William Knibb was the closest, so he accepted the scholarship.'

That meant daily taxi rides. Apparently Mr Bolt would wake his son at 5.30 a.m. 'Yes,' he nods, 'I don't believe in lateness to school. You go to school and you must get every ounce of your lesson.' Wellesley has an older son and a daughter, each to a different mother, but he kept a very close eye on his younger son, turning up in Falmouth randomly and unannounced. 'I always go to William Knibb once per week to see him train,' he says. 'In the early part he would try to skip training sometimes to go and play those video games in Falmouth. So I always had to be on top of that.'

He kept on top of that by not telling Bolt when he would turn up. 'After a while he realised that's what I was doing.' Wellesley slaps his hands together. 'He couldn't take the chance. Coz I was vicious, then.'

What was the punishment when Wellesley caught his son skipping school or training? 'I would strap him. Because I told him, "It's difficult to find money to send you to school." He was wasting that. He didn't like it. But now he say I'm the best father. He said if I was the type of father who let him do that, probably he wouldn't be where he is now.'

For a thirteen-year-old boy from rural Trelawny, Falmouth represented the bright lights, the big city.

I went to Falmouth a couple of days earlier. It's a twenty-mile drive up the coast from Montego Bay, Jamaica's second biggest city and a busy, bustling place, popular with tourists. The road to Falmouth is dominated by large luxury resorts, where security guards prowl the grounds and patrol the gates, with the beach divided up and enclosed by fences. Presumably to keep the locals out.

You turn off the main highway at a junction marked with a huge billboard showing Bolt from behind, topless, arms outstretched against a backdrop of the Jamaican flag. 'Living Legend', it reads: an advert for Digicel. Ten minutes later you enter the town of Falmouth, the capital of Trelawny Parish, and it's like stepping back in time. It resembles a nineteenth-century film set, with dusty, bumpy roads, crumbling buildings and hand-painted signs above the shops. You half expect to find horses and carts instead of cars.

As I drove into Falmouth, there was another sight, one that was utterly incongruous. Sitting in the harbour, towering over the town, was the *Freedom of the Seas*: one of the world's largest cruise ships, capable of holding over 3,500 passengers. Two days later, there were two of these Caribbean cruise behemoths moored in the harbour. That should have meant up to 6,000 visitors, yet the streets of Falmouth were virtually empty.

There are market stalls, shops and restaurants, all empty. Locals beckon you to their stalls or into their shops, not aggressively, but with an air of desperation. An old man with white dreadlocks and gold teeth sneered when I said 'No thank you' to his offer of accompanying me to the shop selling Falmouth's best jerk chicken. 'This is Jamaica,' he pleaded. 'People friendly here. Don't be unfriendly.' He continued shouting as I walked away. But he was right – people were friendly, though many seemed to have given up and sat slumped in the shadows, escaping the heat. It was a mystery. Where were the tourists?

It was as if the clock had stopped around 1810, when Falmouth had its heyday as a busy port. In one direction went sugar and rum to Britain; in the other came slaves from Africa: up to thirty boats a day sailing in and out of the harbour. The town, built on a grid system similar to New York's,[1] boasts the finest Georgian architecture in the Caribbean, the *pièce de résistance* being the courthouse, the first building you would see when you arrived in Falmouth by sea. Not a coincidence, perhaps.[2]

Close to the courthouse is Market Street. This is where Ben Johnson lived before moving to Toronto when he was fifteen. It's one of the main streets in Falmouth, with shops and businesses as well as homes. The businesses are eclectic: there's a 'Miracle Medical Lab' (which might have been of interest to Johnson in his drug-fuelled pursuit of glory), as well as a 'Dr C. A. L. Behasse, Clinical Christian Psychologist'.

I had arranged to meet Devere Nugent, pastor of the William Knibb Memorial Baptist Church: the man who spotted Bolt's talent, and who, as Bolt says in his autobiography, bribed him with food ('jerk chicken, roasted sweet potatoes, rice and peas') as he encouraged him to swap cricket, which he loved, for athletics, towards which he was initially indifferent.

On the phone, Nugent had told me to meet him across from the church in the William Knibb Educational Centre. But it appears to be a building site, all bare concrete and exposed metal rods, with workmen adding a second floor. On closer inspection, however, the ground floor is intact – and in here, despite the noise and commotion overheard, it is business as usual.

The pastor's office is in a small room in the corner of a big hall, where I wait while Nugent finishes a meeting. He is well turned out in jeans and a Ralph Lauren shirt, and when I am called to see him,

---

1 Falmouth was different in one respect: it had piped water before New York. The town had the first piped water in the western hemisphere, introduced in 1799, which only makes the lack of water in Sherwood Content and other rural villages seem more ridiculous.

2 As well as being a major slave port, Falmouth also became a focal point for revolt. A leading abolitionist in the first half of the nineteenth century was the man whose name now adorns the church and the high school, the Baptist minister William Knibb.

he explains that the building we are in hosts an academy, which he set up four years ago. They hold evening classes for schoolchildren wanting extra tuition in, as the sign outside indicates, 'Math, English, Business, Accounts, Human & Social Biology, Social Studies, Physics, Chemistry, and others on demand'. Students attend these classes in their own time – the academy is entirely voluntary, but they struggle to accommodate all the young people who want to come. Hence the extension.

Like Bolt, Nugent comes originally from Sherwood Content. He also went to the same secondary, William Knibb Memorial High School. But he was never an athlete. 'In my mind I was,' he tells me, 'but as a child I grew up with bronchitis and because of that my mother never allowed me to exert myself too much physically. But I grew to love track and field when I got to high school.'

Charismatic and engaging, Nugent continues: 'You know, Usain Bolt is not our first Olympian; neither is he the first William Knibb past-student to have made the 100 metres finals of the Olympics. There's a guy, I don't know if you've ever heard of him, named Michael Green.'

Green, who made the 100 metres final in the 1996 Olympics, was a few years older than Nugent. A new coach also started at the school while Nugent was a pupil there. Pablo McNeil was an ex-Olympian who ran in the Jamaican 4x100 metres team that was fourth in Tokyo in 1964. 'When Pablo came to William Knibb I would sit behind the auditorium,' says Nugent, 'and watch him evening after evening just taking the students through their paces. I began to have an appreciation for that.'

When he finished high school, Nugent returned to Sherwood Content to work as a teaching assistant at Bolt's primary, Waldensia. 'I knew Bolt from when he was a baby,' he says. 'No, before – I've known Bolt from when his mother was pregnant.'

He began to look after the sports programme at Waldensia. It was a big school, 300 pupils from six up to fifteen, and Nugent's goal was the district athletics championships, which they won. But the school then downgraded to a primary, losing the older pupils. It meant that Nugent began to take an interest in the eight-year-old Usain Bolt, who was part of the cricket team but didn't play because he was too young. 'The next year, he was a Grade 4 student and he was batting at number three with the Grade 6 boys. He was my gully fielder and I remember it like yesterday, for two reasons – his height and his athletic abilities. He could cover that span, that area, in absolutely no time and for me had the best square cut. For a schoolboy he had one of the best square cuts that I have seen.'

Bolt played cricket in the first part of the year and did track and field in the second. According to Nugent, he was 'a decent athlete and he liked the competition'. Nugent encouraged the rivalry with his classmate, Ricardo Geddes. 'That for me created the passion inside of him to not allow anybody to beat him.' He admits that he did bribe him with food. It was a way, he says, of saying: 'Give me everything you have, lay it all on the track.' And Bolt did. He had boundless energy. 'That fella never really walked as a child, not a day in his life. He ran to school, he ran to the shop, he ran, he ran. He had a wheel, one of those bicycle wheels where the spokes were removed and he would run it with a stick.'

Nugent coached Bolt until he left for theological college at the end of Bolt's penultimate year at primary school. Despite not being around, he kept in regular contact with the family and took a keen interest in Usain's schooling. Bolt's father told him he was thinking of sending Usain to Cedric Titus school in Clark's Town. Nugent advised against it. 'I told him, "No you cannot send him to Cedric Titus." Cedric Titus never had, in my mind, a decent enough sport programme. The only school in the parish that had a decent programme at the time was William Knibb. So I said to him, "Let me speak with the coach at William Knibb." That would have been Pablo at the time.

'I went to Pablo and asked whether or not he would take a look at him. The next day Pablo had a look at him and got him into school.'

*

Searching through the records of Champs, the first mention of Bolt is in 2000. He was thirteen, running for William Knibb in the Class 3 (youngest) category, and he placed fifth in the 200 metres in 24.03. First was a local rival, Keith Spence, who went to Cornwall College, along the coast in Montego Bay. (These days, Spence is a fitness instructor in a private gym in Kingston.) Otherwise, Champs was notable not for the debut of a boy named Bolt, but for crowd trouble during the medley relay: 'A melee in the bleachers splashed spectators on to the track.'

The following year, 2001, now in Class 2, Bolt was seventh in the 400 metres in 51.16. Veronica Campbell, another sprinter from Trelawny, was the standout performer, winning the girls' sprint double. Still a schoolgirl, she was, incredibly, already an Olympic medallist, having been a member of the 4x100 metres relay team that won silver in Sydney the previous year. She was also the junior world champion over 100 and 200 metres.

Finally, in 2002, in his all-white William Knibb kit, Bolt tasted victory at Champs. The meeting was held not at the National Stadium, which was being refurbished for the world junior championships in July, but at G. C. Foster College in Spanish Town, along the road from Kingston.

The star of the meeting was Steve Mullings, yet another Trelawny product, who won the sprint double in his final Champs before heading to the US and a career as a professional. Bolt, 'the gangly William Knibb Memorial product, was almost as good [as Mullings]', reads *Champs 100*, the commemorative book. Bolt was denied a possible 400 metres record when a power cut stopped the electronic timing. He was hand-timed at 47.4 seconds – the Champs record was 47.49. In the 200 metres he equalled the record, winning in 21.61. Interviewed afterwards, he said: 'I train hard but not as hard as you would expect from one doing such fast times at my age.'

Then, as now, a record at Champs had the whole country buzzing. Already they were asking: what could this kid do at the world juniors,

to be held on Jamaican soil, at the National Stadium, just four
months later?

Lorna Thorpe, head of sport at William Knibb, realised early that in
Bolt the school had a major talent on its hands. She had seen him run
at the local primary school championships, held on the grass track at
the high school he would later attend. 'I was introduced to him, a tall,
lanky young man,' she says.

Thorpe was head of sport at William Knibb for thirty-four years
and retired recently. She now works for the Member of Parliament for
North Trelawny, Patrick Atkinson QC, Jamaica's Attorney General
and a member of one of the country's two main political parties, the
(left-leaning) People's National Party. I meet her in the PNP's Falmouth
office, around the corner from the William Knibb Memorial Church,
where she sits behind a desk, showing admirable patience in dealing
with the issues, complaints and gripes of an ever-renewing line of local
people. Judging from those in the waiting room, they include some of
Falmouth's most colourful characters.

Thorpe speaks about Bolt with motherly affection – Bolt has
described her as his second mother – and, in her gentle way, shrugs off
the wayward behaviour that could earn him a beating from his father.
'That's any teenager. When you're always at training and you see your
friends doing something else – football, basketball – you want to be
part of that. So sometimes Usain would run away from track training
just to be with some of his friends, to play different games.'

Being responsible for the sports programme at William Knibb
meant Thorpe had to 'make sure that they go to training, they get
their meals, they get their uniform, their running spikes. I was always
there for them, to hear their complaints and make sure whatever they
were supposed to get, they get it.' She was also Bolt's form teacher.
'The bond get closer and closer. He would come for advice. I would
encourage him: about track and field, outside of track and field.
Having that relationship with him, telling him that the sky's the limit,

I was always there. We still share that relationship. I am in touch with him a lot. He comes back when he can. Holidays, he comes back, visit his parents, stays at home, like any normal person.'

Bolt was a pupil who needed additional support, the school thought. As his athletic talent shone more brightly, he struggled to balance training and school work. The principal, Margaret Lee, tried to find him a mentor. She approached a former pupil, Norman Peart. 'As the principal saw it, we had this special one, and she wanted to make sure he was on the right path,' Thorpe explains. But Peart resisted the overtures from his old school. He had finished college in Kingston and returned to nearby Montego Bay to work in the tax office. When I speak to Peart, he tells me, 'I was single, no kids, and the principal called me one day. "I hear you're down this side of the island. Why don't you come and help the team?"'

'I said, "No, I'm finished work at five o'clock. You'll be finished training then."' But Lee didn't give up. A few weeks later she called Peart again. 'She said, "There's this special one. Very talented. I want you to help him because I want him to get a scholarship." She wanted him to get a scholarship to the States.' This time Peart said: 'OK, I'll help this guy.'

But first he called one of his old teachers, still at the school. 'Is this guy OK?' asked Peart. 'Because I don't want to fight with no kid now.'

'No, no, he's fine,' he was told. 'Quite humble.'

Peart is thirteen years older than Bolt. Did they connect? 'Erm, no,' he laughs. 'Not really. He wasn't a talker . . . then. He saw me more as a second dad. I let him do things his dad didn't.'

Mainly Peart helped him with his school work. 'He did OK in his studies but had his troubles. I didn't realise when I got to him, but I don't think he was ready to go to college, for more reasons than one. But pretty much the big decisions for him came within twelve months of knowing him, because I met him in February of 2002' – a month before his success at Champs, and five months before his first major meeting: the world junior championships in Kingston.

Thorpe says that she didn't ever believe that going to a US college would be an option for Bolt, even if the principal thought otherwise. She is adamant that he would never have become the athlete he became if he had left Jamaica. American colleges started approaching him; sending brochures, care of the school. Most ended up in a drawer in Thorpe's desk – some might still be there, she says – or in the bin. 'As soon as they come he would pass them to me. He just did not want to leave Jamaica. He loves Jamaica.'

It was July 2002 when Bolt announced his talent to a wider audience, though the most passionate one was packed into the National Stadium in Kingston. The stands were predictably full, the bleachers bouncing – unusual for a world junior championships. And on the new track, in lane three for the final of the 200 metres, was the home favourite: the Champs hero.

The TV camera panned along the eight finalists, but leapt up when it reached Bolt's lane and found only his chest. He looked about a foot taller than the other athletes. Already six-three (though accounts vary about his height at the time; in some he is already six-five) and with the build of a bean sprout, he was just a frame, with no muscle.

Bolt was introduced to the crowd. There was no showboating. He cracked his knuckles. He looked serious and nervous, even a little afraid, rocking from side to side, fidgeting, unable to keep his hands still. But when the race started, he was quickly up, stretching to full height, accentuating his height advantage – though it seemed like a disadvantage on the bend as he drifted to the outside of his lane, as though his head, which was cocked to the right, was pulling him.

Entering the straight, he was alongside the runner on his inside. He was ungainly, ragged, head tilted back as the runner in lane five, Brendan Christian of Antigua and Barbuda, began to challenge.

Christian was catching; he almost drew level. But Bolt held on, winning in 20.51. At fifteen, against runners up to three years older, he was the junior world champion – the youngest in history.

He was watched from one of the boxes at the back of the stand by the country's prime minister, P. J. Patterson, a former Calabar High School pupil and keen athletics fan. Patterson was sitting with Donald Quarrie. 'I said to Quarrie, "You've got to take this fella under your wing,"' Patterson recalls. 'Because if he can run a curve like that he'll be a world beater.'

Now it wasn't just colleges that were after Bolt, but big companies too. Another observer was a French marketing executive from a German company. Pascal Rolling was there representing Puma because the sportswear brand was interested in aligning itself with Jamaica; or more accurately with the Jamaican culture and lifestyle. They were on the verge of signing deals with the Jamaica Athletics Administrative Association (JAAA) and Jamaica Olympic Association. 'At the same time,' says Rolling, 'we were looking for an athlete we could use in our communications.'

And there before him was a fifteen-year-old world junior champion who, after winning, seemed in his celebrations to forge a bond with the crowd. There was a connection there, thought Rollings. 'I had seen Usain before, but at the world championships he not only made the show on the track but also off the track, after the race. I thought, This is the perfect ambassador to represent our new relationship with Jamaica.'

They didn't set out to sign someone so young, Rollings continues: 'It wasn't a specific age we had in mind, just someone who could represent the brand. Usain, with his charisma off the track, was a perfect representative. You didn't have to be a genius to see that this guy has market potential because of his size and how he dominates the junior level. But equally important for us was the fact that this fifteen-year-old kid had such a connection to the public and a way to entertain.'

Jamaica attracted Puma because the sportswear company was interested in more than sport and elite performance. 'We were balanced between sport and lifestyle,' Rolling says. 'Jamaica had a culture of track and field since the late forties, and consistently produced top sprinters, but we were interested in the culture of Jamaica, too. They are everybody's second favourite team at the Olympics, aren't they?'

Within a few months of his world junior title, Bolt had signed with Puma. Lorna Thorpe recalls, 'When he signed his first contract he put in a clause where a certain amount of goods would come to William Knibb each year. From 2002 the school has not bought a pair of spikes because of Usain Bolt.'

Bolt was far from being the first world-class sprinter to emerge from his corner of Jamaica, but his junior world title was the biggest thing to happen to Falmouth since Ben Johnson won the Olympic 100 metres in Seoul in 1988. Thorpe recalls that night well. 'Oh boy, that was a night. I know Ben Johnson quite well; his father, his sisters. When the holidays are here, he comes. William Knibb is where Ben come and train, still.'

Thorpe said I should visit the high school. It's on the outskirts of town, a collection of purple-and-cream buildings – the school colours – with a guardhouse at the entrance, and a sign: 'Ignorance Enslaves. Knowledge Liberates.' I had been told to visit during lunch break; somebody from the sports department would see me then.

Gloria Grant appears, munching a sandwich. She graduated from G. C. Foster College in 1985 and coaches the girls' athletics team, but she remembers Bolt, especially his first Champs. 'He was late for one of his races, so he ran from where we stayed. I think that was why he did not win.' They were staying, as they usually do, in the theological college, close to the stadium.

She plays down the school's part in making Bolt. 'Usain was just natural. He just developed. He used to hide from training sometimes, because Pablo McNeil took training very, very serious. He was firm with them; he would push them. He was a disciplinarian. But I don't think Usain was pushed after a while, because he was motivated.' McNeil, who refused to let Bolt see his stopwatch when he was training, died in 2011. He had been in poor health after suffering a stroke in 2007 (he had been working on a book, *The Bolt of Lightning and Me*, which has never been published). Bolt had another coach at William Knibb, Dwight Barnett, who is said to be at another school in Jamaica – strangely, nobody I spoke to seemed to know which one.

I ask Gloria if there are currently any promising young athletes at the school: anyone to follow in Bolt's footsteps. There are some boys nearby, all in the khaki uniform that every Jamaican schoolboy wears, with purple-and-white epaulettes denoting William Knibb. She looks up. 'Come here, Ben!'

One of the boys comes over. 'Hi, Ben,' I say.

'Bent,' Gloria corrects me.

'Christopher Bent, sir,' the boy says. He says that he's a sprinter too. How did he get on at Champs? 'It wasn't that impressive.' He speaks hesitantly. 'It could have been better. I have to work on certain areas. Go back to the drawing board.'

He was fourth in his heats in the 200 metres, so didn't qualify, though his time of 22.34 was nothing to be ashamed of. And still he hoped that athletics would be his passport to a college in the US or Canada. 'I would like to get to a college overseas to do studies and track and field.'

Bent met Bolt when he returned to the school to donate a bus in December 2012. 'But I've not had a conversation with him. It's a great thing, you know. Usain Bolt has given us a lot of motivation. The way he performs, he's a great man to look up on in terms of achievement.'

Bent seems as reserved as Bolt is outgoing: what does he make of his showmanship? 'I don't really enjoy his showman stuff. His performances are great, that's what I like.' He seems a little embarrassed about Bolt's excesses, which doesn't surprise me. Jamaican schools like William Knibb were modelled on British public schools, and many of the traditions – the deference, politeness, restraint – seem to have been preserved.[3]

Gloria Grant regards Bolt's pre-race and post-race exhibitions with the kind of amused bemusement that a parent might demonstrate towards a child showing off. 'Oh, his antics!' She explodes with laughter. 'I think that is what helps to calm him down. When he does that, I think he gets more relaxed. But Usain wasn't like that at school.'

Back in Devere Nugent's office, across the road from the William Knibb Memorial Church, the pastor shares a secret: 'I have a theory that I have not necessarily brandished about the place.' Then he leans forward, putting his elbows on the desk. 'Usain went through something that a lot of folks did not go through. If you are a doctor practising surgery every day for fifty years, after fifty years you are going to be good at what you are doing. Well, since this fella has been about eight or nine years old, he has been running at the highest level of his age group.

'Since he has been eight years old he would have been running at the National Stadium every year. I don't think there's another athlete in the Jamaican set-up right now with that kind of experience under their belt. I don't think there is.' These were the formative years, says Nugent. 'Because if you look at him as a [sixteen-year-old] Class 1 athlete, he's a very lanky fellow with no muscles, which indicates that up to that point he was just running off raw talent: raw, raw talent.

'There's a second aspect to him that is under-discussed,' Nugent

---

3 In *Beyond a Boundary*, his memoir of growing up in Trinidad in the early part of the twentieth century, C. L. R. James writes: 'I learnt and obeyed and taught a code, the English public-school code.' This code manifested itself in particular in sport: 'We lived in two worlds. Inside the classrooms the heterogeneous jumble of Trinidad was battered and jostled and shaken down into some sort of order. On the playing field we did what ought to be done.' That translated as fair play, sportsmanship, respect for authority: something I observed at Champs, even if it was not always apparent elsewhere in the 'heterogeneous jumble' of Jamaica.

continues. 'I call it a reverse preparation. When he was in primary school he ran 100 and 150s at his age. So when he went to William Knibb he went feeling in his heart that he was a 100 metres runner. But the coach, looking at his height and his physique, decided that this fellow is not suited for the 100. So he takes him from the 100 and pushes him up to the 400 and says, "Now you've got to run the 400 or the 200." But in his heart and in his belly as a child he's always been a 100 metres runner.'

Running 400s built a foundation of strength and endurance that Bolt wouldn't have had if he'd always focused on the shorter events, Nugent believes. 'I think what that did was to somehow – and while I cannot prove it from a scientific perspective, it's just my layman's theory – develop him in another kind of a way. He always had the speed, but that kind of endurance built up the muscles, developed him in a kind of different way. Which is the reason he does not break down as easily as most sprinters.'

Yet, as several people observed, Bolt was not at one of the major schools. Although exposed to the highest level of schoolboy competition in Jamaica, he was at a school that did not measure itself by how well it did at Champs, perhaps for one simple reason: they had no chance of winning. 'There was a big to-do at one stage because when he began to be seen as a good athlete, some schools in Kingston wanted him,' Nugent says. The likes of Calabar and Kingston College were sniffing around, trying to recruit him, but Nugent felt that he would be better off staying where he was. 'I explained it in this way: 1988 boys' championship, Daniel England, Calabar, is in the 100 metres finals. Michael Green of William Knibb is in the 100 metres finals. Michael Green runs eighth in the final. Daniel England wins. But more than that, Daniel England won that year the 100, the 200, the 400, he won the 4x100 and the 4x400 for Calabar. Jump to 1996: Michael Green is in the Olympic finals in Atlanta. Daniel England is yet to make an Olympic team.'

When approaches were made by the big Kingston schools, Nugent continues, 'I told Bolt's father, "If you are going to send him to a school in Kingston he is going to board with somebody else. You don't know what he does, where he's going."'

He says he wasn't worried about Bolt going off the rails or falling in with the wrong crowd. Despite perceptions, he was always level-headed. 'A lot of people will look at him and see him playing around and even behaving as if he's an imbecilic person. He's not – he's a very disciplined guy. If he respects you he gives you 110 per cent. If you have not earned his respect, you can't get anything out of him. To this very day, even though he's a big superstar, when he sees me he still says "Mr Nugent" as if he was a student of mine. Still says "Mr", and he's still very humble and cordial with me. Even with the colossal-ness of his . . .'

Nugent can't find the word, but he adds that Bolt's success can be attributed to three things: talent, parents and discipline. 'I don't think he understood his talent and that probably was a good thing. Because very often when they know how good they are, they see the light even before they reach it.'

You wonder if there is a fourth factor, too. The coaches and teachers who worked with the young Bolt, then passed him along to the next one, like a sprinter handing over a baton. Nugent and Thorpe, both formative influences, come across as fundamentally decent, sensible people; moreover, people whose lives are devoted to helping others – it is what they still do, sitting in their offices, dealing with others' problems.

These days, Nugent is too busy with the church and his academy to do any sports coaching, which is a source of regret. 'It's something I've missed. Especially cricket coaching, because I think you get a chance to pass on valuable tips and not just about the game but about this game called life,' he says, adding that he enjoyed telling people 'they can', and 'watching the light bulbs come on in their heads'. It is often just a case of believing, he thinks, telling anecdotes about children he has helped make something of themselves by planting an idea in their heads – Bolt isn't his only success. 'We get so much opportunity I believe to help children believe in themselves,' Nugent says. 'I never understood it until a few years ago. One of my former students from Waldensia came to me and he said: "Sir, I want to thank you." And I said: "For what?" He said: "Do you remember the day you came to class? You came into the class and you began to tell us what you saw us doing in the future."

'And I said: "Yes, I remember," but I didn't remember what I told him. He said: "Yeah, you came in the class that day and you told me that you saw me as a businessman in my jacket and my tie going into my office to work. That was the day you put it in my head. So I did business in high school. I went to UTech [University of Technology in Kingston], I did business because you placed it in my head. Now I am working with Scotia Bank, where I have to wear my jacket and tie to my office." '

Before leaving Nugent to deal with the lengthening queue of people outside his office, all waiting in the hall with the building work still going on overhead, I ask him the question that's been bothering me about Falmouth. With two cruise ships in the harbour, why is the town deserted?

'Oh,' he says, 'that's a different thing.' For the first time he looks deflated and downbeat. What happened, he explains, is that Royal Caribbean International (a cruise company based in Miami) approached the town with a proposal: they would redevelop the old pier, which was dilapidated. The quid pro quo, the town assumed, was that the boats would sit there for days and the passengers would disembark. Local people were encouraged to open restaurants, shops and market stalls for all the tourists who would throng the old streets.

'I knew from day one,' Nugent says. 'I recognised that the persons who were leading the process have never been on a cruise ship, so they really never knew how a cruise ship would work. Now, when you pay

$600 for a cruise, it's all-inclusive, so why would people come into the town and pay more money?'

But it turned out to be worse than that. When the pier was redeveloped, shops and restaurants were built in what Nugent calls 'a demilitarised zone'. It's a mini-town, modelled on Falmouth, built in an enclosed area on the pier. 'It is literally a replica of the town of Falmouth. It is basically designed like Falmouth. It has the square and it has the . . .'

A fake Falmouth on the pier itself? 'On the pier itself. Ten acres. So the people on the boat don't really have to come into Falmouth.'

The shops and restaurants in the replica town are staffed not by locals but by employees of the cruise company. A fence keeps tourists in and locals out. As in the expensive resorts, fear is driven into tourists; it is fear that keeps them (and their money) within the confines of the hotels, the ships and the replica town. 'I can understand the security concerns,' Nugent says. 'But I think the days when ships are not in, the pier could be open even if it's at a cost. So that folks could walk over there and enjoy the aesthetics, even; just enjoy the aesthetics of the pier. The other problem is that there are not too many attractions in Falmouth.'

Well, other than the fact that it is where the fastest man in history went to school. Nugent says that the town – like Bolt himself – does not really appreciate what Bolt could and should mean to Falmouth. 'Those who come in on the boats and really want to see Jamaica are bussed out of the town,' he says sadly. 'Falmouth has become a dumping ground.'

It literally has: the boats dump their waste and stock up on water. How depressing, I say.

'We will overcome,' says the pastor as he stands to see me out.

4

THE BROTHERHOOD

There's no miracle in Jamaica. We've always been doing this.
Albert Corcho

The name was ubiquitous at Champs, sounding particularly resonant in the precise, lilting Jamaican accent of the stadium announcer, his emphasis on all three syllables: Cal-a-bar.

Calabar athletes looked a cut above the others in their green and black Puma kit. They were slick, professional, menacing – especially the captain, Romario McKenzie, who wore a black Batman mask throughout in homage to his older brother, Ramone, who used to do the same.

There was an air about Calabar. As Champs built towards its climax, they seemed to win virtually everything; they had momentum behind them on the track and in the stands, where their supporters were the loudest and most passionate. They had an aura that other schools lacked. I found myself intrigued, fascinated, impressed. By the final day I even found myself quietly rooting for Calabar.

I began to look into the school's history. Its athletics pedigree is astonishing. When Jamaica won a gold medal in the men's 4x400

metres at the Helsinki Olympics in 1952, three members of the team – Herb McKenley, Arthur Wint and George Rhoden – were from this one school. Since then there has been a steady stream, the legacy continuing all the way to the present day, with 200 metres runner Warren Weir, the bronze medallist at the London Olympics, the latest star alumnus. And yet, as I was repeatedly told at Champs, the current crop of schoolboy superstars may turn out to be the best yet: Javon 'Donkey Man' Francis, Michael O'Hara, fourteen-year-old Christopher Taylor, to name a few.

They were visited by Weir on the eve of Champs. It was dark and flash bulbs illuminated Weir, who wore a white Adidas tracksuit top as he addressed the athletes. Impossible to believe he was only twenty-four; he spoke with the authority of a veteran coach; with the motivational qualities of Martin Luther King. 'My favourite time of the year,' he said. He sounded serious and statesmanlike, and was confident enough to pause after important points, to let them sink in. 'Favourite time of the year, no matter how old or young you are.

'One thing we go out there for, and that's to win. To win. To win. To win. To win. To dominate. To crush them.' He said 'dominate' the way the stadium announcer said 'Calabar'. *Cal-a-bar, dom-in-ate*. 'To repeat also,' he continued, 'and carry on the legacy, the big legacy of *Cal-a-bar*. Win. *Dom-in-ate*. Make people inherit that this week – this weekend – nothing shy of that. Go out there and represent yourselves good . . . As Martin Luther says, be the best you can be. Never stop being that. The best sprinter, best middle distance, best hurdler. The best you can be.'

Weir was interrupted by a shout from the crowd, which was the cue for wild chanting, ending in the Calabar Lions' motto: 'The utmost for the highest.' The passion and intensity – the fervour – was comparable with that surrounding high school football in Texas, as depicted in the book *Friday Night Lights*, 'where high school football went to the very core of life'.

Two weeks after Champs, I meet Weir for lunch in one of the plush hotels in Kingston's business district. He is softly spoken, boyish-looking and seems even younger than twenty-four. He turns up with his girlfriend. She snuggles close to him, while he turns and speaks quietly to her at regular intervals. (Efforts to market Weir as 'the Weirwolf', not least by Weir himself, seem a bit ambitious. Similarly with Yohan Blake's nickname, 'the Beast'. Perhaps only Bolt has the profile and the personality to carry off such a nickname – the irony being that he is so transcendent he doesn't need one.)

Weir is one of the new breed of Jamaican athletes, those who eschewed the US colleges to live and train at home. He lives in a smart area in the Kingston hills overlooking the National Stadium, drives a nice car, has some of the trappings of modest wealth: expensive-looking watch, jewellery, smartphone. He is sponsored by Adidas, but, like most professional athletes, he is not a millionaire. The $40,000 that came with winning the Diamond League 200 metres title in 2013 would have been quite a windfall.[4]

Like Bolt and so many other top athletes, Weir comes originally from Trelawny. There is actually a small community in Trelawny called Calabar, where Calabar Theological College was established in 1839. It was named after the slave port in Nigeria; the community in Jamaica was close to Falmouth, one of the major ports of embarkation for the thousands of slaves shipped through the Middle Passage from Africa. In 1868, Calabar College moved to Kingston, and in 1912, Calabar High School was established in the city by two Baptist ministers for the sons of other ministers and for the ever-larger population of poor Jamaicans, many of them descendants of former slaves, living in ghettos – or garrisons, as some areas would eventually come to be known. In 1952, Calabar High School moved to its current grounds at the foot of Red Hills Road, in west Kingston.

It was here that Herb McKenley, the hero of Helsinki – still the only athlete ever to reach the finals of the 100, 200 and 400 metres at an Olympic Games – was head coach for more than thirty years. Here that he led the school to no fewer than eighteen Champs titles. And here that, upon his death in November 2007 at the age of eighty-five, his body lay in an open casket.

McKenley is the one they all talk about, yet his career as an athlete is only the beginning of the story. It is as a coach and motivator that he is recalled with even greater reverence. 'People tell you that if you go to your grave having not heard Herb in his final pep talk before boys' Champs, especially if he has a glimpse he can win, you haven't heard the best of Herb,' said Neville 'Teddy' McCook, one

---

4 How much athletes earn is shrouded in mystery with shoe deals generally undisclosed, with the exception of Usain Bolt's $10m-a-year from Puma. A 2014 survey by the Track & Field Athletes Association and the USATF Foundation revealed that more than 50% of athletes ranked in the world top 10 in their event earn less than $15,000 a year. It is worth putting that in the context of earnings in Jamaica, however, where the minimum wage is £31 per week and the average worker earns £2,600 a year.

of Jamaica's great sports administrators, who died in 2013. 'He saw his athletes right to the gate, telling them, "You can win, you can win, you can win."'

In his pre-Champs talks, McKenley would sometimes reduce himself to tears. 'The boys would realise that, they would see the tears trickle,' said McCook.

Warren Weir was McKenley's final gift to Calabar: one of the last athletes he recruited. 'Mr McKenley got me in 2001, when I was in primary school, then he got a stroke in the summer, so he was mainly in the background,' Weir tells me. 'I didn't get to know him personally, but the little words he spoke to me was very encouraging. No matter how down you were feeling he'd always have words of encouragement.'

The curious thing, says Weir, is that he was not an outstanding athlete at primary school. As well as Calabar, other leading schools, such as Kingston College, Wolmer's and St Jagos', have highly active recruitment programmes run by alumni, sometimes offering inducements (refrigerators, for example) for the parents of talented athletes. But no one showed much interest in Weir. 'I was pretty much a normal athlete, but Mr McKenley saw something.' He was a hurdler at the time rather than a 200 metres runner, but at Calabar, under head coach Michael Clarke, Weir began to blossom. He ran at Champs, experiencing the extraordinary atmosphere and finding it terrifying, but also inspiring. Where does it come from, I ask him: the tribalism, the intensity?

It comes from the high schools wanting 'bragging rights', he says. 'Everybody wants to be the top school. Even if you don't attend one of the top schools, you tend to be a fan of that school, because there's a hype and a certain tension. And that's what drives us Jamaicans to be so successful, because even after the high school level, we're still driving for that . . . bragging rights, or driving for that goal.'

Weir was at Champs in 2014, in a box at the back of the stand with his Racers clubmate Yohan Blake, watching some extraordinary performances. He is still processing what he saw. 'To see high school kids run 10.1 seconds [for 100 metres], 45-zeros [400 metres], the four-hurdles in 49; to see fourteen-year-olds running 21.7 [200 metres]; to see fourteen-year-olds running the four by one in 41 . . . that's really, really fast. Extremely fast. A fifteen-year-old ran 10.3. That's quick.'

But best of all, Calabar won. The school is like a fraternity, says Weir. And it endures; his status as a Calabar old boy seems even more important to him than his national identity, or his membership of Glen Mills's Racers Track Club. 'Every year I go back there, because I left maybe, like, four years, five years ago, and so there are still students there that I knew. I'm still familiar with some of the athletes, but even when I don't know anybody there, I'll still go back and support them, because it's like a brotherhood.'

He echoes McKenley, who said, in a documentary film made shortly before his death, that when he was approached to become a pupil at Calabar, the headmaster 'told me how important it was to have a sense of belonging to Calabar . . . that I should feel about Calabar the way I feel about my parents and brothers and sisters'. And yet, like Weir, McKenley did not strike many as a world-class athlete: he was consistently in the top two or three, but lost his first ten races at Champs.

There is footage in the film of one of McKenley's famous pre-Champs motivational speeches. What strikes you, apart from the logic of what he says, and the sense of morality underpinning it, is his sincerity – that, and the boys' rapt attention. 'Remember to do your best,' McKenley tells them. 'Your best does not necessarily have to be better than somebody else's. But your best is what you have. Your best today can be superseded tomorrow because of what you do between now and then. Your best in every way: in academics, your behaviour.'

Then he recites from memory (so not entirely accurately) his favourite quotation: 'Sports is an occupation of the whole man, for it not only develops the body but makes the mind, what, a more refined instrument for the search and attainment of truth and helps man to achieve love, the greatest of them all.'[5]

McKenley's speech is quite different to Weir's, with its emphasis on winning and 'crushing' the opposition. Yet there is the same idea of being 'the best you can be'. McKenley concludes: 'If you do those things, transfer them, then you will be such a great champion in every way. A champion who everyone will admire.'

There were extraordinary scenes at Calabar on the Monday morning after the school's third consecutive victory at 2014 Champs – their twenty-fourth success in total.[6] The celebrations got under way at 8 a.m., when the chairman of the school board, the Reverend Karl Johnson, addressed most of the 1,700 boys – plus parents, family and old boys – during morning devotion. There wasn't room for everybody in the chapel; they had to move outdoors, where the Mortimer Geddes trophy stood on a table draped in the green of Calabar. 'Ever so powerful, ever so strong,' Johnson told them, his voice rising. 'One, two, three, C'bar. Three, two, one, yow!' The address was greeted by a storm of cheers and vuvuzelas.

Then it was the turn of the principal, Albert Corcho, to speak from the stage. 'I am glad the media are here,' he said. 'We want to send a very strong message to all the other schools that participated at Champs that the Mortimer Geddes trophy will live at 61 Red

---

5 McKenley was paraphrasing Pope Pius XII's speech at the Sport at the Service of the Spirit Award in 1945: 'Sport, rightly understood, is an occupation of the whole man, and while perfecting the body as an instrument of the mind, it also makes the mind itself a more refined instrument for the search and communication of truth and helps man to achieve that end to which all others must be subservient, the service and praise of his Creator.'

6 They might have won more Champs titles, but in 1981, while leading, there was a scuffle during the medley relay, when athletes from Calabar and deadly rivals Kingston College clashed, prompting a track invasion by spectators. According to the book *Champs 100*, 'ugly pandemonium' ensued. Both schools were banned in 1982.

Hills Road.' More cheering; more blasts from the vuvuzelas. Corcho continued: 'It doesn't matter where athletes are imported from, one thing I can tell you is that the programme is the best programme in this side of the hemisphere.'

Romario McKenzie, the captain, in his Batman mask, introduced the winning team. 'It was a rough championship,' he said. 'After the first two days without a point, my phone kept ringing because persons wanted to know what was happening. The team was worried, I was worried, but as a leader you can't show signs of weakness, so I kept them motivated.' McKenzie then handed the microphone to Michael O'Hara, which was symbolic: O'Hara would take over as captain in 2015. But O'Hara, who struggled with injury at Champs, wasn't as composed as McKenzie. He began crying and couldn't speak. The microphone was handed back to McKenzie, who ran through some of the heroic performances by the Calabar Lions, saving the best until last, introducing the Donkey Man, Javon Francis, to huge cheers. Like O'Hara, Francis then burst into tears. It fell to his guardian, Andrea Hardware – also the team manager – to speak: 'I am the proud manager of this track team. I am the proud guardian of Javon Francis and I am the proud grandmother of Dejour Russell.' Russell was another promising young sprinter and hurdler.

The celebrations continued, and when I visited Calabar ten days later, there remained a lingering sense that something good had recently happened. There was a feeling of confidence and optimism about the place.

The Red Hills Road compound is on a dusty, arid expanse of land just off Washington Boulevard, the main arterial road that enters Kingston from the west, from Spanish Town, Jamaica's original capital. It was the scene of one of the island's most remarkable and bizarre recent episodes, with gunfights in 2010 involving the police and supporters of the powerful Kingston don Christopher 'Dudus' Coke.

Coke, wanted in the US for gun and drug trafficking, was believed to be protected by one of Jamaica's two political parties, the right-leaning Jamaica Labour Party. (At times it might perhaps have been more accurate to say that the party was protected by him.) Coke was the Don for the Tivoli Gardens garrison, about five miles from Calabar in west Kingston, but during a state of emergency dons and gunmen from other areas took on the police in sympathy with Coke, including men from a garrison near Calabar. At least seventy-three people were killed in a five-week US-led hunt for Coke, not to mention those who over many years were allegedly executed by the don in his makeshift jail, using a hatchet and a power saw. Yet like other dons, some of them still at large in Kingston today, Coke was a hero to many: a Robin Hood figure who redistributed his ill-gotten gains among the poor.

Coke was eventually caught at a routine roadblock, in a car driven by an evangelical priest. He was dressed in women's clothing, wig and all. He said he was on his way to the US Embassy to turn himself in. In 2012, he was sentenced by a New York court to twenty-three years in prison.[7]

Driving into the school compound, I negotiate my way past the guards at the entrance by saying I'm meeting the principal, and park near a green-and-cream building with a large sign. There are signs everywhere in Jamaica, warning against everything from unprotected sex to drunk driving, frequently in patois, often in graphic and blunt terms. The schools are no different. 'Calabar High School Dress Code', reads this one. 'No Setters (Rollers). No Spaghetti Straps. No Halter Tops. No Midriff Blouses/Shirts. No Tights, Shorts. No Low Cut Pants/Jeans.

---

7 During his trial, a link emerged between Coke and schools athletics – though not Calabar. Anthony Brown, a former assistant coach at St Jago, the Spanish Town school with its own great sprinting tradition, thanks to Yohan Blake, Nickel Ashmeade and others, told of a US visa racket between 1997 and 2001. Brown said that he charged $1,500–$3,000 to help people get visas through the athletics programme to travel to the US. The head coach at the time was Bert Cameron, Jamaica's 1983 world 400 metres champion. Cameron said he had no knowledge of the scheme.

No Bathroom Slippers. No Flip-Flops. No Handkerchief on Head/ Around Neck. No Merinos. No Vest. No Clothes Displaying Explicit Graphic Information. No Exposed Undergarment. No Bare Feet.' And underneath, the school motto: 'The Utmost for the Highest'.

I can see, beyond a high fence, the sports facilities: a field with isolated patches of grass and a dirt running track. The buildings are scattered and sand-coloured. Some used to be dormitories, but there are only fourteen boarders now. The pupils, all wearing uniform – the usual khaki, army-style, with Calabar-green epaulettes – stand in clumps, eyeing the stranger with curiosity.

The principal's secretary instructs me to take a seat in the reception area, telling me that Mr Corcho will see me soon. The Mortimer Geddes trophy takes pride of place in here, but it is in good company: the shelves sag with silverware; medals dangle from cup handles. A steady stream of people file in, all of them addressing me – 'Good morning, sir' – until eventually Mr Corcho appears: clean-cut, businesslike, in a tailored light tan suit, offering a universal 'Good morning' as he breezes past.

Once he has seen the other people who have been waiting, I am summoned. 'All right, what can I do for you?' says the principal as I enter his office. 'Welcome to Calabar.' Same lilting pronunciation as the stadium announcer: *Cal-a-bar*.

Corcho has only been at the school since May 2013, when the previous head, Austin Burrell, resigned after receiving death threats. That followed the fatal stabbing of a pupil, sixteen-year-old Narrio Coleman, during an argument with another student. The head of the local police force was angry, complaining that the school failed to report the incident: they learned of it from medical staff at Kingston Public Hospital. As for the death threats, the Ministry of Education took them seriously enough that Burrell, once removed, was only able to retrieve his belongings by sneaking back into the school.

Corcho was principal previously at Munro College, another school with a strong reputation for athletics. Munro have the advantage of boarding facilities, he explains, which means they can attract youngsters from abroad. 'It's something Calabar needs to do in the next couple of years. We have land on this compound.'

The school is not obsessed with athletics, he says, insisting that they strive hard to keep a healthy balance between sport and academic work.[8] But the recent success at Champs is reward for a strategy put in place four years ago. 'Let me give you some history,' Corcho says, bringing his hands together and relaxing into his leather chair. 'Before my time, four years ago, the board sat down. The school celebrated a hundred years two years ago and they wanted to do something long-lasting in terms of the centennial.

'The chairman sat with the coach and said, "Listen, we want to reorganise our programme: we want to win Champs." ' Calabar, in the period after Herb McKenley's death, seemed to lose its way – which only highlighted the great man's contribution. 'So,' continues Corcho, 'they sat and they crafted a programme. It's for five years. What you're seeing now is year three. You saw that we dominated the thing, but more so we dominated Class 3' – the youngest age group. *Cal-a-bar, dom-in-ate.*

The issue of recruiting talented athletes from beyond the Calabar catchment area, and indeed from beyond Kingston, is controversial. But Corcho says that it's just as likely that parents will approach Calabar looking for a place for their son. They call and say, 'We want our son, we want our nephew, to be part of the programme.' But it is true, he concedes, that the school 'may identify an athlete, and say, "Listen, Calabar is available if you're interested." But I can tell you that since Champs I've had about thirty, thirty-five people calling, sending letters, saying, "Listen sir, come September we want to be part of the programme." '

---

8 The academic attainment of boys in Jamaica is a national crisis, with dwindling numbers progressing to further education. According to Corcho, 'only about 10 or 15 per cent of the [Jamaican university] population is male'.

The brightest star in the Calabar stable is the Donkey Man, of course. Javon Francis was recruited. 'We facilitated that,' says Corcho, and he pays tribute to former pupils, the 'old boys' association', who 'do a fantastic job in offsetting some of the costs for boarding, if boys are coming from rural areas. They help provide for books, tuition, food. They do a lot of fund-raising. The old boys love track and field. If we weren't getting the support from our alumni, we wouldn't be able to perform the way we do.

'And we have a food programme. We try to make sure the boys get fed.'

What does the Puma sponsorship provide? I ask, and Corcho springs forward: 'Oh, let me tell you, I'm glad you brought that up. One of the reasons we have done so well is our main sponsors, Puma. Puma provide all the gear.' Calabar have a five-year contract with the German company (I find myself wondering how many British schools have such arrangements), and Corcho is confident it'll be renewed. 'Let me tell you,' he says, 'we have not purchased any gear for the track and field programme. We could not afford it. I feel for some of the other schools who compete at Champs because they don't all have sponsorship.

'We say to our boys, once you put on the Calabar top, it's not just about the school; you're representing our sponsors. I meet with them on a regular basis.'

For some reason, the latest Champs victory sparked the biggest celebrations yet at Calabar. Perhaps it was the quality of some of the individual performances – Francis beating Bolt's 400 metres record stands out – or that they had to come from behind. Corcho is still basking in the warm glow. 'The reception here was enormous,' he gushes. 'Enormous! We couldn't hold it in the chapel, we had to do it outdoors. Un-believable. They stood in the sun. Parents were there, friends, well-wishers, old boys, past teachers. Everybody came back. Because this victory was very special. There was talk that other schools would win. That it was going to be close. But we threw down the mantle and made it quite clear that we were not about to lose our title. We had some hiccups. Some never performed: Michael O'Hara; Javon in the 200. But it shows the depth of our Calabar programme.'

The highlight was certainly Francis's 400 metres. 'He said long before, he said, "Sir, I am going to break Usain Bolt's record. I am going for the record." I watched that race about ten or twelve times. From when the gun went off, you saw it was on his mind . . . On his mind from the moment the gun went. Proud of him.'

I head back out into the blazing sun and suffocating heat to meet one of the coaches, Omar Hawes. He scowls beneath his baseball cap but appears relaxed, peppering our conversation with 'Yeah, man', as most do here, but occasionally seeming exasperated. Then it becomes 'Yes, man!'

Omar has promised to talk me through the programme and show me the facilities. I meet him on the sports field; the running track is just about visible: an oval of scorched dark lines on a grass track without much grass. Really, it is bumpy, dry mud. 'The track,' I say to him, 'it's—'

'Bumpy,' he interrupts. 'Yeah, man. But this is where we start. What it does for us is show . . . Not blowing our own trumpets, but I think we're doing pretty well in terms of the techniques we use, and how we utilise what we have . . .'

He can say that again. It is frankly amazing to think that athletes who are already world class train here. Not just Javon Francis, but also Jason Livermore and Romario McKenzie, both now professionals who continue to train under the Calabar head coach, Michael Clarke.

Sometimes, when speaking to someone like Omar, you are brought up short. The smart Puma gear – the slick green-and-black vests, shorts, tracksuits and rucksacks – and the professional air of Calabar at Champs is misleading. 'A youngster can be running well but he doesn't have shoes,' Omar mentions. 'Once he earns the shoes, there's a lot of shoes for him from the sponsors . . .'

'Some of the kids don't have shoes?' I say.

'Yes, man!'

'Silly question?'

'YES, MAN! A lot of kids come here and they'll train, but they don't have shoes. But they want to be part of the Calabar team. And once they earn the stuff, we give it to them. Everything in life, you have to earn it.'

It must be an ambition to have better facilities, I say. 'Yes, man! For years. For years. We just need somebody to push it forward. Probably a Javon Francis. If he goes out, it can make a difference, because this is where it started for him. And Warren Weir is very, very passionate.'

I tell Omar that I met Weir, and that he said he was surprised to be recruited by Calabar; that he considered himself only modestly talented. 'Warren came here with a youngster by the name of Roger Tennant,' Omar explains. 'We went to Waterford [primary school] for Roger Tennant and he say he has a friend called Warren. Warren wasn't the prime target.' What happened to Tennant? 'He got an injury.'

Omar, himself a Calabar old boy, recalls McKenley with fondness and reverence, as they all do. 'He was more of a motivational person than a coach. A coach too. But he made persons do things they couldn't have done otherwise. Brought the best out of persons. He was great at bringing talent to the forefront; and he had an eye for talent.' And when he decided he wanted an athlete to come to Calabar, he 'went all out. He was a person that came to your house, Mr McKenley. You saw him at your church.'

When it came to recruiting Javon Francis, Omar says that he was identified at Junior Champs – the primary schools' championship. 'For the most part, he . . . how would I put it? He was a bit, um, more talented than the other athletes there; he stood out in terms of talent. But when most schools have gone to recruit him for their institutions their response to him was . . . inferior, because he wasn't as articulate as some persons. But,' Omar quickly adds, 'very talented.'

The plan with Francis was to develop him, to work on his running and his education. 'Over the years he has moved leaps and bounds in terms of how he answers a question,' says Omar. 'You speak to him; he can answer a question properly.'

I had spoken to Francis, the so-called Donkey Man. The nickname had in fact been the subject of some discussion in the *Jamaica Observer*, and even a little soul-searching (was it derogatory? demeaning?). Noting Francis's tough upbringing in Bull Bay, the newspaper claimed that it originally came from a football coach who said Francis resembled a boy named Donkey. But it really caught on at Calabar, for entirely unrelated reasons. As one coach explained: 'We allowed a younger runner to run off seconds before him and told him to chase him.' Francis failed to catch the youngster, and the coach asked why not. 'Him fast, sir.'

In fact, the runner he was chasing was – unbeknown to Francis – one of the school's most promising young athletes. Again Francis was told to chase him. This time the greyhound almost caught the hare. But not quite. Feigning outrage, the coach asked: 'How you don't catch him?'

'Mi a nuh donkey, sir,' replied Francis ('I'm not a donkey, sir').

From that day on, he was Donkey Man.

5

DONKEY MAN

He knew of no candle that burned out more
quickly than that of the high school athlete.
Friday Night Lights

They rejoiced when Javon Francis took the baton at the world championships in Moscow and, with talent, guts and determination, dragged Jamaica to a silver medal.

They despaired a few months later when, at Champs, he broke down. There was outrage at the decision to put him in the final of the 200 metres just a couple of hours after his beating of Bolt's record in the 400 metres. He had collapsed to the track, at one point being helped on to a stretcher before staging a Lazarus-like recovery.

To see him pull up injured, his face a picture of agony, was heartbreaking. It became a huge talking point throughout the country, even warranting a solemn editorial in the *Jamaica Observer*: 'This newspaper was jarred by the perception that student athletes are being overworked in pursuit of glory.' To underline the seriousness of the matter, he was 'Mr Francis' throughout. Noting that after the 400 metres he 'had to be helped off the track', the article continued: 'It seemed logical that, given this hiccup, Mr Francis would be pulled from remaining competition. Not so. Less than three hours later – with Calabar holding an unbeatable points lead in the race for the boys' championship title – Mr Francis was on the track lining up for the 200 metres final.

'To the utter dismay of most of us watching, Mr Francis pulled up, grabbing his hamstring 20 to 30 metres from the finish line. Jamaicans will be keeping their fingers crossed that this athlete, among this country's most promising, wasn't badly hurt.'

Francis grew up in Bull Bay, nine miles along the coast from Kingston, where children play on the beach and catch fish in the river. To call the dwellings of this community modest would be an understatement: many are no more than shacks with wooden walls and tin roofs.

He went to St Benedict's Primary School and dreamt of becoming a footballer. But in Jamaica, football comes second to athletics. His football coach, seeing his speed, took him aside one day. 'You know, Javon, you have good potential – have you tried track and field?'

'No, sir,' said Javon. 'I don't want to try track and field. I want to be a great footballer like Ronaldinho.'

'But you can be the next Usain Bolt or Herb McKenley.'

'OK, coach, I give it a shot.'

The Javon Francis who relates all this, grinning as he recalls the exchanges, is nineteen and about to turn professional. He sits in the grounds of Calabar High School, where he still trains with his old coach, Michael Clarke, and speaks with an endearing sense of innocence, giggling and opening his eyes wide to convey wonder.

At his sports day, after the eleven-year-old lined up against the school's fastest sprinter, and beat him, it was the turn of the athletics coach to have a word. 'Bwoy, you really fast! Footballer, come to track and field.'

'Sir,' said Javon, 'I am going to sit down and decide what I want to do.'

He talked to his father. 'Whoa, dad, it's hard. I want to be the next

Ronaldinho.' His father told him it was up to him. 'Then I go round,' says Francis, 'and ask lots of questions, make people tell me how it feels to do track and field. My cousin used to do track and field and he said to me, "Well track and field, it's nice, but the training is very hard. But you can go to places, the Penn Relays, the Miami Classic."

' "Wow! Those places? Cuz, if you go on a plane, how does it feel?" '

' "Well, it's nice, you go up in the air, look down." '

That was it, says Francis. 'I make up my mind. Track and field is what I'm going to do: be a superstar. But my first day, training hard, I throw up. And say, whoa, this is hard.'

While Francis talks, his guardian, Andrea Hardware, gazes at him and smiles, swatting flies and mosquitoes as they land on him. Beside her is Noel Facey, who recruited Francis. Facey and Hardware are both parents of Calabar pupils or former pupils; Hardware, director of human resources at Digicel (who sponsor Bolt and now Francis too), also manages the school's athletics team.

Facey recalls the moment he spotted Francis. He was sitting watching a meeting with Clarke. 'Michael Clarke has an eye for talent. Not for the winner. He'll look at the boy who comes third or fourth, looking at stride pattern, muscle build-up. I don't question Michael. I was beside him when Javon ran and he said, "Facey, this is the boy I want." '

Facey's job then was to recruit him for the school. 'It's a whole lot of work,' he says, 'but everything we do is with the head coach. He picks them out, and my job is to go and get them. I talk to the parents, tell them about the programme. I generally sell Michael: his track record. But the parents have got to say yes. Javon's parents said yes.'

Omar Hawes had stressed how humble Francis's upbringing was. Francis himself mentioned that the first time he ran the 100 metres, he was in his stockinged feet. 'His parents are not well off, but they're trying to make sure he gets the best out of life,' said Omar. Unusually, his parents are still together. 'Most of the athletes who have talent here in Jamaica, you find they come from broken homes. Most of them have a reason to excel in whatever strength they have. To help the family out and help themselves.'

Francis's father is a fisherman, while his mother, says Hardware, 'does anything she can find herself to do to make a living'. Javon is the youngest of six children: five boys, one girl. Which is interesting. An extraordinarily high proportion of top male sprinters seem to be late-born, or youngest, in their (often large) families: Usain Bolt (youngest of three), Ben Johnson (youngest of five), Carl Lewis (third of four), Asafa Powell (youngest of six), Calvin Smith (sixth of eight), Yohan Blake (seventh of eleven), Justin Gatlin (youngest of four), Maurice Greene (youngest of four), to name just some.

This phenomenon was discussed by Daniel Coyle in his book *The Talent Code*. 'History's fastest runners were born, on average, fourth in families of 4.6 children,' writes Coyle, who argues that 'deep practice' is the key to sporting excellence (excellence in any field, for that matter). The pattern of late-born sprinters suggests, he asserts, 'that speed is not purely a gift but a skill that grows through deep practice, and that is ignited by primal cues. In this case the cue is: you're behind – keep up!'

In a nutshell, speed is honed by younger children trying to keep up with their older siblings.

There may be something in that. Or perhaps not. David Epstein, author of *The Sports Gene*, notes that the leading female sprinters are nearly all first- or second-born in the family. Is it because females are less competitive, less ego-driven? Again, maybe. But Epstein doesn't think that's it. 'To me,' he writes in an email, 'when you see a male/ female disparity – handedness, dyslexia, etc. – it often points to a pre-natal effect.'

The Coyle theory, that the social effect is the determining factor, is also slightly undermined by the fastest man of all time. Bolt was third-born, but didn't really grow up with his older siblings (a brother and a sister). In fact, several of the youngest-born sprinters mentioned above, including Gatlin, did not grow up in the company of their siblings.

Epstein carried out his own informal survey into the phenomenon and considered that the gender of the older siblings seemed to be significant. 'We know that the environment of the womb changes with each successive boy birth, but not each girl, and my survey found that the boys particularly had lots of brothers. So in my opinion, the weight of evidence is for a biological effect, not a social one.' (Although being a good scientist, he is reluctant to draw any firm conclusions, given the limitations of such a small sample.)[9]

So Francis may have got off to the best possible start in his athletics career by being the youngest in his family, especially by having four older brothers.

Although he started out running all the sprint events – the 100, 200, 400, 4x100 and 4x400 – he found himself gravitating towards the one-lap race, or the quarter-mile as people still call it here, in which Jamaica has such a strong tradition – on which the island's reputation was originally built. 'The 400 is an event I love with a passion,' Francis tells me. 'I go out there in Moscow or at Championships, and say, Hey, I want to make a big statement out there, so everyone say: "Young Javon Francis is coming up."

'I wish my idol, Herb McKenley, was alive to sit and talk to,' he continues. Francis was thirteen when McKenley died, and never met him, so presumably he is only aware of his reputation through attending Calabar. 'Yes, sir,' he says. 'I hear that Herb McKenley is a great guy and I look up to him.'

---

9 Epstein adds something else: 'Actually, there's at least one other very well known effect of older brothers, and it doesn't matter at all if the younger bro grows up with his siblings, only that they once occupied the same womb.' This is the 'older brother effect': the more older brothers a man has, the greater the possibility that he will be homosexual. Again, there is no equivalent correlation with women. It's thought to be connected to the hormonal conditions in the womb; as Epstein explains, the idea that 'the mother's body has an immune response only to male fetuses, and there's some imprinting of it with each successive boy', is scientifically unproven, but 'gaining conceptual strength'. A logical follow-up would be to ask: how many leading male sprinters are homosexual? Not many – at least publicly.

When he first started at Calabar, he commuted from Bull Bay by bus: a journey of between forty minutes and over an hour each way depending on the Kingston traffic, on roads that, in the miles close to Bull Bay, deteriorate terribly. It took its toll on the fourteen-year-old. 'Training finishes at six o'clock,' says Hardware, 'so that would get him home pretty late. The affordability was a big challenge for his parents. They're very proud. They wouldn't ask for help and they could only afford public transportation, not a taxi. So he was getting home late. And for development meets at weekends it became a big challenge for them to afford those. So he'd be missing those, and those meets are important; they're where you get ready for Champs.'

Hardware was already acting as a mentor to Francis. 'Each year we take in a cadre of boys. About fifteen of us manage the team and each of us gets two or three boys to mentor. Javon was my mentee.

'We realised that coming to Calabar, he needed all kinds of support: educational support, financial support, and through our committee and myself that was provided for him,' she continues. 'But I got very concerned when I got a call telling me he's coming to school late, he's sleeping in class, he's not keeping up – that sort of thing. Mr Facey said, "You have to do something more for this boy."'

'After Javon came to Calabar,' Facey interrupts, 'Andrea loved him so much she let him move in.'

Hardware nods in agreement. 'It was very easy for me to say, "Come, Javon, stay with me." My sons both went to Calabar, but they were away.'

When she spoke to Francis's parents, 'They were immediately open to the idea. I remember the conversation I had with his mother. She said, "Thank you, God bless you. I know he needs the support and I can't do it for him." She was very, very appreciative.' Francis has lived with Hardware in her home in Kingston for the last four years. She treats him like one of her own sons, and he looks on her as a second mother. 'He calls me Mum,' says Hardware. 'But when I get angry at him he calls me "Andrine". He's part of our family; they

all get along very well. He's quiet, so they pull him out of his shell, take him places.'

There is an innocence about Francis that makes him difficult to read, particularly when he can be such a showman on the track. It's hard to reconcile the quiet, diffident boy with the pumped-up extrovert who appeared in the mixed zone in Moscow, announcing: 'A super donkey just did it!'

'That's just him,' says Hardware. She means the sweet, innocent boy who has jogged away to start training, leaving with a handshake and a 'Thank you, sir.' 'That's who he is,' she says. 'It's one of the qualities he has that really endears him to me. Because he's so humble, so appreciative. I don't think he's aware of the immense talent he has.'

Later, I speak to Michael Clarke, the head coach, who I had met in Moscow at the senior world championships. In smart shirt and trousers, with obligatory baseball cap, he strolls slowly around his athletes as they go through their drills, sometimes pulling them aside to have a quiet word. Then he peels off to speak to me, also very quietly – and with a Zen-like calm. Clarke went to Calabar in 1973, having been recruited by Herb McKenley; then, in 1980, he was among the first batch of students to be trained in sports coaching at the new G. C. Foster College. For the last thirteen years he has been head coach at his alma mater.

The first time he saw Francis run, he recalls, 'he didn't do anything spectacular. He was third, beaten by some distance. He ran 52.7. But I wanted 400 athletes and what struck me was his build: he was tall, sinewy, lanky, but he had some speed. He was sought after by a number of other schools, in fact.'

Clarke can reel off Francis's times, illustrating his improvement once he joined Calabar: 'First race he ran here was 49-something, then he was in the 50-range, then he did a 48, then a 47.'

It was Clarke who took the bold decision to select an eighteen-year-old for the anchor leg of the 4x400 metres in Moscow. Francis, when he found out, went straight to his guardian, who was on the team bus, travelling to the stadium. Hardware recalls how the conversation went: 'Mum, me coach make me anchor for the race!'

'What?' said Hardware.

'Mum, I'm going to run the race, I want to win a medal.'

'If you win a medal, I get you a car,' she told him. ('I still haven't got him that car,' she admits.) 'He said he didn't have a race plan,' Hardware tells me. 'He said he just wanted them to give him the baton in the pack. I was standing in the stand, and when I saw him blaze out, I was like, "No, Javon, you're going too fast!" I was literally shouting, "You're going too fast! You're running too fast!" But when he came off of that third bend, I knew he was going to finish it. He maintained his composure; such a mature thing for him to do at eighteen.'

Now Clarke tells me that he chose Francis for the anchor leg because of the heart he'd shown at the Penn Relays earlier in the season. 'He was coming off chickenpox, and he ran down a guy, Delano Willliams, from a twenty-metre lead. I said, "Wow." It was an outstanding time: 44.6. He has the record for Penn Relays.

'He has something special,' continues Clarke. 'He's a chaser. He displays an intellect on the track that belies his real intellect off the track.' Expanding on this, Clarke explains: 'He's a simple youngster: simple, jovial, very candid about things. He has tremendous charisma.'

He can see similarities with Bolt, as everyone can. They have been looking for the next Bolt or Shelly-Ann Fraser-Pryce: another athlete who can dominate at world level. But so many athletes who seem poised to do just that don't make it, often because they break down with injury. On the comparison with Bolt, Clarke says: 'Both are candid. They both have charisma. They like to perform. Javon is not as eloquent yet, but he's getting there. We're trying to help him. But he has personality. Now in Jamaica when we go out in public everybody – kids, adults – they flock around him. People recognise him, they are endeared to him.'

I was still coming to terms with the quality of the facilities at the centre of world excellence that is Calabar High School. I had asked Omar Hawes how many other coaches there are at the school. 'Let's see,' he said, and began counting on his fingers. 'There's a coach for the throws, horizontal jumps, vertical jumps, hurdles, quarter-mile programme, sprints, distance . . . That's seven. And Mr Clarke is overall coach.' Eight dedicated athletics coaches. But what I only learn later is that they are all volunteers – parents of pupils, or old boys, like Omar. In his day job, I discover, Omar is a policeman.

There is a darker story I want to ask the coaches about. Demar Robinson was a Calabar schoolboy who in 2013 – within weeks of leaving the school – tested positive at the Jamaican national championships for androgen receptor modulator (SARMS), a steroid. Robinson was a high jumper who captained the school at Champs in 2012. He was given a one-year ban: a light sentence for such an offence, but the rumour (unconfirmed by Jamaica's anti-doping agency, because his hearing was in camera) was that he had offered useful information. Robinson is now at college in Kansas.

When had Omar last seen him? 'It would have been at Champs. He came to say hi to the youngsters.'

Omar told me he didn't know why Robinson had tested positive, and hadn't spoken to him about it. 'He had his lawyers. I wish him the best. It was an unfortunate situation. I don't know how that got into his system.' He did speak to him at Champs, but didn't discuss the positive test. 'I asked him how he was dealing with the pressure. He said "All right." It sounded like he wanted to return.'

I want to ask Michael Clarke about Robinson too. It seems like a blot on the Calabar name, and indeed has fuelled a certain amount of suspicion. At another school I visited, Cornwall College, in Montego Bay, the head of sport, Gregory Daley, was critical of what he described as the 'win-at-all-costs' mentality that prevails at some schools. 'It is hard to say, but I am going to say it anyway,' he said. 'Schools like Calabar, KC, JC [Kingston College and Jamaica College] will always have the best athletes. They will do things we won't do or we can't do. There are schools who will come to a parent and say, "The boy can run, and I want him to come to our school – here's a fridge."

'Most often these boys are from the, I don't want to say ghetto, but they are from the lower strata of the financial scale. So the parents will always say, "What? Fridge? Stove? Yeah, man," and the boy's gone.'

On this specific point, Noel Facey, who recruited Javon Francis, says it's not common practice. 'I can say that's a rumour for Calabar. Everything at Calabar is for the boys, not for the parents. So we cannot give the parents this.'

Daley said he had personal experience of Calabar's recruitment policy. When he was at another school, Herb McKenley came for one of the most talented young athletes he had ever seen: Ali Watson. 'Herb McKenley came for him at Grade 4,' said Daley. Watson was eight years old. 'The father and myself, we're very good friends, he came to me and said, "Grade 4? Why's he want a Grade 4?" The fella went to Calabar and in Class 3 at Champs he won the 100, he won the 200, he won the 400 in record times.' Class 3 is the youngest age group. But it was as good as Watson got; he never won again.

As for drugs, Daley said he had not encountered any at schools level. 'But I doubt if it does not exist.'

Clarke says he believes that doping is unlikely to exist in schools, mainly because of the cost. 'Those performance-enhancing drugs are expensive, very expensive, to get initially, and to sustain it is even more expensive. The coaches can't, I certainly can't [afford it]. And even if I could, I wouldn't, because it is unethical.

'I've been coaching for thirty years and I don't think any one boy should risk putting thirty years on the line,' Clarke continues. 'For me that's a no-no.'

Nonetheless, he admits that the Robinson case did leave a cloud over Calabar. 'He had just left school. You hear a lot of discussion about it in terms of what the real truth is; I don't know what the real truth is. But given his humble beginnings, it would be difficult to think that he could afford it. So obviously somebody must have given it to him in ignorance, from what I gather.'

He looks reflective. He is still Zen-like. 'That left a bit of a blemish, yes,' he adds. 'I guess we can hide behind the clouds and say it wasn't during his time at Calabar.'

Now Clarke is coaching not just high school athletes but professionals too – the latest being Javon Francis. Given the positive tests there have been in senior athletics, and rumours that the sport has a serious doping problem at international level, is Javon going to have to make a choice at some stage?

'Well, he listens to me attentively, and to his guardian,' Clarke says. 'We discuss whatever supplements he takes. He doesn't like taking pills, doesn't like taking these things, but he needs to. I get them checked out. We don't push anything. He follows my instruction where that's concerned.'

*

There were other questions for Francis – and for Clarke. I kept hearing about Jamaican athletes who had been high school stars – Ali Watson, Daniel England – only to fade away as seniors. It brought to mind another passage from *Friday Night Lights*, concerning the father of a teenage star who 'saw the irresistible allure of high school sports, but also saw an inevitable danger in adults living vicariously through their young. And he knew of no candle that burned out more quickly than that of the high school athlete.'

There were so many examples of this happening to athletes in Jamaica, I was learning. And it was bound to get worse. The achievements of Bolt, Yohan Blake, Shelly-Ann Fraser-Pryce, Asafa Powell and others only intensified the pressure on the young stars of Champs: the stakes were higher than ever. At Calabar, as Omar Hawes suggested, it was hoped that Francis's success could help the school get better facilities, perhaps even a new track. Bolt, in his minor school in the backwater of Trelawny, had had it easy; he was protected, wrapped in cotton wool, by Devere Nugent, Lorna Thorpe and his parents.

Would Francis be the next Bolt or an Ali Watson? Perhaps the season stretching out in front of us would offer some clues. I said to Francis, just before he joined Clarke for training, that I would be returning to Jamaica in a few months and hoped to see him again. 'Yes, sir,' he nodded.

More immediately, I had another appointment, with somebody at the other end of the age spectrum. I had been told about him repeatedly at the National Stadium during Champs. His name was the answer most frequently suggested when I asked the question: 'Who is responsible for all this?' He was yet another Calabar man, and the original Herb McKenley protégé, and he was known throughout Jamaica as 'DJ'. As Mark Ricketts, the economist and writer, told me: 'Without DJ, there would be no Glen Mills and no Stephen Francis' – the two leading coaches. 'And without Mills, you don't have Bolt,' added Ricketts.

Could he put me in touch with Dennis Johnson? He gave me

Johnson's number. I called and asked if I could come and hear his story. 'Yes, man,' said a voice at the end of the line. 'Come on Sunday at eleven o'clock,' he added, and hung up.

6

THE ARCHITECT

I tell you, man, Jamaica is not going to lose any
sprints for the next fifty years.
Dennis Johnson

His sprawling house sits on the outskirts of Kingston, overlooking the city. It's on Stony Hill, one of the more salubrious parts of the capital, but the steep, hairpinned road leading there is rutted and not so much potholed as cratered, as though it has been shelled.

Several cars are parked in the driveway, some in as poor condition as the road. The garden is a little overgrown and scruffy, and on the large porch, sitting on a chair by a table, is a man who is clearly not Dennis Johnson. For one thing, he is white. 'Looking for DJ?' he asks as I approach, then shouts: 'DJ? Somebody here to see ya . . . DJ!'

As well as the table and chairs, the porch is cluttered with potted plants and large birdcages full of budgies hopping from bar to bar, chirruping.

Johnson shuffles stiffly in, sliding across the hard floor in flip-flops, shorts and a faded yellow T-shirt that says 'Director – Sports'. He has a shock of white hair, a bushy moustache and a tuft of hair below his

lower lip. It is clear that he also has no recollection whatsoever of our appointment.

Before I can explain – even before I sit in the seat he indicates – he launches into an impassioned defence of Asafa Powell and the other sprinters who tested positive the previous year, clearly continuing a conversation he and his friend had been having. 'They took a supplement and in the supplement is a banned thing!' Johnson protests. His friend looks at him with a mixture of bemusement and irritation. 'He can't know that!' continues Johnson, who seems a little breathless. 'WADA, I think, is out of order. The IAAF think so too. You understand?'

The friend shakes his head in quiet resignation. Then Johnson turns to me. 'Now, what do you want?'

Well, I say, I would like to hear his life story. But on the other hand, it sounds like I've interrupted an interesting conversation. (The friend,

I later learn, is David Mais, until recently chairman of the G. C. Foster sports college.) So what does Johnson think happened, and why are the anti-doping authorities out of order?

'It's simple,' Johnson says, settling back in his chair. He speaks slowly and frequently closes his eyes, as though keeping them open is too much effort. 'Let me think of an example.' He tilts his head back. 'OK, I'm from Mars and I don't know what calculus is. What is calculus?'

Fortunately, he isn't really interested in an answer. 'The reason I ask is that even the people who do maths don't know what calculus is. I'm telling you, ask a maths teacher: what is calculus? It's finding the area of an irregular shape – that glass or something.' He reaches for a glass on the table. 'Easy. This?' He leans forward and picks up a plate. 'Easy. But a teapot? A pentagon? A nineteen-a-gon? You get what I'm saying?'

'Um . . .'

'You cannot tell an underdeveloped country to work out calculus when only 10 per cent of the population is literate!'

'Aha, so you think the rules are too complicated? It shouldn't be one size fits all?'

'Yes, man! It should be made simple! You cannot have a universal rule! They want to stop doping so they go to the extreme. It's like the false start rule. Nothing wrong with it, but give people a way out, threaten them. Should be about stopping people cheating, not punishing them if they make a mistake! You understand?'

Johnson's booming voice, his bombastic presence, fills the porch of his house, which, it becomes clear, is where he holds court, receiving visitors much like a member of the Jamaican royal family, if such a thing existed.

He was born in Kingston in 1939 and went to Calabar, where the coach was Herb McKenley. McKenley started the athletics programme there in 1953, the year after his defining achievement as an athlete, when he almost single-handedly won the 4x400 metres relay gold medal for Jamaica at the Helsinki Olympics. He received the baton twelve metres down on the Americans but ran his leg in 44.6 seconds, to hand over to George Rhoden with a one-metre advantage. Had it not been part of the relay, his time would have stood as a sea-level world record until the late 1970s. The wiry, sharp-featured McKenley was credited with revolutionising the 400 metres: he ran the distance flat out, like a sprinter, rather than conserving energy and saving it for the finishing straight.

At the 1948 Olympics in London – Jamaica's first Games – McKenley had been favourite for the 400, but took silver after being overtaken close to the line by his fellow Jamaican Arthur Wint.[10] McKenley said that for years afterwards he was haunted by the sound of Wint gaining on him: 'Boom, boom, boom.' With first and second in the individual event, they were favourites for the relay until Wint collapsed with cramp.

They made amends four years later, when McKenley also became the first – and still the only – athlete to reach the finals of the 100, 200 and 400 metres, winning silver medals in both the 100 and 400. Many

---

[10] Given Herb McKenley's profile, Arthur Wint might be considered the forgotten man of Jamaican athletics, though the National Stadium sits on Arthur Wint Drive (near Herb McKenley Drive), and an enormous statue outside the stadium, 'Athlete' by Jamaican sculptor Alvin Marriott, is clearly modelled on Wint's Bolt-like six-foot-five frame. Confusingly, the head is McKenley's. It was Wint who originally inspired McKenley, when he appeared at Calabar High School in his Jamaican team uniform and panama hat. 'He looked really splendid,' said McKenley. 'Regal.' Wint was a surgeon, an RAF pilot and a diplomat, who served as High Commissioner to Britain, before returning to work as a doctor in rural Jamaica; he was a noble, upstanding and principled man, known as the Gentle Giant, apart from one curious incident. This features in *The Longer Run: A Daughter's Story of Arthur Wint*, Valerie Wint's fascinating biography of her father. In 1941, when he was twenty-one, Wint accidentally shot and killed a colleague: a thirty-year-old woman. He didn't know the gun was loaded and was given two years' probation. It was, perhaps, his most formative experience. Of his sport, he said in 1985: 'Today running can make you well off. In my era it was the thing that taught you about the limits of money. It lifted you to heights and rewards money could never buy.' Wint died in 1992, aged seventy-two.

maintain that he should have been given gold in the 100. He started as favourite alongside another sprinter originally from the Caribbean, the Trinidadian McDonald Bailey, representing Great Britain. Lindy Remigino of the USA later recalled being visited by McKenley before the final in the locker room. 'I was laying on a table, getting my thoughts about the race,' said Remigino, 'when Herb comes up to me. He's a very jolly fellow, and he said: "You know, Lindy, McDonald Bailey is ready to be had, he's so nervous. I think we've got him out of the way."'

McKenley got a poor start while Remigino, in the lane alongside him, was off to a flyer. But McKenley finished fast and was closing the gap when Remigino dipped too early. They crossed the line together: a photo finish. Remigino was convinced McKenley had won. 'I went up and congratulated him. I said, "Herb, I think you won this doggone thing."'

'It was close,' McKenley replied, 'but I think I got it.' Meanwhile the officials were still studying the photo finish, and eventually showed it to the two athletes. 'It was the closest thing I ever saw in my life,' said Remigino. He got the verdict and the gold medal. 'When I look at the film,' said McKenley fifty years later, 'I still think I won.'

One remarkable aspect of Jamaica's first two Olympic Games is that they foreshadowed Beijing and London by sixty years. In 1952, for the second Games in a row, there was a Jamaican one-two in the 400 metres, George Rhoden winning, with McKenley second again. The athletics medals table in Helsinki makes for surprising reading. With its population at the time of 1.5 million, Jamaica took silver in the men's 100, gold and silver in the 400, and gold in the 4x400 (and Wint also claimed a silver in the 800).

On the night of their triumph, the relay quartet celebrated in their living quarters with a bottle of Scotch and a member of the British royal family, Philip Mountbatten, the Duke of Edinburgh.

At Calabar in the mid-1950s, Johnson the schoolboy athlete and McKenley the coach formed a close bond. 'We became friends, Herb

and me. He would take me to his house in Mona.' Mona is at the foot
of the hills on the other side of Kingston. 'I had dinner at Herb's. I
had a bed there. If he was going to a picnic with his family, they would
take me, and after training he'd go buy me a milkshake. You know? We
became friends for life.'

Johnson echoes everyone else when he describes what McKenley
was like. Warm, enthusiastic, encouraging, driven by a passion for
athletics and coaching. 'Herb was something else. You'd like him
immediately. Charming; a beautiful guy; just a fine human being.
But no nonsense. I took my dog to the vet one Saturday morning and
he came storming in. I was missing training, you see. He had made
arrangements for the dog, but I didn't know that. I was sitting at the
vet's having an ice lolly. "Not on my time!" he said.

'We were friends, but he was very strict when you were working.'

Before Champs in 1957, Johnson was the favourite for the sprint
events. Mark Ricketts was also competing, and remembers his teacher's
response to Johnson's final leg in a relay: 'That was a lightning bolt.'
In his book Ricketts recalls Johnson as 'a cocky young man . . . As he
walked, he half rotated his upper torso, swinging it from side to side.
This confident swagger, this peacock-like strutting, was reminiscent of
wrestlers readying for battle and fearing no one.'

'A very bossy young fellow' is how P. J. Patterson, another Calabar
old boy, remembers Johnson. 'You would hear him before you saw
him, but he's one of the early great successes of Jamaican athletics. I
don't think he gets his due.'

Despite his confidence, Johnson could only finish fourth in the boys'
100 yards and third in the 220 yards at 1957 Champs. But there was
a reason for that. He had a broken arm. With the rest of the Calabar
team, he had been at McKenley's house on the eve of the final day
of competition to 'map a winning strategy'. He and a friend left at
10 p.m. to drive home, but they were involved in an accident; their car
overturned. Johnson was taken to the nearby University of the West
Indies hospital for surgery. The surgeon was Arthur Wint.

A year later, Johnson made amends, taking the sprint double. His winning time for the 100 yards (about 91 metres) was 9.8 seconds, then a Champs record.

McKenley had been the first Jamaican – the first from any Caribbean island – to get an athletics scholarship to a US college, in his case to Boston College in 1942, before transferring to the University of Illinois in 1945, coming under the spell of an influential coach, Leo Johnson. McKenley encountered racism, even if it only dawned on him slowly – during a train journey with segregated carriages. He said he overcame it thanks to his British passport.

It was as a coach himself that McKenley helped to open the floodgates. It is said that he arranged college scholarships for 1,000 Jamaican school-leavers. After his Champs double, Johnson was one of the first. He had little say in the matter. McKenley had contacts all over the US and set it up for him. 'All right, Dennis,' he told him, 'you are going to Bakersfield.'

So Johnson went to Bakersfield, California, on a scholarship that was not as glamorous as it might sound, nor as generous as those being offered by Keith Barnier of ACU at Champs in 2014. 'The old boys put you up,' Johnson tells me. 'In my case, in a fire station. My job was to clean the place, do odd jobs, and you'd get your meals and fifteen dollars every couple of weeks.'

At a track meeting in his first year at Bakersfield, Johnson was approached by a coach from another college. He had caused a stir, winning the national junior college title, and he was getting offers from some of the top universities – Stanford, UCLA, USC. But it was a coach from San José who said to him: 'Come up to San José and see if you'll be comfortable.' The coach sent Johnson an air ticket, met him at the airport, and took him to dinner. Then he made a formal offer. Johnson accepted immediately.

The coach was Bud Winter, one of the most famous names in sprint coaching. Winter worked at San José State College for twenty-nine years, from 1941 to 1970, building his reputation as his athletes sped to thirty-seven world records. The stadium at San José became known as 'Speed City'. Thanks to Winter, it was also the first to have a synthetic track – initially just a single lane – years before the rubberised material was used in competition.

Winter was progressive in lots of areas, but particularly when it came to coaching black athletes. After Johnson, he coached Tommie Smith and John Carlos, the 200 metres gold and bronze medallists at the 1968 Olympics in Mexico who became even better known for their Black Power salute on the podium. It took courage for Winter to actively recruit not only African Americans (and Jamaicans), but also Hispanic athletes. Johnson says his old coach was colour-blind; when it came to athletes, he only saw ability.

Once he had them, what was his secret? I ask Johnson. Was he scientific? 'No, man! Bud was a journalist. Then he was a social professor at the school. When it came to coaching, Bud was simplistic. Very simple. The strange thing about Bud was the things he thought was good, the method he came up with, they were hunches. And it turned out, as time went by, that he was right.'

Winter focused on the mechanics of sprinting: correct form, and the importance of maintaining it over the course of a sprint, blowing his whistle at eighty metres, at which point the runner would have to snap back into shape. The mechanics of sprinting are something Johnson is also obsessed with; he points out that it is not simply about moving one's legs quickly; that the sprinting action is not natural, but has to be learned. In fact, he adds, sprinting is not really about moving the legs quickly at all: it's about minimising contact with the ground while applying as much force as possible.

Form depended on 'a half-dozen or more essentials', said Winter, 'starting with high knees'. As he put it: 'A man doesn't walk with his knees up, so first you have to develop the muscles for it. The second and most important essential is foreleg reach. The knees have to be pumped high; but they can't be pumped straight down unless what you want is to run in [one] place. Watch a whippet sometimes, or a racehorse. They're extending their legs as far as they can.' Then there was 'Good arm action, lean forward, run tall, and "dig a hole" in the track with each foot as it comes down.'

But Winter was concerned with more – far more – than the mechanics of running. He was equally focused on the mental approach of the sprinter.

'Bud had an interesting job in the war,' Johnson says. 'He used to teach pilots to relax.'

How? Johnson blows out his cheeks, exhales, shakes his head. 'Read my book,' he says. 'You'll learn something.'

I couldn't find Johnson's book, but I did find Winter's – not his most famous, *Relax and Win*, but his other one, *So You Want to be a Sprinter*, where he explained his wartime job. 'In the Navy we were dealing with the cream of American youth,' he wrote. 'We provided them with the best planes in the world, the best education in the world, but at no time were we shooting live bullets at them. In their first mortal combat some of them tied up mentally or physically, or both. We lost the man and the plane.'

Winter could see that they needed to be as relaxed in combat as in drills, but this, of course, was easier said than done. So he set about devising a relaxation programme in consultation with 'the best minds in the country on the subject'. It had 'startling results'. Winter explained: 'Fatigue was alleviated, coordination got better, speed and reaction time improved, the learning of physical skills was accelerated and self-confidence was established.'

In a 1959 interview with *Sports Illustrated*, Winter went into more detail about his wartime work. He explained that they were losing pilots who were good in training because they tensed up in combat. They were sleep-deprived thanks to 'nuisance bombers' sent at night by the Japanese to fly over their Pacific base. They were understandably tense. And when they were tense, their physical coordination deteriorated.

'We had to figure out some way to relax them,' he said. 'We worked out a programme that taught pilots how to relax themselves, and we ran a test on two platoons, 60 men in each platoon. The 60 who learned how to relax did better in everything which requires physical coordination.'

There was no secret or quick fix, claimed Winter in his book: 'The course took six weeks, three hours a day. It taught you progressively how to relax every muscle group in the body. Then you were given a conditioned reflex with one word, "CALM". By repeating this word, you could elicit a relaxed state immediately . . . You could get to sleep in two minutes any time of the day or night – even with amplified machine gun noise in the room.'

After the war, working with sprinters, Winter noticed the same inability to relax under pressure, with the same effects on physical coordination, albeit with less catastrophic consequences. He paid special attention to the jaw and hands. When the sports writer Tex Maule spent time with him in 1959, observing a training session involving Ray Norton, Winter told Maule: 'Watch his lower lip. That's what we work on. The lower lip and the hands. If his lower lip is relaxed and flopping when he runs, his upper body is loose. If his hands are relaxed, his arm muscles are relaxed. You got to run relaxed to get maximum speed. If you have antagonistic muscles working against each other, you're working against yourself.'

Maule described Winter as 'a sun-scorched, intense man who talks very rapidly, as if his ideas outpaced his words'. There is footage of Winter: he fizzes with energy, though in his breeches and hat he looks more Victorian dad than pioneering coach. He told Maule that his favourite exercise was to time a sprinter making three efforts over thirty yards, then tell him to do it one more time at four-fifths speed. Flat-out, a good sprinter would do thirty yards in three seconds.

'Don't strain,' he would instruct his athlete before their final 80 per cent effort. As he told Maule: 'So he runs it at four-fifths speed, and we time him and he comes up to me and I say, "What do you think your time was?" And he'll say, "Oh, maybe 3.4, Coach," and

I'll show him the stopwatch. You know what? Nine times out of ten, he's run it two tenths of a second faster. He's run 2.8. You believe that? It's true.'

Relaxation did not appear to be much of a problem for Johnson.

'A New Sprinter for the Speed Master' read the headline in the 22 May 1961 edition of *Sports Illustrated*. The subject was Johnson, 'the latest of a long string of distinguished runners whom persuasive – and sometimes hypnotic – Coach Bud Winter has attracted to California's San José State College'.

Johnson quotes the introduction of the article to me from memory: 'At 8.24 last Saturday night, a tall, lithe Negro from San José State College . . .' The description seems to tickle him, still. The article carried on: 'Dennis Johnson jogged easily in the dim light behind a wire fence set at the head of the 220-yard straightaway in Fresno (Calif.) State College's Ratcliffe Stadium. When Starter Tom Moore called to the eight finalists in the West Coast Relays 100-yard dash, "Runners to your blocks," Johnson took off his sweat suit, stepped through a door in the fence and walked slowly to the starting line. The man who many now think may be the fastest runner in the world was the slowest to get ready.'

Johnson remained relaxed as they were called to the 'set' position. While the others got ready, he stayed on his haunches. Then, just before the gun, he sprang up and launched forward. The starter called them back. But this was Johnson's style: a style that, according to the magazine, 'made him as controversial as he is fast'.

A rival coach, Chuck Coker, accused Johnson of a 'rolling start'. 'Oh, that was ridiculous!' Johnson says now, throwing his head back and closing his eyes. 'There was no rolling anything. When the man said "On your marks, get set," I did not listen to the instructions immediately. I got up slowly. When everyone is in the set position the starter fires the gun, unless the starter is an idiot.' But why did he get up so slowly? 'I couldn't hold the set position because I broke my arm three times.'

At the time, Johnson didn't mention his arm, responding to the accusation of a rolling start by saying: 'It's so stupid. Rising slowly has very little to do with my style. It just keeps me relaxed by leaving me straining at set for less time than the others. The short piston arm stroke is what's important.'

Now he says, 'Oh, one guy, Coker, made heavy weight of it. Did I ever get kicked out of a race for false-starting? Never. Not once.' (Well, there was that one time at Fresno State, I think, but he wasn't kicked out of the race, so I don't bring it up.) 'I was a good starter. But starting doesn't mean moving first. It means accelerating quicker than everyone else, which involves mechanics and leverage. You cannot move without levers. Levers! It all depends on that.'

Johnson never scaled the very highest peaks in major champion-ships: at the 1960 and 1964 Olympic Games he reached the 100 metres quarter-finals; and alongside Pablo McNeil, who later coached Bolt at William Knibb, he helped Jamaica to fourth in the 4x100 metres relay in Tokyo in 1964.[11] But in a six-week period in 1961, he equalled the then world record of 9.3 seconds for 100 yards on four occasions.

'Jamaican Fast as a Jet' read the *Toledo Blade*'s headline after his second run, at Stanford on 15 April. The article noted that 'an oversight by the Stanford hosts – failure to have a wind gauge alongside the track – was the only thing that prevented the San José State sprinter from getting his world record equalling time into the books. There was virtually no wind . . . two of the three official clocks had him at 9.3 [this being before electronic timing and times to a hundredth of a second]. The third showed 9.2.' That would have

---

11 A teammate at the 1964 Olympics was Vilma Charlton, who says that Jamaica's reputation for track and field was already established – in Japan, anyway. 'We went to the opening ceremony and the Japanese children, who ran alongside our bus, knew about Jamaica and knew about Herb McKenley. So this was their chant: "Jamaica, Jamaica, McKenley, McKenley". That made me feel special. We were resting on their shoulders: they were the giants.'

been an outright world record, but Coach Winter was – as you would expect – relaxed. 'He'll get the world record sometime this year,' he said. 'He's a wonderful fellow to work with – eager to learn and very pleasant.'

Johnson never did get the outright world record. Still, the figure sitting before me now, his hair white and bushy, his paunch straining at his T-shirt, his atrophied legs and flip-flopped feet below the table, could once claim to be the equal-fastest man in the world.

Back in 1961, Johnson was twenty-two and was, as he says, as close to Winter as he had been to his first coach, Herb McKenley. In the *Sports Illustrated* article the reporter observed this closeness first hand, writing that athlete and coach had a tendency to 'smother each other with verbal posies'. Johnson's scholarship was worth $160 a month and covered his tuition; he also had a job, working in the Santa Clara Youth Village. He needed the money because he was married and had a baby daughter. They had managed to rent a small apartment near the campus; before that, they lived in a hotel. 'No one wanted to rent to Negroes, because "the neighbours might object",' Johnson said, with, the reporter noted, 'some bitterness'.

Johnson's wife has passed away. 'She's over there,' he tells me, gesturing at one of the plant pots.

In 1966, Johnson finished at San José and returned to Jamaica to be interrogated by his father. 'What are you going to do?' he asked. 'Teach people how to run,' Johnson replied.

'The man laughed,' Johnson says. 'He had a fit! Then he said, "How?" I said, "Watch me."'

Johnson's plan was to introduce Bud Winter's techniques to Jamaica by holding training sessions around the island. He wrote a proposal that he presented to one of the island's cigarette companies, Carreras, asking for sponsorship for an island-wide athletics programme. His goal was 'to have workshops and clinics in every school. The guy said, "Does that sell cigarettes?" I said, "No. It's what you call niche marketing. PR. You're getting PR from me, a world record holder. And you're doing a good thing for the country."'

But he told them he could sell their cigarettes, too. 'Give me six vans with cigarettes and I'll take them to the shops as I go around the country. And in the evenings I'll show track and field films.' Carreras went for it, and so was born the Carreras Sports Foundation, as well as Johnson's mission.

A common sight in Jamaica these days is large marquees hosting temporary churches, often Jehovah's Witnesses or Seventh-day Adventists, attracting new recruits with lively, impassioned services. Perhaps there are also parallels with the Jamaican music scene, which began to thrive from the late 1950s, when the 'sound men' took their equipment out of Kingston and toured the island, finding big and appreciative audiences in the most remote communities.

Johnson was no less evangelical as he travelled round the country in the late 1960s, visiting schools by day, showing films from his van-cum-mobile-cinema in the evening.

But as he's telling the story of how he founded and ran the Carreras Sports Foundation, Johnson is interrupted by his friend David Mais. Mais says it was in fact his uncle who started the Carreras Sports Foundation. Johnson is having none of it. Mais protests, but Johnson butts back in: 'Anyway, that's neither here nor there. What is here or there is the VISION. You need to know what you're doing.' And Johnson was using Winter's techniques, focusing especially on relaxation and the mechanics of movement, to teach Jamaican youngsters to run with grace, style and speed. And form. Nobody slipped through the net, he says. Anybody with talent would be discovered.

After a year of his running roadshow, Johnson was called into the offices of his Carreras paymasters to be told: 'Dennis, we no longer need your services.' Yet the man was smiling as he delivered the message. 'Dennis,' he continued, 'when you took over, we had 33.3 per cent of the market. Now we have 66 per cent.'

'Why are you firing me, then?' said Johnson.

'We need you at the Rothmans Foundation.' Carreras had merged with Rothmans in 1958, and the company eventually became Rothmans International. For Johnson, it was a promotion. 'I had this dream,' he says. 'I wanted to be like Herb. I wanted to become like him. I said to people, "We're going to produce international runners right here." Because I had this vision. That's what sustained me and kept my sanity. And I did it! You understand?'

Something else Johnson did once he was back home was invite his old San José mentor, Bud Winter, to Jamaica to take part in a two-week conference on coaching. 'And you know who came to Bud's seminar?' Johnson says. 'Glen Mills and Stephen Francis.'

In 1971, Johnson was appointed part-time lecturer and director of sport at the University of Technology in Kingston. In the 1970s, Ricketts had told me, Johnson became known on campus for his 'ever-present smile and his swagger'. He was a maverick with a rebellious streak who always said that his dream was to produce world-class Jamaican athletes right there in Jamaica.

There were obstacles, but Johnson was enterprising and resourceful. Before one of his first big meetings as a coach at UTech, he asked if his athletes would be allowed to train at the National Stadium. No, he was told. (For a country famous for being laid-back, there is a lot of petty bureaucracy in Jamaica – another legacy of British colonial rule, no doubt.) Regardless, Johnson instructed his athletes to meet at the stadium at 4 a.m.; they scaled the walls and, before the sun crept over the Blue Mountains, did their training before making their getaway.

Johnson remained at UTech until 2006, by which time the university had fulfilled his vision, becoming the base for the world's top track and field club, MVP (Maximising Velocity and Power), with its stable of home-reared global stars. The club was – still is – run by Stephen Francis, who became Johnson's assistant at UTech, taking over as head coach at the university when Johnson retired in 2006. A partnership began between the university and Francis's club, building on what Johnson had established: namely, home-based support to rival – or improve upon – what was available elsewhere. It was the first programme designed to support world-class athletes who wanted to live and train in Jamaica, finally offering an alternative to a US college scholarship. In 2001, Asafa Powell declared: 'I am going to stay in Jamaica and beat the world naturally.' Four years later, when he ran 9.77 seconds in Athens, MVP and UTech had the fastest man in the world: proof that it was possible.

Yet that was only the start. At the 2008 Olympics in Beijing, ten MVP athletes made the Jamaican team and seven won medals. The most impressive single result was in the women's 100 metres, won by Shelly-Ann Fraser, with Sherone Simpson and Kerron Stewart both awarded silver medals: one-two-two in the women's 100 metres for Jamaica, and Fraser and Simpson from the same club.

There is no false modesty from Johnson, who argues that it is merely the realisation of his original vision. 'We established a programme here that's probably the best in the world,' he reflects. 'I don't know if there's another college anywhere that's produced the world-beaters we have. Can you think of one?'

'Not off the top of my head,' I reply. Wrong answer. 'Try six months of thinking!' Johnson blasts back. 'Think of the Olympics: one-two-two. This isn't a backyard thing! The Olympics! That's where it all started, and the high performance centre, with Bolt and everything. All the sprinting technique, all came from there. I tell you, man, Jamaica is not going to lose any sprints for the next fifty years.'

'Fifty?'

'Yes, man.'

Johnson enters an almost meditative state, even becoming a little glassy-eyed, when he talks about the top sprinters who have emerged from Jamaica in the last decade, partly because he appreciates their talent, but also because he views this golden generation as his legacy (his Wikipedia page describes him as 'the architect of the Jamaican athletics programme'). He says he coached Usain Bolt briefly – he isn't specific about when – but the emotion isn't far from the surface when he speaks about Mills, the coach who led Bolt to greatness. And he explains that he can tell a Mills-coached sprinter simply by watching him run. 'Oh yes, easily, easily. When Mills's sprinters run, when they perform, if you're into sprinting, you'll cry.

'The feet just touch the ground. They just kiss the ground. The people don't look haggard, they look like they're dancing. If you appreciate movement, the dance, anything poetic, like I do . . . When I watch Champs, I cry sometimes. Where in the world do you see movement – form – like that?'

Like all the best coaches – like Winter – Mills is a hypnotist, says Johnson. 'Coaching is hypnosis. When you believe in a coach, you go out there with all sorts of confidence.' As an example, he cites a schoolboy athlete he coached. It was Champs, and Johnson needed the athlete to finish the 5,000 metres to score the one point his team needed. The athlete started the race in a suitably hypnotic state, with one thing on his mind: to finish. Even when, mid-race, he suffered a sudden, violent attack of diarrhoea, his focus didn't waver. 'He was dehydrated,' Johnson explains. 'Started shitting himself all the way around the track. Plop plop plop plop. The most embarrassing fucking thing I've ever seen. And people saying, "Stop him; take him off," and the boy says, "DJ says I need one point, one point, one point." ' Recalling the episode, Johnson wheezes with laughter.

On Mills, he says: 'Mills is more Bud Winter than Bud Winter. Glen Mills used to come here every Sunday and listen how you're listening now.'

I had read that Mills was interested in maths and numbers. 'No,' says Johnson abruptly. 'He's not that intelligent. He's got street smarts, and his sprinters look beautiful. He got that information from me, not in a formal way. So did Stephen Francis; they learned at the same time. It all started when I brought Bud over to Kingston.'

Francis is better known than Mills as a Johnson protégé. He certainly was interested in maths and numbers, having worked in corporate finance. 'Stephen is not intelligent,' Johnson says. 'He's super-intelligent. I wish I was as bright as him. First-class honours; a scholar at Michigan [where he did an MBA]. He has a computer in his head. Super-bright. I have a good library. One of the best. And Stephen's library is bigger and better than mine.'

Francis also seems more versatile than Mills, and he has developed a reputation for polishing rough diamonds. 'Hurdlers, triple jumpers, high jumpers, women and men. Mills just teaches sprinters. Good sprinters. But most of Stephen's people – like Asafa – are people who never won Champs.'

Johnson describes himself as a 'connoisseur of sprinters'. He explains: 'Frankly I don't give a shit about nothing else. I like sprinting. Like the idea of getting from one point to the next as fast as possible. I think outside the box as far as sprinting is concerned. For example, energy.' He looks thoughtful, unsure whether he should carry on. Then he carries on regardless, explaining a theory he has been developing (if only in his own mind). 'If you're in the desert dying, if the first energy source dies – the glucose system – fat takes over. And we store more fat than Carter has peanuts. I'm trying to figure out how I can get to that energy source.'

This sounds interesting, if ambitious, but Johnson dismisses it. 'What I'm saying is foolishness, madness. Because right now it's impossible. But that is where my eyes are.' It would mean, he thinks, 'tricking the body into saying, "We need this energy"' – the energy stored in fat.[12] 'I don't have any secrets, but I've been discussing this with the Prof, Errol Morrison. He's the best physiologist in the world.'

---

[12] Perhaps it isn't madness. In early 2015, it was reported that scientists at the University of Oxford have been developing an energy drink using ketones, chemicals produced naturally by the body, which encourage the burning of fat as an alternative to glucose.

Morrison, the president at UTech, has worked with the physiologist Yannis Pitsiladis, originally of Glasgow University, more recently of Brighton, in studying the Jamaicans' sprinting success, including trying to identify a gene that might explain it – a speed gene. I mention to Johnson that I'd like to meet Morrison; is he easy to contact? 'Yeah, man,' says Johnson, reaching for his phone, dialling his friend's number. 'Prof, got someone wants to speak to you . . .' – looking up, addressing me. 'What's your name, my friend? . . . Richard. Here,' and he hands me the phone.

'One final question,' I say to Johnson when I've arranged a time to meet Morrison, but he interrupts: 'No, relax! I'm not in a hurry.' And on cue, a teenage boy appears with a tray of cold drinks. His son, says Johnson. A promising sprinter.

One thing that Johnson has been insistent on is that as well as technique (the number one thing), the physiology of the sprinter is important, and that the physiology of humans has not changed over the years. Therefore, training and coaching hasn't changed. A curious but related claim he makes is that sprinters are not any faster now than in his day, despite the times coming down. What does he mean? 'The fundamentals are the same,' he says. 'Physiology doesn't change, unless we grow horns or fins.'

But times do seem to have improved; how does he explain that? 'That's a very interesting question,' Johnson says. 'Are you ready for the answer?'

'Yes.'

'Nothing has improved since 1948.'

He thinks the faster times can all be explained by improvements in tracks, shoes, timing methods and other non-physiological factors. So, I ask him, who would win if both were at their peak – him or Bolt? He takes a circuitous route to the answer – hardly 'getting from one point to the next as fast as possible'. 'I was the first man in the world to run on an artificial track – a Tartan track. The Minnesota Mining and Manufacturing Company [these days known as 3M] came to

San José and put down one lane. One lane! Sixty yards long. The guy wanted to know how fast I ran. I alone ran along this track. I also had the world record for 60 yards: six-flat. Hand-timed. But when I did this experiment, with a guy called Arthur from Los Angeles, he had an automatic timer, but not like a stopwatch – it was one of those computers that fill a whole room. Anyway. The long and short of it is that I run 5.8 seconds. That means the track is two tenths faster than the dirt.

'Now, sixty yards is about fifty-five metres,' Johnson continues. 'The world record as we speak is 5.80. You can check that on your Google. So I ask myself the question: how much longer would it take me to do the next forty-five metres, bearing in mind I'm going at twenty-five m.p.h.? I'm asking you – I have forty-five metres left, I've passed the point at 5.80. My time for 100 metres. Come on.'

'I'll say around 9.8,' I suggest.

'Exactly!' says Johnson. 'And that is the ballpark in which they run today. When I did it, my shoes don't resemble what they look like today. We were running on dirt. I was a student with a job. You understand?'[13]

But Bolt has gone quicker than 9.8, I say – 9.58 is his world record. 'Bolt doesn't run 9.5 again,' Johnson says, 'or anywhere near it. Nobody is running that or close to it every day. Nine-point-eight is the ballpark.

'But Bolt is the best,' he concedes. 'The best ever. Undoubtedly. I know him fairly well. What is good about Bolt is not his blinding speed. What is good about him is his head. You understand? You can't beat somebody like that.'

Before I leave, Johnson mentions a sports science conference in the Pegasus Hotel in Kingston in a couple of weeks. 'The Prof', Errol

---

13 Once again, Johnson may be on to something. An academic study attempted to compare times set today with those of yesteryear. Allowing for the cinder track, shoes and other factors, Bob Hayes' 1964 world record of 10.06 seconds is equivalent to 9.66 (9.72 with no wind), reckons Dr Brian Maraj of the University of Alberta.

Morrison, will be there, among others, and he says I'm welcome to come along.

A fortnight later, I take up his invitation. During a break in the conference, I spot Johnson deep in conversation with a young man in a suit. It looks pretty one-way, with Johnson doing all the talking. And as I get closer, I can hear what he is saying: '... a sixty-yard track, about fifty-five metres, and I did it in 5.8 seconds. Five-point-eight-zero. The world record today is 5.80. Check that on your Google.

'So I'm asking you . . .'

7

CUBAN SWIMMING POOL CRISIS

Jamaica's prowess in global athletics is no fluke . . . or, as some would wish to convince the world, the result of officially blessed and systematic cheating . . . That dominance rests on natural talent, a tradition of excellence that has its roots in more than a century of Champs and the return on investment more than three decades ago in establishing the G. C. Foster College for Physical Education and Sports.
Editorial in the *Jamaica Gleaner*, 2 April 2014

If Dennis Johnson did more than any other individual to take sprint coaching around the country, and Herb McKenley developed a culture of excellence at one school, it needed something else, an institution, to bolster, spread and sustain their work.

Heading out of Calabar High School, turning right on to busy Washington Boulevard, takes you in the direction of Spanish Town. And when, after half an hour, you reach Spanish Town, you find G. C. Foster College.

Or you try to find it. It isn't easy. It's actually in the north of Spanish Town, in the Angels district. The college sits in expansive grounds, but these grounds are hidden on the other side of a railway line, in the middle of a community that resembles a shanty town: houses and shops constructed from wood and old bits of metal. You get lost in a maze of small, bumpy streets, until, about to give up, you abruptly emerge into open space, with plains and sports fields stretching out in front of you.

'It's in a terrible place,' I was told by Hugh Small, a judge and former politician who served as youth sports minister. 'It's not what it was or what it could be. But it needed a significant amount of land and the only available land was in Spanish Town.'

Small was one of the politicians who in the late 1970s worked on the plans to establish a sports college in Jamaica modelled on the centres of excellence that existed in Cuba, East Germany and the Soviet Union; centres integral to the systems that brought these countries phenomenal success at the Olympic Games. It was no coincidence that inspiration came from behind the Iron Curtain.

Jamaica in the seventies had a socialist government, led by the charismatic five-times-married Michael Manley of the PNP, the People's National Party. Manley forged a relationship with Fidel Castro's Cuba that alarmed the US, who feared the spread of communism so close to their shores. As a consequence, the CIA increasingly involved themselves in Jamaican politics, backing the rival right-leaning Jamaica Labour Party (JLP), led by the reggae-loving Edward Seaga (also a record company owner who contributed much to the burgeoning music scene). Less than two decades after gaining independence, the island was becoming bitterly split along party lines. Communities in Kingston were turned into garrisons affiliated to one political party or the other; guns began flooding into the country; gangs were allegedly armed by politicians.[14] The violence kept escalating

---

14 Almost inevitably, a culture developed where local 'dons', like Christopher 'Dudus' Coke, became all-powerful in the garrisons. As Mark Shields, a British police officer seconded to Jamaica in 2004, told the *Guardian* in 2012: 'It's criminal terrorism. People literally live in fear. If they run a shop, they have to pay protection. If the don wanted their youngest daughter, they would have to give her up so he could take her virginity. The community was completely under the control of the local don, and the police were deeply frightened about going in there.'

even as Bob Marley, living in exile in London after being shot in his home on Hope Road in 1976, put Jamaica on the world stage with his songs about love and peace.

Marley's One Love Peace Concert at the National Stadium in 1978 was intended to signal his return to Jamaica and put an end to the violence. At one point he called the two political rivals on to the stage to stand alongside him, joining their hands above his head, the politicians stern-faced and awkward as they towered over the diminutive singer. 'We gotta be together,' said Marley. 'I just want to shake hands and show the people that we're gonna make it right, we're gonna unite, we're gonna make it right, we've got to unite . . .' (It didn't have the desired effect: in 1980, when Seaga replaced Manley in a bitter election, 800 people were murdered in the course of the campaign. The violence was shocking. But it has since got worse: there are around 1,500 gun deaths a year in Jamaica, almost a fifth at the hands of the authorities: in 2013, 258 people were shot dead by police, though, encouragingly, it was closer to 100 in 2014.)[15]

The Manley name is synonymous with Jamaican politics. Michael Manley's father, Norman, who founded the PNP, was hailed in 1962 as one of the founding fathers of independence. It seems more than a coincidence that he was also one of Jamaica's first world-class sprinters, whose national 110 yards record of 10 seconds flat, set at Champs in 1911, stood for forty-one years. Later, as a barrister, he represented future Olympic champion Arthur Wint when the young Wint was on trial after accidentally shooting and killing his female colleague. Yet Norman Manley, having fought so hard for Jamaican independence, never served as prime minister. His cousin, Alexander Bustamante, who set up the rival JLP, was the country's first elected leader, serving from 1962 to 1967. Manley's son, Michael, was then elected in 1972.

Michael Manley was inspired by the strong emphasis Cuba put on sport, with athletes identified at a young age – a Junior Olympic Programme was established in Cuba in 1963 – and given specialist coaching. Results followed. By the seventies, Castro's Cuba was an Olympic powerhouse.

Hugh Small told me that in the late 1970s, when he was Jamaica's youth sports minister, he visited Cuba to inspect their then state-of-the-art sports facilities. He also travelled to East Germany and the Soviet Union, and to one non-communist country: Great Britain. 'I went to Loughborough,' he recalled. 'I met Seb Coe and his father, Peter.'

Even back then Jamaica already had a disproportionate number of world-class runners: after McKenley, Wint and Rhoden came George Kerr, a double Olympic bronze medallist in 1960, Lennox Miller, an Olympic 100 metres medallist in 1968 and 1972, and Don Quarrie,

---

15 According to Laurie Gunst in *Born Fi' Dead*, her disturbing and controversial 1996 book about gang culture in Jamaica: 'The politicians and their gunmen took over where the slave masters and their overseers left off: the practice of intimidation was a logical outgrowth of the brutal intimacy that had always prevailed between the powerful and the powerless.'

the 1976 Olympic 200 metres champion. But Manley wanted to establish a system, open to rich and poor, but especially poor, to put Jamaica on a par with other small nations – Cuba and East Germany being the obvious examples – that didn't just punch above their weight but were sporting superpowers.

P. J. Patterson, the foreign minister in Manley's government, recalls a visit by Castro. 'Fidel offered six schools,' Patterson told me. 'Michael said he wanted one for people to be trained in physical education. That became the G. C. Foster College, and out of it has come a flow of coaches.'

You enter its grounds and drive past a disused Olympic-sized swimming pool and diving pool. Both are fading white edifices, dry as a bone, with weeds sprouting through the cracks. The sports fields are large, but they too seem neglected. The buildings that make up the campus look as though they were built in 1980 and have barely been touched since. A large sign at the entrance, with a picture of a smiling Gerald Claude Eugene Foster, offers some historical background. The first sports college in the English-speaking Caribbean opened in September 1980, 'the original buildings and equipments [...] gifts from the government and people of Cuba to the government and people of Jamaica'.

Foster, after whom the college is named, is another major figure in Jamaican sport. Dennis Johnson mentioned him as the only coach, apart from Herb McKenley, worthy of the name when he returned to the island in 1966. He was an old man then; he died that same year, aged eighty.

Foster is best known for his efforts to compete at the 1908 London Olympics, crossing the Atlantic in a banana boat only to be denied the opportunity because Jamaica, as a British colony, was not a member of the IOC in its own right. Foster remained in England and took part in post-Games meetings, where he showed his talent, beating some of the sprinters who had excelled at the Olympics. He had attended

Wolmer's Boys' School – still a powerful force at Champs – and was marked out as a gifted athlete when, as a fourteen-year-old, he was given a ten-yard handicap against Kingston's best sprinter, M. L. Ford. He won by three yards. When he was eighteen, he ran 100 yards in 10 seconds: comparable with Archie Hahm's 11 seconds over 100 metres to win the Olympic title in the same year, 1904.

While I was in Jamaica, staying in Bull Bay, I mentioned that I was researching a book on athletics and was asked if I had heard of G. C. Foster. 'His daughter lives two doors down,' I was told. Pat Lightburn was her name, and she was eighty-eight and frail, living in a small, run-down house by the beach, surrounded by family – four generations at least, with a not untypical mix of ethnic influences, from the pale-skinned Mrs Lightburn to her black great-granddaughter.

Here was a living link to the original roots of Jamaica's sprinting culture. It was quite mind-blowing, especially to realise that it was almost fifty years since G. C. Foster had died. His daughter recalled him as vividly as she could: as an energetic, enthusiastic and relentlessly positive man who poured all his energy into sport. He was also a first-class cricketer before becoming an athletics coach, but he coached everything – she remembered him firing the starting pistol at the cycling track at the National Stadium to cries of 'Let them go, Mr Foster! Let them go!' She added: 'He coached at every school at one time or another, and they all won Champs when he coached them.' Indeed, he led Calabar to their first Champs title in 1931, then took Jamaica to the island's first international games, the 1935 British Empire Games in Hamilton, Canada, and to the 1948 London Olympics.

At the entrance to the college posthumously named after Foster, I am met by Maurice Wilson, the head coach, who takes me on a tour, pointing out, beyond the running track, a curious structure that looks like a funfair ride made out of Meccano. '*Cool Runnings*,' he says. This was where the Jamaican bobsleigh team trained for the 2014 Winter Olympics.

Wilson tells me that he has been head coach at G. C. Foster for eleven years. But like so many other coaches in Jamaica, his responsibilities range from schoolchildren to the best in the world. He is technical director of the country's governing body, the JAAA, and acted as head coach at the 2002 Commonwealth Games in Manchester, then again at the 2014 Games in Glasgow, having done the same job at the 2011 senior world championships in Daegu, South Korea. At G. C. Foster he is also principal lecturer in sports and recreation. 'But I'm a specialist track and field lecturer,' he adds.

Wilson talks the way an athlete limbers up, stretching his vocabulary. 'The persons who come under my guidance are versed in the major disciplines of track and field,' he explains when we are in his office. 'They must be able to coach to a level, and to pass on the information to other coaches.' His office is next to a classroom in which the students are becoming rowdy. 'I need to talk to them,' he says, and disappears, then quickly reappears, closing the door. 'My job is to make sure they become experts in the different disciplines; they are then distributed and dispersed all across the island to spread the philosophy of G. C. Foster. So it filters through the system.'

How would he sum up that philosophy? 'The basic techniques, the basic training methods, are given to these youngsters early. This is why you're seeing these performances. We do not leave, for example, technique, and mobility, and coordination, just to be learned. We help to correct deficiencies, and so on. This is done at an early stage. This is why Jamaicans are able to pass a baton without even having a training camp. It's drilled into them; from primary school.'

He echoes Dennis Johnson when he says that as far as he's concerned, it's all about technique. Not that Jamaicans know how to sprint while the rest of the world does not, but that the correct techniques are so ingrained because they are taught so early.

I was struck at Champs by the fact that the schools all had coaches who were, clearly, coaches, as opposed to teachers performing extracurricular duties. It is difficult to explain why this was obvious;

it just was, from their uniform – baseball cap, polo shirt, stopwatch, whistle – to the way they carried themselves, to the deference shown by their student athletes. The coaches took what they did – and by extension their athletes, and themselves – seriously. Wilson says that all of them will have passed through G. C. Foster; indeed, it is now a requirement of the secondary schools' association that organises Champs that school coaches must have a G. C. Foster qualification.

The college doesn't just churn out coaches. It produces people with other sports-related qualifications: sports masseurs, for example. Usain Bolt's personal masseur, Everald Edwards, trained at G. C. Foster. So did Shawn Kettle, who works for Yohan Blake, and Patrick Watson, a long-time member of Asafa Powell's team.

Wilson himself was a 400 metres runner at school, but, like Glen Mills and Stephen Francis, he was not an exceptional athlete. He excelled academically; he has a masters degree in science, as well as an undergraduate degree and a teaching diploma. This is another feature of quite a few of the top coaches: they are highly educated. Wilson believes that as well as being good athletes, his countrymen have a flair for coaching: 'I think we're naturally good coaches. Like Englishmen are good bankers . . . or seafarers.'

Where does it come from, this aptitude for coaching? 'I think although sometimes we don't pay attention to detail, anything that intrigues us we do well at. And running is a national obsession.'

On a tour of the grounds, Wilson laments the state of the running track and hopes a new one can be installed soon. He seems apologetic or embarrassed by the non-pristine condition of the place, and doesn't lead me anywhere near the swimming pool. But even if the infrastructure is crumbling, the wide-open space is invigorating. And compared to the facilities at Calabar, this is state-of-the-art.

We arrive at the office of the principal, Edward Shakes. He too speaks slowly, deliberately, in similar velvety tones; but initially, and at some length, about British football. 'I'm a Man U fan,' he says sombrely. 'Me, Chelsea,' offers Wilson, who sits in the corner of the principal's office and inspects his phone.

Shakes's background is in engineering – he studied in Britain for a while. 'I didn't come here as an expert in sport,' he says, 'I came in as an education administrator.' There are around 500 students at G. C. Foster, slightly more men than women. All will leave as certified coaches, and in many cases, as qualified teachers too.

'Prior to the college, there were only a few schools who performed very well and most of the outstanding athletes came from those few schools,' Shakes explains. 'Kingston College, Calabar and so on. But with the advent of G. C. Foster College, we train and disperse persons right across the country. We have trained persons placed in the schools in very rural areas. So someone like Usain Bolt, for example, who comes from rural Trelawny, he would have been exposed to a G. C. Foster coach at a very young age, and it would have been that person who discovered his talent and gave him all the early grooming.'

Shakes acknowledges the benefits of having an international coach on his staff – one of Wilson's athletes, Rasheed Dwyer, would go on to be crowned Commonwealth 200 metres champion in 2014, winning ahead of Warren Weir. Wilson is a Level V IAAF coach: the highest qualification. 'When you have that combination – someone like Maurice who is an academic as well as an internationally qualified coach, and a practising coach – you ensure your standards remain relevant. We have other international coaches on staff. We try to maintain standards. And they are practising what they teach.'

In a sense, the college has achieved what it set out to do, training coaches to a high standard and, as both Shakes and Wilson say, dispersing them around the country, like seeds blowing off a dandelion. Naturally it took a few years for these seeds to find fertile ground and flower; then a little longer for the athletes to progress through the schools system and emerge on the international stage. But it certainly happened. And now the challenge, for Shakes, is maintaining standards, keeping G. C. Foster College fit for purpose – not letting the Jamaican system, of which the college is such an integral part, decline as the Cuban one has.

Shakes mentions the swimming pool, describing it as 'one of two big projects', along with the athletics track, requiring attention. He says he wants to 'resuscitate our pool. One point I was making was that we have the opportunity to do in swimming what we have done in track and field.'[16]

I ask when the pool was last used. Shakes sighs deeply. 'Interesting story. It was built by the Cubans. But as happened in the UK, governments change. And in 1980, the socialist government in Jamaica was voted out and a more conservative government was voted in on an anti-communist, anti-Cuba platform.

'So immediately after the election, the new prime minister [Seaga] ordered the Cuban technicians that were here to go home. And so, although the pool was built, it was never commissioned.'

'You mean it's never been used?'

'No. It was well built. And now, refurbishing it and getting it going is what we want to do.'

The Cuban technicians were just days away from completing their work. Could Seaga not have let them stay to get it finished? 'In the Cold War, a lot of crazy things happened, you know,' Shakes says. There was considerable pressure on Seaga from the US, he adds. 'If you wanted their money . . .' So it was American money or a swimming pool? 'I wouldn't put it that way, but the government acted because of pressure from the US.'

*

16 Why not? In December 2014, a Jamaican, Alia Atkinson, became the first black woman ever to win a world swimming title, at the world short-course championships in Doha. Atkinson won the 100 metres breaststroke. She trains in Florida.

'Irrespective of what you may think of Jamaica, you have to come here to see,' Maurice Wilson tells me after we have left the principal's office. 'We have many more Usain Bolts. It is not a fad. It is something that is ingrained in us. You have to be at boys' and girls' Champs to understand it.'

I tell Wilson that it's all very well me reporting back on Champs, and the extraordinary performances I witnessed, but many have made up their minds – that the explanation for Jamaica's success is drugs.

'Let me say something on that,' he replies. 'When you look at the drugs that was involved [in recent cases], let us be reasonable. When you talk about a stimulant, that has no effect on you during competition . . . yes, you have violated a rule, but why make it appear as if those guys are on steroids? There is no distinction made!'

Wilson, like Dennis Johnson and others involved in the sport in Jamaica, is frustrated at the perception that their athletes are systematically cheating. He does not think the transgressions are the 'tip of the iceberg', as one Jamaican drug-tester has claimed. 'We have never had a top-notch athlete coming out of Jamaica that has tested positive for a hard drug, like steroids, where you know that they definitely went out there to cheat,' Wilson says. 'And I know that a lot of times people throw cold water on performances. In other words, "I cannot believe that in a population of three million these guys are topping the world." But I do believe that Scottish people are great bankers . . . I do believe that the Irish do well in business. So how is it that you cannot believe we are great athletes?'

Perhaps it was a natural evolution from G. C. Foster's production of so many home-grown coaches to have home-grown stars too. 'It was Stephen Francis', Wilson says, 'who decided, after Carl Lewis made a statement that they [the US] were training our athletes, that the job could be done here.'

8

SHIFTING THE PARADIGM

We no longer saw track and field as an individual sport. We saw
it then and still see it today as a team sport.

Bruce James, President, MVP

They meet at 5 a.m. at the East Stadium, which sits beside the National Stadium like its little brother. This was the warm-up track – the 'boiler room', my American coaching friend called it – during Champs.

The first question is: why so early?

'I do this', Stephen Francis has explained, 'to control the night-time activities of my athletes.'

By 7 a.m., the sun is creeping up from behind the Blue Mountains, casting long shadows across the faded red track and patchy grass of the infield. The light is pale gold.

Sitting watching in the stand, it's like observing a factory floor, with groups of workers performing highly specific tasks, watched over by the foreman, Francis. There are close to 100 athletes, all in little knots: a hive of activity and noise, the coaches' whistles providing regular, jarring variations to the hum of the morning rush hour.

Francis is slumped on a bench in the infield wearing ill-fitting black tracksuit trousers, a green polo shirt and a sun hat. He has a black 'man bag' slung over his shoulder. The bench faces away from the track, but Francis has twisted his body – no mean feat, given his build – to be able to see the home straight. But as waves of athletes pass, sprinting or running with exaggerated knee-lifts, Coach Francis seems hardly to notice; he looks indifferent. Eventually he gets up and lumbers towards a group of four female sprinters gathered at the bend. Four other sprinters pass him and, without appearing to be watching them, he barks, 'Shoulders, Shamira!'

A sprint hurdler is next down the straight and past the slow-moving Francis. 'Trail leg!' he shouts after her, again without turning.

But now he goes to work, helping the female sprint teams prepare for the upcoming Penn Relays: a huge date in the Jamaican athletics calendar ever since Herb McKenley began taking teams there in the early 1960s. Today, in one of their final sessions before Pennsylvania, the baton changes are not as slick as they could be. 'Reach!' yells Francis after one sloppy change. After another failure, he stretches to full height with his hands in the air, then places them slowly behind his head in an attitude of pure exasperation. He raises his voice again: 'Tell her to reach!' When the men have similar problems, he seems to lose his temper: 'What did I say? What did I say?'

Francis turns his attention to a young male sprinter. 'Relax your shoulders, man . . . Let's go, boy. Heels!' Then, to a female sprint hurdler: 'Lean forward! Forward . . . Forward . . . Forward! . . . Good, I like that.'

The track is full of sculpted, muscular bodies, now starting to overheat as the sun rises further in the sky. It's still only 8 a.m., but Francis blows for a final time on his whistle, the activity abruptly ceases, and he wanders into the bowels of the stand. Soon he will make his way to the car park and his gleaming white BMW X5 to drive to his home in the surrounding hills, where he will read scientific papers or pore over data on his computer. Training will resume at 3 p.m. with a weights session in the gym at UTech.

The fifty-year-old Francis's reputation precedes him. In reports his name is frequently prefixed with 'controversial', mainly because he seems to be permanently at war with the administrators: the Jamaica Athletics Administrative Association, the Jamaica Olympic Association, the government; pretty much anyone in authority. 'We have never received one cent from any of them,' he once complained. In interviews he comes across as blunt and outspoken but not rude or aggressive. In contrast to Glen Mills, with whom Francis has a strained relationship, at least he *gives* interviews.

Watching Francis with his athletes, blasting on his whistle and barking instructions, the impression is of a formidable, imposing and intimidating figure. Not somebody you would pick a fight with. Then again, perhaps his reputation owes too much, and unfairly, to his physique. He is a generously proportioned man. A 2009 article in the Australian newspaper *The Age* described him, a little unkindly, as 'one of the unlikeliest sights in sport . . . A bear of a man who can barely manage a brisk walk, he spends his days bellowing through a megaphone at some of the fleetest athletes on the planet. They appear terrified of him.'

That was tame. In 2013, the *Gleaner* published a comment piece about Francis, under the headline 'He ain't pretty but he's pretty damn good.' It opened with some general observations on the relationship between a person's looks and their popularity, in particular the unfortunate fate of the 'ugly man'. It went on: 'It can be argued that Stephen Francis, a genius of coaching and moulding athletic talent, does not get due respect and acknowledgement from the Jamaican public, perhaps because he's not a pretty boy.'

The article continued: '"Frano" could hardly have been more unfortunate in the looks department. A corpulent man who makes the shade black look black,[17] Francis knows what it takes to make athletes run pretty quickly with poise and beauty. Much of the reason for some people disliking him is the fact that he's often brusque with the media and doesn't indulge their prying into the business of him and his athletes.'

It ended with a plea for respect. It was an article in *defence* of Francis.

First impressions can be misleading. The day before my early-morning appointment at the East Stadium, I visited Dr Rachael Irving, a scientist at the University of the West Indies. From her office on the sprawling, well-maintained Mona campus we could just about see the pristine blue track where Mills and his Racers Track Club, including Bolt, train every morning.

Irving has been involved in a project to find the 'speed gene' that might explain the Jamaicans' success, though originally she was more

---

17 The remark about Francis's colour provoked some angry responses in the *Gleaner* but it hints at an enduring preoccupation with the colour, or shade, of someone's skin, and some of the complex, contradictory attitudes surrounding this issue in Jamaica: attitudes exemplified by the dancehall star, Vybz Kartel. In 2011 he bleached his skin and launched a range of skin-bleaching products even while singing that black people should be proud of their colour. During my first visit to Jamaica the news was dominated by Kartel's conviction for murder; he was sentenced to thirty-five years in prison.

interested in the original trailblazers, Francis and his MVP club, than in Mills's Racers Track Club. She was charged by scientist Yannis Pitsiladis with collecting DNA samples from some of the top athletes, including those at MVP.

She only knew Francis by reputation. 'I was a little afraid. I went there to watch them training, the early mornings. I sat there in the stand for a month and just watched. Stephen came to me one morning and said, "Why are you here every day looking at us?"

'I said, "Well I'm supposed to be involved in this project but I'm afraid to talk to you."

'Stephen said, "Why are you afraid of me?"' She explained the project and Francis, to her surprise, was curious. He told her to phone him when he returned from a trip to Europe. She would do that, she said, adding that she already had his number. 'That's the number I give to people I don't want to talk to,' said Francis.

When it came to collecting the samples, Francis couldn't have been more obliging. While Irving hovered with her swabs to collect saliva samples at the end of training, Francis ordered his athletes, including Asafa Powell and Shelly-Ann Fraser, to assist her. 'Give Dr Irving some support!' he barked if they showed any reluctance.

'We developed, I wouldn't say a friendship, but he's somebody I can talk to,' Irving told me. 'He has a rough exterior. Well, persons say that, but they don't know him. I think he's fantastic!'

Beneath the stand, in the shade, the athletes file past, panting and sweating, in various states of distress. Francis, having stopped to speak to a couple of his assistants, watches them, offering words of encouragement or mild, tongue-in-cheek rebuke. The athletes include some of the best in the world: double Olympic 100 metres champion Shelly-Ann Fraser-Pryce; Nesta Carter, a double Olympic 4x100 metres gold medallist and 9.78-second 100 metres man; Shericka Williams, an Olympic relay medallist.

Francis looks relaxed. It might be a good time to approach. Can he spare some time? 'Sure,' he says.

Like Glen Mills, Francis was not a star athlete as a schoolboy (another thing he has in common with Mills is that he is a bachelor. He explained in 2006: 'In my twenties I was too much of a party person to marry. In my thirties I could not afford it. Now that I am in my forties I travel too much').

'I was a thrower at school,' he tells me, 'but not very good.' He was a pupil at Wolmer's Boys' School (the first ever Champs winners, in 1910). He was more academically inclined, captaining the Schools' Challenge Quiz team (a big deal in Jamaica: basically Champs for brainy kids). He went to the University of the West Indies in Kingston to do management studies, with accountancy and economics. Later he went to the US, to the University of Michigan, to do an MBA in finance. Bright, then.

While doing his undergraduate degree in Kingston, Francis began to take an interest in the athletic career of his younger brother, Paul, who was also at Wolmer's, and a decent thrower. He volunteered to help coach at the school. 'I got the coaching bug after a while,' he says. 'I went to the US to do my MBA, then returned and started coaching again part time at the school.'

Back in Kingston, he worked as a management consultant for KPMG. But it was increasingly coaching that consumed him. He would go and watch Dennis Johnson's training sessions at UTech. A voracious reader, he devoured books on athletics and coaching. He was interested in the theoretical as well as the practical. (Which brings to mind a Ronald Reagan quote: 'An economist is someone who sees something that works in practice and wonders if it would work in theory.' Francis is an economist.)

'You start first by reading books on track and field,' he says, his voice so deep that you can almost feel the stand vibrating. He has a tendency to refer to himself in the second person. He says he read 'Sprinting books, throwing books. Um, and then you realise you have to move to different areas: physiology, biomechanics, anatomy. To be a really knowledgeable coach you need to read a lot more than one would think necessary.'

Any key books? 'A lot,' Francis nods. 'I think the most important book in my early career . . . I had a friend at Wolmer's who went to study coaching in Cuba. He came back with a book about coaching that he said had all the secrets. But it was in Spanish.' Which Francis didn't speak. So how did he read it? 'I sat down with a dictionary and a typewriter and translated it over a period of a month or so.'

It didn't contain all the secrets, but it had some useful information on 'the whole question of recovery; how they did periodisation; increasing [training] load. Those things were not as clear in most of the American textbooks I was reading at the time. You had other people like Frank Dick in Britain, who wrote some good books, and some American authors. A wide variety. Now a lot of the reading I do is research papers, research journals.'

It's not all he reads. 'I'm a very avid fan of novels. I read a lot of non-fiction, mainly legal, mystery-type theories. I do a lot of reading.'

As for favourite authors: 'I like to think I discovered Michael Lewis,' Francis says, 'because I read his first [*Liar's Poker*] in 1989.'

This is interesting, because Lewis's books are concerned with the worlds of finance and money, or, as in the case of *Moneyball* and *The Blindside*, sport. There are differences between them, though. In his books about finance, he is concerned with exposing corruption, greed and nefarious practices; in his books about sport, he tends to be more interested in innovative coaches who discover and develop previously hidden, underrated or underperforming talent (the subtitle of *Moneyball* is: 'The Art of Winning an Unfair Game').

In fact, you could say that most of his books are essentially about people who beat or subvert the system: schemers. In the world of finance they tend to be malignant; in sport, benign. It could be a coincidence, of course. But there seems to be a moral distinction, one that maybe says more about Lewis's cynicism towards the world of finance (a world he knows well having worked as a bond salesman) and his idealism when it comes to professional sport, with which he is perhaps not so intimately acquainted.

By the late 1990s, Francis had itchy feet. His job at KPMG paid well, but his passion was for athletics, or rather coaching. He believed that Jamaican athletes were being lost, slipping through the cracks in the system, although his main bone of contention was that there was no system in the first place. He felt that complacency reigned. (In the best tradition of those who see themselves as operating outside and against the system, he cannot resist digs at the Jamaican sporting establishment, even as he praises Champs as the island's greatest institution: 'Jamaica's athletics success has always been about Champs. It was not designed by anybody, though the British have a lot to answer for. And so far Jamaicans have not been able to destroy it – but I think they're working hard at that.')

Jamaica's problem was that they had always done so well: they consistently won more medals than an island their size had any right to expect. Francis believed that success bred complacency. There was a reluctance – a refusal – to think about how they could be even better.

Jamaica was a good nursery, but the finishing schools were in the US. As well as the home-grown, overseas-reared athletes, the success of other expats – including the Olympic 100 metres winners from 1988–96, Ben Johnson, Linford Christie and Donovan Bailey, even if the first two now have doping offences against their names – reinforced the idea that the existing model worked: teach kids how to run, then send them away.

Francis thought differently. He wondered if, in fact, talent was being lost. 'The research thing for me', he explains, 'was to compile a list of people from Jamaica and see what happened to them four years down the road compared to Americans, Kenyans, Australians . . . whatever. It was always something I discussed at various levels with the

JAAA and with other coaches. At the time, everyone was very fearful of taking the step [of coaching Jamaican athletes at home], because it was all they knew: they run, they get a scholarship, and if you do hear from them again you get them to run for Jamaica as seniors. That was how it was.

'DJ tried to change that up at UTech, but there was something missing when he was there in terms of connecting what he was doing at UTech to the top level of the sport.'

The frustration for Francis came in realising how many talented athletes had left for the US and then disappeared. 'It was difficult to understand. I mean, I believed that a lot of the kids who didn't make it in the States were either sidelined or there was maladjustment: missing their parents, missing their food, being stuck in the cornfields of Iowa, or the cornfields of Kansas, or being in the city and being caught up in the whole gangster and drugs stuff.'

There were advantages in the States in terms of facilities and regular competition. But not coaching – he believed they could be coached better in Jamaica, where their focus wouldn't be running all over the US chasing points for their universities in the national colleges competition. Moreover, he adds, 'I felt that if you could give them a relatively comfortable situation, the fact that they are where they're accustomed to would more than make up for the deficiencies in proper weights facilities and so on. It would at least give them an equal chance. The problem was to get people to try it out.'

In September 1999, the Francis brothers and two friends, David Noel and Bruce James, who worked at Citibank, sat discussing the issue in James's flat in Kingston. From this discussion they decided to start their own club. They called it Maximising Velocity and Power (MVP) Track and Field Club. At the same time Francis made a major decision: to quit his job and try coaching full-time. A radical, bold – or foolish – step. 'Oh yeah,' he says, 'a big move. There were many ramifications. A lot of lifestyle changes and questioning as to whether it was a sensible thing to do.'

Presumably it meant a big drop in earnings, too. 'Oh, huge, because up to that point nobody had made a living out of full-time coaching seniors in Jamaica. The only person at the time who'd made a living as a coach was the national football coach, who was a Brazilian.' That was René Simões, who led the national team, known as the Reggae Boyz, to the 1998 World Cup finals in France.[18]

For the new MVP, the challenge was to recruit athletes. Was it a hard sell? 'It was a no sell,' Francis says.

The first member was Brigitte Foster, a twenty-five-year-old sprint hurdler who had followed the familiar path. She had been a promising schoolgirl – though she never won at Champs – but had lost her way when she went to university in the US. In 1999, after four years away, she was back in Jamaica. As Bruce James explained in a TEDx talk in 2011 about the origins of MVP: 'She was in search of a coach, and we were in search of an athlete.'

Francis began working with Foster, and within a year she was an Olympic finalist. She finished eighth in Sydney after hitting a hurdle, but the telling statistic was the improvement she made in twelve months, her time dropping from 13.30 for the 100 metres hurdles to 12.70. Foster said that what most impressed her about Francis was his 'constant grasp for knowledge'.

Francis thought Foster's performance in Sydney would put MVP on the map. Instead there was resistance at home to what they were trying to do. Bruce James believed that their vision, to coach senior Jamaican athletes in Jamaica, was actually unpopular with the powers-that-be: 'We soon discovered that not everyone loved our idea. In fact, they

---

18 Dennis Johnson was absolutely scathing of the Reggae Boyz. 'The Reggae Boyz!' he spluttered. 'The Reggae Boyz was born to lose. When countries go to the World Cup, them eyes on the prize! You know what we went to do? Get on to the field of play!' Johnson overlooks the fact that Jamaica became the smallest nation ever to win a World Cup Game, beating Japan 2–1 in their final group match. The Reggae Boyz might not have been in France thinking they could win the tournament, but they were hardly *Cool Runnings*.

didn't even like it . . . the Jamaican power brokers thought, How dare these four men try to wreck a great thing that Jamaica has going on.' He thought the 'biggest hurdle was the Jamaican mindset. In Jamaica, Jamaicans were convinced that what we had achieved at the world championships and Olympics was so amazing it was remarkable. What were you going to change?' (And indeed, why?)

In their first few years they trained on the dirt track at Wolmer's. But the club began to struggle financially. Francis sold his car to keep MVP afloat. 'My credit rating was so bad I could not get a credit card.' Then he had an idea. He went to Johnson at UTech with an offer: he would coach their athletes for free (he was by now an IAAF-accredited coach) if MVP could use their facilities. He thus became Johnson's unpaid assistant. And now, well over a decade later, the partnership between university and club is, says Francis, 'hugely symbiotic. Most athletes who come to UTech know they'll be in MVP. It's almost like it's one; we are known as UTech/MVP. We share everything.'

The founding principles of the club they discussed in James's flat in 1999 remain paramount, however. James, in his talk in 2011, called them the 'three philosophies' of MVP:

1. We no longer saw track and field as an individual sport. We saw it then and still see it today as a team sport.

2. The option to stay and train in Jamaica is just that: an option. But it is critical to have this option.

3. Confidence. A Jamaican national hero, Marcus Garvey, said: 'If you haven't confidence in self, you are twice defeated in the race of life. With confidence, you have won even before you have started.'[19]

---

19 Garvey (1887–1940) was a political leader, skilled orator and hero to the Rastafari movement, who consider him a prophet. Ironically, given MVP's mission to

When they were getting started, says Francis, 'we were just looking for people we could get. There were some who I coached at Wolmer's. They would be more likely to believe in me and say, "OK, we'll give Coach a chance." The majority of the time we had to look for people who the coaches in the States were not going to be pursuing.'

Francis was also setting out to coach adults rather than kids. This posed a new challenge and required a different approach. Schoolchildren would, he explains, 'finish training in May and come back in September taller, stronger, faster, without you doing anything. As long as the youngster grows you don't have to pay too much attention to technique or anything like that because their body's natural progression . . . is ensuring that some kind of improvement occurs.

'When, at eighteen, nineteen, the growth slows – or for females when they're sixteen, seventeen – then it becomes a lot more difficult for them to improve. You no longer get the physical help from their bodies. For them to [improve] you need to ensure they do the right kind of work. So it's vastly more difficult – it's part of the reason why there is such a very low transfer rate in terms of talent as juniors to success as seniors.'

Francis, in any case, was not looking for the best high school athletes, mainly because he didn't think they'd be interested. 'At first we didn't dare approach anybody who people thought was good. With Asafa we directly picked him out because he came last. He looked OK but we knew there'd be little or no competition to get him.'

Asafa Powell was eighteen when he joined MVP. He had grown up in Linstead, in St Catherine Parish, twelve miles inland from Spanish

---

encourage Jamaican athletes to stay in Jamaica, Garvey was the founder of the Black Star Line, which promoted the return of the African diaspora to their ancestral lands. 'A people without the knowledge of their past history, origin and culture is like a tree without roots,' he said.

Town. He went to Charlemont High, not a leading force at Champs – often they didn't even qualify.[20]

At Champs in 2000, Powell was third in the first round of the 100 metres in 11.45 and fourth in his 200 metres in 23.07; he didn't progress beyond the heats. A year later he reached the 100 metres final, after running 10.77 in the semi, but false-started. The race was won by Marvin Anderson of St Jago in 10.40, ahead of another red-hot talent, Steve Mullings.

Francis didn't see Powell's talent (nobody did), but he did see his potential. His technique was so ragged – 'I used to lean way back,' Powell has said. 'My arms weren't going up; my knees were going too high; everything was wrong' – that Francis believed improvements were possible in every department. To be fair, few would have disputed that.

Something that counted in Powell's favour, perhaps, was that he hadn't been through the kind of regime that athletes at schools such as Calabar and Kingston College were exposed to. Francis might also have imagined there was something in his genes. He was the youngest of six boys (of course) born to William and Cislyn Powell, both pastors in the Redemption National Church of God. His parents had been decent sprinters in their youth, his father running 10.2 seconds for the 100 yards, his mother 11.4, but the talent seemed to have passed to another of their sons, Donovan, who was eleven years Asafa's senior. Donovan's personal best for 100 metres was 10.07, in 1995, but he is even better known in Jamaica for inflicting the only defeat in four years on Calabar's Daniel England at Champs, in the 200 metres in 1990. Donovan Powell attended one of the sprinting powerhouses, St Jago (where Yohan Blake went to school). He also had a positive

---

20 Powell might be one of Charlemont High's most famous alumni, and was for a while arguably the most popular man in Jamaica, but his popularity had its limits. A proposal in 2010 to change the name of his former school to the Asafa Powell High School, which seemed to be led by the Asafa Powell Foundation, was opposed by other ex-pupils, and over 800 objections were reportedly posted on Facebook.

drugs test against his name, for ephedrine (a stimulant common in cold treatments) in 1995.

Asafa began working with Francis a week after Champs in 2001. The improvement was immediate. Three months later, on 22 June, he won the national under-20 100 metres in a personal best, 10.50 seconds. The next year he represented Jamaica at the Commonwealth Games in Manchester. He didn't make the final but did record another personal best, 10.26, in finishing fifth in the semi-final. In the relay, with Powell running the anchor leg, Jamaica took a silver medal behind England.

In the same year, the Powell family suffered the first of two tragedies. Asafa's brother Michael was shot dead by a mugger as he sat in a New York taxi. The next year, another of his brothers, Vaughn, dropped dead while playing American football. A heart attack was the verdict. Powell suffered a loss of confidence. 'I started to wonder,' he said, ' "Who's next?" '

But he carried on running, and training with Francis, and improving, becoming Jamaican national senior champion in 2003. A year later, he went below 10 seconds for the first time, running 9.99 seconds on G. C. Foster's threadbare track. Then he defended his national title with a sparkling 9.91 at the National Stadium: one of nine sub-10-second runs he recorded that season.

He was on his way.

Francis and MVP were on their way too. With Brigitte Foster winning a silver medal at the 2003 world championships, their reputation was burgeoning, even if some local resistance remained. At least now they didn't have to chase second-tier athletes. 'Eventually it became an option for athletes who people thought were good,' Francis says.

And people were paying attention, because Francis was asked to coach one of the island's brightest young prospects. He was from rural Trelawny, on the other side of the island, and his name was Usain Bolt.

'I was asked to coach Usain in 2003. But, well, I was told he was an extremely hard worker and I felt that most of his success at the time was due to the fact that he was training hard.'

In something of a mumble, Francis adds: 'Which was inaccurate.'

So he is the coach who turned down Bolt – though he insists he has no regrets. 'I wasn't put off by this,' he adds, referring to his belief that Bolt could be one of those athletes who peaked in his teens. 'What I was put off about, really, was the amount of people who were trying to claim a piece of him.' There was a growing entourage – Bolt's sponsors, Puma; his manager, Norman Peart; a European agent, Ricky Simms. 'I told the Puma people, "Look, if I'm going to coach Usain, most of these people are not going to have any influence, so it might not be a good thing,"' Francis says. He told them who he did and didn't want to be involved. But it was the constellation forming around him that he really found off-putting. 'I have never been a person who gravitates to an athlete because he is the best. It's more of a challenge to me to look at those people who others are ambivalent about, or who they don't think are any good.'

As per one of the MVP philosophies, he also believes in the idea of creating a team without major stars who stand head and shoulders above the others. It is all part, he says, of fostering a culture in which people are motivated – indeed, compelled – to improve. Almost any-body who commits to his programme will improve, he states, 'unless they are really, really, really, really bad'. Moreover, he adds, 'It is hard not to commit, because right now we have almost like a treadmill going downhill. Once you get on it, it's hard to stop because the whole environment, the whole culture, forces you to fit in.'

What he looks for, says Francis, 'are people who, based on their trend so far, look like they have some sort of upside. They've not been killed in high school; there's still something there to be got out. We try to work with them. To me it's a much better feeling taking an also-ran to the top.'

On the eve of the 2004 Olympic Games – the second of MVP's

existence – that is where the club's flag-bearer was. Asafa Powell ran in a star-studded 100 metres at the Weltklasse in Zurich, part of the IAAF's Golden League and traditionally the most prestigious meeting on the circuit. Olympic champion Maurice Greene was there, as was world champion Kim Collins and a young American prospect, Justin Gatlin. The tall figure of Powell (he is six foot three) was in the lane alongside Greene, and these two emerged at the front, Greene drifting towards Powell, emphasising that they were locked in battle. Their arms brushed but Powell didn't flinch; he remained focused on the line to win in 9.93, a hundredth of a second ahead of Greene, with Gatlin a distant third.

It was no longer a surprise. Powell was now being talked about in the same breath as Greene, Gatlin and Collins. With every passing race, Francis and MVP were demonstrating that they could produce world-class athletes at home in Jamaica. In Powell, they had the favourite for the blue riband event at the Olympic Games in Athens, the men's 100 metres. They were close to reaching their Everest; they could look up and see the summit.

9

JETS AND SHARKS

Well, we don't really have a relationship.
Stephen Francis on Glen Mills

It was October 2003 when Usain Bolt moved to Kingston, sharing a house with Jermaine Gonzales, a 400 metre specialist from the St Catherine Parish. A few months later, in January 2004, both runners moved in with Norman Peart, into a house in the Red Hills part of the city – at the salubrious end of a street that had Calabar High School at the other end.

Peart, the mentor appointed by Bolt's old school, had moved back to Kingston from Montego Bay at the same time. Now he wasn't just tutoring Bolt, but living with and looking after this kid just out of school, plucked from rural, sleepy Trelawny and parachuted into vibrant, violent Kingston.

'It was like becoming a dad for the first time,' he tells me. 'A parent entrusted with the golden treasure of Jamaica.'

Peart headed the rapidly expanding Team Bolt: the seventeen-year-old was sponsored by Puma, he attended the newly opened IAAF High Performance Training Centre in Kingston, where he was coached by Fitz Coleman, and he had a European-based agent, the Irishman

Ricky Simms. Another member of his entourage, then and now, was his best friend from school, Nugent 'NJ' Walker.

The headquarters of Team Bolt is a nondescript building from the outside, round the back of an auto insurance assessor's office, but with a cool interior, upholstered in dark green and yellow, a bit like the VIP area of a nightclub. When I was there, NJ was hovering in reception. His rather grand title is 'executive manager', but the impression is that his job description might more accurately read 'Usain's mate'.

As for Bolt himself, he was absent from HQ, though I could feel his presence, as I did elsewhere: at the track named after him at the University of the West Indies; the sports bar he owns in New Kingston, Tracks and Records; his favourite nightclub, the Quad; his parents' house in Trelawny; the Spartan gym where he trains.

When I asked Simms about doing an interview with Bolt in Jamaica, I was told: 'Usain hasn't done an interview in Jamaica since 2008.' So what about now? 'Usain hasn't done an interview in Jamaica since 2008.' No chance, then? 'Usain hasn't done an interview in Jamaica since 2008.' (Not actually true: Donald McRae of the *Guardian* did one in March 2010, organised by Puma, and Bolt spoke to a French documentary crew in 2011. But in 2014, when a crew making a film about Bob Marley asked for a short interview, they were told he would only do it for a price: £30,000.)

My contact with Bolt came in Europe rather than Jamaica, but in Jamaica I did feel close to him. It's a small place, so perhaps it was impossible not to. But it could be a bit freaky. One day, I had a call from Michelle, whose Stony Hill guest house I was staying in. 'I'm in the bank and Usain is here with me – shall I ask for an interview for you?' (I'm not sure if she did ask for an interview or just a selfie. She came home with a photograph, but Jamaicans tend to be laid-back even in the presence of their most famous countrymen and women. Which is partly why Bolt enjoys living there so much. Although he usually spends part of the summer in London, life is less stressful in Kingston because fewer people hassle him, which chimes with something Ziggy Marley said, that 'in Jamaica, you just someone, not nobody big'. Or as Bolt told McRae in one of his favourite nightclubs, Fiction: 'Most people know I'm there. But they also know I go to the clubs a lot, so they're relaxed. They're used to me in Kingston.' McRae is deservedly known as one of Britain's best sports writers, with a knack for prising open his interview subjects. He trailed Bolt for a few days, but the most revealing bits of his story are his own observations. In conversation, McRae found Bolt obliging but unreflective.)

I loitered in the vicinity of the Usain Bolt Track at the University of the West Indies, but although the campus is open, the track has a perimeter fence, with security staff at the entrance. Even if you drive towards it and look like you know what you're doing, they still stop you and turn you back.

Another day I visited the Spartan gym – I had just missed Bolt, said Steve Ming, a personal trainer there. He had been for an hour of free weights; the previous day he'd taken part in Ming's kick-boxing class, lurking at the back of the room. 'Sometimes a new person will say, "Is that Mr Bolt? Can I take a picture?"' Ming says. 'But most are accustomed to seeing him, Yohan Blake, Warren Weir and the others on a daily basis. We don't have a policy for members. We don't need one.'

Does Ming sometimes sneak a look at what weights Bolt is squatting? 'I don't have to sneak a look. At the moment he's squatting a lot – 345 pounds on each side.' (That's 156 kilograms, or 312 kilograms in total, though these are partial, not full, squats.)

When Bolt first moved to Kingston, the entourage that today forms a protective cocoon around him was pretty much as it is now – the key people are the same. Simms first became aware of him during the 2002 world junior championships in Kingston, though the Irishman wasn't actually there. 'He was the one everyone was talking about,' he recalls. 'You could see his technique was ragged, but everyone was very excited about this big Jamaican guy.

'I was asked if I wanted to have a meeting with his people in 2003. He didn't want to go to the US – he wanted to stay close to his mum. He wanted to turn professional right away.'

By 'his people', Simms means his parents, plus Norman Peart, and Pascal Rolling at Puma. Peart tells me that he approached Simms after 'checking with people in the business'. It was necessary to have someone based in Europe because Peart didn't want to spend his life travelling, and Simms, a former middle-distance runner who took over Kim McDonald's athletes' agency when McDonald died suddenly in 2001, seemed like the ideal candidate. Simms, still only in his mid-thirties, is calm and understated, the antithesis of the flash sports agent (even if he does now live in Monaco). 'Ricky had an established business, a place to stay in London,' Peart explains. 'He wasn't operating out of a suitcase.'

It was a period of transition, says Peart, for him and for Bolt. He doesn't sugar-coat it, admitting it wasn't easy. Even before Bolt moved to Kingston, there was some controversy back in Trelawny, at his old school in particular. They considered that he was leaving a year early. 'The teachers didn't want him to leave,' says his father, Wellesley. 'They wanted the school name to be on top, but he'd outgrown all those so it was necessary for him to go. With Norman Peart, we decided it was best for him to go to Kingston.

'We went to Kingston to see where he would stay,' Wellesley continues. 'Gonzales stayed in the same house and every week I would go to see if things were OK. Well, he probably wasn't happy to go, to leave the house here. But after a few weeks, with the excitement in Kingston – he found what he did not have here.'

Bolt's move to Kingston seems preordained. It was certainly orchestrated at the very highest levels of Jamaican government, which goes to show how central athletics is to the country, and how central Bolt was to their future ambitions. P. J. Patterson, the prime minister, had sprung into action after the world junior championships, when he instructed Donald Quarrie to take Bolt under his wing. That wasn't realistic; Quarrie spent most of his time in Florida. Getting Bolt to Kingston became the priority. 'Obviously he had nothing to gain by staying at William Knibb,' says Patterson, sitting in his plush office on the twelfth floor of the Sagicor building in New Kingston, with views all the way down to the waterfront. 'He had to be moved.

'I met him,' Patterson continues. 'He was brimming with confidence, obviously a super-talent. We have a word in Jamaica, "brought-upsy". He was brought up properly; has two very good parents. He was disciplined, easy, humble.' Patterson confirms that he helped as 'arrangements were made for Bolt to move in with Gonzalez'.

Aside from his living arrangements, Bolt was installed in the High Performance Training Centre – one of several centres set up by the IAAF in developing countries, and the only one to focus on sprinting. His coach there was the well-respected and highly experienced Fitz Coleman. But within weeks it became clear that coach and athlete did not see eye to eye. Bolt wanted to focus on the 200 metres but felt Coleman's training was weighted towards the 400: 'Coach Coleman had me running 700, 600 and 500 metres all the time,' Bolt wrote in his autobiography. 'I hated waking up in the morning because that's when I reacted to the work the most. I was in agony; everything felt wrong.' For the first time, he was also doing weight training – a development that began to add muscle to his skinny frame. (By 2008 he had added 18 kilograms to his recorded weight in 2003, bulking up from 75 to 93 kilos.)

Jermaine Gonzalez, his housemate and sometime training partner, says that the impression of Bolt as laid-back, even lackadaisical, was never accurate. 'Not true. Not true. A lot of people think that he doesn't work hard. If you think he doesn't work hard, go and train with him. You cannot do what Usain do. He's not the most disciplined guy, I can tell you that, but when he comes to work, he's working and he's working really hard. Because he's jovial people think he's just doing what he does because he's talented. Not true.'

Wellesley Bolt backs up his son's claim that the training under Coleman was brutal. During one of his weekly visits to Kingston, he attended a session. It harked back to his unannounced journeys to Falmouth, the difference now being that instead of beating Usain for skipping training, he was concerned that he might be training too hard.

'Oh my God, it was rough,' Wellesley tells me on the porch of his house. 'I said, "Son, I didn't know it was that hard." I said, "You seems to be lazy, not training hard." But when I watched him train, I realised it was hard, hard work. When you see him race, you don't realise.' What kinds of things was he doing? 'They have those big [medicine] balls, carrying it up and down. It's rough. He vomit one time when I was there. He would say, "Dad, you see? You thought I had it easy." '

It wasn't all hard work. The lively Kingston club scene was a distraction. 'Movies, dance: in Kingston it was all there,' says Wellesley. 'Then Norman had to put his foot down, to keep him focused from the distractions.'

'He was a party guy,' says Peart, who was not exactly Mr Popular when it was time to curb Bolt's nightlife. 'He was not amused with me, because, you know, he got to the magical eighteen years. At that age they're trying to find themselves.'

Bolt has never been a big drinker – a pint or two of Guinness at most – but he liked a late night. He still does. 'The thing is, he's a single man,' says Simms. 'He's not doing anything wrong, it's something everyone else does.' On nights out these days, Simms adds, 'we normally have someone with him, and he often goes out the back door straight into a car. You try to make life as easy as possible for him. Though sometimes he likes to go out the front door . . .'

Before he moved to Kingston, the highlight of Bolt's 2003 season, his last as a schoolboy, was his 200 metres title at the world youth championships in Canada in a championship record 20.40 seconds. A close second was his final Champs, where he did the 200/400 double, setting records in both, with his 20.25 in the 200 still surviving.

In August, he went to Paris for the world senior championships. He was sixteen – turning seventeen while he was there – and thought he might be capable of making the 200 metres final, maybe even challenging for a medal. In the build-up to the championships, however, he was laid low by conjunctivitis (at least this was the official reason; I was told that he was not in good enough shape) and it was decided that he shouldn't race. But in an example of the forward thinking being applied to the 'golden treasure of Jamaica', he travelled with the team to gain experience of a major championship.

In Paris, *Trans World Sport*, the eclectic magazine-style TV programme, did a mini-feature on the prodigy. This shows a Jamaican party by the Seine, complete with a band that launches into a birthday tribute. Bolt, a gangly teenager looking like he's on a school trip, rucksack on his back, shuffles on to the stage; he seems uncomfortable being the centre of attention and mumbles along self-consciously to 'Happy Birthday'.

Patrick Anderson, part of the Jamaican delegation, was interviewed for the feature. 'He is one of those beautiful young men that is so talented it's unbelievable,' he said. 'Now, in a crowd, he's so modest and humble, he doesn't stand out, like some of these pretenders. That made me really warm to him. The kind of talent he has, you really have to nurse him.' Although Bolt wouldn't be competing in Paris, the experience would be useful, added Anderson, 'because we're expecting wonders at the Olympics next year, that's the big one'.

So enamoured by Bolt were the *Trans World Sport* team that they followed him to Jamaica a month later, turning up at his home in Trelawny. 'I really am proud of myself for doing so well and making Jamaica proud,' Bolt tells them, adding that Michael Johnson is his hero for 'always staying relaxed, no matter what kind of pressure he is under'. He confirms that his sights are firmly fixed on becoming a 200 and 400 metres runner; there is no mention of the 100 metres.

Perhaps the most revealing titbit in the footage from Trelawny has nothing to do with Bolt-the-athlete – or not directly. We see Bolt in his track gear standing by the side of a small road near Sherwood Content. When the camera pans out, a very different scene is revealed: there are cameras, vehicles and a large film crew. It looks like the set of a movie with a decent budget. They are shooting a Puma commercial. Bolt has just turned seventeen, yet he is somebody in whom, evidently, much is invested.

Simms, whose first visit to Jamaica wasn't until the winter of 2004, was not opposed to Bolt remaining on the island. 'The timing was good for him. There were good structures in place, with the IAAF High Performance Training Centre in Kingston. The problem at the start was that he was injured a lot, which meant he didn't train a lot. And his appetite for training wasn't that great, especially when he was getting hurt a lot. But he was such a huge talent he was able to get by on talent and a bit of work.'

This created something of a problem for Bolt in early 2004, when, at the CARIFTA Games in Bermuda, he ran 19.93 seconds to break the world junior record for 200 metres. It was a sensational time: he was the first teenager ever to go under 20 seconds. The race is extraordinary to watch: Bolt's winning margin is most of the finishing straight. Or as Robert Johnson, writing on the LetsRun website some years later, put it: 'Watching that made me feel like it was just unfair to make the other competitors even try to race Bolt. It's what you'd get if you filmed a horse racing humans.'

'The young Goliath of 200-metre running has installed himself as the gold-medal favourite for the Athens Olympics this summer,' said the *Bermuda Gazette*, which praised Bolt's 'ruthless demonstration of power and speed'.

For Bolt, however, it was a double-edged sword. The fact that it came on the back of Fitz Coleman's diet of endurance training seemed to validate the veteran coach's methods. 'You see?' Peart told Bolt, who had been complaining all winter about Coleman's training. 'You should believe in Coach's programme.' It only made Bolt more frustrated. He was annoyed that he had inadvertently endorsed Coleman's approach with his fast time.

Two weeks later, he broke down in training with a pulled hamstring. 'I was in agony, I could barely walk off the track and as I waved out for help the anger bubbled up inside. I felt pissed at the schedule, pissed at Mr Peart for telling me I had to suffer the pain, pissed at everybody for not listening to my complaints.'

Blink and you might have missed Bolt in Athens. His Olympic debut passed almost unnoticed: in the fourth first-round heat he was fifth in 21.05 – considerably slower than the 19.93 he recorded earlier in the season, which would have been good enough for a silver medal in Athens. Bolt knew he was in no fit state to challenge – in addition to his problems with his back and hamstring, he sprained his ankle a few days before the Games got under way – though the expectations on him in Jamaica were huge, which, he said, 'messed with my head'. In the heat itself, he felt capable of fourth, which would have meant qualifying for the next round, but he eased up, knowing he would go no further. Among the criticisms made following his Greek failure was that the crucifix he wore around his neck – a gift from his mother – and clamped in his teeth while he was sprinting was a distraction: how could he concentrate?

As the Jamaican press and public turned on Bolt when he returned home, the crucifix became a symbol of his failure. It seemed to many that he was following the path of Daniel England, Ali Watson and other prodigies who had shone as schoolboys then faded into obscurity. 'We keep hearing that Usain is young and we should give him a chance to improve,' one correspondent wrote to the *Gleaner*. 'The trouble is Usain Bolt has not been improving. He needs to get his act together and start achieving the results that his talent so desperately demands.'

There were also questions at Puma, Bolt's main sponsor, about the athlete in whom they had invested so much, both financially and as the figurehead of their association with the country. Apart from his poor performances, there were doubts about the wisdom of backing an athlete who many struggled to understand when he was speaking. 'I mean, in a big company you always have people who question stuff,' says Pascal Rolling, the marketing man who had a major stake in Bolt, since he had signed him. 'But I think from the sports marketing and the chairman's point of view we wanted to continue with Usain because we knew the potential he had.'

There was work to do, though – and not only on the track. 'At the time he was, like many Jamaicans, talking more in patois,' Rolling says. 'He was very difficult to understand. He needed to improve his English.' This is confirmed by Simon Lewis, an English communications executive whose job it was, in the run-up to the 2004 Olympics, to give Bolt media training at the Jamaican training camp in Germany. Of the Jamaicans 'Bolt had the broadest accent,' says Lewis. 'He was also extremely shy. When it was time for our sessions he would hide from me. He would eventually emerge laughing and joking – he was very playful, very likeable – but media training wasn't something he particularly wanted to do.'

Rolling and Puma planned more English and communication lessons for Bolt. But they never happened. 'We realised after a while that he was doing so many interviews and getting better so quickly that there wasn't any need for training.'

As soon as he returned to Jamaica, it was reported that Bolt would change coach. Out would go Fitz Coleman, in would come Glen Mills, who for seventeen years had been national coach. Mills had also coached Raymond Stewart, Jamaica's top sprinter of the eighties, and, more recently, Kim Collins of St Kitts, the 2003 world 100 metres champion.

Mills had wanted to be a sprinter himself but at the age of thirteen had realised it wasn't meant to be. 'I was disappointed that I wasn't able to measure up to the others,' he said. He would go and watch training instead, under Henry McDonald, the coach at his school, Camperdown. Eventually McDonald called him over: 'Come here, little man. I see you here every evening and you are not training any more. Why?' Mills told him he was interested in coaching, and McDonald appointed him his assistant. He started by taking the register, but by the age of sixteen he was coaching thirteen-year-olds. He soon had success with his sprinters, but his star was Stewart, who went straight from school to the Los Angeles Olympics, where he made the 100 metres final, then anchored the Jamaicans to a silver medal in the relay.

In early October 2004, with his partnership with Bolt confirmed, Mills told the *Gleaner* about his hopes for the eighteen-year-old. One of his first decisions was to restrict media access. 'While I can understand that Jamaica is interested in his well-being and development, he's constantly in the press and I think he needs less press attention,' he said. 'I've noticed over the last two years that every detail of his life is news and this puts pressure on him. While I've no intention to hide him from the media, I'll definitely be making an effort to reduce press attention. He needs a break to settle down and train in a serious way.'

Mills confirmed that the 200 metres would remain Bolt's priority, 'but I can see in the future the 400m could become his most dominant event,' he explained. 'He's 6ft 6ins and growing.'

In another interview Mills said, 'There are a number of challenges which have to be given equal importance, the first of which is to restore his confidence. This is the first time in his young career that he has experienced disappointment.' As for the two of them, 'We have to develop a coach/athlete relationship and understanding as early as possible. I have to learn about him as a person and he has to adjust to my coaching methods and demands because each coach has his own signature. I have to get a greater understanding of him because that's important in any relationship.'

Mills, who was fifty-five when he began coaching Bolt, spoke of his 'immense potential', but stressed that that was all it was – potential. And he made the point that Bolt's height (six-five, despite Mills thinking he was an inch taller) had perhaps tricked some into believing that he must be closer to reaching his potential. Just because he was tall didn't mean he was the finished article – he still had to fill out, to develop physically. This was happening, he was changing shape, but it meant 'his whole skeletal structure is fragile. Once the growth process slows down he will start to experience greater muscular density and significant increase of the muscular structure and will have less injuries related to the growth process.

'My experience working with athletes doesn't follow an upward graph from season to season,' added Mills, 'but there's no doubt he'll fulfil the expectations.'

There were also technical issues that Mills felt he had to address. Bolt had been a teenage phenomenon, and yet, Mills said later, 'one of the things that stood out like a sore thumb was his poor mechanics'. He was off-balance, which put pressure on his lower back, his hips and hamstrings. Mills videoed his training and analysed the angle of his back; he wanted 'a forward lean of somewhere around five to ten degrees'. He was not able to hold that optimum position at top speed, so Mills got him doing core strength work. He also got him to shorten his stride. He was over-reaching – a legacy, perhaps, of his 400 metres running, where the stride pattern is different. Mills thought it would take him up to two years to learn how to change the pattern and take shorter strides.

Wellesley Bolt had no say in his son's switch from Coleman to Mills. But he supported his decision. 'He said he doesn't like how Mr Coleman train him. I didn't see it that way, I was just seeing that he didn't want to train. He made up his mind himself, to leave Mr Coleman and go to Mr Mills. So I said, "He's the one doing the training, let's go along with it."

'He has some problems with Mr Mills in the early days,' Wellesley continues, 'because he was lazy. Mr Mills had to get under his skin.'

Mills told Bolt they would be working to a three-year plan, aiming to peak at the Beijing Olympics. He arranged for a masseur, Everald Edwards, to work with him; each training session would begin with a session on the table, having his muscles kneaded and manipulated, getting his body ready for the punishment. Most importantly, Mills got to know him and would visit him at home if he saw that he was down or distracted in training. When that happened, 'I'd go quiet,' Bolt said, and a visit from Mills would follow. Over a game of dominoes they would discuss what was on his mind and agree on a course of action; usually the course of action advised by the coach. 'I like to help them develop into total human beings,' Mills said. 'You try to be involved in the rest of their lives as much as they let you.'

Mills was keen to impress upon Bolt the importance of committing to a long-term plan: 'To educate him about the journey, not so much the destination . . . because if you're on the wrong road, you're going to end up in the wrong destination.'

Norman Peart says that one of Mills's great talents is the art of gentle persuasion. 'He says: "It's your choice. This is my advice. But it's up to you." Glen has an ability to deal with teenagers, youngsters.' Despite not being a father himself, 'he's like a father figure', Peart says. 'He tries to help them. There are some who have different problems: could be family matters or problems with a girlfriend or financial problems. He reaches out to them. He's more than a coach. But he tells them it as it is: "You wise up or you drown."'

'Sure, he's strict,' Peart adds. 'But they're not afraid of him like he's a monster.'

At the Athens Olympics, Stephen Francis's rough diamond, Asafa Powell, who had been discussed as the favourite for the 100 metres, went below 10 seconds again, but his 9.94 was only good enough for fifth behind Justin Gatlin. It was a disappointment. In his breakthrough season, it was also an early indication of his fatal flaw: his failure to produce his best performances on the big stage, when it truly mattered. As if to emphasise the point, less than two weeks after the Olympic final, Powell won the Golden League in Brussels in 9.87, a personal best.

How Bolt might have fared under the other top coach, working a little over a mile away at the UTech campus, is a fascinating question. Francis and Mills are quite different. While Mills is a sprint specialist, Francis says he most enjoys coaching jumpers. Mills has had his greatest successes with male athletes, Francis with both men and women, though especially women.

Mills gets close to his athletes; Francis likes to maintain a distance, saying he avoids being 'too pally-pally because there has to be a level of authority'. He is not the father figure that Mills appears to be. 'It operates best,' he says, 'if there is at least a certain gulf. I am not in the European mode of coach as best friend.' The challenge comes, he adds, when athletes do well. 'Obviously you have difficulties when people are successful, because as they get more successful they start to look more to themselves and doubt what you tell them.'

One of the most intriguing, compelling aspects of the two camps of sprinters in Kingston is the antipathy between them, which seems to have its roots around the time of Powell's emergence and Bolt hooking up with Mills, which put his Racers Track Club on the map. Since then, MVP and Racers have kept up a rivalry that is always fierce and at times acrimonious. They resemble two gangs, like the Jets and the Sharks of *West Side Story*.

Perhaps it is because there just isn't room for two world-class clubs in the same city. But it also seems to have something to do with the relationship between Francis and Mills – despite once being good friends, these days they do not get on. Dennis Johnson told me about their friendship but couldn't shed much light on their falling-out. 'Mills and Francis are both from the ghetto,' he said. 'Mills is from Waterford, Francis from Mountain View Road: that's where they're from and you can't take that out of them. They used to be very good friends.'

What does Francis have to say about his relationship with Mills? 'Well, we don't really have a relationship,' he tells me. Then he concedes that 'We used to be good friends at one point in time.' How does he explain the fact that they don't speak to each other any more? 'I guess he's a bit busy and I'm busy.'

Francis and I are talking by the side of the grass track at UTech following another MVP training session. Francis continues explaining that he doesn't mix with many other coaches: 'I tend not to spend a lot of time at the local meets early on. I work away from the track at home, analysing data . . . I tend to be extremely busy.' But he and Mills didn't fall out because they are both busy, of course they didn't. Eventually Francis says it was because of 'leakage' – the alleged passing of MVP secrets to the Racers camp. There were 'transfers of personnel and systems and so on', he claims, 'which I think we, over here, were not happy with. So we decided, I think, that we had to act to stem the leakage. Put it that way.'

He insists it didn't go the other way; that he has never tried to find out Mills's secrets. He wouldn't be interested, he says. 'I don't have any curiosity at all.' But the alleged leakage upset him, and offended a code of honour. 'You know, I am still a believer in the old coaching creed. I don't believe in recruiting people who leak. I don't believe in bad-mouthing a coach.'

Is the rivalry with Racers healthy? I wonder. It is tempting to conclude that it must be, for all that Francis says MVP are 'kind of like an island over here'. There are parallels with the music scene in Jamaica from the late 1950s into the 1960s, which was built on and fuelled by intense rivalry between the 'sound men', each competing to be louder, to play the latest ska, rocksteady or reggae to the biggest audiences.

Francis's main issue, he says, comes when he has to persuade his own assistant coaches not to worry about Racers' recruitment of the latest teenage stars. 'All my assistant coaches believe that we must try and get the kind of high school talent which Racers acquires. They are upset that Racers cream off that talent, and they don't understand why it doesn't faze me. But, so, you do have tension in terms of that.'

But as his lack of regret over his decision not to work with Bolt illustrates, Francis prefers to polish rough diamonds. His favourite coach is Bill Belichick of the New England Patriots, who is famous for his gruff demeanour. ('Yes, it's true,' read a *Sports Illustrated* headline, 'Bill Belichick actually smiled.' This, the magazine went on to say, 'is akin to seeing Halley's Comet'.)

'I love Bill Belichick, I'm a big fan of his,' Francis tells me. He explains that he likes coaches 'like Jose Mourinho, who overcome the bias of not being good players'. These are the coaches who have to use their brains. Alex Ferguson is another, because of his knack of building and renewing teams. 'I'm inspired by coaches like those,' says Francis.

I put it to him that if MVP and Racers were football teams, they would be Barcelona and Real Madrid: one rearing home-grown talent, the other importing expensive Galácticos. He smiles (which he does a little more often than Belichick). 'As I said, I love to see somebody become great who nobody knew about. That's why Bill Belichick is my favourite coach. I mean, he can make good of people who nobody had a clue could be good. He does it year after year after year. He does it through preparation, through imagination, through all those intangibles which I think is essential for good coaching.'

I was keen to speak to Mills, of course. But I was familiar with his reputation and his reluctance to speak to journalists. He seemed something of an enigma. I was told that he is a deeply religious man, who attends Swallowfield Chapel in Kingston every Sunday, and who is not interested in material wealth; when he receives gifts from sponsors, he gives them away (including cars, apparently). He is also a confirmed bachelor. 'I've had my admirers,' he said in 2011, 'but marriage for me now, at 62? Well, I'll finish my life in serving my God and coaching my athletes.'

When I asked Bolt's manager, Norman Peart, about an interview with the coach, he laughed. 'Good luck,' he said. Ricky Simms, Bolt's agent, was no more encouraging. I asked if Mills's reticence stemmed from the fact that he was a man of few words. 'No, he has a lot of words,' said Simms. 'He's the heart and soul of training sessions.

'For Glen coaching is an art,' he continued. 'It's not magic. He looks at an athlete and sees what they need to do. There's no messing about, no big words. I sometimes laugh when you see American high school coaches come in with a load of big words and phrases.'

I paid a visit to Racers Track Club, at the University of the West Indies. They have an office in a hut by a grass running track, a short distance from the Usain Bolt Track, a gift from Puma and German firm BSW Regupol. The well-appointed campus seems to be surrounded on all sides by the Blue Mountains. It is a lush green paradise.

At Racers HQ, the door was opened by Cynthia Cooke, who helps run the club (and is a former head teacher at Mills's old school, Camperdown). Mills was not in, she said. She told me to email my interview request. She said she would ask Mills, but explained that 'he hates interviews'.

To try and convince Cooke – and by extension Mills – to give me my interview, I attached a newspaper story I had recently written about one of Mills's younger athletes, Zharnel Hughes, the 100 metres winner at Champs. Hughes, based at the IAAF high performance on the same university campus in Kingston, was eloquent and engaging and clearly a great prospect. Cooke emailed back that she had enjoyed it. I felt a warm glow. 'However,' read the final line of the first paragraph, 'it was offensive in parts.'

Offensive? I read on.

'You may wonder what on earth could be offensive,' Cooke continued. 'I am one of the many passionate, loyal, patriotic Jamaican track and field fans, or maybe fanatics. We find that the British media consistently seek to promote a negative image about our country, in every story they write about us.

'During your trip to Jamaica, I am sure you did not experience any violence except in the media' – this was actually true. 'Why was it necessary to mention that it was the most violent city in the Caribbean? What does that have to do with Zharnel's exploits on the track? Mentioning the scantily furnished apartment is redundant if the objective was to place Jamaica's significance in the grand world of wealth.

'Yes, I have said a lot! I guess you now understand our view of British journalists. (You are free to accuse me of doing the same. Finding one little negative in a slew of positives.)'

There goes my interview with Glen Mills, I thought. (Though in further emails, relations improved with Cynthia Cooke, especially when I told her that my wife had agreed with parts of her email: 'Thank God for women,' she wrote. 'It is instances such as these that make us understand why God saw it fit to complement man with woman. It took myself and your wife to "enlighten your darkness" on this topic, while having no ill feeling towards you . . . Again, in spite of my "touchiness", it was a good article.' Great, so how about that interview with Mills? She replied again: 'Having Coach Mills agree to any interview is very difficult. He hates interviews.')

Then, out of the blue, I got an email from Mills. It followed a question to Cooke about Francis's allegations of 'leakage': of the passing of secrets from MVP to Racers. 'Laughable,' Cooke replied. Indeed, she was so incensed that she said she would ask Mills for a full response. And a full response is what followed. Mills wasn't just angry; he was deeply offended:

Hi Mr Moore, please accept my best wishes. Thanks for your attempt to be balanced in writing your book and I wish you success.

I have read the allegations which Coach Francis is making that his training secrets have been leaked to Racers Track Club by former members of his club. This is one of the most absurd allegations to be made by him and his organisation. It is a fact that members from his club were accepted into Racers Track Club but it is totally false that they divulge secret methods that Mr Francis may have developed. Let the record show that I have never questioned nor interviewed any of these individuals which entered Racers from MVP about any aspect of their training programmes while they were being trained at MVP.

I have my own philosophy and methodology of training which I am willing to share with anyone. Before MVP was formed I had already acquired over thirty years of coaching knowledge and experience at the local and international levels.

I started coaching in 1964 at my alma mater Camperdown High School where I developed my philosophy and methodology while attending many international courses and seminars. My tenure at Camperdown developing programmes and methods of coaching sprinting was marked by extraordinary success that earned the school the title 'Sprint Factory'.

By 1983 I was appointed assistant national coach to the incomparable Herb McKenley and the following year [as] one of the coaches to the 1984 Olympic team of Jamaica. In that year I coached nineteen-year-old Raymond Stewart to be the fastest Jamaican and the fastest junior in the world. Stewart went on to place sixth in the 100 metres final at the Olympics in Los Angeles, [and] incidentally he was unbeaten at the Olympics up to the final of the 100 metres. I coached Kim Collins to Commonwealth and world champion titles long before any transfer of personnel from MVP. I could enumerate so many other achievements in coaching sprinters before the advent of MVP that makes Mr Francis's allegations utter rubbish.

I am mystified what are his reasons for such mischief or his desire to try to discredit Racers and my achievements but whatever they are it is not possible to remove the imprints I have made in sprinting history.

Best regards, Coach Mills

10

HEALING HANS

A Frankenstein-type experiment.
Travis Tygart, United States Anti-Doping Agency

One of the first things Glen Mills did when he began working with Usain Bolt was to try and understand the injuries that had afflicted him in the run-up to Athens. Bolt had been troubled by hamstring and back problems, and not long before the Games got under way, he was diagnosed with scoliosis – curvature of the spine.

Mills studied Bolt's medical notes. They were detailed and made a big deal of the scoliosis, as though this was the root of all his problems. There were suggested exercises and stretches to get his body ready for training and alleviate the symptoms. It was perhaps unusual for a doctor to offer such detailed advice – this was encroaching on the coach's territory.

But the doctor was not just any doctor. Bolt's meeting with him had been arranged after he broke down in training, when his participation at the Athens Olympics seemed in the balance. He and his entourage had been desperate. It was time for an addition to Team Bolt.

*

Dr Hans-Wilhelm Müller-Wohlfahrt is one of the most important men in world sport. That is the only conclusion to draw from scrolling through his list of patients. Boris Becker, Paula Radcliffe, too many footballers to mention, including Diego Maradona, Cristiano Ronaldo, Steven Gerrard and half the English Premier League, as well as those of the club and national team to which he is official doctor: Bayern Munich and Germany. Other patients include 1987 Tour de France winner Stephen Roche and golfer José María Olazábal. The sprinters Linford Christie, Donovan Bailey, Maurice Greene, Tyson Gay and Asafa Powell have all been treated by him. And, since the summer of 2004, so has Usain Bolt.

'It was arranged for me to visit Dr Hans Müller-Wohlfahrt,' Bolt writes in his autobiography, without elaborating on who organised, or paid, for a seventeen-year-old wunderkind to travel to Germany and see the world's most renowned sports doctor. The connection was made through his German-based sponsor, Puma. 'I mean, Dr Müller-Wohlfahrt is one of the best sports medicine doctors in the world,' Pascal Rolling, the marketing man who signed Bolt, tells me, 'so when Usain had his recurrent problem, we said we need to bring him there to evaluate exactly how serious it was, and what could be done to stop the injury coming up all the time.'

When he arrived at Müller-Wohlfahrt's clinic, Bolt 'was laid out flat on a bed, as his fingers felt along the bumps and grooves of my spine, and he pushed against my hamstrings. When I glanced up, I noticed his eyes were closed. The man was feeling, sensing my injuries . . .' When Müller-Wohlfahrt was interrupted by a nurse, he reacted angrily, as though a spell had been broken. He started again. Thus the impression immediately formed is that of somebody with special, mystical powers, which can only be summoned by deep concentration. And yet in this instance the diagnosis came from an old-fashioned X-ray. Bolt was informed that he had scoliosis; quite a serious case of curvature of the spine. Müller-Wohlfahrt told him that it need not prevent him fulfilling his potential, but his training should be adapted accordingly.

For Bolt the diagnosis was the start of his journey back to fitness. It was also the first of dozens of trips to Munich and Müller-Wohlfahrt's clinic on the second floor of the Century Alte Hof building, originally built in the twelfth century and once Germany's imperial residence.

Müller-Wohlfahrt is not just a doctor to celebrities: he is a celebrity doctor. His high profile is due mainly to his work with sports stars – though his patients have also included Bono and Luciano Pavarotti – but he is also one half of a famous couple. His wife, Karin, is a well-known artist in Germany. His daughter, Maren, used to date Germany's most capped footballer, Lothar Matthäus. Those who have met Müller-Wohlfahrt in his lair tend to all emerge with the same breathless reaction. He is incredibly charismatic, they say; relentlessly positive and upbeat, and quite brilliant at breaking down the normal barriers that stand between doctor and patient, establishing an instant connection, a powerful bond. Typically he greets patients with either a bear hug or the kind of handshake preferred by teenagers: hand up, thumb out, while his other hand grasps your elbow. With dark shoulder-length hair, smooth caramel skin and lively eyes, he looks at least two decades younger than his seventy-plus years. And he is dapper, often sporting a black suit, white shirt and black tie. His all-female staff, meanwhile, wear immaculate white outfits. 'They look like angels,' says one sports doctor who has visited him. 'They're all absolutely beautiful.

'And he has a chef. You eat downstairs in a private dining room.'

Müller-Wohlfahrt qualified as a doctor in 1971, completing his training at the orthopaedic clinic of the Rudolf Virchow Hospital in Berlin. His entry to the world of professional sport came when he was appointed team doctor at Bundesliga side Hertha Berlin in 1975. He switched to Germany's biggest club, Bayern Munich, two years later and began working with the national team in 1996.

For forty years, then, he has worked at the highest level of sport, in which time there has been intrigue and mystery, scepticism and suspicion – even, or especially, within the medical profession – over his methods. Partly it is due to his reluctance to write scientific papers about his methods, or subject his work to peer review. Partly it might stem from the fervour of his patients, who can seem like disciples. But there is also envy. Plenty are jealous of the dashing doctor known as 'Healing Hans'.

Müller-Wohlfahrt describes his treatments as homeopathic. Consciously or not, there appears to be an Eastern influence to his practice of medicine. He relies heavily on injections of products that for some raise ethical questions, and for others provoke a squeamish reaction. For muscle injuries he swears by Actovegin, a calf-blood extract that is not banned under the World Anti-Doping Code, but is also not approved for sale in some countries, including the US and France. He uses products containing blood from goats,[21] and prescribes Hyalart (made by crushing the fleshy pink comb on a cockerel's head) for knee injuries, preferring these treatments to surgery wherever possible.

---

21 'St Johnstone star Peter MacDonald gets goat blood injections to cure hamstring problem,' was the unlikely headline in the *Daily Record* in early September 2009. 'At times it was uncomfortable because I had an epidural and more than 50 jags over four days,' said MacDonald, who reported that Arjen Robben, the Dutch star, had been in the next room having the same treatment.

According to one sports doctor familiar with his work, he has also used X-rays to treat ligament damage, killing the nerves with radiation. I asked this doctor his view of such treatment, and he said it wouldn't be allowed where he works, in the UK – the levels of radiation would be over safe limits.

'Nearly every one' of his injections contains Actovegin, Müller-Wohlfahrt has said, estimating that he has administered the calf-blood extract over a million times. But many in the medical and sporting community are unconvinced of its supposed healing properties. Patrick Arnold, the chemist at the centre of the infamous Balco drugs scandal of the early 2000s, has tried Actovegin and considers it a placebo, no more. Arnold describes Müller-Wohlfahrt's methods as 'pseudoscience', while Travis Tygart, head of the US Anti-Doping Agency, has claimed that those who subject themselves to such treatments are taking part in a 'Frankenstein-type experiment'.

This might be a little extreme. Others take a more nuanced view. Mike Davison, who manages Isokinetic Medical Group, a specialist sports injuries centre on Harley Street in London, is an admirer of Müller-Wohlfahrt, though he concedes that he is 'provocative', an 'agitator'. Says Davison: 'He's an outlier in the artistry of medicine. He's not accepting of conventional wisdom and science because he believes that is looking in the past rather than the future.'

Davison talks about Müller-Wohlfahrt as a genius who has pushed back the boundaries of sports medicine through a combination of 'instinct and infiltration'. 'My sense is that in Europe if not the world there's no individual in the last twenty-five years who has made a greater contribution to sports medicine for elite athletes.' Nobody gets athletes back training or competing quicker, stresses Davison. 'Yes, he will take risks. He doesn't admit to always having a 100 per cent success rate. But he binds athletes closer to him than any other doctor I've come across.'

It is his use of Actovegin that raises a red flag for many. I ask a sports doctor friend about Actovegin. He explains that it is 'the whole blood, spun down to remove the white blood cells and the red blood cells, so you're left with serum. It has all the tissue factors, the growth factors that circulate in the blood. They de-nature it to remove the large proteins, which can have transfusion reactions, particularly cross-species.'

The serum is a clear, sterile liquid. But what does it do exactly? What are its magic properties? 'That is complicated,' says the sports doctor. 'I believe it has a whole variety of activation factors, interlukins, growth factors, and when used in torn muscle it might accelerate the biological process [of healing]. Which I believe it will do, to some extent.'

There is a grey area in discussing doping: where does performance-enabling end and performance-enhancement begin? Tyson Gay came out with a fascinating, hugely revealing line when he explained why he consulted Müller-Wohlfahrt: 'I run too fast for my body.' Could Actovegin be described as a performance-enhancer, or is it simply used to repair damage? 'I personally think it's used in body repair,' says my doctor friend. 'I know people have given it intravenously, thinking it's helping recovery, but there's no science there and no scientific logic to think that would help.'

Would he use Actovegin? 'I wouldn't use Actovegin. I would use the person's own blood and spin it down.'

But this is banned under the anti-doping rules. 'Correct. But if you're a non-athlete, and you need treatment, it's fine. In hospitals, this plasma-rich distillate is used in mainstream medicine.'

Where many seem to agree, including Travis Tygart and Mike Davison, is on the notion that Müller-Wohlfahrt's personality goes a long way to explaining his appeal. His charisma is part of the treatment. 'He has an aura about him,' Davison says. 'I think he fundamentally loves his patients. No one should confuse their personal experience of health care with what he offers. In some ways we should encourage, in general health care, the warmth, love and care he shows towards his patients.' There is usually a boundary between doctor and patient.

'But in elite sport that boundary gets blurred because of the emotions involved,' Davison says. 'As is proved a lot in science, the placebo effect provides comfort and security for individuals who are vulnerable.' You don't often hear of world-class athletes being described as vulnerable. But an athlete with an injury, or who thinks he has an injury, is very vulnerable indeed, Davison says.

Tygart takes a less benign view. 'These sorts of gurus get a reputation within athlete populations,' he told ESPN. 'And these high-dollar athletes who are desperate to do anything and everything to win, even at the jeopardy of their own health, go to these guys. That is the culture. It is not right, but that is the culture.'

Yet in over four decades, even as some of his patients have fallen foul of the anti-doping authorities, Müller-Wohlfahrt's reputation has remained intact and unsullied. 'No one has ever pinned anything bad on him,' says Davison. 'I think he may have taken some risks early on.' But sports medicine – into which there is so little research – almost requires this, he argues. I can see Davison wrestling with this, in the way that medical people sometimes do when trying to describe something that is hugely resistant to simple, black-and-white interpretation – and sports medicine evidently comes into this category. 'Medicine is the application of scientific principles in a world of values,' he says. 'It's not just science, there's an artistry to it, and within muscle and tendon injuries Müller-Wohlfahrt has some of the greatest artistry skills in the world.'

He offers an example. 'A lot of people will send a patient for an MRI and then interpret the results. Dr Müller-Wohlfahrt will put someone in a functional position – maybe Bolt in a starting blocks position – and he will feel the tension of the muscle himself, and match that with the commentary from the individual, remembering that athletes probably know their body better than anyone else.'

Linford Christie, when he won the 100 metres at the 1992 Olympics, suggested that Müller-Wohlfahrt was more ethical than other doctors he'd consulted, who all recommended cortisone. Noted anti-doping crusaders, like Paula Radcliffe, have also endorsed Müller-Wohlfahrt's methods. The marathon world record holder was in Müller-Wohlfahrt's Munich clinic when Mike Fish, an ESPN reporter allowed a rare interview in 2011, paid a visit. Fish described the scene:

'... the doctor spent an hour listening patiently while tending to Radcliffe. As she lay on a treatment table, the sinewy, muscled distance runner gradually morphed into a human voodoo doll. The doctor went about sticking her with a bevy of needles, injecting a numbing agent and then leaving the needles in place. Into the needles' plastic base or hub that remained above the skin, he followed with injections of natural lubricants and hyaluronic acid.

'Radcliffe sighed as the initial injections penetrated deep beneath the skin, with some needles 2 to 3 inches long. Müller-Wohlfahrt used his right hand to deliver 14 injections into her lower back. Another two were directed into the front of her right hip, followed by four into the top of her left foot. He then manipulated her legs wildly – left and right, up and down.'

Radcliffe told Fish that she visited Müller-Wohlfahrt every two or three months for similar treatments. 'I call it coming for a tune-up or checkup,' she said. 'He is someone [athletes] trust.'

Despite his reluctance to give interviews – which he blames on a full diary; also the reason, he says, for not writing scientific papers or subjecting his work to peer review[22] – Müller-Wohlfahrt is hardly a shadowy, reclusive figure. He could hardly be more visible, because he often sat on the bench for Bayern Munich's matches; even as managers came and went, he remained. [23]

---

22 In 2012 Müller-Wohlfahrt did produce a book, *Muskelverletzungen im Sport* (*Muscle Injuries in Sports*). In it he acknowledges the lack of studies of muscle injuries, and that much of his information 'is thus admittedly based more on empirical knowledge than scientific data. But isn't it also true that other medical classifications are evidence-based only to a limited degree, due to a lack of scientific research?'

23 Until April 2015 when he abruptly quit after falling out with manager Pep Guardiola. Guardiola had been publicly critical of Bayern Munich's medical team.

In 2012, the club threw a lavish party for his seventieth birthday, with 190 guests, including German football legends Karl-Heinz Rummenigge, Franz Beckenbauer and Gerd Müller. In his toast, Rummenigge described Müller-Wohlfahrt as 'one of the most important people at the club for thirty-five years, exactly half his life so far. He may never have scored a goal for us, but he's made countless goals and triumphs possible in the first place.'

Nor does Müller-Wohlfahrt, unlike some sports doctors, appear reticent when it comes to his work with some of the world's leading sportsmen and -women – on the contrary. 'It's curious how many sports people talk about him,' says Daniel Drepper, a German investigative reporter who has written extensively about doping in football. 'I suspect he asks them to mention him.

'Some view him as a bit controversial,' Drepper continues, 'but in general the media reporting is really positive. He's seen as a genius. And he's a seventy-year-old guy who looks fifty-five.'

Despite his work investigating doping in football, Drepper has turned up nothing on Müller-Wohlfahrt. Not that he isn't sceptical, or doesn't have questions. But the doctor has been reluctant to engage.[24] 'We asked Müller-Wohlfahrt normal questions but also included questions about doping,' Drepper says. 'He directly responded through his lawyer, Christian Schertz, the most famous and expensive media attorney in Germany.'

Drepper continues: 'We are not sure if he does anything illegal, or whether he operates on the edge of illegality. People tell us that he talks to the anti-doping authority every year.' In the ESPN article, Fish said that Müller-Wohlfahrt 'routinely communicates with WADA about his treatment methods, including his use of Actovegin'. Fish also said

---

24 I emailed Müller-Wohlfahrt's clinic requesting an interview. Next morning a German number appeared on my mobile phone. 'Hello,' said the female voice, 'this is Dr Müller-Wohlfahrt's clinic.' 'Hello!' I said, impressed by their efficiency. 'Yes, well, I am calling to tell you that I am afraid Dr Müller-Wohlfahrt is too busy to give you an interview.'

that WADA's science director, Dr Olivier Rabin, 'vouches for Müller-Wohlfahrt's operating a clean practice, but he isn't ready to speak to the purported healing qualities of Actovegin'. Müller-Wohlfahrt told Fish he doesn't have any secrets, or use unknown, undetectable products: 'You risk your career. They [keep] the urine sample for years. So if they have technique to detect it later, then it will be found.'

The worst Drepper can say is that Müller-Wohlfahrt's methods are 'voodoo' and that his success could rest heavily on his charisma. It chimes with Davison's mention of his aura ('Medicine is an industry of the cult,' Davison says. 'There are no kite marks of quality') and Tygart's talk of gurus and the importance in elite sporting circles of reputation. It becomes a self-fulfilling prophecy, or a virtuous circle, whereby the very act of being on the books of the world's most famous sports doctor can imbue confidence; where little more than his personal attention can leave an athlete feeling restored, walking out of the clinic a little taller and stronger. Perhaps that is as potent as anything found in a bottle or syringe.

In 2013, Müller-Wohlfahrt spoke about medical strategies for muscle injuries in football at Isokinetic's Football Medicine Strategies Conference in London. In his trademark smart black suit, white shirt and black tie, he was hesitant and halting. The charismatic healer described by those who have visited him in his clinic was not discernible in the handsome but almost diffident figure who read in heavily accented English from his script, only occasionally glancing up.

It was one of the rare occasions when he has discussed, in some detail, his work – and he was candid about his use of Actovegin. 'I have changed my therapeutic approach only marginally since the seventies,' he told his audience, 'since it has been proved highly effective.'

He continued: 'Since the seventies I use Actovegin together with Traumeel [a homeopathic painkiller] in the treatment of muscle injuries. Actovegin is a deep-proteinised hemoderivative obtained by ultra-filtration of calf blood. It is constituted mostly of electrolytes, essential trace elements, a mixture of amino acids and intermediary products of carbohydrates.

'I know that there is still controversy about its biologic actions, especially in muscle tissue. But I'm still convinced that Actovegin is the most helpful and highly effective medicine in our treatment. The daily experiences of athletes, some [of whom] were treated not successfully elsewhere, support this. In over thirty-six years I have never experienced any side effects. No complication has occurred.'

He went on to argue for the 'conservative treatment' of injuries, explaining that surgery can be avoided with injections – or 'infiltrations', as he prefers to call them. Some of his critics object to this, saying that his treatments address the symptom, not the cause. Indeed, some of those critics were in the audience in London, judging by the tuts and shaking heads. Müller-Wohlfahrt explained that his priority is minimising the disruption to an athlete's training; the treatment itself is active. Rest may sometimes be necessary, but it seems to Müller-Wohlfahrt – like it does to every elite athlete – anathema. In this, he is squarely on the athlete's side. Perhaps that is why they get along so well.

As Müller-Wohlfahrt admitted in London, Actovegin is controversial. During the 2000 Tour de France, it was found in waste dumped by staff members of Lance Armstrong's US Postal team, prompting an investigation by the French authorities, and in 2009 the Canadian Anthony Galea, another sports doctor with a stable of stars – including Tiger Woods, Alex Rodriguez and Mark McCoy – was charged by Canadian authorities with selling an unapproved drug: Actovegin.

However, it is incorrect to say that Actovegin is illegal for sportspeople. It was briefly placed on the WADA banned list in 2000, then taken off; a WADA official compared it to a 'super vitamin for the blood'. It is not banned in the US, either; it has simply never been approved for sale by the Food and Drug Administration.

*

As Paula Radcliffe says, athletes trust Müller-Wohlfahrt – and given his track record, why wouldn't they?

Perhaps Radcliffe knows exactly how she is being treated, and what with. You could argue that her trust is implicit but well placed. Others might not be so well informed – or even interested. In talking about his visits to Müller-Wohlfahrt, the former footballer Jamie Redknapp recalled being told only that he was being given 'high-quality oil for the engine of a car'. Another footballer, Michael Johnson of Manchester City, said in an interview that he too had been treated by Müller-Wohlfahrt: 'I stayed a week in Germany and had a course of injections into my back and spine. I don't know what he put in there, but it worked.'

Asked by Mike Fish in 2011 whether he told his athletes what was in his needles, Müller-Wohlfahrt said: 'I try to explain to them, but they don't understand.'

One of the more inquisitive of his athlete patients was Stephen Roche, the 1987 Tour de France winner who began seeing Müller-Wohlfahrt in 1988 after three operations failed to clear up a knee injury. The loquacious Roche and the charismatic, attentive Müller-Wohlfahrt (who once took a private plane and helicopter to the Pyrenees to treat Roche at the Tour, staying for less than an hour) got on well. But they almost fell out early in their relationship when, as Roche explains it, 'I wanted to know what exactly he was injecting into my knee.'

After one injection, Roche observed the doctor putting the empty ampoule in the bin. He fished it out when Müller-Wohlfahrt was out of the room, slipped it in his pocket and took it back to his home in Paris, where he gave it to a doctor to analyse it. 'And it turned out it was extracted from calves' livers.' When Roche told Müller-Wohlfahrt what he'd done, the doctor 'froze and stood back'. 'Stephen,' he said, 'I'm very disappointed. I've been a doctor for twenty-five years and no athlete I've ever worked with has been involved with doping or even suspected of doping. My office has never had a hint of scandal. Everything we use is a natural product. I don't know how you could have thought that we might have used anything suspicious. No one has ever questioned me before. No one has ever taken anything from my office.'

In September 2013, Usain Bolt was asked by the French newspaper *Le Monde* about his relationship with Müller-Wohlfahrt. There had been controversy in France during the 2006 World Cup when a French player, Patrick Vieira, was prevented by the national team doctor from consulting with Müller-Wohlfahrt because Actovegin is banned in France.

'I do not know what it is,' said Bolt when asked by *Le Monde* whether Müller-Wohlfahrt had given him Actovegin. 'But let me tell you this: if he had given me something illegal, I know.' (In his book, Bolt writes: 'I'd heard through other athletes that calves' blood injections were a common prescription for his patients, and that sounded freaky to me. Still, everything that was used on my back was carefully administered within all the legal guidelines – nothing sketchy was injected – and Dr Müller-Wohlfahrt's syringes took away the pressure and pain from my spine.')

There are few athletes with whom Müller-Wohlfahrt has had such a long and fulfilling relationship as Bolt. The doctor has even said that his remit extends beyond treating Bolt's injuries, and giving him specific exercises to prevent problems with his fragile back, to 'analysing his sprint mechanics during track workouts when he's in town'.

It wasn't just scoliosis that was diagnosed in Müller-Wohlfahrt's Munich clinic in early summer 2004. In his examination, Müller-Wohlfahrt also observed the discrepancy in Bolt's legs: his right one is 1.5 centimetres shorter than the left. Not ideal for running round the bend of a track. It also makes his stride pattern asymmetrical – hardly unusual, but in Bolt's case it can be quite extreme, leading to extra stress on what is the most vulnerable part of a sprinter's body: his hamstring. In Bolt's case, his left hamstring.

Ever since that first visit when he was seventeen, Bolt has been a regular. He has said that he typically visits Müller-Wohlfahrt three or four times a year. 'He gives me the impression that he loves me,' he says. 'He's not just a doctor, he is a friend, almost family.'

The feeling is mutual. Of all the names in the visitors' book that sits in the reception of the Munich clinic, Bolt is Müller-Wohlfahrt's favourite, the star who shines brightest. It is Bolt's name that he invokes most frequently in conversation (taking huge delight in introducing him to the footballer Joe Cole, who on his first visit was kept waiting three hours. 'Joe!' said Müller-Wohlfahrt as he wrapped his arms around him. 'There's somebody I want you to meet . . . Usain?')

'The first time he came, nobody knew him,' Müller-Wohlfahrt told ESPN in 2011, 'but his coach sent him here to ask me whether it was worth it to train him. He was not sure whether he was able to train very, very hard. I said, "If he does this and this exercises – yes, then he can." So he started to do exercises and then the success grew more and more. For example, yesterday he phoned and he does his exercises. We have a very good connection, very good correspondence.'

In his office, a pair of Bolt's spikes have pride of place, displayed in a glass case. 'I have many trophies and items, but I don't display,' Müller-Wohlfahrt said. 'These are special.'

11

REAL AS IT GETS

The majority of them come from the same housing projects and were
singing in large part to get out of them. Partly it's this yearning,
a brilliant hungriness, that you hear.
John Jeremiah Sullivan on Jamaica's musicians

Shelly-Ann Fraser grew up in Waterhouse, a suburb of Kingston, one of Jamaica's poorest and most violent garrisons. A ghetto so notorious that it was name-checked in Jay Z's 'Real As It Gets'.

Shelly-Ann's mother, Maxine Simpson, who was one of fourteen children, worked as a street vendor, or 'higgler'. The family – Shelly-Ann, her mother and two brothers – lived in one of the zinc-roofed dwellings known as tenement yards.

It was a tough place to live. Two gangs had been engaged in a battle for control of Waterhouse since the 1970s: the Buckers, affiliated to the PNP, and the Yap Sam gang, claiming to represent the JLP. It was where Vybz Kartel, dancehall star and convicted murderer, grew up. Violence was an everyday reality (which, presumably, is what Jay Z means by 'real'). One day while Shelly-Ann was at school, her cousin Dwayne was shot dead; three days later his baby was born. Another day, her uncle Corey was gunned down.

At the age of ten, running for George Headley Primary School, Shelly-Ann was second in the 100 metres at Jamaica's primary schools Champs. She competed in bare feet. She had honed her sprinting in Waterhouse by running past the gangs of men, as her mother told her to do. They called her 'Merlene', after Merlene Ottey.

Speed was in her genes, thinks Shelly-Ann. Her mother was a good runner but 'she went to a mixed school and she got pregnant with my older brother when she was sixteen. That was it for her when it comes to athletics. But she was very fast; I would try to outrun her. I spoke to her coach: she was very good. So I knew I got the talent from her. And my mother tried to spark that interest in me. She was always the one person to tell me that if I was good at what I did I should be focused on it.'

Her mother's work was erratic and irregular. 'She would sell whatever was "in", so if it was Valentine's Day she was selling roses; if it was Christmas she was selling toys and firecrackers; it just depended what season it was.' It meant Maxine was rarely around for family occasions, and she missed most of Shelly-Ann's races once she started competing. Athletics meetings were on Saturdays, when 'she'd be in the country selling, and come back very late. At Christmas she'd be away all night so it would be me and my two brothers would have to look after ourselves.'

Shelly-Ann paints a vivid picture of a childhood that is all the more striking because of where she is sitting as she describes it. We are in an expensively equipped hair salon in a gated business park in New Kingston. The salon, Chic Hair Ja, belongs to her. It opened two months earlier. 'I get very bored with my hair,' says the woman famous for her colourful, adventurous hairstyles. 'I want to do so many things with it. This business was born from that love.'

The smart reception area is roughly the size of the house she shared with her mother and two brothers. It is decorated in pink and black, with floor-to-ceiling mirrors and leather sofas. Positive messages abound (a bit like her Twitter feed. Typical example: 'When no one celebrates you, learn to celebrate yourself. When no one compliments you, learn to compliment yourself! Good morning #Pryceless'). A sign in reception reads: 'It's all fun and games until someone breaks a nail.'

The salon is a symbol of how far she has come, of course. In the house that was the same size as the reception area, Shelly-Ann, her brothers and mother all shared one bed. She recalls that 'We had a small TV, a small fan, a couch, and a desk for the plates and stuff. And one bed. Four of us sleeping on the bed; we had to turn different ways so we could all fit. Sometimes I had my brother's feet in my mouth, or in my head.

'But I think it was still fun,' she adds. 'We had good times.'

There must have been . . . safety issues. 'Yeah, there were lots of safety issues,' she nods. 'I had to go to school early. I was coming out once, there was police in the yard because there was a lot of violence and a lot of shootings at that time. We had a curfew imposed on the community: nobody could come out until a certain time. But I had to get to school, so they let me pass.'

There were other unscheduled interruptions. 'We didn't have a wall structure to separate the houses, we had a fence, so men could come over. You had men coming over, walking through; sometimes we would hear them, I would say to my mum, "There's someone there," and she would say, "Sssshhhhh." But we survived.'

She is, as should now be clear, a survivor and a natural optimist. Waterhouse has improved, she thinks. 'I still go home every Sunday. I go to church there. It has gotten a lot better. There are a lot of times I would not dream to go down there at night; nine or ten o'clock at night you would not catch me there. But there's more peace now. I don't know if it's because a lot of the men who so-called ran the area have passed away . . .'

Fraser, who became Fraser-Pryce in 2011 when she married her boyfriend, Jason Pryce, attended Wolmer's High School for Girls. 'It was a very good school,' she says. For her it was also a way out of Waterhouse. 'You had persons say, "Oh, you'll never make it, you'll end up pregnant."[25] I felt I had something to prove.'

Where did it come from, her drive? 'I saw the struggles my mother had,' she says. 'And I had persons who believed in me.

'When I started high school, I went to the Penn Relays for the first time in 2000 and I met a lady who was part of the old girls' association. And she just started to take a liking to me. She paid my school fee for the following year, she bought my books and my uniforms. I asked her why, and she said, "You're going to be very good one day, I believe in you."' The woman's name was Jeanne Coke, then president of the Wolmer's Alumni Association, New York chapter.

At Champs in 2004, Shelly-Ann won the Class 2 girls' 100 metres in 11.73 seconds. A year later, she was second in Class 1; the winner, Anneisha McLaughlin, was the big star, the sprinter who seemed destined for great things. There was little to suggest that Fraser was

---

25 Nearly a quarter of babies in Jamaica are born to teenage mothers. Although many are unplanned, in the ghettos there can be an expectation of childbirth in young women; a childless girl may be stigmatised – called a 'mule' – when she is barely out of her teens.

even an Anneisha McLaughlin, never mind a Usain Bolt, the schoolboy who was four months older than her and already a household name in Jamaica. 'I wasn't a super-athlete, or a superstar at high school, I was just a normal athlete. I won once at Champs, when I'd almost finished school. I came second and third as well. You had a lot of talented athletes. Anneisha McLaughlin was so talented. It was fierce competition.'

When Fraser-Pryce left school, she thought about going to the US, as McLaughlin did. She was good enough to get an athletics scholarship to one of the smaller colleges. 'I had a few options.' Iowa was one of them. 'I knew the coach very well, he was a Jamaican.

'But one night I went to KFC here in Kingston and met Paul Francis.' He was running MVP with his brother, Stephen. 'When I saw Paul, he was saying, "What's happened, we're expecting you to be at UTech."'

Fraser replied: 'Oh, I don't know.'

'Come,' said Paul Francis, 'because Stephen wants you at UTech.'

'I went, sat down, had a conversation with Stephen Francis, and then I went home and said to my grandmother, "I'm going to UTech." I had made up my mind. I thought I would try it. If it didn't work out, I could go overseas.'

What convinced her? 'I don't think Stephen Francis convinced me, though I knew he could take me far if I listened. I think what sold it was that he had other athletes in his camp who were doing very well: he had Sherone Simpson, Asafa Powell, Bridget Foster, Michael Frater. I saw the progress they were making and decided, "I'm going to give this a chance."

'But I knew I had to be 100 per cent in; I couldn't have just one foot in.'

Francis had missed out on coaching Bolt two years earlier. But in Shelly-Ann Fraser he got the kind of athlete he loved, and the sort of challenge he relished. She was somebody few people rated and the opposite of Bolt in many ways: diminutive – five foot in bare feet – and shy, but with a big, infectious smile, and from the inner city rather than the country.

Francis discerned other strengths: her gritty determination to escape Waterhouse; her bubbly optimism; her independence; and the intelligence to realise an opportunity and seize it. Not that Shelly-Ann believed everything Francis told her. Early on he said that he thought she could make the team for the 2008 Olympics in Beijing. 'But I wasn't listening to that, I wasn't buying that kind of thing. The Olympics? Oh yeah?!'

In her first year with Francis, her personal best dropped from 11.7 to 11.3 between October and June. What changed in those months? 'I did a lot of technique training. If I didn't do something correct, I would be the one left on the track doing a hundred knees-up or arm swings; technique work until I was crying. He spent a lot of time on that.'

As a coach, Francis was strict. Fraser didn't always appreciate his gruff manner. 'I would say sometimes he's a dictator. He says he needs to be a dictator because athletes think they know best. He says if I know best I should coach myself, and I can't coach myself. But sometimes he is very harsh.'

And unlike Mills, he kept a distance. There was no 'pally-wally'-ness. Yet he and Shelly-Ann did establish a rapport, she says. They 'connect well', but only perhaps because she cedes total responsibility to him. 'For it to work for me, I have to be submissive in a sense,' she explains. 'If he says to do something, I do it, because he is in control.

'You can talk to him and he'll listen,' she adds. 'He understands . . . He might look very aggressive and unapproachable from the outside, but once you get close to him and talk to him one-to-one, you realise it's a shell.'

In 2007, her second full season with Francis and MVP, Fraser was selected for the Jamaican team for the world championships in Osaka.

Osaka was a prelude to Beijing: Powell took bronze in the 100 metres; Veronica Campbell won the women's 100 metres and took silver in the 200. And finally Jamaica got what it had been waiting for: twenty-year-old Usain Bolt won a senior medal – silver behind Tyson Gay in the 200 metres, in 19.91 seconds. Bolt was also part of the 4x100 metres relay team that was second to the USA. The American men remained dominant. Meanwhile, the Jamaican women won silver in both relays.

Fraser went to the Osaka world championships as a member of the sprint relay team. She didn't run, but 'seeing everybody competing and winning medals, that was my inspiration. The glory, the energy they felt when they won medals, that was my inspiration. I came back to Jamaica, I got my body fat down, I went to Juliet Cuthbert's fitness club. I went there and I worked out. I would be on break but I would be working. I worked very hard.'

She made more dramatic improvements over the winter before Beijing. And at the Jamaican trials in June she sprung a huge upset, beating the golden girl, the world 100 metres champion, Veronica Campbell-Brown (who had married Omar Brown, a fellow Jamaican sprinter, in November 2007). The top three in the trials qualified: Fraser was second, Campbell-Brown fourth. The backlash began immediately – who was this Shelly-Ann Fraser to be taking the place of the world champion? She was advised to give up her place for the good of Jamaica.

Francis weighed in on his athlete's behalf. 'They can't take you out,' he told her. 'You earned your spot.' It was the media and public campaign to oust her that really bothered Shelly-Ann. 'I was upset at my country. Here am I, a young athlete, making my first Olympic team, and you're telling me I should pull out because I don't have experience? Now, how do one get experience if you don't get the chance? It was very hurtful that they said the things they said.' As well as the media coverage, the selectors seemed to be prevaricating, waiting to see if one of the top three sustained an injury – as though they were trying to leave the door ajar for Campbell-Brown.

'In Jamaica we have diehard track fans,' says Fraser-Pryce. 'They take it very serious and personal. You can't have a bad race. If you run horribly they will slaughter you.'

There were no last-minute reprieves for Campbell-Brown. In only her second full season with MVP, Shelly-Ann Fraser was – as Stephen Francis had forecast – going to the Olympics as part of a fifty-one-strong Jamaican team (of whom thirty-nine were sprinters).[26]

When the team arrived at Beijing airport for the Games, on 1 August, they were met by Jamaica's ambassador to China, Wayne McCook. With his diplomatic status, McCook was able to enter the airport to give the athletes their official accreditations, which acted as a visa for the duration of the Games. But Francis refused to accept his accreditation. He wanted nothing to do with Team Jamaica. The bad blood hadn't just been caused by the controversy over Fraser's selection. A row had been simmering between MVP and the JAAA over the governing body's insistence that all Jamaican athletes attend a pre-Olympic training camp in Tianjin. 'The way that the JAAA is forcing us to prepare for the Olympics is not what we had in mind,' said Francis. 'We don't believe this is the ideal preparation.'

Pouring oil on the flames, he continued: 'I guess because they want to ensure that the athletes who I coach don't do well, they decided to come up with this camp and this mandatory thing. I guess they know that the preparation I have in mind doesn't involve a camp. So I guess there's a debate.'

At the heart of Francis's complaint was his fear that he would be prevented from coaching his own athletes in the build-up to the Games. Moreover, he believed that the JAAA organised their camp in Tianjin 'only after hearing in February that we were planning to have our own'. The governing body denied this, claiming that arrangements had been

---

26 It was reduced by one shortly before the Games when Julien Dunkley, a US-based sprinter who made the 4x100 metres relay squad, tested positive for an anabolic steroid at the Jamaican national championships.

made over a year previously. They also pointed out that they had held a pre-Olympic camp for every Games since 1984. 'The suggestion that our training camp was belatedly undertaken to "obstruct" Mr Stephen Francis's own camp cannot be substantiated,' the JAAA responded. The problem, they suggested, was Francis's general hostility towards the governing body.

The head coach to the national team was Glen Mills, and it is impossible to avoid the suspicion that the feud had something to do with the underlying rivalry between the Racers and MVP. It also reinforced the notion of Mills and Racers as establishment, Francis and MVP as outsiders.

I asked the JAAA vice president, Vilma Charlton – herself a former Olympian – for her take on the relationship between Francis and the governing body. She was inclined to a charitable view. 'I understand him,' she said. 'He wants the best for his athletes. He's a bright fella, very brilliant; it's just his personality and we have to work with it.' She looked thoughtful. 'He is very, very different. A peculiar person, but that's because he's bright.'

Francis backed down after a few days when he said he would accept his accreditation after all. But he wouldn't pick it up himself, instead sending an athlete (unnamed). The message relayed to the athlete was that Francis should collect it in person. Which, eventually, he did.

Thus did the Jamaican athletics team's Beijing Olympic campaign get under way.

On the night of Sunday 17 August, Shelly-Ann Fraser was one of three Jamaicans who lined up for the final of the women's 100 metres in Beijing; Kerron Stewart and Sherone Simpson, her MVP clubmate, were the others. There was no clear favourite. Although Shelly-Ann had won all three of her qualifying rounds, she was still a rank outsider. Few had heard of her before the Jamaican trials two months earlier. But the heats had shown that she was a tremendous starter. Her height – or lack of it – meant that she seemed to spring out of the blocks.

As they were called to the start, Fraser wore an expression of wide-eyed surprise – perhaps she was as shocked as everybody else that she, little Shelly-Ann Fraser from the Waterhouse ghetto, was in an Olympic final. She was in lane four. As they waited for the gun, Torri Edwards, the 2003 world champion, twitched; but no false start. Fraser, in any case, was entirely focused on her race: her eyes, opening gradually wider over the 10.78 seconds it took her to cover the distance, locked on to the track ahead of her; her cheeks puffed out and mouth open in a small 'O'.

She was fastest out of the blocks, but seemed to find another gear in the second half of the race and the gap opened to two metres by the line. Fraser smiled her way to victory: it crept gradually across her face as she homed in on the line and punched the air. There was no stopping her then. She bounced up and down. And she kept smiling. 'I can't stop smiling,' she said once she made it around the track. 'My braces are hurting me.'

Behind her, Stewart and Simpson emerged from the pack and could not be separated by the photo finish: they were both awarded silver medals. A Jamaican clean sweep, a one-two-two. 'The Jamaicans showed up, and we totally didn't,' said Lauryn Williams, the American who was fourth. 'It's very humbling.' And this with Veronica Campbell-Brown, the world champion, missing.

Six years later, in her hair salon in Kingston, Shelly-Ann beams as she recalls the night she became the first Jamaican woman to win the Olympic 100 metres. 'Yeah, yeah! I felt so good because I said before that if I won I'd be jumping and screaming because I wouldn't know what to do with myself. It was awesome.'

What was going through her mind? She was thinking about how far she had come, where she had come from, and the hard work she had put in over the previous two years. 'I remembered the struggles, I remembered growing up, the fact no one wanted me to run, telling my coach I was too tired, that I couldn't do it. I remembered all that.'

Winning the Olympic 100 metres title didn't change Shelly-Ann Fraser, says Stephen Francis.

There were no invitations from David Letterman, no multimillion-pound sponsorship deals. It raises the question of whether she has the profile and recognition she deserves. 'Deserves, yes,' Francis says. 'But most people don't realise how good she could be if she got opportunities. She's a very good speaker, a teller of stories; a natural chatterbox who likes to perform, even more than Bolt.'

The upside was that after Beijing she remained hungry for more; her appetite for training was certainly undiminished. 'Yeah,' says Francis, 'because the difference is that Bolt has always thought he is getting what he deserves. Shelly-Ann always questions whether she deserves what she has.'

12

SHOCK AND AWE

When I saw the time, I knew I had to go out and catch him.
But even after the finish I couldn't catch him.
Asafa Powell

'I wanted to run the 100, not just the 200,' Usain Bolt said. 'My coach told me if I broke the national record for the 200, I could run a 100.'

At the Jamaican national championships in June 2007, he ran 19.75 to beat Donald Quarrie's thirty-six-year-old Jamaican record. 'After the race he didn't even say thank you,' said Mills. 'He just said, "When is the 100?"'

In his first professional 100 metres, a month later, in Rethymno, Greece, Bolt recorded 10.03. It was hardly earth-shattering, but his head had been turned; over the winter he worked at his start and explosiveness. Mills was fine with that; he believed that to win the 200 metres he had to be faster anyway. 'We mapped out a programme to improve his speed in the first part of the season,' he said, 'and then we would switch over to improving his 200 metres for the Olympics.'

When Mills began working with Bolt, everybody in Jamaica had an opinion about why he wasn't delivering on the promise he showed as a fifteen-year-old. He was too tall, he couldn't run the bend; or he suffered the curse of the sprinter: his body wasn't robust enough and was prone to breaking down. And he was lazy. 'I took it all on,' Mills said in a rare public speaking appearance at the IMD business school in Switzerland in 2009. 'But I like to do my own analysis, too. I did my own assessment and came up with something different.'

Sitting alongside his star athlete, wearing a white Adidas polo shirt and his usual jeans and trainers, shaven headed and rotund, Mills spoke slowly, deliberately, seeming not so much laid-back as verging on horizontal. Such a state lends itself to deadpan humour. 'I think the problem', he continued, 'was that he was not fast enough.'

In the first part of the 2008 season, they worked together on his 100 metres, to hone his speed. But Mills was clear on the reason why: to improve his chances in his main event, the 200 metres.

Then everything changed. On 3 May, Bolt entered the 100 metres at the Jamaican Invitational at the National Stadium in Kingston. With a just-legal tailwind of 1.8 metres a second, and after two false starts, he ran 9.76: the second fastest in history, behind Asafa Powell's world record 9.74 in Rieti eight months previously. Bolt's time caught everybody by surprise. 'Usain said he was shocked,' said Michael Johnson, the US's 200 and 400 metre world record holder. 'I'm shocked too. I never would have predicted he could run that fast over 100 metres.'

Twenty-eight days later, the sense of shock was even greater. With another tailwind – 1.7 metres a second this time – Bolt sprinted in New York's Icahn Stadium to a world record 9.72 seconds. He had become the fastest man in history in only his fifth attempt at the distance. Gay, the world champion, was second. He was stunned not only by the time but by Bolt's ability to overcome what was considered his disadvantage – his height – to move so fast. 'It looked like his knees were going past my face,' he said.

Now, said Bolt, he would go for the double in Beijing: the 100 and 200. Mills, speaking in New York after the world record, reflected: 'Over the past three years we've had our differences and we've had our ups and downs. But I can say for him he never lost sight of what the big picture is and although we differ in what is hard work, we are always able to get things done.'

Powell was one of the first to phone Bolt. 'You've made things rough on me now,' said the now former world record holder.

Back in Falmouth, Bolt's first coach, Devere Nugent, watched the world record in New York on television. 'I always knew, and probably outside of Glen Mills, I might've been the only one who knew that he could run a 100 metres. And what Glen did was what I did with him as a child: he bet him; he challenged him.' Nugent was not surprised that Bolt was so fast. 'If you keep a horse that wants to run locked up for fifteen years, once you release that horse, it's going to run.'

Early on the morning of the men's 100 metres final in Beijing – 9.30 a.m. Jamaican time – Nugent drove the thirty minutes from Falmouth to his and Bolt's home village of Sherwood Content, where he joined Wellesley Bolt and others – Bolt's mother Jennifer was in the 90,000 crowd at the Bird's Nest stadium in Beijing.

Inside the stadium, away from the camera lenses, the finalists waited in the call room. It is half-sanctuary, half-purgatory in there. 'I love the call room, the pressure that you feel,' said the British sprinter Dwain Chambers. 'You want to vomit. You think to yourself, why am I here? Why do I put myself through this stress? . . . It's like your driving test and wedding combined.'

It is here that races are won and lost, say athletes. Carl Lewis would shake opponents' hands and get in their faces, killing them with kindness. Maurice Greene would flex his muscles. Some athletes snarl and pout, sometimes to disguise the fact that they are shaking with nerves. Asafa Powell, crippled by self-doubt and fear, can't seem to act the part of the macho sprinter; he disappears into his own world.

In the call room in Beijing, Bolt did what he always does: laughing, joking, chatting to his rivals. 'They don't always talk back to me. Just stare back. I try not to focus too much on the race. I may sing a song.

My method is to stay relaxed. And not think about the race until the starter says, "On your marks." Then I take a deep breath, refocus, think, Let's get it done. It's all about staying relaxed.

'But some are really tense,' Bolt told an IMD business school seminar in 2009. 'Like, they're going to strangle you. Crazy, are some of them in the call room.' Describing the scene, he mimicked his rivals, leaning forward, narrowing his eyes, staring intently. 'They're ready,' he said. 'Ready to take you apart.'

Bolt was one of three Jamaicans in the final in Beijing, along with two of Francis's MVP athletes, Powell and Michael Frater. 'He's got a bit of a swagger,' said the BBC commentator, Steve Cram, as Bolt ran through his routine, smoothing his hair (what little there was: he was shorn, looking as youthful as his twenty-one years), smiling, then pointing to his face with a mock-serious expression. 'He's enjoying himself.' While the others looked as though they were on their way to their own execution, Bolt 'looked like he was heading to the beach', said Cram.

On an airless Beijing night – the wind gauge read '0.00 m/s' – they settled into the blocks and the stadium hushed, the only sound that of anticipation – echoey bangs and clatters, nervous giggles. In the set position, Bolt, in lane four but with only two runners on his inside, remained bigger and taller than the others, his backside sticking up.

Richard Thompson alongside him gets off to a flyer. As he drives out of the blocks, Bolt's left foot gently scuffs the track; the laces are loose on the same shoe and will gradually come undone over the next nine seconds. He drives for ten metres, head down, gradually unfolding. Then, once he's fully extended, comes the acceleration. Only there is no acceleration. Of course there is no acceleration. Dennis Johnson drilled this into me.

'Have you ever seen 100 metres run?' DJ asked.

'Yes,' I replied.

'Sure?'

'Is this a trick question?'

'No.'

'Yes, I have seen 100 metres run.'

'OK, we've established you've seen 100 metres run. OK. Have you ever seen one guy come from the back, speed up and win?'

'I think so, yes. Yes, Bolt in Beijing.'

'Bolt, yes.' Johnson allowed a long pause to hang between us. 'Are you sure you've seen that?'

'Erm, well . . .'

'You didn't see that,' DJ said. 'What you saw was some tiring before others. You can't speed up after six seconds. That's a physiological impossibility. So it's the guy who tires least who is going to win. What you see is the guys who finish second, third, fourth tiring and slowing down at a faster speed.'

At forty metres in the Bird's Nest they are just about level: Thompson, Bolt, Frater, with Powell a fraction behind. Bolt, having worked through the gears, doesn't speed up; he hits cruise control. It's his height, his long legs; they seem to give him an unfair advantage. He gobbles up the track while the others fall away.

At sixty metres, Bolt glances right. 'He's looking for Asafa,' says the commentator. 'Asafa isn't there.' Then he glances right again. 'He's looking for Thompson. Thompson isn't there.' Still looking to his right, he begins to ease up a full fifteen metres from the line, stretching his long arms like an enormous bird of prey coming in for landing. Then he thumps his chest and yells. The winning time, 9.69 seconds, is astonishing, not that Bolt notices that he has broken his own world record as he carries on sprinting, cavorting, around the track. The winning margin – several metres – is immediately declared the biggest ever: it wasn't necessary to check.

Watch Bolt's Beijing 100 metres final and his world junior 200 metres race in Kingston, six years apart, and it is as though you are watching a different athlete; the twenty-one-year-old Bolt had added muscle and technique: what they call 'form'. He had added one or two inches in height and eighteen kilos in weight. He was smoother; the

lolling head had gone. He was graceful but at the same time powerful and strong. Watching it brings to mind DJ's poetic description of Mills's sprinters' ability to dance across the surface of the track, their feet kissing the ground, all the more surprising in someone of Bolt's size, as though he defied the laws of physics.

'You couldn't hear, it was deafening,' Devere Nugent recalls of watching the 100 metres final in Sherwood Content. 'The noise in the room was absolutely deafening. Everybody came out to watch because I think we recognised that we were witnessing a moment in history that as long as we live probably will never happen again: that out of the belly of a small, rural village comes one that has stamped his mark on the world.'

Wellesley Bolt was watching at home because he was scared of flying. He recalls, 'It was tense moments for me. To be honest, I don't like flights. The mother enjoys. So I wasn't there for the 100. I said, "I'm not going." But after the 100, Digicel were Bolt's sponsor, they insist I have to go. I said, "OK, let's go."'

So Wellesley set off from Trelawny, bound for Beijing. 'I didn't think I'd catch the 200. Because the 200 was run while I was in the air.' Of course Bolt was unbeatable in the 200 metres. 'You're Usain's dad?'

said the security official to Wellesley in Beijing, when he landed. 'Oh God, he broke Michael Johnson's record.'

The 100 and 200 metres in Beijing were the last major races of his son's that Wellesley Bolt missed.

Asafa Powell cut a forlorn figure as Bolt carried on around the track, milking the acclaim, launching his 'To Di World' routine, dancing, establishing himself not only as a great athlete but also a showman.

While Bolt celebrated, Powell, fifth in his second successive Olympic final, stood dejected, hands on hips as he stared up at the replay on the big screen, the folds in the back of his neck making him look like a defeated boxer. Interviewed after the race, he couldn't bring himself to look at the camera; he stood with his back to it. 'Well, um, I messed up big time,' he said. 'My legs died on me. Usain ran an awesome race and I'm very happy for him.'

What went wrong? he was asked by the trackside interviewer, Phil Jones, who had his arm around Powell as though comforting him. 'I'm not sure what happened. I just have to live with it. I'm happy for Usain.'

Did it prove that he couldn't handle the big stage? 'Well, you know, it's really for myself I wanted to get the gold medal,' he said. 'It's quite obvious that I wasn't ready for the big stage.'

Powell left Jones and the media area to congratulate Bolt, and found himself swept up in his celebrations; it was irresistible, even for someone as defeated and deflated as Powell. Bolt performed a couple of Jamaican dancehall moves, the Gully Creepa and Nuh Linga – typical of the expressive, suggestive routines made popular by dancehall culture – and Powell joined in. Watching back home, Powell's parents were unimpressed. 'God gave [Asafa] those feet to bring joy to the world, but not in that form of dancing,' said his mother, Cislyn. 'We don't want Nuh Linga, we just want Jesus.'

She wasn't the only one who disapproved. Jacques Rogge, the IOC president, said that he thought Bolt's celebrations were unbecoming of an Olympic champion and showed a lack of respect for his opponents. 'That's not the way we perceive being a champion,' he said. Bolt, he added, should 'show more respect for his competitors and shake hands, give a tap on the shoulder to the other ones immediately after the finish and not make gestures like the one he made in the 100 metres'. On the US channel NBC, Bob Costas echoed Rogge, saying Bolt was 'disrespectful to his competitors, to the Olympic Games and to the fans'.

It was a baffling reaction to an outpouring of what looked like spontaneous joy from a twenty-one-year-old. Bolt wasn't making a political statement. Not that he was aware of, anyway. But perhaps that is exactly what he was doing – a cultural if not a political statement, at least. His very Jamaican celebration and the reaction to it intrigued and concerned some commentators, who detected a whiff of resentment that Bolt, the first Jamaican-born and Jamaican-trained gold medallist, was so brazenly flaunting his culture on such a hallowed stage. It was a clash of cultures between Bolt's exuberance and the conservatism of the Olympic movement. 'Bolt's display is an affront to both the imperial conquests the Olympics are supposed to honour and the colonial ethos and discipline that sport is supposed to instil into "natives",' a trio of academics, James McBean (a Jamaican), Michael Friedman and Callie Batts, would later assert in a book, *Beyond C. L. R. James*.

There was even some negative reaction in Jamaica, as Cislyn Powell's comments illustrated. But perhaps it is more accurate to describe it as shame, or a sense of embarrassment, owing less to the extrovert display – the showing off – than to the dancehall origins of the Gully Creepa and Nuh Linga, and their associations with the Kingston ghettos. And for the IOC establishment, perhaps Bolt, with his 'creolised display of exuberance', was getting above himself, offending Olympic ideals 'steeped in the ethos of the elite British boarding schools', as the academics put it, 'which [Olympic founder Pierre] de Coubertin believed were at the foundation of the British Empire's global domination'.

Bolt's lap of honour in Beijing was an expression of individuality and cultural identity. But it was only the start. Before too long, the victory laps would be accompanied by a prolonged blast of Bob Marley in stadiums from London to Moscow, Rome to Zurich. Puma, the German sportswear manufacturer so keen to align themselves to Jamaican culture when they signed Bolt, would later use the dancehall moves in an advert.

As for Bolt, he seemed to be doing what came naturally, though perhaps he was not completely oblivious to the significance of show-casing some of the moves he'd learned in the Quad nightclub. 'I love taking dances from Jamaica and putting it out to the world,' he said.

Bolt's win came twenty-four hours before Shelly-Ann Fraser became the second Jamaican 100 metres champion. Her motivation, she said, was not Bolt, it was her clubmate, Powell. She wanted to make up for his disappointment. As Stephen Francis puts it: 'Well, there is no reason for her to be overly elated at Usain Bolt, because after all she hardly sees Usain Bolt. Usain Bolt may as well live in England for all the time she sees him.'

There was more, much more: Bolt's golds and two more world records in the 200 metres and the 4x100 relay; Veronica Campbell-Brown's successful defence of her title and Kerron Stewart's bronze in the 200 metres; Shericka Williams's silver in the 400; Melaine Walker's gold in the 400 hurdles; bronze in the women's 4x400.

It was too much. It didn't merely invite suspicion. It opened the door and ushered it in.

The men's 100 metres was the show-stopper: the most sensational since Ben Johnson shot to a world record 9.79 seconds in Seoul in 1988. That fact alone was enough to give pause, to temper the euphoria. Johnson's run was seared into the consciousness, but so was news of his failed test for steroids a few days later. Since then, it was difficult to know how to react to incredible performances. If the heart rejoiced, the head urged caution.

Bolt's brilliance could be explained: he had been brilliant at fifteen, then held back by injury. His height advantage – his ability to move his long legs as fast as the shorter guys – helped rationalise his performance; after all, he required fewer steps, only forty-one compared to forty-five for most others.

With Fraser, the Pocket Rocket, it was more difficult to find a reason, or to accept that she had apparently come from nowhere. Watch and listen to the footage of the women's 100 metres in Beijing and you can hear the stunned reactions of the commentators: their failure to reach for the same superlatives they had used twenty-four hours earlier is striking. Her win was the kind of upset that keeps sport interesting. Unpredictability is supposed to be part of the appeal. But athletics, the 100 metres in particular, has had a habit of throwing up nasty surprises. Fraser's improvement in a year, from June 2007 to June 2008, was almost half a second: 11.31 to 10.85. And in Beijing she shaved off another seven-hundredths. It added a question mark to that Jay Z lyric. Real as it gets?

Carl Lewis, the US's nine-times Olympic gold medallist, said he had questions about the effectiveness and integrity of the anti-doping programme in Jamaica. More accurately, he wondered if there *was* an anti-doping programme in Jamaica. Although the IAAF insisted they were regularly testing the top Jamaicans (they said only four countries had been subject to more out-of-competition tests),[27] locally it was a different story, alleged Lewis. 'No one is accusing anyone,' said the sprinter who inherited Ben Johnson's gold medal in 1988. 'But don't live by a different rule and expect the same kind of respect. They say, "Oh, we've been great for the sport." No, you have not. No country has had that kind of dominance. I'm not saying they've done anything for certain. I don't know. But how dare anybody feel that there shouldn't be scrutiny, especially in our sport?'

---

27 According to Herb Elliott of the JAAA, in 2008, prior to the Olympics, Bolt was tested out of competition by the IAAF on four occasions, Powell six and Fraser three.

Lewis went on to say that if he were still competing, he would expect questions. He conceded that Bolt 'could be the greatest athlete of all time . . . But for someone to run 10.03 one year and 9.69 the next, if you don't question that in a sport that has the reputation it has right now, you're a fool. Period.'

It was true that Bolt had made a huge leap, but then again, he had only run one 100 metres the previous year. It was more useful to study his progression over 200 metres. He was somebody who had run a sub-20-second 200 metres as a teenager, and following the Beijing Olympics, *Athletics Weekly* charted his progress over five years in the longer event. Tracking his times from the age of sixteen, his improvement, culminating in Beijing with his world record 19.30, was 1.28 seconds, or 6.22 per cent. Of seven of his peers selected for the study, Bolt's improvement was, in percentage terms, ranked only sixth. The British runner Christian Malcolm had made the most dramatic gain: 1.50 seconds (6.95 per cent). John Regis, the retired British sprinter, had made a 7.50 per cent improvement over a similar period, while Michael Johnson made a bigger gain – 6.81 per cent – in a shorter period between eighteen and twenty-one. The magazine's conclusion: there was nothing exceptional about Bolt's improvement over 200 metres from the age of sixteen to twenty-one. The implication: he shouldn't be judged guilty on performance alone.

But apart from his credulity-stretching speed, the other problem for Bolt was that so many of his predecessors had associations with doping. 'Let's be real,' Lewis continued. 'Let me go through the list: Ben Johnson, Justin Gatlin, Tim Montgomery, Tyson Gay and the two Jamaicans [Bolt and Powell]. Six people have run under 9.80 legally, three have tested positive, and one had a year out.[28] Not to say [Bolt] is doing anything, but he's not going to have me saying he's great and

---

28 Lewis was speaking in 2008: since then, Tyson Gay has also tested positive. Now, of the nine who have gone under 9.80, only Bolt, Maurice Greene and another Jamaican, Nesta Carter, have never tested positive.

then two years later he gets popped. If I don't trust it, what does the public think?'

Lewis praised the drug-testing in the US, which he said gave him confidence in Veronica Campbell-Brown. 'Veronica Campbell-Brown lives in the United States and has been transparent and consistent. She won the worlds last year in the 100 metres and this year can't even make the team. Are you going to tell me that shouldn't be questioned?'

Bolt returned to Jamaica and to a party in the grounds of the William Knibb Memorial High School in Falmouth. Twenty thousand people turned up: three times the population of the town. Bolt appeared on the stage at 10 p.m., introduced by the dancehall reggae star Tony Matterhorn. 'One Carl Lewis wonders why we so fast,' Matterhorn addressed the crowd. 'I guess maybe he'll come to the islands and meet and greet the Jamaican mothers who make the greatest food in the world.'

Taking the microphone, Bolt struck a different note. An interesting one, before a captive audience. 'If you guys in the country don't act better, then people will still look down on the country,' he said. 'You guys try to do better. Start to look at yourself. Think before you act. Because Jamaica is a great place. People love coming here, but you have to stop the crime to let them want to come back. A lot of people say, "I'm coming to Jamaica, but I'm wondering about the crime." I say, "Don't worry about it. Jamaica is wonderful. It's nice. The vibe is . . . look at me: I enjoy myself every day."'

Shelly-Ann had a similar homecoming, with murals painted on the crumbling walls of Waterhouse in her honour. As the crowd waited for her, her mother, Maxine, in front of banks of speakers, with a thousand people gathered around her, picked up the microphone and sang, 'God is goooood, God is good to me,' before launching into a prayer. When her girl finally arrived, there was pandemonium. The only sadness for Shelly-Ann was that Jeanne Coke, the Wolmer's 'old girl' who had supported her financially at school, couldn't be there.

Coke passed away in March, five months before the Olympics. 'It hurt,' says Shelly-Ann now, 'a lot of hurt – but I'm glad she saw me . . . she knew what was coming.'

Fraser was joined at her homecoming by a journalist from *Sports Illustrated*, who asked her about Lewis's comments and the scepticism that had greeted her win. 'I would want Mr Dope-Man to come test me every day,' said Fraser. 'I want him to test me in the morning, before I train, after I train, because I'm not hiding one thing and I'm not taking anything. I'm a nervous type of person. Whenever I do something bad I'm just going to tell you, because my conscience is going to hurt.

'I can tell you one thing about my teammates,' she continued. 'I know we are 100 per cent clean. Hard training— we are vomiting. I mean, US athletes are so privileged, they get everything they want. And when it doesn't work their way, they cry. They don't understand. We have to do good with what we have here. They have to come here to live it, to see it.'

Her words seemed heartfelt. But surely Carl Lewis was right to be sceptical. He wasn't the only one; we were all more inclined to ask questions than to acclaim unreservedly. I remember the atmosphere in the press room in Beijing as Bolt's time flashed up. Incredulous.

How credible was it that this tiny island had turned up in Beijing with their home-trained athletes and dominated the Olympic Games? They had wiped the floor with the Americans. No wonder Lewis was searching for answers. He claimed no country had ever dominated to the extent that Jamaica did in Beijing. One had. His very own USA, who routinely dominated (including in Lewis's day) and in 2004 won gold and bronze in the 100 metres, and gold, silver and bronze in both the 200 and the 400, as well as silver in the 4x100 and gold in the 4x400. But the USA had a population of over 300 million. Jamaica had fewer than three million.

Yet Beijing was only the start. Next was Berlin.

*

Bolt began 2009 with a dreadful car crash. At 1 p.m. on Wednesday 29 April, he was driving his black BMW M3 – a twenty-second birthday gift from Puma delivered to Jamaica only seventy-six days earlier – along Highway 2000, which cuts through the middle of the island, from Ocho Rios in the north to Spanish Town in the south.

Most of the roads in Jamaica are terrible: narrow, potholed, twisting. One of the few decent stretches of dual carriageway is Highway 2000, on the approach to Spanish Town. It was here, as he accelerated in torrential rain, that Bolt skidded, left the road and smashed through a barrier. The car rolled three times before ending on its roof.

Somehow Bolt and his two female passengers – nineteen-year-old Venecia Crew and twenty-year-old Latoya Taylor – were able to clamber from the car. They had only minor injuries – Bolt sustained his, thorns in his feet, thanks to his shoeless state. He believed a higher power had intervened to save him. But he had God in mind, not a German automotive manufacturer. As images of the squashed BMW flashed around the world – it looked as though a heavy object had landed on the roof – the company was keen to point out that the accident had highlighted the car's safety features.

Bolt hobbled painfully out of hospital two hours later, his still bare feet heavily strapped. Local reporters were there, and Bolt, speaking in the patois we don't usually hear, reassured them. 'Mi good, man, mi good,' he said, affecting a casual tone, though he must still have been in shock. From the passenger seat of the waiting car he continued: 'Am a good, man. A'm all right. A few talks, a'm good, man.'

He seemed anxious to get away, telling the reporters: 'We talk, man, we talk, we talk, we talk, all right? A'm all right man.' He was due to compete the following weekend at the National Stadium – would he still be able to run? 'Mi talk to mi coach about that. We talk, we talk.'

Fifty-nine days after his crash, Bolt ran 9.86 seconds at the National Stadium to win the Jamaican trials ahead of Powell. In Paris, twenty days after that, he won in 9.79. And at the world championships in

Berlin, 108 days after the car crash, he did what he hadn't done in Beijing, running all the way to the finish.

He stood at the start of his first world 100 metres final with a twinkle in his eye, a smile playing on his lips. He launched his arm up straight like an aeroplane taking off. Taking a few steps forward and shaking out his shoulders, he caught Powell's eye and invited him to join him in a bout of shadow boxing. As they swayed and threw mock punches at each other, it looked as though Bolt was consciously trying to get his uptight, nervous countryman to relax. It came naturally to Bolt, less so to Powell, but he joined in.

There were five Caribbean men in the final. Two of them were Jamaicans; the others included Daniel Bailey of Antigua and Barbuda, also coached by Glen Mills. It was telling that several of the finalists indulged in horseplay, as though Bolt, in Beijing, had established a new trend. The menacing, pumped-up machismo of Maurice Greene or Justin Gatlin now looked outdated, comical. Only Tyson Gay, the defending champion, looked serious, but not for show; in the lane next to Bolt, he appeared to be talking to himself. Beside him, Bolt was an overgrown child as he once again launched his long arm down the runway. He smoothed his hair and eyebrows, pursed his lips.

Berlin was a slow track, they reckoned. But there was a tailwind: 0.9 metres per second, compared to the perfectly still conditions of Beijing. Bolt reacted to the gun in 0.146 seconds (as opposed to 0.165 in Beijing). Only 0.89 seconds into his run he reached maximum power: 2,619.5 watts. From zero to twenty metres he was 0.02 seconds slower than he had been in Beijing; from twenty to forty metres, faster by 0.03.

In Beijing, he reached sixty metres in 6.32 seconds; in Berlin, 6.31. It was between sixty and eighty metres that he began to pull away (from his Beijing shadow), reaching his maximum speed, 27.44 miles per hour.

From eighty to a hundred metres he pulled away from the others as well as the Beijing Bolt, going 0.11 seconds faster than in the Olympic final. Did that help settle the debate over how much time he had lost by thumping his chest and coasting the last ten metres in Beijing? In Berlin, as Bolt ran all the way through the tape, Gay was closer than anybody had been in Beijing. Gay's 9.71 seconds was a personal best and would have been a world record had the man in front of him never existed.

Bolt's time seemed fantastical; it pushed the boundaries of what was thought possible: 9.58 seconds. A demolition of his own world record, and all the world records that came before it – when, for the best part of twenty years, a time of around 9.80 seemed to be at the threshold of human performance. 'I knew it was going to be a great race,' he told the BBC, 'and I executed it. It's a great time, a great feeling, I feel good in myself and I knew I could do it. There was a big build-up, great atmosphere. It wasn't going to be an easy race, but I had a perfect start and just went from there. I came out here to do my best and I did what I had to do.'

'When I saw the time,' said Asafa Powell, 'I knew I had to go out and catch him. But even after the finish I couldn't catch him.'

Looking at Bolt's ten-metre splits in Berlin with Dennis Johnson's words in mind – they all slow down, the one who slows least wins – confirms the wisdom of his mantra. Bolt accelerates all the way to seventy metres: his fastest ten-metre split is from sixty to seventy metres (0.81 seconds), then he hardly slows at all, recording 0.82, 0.83 and 0.83 for the final three ten-metre splits. Slowing down, maybe, but not so the naked eye would see.

His ability to minimise his deceleration over the final thirty metres sets him apart. But it is not the only thing. Tom Tellez, who coached Carl Lewis throughout his career, identified five phases of sprinting and what each phase is worth as a percentage of a 100 metres race. Reaction time, he reckoned, accounts for only 1 per cent – which seems to make a mockery of the emphasis put on the start (though it is impossible to look at each phase as a disparate part: one affects the other).

Block clearance is the next phase: 5 per cent. The third, the 'speed of efficient acceleration', is believed by Tellez to be the most important: 64 per cent. It is also the longest, taking top sprinters to, in most cases, sixty metres. Maintaining top speed is worth 18 per cent. Finally, the deceleration phase is 12 per cent.

In terms of top speed, there might be little difference between Bolt and the others. But he reaches his top speed later than most. According to Jimson Lee, a coach and physiologist, Bolt and Tyson Gay are the only sprinters in history who have been able to accelerate all the way to seventy metres.

The received wisdom is that sprinters accelerate up to sixty metres then slow, with the final forty metres largely about damage limitation. 'You want to "delay" your top speed as long as possible,' Lee says. 'You want a smooth acceleration: the longer, the better.' Because of his longer training efforts (perhaps also his background as a 400 metres runner, as Devere Nugent suggested), Bolt is conceivably more accustomed to and better equipped for a smooth, gradual acceleration. Yet he also has explosive speed.

Lee has, along with many others, given a lot of thought to Bolt's training. Although they are cagey about their methods, it is understood that the Mills camp follows a 'short to long' programme, starting with short efforts and progressing to longer distances. In this context, short means pure speed – thirty to fifty metres – while long means speed endurance – 250 to 400 metres. Mills's thinking is that you are not going to be one of the fastest in the world if you are not one of the fastest in the world over thirty metres. As he has put it, 'We tend to train the speed then stretch it out.' Or: 'I believe in speed, from a yard to a mile, as my number one objective.' Interestingly, Stephen Francis prefers the opposite, 'long to short': 'High volume, short recovery' in the pre-season, 'leading on to low volume, long recovery, high intensity'.

*

Back in Jamaica, in the midst of the off season (pre-season, if you're an athlete), I ask Francis about the two philosophies, short to long and long to short, and the thinking that underpins each. He admits he prefers long to short. His athletes do the kind of training that Bolt so hated doing with Fitz Coleman – long efforts, up to 400 metres. 'Most sprinters wouldn't want to train with us because we do stuff that they don't do,' Francis says. 'I'm a big fan of sprinters running 300s, and they run them from the start of training until February or thereabouts. And then they go out and have to run a 400 at a meet.'

Francis's belief is that the benefits are mental as well as physical, building 'a certain commitment in my sprinters. When you have had to do that kind of work you become more committed because of the suffering that you've had to go through.' It is almost as though the 100 and 200 metres races that make up a sprinter's diet in the summer are a reward for the gruelling winter.

Mills places more of an emphasis on shorter intervals: honing his sprinters' speed, worrying less about endurance. His philosophy seems similar to that of the late Charlie Francis, Ben Johnson's coach. Charlie Francis's name may have been forever sullied by Johnson's positive test, and his subsequent admissions about his doping regime, but he was a visionary, whose book, *Speed Trap*, is still acknowledged as a bible of coaching and training.

Charlie Francis dismissed the accepted wisdom, which he said was prevalent in the US, that sprinters had to build an endurance base before working on their speed. He equated it to a pyramid, but added that 'If these people had designed the Great Pyramid, it would have covered 700 acres and topped off at 30 feet.'

For sprinters, reckoned Francis, it was the sharp point – representing pure speed – that mattered, not the endurance base. If the goal is to go as fast as possible in less than ten seconds, then why train over thirty, or forty? Why train to go longer, slower?

Stephen Francis understands this thinking, but says that it isn't an either/or question. 'We have a number of different things going on at any given time.' Mills would doubtless say the same. One of his athletes, the promising teenager Zharnel Hughes, told me of a typical session. 'I'm working right now on speed endurance,' he said – it was December. 'Like today, we had something called the diagonal. We run sixty metres across the field, walk forty-five metres, ten times. Tomorrow we do ten [intervals of] 300 metres at 44 seconds pace, with five minutes recovery. That's very rough. But Coach says this is the easy part: "Wait until the season starts!" We train six days, with Sunday off.'

As I watched MVP train at UTech in early December, Shelly-Ann Fraser-Pryce, Nesta Carter and the other sprinters were doing explosive thirty-metre intervals, with harnesses around their waists, dragging weights (each pulls about 20 per cent of their bodyweight, Francis told me). 'I don't think our methods hamper the results we get,' Francis explained. 'It means our athletes have to work a little bit harder, but as I said, until there is some research which tells me that [running longer intervals] is definitely hampering the athletes then I think it works well for us – it may not for somebody else.

'We pretty much believe that sprinters are athletes who need to get fit, to suffer a bit, rather than just go out there and run thirty metres day in, day out.'

At the Berlin world championships, as Bolt raced to his outrageous world record, Powell provided more evidence that Francis's methods were effective. He was third behind Bolt and Gay – his first individual medal in a major championship. Perhaps the shadow boxing with Bolt did help after all.

But most were preoccupied with Bolt and his 9.58 seconds. And the question: how did it compare to his run in Beijing? The following wind was worth a tenth of a second, it was estimated, so on a still night in Berlin he might have run 9.68 (while with a just-legal 2.0m/s tailwind he would have done 9.46). By this reckoning, there was only a hundredth of a second between Beijing and Berlin. Yet in Beijing he coasted the final ten metres. Had he not done so, claimed some, he would have stopped the clock at 9.64. So was Beijing a superior Bolt performance? Jimson Lee thinks not. When I ask him which was the better run, he doesn't hesitate: 'Berlin.'

Four nights later, in the 200 metres, Bolt's reaction time is even quicker than in the 100: 0.133 seconds. That makes the outcome inevitable. Emerging from the bend, the other Jamaican in the final, the US-based Steve Mullings, is second, while Bolt, running into a 0.3m/s headwind, pushes all the way to the line. He has the kind of lead – at least ten metres – he had in 2002 at the junior world championships, but here he isn't just racing for the win. His eyes are locked ahead – no looking right and left for opponents – until he crosses the line and glances to the left, to the clock. It reads 19.20 – before being adjusted to 19.19 – and Bolt's grimace cracks into a smile. Another world record, one that is, if anything, even more remarkable than his 100 metres mark.

Anything Bolt could do, Shelly-Ann Fraser could almost match. She won the 100 metres ahead of her MVP clubmate Kerron Stewart in a world championship record 10.73 seconds. She didn't emulate Bolt by going faster than any of her predecessors – that might be impossible. With a tailwind of just 0.1 m/s, Fraser's time in Berlin was over two-tenths slower than a twenty-one-year-old world record that is so out of reach it might as well be on the moon.

'Well now, I've heard things about that record,' says Shelly-Ann in her hair salon in Kingston. The record is infamous for more than one reason. It is held by the late Florence Griffith-Joyner, set at the 1988 US Olympic trials in Minneapolis. The wind blew hard that weekend, assisting Carl Lewis as he ran to a world-best 9.78 seconds in the men's 100 metres; but at 5.2 metres per second it was well over the legal limit so didn't count. Yet as Joyner lined up for the women's 100 metres, and the flags blew, the wind gauge read 0.0. Over by the long jump pit, meanwhile, another gauge read 4.3. Joyner blasted to the win in

10.49 seconds, quarter of a second faster than Evelyn Ashford's world record.

Most of the questions about Joyner – who went on to win the 100 metres at the Seoul Olympics – concerned how she had been transformed, at the relatively advanced age of twenty-eight, from decent 200 metres runner to fastest woman in history. The British athletics writer Pat Butcher wrote at the time about this transformation, which encompassed more than just her speed on the track. When Butcher first encountered her, in 1985, Flo-Jo was 'one of the most beautiful women I had ever seen, petite, oval-faced with unblemished skin. It would be three years before I would get as close to her again, in Seoul 1988, by which time she had metamorphosed. Apart from the overall muscular definition and diminution of breasts, her jaw had elongated, a condition called acromegaly, known to be an effect of human growth hormone. She wore thick pan-stick make-up, to cover the widespread acne, a side-effect of male hormones, and her voice had deepened substantially.'

Butcher also recalled a press conference in Tokyo, following the Seoul Olympics, when Flo-Jo's predecessor as Olympic champion, Evelyn Ashford, turned on the journalists, asking: 'Why don't you guys write the real story?'

Even more questions followed Flo-Jo's abrupt retirement after Seoul. Ten years later, she suffered an epileptic seizure in her sleep and died. She was thirty-eight.

Stephen Francis shakes his head at the legacy Flo-Jo left female sprinters. 'Shelly's unlucky,' he says. 'If circumstances had not allowed a wind-assisted record to be world record . . . She's also unlucky because almost all her 10.7 races have been in headwinds. You keep telling her, "Don't worry about it, you'll get the conditions." '

The lack of a world record is one reason why Fraser-Pryce doesn't have anything like the profile of Bolt. Does she resent the fact that while Bolt is one of the world's most famous athletes, she struggles for recognition outside Jamaica? Not to mention missing out on the multimillion-dollar deals, the American talk show appearances, the celebrity lifestyle. 'Well now, I'm a very down-to-earth person,' she insists. 'I'm OK with it. I'm fine.'

13

THE BEAST

We are humans, we are bound to make mistakes.
Yohan Blake

I have arranged to meet the man who calls himself 'the Beast' in Hope Gardens in Kingston, where – just as in Shelly-Ann Fraser-Pryce's hair salon – another side of the city is very much in evidence.

The botanical gardens are spread over 200 acres, with palm avenues, manicured lawns, a bandstand, lush green hills rising up in the distance, a zoo next door. It is a place that reeks of affluence, the tranquillity pierced only by the cries and screams of young children – a primary school sports day. Yohan Blake's agent, Timothy Spencer, whose son attends the school, tells me not to worry that his client is late: he is on his way. 'This is really unlike Yohan. He's not usually late.' Turns out Blake had taken the wrong road and got lost in the neighbouring zoo.

While we wait, I chat to Spencer, who, in his shades, designer jeans and white shirt, top two buttons undone, looks like he might have stepped out of a wine bar in Chelsea. He's chatty, friendly, and wonderfully indiscreet. When he hears that I write about cycling, he is particularly interested in talking about Lance Armstrong's doping, mouth opening and head shaking slowly as he hears about the extent and sophistication of Armstrong's cheating. Spencer is a member of the Jamaican middle class: a successful businessman in Kingston, who seems to help Blake as a favour. He tells me that he's more involved in running Blake's foundation than in acting as his agent on a day-to-day basis (Blake has a US-based agent, Cubie Seegobin). Spencer seems more like a big brother, an impression confirmed when, on a later visit to Jamaica, I met him in a hotel bar. On that occasion, Blake phoned him in a state of panic: he'd heard a noise outside his house and wanted Spencer to call the Ministry of National Security. Spencer shook his head, laughed, and told Blake not to worry.

This didn't seem very Beast-like. The nickname dated back to the autumn of 2008, when Blake began training with Glen Mills and Bolt said he was struck by the eighteen-year-old's work ethic: 'Watch out for Yohan Blake. He works like a beast. He's there with me step for step in training.' 'You know why Usain calls me the Beast?' Blake said. 'Because when you're sleeping, I'm working, I'm toiling through the night. It's what great men do.'

Finally Blake appears, ambling self-consciously towards the grass where the kids are holding their races. The MC excitedly introduces him: 'It's our Olympian – El Centro's favourite! Uncle Yohan "the Beast" Blake!' Children swarm around him, and Blake signs autographs and poses for some pictures with their mothers, all the time looking distinctly uncomfortable.

He is no more relaxed when he breaks off and saunters over towards Spencer and me. He wears baggy jeans and trainers, an oversized baseball cap covering his cornrow hair. He keeps a Bluetooth device in his ear, like a cab driver. As we sit on a bench, I tell him that I was in his home town, Montego Bay, a couple of days earlier. 'Montego Bay is where it all started for me,' Blake says intently. 'The wanting to get to the top, this drive for what your parents is going through, the suffering, and you want to take your parents out of that. I said I wanted to do something and God answered my prayer.'

Blake's shyness is apparent as his eyes flicker and then focus straight in front of him; he avoids eye contact. He seems more cat than beast; graceful and feline, with small, gentle features and dark, sparkling eyes.

Blake's parents, Veda and Shirley, are still together, though there have apparently been some rocky moments (and children with other people). 'My dad was a drinks mixer,' Blake says, 'my mum was a domestic worker: that was the jobs available at the time and that's what they did.'

It was cricket Blake loved when he was growing up – he still does. In fact, he gives the impression that he would rather be a cricketer than an athlete. When he was twelve, the family moved to Clarendon, on the same side of the island as Kingston, though his parents are back in Montego Bay now. 'In a nice home that I bought for them,' Blake says. 'That was the plan, you know? But they don't like the whole glamorous thing; they stay humble, quiet.'

They must be proud of him. 'Every day,' he says softly.

In Clarendon, Blake went to Green Park all-age school. 'I wasn't an athlete then, I was a cricketer. That was my focus. I didn't know anything about track and field. Then I was running up to bowl really fast, and my teacher said, "You know, man, this boy can really sprint." '

The principal told him he should go to one of Jamaica's top athletics schools – Calabar, Kingston College or St Jago. He recommended St Jago on the basis of the coach there, Danny Hawthorne. 'Mr Hawthorne is a very good coach,' Blake says. 'He took me under his wing and made me run a Champs record and a national junior record.'

Blake missed cricket, but seemed, at a very young age, to take a pragmatic view, seeing athletics as a means to an end. 'Track and field was what was presented to me at the time, and I was getting what I wanted really fast. I was running really fast, so I used that as a drive to help my family. They needed help and they needed it fast.'

So the motivation was to earn money to help them? 'Yeah, that was it. That was the drive: to get my mum out of poverty, to get myself out of poverty, to help poor people.' And running fast, even training hard, beats collecting empty beer bottles to sell, which is how he raised money as a kid. How big is his family? 'In all there's eleven of us kids,' he says, and giggles. 'Back in the day there was nothing to do but have fun.' Naturally, he is one of the youngest – with lots of older brothers. 'I'm seventh – somewhere in the middle.' Three are half-siblings. Shirley Blake is father to eleven children, Veda is mother to eight.

It was Asafa Powell who inspired Blake. The schoolboy was fifteen when Powell, still living and training in Jamaica, broke the world record. Around the same time, Blake ran 10.65 seconds in the final of the world youth championships in Marrakech as he trailed in seventh, three tenths behind the winner, Harry Aikines-Aryeetey of Great Britain. The next year saw a big improvement: Blake ran 10.33 to win the Central American and Caribbean junior championship, then he took a bronze medal in the world junior race in Beijing. But 2007 was the breakthrough, when he claimed Raymond Stewart's twenty-eight-year-old national junior 100 metres record by a hundredth of a second with 10.18 in the first heat at the Carifta Games. In the final he lowered it further, to 10.11. He was still only seventeen. 'My first time at the world juniors, when I came third, I thought: There's a future for me. You see Asafa Powell and all them running and I think, You know what, I can do something in track and field.' But the following year he returned to the world juniors and slipped down a place, finishing fourth. There was a silver lining to that disappointment, says Blake. 'It teach me how to lose.'

The programme and workload at school was intense and punishing for a seventeen-year-old. 'I was running the 4x100, the 200, the 100 and 4x400. That was a lot for my body to take.' In 2007, when he set a new record at 100 metres (10.21) and won the 200, Blake also helped St Jago to a record in the 4x100 – their time of 39.80 beat the Glen Mills-coached Camperdown, and was the first time any Jamaican school had gone below 40 seconds – and then he anchored the triumphant, record-breaking 4x400 squad. With his hair shorn, it was a youthful-looking Blake in the yellow vest and green shorts of St Jago, far less muscular than the powerful-looking senior athlete of a few years later.

In his final year at school, Blake was approached by Jamaica's national coach, Glen Mills. 'Coach Mills said to me, "There's a future for you but you need to know what you're going to do." He didn't say, "Come train with me." But I made a choice from there.' The choice was to join Mills's club, Racers. 'And up to today I don't regret it,' says Blake, 'because I'm the second-fastest man not only in the world but in the universe.'

Blake joined Mills in the summer of 2008 – just as Bolt was rewriting the record books in Beijing – but in doing so he walked out on Hawthorne, quite literally. He had been living with his high school coach for three years, and Hawthorne was planning a future for the pair of them: he wanted to look after his star sprinter as he entered the professional ranks – he was convinced Blake was going to be bigger than Powell, bigger than Bolt. But 2008 had not gone as well as 2007: Blake was beaten in the 200 metres at Champs by another St Jago sprinter, Nickel Ashmeade. This, perhaps, was why Mills was concerned, and also why Blake was receptive to his approach.

Hawthorne, still head coach at St Jago today, was devastated when Blake left him. 'I don't know anything,' he told the local press on being informed that Blake had teamed up with Mills. 'Nobody has said anything to me.' Hawthorne was called later by Blake's parents explaining their son's decision.

When Mills first cast his eye over Blake, he was not impressed. 'The first thing when we got him, he had a back and a hamstring problem that we had to attend to,' Mills said. Perhaps all the training and racing at St Jago was catching up with him. Then, in his first outing as a Racers Track Club athlete, Blake seemed to suffer stage fright. As Mills put it: 'When he started in his first meet, he froze. The gun fired and he didn't run. So we had to be patient with him and work on him both mentally and physically. We corrected his back, strengthened his hamstrings and then once that was in place, we started to work on him bio-mechanically.'

The effects were almost immediate. 'What I achieve in one year with Coach Mills,' Blake shakes his head, unable to find the words to describe his transformation. 'I was nineteen when I ran my first 9.94' – in May 2009 in Paris – 'the youngest man to go under 10 seconds. That proved the decision I made was right.'

What is Mills's secret? 'His secret is the love for the athletes,' Blake says. 'The time he puts in and the technical stuff he do. Every day he say: "Yohan, you need to eat this, you need to do that, you need to keep ahead of that." He draw a diagram of all you need to do; little things. It's twenty-four hours. He drives to every athlete's home and talks to them. That's the kind of person he is.'

Mills also suggested some changes to his technique. 'Yeah, because in high school I ran with my arms at my chest. I didn't move them. Technically now I'm getting really good.'

I spoke to Zharnel Hughes, the eighteen-year-old who is also coached by Mills and who broke Blake's 100 metres record at 2014 Champs. Hughes said that he can be training and unaware that his coach is watching him when, as if from nowhere, he will hear a voice:

Mills's. Blake smiles at that. 'Coach Mills is like a ghost. He appears when you don't expect him, or you hear him when you don't even know he's there. "Lift your knees!" That's all you hear, and you don't even see him.'

Blake says he enjoys training. 'I love it. If you don't love it, you won't do it. I try to enjoy it even when the programme is hard. We're human and I would tell a lie if I said I don't get moments of not wanting to do it. But every time I get that moment I have to remind myself why I do it.'

A month after his sub-10-second 100 metres in Paris, the Beast was derailed. At the national championships in June, which served as a trial for the 2009 world championships in Berlin, he tested positive for methylxanthine, a stimulant in the same family as caffeine, though also a drug that can dilate the airways to aid breathing. The substance wasn't on the banned list, but was closely related to one that was, and after some deliberation, it was considered a doping offence. Another four Jamaican athletes, including the sprinters Marvin Anderson, Allodin Fothergill and Lansford Spence, tested positive for the same substance. Fothergill and Spence were also members of Mills's Racers Track Club. They were initially cleared by Jamaica's anti-doping disciplinary panel. The Jamaica Anti-Doping Commission (JADCO, which had only come into existence on the eve of the Beijing Olympics) then appealed the decision of the disciplinary panel. In the end the athletes were suspended for three months. For Blake, it meant missing the world championships. It also left a blot against his name.

Even more worryingly, Blake was a member of Racers. He was coached by Mills. The bottom line: he trained with Bolt, the man single-handedly restoring the lustre to a sport tarnished by a succession of scandals, from Ben Johnson to Marion Jones and Justin Gatlin.

The headlines said it all: 'Usain Bolt's training partner linked to positive Jamaican drug tests' (*Guardian*), 'Bolt's friend Blake named as one of five athletes to have failed a drugs test' (*Daily Mail*). Patrick Collins in the *Mail* compared the news to a dark cloud appearing over athletics: 'And the entire sport of track and field shivered in apprehension.'

It was a red flag: others would follow.

It was September 2010. Shelly-Ann Fraser was at UTech, coming out of an advanced communication course, when her phone rang. She glanced at the screen: her coach, Stephen Francis. 'Where are you?' he asked. She told him she was at university. 'That painkiller you took in China,' said Francis. 'Did you write it down?'

'No, I didn't write it down because it was a painkiller.'

'You tested positive.'

'No, you're crazy.'

She hung up and nearly collapsed. 'I remember my legs went weak. I sat down and I called my husband: "Where are you, I need you to pick me up." I was crying, I was hysterical. No, this is impossible! At that time I questioned my faith, I questioned everything. I told myself, but I'm not cheating! It was unfair.'

What happened, she says, was that she delayed dental treatment before a Diamond League meeting in Shanghai in May. 'I had braces at that time and needed root canal [work]. But because I was flying to China the next week my dentist told me she couldn't do full root canal. I had semi root canal so I could travel.'

On the plane to China she began to suffer from severe toothache. She had some Aleve with her, but it did nothing. When she arrived at her hotel she turned the lights off, put a hot towel on her face, then went to see the doctor. By now her face was swollen. The doctor gave her antibiotics and painkillers. These didn't work either.

'I went to Coach,' she recalls, 'and said, "I'm in such pain."' Francis gave her a painkiller he was taking for kidney stones. That did alleviate the pain, though she ran poorly, finishing second to Carmelita Jeter in 11.29. But the painkiller contained oxycodone: a powerful opioid-based narcotic, sometimes used as an alternative to morphine, that isn't considered to be performance-enhancing but is on the banned list. When she was drug-tested after the race she was given a form on which to list any medications she was taking. She neglected to write the painkiller Francis had given her.

When the Jamaican athletics federation notified her that she had tested positive, they asked if she wanted her B-sample tested. She said no. 'There was no point; it wasn't a mistake, I remember vividly taking the painkiller. I just didn't think to write it down.'

The worst part of it, she says, was the coverage of her case. She published a statement, but few seemed prepared to believe the one about the athlete who took her coach's painkiller. 'I went on every media, I read every newspaper article, and I saw "Jamaican sprinter tests positive for doping". I was like, "doping"? That sounds like I test positive for steroids or something. No, they can't report that. My coach sat me down and said, "Shelly-Ann, you can't stop persons from saying what they want to say. Even before this painkiller thing came about, the fact you won the Olympics in 10.7, the fact you ran 10.8 and persons didn't know who you were . . . they were saying you were on drugs."

'But I was so hurt. This is not supposed to happen to me. I worried what persons would say about me, what my sponsors would think. I sat there in front of the federation and told them what happened. I didn't want them to feel sorry for me. I was young and I think I was very naive. I said to myself, There's no need to hide because I'm telling the truth. But it was hard.'

She was given a six-month suspension. She recognised she had made a mistake and knew that another one would cost her her career. 'For me, I tell you, when that thing happened, I didn't want anything to come near my mouth, I swear. If something happen to me, God forbid, that's it for me.'

As with Blake, a second doping offence would see her banned for life. 'So I can't be careless. The only thing that passes my mouth are vitamins and that's normal vitamins because I'm so scared about what's out there. You never know.' She says she doesn't take any supplements.

Her case was one of six in Jamaica in the space of a year. And since then there have been others, many of them, according to the athletes, because of 'mistakes': mainly, as in Blake's case, supplements that don't list any banned substance in their ingredients.

Some excuses seem as far-fetched as 'the dog ate my homework'. Yet the cases of Blake, Fraser and others in Jamaica have seemed less than clear-cut. The result of carelessness and cock-ups rather than part of some wider, more sinister conspiracy. Or is that too charitable? Or just plain naive? Blake explained at the time that he had taken energy-boosting tablets whose ingredients did not list methylxanthine (in any case, the stimulant was not banned – though it was later added to the WADA list).

He says that he had checked it out and believed it was a legal supplement. But he concedes it was a mistake. 'We are humans, we are bound to make mistakes. You can't kill yourself about it. But my mother say prevention is better than cure, if you know what I mean. Before you do anything, just be careful.' He says that since then he has been ultra careful about what he puts in his body.

'When you see these cases happen, it heightens your awareness,' Shelly-Ann tells me. 'You hear athletes taking supplements that are contaminated. I read a story about someone, not an athlete, taking a B12 vitamin and they got facial hair and everything; they found it was contaminated. Now, if an athlete took a contaminated B12 and that happened, would you say they were doping?'

14

THREADS

When you run a 9-second 100 metres or 19-second 200 metres
your body is gonna be ripped up.
Tyson Gay to Steve Mullings

'It's so obvious that they're up to something,' Victor Conte says of the Jamaican sprinters. But up to what? 'State-sponsored doping.'

You would assume that Conte would know what he is talking about. His name is synonymous with doping, since he was the man who ran the Balco operation: a doping ring that in the early 2000s included the world's fastest woman and man, Marion Jones and Tim Montgomery. He has been saying since 2008 that he thinks the secret behind the Jamaicans' success is doping. He gets exasperated that nobody seems to listen. I suppose this comes with the territory of being a convicted drugs cheat, though these days, in his new guise as boxing trainer, Conte insists he is committed to the cause of clean sport. He is certainly a vocal proponent of fair play, and a crusader against drugs cheats.

But state-sponsored doping? That is some claim.

According to the IAAF, drug-testing at the 2009 Berlin world championships represented a big step forward. A thousand urine and blood samples were collected. The IAAF president, Lamine Diack, said that the samples would be stored for future analysis, using new testing methods as they were developed.

According to others, the testing was – and always has been – ineffective. Around 2 per cent of tests turn out positive – year after year that figure is fairly stable – which is either a sign that not many athletes are doping, or that most cheats are not caught. It is widely understood that in-competition tests are unlikely to yield many positives. The reasons are obvious: athletes know they are likely to be tested; drugs are of most benefit in training, not in competition. Failing a test at a major event is akin to failing two tests, says Dick Pound, the former head of WADA: 'A drugs test and an IQ test.'

Pound estimates that 10 per cent of cheats are caught – which means he thinks that around one in five competitors are doping. The athletes themselves, when asked on the eve of the 2012 Olympics, said they thought it was around 10 per cent. Conte says it's more like 60 per cent.

The truth is this: nobody knows.

Into the vacuum of knowledge, speculation floods. In the absence of facts, guesswork is all we have. We grasp at anything – rumours or threads, however tenuous, connecting an athlete to a notorious coach, chemist or doctor. And of course performances. In an event with the history of the 100 metres, a great performance is enough to elicit suspicion.

There are some who contend that there is a natural threshold: that anyone running below a certain time must be doping. But this is hugely problematic. Can anybody claim to know the limits of natural human performance? Or quantify how much of a difference drugs can make – what they are worth in terms of times?

Conte believes he has a reasonable idea. When he was running the Bay Area Laboratory Co-operative (Balco) he gave his athletes 'the full enchilada' of doping products – the blood booster EPO, testosterone, human growth hormone, insulin, as well as a 'designer steroid', tetrahydrogestrinone (THG). This was his secret weapon, known as 'the Clear' because it was undetectable. And for years he got away with it.

He and his athletes, including Jones and Montgomery and Britain's Dwain Chambers, might never have been caught. They were rumbled not by conventional drug-testing, but because in June 2003 a rival coach, Trevor Graham, a US-based Jamaican, sent a syringe containing traces of THG to the US Anti-Doping Agency (USADA). With the syringe he included a note explaining that Conte's athletes were using this mystery substance. The agency sent the syringe to an anti-doping lab in Los Angeles, which analysed its contents, identified its anabolic properties and developed a test for it. Then they retested Conte's athletes, catching Chambers, among others, and setting in motion a chain of events that led eventually to the imprisonment of Conte and Jones.

Two days after Graham's package arrived at USADA, Jeff Novitsky, a federal agent who had been carrying out his own (separate) investigation into the activities of Conte and Balco, discovered a letter while going through Conte's rubbish. It was written by Conte, addressed to USADA and the IAAF, and accused Trevor Graham of systematically doping his own athletes with the help of a Mexican contact. Conte had obviously had second thoughts about sending it.

When Graham was outed as the anonymous syringe-sender – partly because he couldn't help boasting about it – he accepted the praise that followed with humility. 'I was just a coach doing the right thing,' he said. 'No regrets.'

But eventually he too was charged with doping his athletes (who included the 2004 Olympic 100 metres champion Justin Gatlin). Graham ended up with a year's house arrest and a lifetime coaching ban. Another Jamaican who became embroiled in the fallout from the Balco scandal was Raymond Stewart, the coach to another Jamaica-born athlete, Jerome Young, who ran for the US. Stewart also ended up with a lifetime coaching ban.

Of the two Jamaican-born coaches, Stewart is far better known than Graham as an athlete. He ran in four Olympic Games, making the 100 metres final a record three times in a row. In the most notorious final of all, in Seoul in 1988, he pulled up injured mid-race – something he blamed on the Jamaican team not having adequate medical or physio support (he was treated before the final by a member of Ben Johnson's entourage).

Stewart's personal best of 9.96 seconds makes him the fifth-fastest Jamaican of all time. He first emerged at Camperdown High School, which developed an enviable reputation for sprinting from the late 1970s under its coach, Glen Mills – it was the 'sprint factory' as Mills himself told me. It was Mills who coached Stewart before he left Jamaica for Texas Christian University in Fort Worth in 1985. In 1983, running for Camperdown, Stewart won the 100 and 200 metres at Champs, held at its temporary home of Sabina Park in Kingston, winning the 100 in a record-equalling 10.3 (on grass). In 1984, he repeated the sprint double at Champs and later that year helped Jamaica to one of their most significant results – a silver medal in the men's 4x100 metres at the Los Angeles Olympics.

Graham didn't have the same distinguished career (I could find no record of him even running at Champs), though he did represent Jamaica, alongside Stewart, at the Seoul Olympics. He was a member of the 4x400 relay squad that won a silver medal, though he didn't run in the final. He too left Jamaica for an American college – in Graham's case St Augustine College in North Carolina.

When the Balco case exploded, and then Graham was found to be as guilty as Conte of doping his athletes, it was a former discus thrower from Mexico (Graham's 'Mexican contact') who appeared to be the thread connecting many of the world's leading coaches and athletes. Ángel Guillermo Heredia Hernández, also known as 'Memo', the son of a chemical engineer from Mexico City, was part guru, part supplier. Although largely self-taught, what Heredia didn't know about drugs and how to pass drug tests didn't seem worth knowing.

Graham was the coach with whom he worked most closely, but Heredia's introduction to the world elite originally came through Stewart. The pair met when Heredia went to Texas A&M University-Kingsville to study kinesiology. Stewart was launching his coaching career, and Heredia told him he could help his athletes. He took Stewart to Mexico City to visit a laboratory where a member of his family worked; it was here that some of the world's top athletes would later have their blood and urine screened to ensure they would pass drug tests.

Heredia began working with other coaches, too. In 1996 he was contacted by Graham, who drove to his home in Laredo, Mexico, with two of his less well-known athletes during the Christmas holiday. They stayed, said Heredia, for four or five days.

Now Heredia had access to some of the fastest sprinters in the world, including Montgomery and Jones, who at the time were both coached by Graham (they would link up with Conte later). Later, Heredia claimed that he also worked with Graham's cousin, Winthrop Graham (another Jamaican), as well as John Smith (who coached Maurice Greene) and Dennis Mitchell. Thus did he spin a web connecting many of the world's top sprinters from the late 1990s into the early 2000s. Between them, Heredia's clients won twenty-six Olympic medals and twenty-one world championship medals. 'At one time, between Victor Conte and me, you could say we had the whole of US track and field in our pocket,' he told the journalist David Walsh in 2008.

It was inevitable, then, that Heredia's name would become familiar to the federal investigator Jeff Novitsky, a toweringly tall, bald figure. When Novitsky finally tracked him down and confronted him, he knew as much about Heredia as Heredia knew about performance-enhancing drugs. Novitsky presented him with a choice: turn informer or go to prison. Heredia took the first option, becoming the prosecution's star witness (Source A) and testifying against Raymond Stewart, Trevor Graham and the athletes he had helped to cheat. 'Even at the last moment, I felt I was betraying my oath, the underground oath among athletes,' he said later. 'What hurt me was that, deep down, I didn't want to put all this stuff on the table. I truly felt sad about it, but Trevor sent that syringe and in the end, I had no choice.'

In the end, Travis Tygart, the head of USADA, was less than impressed with Heredia. After the initial slew of information, he 'went quiet'. He disappeared back to Mexico for a while. Then he reappeared in the sport of boxing with a new name, or a variation on his actual name: he was now Ángel Hernández. The man who identified the trainer formerly known as Ángel Heredia was Victor Conte (on Twitter). When he was outed, Heredia explained that Hernández was simply easier to spell to reporters. But to Conte it looked like he was trying to hide his identity. He wanted to know why.

Since his re-emergence, Hernández/Heredia has worked with some top boxers, including his fellow Mexican Juan Manuel Marquez, insisting that his methods have changed, that he is in favour of clean sport and that his fighters are drug-free. But in a sport that has traditionally had something of a lax attitude to doping, some are reluctant to take him at his word – his old nemesis Victor Conte foremost among them.

There have also been rumours – many of them fuelled by Heredia himself, through a series of tantalising, provocative tweets – that he still works with track and field athletes. In August 2008, during the Beijing Olympics, he gave an interview to the German publication *Spiegel*. This was instantly notorious; and for athletics fans it made for grim, depressing reading. Asked if he would watch the 100 metres final in Beijing, Heredia replied: 'Of course. But the winner will not be clean. Not even any of the contestants will be clean.' There is no way to prove this, pressed the reporter. 'There is no doubt about it,' replied Heredia. 'The difference between 10.0 seconds and 9.7 seconds is the drugs.'

It was a long interview, 3,000 words, presented in its entirety as a

Q&A. In it, Heredia buried the myth that drugs can transform athletes:
'In reality you have to train inconceivably hard, be very talented and
have a perfect team of trainers and support staff. And then it is the
best drugs that make the difference. It is all a great composition, a
symphony.'

He went on to explain why athletes take drugs: 'Athletes hear
rumours and they become worried. That the competition has other
tricks, that they might get caught when they travel.' He said when
they take drugs: 'When the season ended in October, we waited for a
couple of weeks for the body to cleanse itself. Then in November, we
loaded growth hormone and EPO, and twice a week we examined the
body to make sure that no lumps were forming in the blood. Then
we gave testosterone shots. This first programme lasted eight to ten
weeks, then we took a break.' He revealed how they circumvented the
tests: 'I had to know my athletes well and have an overview of what
federation tested with which methods'; he gathered information by
using 'vigilance [and] informers'. And he explained what he used: 'I
always combined several things. For example, I had one substance
called actovison that increased blood circulation – not detectable. That
was good from a health standpoint and even better from a competitive
standpoint. Then we had the growth factors IGF-1 and IGF-2. And
EPO. EPO increases the number of red blood cells and thus the
transportation of oxygen, which is the key for every athlete: the athlete
wants to recover quickly, keep the load at a constantly high level and
achieve a constant performance.'

Asked why he seemed to lurk in the shadows, Heredia said: 'I
rarely travelled to the big events, but that was because of jealousy:
the Americans didn't want me to work with the Jamaicans and vice
versa. But shadows? No. It was one big chain, from athletes to agents
to sponsors, and I was part of it. But everyone knew how the game
worked. Everyone wanted it to be this way, because everyone got rich
off it.'

The only way drug-testers could win, he added, was if they invested all the money generated by the sport and tested every athlete twice a week – 'but only then. What's happening now is laughable. It's a token. They should save their money – or give it to me. I'll give it to the orphans of Mexico.'

He concluded: 'Peak performances are a fairytale, my friend.' Which might be the only thing on which he and Victor Conte agree.

I am speaking to Conte, or rather, Conte is speaking to me down the phone from California. You don't ask Conte many questions – you simply tee him up, and off he goes. The former rock guitarist, who looks a bit like a TV magician with his slicked-back dark hair and pencil moustache, lives up to his reputation as a larger-than-life figure. Or, as some have described him, a publicity-hungry big-mouth whose regular briefings of reporters during the Balco investigation infuriated his own lawyers and perhaps helped land him behind bars. Yet he is also engaging, curious – and deeply suspicious.

After spending four months in prison in 2007, he too re-emerged as a boxing trainer, also professing to have changed his ways – to be fair, Conte has continued to cooperate with anti-doping organisations – and as the owner of a nutrition company. Conte hates Heredia, or Memo, as he insists on calling him. The reason for his animosity, he explains, is simply that while he opted 'to accept the full consequences for my mistakes and not testify against anybody in the case, Memo chose to throw all his athletes under the bus . . . He was their leader and when caught, Memo ratted his athletes out.' (Their animosity plays out on Twitter, where Conte interrogates Heredia and Heredia goads Conte in response, sometimes, just to rub it in, adding #felon to his tweets.)

Conte claims that in 2009 he was told by a track and field insider (a former athlete turned agent) that Memo was working 'with twenty-five track athletes, most of them Jamaicans', including Usain Bolt. The allegation that Bolt was involved with Heredia was published by Deadspin, the sports website, in August 2011 ('What Do Usain Bolt

and Juan Manuel Marquez Have in Common?' read the headline. 'They Train With the Same Admitted Steroid Dealer'). This was flatly denied by Bolt's agent, Ricky Simms. 'I have no idea why Usain's name was brought up,' he said. 'Usain has no connection with any of these people. Nobody from Team Bolt has any connection or knows any of these people.'

'They would say that, wouldn't they?' says Conte. His conviction that the Jamaicans are up to no good is unwavering. He says he first became suspicious when he saw the results of the Olympic trials in 2008. 'First thing that caught my attention: the most decorated Jamaican athlete, Veronica Campbell-Brown, ran 10.88, got fourth and didn't even make the team. Then those three girls ahead of her got all three medals. I looked up Shelly-Ann Fraser. She ran 11.3 the previous year and I don't believe it's possible, based on what I know, to run five metres faster in the course of one year.'

But how can he know that? 'Look, here's the comparison I use. Kelli White [100 and 200 metres world champion in 2003] could run 11.19. With all the sophisticated drugs I was giving her, with some of the best coaching in the world – and she was a hyper responder – she went from 11.19 to 10.85 legit and 10.79 wind-aided. I mean, this is a really sophisticated doping programme with excellent coaching. Do I believe it's possible to make those types of gains in a period of one year without the use of performance-enhancing drugs? I personally don't believe that's possible.'

There is one significant difference between White and Fraser-Pryce. White was twenty-three when she ran 11.19 in 2000. She was twenty-six when she made the leap to 10.85: an unusual age at which to suddenly improve – and as we now know, it was drug-fuelled. When Fraser-Pryce made her big improvement, she was twenty-one: an age at which sudden gains are not so unusual, albeit hers was dramatic. Fraser-Pryce explains it by saying that the previous winter was the first she trained seriously, lost weight and added work at Juliet Cuthbert's gym to the technical training she was doing with Francis and MVP. (And despite Conte's example of White, it remains difficult to quantify the effect of drugs. Chambers, with 'the full enchilada', actually went slower.)[29]

Conte says that he watched events in Beijing and Berlin in a state of bewildered curiosity, partly because he didn't see the Jamaicans coming. For almost two decades he had been a fixture on the global athletics circuit: he was trackside as Ben Johnson blasted to the gold medal in Seoul in 1988, and subsequently he became a regular behind-the-scenes fixture at athletics meetings, with his little black bag full of pills and potions. He says that throughout his period at the top of athletics

---

29 In 2013, a paper by Aaron Herman and Maciej Henneberg of the University of Adelaide titled 'The Doping Myth: 100m sprint results are not improved by doping' was published in the *International Journal of Drug Policy*. After studying performances by top sprinters from 1980–2011, including known doped ones, they found that 'No significant differences ... between dopers and non-dopers were found in their average results,' and concluded that either '(1) "Doping" as used by athletes so detected does not improve results, or (2) "doping" is widespread and only sometimes detected. Since there was no improvement in overall results during the last quarter of the century, the first conclusion is more likely.' Victor Conte and others might argue nevertheless that (2) is more likely.

he was not really aware of the Jamaicans, apart from the individuals –
such as Raymond Stewart, Merlene Ottey and Bert Cameron – who
emerged from some US college or other.

He had never even heard of – far less met – the coaches behind
the Jamaican gold rush. 'My sources were telling me that what's so
strange about all this is that they were not all that high on Glen Mills
as a coach,' Conte says. 'They just don't think he's all that good as a
coach. They think Stephen Francis is a much more scientific and much
better coach.'

Conte wasn't the only sceptic. Immediately after the Berlin world
championships, Stephen Francis was also sounding a warning bell.
In a remarkable interview with a Jamaican journalist, Kayon Raynor,
Francis was spitting nails after his latest falling-out with the JAAA.

It was Beijing all over again: a dispute with the governing body
over the pre-competition training camp. Before the championships
it was reported that Francis's athletes – including Asafa Powell and
Shelly-Ann Fraser – would be sent home for missing the camp. They
eventually ran, won their medals then returned to Jamaica to the news
that they could face fines over the training camp fiasco. Francis was
livid, particularly, he told Raynor, when he believed the JAAA should
be focusing their attention on more important matters.

'The problem the JAAA have is that they are sitting on top of, in my
opinion, a serious drug problem,' he said. 'I think that is the problem
they should be addressing. They have three athletes, five athletes,
who have tested positive for a fairly serious substance which could be
covering up bigger substances.' He was talking about Yohan Blake
and the others who tested positive at the national championships.
Francis said that by selecting these athletes for Berlin, the Jamaican
federation 'made a fool of themselves', and then 'embarrassed
the country' when, on being sanctioned, the athletes were later
withdrawn.

Five years later, I am speaking to Francis after a training session at UTech. I mention this interview and ask if he still believes Jamaica is sitting on top of a big drugs problem. 'I don't think . . . I don't see the signs as much now as I saw then. I suspect that for there to be a continual drugs problem you have to have the science to keep up. Anything that you have has maybe a two-year window before they catch up with you and people move on to something else.'

He repeats a familiar refrain, one you hear all the time on the island: that serious doping is a problem in the US, not in Jamaica. Bert Cameron, the 1983 400 metres world champion who now coaches in Jamaica, told me that it has always been an American phenomenon: 'I am totally against anybody who takes an enhancing substance because of what I went through in the eighties and nineties. People who were not better than me, I see them running faster. But we couldn't say anything. If we do, we get blacklisted, and can't go to Europe. Now it's different, you can speak out now.'

Have things changed? Francis shrugs. 'I am no longer worried too much about the drugs, because guess what: most of the time someone gets a one-year boost then they have to back off because they're on the testing list.'

At MVP they are strict about drugs and supplements, insists Francis (though as we shall see, there are limits to how much they can control what athletes do of their own accord). But how, when drugs appear to be so prevalent, does Francis convince his athletes they can reach the top without doping? 'Because most of them see that the people who they train with, they see how the success comes about, right? The supplements we use here we have been using since 1999. We haven't had a change, mainly because I can't trust any other companies to not put stimulants and that kind of stuff in, to give you a buzz. So therefore we take the same thing as all the high schools are taking. So everybody here eventually sees "Oh, it has nothing really to do with what you take."

'When Asafa was coming up he used to take nothing,' Francis continues. 'You had to fight him to take a little creatine. You had to follow him. The drug-testing form would come in and he'd have nothing on it.'

Francis admits that he does understand the temptation. 'Let's face it, if you're faced with something that you know is going to make you better, and you know the chance of being caught is very small, then you're probably going to take a chance. But we operate a closed shop. We don't let anyone in from outside. We don't go to gyms. We use our little ragged gym here to do our weight training. We are self-contained.'

Many of the more recent cases of doping seem to come about when athletes hook up with freelance 'gurus' – budget or low-rent Müller-Wohlfahrts who describe themselves as sports doctors, chiropractors or anti-ageing specialists, and who convince athletes they can help them with legal potions and treatments that often turn out not to be legal after all. Usually it is the athlete who faces the consequences alone, with the 'guru' free to carry on their business. Has Francis been approached by such outsiders with offers of help? 'Oh yeah, I mean, over the years people come to you and say, "Bwoy, I have this thing that can do this . . ." You tell them: "Send me an email." '

Are these people from Jamaica or overseas? 'Mostly overseas. You tell them, "Send me an email", and the email come in and you don't answer and it more or less stops.'

Victor Conte is convinced that one overseas 'guru' who has links to the Jamaican athletes is his old bête noire Ángel 'Memo' Heredia. He is not the only one who is suspicious. But Heredia is a perplexing, enigmatic figure. He regularly tweets that he is in, or on his way to, Jamaica. I was told that he lives these days in Florida – only a two-hour flight away. In November 2014 he tweeted: 'Thank you Jamaica!!! Nice training gear', and attached a picture of a Puma top.

Conte tweeted back: 'Interesting that Usain Bolt is a Puma athlete.'

Which is exactly the point. Why would Heredia send out tweets like this if he really was working with Bolt? 'Why tease people, you mean?' Conte replies. 'Because he really wants to be associated with the success of Usain Bolt. He wants that credit. That's the reason.'

That might be the reason – but it doesn't mean he is working with Bolt. It makes little sense. When he gave his interview to *Spiegel*, he claimed all the Olympic 100 metres finalists were on drugs. Does that suggest he was working with any of them? One theory is that he began working with Bolt between Beijing and Berlin. But why would the Olympic champion and world record holder – the fastest man in history – decide to hook up with a man intimately involved in the sport's biggest ever drugs scandal? (Moreover, a man who threw his athletes 'under the bus' when he was caught.)

I tried phoning Heredia, then emailed him, and eventually he responded: 'Congratulations on your upcoming book, can you brief me more about your project? Such as questions, topics, etc. Best regards, Heredia.' I replied to his email but didn't hear back. I tried calling again – he appeared to be in Puerto Rico.

Conte is desperate to expose Heredia, partly because they are rivals once more, in boxing now, partly because he thinks he's up to no good – mostly, I suspect, because he despises him. Interestingly, they have never met. 'People wonder why I'm out there doing this,' he says of his public feud with Heredia. 'It's because I'm trying to put a spotlight on the cockroaches so they gotta go back into hiding.'

Conte has little faith in the anti-doping agencies, including WADA, though he does concede that the game has changed. He echoes what Francis says, that testing has improved. It has become more difficult to dope; it requires more sophistication (which doesn't mean doping has been eliminated; it hasn't). He doesn't think there are new, undetectable steroids, like 'the Clear'. 'No,' he says. 'I'm convinced there isn't. Lemme tell you the reason why. All anabolic molecules, steroids and other molecules, have a very similar, what they call mass spectrogram fragmentation pattern. These sit on a graph like mountain tops going up, so they know where these peaks are in the graph.

'Therefore – and I'll explain exactly why I say this – if you have these peaks that are in a certain range as testosterone – and every single anabolic steroid is similar in structure to testosterone – well, it triggers an alert to go back and look closer at this sample.'

Under anti-doping rules introduced post-Balco, the labs no longer have to know what a substance is – all they have to show is that it is similar to testosterone, i.e. that it is an anabolic steroid. 'That sucked out the designers; it shut it down,' says Conte.

But there are still major loopholes, he says, such as the rule that says an athlete's ratio of testosterone to epitestosterone (its 'mirror') must be no higher than 4:1. 'A piece of cake to beat,' Conte claims. 'You get these fast-acting gels and creams and if you take this stuff after the tester has come, in a matter of hours you're back down below the 4:1 ratio.' Under the 'whereabouts' programme, whereby athletes nominate a one-hour daily window to be tested, they can be confident they will not be tested for another twenty-four hours, at least. 'So these guys can use testosterone on a daily basis and beat the test,' says Conte.

But not necessarily. Not with a more advanced (and costly) method – the carbon isotope ratio (CIR) test. 'We know, for example, that Lance Armstrong was using testosterone during the Tour de France,' Conte says. 'They'd have busted his ass if they'd used the carbon isotope test. But in all his career they never tested his urine using the CIR method. Why?'

Conte wants the samples collected in Beijing and Berlin tested using this method. The samples can be kept for up to ten years, then tested using the latest technology – so the IAAF and IOC have until 2018 and 2019. There seems to be no will to test before then, though Conte has tried. 'I gave Dick Pound lots of information about who I thought was using performance-enhancing drugs and who their coaches were. He presented this to WADA and specifically asked them to test the samples from the Olympic Games in 2008 and the world championships in 2009 and they absolutely refused to use carbon isotope ratio testing for synthetic testosterone on those samples. They didn't want anything to do with that.'

I checked this with Pound, the former WADA president, and he clarified and corrected Conte's claim in an email: 'The samples at the Olympic Games are "owned" by the IOC and the IAAF and they are the only organisations that can retest. WADA has no rights to retest such samples. I have no specific recollection of speaking to [WADA director] David Howman on that matter, but I expect that if I had, that is what he would have reminded me.'

Pound did add, though, that, 'WADA had tried to get more testing done on the samples from Athens, but the IOC refused to do so.'

Conte doesn't believe the samples will ever be tested. 'Because if they go back and do the tests, what does this do to the credibility of the Olympic Games? It would make everybody question everything. It would be bad for business.' But there is conflicting evidence for this. Appearing to support Conte's argument, a WADA-commissioned survey of athletes at the 2011 world championships claimed, staggeringly, that 29 per cent admitted doping in the past year. The findings were never published but were leaked in 2013 to the *New York Times* by three of the researchers, who said that when they presented their results to WADA, they were told that the IAAF would need to review the final draft. Nick Davies, the IAAF spokesman, told the paper that the study 'was not complete for publication' and was 'based only on a social science protocol, a kind of vox pop of athletes' opinions'. However, he 'indicated blood tests from the world championship [in August 2013] in Moscow would be combined with the previous research to produce what the IAAF believed would be a more comprehensive study'.[30]

But Conte's claim that the authorities will never do retrospective testing is not quite accurate: in 2013, the IAAF announced that after

---

30 When I asked the IAAF about this, I was told: 'The IAAF is working on another prevalence study based on the analytical data collected at the IAAF World Champs in Daegu 2011 and in Moscow 2013. The IAAF is the only sports federation to have conducted such a prevalence study.'

testing 100 samples from the Paris world championships in 2003, five medallists had been caught. 'We have an eight-year statute of limitations on anti-doping, so seven years past the event is really when you want to test, using the most up-to-date equipment,' Davies told the BBC. 'The message we're trying to give out is: "Don't even think about it, because even six or seven years down the road, something you think you got away with you won't."' In the new WADA code, introduced in 2015, the statute of limitations has been increased to ten years.

The anti-doping fight has been stepped up considerably since Conte was up to his tricks with Jones, Montgomery and the rest. Back then it was easy to beat the system, mainly because there wasn't really a system. WADA was only established in 1999, and it was a couple more years before it became operational; the national agencies followed.

Now, for the top athletes at least, there is the 'whereabouts' programme of out-of-competition testing – if not by the athlete's own national anti-doping agency then by the international governing body. 'Well, even that's possible to circumvent,' Conte says. 'Here's the big loophole. You're allowed two missed tests in any eighteen-month period, right?' Three missed tests constitutes an anti-doping offence. 'So, for whereabouts, you say you'll be at training centre X, then go instead to training centre Y. They miss you: strike one.'

True, though the testers could return the next day, and the day after that, and if they miss you each time, that's three strikes, which means a doping offence. Conte counters that the athlete could have used the fast-acting, quick-clearing testosterone cream on day one, and have no concerns.

State-sponsored doping? Conte's allegation is extraordinary, but the fact of what he alleges is not, of course, unprecedented. The programmes in East Germany and the Soviet Union in the 1970s and '80s are well known, but there must be other countries in which sporting authorities covered up positives, or turned a blind eye, or actively helped their athletes to pass tests. The USA stand accused of doing exactly that before the 1984 Olympic Games.

What does 'sponsored' mean, exactly? I am not too sure. It's not quite state-organised, or state-sanctioned. But it suggests something more than turning a blind eye.

In Jamaica, the national anti-doping agency, JADCO, did find positive tests almost from the moment they came into being in 2008. There was a steady stream, in fact, mainly for relatively minor offences, including Yohan Blake and the others in 2009. Then, at the 2011 national championships, they caught Steve Mullings for a second time, which meant a life ban.

Mullings had been a Champs star – a contemporary of Asafa Powell but considerably better as a teenager – who lived and trained in the US with Tyson Gay and his coach, Lance Brauman. He was a member of the Jamaican team at the world championships in Berlin, part of the quartet that, with Bolt, Powell and Michael Frater, won gold in the 4x100 metres relay. He then struggled with injuries but in 2011 made a dramatic improvement, running 9.80 seconds in Eugene, Oregon, in early June. Previously his best was 10.03, but in 2011 he beat 10 seconds on no fewer than seven occasions. He was twenty-eight.

At the Jamaican national championships a few weeks after his 9.80-run in Eugene, he tested positive for furosemide, a diuretic suspected of being used as a masking agent. It was his second positive, after failing a test for testosterone in 2004 – also at the Jamaican national championships. News of his latest positive broke just days before the 2011 world championships in Daegu.

I spoke to Mullings thinking that, with nothing to lose, he would offer some insight into the world of athletics and doping. But he is more interested in clearing his name and remains furious with JADCO, who, he says, made a number of mistakes in his case, and showed a reluctance – suspicious, he claims – to allow him to submit to a DNA test. Despite all the apparent evidence against him, and the suspicion generated by his sudden improvement in 2011, Mullings could actually have a point, certainly in the case of his first positive test in 2004. On that occasion, he was tested twice, after the 100 and the 200 metres: only the 100 metres sample came back positive.

Another of Mullings's gripes is his claim that by 2011, a new orthodoxy existed in Jamaica. He says that US-based athletes, once the golden boys and girls, were now discriminated against. 'It's now not Jamaica versus the world; it's Jamaican athletes who train in Jamaica against those who train in the US,' he tells me. 'It wasn't a surprise to me when I tested positive. I had a feeling they were going to get me; I told Nickel Ashmeade [his Jamaican training partner] that.' He adds that there was resentment when he took a Jamaican-based athlete's place in the national team for major championships. 'The 200 metres was OK, but in 2011, when I got one of the spots in the 100 metres, they didn't want me taking that.'

When he was positive a second time, he says he had been tested in the US numerous times, including after his 9.80 run in Eugene. 'Why would I wait till I go to Jamaica to take some drug-blocker? You telling me the US [drug-testing] system isn't good, but the Jamaican system is the best?'

Mullings maintains he was clean and that he avoided drugs. 'I wanted to go to the Trevor Graham group and people said, "Man, they all take drugs over there." You go to the Brauman group and the only thing Coach Brauman recommends is coaching, protein and amino acids. That's it. I never had drugs around me, never, ever.' He says he was careful with supplements, sticking to 'vitamins'. 'The IAAF makes it clear you're responsible for what's in your body, so you have to have supplements tested.'

Besides, he says, drugs don't make you faster; it's all about recovery. 'Some athletes recover like they're superhuman. Everyone wants to recover; they want to have doctors who know what they're doing, who give you legal stuff to help you recover.'

His training partner and friend Tyson Gay told him: 'When you run a 9-second 100 metres or 19-second 200 metres your body is gonna be ripped up. I don't know how these people recover.'

'It's true,' Mullings continues. 'When I ran 9.80, my body was ripped up. I remember when Tyson ran 19.5, we were in New York, and he fell off the chair. In 2009, in a restaurant, he falls off the chair because he was so ripped up. But I've seen people run these times and walk away like nothing happened.'

When he tested positive a second time, Mullings says he was offered a deal by the Jamaica Athletic Administrative Association. 'They had a doctor contact me wanting me to confess. They said they could give me six months if I confessed. But how could I confess to something I didn't do?'

Instead, having taken a lie detector test (which he passed) and requested a DNA test, he appealed to the Court of Arbitration for Sport in Lausanne. 'No guilty man asks for a DNA test,' he says. 'Jamaica took six weeks to give them the paperwork, then wrote them a letter saying I shouldn't get a DNA test because no one else has had one, and if everyone asks for one, we can't afford it.'

Mullings is convinced dark forces were out to get him, 'to get me off the team' for Daegu so that his place could be filled by a Jamaica-based athlete instead. Ultimately, he says, 'I wasn't big enough. If you don't have money, you don't get no justice.'

So if he was set up, by whom? 'I don't really want to call anyone's name out,' he says. 'They know themselves. For my hearing, they said, "You have to come to Jamaica." I know Jamaica; people will tell you about Jamaica. If people want to get rid of you fast they give you a ticket to Jamaica. I feared for my life, but I went there. Then it took them ten minutes to give me a lifetime ban.'

I also wanted to speak to Raymond Stewart. His lifetime ban was based on Heredia's testimony, and money transfers that Heredia said were for steroids and EPO.

In the USADA arbitration hearing against Stewart, it was claimed that he acquired drugs for his wife, Beverly McDonald – a fellow Jamaican, also an athlete – and that he sent her to be blood-tested by Heredia in Mexico prior to the 2004 Olympic trials. McDonald was a member of the Jamaican 4x100 metres relay teams that won silver in Sydney in 2000 and a memorable gold in Athens in 2004; she was also a bronze medallist in the individual 200 metres in Sydney.

Stewart lives in Texas and works for a life assurance company. He doesn't return to Jamaica often. 'When I go I might go to the north coast [the opposite side to Kingston], in and out. My mum is still there, my dad passed away a while back, and I have one brother still there.'

But more than his doping ban, I wanted to speak to Stewart about the young coach who recruited him in the 1970s: Glen Mills. Stewart recalls interest from other schools – Jamaica College, Calabar. 'But I wasn't into all-boys stuff.' He also wanted a couple of friends to go with him, and Mills was willing to accommodate them.

Stewart says that Mills was 'more like a mentor, a dad'. He would only have been in his mid-thirties at the time, but as Stewart says, father figures were in short supply. 'You notice in Jamaica there are not too many kids around with a dad that can guide them on the right track. I have to admit I learned a lot from Mills discipline-wise. It helped when I left Camperdown and moved over to the States here. He was good at teaching me not to get too distracted; to take advantage of my scholarship and not waste it.'

Mills was not, says Stewart, a great technician – at least not when he worked with him. Before he went to Camperdown, Stewart worked with another coach who 'had me doing high knees, high knees, high knees, every day. I said, "Hey, man, when am I going to actually run?" It was all technique. That played a big role in how I ended up as a sprinter.' At Camperdown, 'Mills polished what I already had.'

Perhaps Mills also learned from Stewart, who was clearly a phenomenal talent. After Stewart left school and went to college in the US, their paths kept crossing when Stewart was selected for the national team. 'Mills was always travelling with the national team – he was one of the coaches on every national team I was on.' Stewart bursts out laughing. 'In Jamaica, nothing changes; every championship they think those are the only guys who can get the job done.'

You get the impression, talking to Stewart, that his respect for Mills is limited. When I ask him if he is surprised at what his old coach has achieved, that seems to be an overstatement. 'His success comes through not just Bolt, right,' Stewart says. 'If I hadn't come through track and field back then, there wouldn't be no Glen Mills.

'One of the reasons for him to be where he's at right now, it's my name that kept him floating. He will not admit that to a lot of people.' Not that Stewart bears a grudge. He says he and Mills are no longer in contact, but if he spoke to him now he'd say: 'Hey, great job, big respect to you and all that stuff.'

Stewart continues: 'He's at the point right now where he's got the fastest man in the world and he's producing a few behind him as well, so he's learned the game. He can actually keep continuing to repeat.' Like a production line at a factory? 'Right. That's what they used to call Camperdown: the sprint factory.'

On the case against him, Stewart can talk and talk. He feels he was stitched up by the US authorities, that it was political, anti-Jamaican ('They tend to go after foreigners; their own people got a slap on the wrist') and that in any case, the charges against him were false. 'I don't care about track and field any more. It has nothing to offer me, not a damn thing. Those guys can kiss my ass. I'm outta here.' Even if the accusations were true, Stewart says he was harshly treated. 'They paint you as if you blew up the Twin Towers!'

Then there's Heredia, his former friend. 'Man, that kid . . . that guy lies so much people just don't understand.' He can't believe that it was Heredia's testimony that led to his punishment. 'They take the guy who is a drug dealer, make him make phone calls, set people up on the phone.' Stewart claims – improbably, I feel – that when he was recorded asking Heredia questions about drugs, he was simply curious.

'If a guy is picking your brains, asking you questions, is there a crime to that? Does it mean I'm going to do what you tell me to do?'

Stewart is far from stupid ('Some people want to achieve something in life, and others think they want it' is one of several profound observations), and his perspective on the current state of Jamaican athletics is fascinating. He has watched from afar as they have risen to the top by staying at home – something that was never an option for him, because he wanted to gain an education, to earn money and have 'a better life'.

'We were drinking water out of a little pond,' he says. 'Now they have companies going in there – companies are going down, sponsoring athletes. Nutrition companies. These guys have nutrition – we didn't even know where the next meal was coming from.'

There are clearly advantages to the new orthodoxy. It has worked spectacularly for Bolt, Fraser-Pryce, Blake, Powell and others. But it isn't all milk and honey. Stewart thinks there are dangers in the new system, where every kid thinks they can be Bolt or Blake when, clearly, they can't. 'A lot of kids who are there can come here [to the US] and further their education and still perform on the track, but the coaches in Jamaica are telling them, "Don't go, stay home." But if they don't do anything within another two, three years their career goes sour; they go to the countryside where no one talks about them, you know what I mean?'

The coaches are to blame, he says. Not Mills and Stephen Francis, but those who aspire to be Mills or Francis. 'They figure, "OK, I've got a superstar, I can become the next Glen Mills coaching this guy." The kid is brainwashed and the coach doesn't think about what's best for the kid.

'They don't let him go and do something for himself, you know what I mean? That's the problem plaguing Jamaica now.'

15

THE TESTER

Everybody's against drugs, in every country, until one
of their heroes tests positive.
Paul Wright

'I put it this way,' Paul Wright tells me. 'In the medical profession you have doctors who sign sick leave for people who are not sick. You have bad doctors. And lawyers. And journalists! You have people who take money from housing sales and don't turn it over. You have people who murder children. You have people who behead women.

'But in athletics,' he adds, 'no bad people in athletics. Everybody in athletics is related to Pope Francis!'

Just as people asked questions about the Jamaican athletes in Beijing and Berlin, so questions were asked about the competence of the Jamaican sports authorities, the athletics federation and, in particular, the national anti-doping agency.

The Jamaican anti-doping agency? It conjured up images of a hut on a beach with the testers lying in hammocks smoking ganja, saying, 'Yeah, man.' A patronising stereotype? Of course. But it was reinforced by Victor Conte, who told me of one story that reached him. 'I heard that Herb Elliott, the guy in charge of Jamaican anti-doping, was in Beijing chest-bumping the Jamaican athletes in the mixed zone!' So not just too laid-back, as the stereotype has it, but too close, too chummy, to the athletes, and in a country that is no stranger to corruption. It didn't exactly inspire confidence.

In fact, when the Jamaica Anti-Doping Commission (JADCO) was set up in 2008, the island did have one person who had been at the vanguard of drug-testing in sport.

Dr Paul Wright's interest in the subject went all the way back to the 1970s. But the sport was different then, and so were the drugs. As a student at the University of the West Indies in Kingston, Wright was a footballer, a goalkeeper. He finished his medical studies at the Royal Free Hospital in London, and on returning to Jamaica in 1976 was asked by his old coach to go with the national youth team to a tournament in Puerto Rico. They needed a doctor, so off went Wright, fresh out of medical school and not even fully qualified yet, as the official team physician.

These days Wright is a large, white-bearded, avuncular fellow who, in his cluttered office at the Nuttall Hospital in central Kingston, keeps half an eye on the small TV sitting on top of a filing cabinet, showing a football match involving Chelsea. His desk is covered in papers and other surfaces with trophies – he owns two racehorses. The phone rings incessantly – each time it's the media seeking comment on the cases involving Asafa Powell, Sherone Simpson and Veronica Campbell-Brown. Wright refuses each request. Yet he seems happy to sit chatting to me about the same subject.

'Where were we?' he says, returning his phone to the desk after the latest call. The late 1970s, I say – Puerto Rico. 'Yes! So I went as team physician – and realised that I knew absolutely nothing about sports medicine.'

It was a subject that interested him, so he did some research, discovering 'a thing called the American Academy of Orthopaedic Surgeons in Sports Medicine. And that's what I always wanted to do – orthopaedics.' He got in touch with this organisation and was invited to Virginia to a conference, where he learned that there was also an American College of Sports Medicine. 'So I promptly joined. They had courses, team physician courses, the works. So I did those things. As I did more and more, I realised, um, there's drugs here.'

With his growing experience – including a two-month stint studying sports medicine at Leipzig University in East Germany – Wright became the doctor to the Jamaican national football team. The Confederation of North, Central American and Caribbean Association Football (CONCACAF) then made him vice president of their medical committee. He also chaired the medical committee of the Caribbean Football Union. 'And there was no drug testing going on,' he says.

He felt that a few of the players were using drugs. Not performance-enhancing ones, but the drug that is as common as coffee in Jamaica: marijuana, or ganja. In other words, it wasn't performance-enhancing drugs that concerned Wright, but performance-inhibiting ones.

He contacted a company in the States that manufactured a kit that screened for three substances: amphetamines, cocaine and marijuana. 'Just a drop of urine would tell you if they were positive,' Wright says. 'I bought a set of kits with my own money and told them I was going to start this programme of drug-testing.' There was only one laboratory in Kingston equipped to test the urine: the police forensic lab. 'I told them I had absolutely no money. They said they couldn't do it for free, would I get sponsorship?'

Wright approached Carreras, the cigarette company who backed Dennis Johnson's athletics roadshow, and they said yes. Now Wright was up and running: a one-man WADA. It was the early 1980s, when the concept of drugs in sport was a vague, barely acknowledged scourge. Next, the Caribbean Football Union asked him to test all the islands' teams.

But as Wright says, his concern wasn't cheating. He was more worried about the 'corner culture' that existed in Jamaica. He explains: 'In a community, the group would gather under a streetlight. And the

kingpins were people that sell drugs, the murderers, the hit men and so on. And the kids would be drawn to these things, because these are really big guys. In those days the club football was communities versus communities. I believed that if I could get the community to have an interest in the young men who play for the team, not to use cocaine and marijuana, I would be winning a . . . a bigger picture: keeping the drugs out of the hands of the vulnerable kids, the marginalised kids in the community.'

One Sunday morning, Wright 'packed my little case and drove to Alligator Pond, out in Manchester' – a fishing village on the south-western coast of the island, where the Jamaican football team were training. He told the manager he was there to drug-test the whole team. The manager was 'uncomfortable' with this, 'but I stood my ground', says Wright, 'because I was in charge of the medical committee. So I tested the whole team and six people failed the test.' There wasn't a punishment, as such. For a first offence the player had to register in an anti-drug programme. A second offence meant they had to actually join the programme. 'But the third time,' says Wright, 'you were gone.'

This was the agreed protocol. But there was a problem: a severe backlog at the forensic lab in Kingston. It meant a six-month delay in confirming those six positives, by which time the football team was at a training camp in Brazil. This is where it got complicated, because the powers-that-be, a sponsor in particular, didn't want six of the players pulling out of the camp to check into drug rehab. Again Wright tried to stand his ground, but this time he met his match. 'I was fired publicly on television,' he says. The tests were ridiculed. 'They said, "These people have never used drugs in their life!"' Excuses included that 'One of them had drunk ganja tea which his grandmother gave him because he had fever.' Following Wright's dismissal, it was announced that a new drug-testing programme would start in two weeks. 'It never restarted and they had no intention of doing that,' he says.

He turned his attention to racehorses. Or rather the jockeys. Again he was looking for the holy herb, marijuana. 'I selected them randomly. Same rules: fail one test, you register; fail two, you join the programme; fail three times, you're out.

'The number one and number two jockeys tested positive.' Wright rolls his eyes. It was déjà vu. 'Big uproar! They have never used drugs in their life; I am the wickedest person that has ever lived; I must have done something to the urine; they don't know what I did to the urine when they leave it with me . . . and I was fired, boom!'

That wasn't the end of Wright's interest or involvement in sport. He is a Wolmer's old boy (like Stephen Francis) and has always helped out with the school's sports teams, including the athletics team. Unusually for a drug-tester, his is a prominent voice in Jamaican sport: he writes a regular column for *Sport Globe*, a weekly paper. It was here, after Champs, that he criticised Calabar for allowing Javon Francis to run the 200 metres a couple of hours after his record-breaking 400 metres. His verdict? 'Child abuse!'

Wright has also worked at the highest level, acting as doctor to Jamaican athletics teams in international competition. In 1998 he was doctor to the Americas team at the IAAF World Cup – an intercontinental championships now known as the IAAF Continental

Cup – in Johannesburg, South Africa. The experience gave him a revealing insight into the mindset of the elite athlete – or at least some of them.

Looking after the Americas team was a big responsibility, though it did not include the USA, who had their own team. 'I said I would be doctor on one condition – that the team has to go to similar elevation for three weeks before the games,' Wright says. Johannesburg is at 5,700-feet altitude. 'They never heard of this, but they agreed. So we went.' They stayed in a 'kind of safari place' for three weeks, during which time one of the Canadian athletes strained his hamstring. A replacement was called up: Obadele Thompson, the 100 and 200 metres specialist from Barbados. But when Thompson got there, he was exhausted. He had travelled to South Africa straight from Moscow, where he finished second in the IAAF Grand Prix final in 10.11 seconds. Wright met him at the airport on the Wednesday evening and could see how tired he was, which was a problem. His race was just forty-eight hours later. 'He was dead,' says Wright, 'so at dinner, everyone's there, and I say, "When you go upstairs, take this, right?" and I gave him a blue tablet.

'Next morning he comes down the stairs, I'm at the back of the line for breakfast. He says, "Dr Wright!" and jumps on my back. "What is wrong with you?" I say.

' "What did you do?" he says. "I have never felt this good in my life! Doc, I cannot wait to race!" '

When it came to the 100 metres, Thompson ran 9.87 seconds, a personal best, to win. Wright was in his hotel room that night. There was a knock at the door and he opened it to another athlete. 'Doctor, could I have a blue pill, please?' That was only the start. 'Everybody's coming for a blue pill!' Wright says. 'These people believed I drugged the guy – they thought I was doping him!'

What was the pill, then? 'Halcion,' says Wright. 'He needed to sleep. That is all this guy needed. I gave him two five-milligram halcion pills. He slept the whole night and he was a new man.' Halcion contains benzodiazepines, also found in valium. It's a relaxant and sedative with no performance-enhancing effects (if anything, the opposite).

'I tell people the best aphrodisiac in life is sleep, you know?' says Wright. Some remained convinced, however, that he had doped Thompson. Particularly, Wright adds, because 'Obadele never ran that fast again.'[31]

A year later, the Jamaican team was rocked on the eve of the world athletics championships in Seville when Merlene Ottey, thirty-nine years old but hoping to compete in her sixth Olympic Games in Sydney, tested positive for nandrolone after a meeting in Lucerne. Ottey was one of a spate of positives for this steroid at the time, along with fellow sprinters Linford Christie, Dennis Mitchell, Javier Sotomayor of Cuba and European 200 metres champion Dougie Walker, as well as dozens of footballers and tennis players. Ottey was outraged. 'I have lived my personal and athletic life with the utmost honesty and integrity,' she said. She denied ever using a banned substance.

Jamaica leapt to her defence. Herb Elliott, the chest-bumping doctor in Beijing who would later be at the helm of JADCO, described it as 'a travesty of justice'. Elliott's main gripe was that Ottey's name had been made public before her B sample had been tested. But he seemed in no doubt as to her innocence. 'This is a shock for all of us,' he said. 'I have known her since she was seven. I have never known her to be on any substance.'

Reading press reports from this time, it seemed that there was only one prominent Jamaican who was prepared to believe the worst. 'We've always held Merlene as an icon, a drug-free track queen,' said Dr Paul Wright. 'Now that's all crumbled to dust.'[32]

*

---

31 Obadele Thompson later married Marion Jones.

32 Ottey was initially cleared of a doping offence by the JAAA, though the IAAF appealed that decision. Eventually she was exonerated. The Court of Arbitration for Sport ruled that the retesting of her sample was not completed in time.

Before the 2008 Olympic Games, there was an ultimatum from the World Anti-Doping Agency. Jamaica was a signatory to the WADA code, introduced in 2004, but had done little to implement it. 'WADA told them, "If you don't implement the thing, nobody is going to the Olympics",' Wright recalls. 'So within two weeks the law was drafted and pushed through parliament. One parliamentarian, Ronald Thwaites, got up and said, "How am I asked today to write something into law that I haven't read? This is crazy!" The prime minister gets up and says, "We know what's good for you – sign it, because we're going to the Olympics."'

JADCO came into existence later that year.[33] They needed people with experience in drug-testing, and there was one obvious candidate: Dr Paul Wright. Despite having been fired twice from previous drug-testing roles, he was, like the 'eight or nine' other testers, employed on a freelance basis, paid a modest day rate (around £55, he says) to conduct tests on behalf of JADCO.

Among the new organisation's responsibilities was to run a 'whereabouts' programme. This meant that athletes had to nominate a daily one-hour window when they would be available for testing. They had to submit this information three months in advance, though changes were allowed if the athlete informed the agency. A lot of athletes nominate their home as the place and early in the morning as the time. Wright says that he tended to turn up early. 'If the athlete said 7–8 a.m. and I turned up at 5.30, it created panic. I thought, This is very suspicious. They would refuse to pass urine until seven o'clock.'

I am not sure that it is necessarily suspicious to react with alarm if somebody appears at your home at 5.30 a.m. But Wright says it would

---

33 Not only did Jamaica not have its own agency, it had also opted out of the WADA-approved Caribbean Regional Anti-Doping Organisation (RADO). RADO's head, Dr Adrian Lorde of Barbados, when asked if testing was sufficient in Jamaica, said: 'I don't get that impression. I would like to think they do that testing there but I really don't know . . . We really don't know what is going on in Jamaica.'

be the same in the evening: he thought one or two athletes' panic was due to the fact that he appeared at all. 'Sometimes they would switch to nine o'clock at night and I would turn up. One athlete couldn't believe that I would really come at nine o'clock at night. I said, "But you put nine on the programme." "Yes, but I never knew you would really come!"' Wright shakes his head. 'They would be extremely angry if I came, even though I would point out to them that "You said that this is the time I could come."

'So I was an outcast, really. They just didn't like me.'

Wright says he tried hard in his testing role with JADCO, at least initially, not to create an 'us and them' mentality. He didn't want to be seen by the athletes as the enemy – and besides, why on earth would he be? Surely a clean athlete would regard him as a friend. In a spirit of solidarity, he tried to help with advice. When he turned up to test some of the MVP athletes, he noticed that during training, their drinking bottles, each with the athlete's name on it, would be left on a shelf out of sight of the athletes and coaches. 'You can't leave these unattended,' he told the club, 'because these are the biggest sprinters in the world, and there are people can watch them train. What if it suits somebody to come and put something in the bottle?'

Wright was enterprising and came up with a novel solution for testing for EPO. To do that, he had to send the urine overseas, to a lab with testing equipment for the blood-boosting drug, but the problem came with storing the urine at a cold enough temperature. 'I would take the urine to the local ice cream factory, pack it in dry ice and ship it to the lab,' he says. 'I found ways to do these things.'

Another hurdle he had to overcome was an unexpected one – at least to me. One of WADA's rules is that the tester must observe the athlete giving the sample: in other words, watch him pee (for obvious reasons, female testers collect samples from female athletes). This is to prevent any sabotage or swapping of samples – it is not unknown for athletes to have bulbs or condoms of 'clean' urine hidden on (or even in) their person. (An apocryphal tale has a Belgian cyclist being informed that he hadn't tested positive but that his sample indicated he was pregnant. He had used his wife's urine.)

'Some people thought I was helping but the athletes got the impression that, number one, I was a pervert,' says Wright. 'That I just wanted to look at men's penises, that was my biggest aim in life, I got a sexual kick out of that.'

Really? 'Yeah! I was a batty man, I was a pervert. They would say all these things but it don't bother me.'

Homophobia in Jamaica seems deeply ingrained, though I was told that virulent anti-gay attitudes are a fairly recent phenomenon. Dancehall music, which exploded in the early 1990s, has contributed to it. 'It's like boom bye bye/Inna batty boy head,' sang Buju Banton, urging that gay men be shot in the head. Casual homophobia can be found in mainstream media too. In a 2006 *Jamaica Observer* article about a male prostitute, the (female) reporter asserted: 'We are led to believe that people are born with gay tendencies . . . the subject will continue to aggravate many heterosexuals who think that it is downright nasty. And to be labelled as a "b . . . [batty] man" while in the wrong crowd may almost certainly lead to death.'

There are various theories about the roots of such attitudes, from the hold of religion to perceptions of masculinity. But any attempts to deconstruct homophobia would not have got Dr Wright very far with athletes reluctant to pee in front of him. 'They say that when they're tested abroad they turn their back and the guy doesn't stay and watch them pee,' Wright says. 'I say, "No, no, no, no. I have to see where that urine comes from."

'And they say, "Boss, you must be a pervert. All those children that you say are yours, they really yours?"'

How does he respond to that? 'I laugh. I laugh, because in Jamaica if you get upset it's because it's true.'

Although he encountered some obstacles, Wright does not subscribe to the view that the only explanation can be that Jamaica's athletes are all part of a sophisticated, systematic doping programme. He is neither a cynic nor a conspiracy theorist. But that doesn't mean he assumes they are all clean. That would be foolish, he says, as he reels off his list of doctors, lawyers and, yes, journalists, who give their colleagues a bad name. Whereas 'everyone in athletics is related to Pope Francis!' 'You got to be kidding me,' he adds.

Wright recognises the responsibility of Jamaicans themselves to have an anti-doping programme that the rest of the world believes in and trusts. 'Dick Pound [the former WADA president] has said, publicly, that we make sure that when our athletes leave Jamaica they are drug-free.' In other words, Pound has alleged that the athletes are screened before they leave the island, to ensure they pass drugs tests when they compete abroad. 'He has said it,' Wright continues. 'And the chairman of JADCO, Herb Elliott, called him a racist. And I wrote to him, I said, "You can't call the man a racist, because we're not doing the job, Herb." If we don't do the job, these people are going to say these things. All we have to do is do the job. Do the job. We have to have people who understand drug testing and who cannot be bought and don't worry about doing this for Jamaica – you're not doing it for Jamaica, you're doing it for track and field.'

A claim that has often been made is that if a big-name athlete tested positive in Jamaica, they would be ostracised, banished from the island. Glen Mills said as much in 2008. He stated that Jamaicans were proud of their clean record: 'It is something that we guard dearly, and it is something that [if an athlete tested positive] the country would turn on you. They would turn on you so strong. It's something they would never forgive. And athletes are aware of that and try to walk the tightrope.'

Does this claim stand up to scrutiny? I am not sure. When Yohan Blake and the other four athletes tested positive at the national championships, the athletes were not ostracised.

Wright dismisses the idea that Jamaica would turn on a drugs cheat with a wave of his hand. He knows that in the event of a positive test, the anger is often directed not at the athlete, but at the testers. There can be a sinister dimension to this, he claims. 'People test positive, right? Big people test positive. The phone rings. "I am such and such" – a big person – "how can we help?"'

Wright's response: 'We? We?! You're on your own, boss.'

He continues: 'I knew that the moment a prominent athlete tests positive – they coming for me. They're not coming for the athlete.'

He has first-hand experience of this? 'Yeah, twice.' The parallels with his experiences with football and horse racing are uncanny. Wearily he trots out the old lines: 'I was the one who put something in the urine; I was the one who did all these things; I was the one who gave them the drugs.'

In his years as a drug-tester Wright says he has received threatening phone calls, and worse. On one occasion he returned home, entered the living room, turned on the light switch – and nothing happened. 'They broke into my house and stole one light bulb. One light bulb.' It's a popular tactic of intimidation, he says. 'I got the message. I got the message.'

It isn't that people are against drug-testing, he adds. On the contrary: everybody with a stake in sport – fans, media, politicians, athletes, coaches – is anti-drugs and firmly in favour of robust testing. It isn't testing that people object to. It's positive tests. This is not unique to Jamaica.

As Wright puts it, 'Everybody's against drugs, in every country, until one of their heroes tests positive.'

16

GENES AND YAMS

Slavery runs through Jamaican life today like the black line in a lobster.
Ian Thomson, *The Dead Yard*

If the doubting world had questions about the Jamaicans' sprinting domination, the answers, believed Professor Errol Morrison, could be found in Jamaica: in the place, the people, and what was on their dinner plates.

Morrison is an eminent scientist, a former president of UTech and an expert on diabetes, which is a major health problem in Jamaica.[34] His sunny disposition belies his work in this field. I meet him at his clinic in the Diabetes Centre just off Old Hope Road in New Kingston; he smiles as I enter and doesn't stop smiling the whole time I am there. If his enthusiasm could be bottled and sold, it would be potent stuff.

Perhaps that is because what we are talking about is, for Morrison, an interesting sideline rather than the life-or-death stuff of his daily

---

34 Especially, it seems, among former athletes; of the island's retired Olympians, it has been estimated that around 30 per cent have type 2 diabetes. A high proportion of fast-twitch glycolytic fibres and a decreased number of slow-twitch oxidative fibres are associated with type 2 diabetes.

work. Nevertheless, the subject – why does Jamaica produce so many good sprinters – has appealed to his curiosity since a journalist, Patrick Cooper, approached him in the early 2000s with his theory about why people of West African descent seemed to be faster than non-West Africans. Cooper's research, over many years, had led him to the conclusion that the sickle cell trait – common in those of West African origin, where it offers protection against malaria – produced 'physiological adjustments' and 'compensatory mechanisms', including a higher proportion of fast-twitch muscle fibres.

Cooper turned his thesis into a book, *Black Superman*, published in 2003. Together, he and Morrison then contributed a paper expanding on some of these ideas for the *West Indian Medical Journal* in 2006. Cooper was battling cancer at the time: he died in 2009.

If it is the case that those with the sickle cell trait do have a higher proportion of fast-twitch muscles (and lower haemoglobin, making them less well suited to endurance events), the reasons why have proved elusive. But Morrison became more interested in the subject, especially when another eminent scientist, Professor Yannis Pitsiladis, began visiting Jamaica.

Pitsiladis first came around the same time as Morrison and Cooper's paper was published. Morrison was not the only one who welcomed him. Vilma Charlton, the Olympic sprinter turned academic, had wondered about the existence of a 'sprint gene'. She felt that Pitsiladis, of the biomedical and life sciences faculty at the University of Glasgow, could be just the man to identify it. 'We got so excited,' she says. 'We thought, Now we can find the answer!'

Dennis Johnson also welcomed Pitsiladis; they got on like a house on fire, and in 2011, Pitsiladis, Johnson and another Jamaican sprinter-turned-academic, Anthony Davis, published a paper together, 'The Science of Speed: Determinants of Performance in the 100m Sprint'. This appeared in the *International Journal of Sports Science & Coaching*.

I first met Pitsiladis when he was about to embark on his Jamaican odyssey. He had spent years studying the world's best endurance

runners in Ethiopia and Kenya from his office in the West End of
Glasgow, where he ran the International Centre for East African
Running Science (ICEARS). It was March 2007, and Pitsiladis told
me that he was preparing to expand his research, turning his attention
to sprinters. Even then, a year before Beijing, Jamaica was the obvious
place to go.

Pitsiladis, like Morrison, was a bundle of energy: fast-talking, fidgety
and restless. Of Greek origin but with a gentle South African accent,
he quickly – like Dennis Johnson – turned the tables, firing questions
at me. 'Every sprinter who has run 100 metres in under 10 seconds is
black,' he said. (Since then, one white man, Christophe Lemaitre, has
accomplished this feat.) 'Why do you think that is?'

This was a difficult question to answer. The problem is that most
answers run the risk of sounding, well, racist. Which was a problem
acknowledged by Cooper, who wrote in *Black Superman* that the debate
(or non-debate) around the subject was 'shaped by two powerful and
related fears: those of racial biology and "the dark history of eugenics" '.
David Epstein, in his book *The Sports Gene*, spoke to scientists who
said they had researched the subject, and thought they could make
a contribution to the (non-)debate, but chose not to. Their reticence,
thought Epstein, stemmed from an essentially irrational idea: that 'any
suggestion of a physical advantage among a group of people could
be equated to a corresponding lack of intellect'. It was, he said, 'as if
athleticism and intelligence were on some kind of biological teeter-
totter'.

Which is balderdash. In fact, it is an idea that developed in the US
only as black athletes began to excel at sport. 'The idea that athleticism
was suddenly inversely proportional to intellect was never a cause of
bigotry,' said Epstein, 'but rather a result of it.'

Yet the idea that black people are athletically superior has taken a
firm hold, to the point where now there is an assumption that a white
man cannot win the Olympic 100 metres. The last one was Allan Wells
in 1980: he was also the last white man to make the final.

On one of his visits to Jamaica, Pitsiladis gave a lecture entitled 'White Men Can't Run' (subtitle: 'Where's the Scientific Evidence?'). In this, and in his paper with Johnson and Davis, he identified a problem that follows from the idea that black athletes have a genetic advantage. The stereotype might lead to a self-fulfilling prophecy. Black athletes believe they can win, white athletes believe they cannot and therefore exclude themselves, thereby reinforcing the stereotype 'to the extent that the unsubstantiated idea of the biological superiority of the African or "black" athlete in these athletic events becomes dogma'.

Unsubstantiated it may be, but the perceived superiority of black athletes in sprint (and endurance) running events remains, as Epstein's reluctant scientists seemed to confirm, a sensitive issue. And one that I, being quizzed by Pitsiladis in his office in Glasgow, felt ill-equipped to answer. He eventually broke the silence: 'You are thinking,' he said, 'that the black person has some kind of advantage over the white person?'

I nodded. 'Hmmm,' he said. 'I may disagree. I would say that you should speak to a sociologist. I could say that it has nothing to do with biology.'

Almost eight years after meeting Pitsiladis in Glasgow, I visit him in Eastbourne: in 2014, he became Professor of Sport and Exercise Science at the University of Brighton, taking with him the world's largest DNA 'biobank' from world-class athletes (containing genetic material from over 1,000 individuals).

He is more interested in Jamaican sprinting and East African endurance running than ever. When we meet, he has just launched a project to break two hours for the marathon (the world record is 2.02.57). Once he has overseen that, with an as-yet-unidentified (clean) athlete supported by experts in every imaginable field, he wants to set a similarly ambitious target for the 100 metres – but more on that later.

Pitsiladis had many years' experience of research in Africa before he travelled to the Caribbean, but he found Jamaica a far more challenging place to work. 'Ten times more difficult,' he tells me. There was a huge amount of resistance and suspicion, and not just in the groups of athletes but among the wider population too. He was keen to collect genetic material from the Maroons – the descendants of escaped slaves renowned for their resilience and toughness, who still live in isolated hilltop villages in Trelawny – and other communities. But there was, from some, fierce opposition, hostility and myriad rumours about his real purpose. A story spread in one community that with his swabs he was infecting people with HIV.

Then there was Stephen Francis, who 'didn't want us walking round swabbing people'. Pitsiladis understood that. 'It's a pain in the butt having anyone hanging around, and what could we give back?' But he believed he did have something he could offer Francis: sports science support. He envisaged setting up an institute of sport in Jamaica with his own lab (an idea he hasn't given up on completely, and thinks could happen once the sub-two-hour marathon project is completed).

Then Pitsiladis met Dennis Johnson. 'A fantastic guy, we got on so well,' he enthuses. 'An evidence guy, and the person who is closest to the truth of the Jamaican sprinting phenomenon.' Johnson helped prise open the door to Francis's MVP club. These days, Pitsiladis and Francis are firm friends (Pitsiladis mentions a recent visit to a Kingston nightclub in the company of Francis, who I struggle to imagine in a club).

Then, through Anthony Davis, a Jamaican who came to study under Pitsiladis in Glasgow, Pitsiladis gained an introduction to Glen Mills's Racers Track Club. For reasons of medical confidentiality, he cannot say whose DNA he has collected. If he could, it might be quicker to say which top sprinters' DNA he has *not* studied.

Pitsiladis began his project in Jamaica at just the right time, months before the Beijing gold rush. He began to make regular visits, funding his research with help from journalists eager to learn about his work, and on one occasion thanks to the owner of his local curry house, whose son wanted to accompany him and meet Usain Bolt. It has afforded him a remarkable view inside the Jamaican sprint factory.

For Pitsiladis, it was never all about genetics, or finding a particular gene. As he explains, 'Genetics is one of the tools I use, and allows me to get evidence.' With his own eyes, and through talking to Johnson, Vilma Charlton, Mills, Francis, and many others, he gathered more evidence. He was interested in identifying all the different pieces that contributed to Jamaican success. He went to Champs, obviously. He visited Maroon communities. He collected biological material. When he came to study the athletes, he was interested in – but not obsessed by – the doping question. A keen athlete himself, he watched training sessions and studied Francis and Mills, noting that they had different approaches and methods. 'And they both work,' he tells me now. 'Which tells you they're probably both wrong.

'When I say wrong,' he clarifies, 'it's probably wrong for some of the athletes and right for some others.'

Pitsiladis still likes to turn the tables. 'Did you see sophistication in Jamaica?' he asks me. 'In terms of the training?'

I tell him that I saw sprinters pulling weights, doing technical drills, doing two-legged jumps into a sandpit. 'No sophistication!' Pitsiladis says with such excitement that he is almost shouting. 'In athletics, in a lot of sports, I see total amateurism.' Yet it seems to work – for some. Which is his point – he thinks it's quite random; that the science is lacking. 'But even if there's no science in it, no scientific basis to what they do, and you're leaning on natural instincts, you will see people getting faster.'

Just think – he doesn't say, but is clearly wondering – how much faster they could go. Yet they go fast enough to win at the very highest level, which leads many to conclude that Jamaica is at the cutting edge in terms of training, preparation and, ultimately, performance. But what if they aren't? Pitsiladis makes a point about athletics that is often overlooked. It is *the* Olympic sport; the blue riband; the one people most closely associate with the Games. And from this comes the idea that track and field, as it is known in the US and increasingly in Jamaica, is a global sport, and that it attracts the crème de la crème.

But what if it doesn't? In their paper, Pitsiladis, Johnson and Davis remark upon the 'appreciable world-wide demise of elite sprinting' over the last couple of decades. It has something to do, they suggest, with the fact that so many fast white runners may be excluding themselves (based on the stereotype mentioned earlier), but even more to do with money. Specifically, the 'defection of the most talented sprinters to more lucrative sports such as football'. They identify talented sprinters who opted instead for American football. The system is changing, too, with the number of track scholarships on offer at US colleges declining markedly in recent times: in 2011 it was one for every eight or nine in American football. 'Sprinting', they write, 'is threatening to become simply a means of training for the football season rather than a sporting choice.' Pitsiladis and others speculate that there are football players, basketball players, soccer players, who might, with proper sprint training, be faster than Tyson Gay or Justin Gatlin . . . or Usain Bolt.

All of this has only pushed Pitsiladis further towards the conclusion that the Jamaican success has little to do with genes – or rather, with a specific gene. In this sense his mind hasn't altered since we sat in his office in Glasgow in 2007. But it is surprising to hear from somebody who, while not a geneticist himself, has devoted so many years to searching for a genetic explanation.

Originally Pitsiladis began his study of elite athletes because the existing research, especially concerning genes, 'was a little woolly'. That is being generous: 'Not a single African's genetics had been looked at from the point of view of performance. No black athlete had given DNA and had their genes looked at. So all the knowledge we thought we had about genetics and performance was based on an assumption.'

The assumption being that athletic ability must be down to genes.

'Then where are they?' Pitsiladis asks. 'It wouldn't be good enough for me, as a scientist, to repeat the myth – sorry, I mean the view: it's not a myth until it's been dismissed – that black athletes are simply naturally superior. I needed evidence. And if I found the "magic gene", I would patent it.'

He started looking in Ethiopia, where initially he encountered some resistance. But before too long, both there and in Kenya, he earned the trust and enjoyed the cooperation of most athletes, who let him collect 'biological material' – all it needed was a swab of saliva. Then he 'searched and searched and searched, and I haven't found' any magic gene. His conclusion: 'There is no compelling genetic evidence that there are race-related genes to explain this phenomenon.'

Through his visits to Africa, Pitsiladis began to believe that sociological or cultural factors were more decisive. He learned that there were around 3,000 Kenyans who made a living through running. It was seen not necessarily as a lucrative career, but it was a viable one. And for kids growing up in poor communities, there were thousands of role models. On his visits, children and parents would flock around Pitsiladis, assuming he was an agent.

Such experiences encouraged him to look beyond genes. The sheer complexity of the task is another reason to look further afield. If humans have somewhere between 20,000 and 30,000 genes, he explains, 'and 95 per cent of them are the same as a chimpanzee's, and between humans there is 99.9 per cent commonality, then we can isolate those genes that we suspect might be significant but there's a lot of work to do. We can spend one year studying a single gene . . . and I'm not going to live to 30,000.'

Then there is the fact that studying a single gene in isolation can be meaningless. Epstein compares the 23,000 genes in a human body to a 23,000-page recipe book, which in theory 'provides directions for the creation of the body . . . but if one page is moved, altered, or torn out, then some of the other 22,999 pages may suddenly contain new instructions'.

It seems that searching for a 'speed gene' isn't like looking for a needle in a haystack. It's like looking for a particular piece of hay in a haystack.

The antithesis of Cooper and Morrison's argument – that there are genetic characteristics unique to people of West African origin – is the 10,000-hour rule, made popular by Malcolm Gladwell. In his 2008 book *Outliers*, Gladwell argues that what separates Usain Bolt from his peers, or Tiger Woods or Bill Gates from theirs, is a combination of environment, opportunity and, crucially, lots and lots of practice: 10,000 hours, to be precise.

Pitsiladis has been coming to a not-dissimilar conclusion, but with a major caveat. Ten thousand hours' practice might be necessary (in fact, Pitsiladis thinks that a world-class athlete needs 'massively more than that'), but it is not sufficient. That is to say, not everybody can achieve greatness simply by doing a lot of training. First and foremost you need, as Pitsiladis says, the 'right parents'. Which, he concedes, means the 'right' genes.

For sprinters, there is a gene that does seem to be essential: a variant of the ACTN3 gene, which produces a protein, a-actinin-3, in the fast-twitch muscle fibres. In Jamaica, around 70 per cent of the population have this gene variant; in the US, the figure is 60 per cent. The only conclusion, however, is that without it you will probably not reach an Olympic 100-metre final. Even with it, there is no guarantee that you will. Billions have it. Most cannot run 100 metres in 9.9 seconds.

Errol Morrison clings on to the idea that one of the main explanations for the Jamaicans' success is genetic. Back in his office in Old Hope Road, he tells me, 'The specific genetic manifestation is still eluding us.' But he doesn't doubt that it is there.

In fact, he and Pitsiladis are not that far apart in some crucial respects (and they have considerable mutual admiration). Morrison insists that one manifestation of the genetic influence is staring them in the face: the runners' bodies. The narrow hips, long legs; even, he says, the shape of their backs. 'I've said to Yannis – but he's stubborn – I said, "Yannis, the performance is not genetically driven: the performance is facilitated by the anatomical structure."

'You look at all of our athletes, you will see them with what they call the scoliosis of the spine.' It is the condition that Bolt was diagnosed with in 2004. 'They all have that!' insists Morrison. 'Look at our Shelly-Ann: the spine has that curvature. But it helps with the knee lift.

'Then of course,' he adds, 'you have the environmental impacts: coaching, food and so on.

'Yannis would like to see something in the musculature that says, "Here is a fast runner, here is an endurance runner," and he's not picking that up. But I really don't think that is where you have to look.'

Where should you look, then? 'I don't think there's a gene for performance; genes make structure, they're proteins, but there's predisposition. And there's environment, and there's also our diet!' Morrison says.

The significance of the Jamaican diet has been frequently cited and often dismissed with a scornful laugh. Usain Bolt is a product of eating yams, you say? Why, yes, of course. Morrison urges me not to dismiss the idea completely. He says the staple diet in Jamaica – including yams, sweet potatoes, green bananas – is steroid-based. If youngsters are reared on this food, and pushed hard in training (as many are), they can develop into strong athletes. He goes into some detail about diosgenin, the steroid molecule in yams, and its anabolic (muscle-building) properties. Eating yams is not like pumping yourself full of testosterone, he makes clear – the effect is only relative to other foodstuffs. But, fascinatingly, the chemical structure of the yam is identical to human testosterone: yams were used to produce the first synthetic testosterone in the 1930s. And the yams in Trelawny, where Bolt and so many others are from, are said to have special properties. (P. J. Patterson, the former prime minister, also proposed the yams theory to me, then admitted rather sadly: 'I'm not sure Usain Bolt likes yams, though.')

I find myself agreeing with Morrison that there might be something in the diet theory: if not for performance-enhancement then simply because so much food is so particular and peculiar to Jamaica. Its distinctiveness took me by surprise: fruits I had never heard of, along with the daily staples of jerk chicken, dumplings, boiled green bananas, yams with the weight and density of cannonballs, breakfast of ackee and saltfish. There's a world of difference to the US, even though it's so close. It might be another reason why staying at home works for so many athletes.

'Slavery runs through Jamaican life today like the black line in a lobster,' wrote Ian Thomson in *The Dead Yard*. He was referring to slavery's violent legacy, but another one, according to a popular theory, gives the descendants of slaves a genetic advantage.

This was a theory explored by the US's four-time Olympic gold medallist Michael Johnson in a 2012 television programme, *Survival of the Fastest*. 'It's impossible to think that being descended from slaves hasn't left an imprint through the generations,' Johnson concluded. 'Difficult as it was to hear, slavery has benefited descendants like me – I believe there is a superior athletic gene in us.'

It is a seductive, if uncomfortable – not to mention grotesque – proposition: slavery as the ultimate Darwinian 'survival of the fittest' human experiment. So brutal was the Middle Passage from Africa to the Caribbean that all but the very strongest survived – boats were packed with more slaves than required, allowing for 'wastage' on the crossing; dead bodies were thrown into the sea, but so were people who were sick. One in four people transported across the Atlantic for slavery died before reaching their destination. Countless others, if they made it to the sugar plantations in Jamaica, perished in the terrible living and working conditions. One estimate is that between 1702 and 1808, around 840,000 Africans were shipped to Jamaica and into slavery.

There is another group reckoned to be significant in the Jamaican athletics story: the ex-slaves known as the Maroons, who escaped to Cockpit Country, in the same corner of the island as Trelawny, and survived in this hostile terrain, fighting off first the Spanish, then the British. If ordinary slaves were tough, Maroons were – are – super-tough. It ties into the theory promoted by Johnson's TV show: that the only African-Jamaicans remaining when slavery was abolished were the fittest, toughest, strongest. And of course their genes, to be passed down through the generations.

Pitsiladis was supposed to be involved with the television pro-gramme, but you will not find his name in the credits. The reason is obvious. As he keeps repeating, he is interested in evidence: 'I don't care about gut feeling.' And as seductive and sensational as the slave theory is – the TV programme attracted lots of press coverage and earnest discussion – Pitsiladis is not aware of any scientific evidence to support it. On the contrary, 'If the idea is that you have survival of the fittest through the slave trade and all that, Jamaicans are going to be similar genetically – and they're not.'

Most serious scientists seem to dismiss the idea that the Jamaicans' success can be traced back to slavery. Still, Pitsiladis does wonder if Africa provides some answers. He has analysed the genes of endurance runners from Ethiopia and Kenya and sprinters from Jamaica to try and establish just how 'African' they are. Are the 'purer' Africans better athletes?

When Pitsiladis looked at Ethiopian athletes, he discovered genes more frequently found in Europe, 'So that dispelled that myth.' In Kenya he found that athletes were 'more African' than the Ethiopians, but there was no difference between the athletes and the general population. So that seemed to dispel another myth.

'But when you look at the sprinters, it becomes more interesting,' he goes on. 'We looked at the Jamaicans. We found that slightly above 99 per cent of the Jamaican athletes are African. We did the same study looking at the US sprinters, and found roughly 10 per cent were non-African.'

The good Jamaican sprinters did appear to be 'more African'. Only there is a catch. As time goes on, they are becoming less African – they are being 'diluted down'. Yet they are also running faster. And there's another problem with the theory. If the explanation lies in Africa, why is sprinting a Jamaican phenomenon? Why not a Nigerian phenomenon? 'The Nigerians are still very good,' says Pitsiladis, 'but although they are more "African" on both [mother's and father's] sides, it's the Jamaicans who have the greater success.'

I have my own theory – that it isn't a specific gene, but rather the combination of genes that might explain the Jamaicans' athletic gifts. You don't need to do genetic profiling, you only need eyes to realise that Jamaica is a diverse place, and surely a diverse gene pool is a healthy gene pool. The country's motto is apt: 'Out of many, one people.' And as P. J. Patterson told me: 'Few Jamaicans are pure anything.' On this island of fewer than three million, there are large communities of African, Spanish, British, Indian, Chinese, Syrian and Lebanese extraction, among many others.

I put my theory to Pitsiladis. 'It is a very diverse place,' he agrees.

'If you speak to some people, they will say the mixed gene pool is an advantage. But I see no evidence for that.'

Oh well.

Environment, then. Pitsiladis stresses the importance of environment, and also of socio-economic conditions. The pockets of excellence in Ethiopia, Kenya and Jamaica all have one thing in common, he says: poverty. 'When I go out to Ethiopia, Kenya, Jamaica, it's so obvious. Wherever you look there are people running, and the African way of life.

'My children live less than a mile from school – we drive them there. In Kenya, a five-year-old will run to school. When we test them, they are fitter than some of our athletes. Is that genetics?'

Another environmental factor – one that Morrison and others highlight too – is the company of other elite performers. The virtuous circle effect. 'In science, if I want to become better, I'll go and work with the better scientists,' says Pitsiladis. 'If you want to become a top athlete, go and work with the best.'

There is, he concludes, no one simple explanation. 'All of it put together explains what we see. Not drugs, not finances . . . But what I would say in addition is that what appears to produce the quality guys, assuming they have the right genes, is how hungry they are. And often that is dictated by how hard their living conditions are. Usain Bolt is incredibly gifted, sure, but he trains incredibly hard.'

Perhaps it is a selfish gene he should be looking for, because Pitsiladis says that what the very best athletes have in common 'is how selfish they are. Every hour of the day is related to how they train harder, nothing else.' It's a part of the equation that cannot be ignored: 'If they aren't training hard like that and they have the right genes, it's irrelevant, it's not going to happen.'

Another common denominator in Jamaica, Ethiopia and Kenya is the extent to which athletics is ingrained in the sporting culture, and the age at which kids start running – and running seriously. 'We believe that starting to run from a young age – especially without shoes – lets them run pretty hard throughout their careers with fewer injuries than would normally happen,' Pitsiladis says. 'You're building a strong foundation.'

The big threat to these countries' culture of high performance could be money – an abundance of it. Pitsiladis reckons that if Kenya, Ethiopia or Jamaica became wealthy overnight, the medals would dry up. 'You may find other, hungrier countries, like Eritrea or Uganda, start excelling.

'And not,' Pitsiladis adds, 'because all of a sudden they have the right genes.'

17

THE G OF THE BANG

All I could hear was something said 'Go' in my head.
Usain Bolt

Yohan Blake is famous for training hard, like a beast. But what does he do when he's not working? How does he spend his downtime?

'Catch wild coyotes,' he says.

'What?'

'That's a joke, man. I play Ludi, I play dominoes, I play cricket with my boys, you know?'

His eyes flicker; he glances towards his agent and friend, Timothy Spencer, and quietly adds: 'Sometimes I read love novels, you know?'

'Love novels?'

'You know, you have *Romeo and Juliet*, you have *The Notebook*. I'm actually reading *The Notebook* every day. You know this love story; this guy and girl were seventeen, you know. Put it in your phone, look it up. I read motivational books, too. Ben Carson.' He shrugs. 'I don't like to sit down. I like to keep active.'

I have no idea if Blake is telling the truth or winding me up. I change the subject. What's the story with his nails? He wears them long. Not just a little bit long, but a good inch: like claws. I tell him that I haven't seen nails like that on an athlete since Flo-Jo.

'Yes, like a beast.' He glances admiringly at them. 'I will cut them at different intervals.'

Spencer interrupts. 'It's a superstitious thing.'

'It isn't,' says Blake.

'It is,' says Spencer. 'He won't cut them before a race. But he cut them for Lausanne and ran 9.69, so I said, "What do you think of that, Yohan?"'

In 2011, the world's fastest two men trained together every day. Blake, still only twenty-one, had progressed rapidly the previous season, whereas Bolt had barely raced and suffered only his second defeat over 100 metres, after his 2008 loss to Asafa Powell in Stockholm. This time he was beaten by Tyson Gay, again in Stockholm. Yet as the 2011 season got under way, it was Blake who seemed to pose the real threat. Bolt must have felt it; he must have been conscious of the younger man on his shoulder, gaining speed, pushing him.

And Blake, too – he must have been measuring himself against the fastest sprinter in history on a daily basis. 'Nothing big, it was nothing big,' he says. 'I was training with Usain from 2009 when I went to the Racers. I waited and waited. Then I was in the big time.'

Even when they became rivals as well as training partners, there was no problem between them in their daily sessions, insists Blake. 'We have good chemistry. He likes to talk to me; he's not that stuck-up guy who don't talk.'

As Blake began to emerge, there were rumours that he and Bolt were training separately, that they weren't talking. The stories annoyed Glen Mills. Asked to compare his two star sprinters, he said: 'One is tall and one is short.' Reluctantly he added: 'I'm happy to speak about each but I don't do comparisons because I coach them and have to maintain balance.'

I asked Zharnel Hughes, the eighteen-year-old Anguillan who broke Blake's 100 metres record at Champs, about the atmosphere at

Racers training. Hughes was a relative newcomer; it was still a novelty to him to be training with the best in the world. 'Bolt is friendly but he doesn't talk much,' he said. 'Blake, you'll hear him talking the loudest. Sometimes when he crosses the finish line he shouts out something funny. He makes you laugh. He's like a clown. Bolt, you really won't find him saying much, but you hear him with Blake, joking, "Come on, man, finish the programme! Don't cheat the programme!"'

Blake says that in Daegu, at the 2011 world championships, when they both qualified for the 100 metres final, Bolt didn't seem any different; he was his usual self. If he was anxious about the race, or wary of the man expected to be his main rival – who also happened to be his clubmate and training partner – it didn't show. Then again, Blake knew that Bolt's schtick was to be relaxed, or to appear relaxed. And what, in the end, is the difference? 'He always creates this atmosphere of being relaxed, it is true,' Blake says. 'Then he goes out and does his tricks before the start. But in the call room he's alive, he's not too serious. When you're not too serious and you're relaxed, there is not a lot of tension in the body.' It echoes Dennis Johnson and Bud Winter and his 'relax and win' philosophy. 'That's good, you know,' Blake continues. 'Usain creates that atmosphere not only for himself but for other people.

'Some guys, you can see the tension. You can see their face tight, their body not loose. You think, All right, Yohan, you've got him covered.'

Daegu saw a decaffeinated final: no Asafa Powell, who had a groin injury, or Tyson Gay, also injured, and no Steve Mullings, the third fastest man of the year, after his second positive test.

At the start, it was business as usual. Salutes from Bolt to a large Jamaican contingent in the crowd – including his parents, sitting with Norman Peart. Bolt stretched his arms. He was in lane four, Blake in lane five; he grabbed his training partner's hand for a loose (relaxed) handshake as they passed. Nesta Carter, the third Jamaican and one of Stephen Francis's men, was in lane seven. As they lined up, Bolt pointed to his left and shook his head; pointed to his right and shook his head; pointed at himself and nodded. Then, just before he stepped towards the blocks, he let out a primal yell. The eight men settled, waiting for the gun, and the stadium fell into restless silence. One moved – Bolt. And then the gun went.

It wasn't a twitch, a reaction to a noise in the stadium or a reflex response to another athlete moving. It was one man breaking the line. It was an unequivocal false start, which meant automatic disqualification. And it was Bolt, there was no disguising that, though a couple of other finalists were sure the officials would find some way to exonerate the culprit. ('I actually thought they were going to blame it on me,' said Kim Collins. 'I really didn't think they was going to throw Usain out,' said Walter Dix, 'because, well, it was Usain.')

Bolt knew what he'd done. As he launched from the blocks, he opened his mouth in another yell, then carried on for a few strides down the straight. In one fluid movement he whipped off his vest and dumped it on the track. He slowed and turned round, walking back towards the blocks. Blake, wide-eyed, stared after him and slowly shook his head. In the stands, Jennifer Bolt's eyes were fixed on the track, her expression one of utter horror. Then she threw herself to the ground, as though trying to hide. 'He take off him clothes, he take off him clothes!' she cried when she got back up. Removing his shirt seemed to be a way for Bolt to spare himself the indignity of being disqualified – it saved the officials the bother of presenting a red card.

Topless, he marched past the blocks, shouting to himself, then slapped the wall beneath the stands and slumped to the ground, sitting there with his arms hooked around his knees, as dejected as he is usually so ebullient. The mask had slipped – here was the other Bolt: anguished and angry rather than relaxed and jovial. It betrayed what he tried to conceal: how much it meant to him.

The question was: why had he done it? To match the kind of time he ran in Berlin? Or because he feared defeat, and couldn't afford to concede even a centimetre to Blake? Bolt had qualified from his semi-

final in 10.05, Blake in 9.95. But in anticipating the gun, rather than reacting to it, Bolt broke Coach Mills's cardinal rule: 'My coach always explains that it's not about anticipation,' he said later.

The remaining finalists were called back to the start. The atmosphere in the stadium was now as deflated as a burst football. Blake settled in the blocks, the empty lane beside him as glaring as a missing front tooth. Thirty-five-year-old Collins got off to a flyer, but Blake, his head down for the first ten metres, powered smoothly along the track – gliding almost, his feet appearing to only dab the surface. He seemed to keep accelerating and crossed the line a comfortable winner, with a Bolt-esque margin over Dix of 0.16 seconds. The winning time: 9.92 seconds. Although it was into a stiff breeze, most believed Bolt would have beaten that even if he had waited for the 'G' rather than going before the 'B' of the bang (a little over two weeks later, in Brussels, he ran a season's best 9.76).

There were parallels with Shelly-Ann Fraser's win in Beijing in the mystery over the winner. Who was this guy Blake? Victor Conte was among those who wondered. 'OK, so initially you hear that Usain Bolt is a genetic freak, that he's very tall, with this stride length which means he takes fewer strides than everybody else. Then here's Yohan Blake – he's not tall!' Yet Conte could, begrudgingly, admire his run. 'Oh, Bolt and Blake are very talented, genetically gifted athletes. They have great technique. They are very well trained.'

Blake was a 'meanwhile' at the foot of news reports: 'Meanwhile, the race was won by . . .' Few were interested in him as the winner, even as the youngest ever 100 metres world champion. 'I've been working hard for this moment,' he said after a lap of honour draped in a Jamaican flag given to him by Bolt's mother. 'I've been dreaming of this moment.' It had cost him restless nights. 'I haven't been able to sleep; I've been up at night praying.'

When his training partner was disqualified, 'For a split second I was breaking down inside,' said Blake, 'but I said to myself, No, you have to get focused, you have to get the job done.' His only sadness was that he and Bolt couldn't go home with the gold and silver medals, as planned. 'The key', he added, 'is Coach Mills and God.'

Bolt, meanwhile, had bolted. He was shadowed throughout 2011 by a French film crew, and they couldn't find him. Neither could Ricky Simms, his agent, who appeared after the race looking bewildered. He gave an interview on Bolt's behalf, then admitted he hadn't spoken to him, nor had he any idea where he was.

When Bolt reappeared, reporters and TV crews stalked him as he strode across a dark car park outside the stadium. He was surly, in a foul mood. 'No comment,' he said. 'Looking for tears? Not going to happen.'

Bolt was sharing an apartment with Blake and Asafa Powell. His first post-race exchange with Blake was captured by the documentary crew. He is slumped on the sofa when Blake appears, and he adopts an announcer's voice: 'The new world champion, Yohan Blake!' Blake smiles. 'It's not a team sport, but if I didn't get it, I'm happy he did,' says Bolt. 'I've seen him train, man. I've seen the work he put in.'

At 1.50 a.m., Bolt is still slumped on the sofa, computer on his lap, phone in his hand. He seems to be the only one up – other than the light from his gadgets, the apartment is dark and quiet – and he looks in reflective mood. 'I was just pissed with myself, man. I just couldn't believe it. You see people on TV false-starting and you say, that's bad luck. Then you feel how bad it is. It's awful to false-start.

'I was in great shape, I was running fast, I was good. I was sure I was going to get the gold medal. So to know it's going to happen and then you lose. Or not even lose, you don't make it to the finishing line . . . Very hard, very hard. I was just frustrated, man.

'You can't dwell on the past, man, you learn that. I grew up in the church. You learn that God has a plan for everyone. I have one more race to go.'

You can see him trying to look forward and put the disappointment behind him. But he can't let go. 'I'm kind of pissed at myself coz I've been working hard on my start especially.' He looks up, addressing the film's director, Gaël Leiblang. 'You've been along the way, you've seen the work I've put in. You've seen what I've gone through. It finally came together at the right time, and I pretty much squandered it, I would say. I don't know what happened. Can't believe it happened; I kept saying to myself, "Why did you false-start, why did you false-start, why did you false-start?" It's never happened. Major championships: that's what I live for.

'All I could hear was something said "Go" in my head and I just went. Then . . . what the hell happened? I guess tonight I was my worst enemy.

'But you can't dwell on the past, mate,' he adds, lurching into cockney. 'Moving on.'

Six days later came the 200 metres, and as Bolt and the other finalists settled in the blocks, an anxious silence descended. There was a look of dread on the face of Jennifer Bolt. When the eight runners rose in unison after the gun, the noise in the stadium was that of relief. Bolt won easily in 19.40 seconds, three-tenths of a second ahead of Dix and Christophe Lemaitre.

'Who's the champion now, uh-uh?' he sang, performing a jig inside the stadium.

Shelly-Ann Fraser-Pryce could only manage fourth in the 100 metres, though she teamed up with Veronica Campbell, the 200 metres gold medallist, to win the 4x100 (the men also won their sprint relay, with two of Mills's athletes, Bolt and Blake, and two of Francis's, Carter and Michael Frater, in a new world record).

It was a minor setback, reckoned Fraser-Pryce. She had problems with injuries after returning from her doping ban. She had other commitments, too: she had got married, and then there were her studies and her family. She had bought her mother a house in a safer part of Kingston and tried to do the same for her grandmother. 'She didn't want to leave,' Fraser-Pryce says. 'It's hard to convince somebody who is that old to move.' Then a solution presented itself. 'My uncle died and that left a big space at the front, so I built her a house there. She's OK there: nobody's going to harm her.

'Helping my family,' she says, 'I think is the most enjoyable and sometimes the most stressful part of everything. You try to see how you can assist with everything, but there are limits.'

It was difficult to keep the same focus on training and competing. There were so many demands on her time. She set up a charity, the Pocket Rocket Foundation, paying for seven youngsters to attend school: buying uniforms, books and food. Each was, like Shelly-Ann, from the inner city. They had been chosen by her, and had targets to reach at their schools; a report was sent to the foundation every month with an update on their progress. 'This is not for publicity, for the TV,' she says. 'I am concerned with them and what they do next. Their parents are poor. If they can understand that I care, outside of the foundation . . . and if they make it, they have a chance of helping someone else. Then it becomes a cycle, it spreads.' The foundation was, she explains, 'born out of what Jeanne Coke did for me. It's about education and sport and linking them to try and

transform individuals' lives, and [have] these people transforming Jamaica.'

Asafa Powell has his foundation, Usain Bolt has his, and after his success, Yohan Blake got in on the act. His is called YBAfraid (Why Be Afraid?) and helps vulnerable young people. He supports the Mount Olivet boys' home: a centre for homeless and abused boys, which includes 'Expressions Through Creativity' workshops in art, music and drama.

Bolt's is focused on helping young people through 'education and cultural development'. I was told that Bolt also helps individuals. While visiting the University of the West Indies one day, I asked for directions from a groundsman, who insisted on jumping in the car to guide me. 'Bolt help a lot of kids,' he said. 'He pay for a lot of kids to go to school in Kingston.'

Bolt can afford it, but the others' ability to keep pumping money into their foundations is entirely dependent on their continuing success on the track. So they end up not only running for themselves and their families, but for lots of other people too: for the poor of their country; for Jamaica. It is another cycle, in addition to Fraser-

Pryce's virtuous one, that puts a lot of expectation, and pressure, on the athletes. Fraser-Pryce's setback in Daegu didn't just affect her profile as an athlete; it affected her earning power, which affected her foundation and, in turn, the seven youngsters whose education depends on it.

She also has her hair salon, of course, where we are sitting in the plush pink-and-black reception area discussing how she recovered from the disappointment of Daegu and the previous season, with her positive test. Her appetite didn't diminish, she tells me, despite the demands on her time and attention. She says that after Daegu, her motivation was even higher. She was determined to defend her Olympic title in London. It was the same as being back at school: feeling that she had been written off. 'People always thought because I was short, and I wasn't very good in high school, I couldn't make it. For them to see me perform as I do . . . when people say, "When I see you running it makes me happy because you're so short but so fast."

'I still go to training as if I've won nothing. My husband said this to me last week when we were driving. I was saying, "People don't get me, they don't get why I always train, why I'm so focused", and he says to me that I train almost as if I am hungry. He told me, "You train as if you've never won anything. You train and if you can't train you sit there and cry – but you're the Olympic champion."'

While the world's best sprinters were preparing themselves for the London Olympics, their country's anti-doping agency was floundering. In July 2012, less than a month before the Games began, JADCO appointed a new executive director.

Renée Anne Shirley had done everything: she was a financial consultant before reinventing herself as a radio and TV presenter and newspaper columnist in the late 1990s; she then became a government adviser and sat on the boards of various task forces. She was chief executive of the Jamaica Rugby Football Union. She had a BA in economics and was the first black woman to graduate with an MBA from the University of Virginia; then there was the PhD in public administration from the University of Kentucky.

It was her work as a government adviser that took Shirley into the field of anti-doping. From 2003–7 she was senior adviser to Jamaica's first female prime minister, Portia Simpson Miller, leading and coordinating the development of Jamaica's Anti-Doping in Sport Programme. She headed the Jamaican delegation at the International Convention Against Doping in Sport in Paris in 2005, attended the International Convention on Doping in Sport at the UNESCO Headquarters, also in Paris, then the World Anti-Doping Code Review in Amsterdam, in February 2007. In November of the same year she was official observer to the Third World Conference on Doping in Sport in Madrid.

She knew her stuff, then. And when she took over at JADCO, she was determined to do the right thing, not necessarily the most popular. She was well aware that the organisation had problems, not least since the order from WADA to appoint a new board. She knew she'd have to roll her sleeves up. 'I am not a believer in patting ourselves on the back and saying, "We believe our athletes are not cheating."'

When she took over at JADCO, 'There were quite a few things I had to sort out and fix up,' she tells me over lunch at Ziggy's, a cafe at Twin Gates Plaza in mid-Kingston that she says offers traditional Jamaican food. It is also a place where the other customers are not likely to be interested in what she has to say: things that have previously got her in trouble.

Shirley's few things to sort out and fix up turns out to be an unusual case of her glossing over the actuality. You don't need to spend too long in her company to appreciate that she is to straight talking what Shelly-Ann Fraser-Pryce is to running quickly. 'JADCO was badly set up,' she sighs. 'The legislation was badly written. There was a lack of staffing, but my main concern was the lack of testing.' The absence of out-of-competition testing particularly worried her. 'Once you're successful – the kind of success that Jamaica had since

Beijing – it called for us to have really strong and rigorous and robust anti-doping.'

She saw immediately that JADCO couldn't do that. There was only one full-time doping control officer, no one in charge of running the 'whereabouts' programme, and the TUE committee (which decided when athletes could legitimately use banned products by issuing a Therapeutic Use Exemption) was without a chairman and had never met. The accounting department was non-existent, and no monthly financial statements had been produced in five years; bills were outstanding.

The situation had been infuriating JADCO's most senior drug-tester, Paul Wright. Yet some of the problems stemmed, Wright told me, from the WADA intervention in late 2010. 'The entire board was dismissed, right? Then the general election came up and the country voted out that government, and a new government was in. The election was in December [2011].' In all that time, JADCO was rudderless. 'I was testing all along,' Wright says. 'Then there was nothing in January [2012]. Nothing in February. We had no board, so there's no testing!'

The statistics for the period confirm this. When it came to out-of-competition tests, in February 2012 there were twelve, in April just one – and that was it. None in March, May, June or July. The Olympic Games in London were fast approaching. 'I was making phone calls,' says Wright, 'I drive to Jamaica House' – the office of the prime minister, who also looks after the sport portfolio. 'I said, "This is Olympic year. We are the biggest sprinters in the world and we can't just stop testing the year of the Olympics. People are going to believe we're hiding something. You've got to get this board in place and restart testing."'

Wright knew the names who were being considered for the new board. He also knew that the same problem would arise – that WADA would object on the grounds that there were too many potential conflicts of interest (perhaps an inevitable problem in a country with such a small middle class: these being the people who volunteer for such positions). When the board was announced, he was dismayed to see who was on it. He called the prime minister to complain and was told: 'Dr Wright, these are our friends, they have spent their life contributing to sports, you must stop maligning people of integrity.'

Still there was no testing. It was only when Renée Anne Shirley was appointed, one month before the Games, that things started to happen. 'I joined after the national trials and started the out-of-competition testing,' she says. 'But they had not tested for six months prior to the London Games. One of the reasons was that their test kits were out-of-date.

'It was a fight from the beginning. Every excuse was that we didn't have the money. But with the money we had, we could have done more.'

Even before she started at JADCO, Shirley had the feeling that more effort could be made to look into some of the darker recesses of sport. She was aware of the threads connecting Jamaican athletes and coaches to doping scandals, and of testimony during the Balco case alleging that Raymond Stewart gave drugs to his wife, Beverly McDonald, on the eve of the Athens Olympics. 'I went to the prime minister,' says Shirley, 'and said that as a signatory to the World Anti-Doping Code, we should at least investigate it. We should call [McDonald] in. What are we going to do: wait for them to take the gold medal away from us? I said, "You should at least be seen to be doing something."

'I can tell you that I got no traction from that at all.

'But listen, my friend,' Shirley adds. 'Jamaica is not unique. Kenya is not unique, China is not unique, Great Britain is not unique. It is the same everywhere. When any country is winning gold medals, they don't want to look too closely. Every country wants to hear their anthem, to see the gold medal around their athletes' necks.'

For Olympic year, ahead of the defence of her title, Shelly-Ann Fraser-Pryce made a renewed commitment to God. Winston Jackson, senior pastor at the Penwood Church of Christ, said that she had always been a 'church girl', and that the church had helped her and her family through 'some early struggles'. Now, said Jackson of Fraser-Pryce's running ability, 'she realises it's not her, it's really God. You can see the change in her.'

She also renewed her commitment to MVP, after reports of discord and several defections over the winter. Ristananna Tracey, Kimmari Roach, Peter Matthews and Darion Bent all left for Glen Mills' Racers Track Club, and there were rumours that Fraser-Pryce might follow them. It saw a deepening of the rift between MVP and Racers, especially when Bruce James, the MVP president, claimed that 'the other club' paid their new recruits. 'Unlike another track club in Jamaica, MVP does not pay our developmental athletes cash,' said James. Former MVP athletes had informed him, he added, 'that the other club pays them cash monthly, in addition to providing them with accommodation in apartments off campus, among other enticements'.

Racers responded with a statement: 'A clear distinction must be made between athlete recruitment and athlete support. Racers Track Club maintains a restrained policy of recruitment and an active policy of support.' It continued: 'Do we seek to support our athletes financially? The answer is, unequivocally, yes. We do try to assist our athlete members to keep body and soul together in the hard times before they become celebrities and before they excite the attention of potential sponsors.'

Fraser-Pryce had a quiet start to 2012. As well as preparing for her Olympic defence, she was finishing her studies; she graduated with a BSc in child and adolescent development and says her degree was as important as her athletics – in many ways it meant more. 'For me it wasn't sport or education, it was both. Both were my way out. It's possible. I lived it. I got my degree while being a professional athlete.' It was her 'greatest accomplishment', she says. Graduation day felt like another Olympic final. 'Everyone came to my graduation, because I grew up in the inner city and some things happen that you don't expect. Young girls getting pregnant, dropping out of school, not going to school . . . that happened to a lot of my friends, too many. Not being part of that statistic feels . . .'

Good? 'Yeah,' she nods.

As the clock ticked towards London, she gained ground. At the Diamond League meeting in New York in early June, she blazed to a win in 10.92 seconds. She was on track. She underlined it two weeks later, at the Jamaican trials, flying to victory in 10.70, a personal best, 0.12 seconds in front of Veronica Campbell-Brown. No arguments over selection this time.

In London, she was bidding to become the third woman to retain the Olympic 100 metres title, after Wyomia Tyus in 1968 and Gail Devers in 1996. When Devers won her first gold medal, in 1992, the woman she narrowly beat was a Jamaican, Juliet Cuthbert. Cuthbert now owns the gym in Kingston where Fraser-Pryce regularly trains. In 1996, when Devers retained her title, it was another photo finish: this time she just got the verdict over Merlene Ottey.

With the Games in full swing, the women's 100 metres, heats and final, are on the first two days of the athletics programme. Fraser-Pryce progresses smoothly, winning her semi-final in 10.85 to make it to the final, twenty-four hours before the men's. It's the night the home crowd are calling 'Golden Saturday', as Mo Farah, Jessica Ennis and Greg Rutherford win gold medals.

Fraser-Pryce is not everybody's favourite: Carmelita Jeter deposed her as world champion in Daegu and is in sparkling form. The American is a thirty-two-year-old enigma, a woman of few words who seems reluctant to engage with the media. She made a sudden improvement relatively late in her career, going from a best of 11.48 in 2006 to 10.97 in 2008. She is coached by Maurice Greene's old coach, John Smith, and her late blooming invites suspicion. 'I'm 32 and clean,' she told *Sports Illustrated*. When people doubt her, 'I pretty much accept it. But it's hurtful, and I'd like to get credit for what I've done.'

They line up for the final and the camera pans along the line.

Muscular and powerful, Jeter looks formidable and serious, frowning and chewing her lower lip. Whereas for Bolt, when the camera reaches him the view is of his chest, when it reaches the diminutive Fraser-Pryce, the view is of fresh air. It has to dip down to find her. She seems as relaxed as Bolt – genuinely, naturally relaxed. When the camera finds her, she flashes a megawatt smile and gives a vigorous wave, but there are no tricks, no showboating. Her only gimmick is a golden ribbon in her hair. She is introduced as the defending champion, an idea that seems to amuse her; her eyes sparkle, her smile broadens and becomes a laugh.

Fraser-Pryce lingers back as they are called to the blocks. Her expression is serious now. She breathes deeply, puffing out her cheeks, narrowing her eyes; she says she has tunnel vision before a race: 'Once I get in my blocks there is nothing in my mind.' The athletes settle and are called to 'set'; she is last to rise but first out of the blocks, though only just – it isn't her best start, which annoys and worries Stephen Francis, watching as critically as ever – 'very messy' is his verdict. At fifty metres, she and Jeter emerge at the front, one lane apart and impossible to separate. Just like in Beijing, Fraser-Pryce's head is tilted back, eyes locked on the big screen: watching the race? If she is, then she is oblivious as she crosses the line. She stops, hands on hips, sucking in oxygen, and stares at the screen again, watching the replay. Her brow is creased; she looks worried.

The time, 10.75, appears first, then the finishing positions. 1. Fraser-Pryce (Jam), 2. Jeter (USA), 3. Campbell-Brown (Jam). When she realises, she throws herself to the track, shouting, 'Thank you, Jesus!'

Back home in Waterhouse, they watch Fraser-Pryce's run in the house she built for her mother. More than ten members of her family squeeze into the living room, watching a small television, cries of 'Go, Shelly!' accompanying her all the way until she dips for the line. That is followed by a brief, stunned silence, and then an eruption of screams and yells and they spill out to join the street party. There are vuvuzelas,

Jamaican flags, one youth dressed as the Grim Reaper in black suit and mask, hanging on to a car, on roller blades. There are shouts of 'That's our Shelly! That's our Shelly!' Children using the lids of pans as cymbals, crashing them against each other. 'Big up to mi sister Shelly,' says Andrew Fraser, her brother, in a red NYC baseball cap, earrings sparkling in his ears, tears welling in his eyes. 'She train hard for this, mi see now, it pay off. Mi sister right now are mi icon. Right now mi don't even know, mi just feel overwhelmed right now, yeah.'

Inevitably in her press conference, with the men's final twenty-four hours away, Fraser-Pryce is asked about Bolt. Is she fed up with being in his shadow? 'I'm not one who loves the limelight,' she says, 'but sometimes I go to the supermarket they ask me questions about Usain. They ask me, "Where's Usain? Where's Usain?"'

Wherever she goes she is asked whether she trains with Bolt. 'I don't.'

As Bolt prepared for his final, the threat, as in Daegu, seemed to be Blake. At the national championships in Kingston at the end of June, their first meeting since the world championships, he had been blown away by the Beast. It was as though the memory of Daegu, and the fear of false-starting, weighed on Bolt's mind. He got a sluggish start and was never in the race. Blake won in 9.75, a personal best and stadium record. Bolt, a desperate look on his face as he chased his clubmate's shadow, trailed in 0.11 behind for second. Powell, back after his injury, was third: the top three qualified for London.

It didn't have the prestige, but winning the Jamaican title was harder than winning the world title. Blake, who after Daegu ran the second-fastest 200 metres of all time, 19.26 seconds in Brussels, also beat Bolt in his stronger event, with Weir third. Defeat in his beloved 200 metres cut Bolt deep. 'I was very sad with my turn,' he said. 'It was awful, but I've been working more on the 100 metres. I can't blame it on that, though. I just have to get my things together and get it done.'

Glen Mills wasn't worried. 'Usain, he has the experience, the ability. He has been there already. He might be a little off at the moment but I'm sure when the time of delivery comes around, he'll be on top of his game.' There were four weeks to go until London. 'We're right where we want to be, going into London,' Mills said. 'We just want to keep them healthy. That's the key.'

It was almost as if Bolt had been playing with people, cultivating a bit of mystery and suspense with the questions over his fitness and form. Keeping everyone on their toes, including himself. Ever since Berlin, when he had a quiet season in 2010, and then the Daegu debacle in 2011, rumours and gossip about Bolt have had a tendency to swirl around Jamaica. When I was there in April 2014, the story was that he had a debilitating foot injury, and that the minor op that had been reported was actually major surgery. 'I wouldn't be surprised if we don't see Bolt run again,' said one athlete's agent. A few weeks later, he returned to competition.

In July 2012, a couple of weeks before the London Games, Bolt did admit, 'For the first time I'm slightly a little bit nervous.' Because Blake was faster? 'I should think I'm definitely faster than Yohan Blake,' he clarified. Always, with Bolt, beneath the facade there lurks a steely competitor.

In fact, Bolt said later, Blake did him a favour at the national trials. 'It was like he knocked on my door and said, "Usain, this is an Olympic year. Wake up."'

When the 100 metres finalists enter the stadium and wait behind the blocks, to be introduced like prizefighters, all eyes are on one man; one man who couldn't have been more comfortable on this stage, with this kind of pressure. 'All right, this is it,' he says. 'It's game time.' He enjoys the crowd's response, the fact that 80,000 pairs of eyes are watching him, expecting another miracle.

Then a brief flicker of fear – a shadow flitting across his face – before he settles into the blocks. It's like the blood drains briefly from

Bolt's face. Daegu isn't on his mind. Or not much. 'First of all, my coach explained to me, it was all about reacting and executing. I got to fifty metres; the last fifty metres are my race.'

Justin Gatlin insisted that he started the race believing he could win. Earlier in the season, in Zagreb, Bolt talked about his American rival's macho posturing at the start: 'I just think that's what he's used to. He's pretty much an old-school athlete and, back in the day, it was all about intimidation.'

Gatlin gets an incredible start and has clear track in front of him. Then he senses Bolt. 'I mean, he's six-five, you can't miss him,' he tells us later. 'When his legs lift, you can see it, you can feel it.'

As Gatlin and Tyson Gay fade, Blake and Bolt emerge, then there is just Bolt. 'The last fifty metres,' says Blake. 'That's when he decided to pull up beside me, and I said, "Wow."'

Bolt wins in 9.63 seconds, beating his own Olympic record, second only to his time in Berlin. Blake's time in finishing second (9.75) and Gatlin's in coming third (9.79) would have won the gold medal in every other Olympic final in history – apart from Beijing. Gay misses a medal and breaks down in tears: 'Ain't nothing else I could do. I don't have excuses, man, I gave it my all. I feel like I let a lot of people down.'

The press conference begins just after 11 p.m., over an hour after the race. This is backstage, shorn of the Olympic sheen: a no-frills, brightly lit conference room, a table at one end, with bottles of (official) drinks, and seats arranged in front with space for about eighty reporters. The three medallists shuffle in together. Bolt smiles and jokes with Blake, who looks nervous, while Gatlin seems out of sorts, as though he wonders what he is doing here. He has a point: few are here to hear from the bronze medallist. Gatlin looks his age – thirty. And as they whisper and giggle to each other, Bolt and Blake look theirs, or younger.

Blake explains, 'Usain Bolt told me to keep calm. This is my first Olympics, so he encouraged me . . . It was just fun out there.

Bolt has a way of keeping me calm. I'm grateful of course, I'm happy.'

Gatlin: 'It feels good to be back here, being part of history. It means a lot to me. I'm really glad to be here.' The elephant in the room: his 'previous' for doping. Or, as Gatlin euphemistically refers to it: 'ups and downs'. He adds: 'You know, watching Bolt, watching Blake, and what they've done, has been the inspiration for me to work harder, to work the angles, to be a better runner.'

Bolt talked on the eve of the Games about attaining the status of 'legend'. 'It's a first step,' he says now. The 200 metres will be another step. He acknowledges one journalist's reference to the only other sprinter to successfully defend the Olympic 100 metres title, Carl Lewis (after Ben Johnson was disqualified). But Bolt is not rising to the Lewis bait. Not yet.

Towards the end of the press conference, a curve ball: 'A question from Germany, Usain. Dr Müller-Wohlfahrt is your doc: how did he help you? And how German is your success?'

'Dr Müller-Wohlfahrt is a major part of my success, a major part of my career,' Bolt replies, suddenly more animated. 'I have been going to him since I was probably nineteen, eighteen, since I first had an injury. He's really done a number, done great work on me. After trials I went to him, he looked at my muscles, he did his treatment, and said, "Usain, you're going to do great, go back, train." He gave my coach the go-ahead. So he plays a very important role.

'He's more than a doctor. He takes us to dinner, he really looks after me. He comes in on weekends to treat me. I thank him and the girls in the office.'

Later, Bolt celebrates his win in his room in the athletes' village with three members of Sweden's female handball team: a moment he captures with his phone and posts on Twitter. The Swedes bumped into Glen Mills in the dining room and asked if they could meet Bolt. He led them to Bolt's room, where they stayed until 3 a.m. 'It was awesome, he wasn't cocky or anything,' said Isabelle Gullden. 'He wasn't drunk, either, he'd just got back from the race.'

If the one-two in the 100 metres was extraordinary, then what was the 200 metres, four days later? Warren Weir had been a decent hurdler at school, spotted by Herb McKenley, and transformed into a 200 metres sprinter by Glen Mills. At Racers Track Club, training with Bolt and Blake, he couldn't cope with the workload initially; he wasn't strong enough, and kept breaking down, partly because of knee problems related – thought Mills – to the strain of hurdling. Weir is slightly built and wiry; in fact, he, Blake and Bolt are all very different shapes. Mills encouraged him to take things slowly. The secret to his eventual breakthrough? 'Patience,' he says. 'I was supposed to go to Daegu, but Coach said, "You're not fit enough; we're going to wait."'

In London, having qualified for the final, Weir was anxious. 'Before all the cameras and before the running was nerve-racking,' he tells me when we meet in a hotel in New Kingston. 'It was my first championship. The first day, I wasn't nervous. I had nothing to lose, but getting into the final, it was a bit nervous.' Yet, having run 19.99 to finish behind Blake and Bolt at the Jamaican trials in June, he believed he should be capable of a medal in his first Olympic final. 'Yes, because when I looked at the times going into the Olympics and the final, I was right in the medals. So I was expecting to get a medal, but at the same time I was saying to myself, "If I don't, it's OK, it's my first Games."'

In the call room before the final, he tried to ease the tension. 'I was laughing and running jokes. I was saying to [Wallace] Spearmon and Bolt and Churandy [Martina]: "In 2008, I was in high school watching y'all guys at Beijing on the couch. And now we're in the same final."'

Weir's game plan was to ignore Bolt and Blake and run his own race. Easier said than done, since he was in lane eight while in lane seven was Bolt. 'I was very realistic out there. I said to myself, I'm nowhere in the range of Bolt and Blake; they are running some extremely fast times. But third place was up for grabs. Everybody with a shout of third place was running pretty much the same time as I was.'

Bolt drew level with Weir in thirteen steps. He and Blake, in lane four, were already out front, running their own race, but Weir led the others coming off the bend. He was aware of Spearmon challenging and lunged for the line – dipping too early, so that his head was down. He didn't see whether he got it. 'I could not judge if I had come third. I had to wait for the replay and the scoreboard. You see people celebrate too early – I didn't want to do that. Then I saw the places and I ran over to Bolt and Blake, who were celebrating up the track. "Yo, I came third."

'It was joy,' says Weir, 'joy all over. To get a one-two-three from the same club, from the same country, from the same coach, and to know that we'd been training for like three years before the Olympic Games was wonderful.'

Is Mills someone who celebrates moments like this? 'I saw Coach after the race because I was in [anti-]doping. So Coach was very excited and he said to me, "Patience." He said to me then, "Patience pays off." Because it was all about building up gradually.'

Weir didn't make the team for the 4x100 metres relay, when Bolt and Blake were joined by Nesta Carter and Michael Frater: once again, two from Racers, two from MVP. Their winning time, 36.84, was a world record. Bolt confirmed afterwards that he was a legend now. But he'd got something else off his chest after the 200 metres, something he had been building up to saying. Flanked by Blake and Weir, he leant forward, into the microphone: 'I am going to say something controversial right now. Carl Lewis, I have no respect for him. The things he says about the track athletes is really downgrading, for another athlete to be saying something like that about other athletes.' Since 2008, Lewis had been voicing his suspicions about the Jamaicans.

Bolt had hinted after the 100 metres that he had something to say, but bit his tongue: 'Patience,' as Mills might say. In footage filmed by Weir in their living quarters in the athletes' village, Bolt can be seen lying on a massage table, muttering about Lewis. But once he finally started, he didn't seem able to stop. 'I think he's just looking for attention, because nobody really talks much about him so he's just looking for attention. So that was really sad for me when I heard the other day what he was saying. For me it was upsetting. I have lost all respect for him. It was all about drugs, talking about drugs, a lot of drug stuff. For an athlete out of the sport to be saying that is really upsetting for me . . .'

Lewis wasn't the only one in his cross hairs – Victor Conte had been in the news claiming that doping remained rampant. 'It is really annoying when people on the sidelines say stupid stuff,' Bolt continued. 'Without a doubt we are drug-free. We train hard. I see us all train together, we throw up every day, we take ice baths, we end up flat out on the track. When people taint us it is really hard but we are trying our best to show the world that we are running clean.'

Beside Bolt throughout the London Olympics, including at his press conferences, Blake smiled, but he wasn't overly happy. He reckoned his 100 metres had been one of his worst – a badly executed race (he would prove his form a couple of weeks later, running 9.69 seconds in Lausanne to make him, with Tyson Gay, the joint-second-fastest man of all time). 'That was my best race,' Blake says of Lausanne. 'At the Olympics I tightened up a bit.' It was a missed opportunity. He believes he could and should have won the Olympic 100 metres final. 'I was leading and I said, Yes, Yohan, you got this in the bag – as soon as I thought that, I tightened up.'

His time would come, Glen Mills was sure of that. Midway through the London Games, Mills confided in another member of the Jamaican entourage. Bolt had been hinting that he might finally give the 400 metres a go, and could do the 200 and 400 at the Rio Olympics in 2016, when he will be thirty. It seemed unclear; up in the air. His coach wasn't sure whether he would try the longer distance.

He seemed certain only about one thing, and it concerned the blue riband event, the 100 metres: 'There's no way', said Mills, 'that any thirty-year-old will beat Yohan Blake in 2016.'

18

AFTER THE HURRICANE

A systematic and knowing failure . . . that is deplorable and gives rise to
the most serious concerns about the overall integrity of the JAAA's
anti-doping processes.
The Court of Arbitration for Sport

The shadows darkened in the twelve months after the London Olympics. Every doping case intensified the pressure on Jamaica and on Usain Bolt in particular. It wasn't just his reputation at stake, it was the whole sport's. After all, they were synonymous. Bolt *was* athletics.

Not that he displayed any signs of being under pressure. In late July 2013 he appeared in a small meeting room at the Grange Tower Hotel in London, the day before he competed in (and won) the anniversary games at the Olympic stadium. With the cases involving the Jamaicans, in particular Asafa Powell, and also one of Bolt's main rivals, the American Tyson Gay, there was only one topic in his pre-race press conference. I sat in the front row, keen to hear what he had to say and to study him as he said it.

A female journalist asks the first question: 'Usain, following the recent doping scandals, only one out of the five fastest men in the world now hasn't failed a drugs test. Lots of people, fans of the sport, will lose confidence – can they trust you?'

'Ah, I was hoping that question would come later,' Bolt laughs. He leans forward and looks in the direction of the reporter. 'I was planning to explain to people. How long have you been following Usain Bolt?'

'A good few years,' replies the reporter.

'2008 maybe?' Bolt continues. 'If you've been following me since 2002, you would know I've been doing phenomenal things since I was fifteen. I was the youngest person to win the world juniors, at fifteen. I ran the world junior record, 19.93, at eighteen. World youth record at seventeen. I've broken every record there is to break in every event that I've ever done. For me, I've proven myself since I was fifteen. I'm just living out my dream now and I've underperformed this season, as my agent would say, and I need to step it up.' He shrugs. 'I was always going to be great.'

There is another reason why the subject of doping seems bigger than ever, and why Bolt is under such scrutiny. Sport is reeling from Lance Armstrong's downfall in the autumn of 2012, which culminated in his confessional interview with Oprah Winfrey in January 2013. There are similarities between Armstrong and Bolt in that both transcend their sport; cycling became reliant upon Armstrong and his remarkable story, just as athletics now seems to depend on Bolt. That bastion of intelligence and measured discussion, *The New Yorker*, in a piece about Tyson Gay, makes the comparison: 'Bolt is in something of the same position that Lance Armstrong was in about 2003: a man dominating a dirty sport as his rivals and teammates fall. It wouldn't be a surprise if one day this summer Bolt starts talking about misreading the label on an herbal supplement – or if, a decade from now, he ends up talking to Oprah.'

Because so many of his rivals have cheated, Bolt is in the firing line. He insists he is different. In London he tells us: 'I was made to inspire people and to run. I was given a gift and that's what I do. I'm confident in myself, my team, the people I work with. I know I'm clean, so I'm just going to continue running and using my talent and trying to improve the sport and help the sport.'

You can see him scanning the horizon for landmines or tripwires. He has prepared for this, clearly – his response to the female reporter's question wasn't spontaneous. He is careful. He doesn't lambast the athletes who have tested positive. Should there be tougher penalties? Up to the authorities, he says, not him. Is the banned list too complicated? 'If it's banned, just don't take it.' When he lines up for a race, he is not thinking that his rivals may be cheating. He trusts his entourage to check that nothing he takes contains a banned substance. 'You have to be careful as an athlete, about what you do, the food you ingest, but I'm not worried because I have a great team around me.' He doesn't take supplements, only vitamins. 'Every athlete takes vitamins. I don't really take supplements.'

Finally he is asked a question that doesn't appear to be about doping, until the kicker, which is. Bolt laughs: 'You almost got there, you almost asked a normal question.'

Then Simon Hart of the *Telegraph*, who has written extensively about doping in athletics, puts his hand up. 'I've got a "normal" question,' he says.

'*You* are asking me a normal question?' Bolt responds. 'All these drug questions and you are asking me a normal question?'

Bolt laughs; everyone laughs. The tone, the mood and the atmosphere are in marked contrast to Armstrong's press conferences. Those were dominated by similar questions but had an edge: an air of hostility and confrontation. With Bolt it's all bonhomie. He seems as relaxed as when he lines up for an Olympic 100 metres final. Is that reassuring, or suspicious? That question is as complicated as asking how anyone can prove that they have *not* done something. You cannot prove a negative: that's what Armstrong used to say. (And therein lies one problem. Armstrong stole all the best lines.)

There is at least one difference between Bolt and Armstrong, however. Bolt says, 'I am clean.' Armstrong used to say: 'I've never tested positive.'

It's December 2014, and Stephen Francis is overseeing an MVP training session at UTech that includes Shelly-Ann Fraser-Pryce and Nesta Carter, but not Asafa Powell or Sherone Simpson.

Fraser-Pryce finishes training, strolls to her gleaming white Mercedes SUV, face glued to her mobile phone. Carter, who arrived late and is still dragging weights as Francis sits in a deckchair and watches him, has a black Honda sports car. It's strange to see the kind of vehicles that wouldn't look out of place in a Mayfair showroom parked beside a dirt running track so worn that the lane markings are not lines, but deep grooves worn into the ground.

When he has finished dissecting the morning's training with one of his assistants, Francis, wearing a floppy sun hat, hoists himself out of the deckchair and makes his way slowly towards the adjacent building, which houses the gym. It's still only 8 a.m., the sun is climbing over the mountains into a perfect blue sky, and he finds shade beneath a tree.

A new dawn beckons after a tempestuous twelve months for MVP. Powell, the man who pioneered the stay-at-home approach for Jamaican athletes, is now training in Texas with his brother Donovan acting as coach. Simpson has also moved to the US. Francis's disappointment is due not so much to the fact that they are no longer here, but to the circumstances of their departures. Their positive tests, he says, were symptomatic of other changes. With Powell, in particular, 'the discipline had started to go'.

He changed? 'Mm hmm, oh yeah,' says Francis, who adds that he told Powell: 'I don't want you to be somebody who you look at and tell the youngsters, "Here is an example of what not to be."'

Francis blames himself, to some extent. 'But if I tell you something five times, if you're not going to listen the fifth time, you're never going to listen. I should have said, "OK, you're on your own."' He says he didn't know Powell was taking up to twenty supplements – he recalls the difficulty in persuading him to take vitamins or creatine. But more than that, it was his attitude. 'I mean,' says Francis, 'you expect some of it because he's had success, he's thirty years old, he feels he's a man.' The problems came when the younger athletes began copying him. 'I said to our youngsters, "OK, stop, stop, stop, stop. When Asafa was your age, he didn't behave like this. What made him good was that he used to conform. I have no problem if you win ten gold medals and decide that you're going to do your own thing, but do not make the mistake of thinking that at nineteen you can behave that way."

'I point out to my kids all the while, even as lackadaisical and idle as somebody like Usain Bolt appears to be, in the year between 2007 and 2008 he was a transformed person. He buckled down, got disciplined, stopped going out, stopped the drinking and so on, and focused on getting himself as good as he was in 2008. So I say to them, "Now, if that applies to someone who has talent oozing out of his ears, then it certainly applies to everyone else."'

Powell's departure means the club can reboot; re-establish some ground rules, 'with an emphasis on punctuality, emphasis on doing everything on the programme, participating fully in assessments and so on', Francis explains. 'A high level of ill discipline had crept into the whole system. The fact that Asafa chose not to be here this year meant that you can apply everything evenly across the board now without people saying: "But look at how Asafa is doing it."'

As for the club's anti-doping policy, it has been tightened up. Francis wants to know 'everything you put in your mouth'.

Yet despite all that, he says he would take Powell back. 'Oh yeah. I mean, as long as I still believe he has more to offer under the right disciplinary situation. But I don't think he . . . he has never understood his role in his demise. If he understands it and wants to come back, I have no problem. Asafa is a very nice guy, very kind, a very lovely person, but too easily influenced. Too eager to be influenced by the last person he speaks to.'

*

I was in Paul Wright's office as a verdict was reached in Sherone Simpson's case, ten months after she tested positive. Powell's would be decided two days later.

The phone rang: Simpson had been given an eighteen-month ban. 'Nobody can take joy out of somebody losing their job,' Wright says after putting the phone down. He takes a zero-tolerance approach: a banned drug is a banned drug and the athlete is responsible for what's in their body. End of story. 'What irks me', he says, 'is that you have prominent, powerful Jamaicans who go on national television and radio and say: "Why are we going about these people who have taken a little supplement: it's no big thing." Completely bamboozling the public.'

By the time of my visit, Wright appeared to have lost *his* job as JADCO's lead drugs-tester after giving an interview to the BBC in November 2013 in which he said the spate of positive tests 'could be the tip of the iceberg'. His main concern was that they were all in-competition positives. He backed up his old boss, Renée Anne Shirley, who argued that out-of-competition testing needed to be stepped up. With in-competition tests, he said, 'Months before, you know the date of the test and the approximate time of the test. You need to be stupid to fail.'

When Shirley wrote in *Sports Illustrated* about the drugs cases being like a 'force five hurricane', 'it went ballistic', says Wright. 'Then the BBC came here and spoke to me, I corroborate everything Anne said, so I was, according to public radio, an enemy of the state. I was vilified in the press. One newspaper had it that I was fired.'

He wasn't fired? 'I was never fired, because to fire somebody you have them on contract. I was just used as needed.'

Since speaking to the BBC, he hasn't been used at all.

Two days later, I go to Powell's hearing. Which is more than Powell does.

In room number five of the Jamaica Conference Centre, on the

Kingston waterfront, are fifteen reporters and four lawyers. Kwame Gordon and Danielle Chai are there to represent Powell. At 10.04 a.m., the three members of the anti-doping disciplinary panel appear. The chairman, Lennox Gayle, opens proceedings: 'I notice Mr Powell is absent, Mr Gordon?'

'I apologise,' says Gordon. 'I hope that will not be a problem.'

The wonderfully officious Gayle shuffles his notes and carries on. 'The defence team of Mr Powell did some real hard work,' he begins, the implication being that the ten months it has taken to reach a verdict owes much to the volume of material submitted in Powell's defence. Gayle speaks slowly for seven minutes, with lots of ominous pauses. 'We reached a unanimous decision,' he says finally, 'and . . . and . . . and it was our decision that . . . we are saying that Mr Powell was found to be . . . negligent.' As with Simpson, an eighteen-month suspension is the verdict.

Powell is devastated. His team had sent one of his supplements, Epiphany D1, to be tested by the US Anti-Doping Agency, who confirmed that it contained oxilofrine. The substance was not listed in the ingredients either on the bottle or on the company's website.[35] The man blamed by Powell and his agent, Paul Doyle, was Chris Xuereb, a Canadian masseur and nutritionist who began working with Powell and Simpson a month before both tested positive. Doyle told the Associated Press: 'Asafa and Sherone have been tested more than 100 times each through their career . . . and never turned in a positive test. Now they change their supplements and the first time they get tested, they have a positive test? It has to be something in those new supplements that has caused it. Chris is the one that provided those.' Xuereb responded: 'It is time the athletes took responsibility for their doping instead of looking around for a scapegoat, whether that person is their therapist, bartender or anyone else.' (The products seized

---

35 In February 2015, it was reported that Powell and Simpson's management company was suing the manufacturers of Epiphany D1 for $8m.

by Italian police when they searched Powell's hotel room included vitamins, Aleve and Actovegin – the calf-blood extract used by Dr Müller-Wohlfahrt. But nothing illegal.)

The hearing in Kingston is not the end. Three months later, Powell and Simpson, having appealed to the Court of Arbitration for Sport, have their suspensions reduced to six months. They are free to return to competition. The CAS takes the view that both were guilty of a minor offence, testing positive for a stimulant with negligible performance-enhancing effects. 'Thank u to the Court of Arbitration for Sport,' Powell writes on Twitter. 'Finally this weight has been lifted off my shoulders. Justice has been served. Now let's run!'

'A complete fiasco,' says Doyle. 'What took CAS ten minutes took ten months in Jamaica.'

There were other blows to the country's anti-doping movement, ranging from the embarrassing to the farcical. While I was in Jamaica in April 2014, the deputy chairman of the anti-doping disciplinary panel, an attorney-at-law, was arrested and charged in connection with a prostitution ring in Montego Bay – a charge he denies. Then the *Wall Street Journal* published a story alleging that JADCO's chairman, Herb Elliott, had fabricated his CV. The paper claimed there was no record of his master's degree in chemistry from Columbia University or his medical degree and PhD in biochemistry from the Université libre de Bruxelles in Belgium. It was an American vendetta against Jamaica, said Elliott, who insisted he did have the qualifications, even if he had mislaid some paperwork after his wife's death in 2010. But after discussing the matter with the prime minister, he stepped down as JADCO chairman. (I was told that Dr Elliott was in poor health and advised not to contact him on my visits to Jamaica.)

Far more serious was the other appeal to the Court of Arbitration for Sport, by Veronica Campbell-Brown. She had initially been given a two-year ban by the JAAA, which was ratified by the IAAF. However, she was cleared by the Jamaican disciplinary panel, who found the results from a polygraph (lie detector) test 'most compelling' and suggested a 'reprimand' would be more appropriate than a ban. But the IAAF Doping Review Board – which adjudicates in the cases of international-level athletes – was not happy, and reinstated the two-year ban. Finally she was cleared again by the Court of Arbitration.

It took several weeks for the CAS to publish the reasons for clearing Campbell-Brown. When they did, the fifty-eight-page report read like a charge sheet against the Jamaican athletics and anti-doping authorities. It detailed a catalogue of abject failings, which began the moment Campbell-Brown was asked for a urine sample at the Jamaican International Invitational meeting in Kingston on 4 May 2013.

She had won the women's 100 metres, which meant a drug test. A JADCO chaperone escorted her to the doping control area, where she met the assistant doping control officer, Danya Williams. It was 8.56 p.m. Campbell-Brown wasn't ready to give a urine sample, so she drank bottles of water and Powerade from a cool box in the doping control area. When she felt able to urinate, she was accompanied to the toilet by Williams. They passed a table with containers in sealed bags; Williams instructed Campbell-Brown to select one. Campbell-Brown washed and dried her hands before passing urine into the container under the supervision of the doping control officer.

She could only produce a partial sample (defined as less than 90 ml). Because of the risks of contamination, there are strict rules about how a partial sample should be stored. It should be transferred to a special container; it should be sealed; it should be kept by either the athlete or the doping control officer; a new container should be provided for any other sample.

None of these things happened. Campbell-Brown returned to the waiting room with her partial sample in a covered but unsealed container, which she left on the floor as she collected more drinks, did stretching exercises and ran her hands under water. Meanwhile, the assistant doping control officer had other athletes to attend to. It was an hour later when Campbell-Brown was able to produce an additional urine sample, and she did so not in a fresh container, but in the one she'd used earlier.

Now that the assistant doping control officer had 160 ml, she was happy. Campbell-Brown selected a storage kit, poured half the urine into one bottle (A sample) and half into the other (B sample). The paperwork was completed, but the box entitled 'partial sample' was left unchecked. It was 10.19 p.m. when the process was finished.

The next day, the sample was sent in a batch of thirteen to the Laboratoire de controle du dopage in Montreal. It arrived on 7 May. On 24 May, the laboratory confirmed it had detected hydro-chlorothiazide (HCT), a diuretic commonly used to treat high blood pressure, but also thought to be used by athletes as a masking agent. On 3 June, the JAAA was informed of the finding; Campbell-Brown was told on the same day. Ten days later, she travelled to Montreal to witness the testing of the B sample, which confirmed the positive. She protested her innocence but accepted a voluntary provisional suspension. (In the same month, two other Jamaican athletes, the discus throwers Alison Randall and Travers Smikle, both tested positive for HCT; Smikle's adverse reading also followed a partial sample collected in violation of the anti-doping rules.)

On 3 July, Campbell-Brown underwent a lie detector test in Orlando, conducted by polygraph expert Donald Harper. 'It is the opinion of the examiner that the subject did not knowingly use hydrochlorothiazide, and further has never used performance-enhancing drugs,' concluded Harper. Campbell-Brown also sent her nutritional supplements to the Aegis Science Corporation in Nashville. They all tested negative for HCT.

Could her urine sample have been contaminated in the waiting area? Could the water in the taps where Campbell-Brown washed her hands be the source? At the CAS hearing in London, this possibility was discussed at some length. Experts were called by Campbell-Brown and the IAAF. They offered contradictory testimony. Campbell-Brown's expert said it was likely that contaminated water was to blame. The

IAAF's expert conceded that this 'cannot be ruled out in theory', but added that it was 'so unlikely that I discount it entirely'.

In the end, it didn't matter who was right. All that mattered was that the correct procedure hadn't been followed by JADCO. Ordinarily, under the strict liability rule, the athlete has to prove how and why a banned substance is in their system. In this case, CAS declared that the burden 'shifts back to the IAAF to persuade the Panel to the requisite standard of proof that the Athlete did consume the prohibited substance'. It was no longer up to Campbell-Brown to prove that a doping violation had not occurred: it was up to the IAAF to establish that it had.

And of course the IAAF could not do that. The CAS, whose panel was made up of Philippe Sands QC, Jeffrey Benz and Michael Beloff QC, had no choice other than to exonerate Campbell-Brown. They also gave JADCO a severe dressing-down. By ignoring the rules on collection and storage, they had 'engaged in a knowing, systematic and persistent failure to comply with a mandatory IST [international standard for testing] that is directed at the integrity of the sample collection and testing process . . . That systematic and knowing failure, for which no reasonable explanation has been advanced, is deplorable and gives rise to the most serious concerns about the overall integrity of the JAAA's anti-doping processes, as exemplified in this case by the flaws in JADCO's sample collection and its documentation.'

The CAS panel was convinced by Campbell-Brown's testimony, too, noting that she had 'given a detailed and materially consistent account of the relevant facts throughout the disciplinary process'. Dr Paul Wright was not involved on the night in question, but in Campbell-Brown's hearing he did concede that the rules were not always strictly adhered to – though he insisted that he had WADA's blessing in his alternative method of partial sample collection, for example.

Wright, for me, had some typical and endearing Jamaican traits. He was a maverick who recognised that solutions to problems were sometimes found by using his imagination and initiative – witness his use of dry ice to store samples for EPO testing, or, going a few decades back, his acquisition of testing kits for marijuana for the football team. What I did not doubt was his sincerity in trying to do the right thing. 'Just do the job' was his mantra, in his daily work as a surgeon as well as in drug-testing athletes. In Jamaica, 'just do the job' can mean trying to get things done despite the problems, challenges, obstacles, as well as the corruption that can seem endemic: circumventing the system, otherwise, nothing would get done.

P. J. Patterson, who helped Campbell-Brown prepare her defence – 'The only person I've represented since I left the bar and entered politics [in 1969]' – felt vindicated by the CAS verdict. 'The fact is, there has to be professionalism at all levels. The consequences for an athlete found to be engaged in those activities is so damning that the rules have to be very strictly applied. And they weren't, they weren't. And the Court of Arbitration confirmed that.'

Renée Anne Shirley resisted saying 'I told you so', but the Campbell-Brown case confirmed her worst fears. It was the reason she had spoken out in the first place. 'I didn't want someone to get off because JADCO did things wrong.'

Sweeping changes followed at JADCO: a new chairman, Danny Williams, a businessman with no ties to sport; and a new executive director, Carey Brown, formerly a financial analyst at the Ministry of Finance. After a couple of visits from WADA, they were also being mentored by the Canadian Centre for Ethics in Sport. 'They are holding our hands, and that is proving very helpful,' is how Williams put it.

The negative headlines were too much for Shelly-Ann Fraser-Pryce. She was fed up with the foreign media – American and British in particular – running their stories fuelled on sensationalism and innuendo, and failing to make any distinction between, say, Tyson Gay's positive test for a steroid and the Jamaican cases. This was like equating a petty thief with a murderer, in her view.[36] She was even angrier with the authorities in Jamaica, the JAAA. 'We are the ones out there competing and yet we read articles and listen to people making accusations about Jamaica, and there's nobody there to take a microphone, be a big person and say, "What you're saying is wrong and it's a lie." ' If the situation didn't improve, she warned, she and her fellow athletes would go on strike – they would refuse to compete for Jamaica.

Glen Mills also felt that the suspicion was part of a vendetta against Jamaica, motivated by jealousy. 'They target Jamaica because of its success. There is no doubt about it,' he told the *Gleaner*. 'Nobody wants to see Jamaica continue its dominance of sprinting at the world level. And the international media – again, one has to question the balance of their reporting. I have read some terrible articles written about Jamaica. I have read some terrible articles trying to insinuate that Usain Bolt's success is false because of all of this.

'We have had some adverse analytical findings for stimulants and those other things,' Mills continued, 'but there are so many cases of steroid use in other countries in the past couple of months, yet there is no sensationalising around those countries or athletes. Yet everyone is banging on the Jamaicans because of our success, and the truth of the matter is that our success has come through hard work, excellent coaches, and making the best use of our facilities that are below world-class standards.'

Fraser-Pryce and Mills had a point in one sense. While Shirley's article in *Sports Illustrated* rightly highlighted the failings of JADCO, it contributed to a misconception that the Jamaicans were not tested at all in the run-up to the 2012 Olympic Games. That wasn't the case.

---

36 In April 2015 Bolt said he thought Tyson Gay should have been 'kicked out of the sport' for his positive test. He told *Runner's World*: 'I was really upset about that. He got a year just because he talked to the authorities about how it was done and who helped him. That sends the wrong message . . . it's the stupidest thing I've ever head. The message should be: "If you cheat you're going to be kicked out of the sport." '

As part of the IAAF's anti-doping programme, forty-seven Jamaican athletes were tested a total of 208 times in 2012. Bolt was the most tested (25 times) then Blake (18), Powell and Fraser-Pryce (both 13).[37] A spokesman for the IAAF anti-doping department told me in an email: 'Please be clear that even if there was not the right level of out-of-competition testing by a national agency (and this is understandable when you consider the limitations of resources and technologies in countries around the world where top athletes originate from), this does not mean that there is a sort of testing "gap" for the very simple reason that the IAAF guarantees a top-level out-of-competition testing system – of INTELLIGENT testing of top-class athletes. Simply put, the top three ranked countries in terms of tested athletes for the IAAF are: Russia, Kenya and Jamaica!

37 Of Bolt's 25 tests, 12 were in-competition, 13 out-of competition: of the former, 3 were blood, 9 urine; of the latter, 6 were blood, 7 urine. The blood tests were a combination of drugs tests and samples for the IAAF biological passport, which monitors an athlete's blood values over the long term and can reveal the effects of doping.

'So all references to deficiencies in the national anti-doping programme of Jamaica should remain in context – in 2012, it was very early days in terms of said agency – perhaps mistakes were made, resources were inadequate, etc., but there was always a powerful IAAF system in the background to cover any deficiency. By 2013, of course, the situation was radically different and the high-profile testing and sanctioning of Asafa Powell was as a result of work done by JADCO.'

I felt there was a guardedness, a wariness and a testiness about some of the Jamaicans when they competed in Europe. It was most evident in Fraser-Pryce, who could seem frosty and unapproachable. She is quite different when I meet her in Kingston. Why is that? I ask her. Is it because she is fed up with fielding questions about doping? 'Ah, sometimes. It depends how many times I get asked.'

She echoes Mills: she argues that there is no serious doping problem in Jamaica, and that people's suspicion is due to jealousy at their success, or a failure to accept that it is possible. It is possible, she says, thanks to the virtuous circle effect. Young Jamaicans see the senior athletes winning at the highest level, 'and they want that success. And we train together. It's not segregated. The fact you have persons doing so well, training with them, it gives the other athletes motivation. The young athletes are so motivated.'

But surely she cannot blame outsiders for thinking there's a problem when there have been so many positive tests? 'I've been in that situation, and you hear what persons are saying,' she says. 'It's heartbreaking. I haven't spoken to Sherone in a long time because she's in the States now, but I speak to Asafa a lot. He was devastated.

'But a lot of our athletes are naive, I think. I think they should read more, research more, try to get more educated in what's out there. Because it is hard. When persons sit and go, "I'm taking this supplement but it's fine because there's nothing in it," you go: "OK." But they think because they're not taking steroids, they're fine. They're not doing the deep research they need to do to protect themselves.

They think, I'm not doping, I'm just taking this vitamin they have on the shelf and it says it's OK. That's the downfall for a lot of Jamaican athletes.' Like Bolt, she says she doesn't take any supplements, only vitamins.

How did her call for a strike go down? Was she called in front of the JAAA? 'No, I wasn't called in.' She remains bitter, particularly over Wright's 'tip of the iceberg' comment. 'When persons make accusations about us, a lot of these persons need to visit Champs. They need to come and see the structure. They need to see how we train. They need to visit our tracks. The fact that a lot of these athletes come from poor communities, that the only way out is track, so the desire and the motivation is high. It's not somewhere where they're used to first-class facilities. Look at the rooms they stay in, the shoes they train in. That's exactly why they are so motivated to do well.'

Much of this chimed with what Yannis Pitsiladis had told me.

It is early 2015, and I am sitting with Pitsiladis in his office in Eastbourne, listening to him enthusing about his marathon project – the quest to break two hours with a clean runner in the next five years. It is a mission that consumes him. But on some distant horizon he sees another project: the first 9.55-second 100 metres. 'It's the logical next step,' he says. 'The sub-two-hour marathon is only the beginning.

'We will get a sprinter below 9.55 seconds. You've heard it first. You're the first person I've told it to.'

He would approach it the same way: identifying athletes who might be candidates, selecting the optimum course or track (more of a challenge with the 100 metres than with the marathon), then surrounding them with experts, analysing their training to the nth degree. He doesn't think much is known about training really – hence his observation that the training in Jamaica is not sophisticated, and that the approaches of Mills and Francis are 'both wrong . . . and both right'. What he means is that training, and adaptations to it, are highly individual. Studies have been done about the effects of exercise on different people, 'where everyone did the same and some got better, some remained the same, and some got worse. Which shows you that everyone responds differently.'

When it comes to elite performance, though, the doping question hangs over everything, casting its long, dark shadow. Pitsiladis has been stung by some of the reaction to his new project, with some claiming that a sub-two-hour marathon could only be achieved with drugs (he makes it clear that he sees the project as a collaboration with the anti-doping authorities; he works closely with WADA). Some have also been dismissive of his work in Kenya because of recent revelations about the extent of the doping problem there.

He is a little bruised, but undeterred. Fundamentally, he doesn't think the drugs issue is very relevant. Although it is difficult to quantify the effects of doping ('I can't at this stage,' he admits, though he is looking at how it might be possible), he believes it is of only minor significance. 'Having done this research for fifteen, twenty years in East Africa, there are so many factors,' he says. 'The drug issue is a tiny component of it that in itself could not have produced this success.'

He points out that 'Other countries have serious drug problems but don't have the success. So that's not the issue.'

Interestingly, he adds that, despite the claims that Jamaica also has a serious doping issue, he doesn't believe it is on the same scale as Kenya. 'Imagine a Kenyan family,' he says. 'No food, suffering, but quite good at running. Running on a track in Eldoret. Trying to find a manager. Someone comes up to them, says, "You're running quite well but I'll give you some EPO." The kid doesn't know what EPO is. The manager says, "I want 20 per cent when you start earning."

'Is that a difficult decision to make?' Pitsiladis asks. 'No, of course not. It's an easy decision.'

So why does he not think the same could happen – or does happen – in Jamaica? 'That's a very good question.' He thinks a long time. 'I'm not talking about Jamaican athletes who leave the island, but locally, in Jamaica, I don't see the same issues.' There are several reasons: there isn't the money in sprinting that there is in road running, with lucrative events throughout the world to support Kenya's 3,000 professional road runners. And he isn't sure what drugs would be involved. 'That would be one of my arguments,' he says. 'The only reason I don't put it at the top is because up until now I haven't had the opportunity to study those drugs. What's the EPO of sprinting? It's not very clear.'

In the end, Pitsiladis explains that his view is informed mainly by his own experiences in and of Jamaica. 'I would argue', he says, 'that the level of sophistication needed to oversee a systematic doping programme is almost beyond what the island could do.

'They'd be caught on day one.'

19

THE IN-BETWEEN

Look out, greatness is coming.
Jaheel Hyde

On my first day back in Jamaica, I ask Dennis Johnson why he thinks his country produces so many top sprinters. He turns the tables. 'You have been travelling around, speaking to people. Why do *you* think we have these sprinters in Jamaica?'

'I think there are lots of factors,' I reply.

'Like what?'

'History, culture, environment . . .'

'All very generic,' says Johnson. 'What empirical evidence is there for these things – history, culture, environment – being important?'

'How about genes, then?'

'A hypothesis. No evidence.'

'All the sub-10-second sprinters bar one originally come from West Africa,' I say. 'Surely that's not a coincidence?'

'So tell me, where are all the West African sprinters? The Ghanaians? No, why are there so many here, in Jamaica? There must be a reason, man! All these sprinters from this island of three million people: from these two groups under Glen Mills and Stephen Francis.

It's total dominance. There must be a reason why that has happened in the last ten years.'

'Well, some would say that it must be drugs,' I venture.

'Bah! The Jamaican cases have been minor transgressions – stimulants, supplements – apart from the ones who train in America. No steroids, not like the Americans. Come on, one reason. It's like Ebola: it's in three countries but no others – why? There must be a reason.'

'You think there's one specific reason?'

'Yes, man.'

Was I any closer to knowing? Before going to Jamaica, I was as sceptical as anyone. Well, maybe not as sceptical as Victor Conte or Carl Lewis. Then along came the positives in 2013, which reaffirmed my scepticism. And yet where were the Jamaicans who made sudden improvements in their mid-to-late twenties? Where was the heavy-duty stuff – the steroids, the blood doping? Most of the cases implicating home-based Jamaicans involved supplements produced by an unregulated industry that preys on athletes desperate for an edge. (Two Welsh athletes tested positive after taking a poorly labelled supplement in 2014; nobody accused Wales of running a systematic doping programme.)

Most of the people I met in Jamaica made a convincing case. Even those who had suspicions, like Renée Anne Shirley and Paul Wright, had no firm evidence of wrongdoing. Yannis Pitsiladis, an outsider, held the view that drugs are not the secret ingredient in the Jamaican sprint factory. 'Don't make it about drugs,' he urged when I told him about this book.

If only it were that simple. You cannot ignore the fact that so many of the fastest sprinters in the world have tested positive. Nor can you overlook the fact that drugs are easily acquired and tests – apparently – easily passed. You are alarmed to hear that a Jamaican schoolboy tested positive for a steroid – and more alarmed that the school didn't appear to investigate. As the journalist David Walsh puts it, when it comes to drugs in sport, there are two choices: to manage it or confront it. Both approaches have been in evidence in Jamaica. Some seem content to manage the problem (and keener still to deny one). Shirley was eager to aggressively confront it. She didn't last long.

So, drugs might be part of the Jamaican success. But they might not be. There could be sophisticated doping programmes in operation, masterminded by Glen Mills and Stephen Francis. But who is helping them? How are they paying for it? Perhaps I was looking in the wrong places, or speaking to the wrong people. Bert Cameron, until recently a member of the Racers Track Club coaching staff, told me that I didn't find the infrastructure because it doesn't exist. But if he was part of it, he would say that.

Pitsiladis's argument is that it is a cultural phenomenon, like Brazilian football, Dutch speed-skating or Austrian skiing. Sprinting is in the Jamaican DNA. In Britain, the country's most promising sprinter, Adam Gemili, is a failed footballer (he was on Chelsea's books). In Jamaica, it's the other way round: Jaheel Hyde walked out on the national football team to be a hurdler.

But the success of Jamaica says something about the state of athletics, too. Its blue riband status at the Olympic Games gives it a veneer that is misleading. For two weeks every four years, athletics has a mass audience; the rest of the time it is the Grand Budapest Hotel of international sport – with its magnificent facade, it looks impressive and imposing, but inside are creaking floorboards, threadbare furniture and a sense of faded grandeur. It belongs to a different time.

It means that Usain Bolt occupies a curious and paradoxical position: a global star whose fame comes from a sport that is beset by scandal and faces a desperate struggle for sponsors, support and relevance.

Apart from in one place: a Caribbean island of fewer than three million people.

*

From the Norman Manley International Airport, perched on the end of a long peninsula, I drove across the narrow strip of tarmac to the mainland, then around the wide bay towards the twinkling lights of Kingston. It was dark, and the Blue Mountains reared up like ghostly shadows behind the city. Along the front, towards downtown, swerving to avoid enormous potholes and people wobbling on bikes, or walking along the unlit road, I passed the huge, imposing prison – high walls, watchtowers, barbed wire – then turned right up South Camp Road. The alternative, Mountain View Road, is more direct, but had also been the scene in recent months of gunfights.

Leaving behind downtown Kingston, with the ghettos of Trench Town, Tivoli Gardens and Waterhouse shrouded in almost total darkness, I reached the bright lights of New Kingston and recognised some of the beggars, windscreen cleaners, banana salesmen and higglers who spend all day (and night) at the junctions. One began cleaning my (already clean) windscreen as I indicated that I had no money. 'Next time, boss,' he said, flashing a gap-toothed smile and finishing the job he'd started. The experience summed the place up: you hear the stories, read the reports about the violence and the murder rate, heed the warnings, feel the edginess and sense the danger, check and double-check that your car doors are locked when you stop at traffic lights, and then find friendliness and good humour in the most unexpected places.

'Think you're in heaven, but ya living in hell,' as Bob Marley sang in 'Time Will Tell'. This was Jamaica: beguiling and maddening; friendly and violent; laid-back and restless; where 'the boiling point is always quite near', as one of their greatest athletes, Arthur Wint, put it. A place where life seems to move slowly while at the same time being home to the fastest humans on the planet. Of course, Jamaicans tire of depictions of the island as a place of extremes. 'You visitors are always getting it wrong,' one local told Ian Thomson for his book *The Dead Yard*. 'Either it's golden beaches or guns, guns, guns, guns. Is there nothing in between?'

I felt the same about the doping question, which is so often presented as one of polar opposites and extremes: as binary, black or white, with only two possible verdicts, hero or cheat. As in many things, perhaps the truth more often resides somewhere in between. There is a vast grey area of supplements, painkillers, prescription drugs, therapeutic use exemptions, creatine, cortisone, caffeine, calf-blood extract, crushed cockerel crest. A 'clean' athlete could be pumped full of all this stuff but be one mislabelled supplement away from 'dirty'. To reduce it to 'clean' or 'dirty' is too simple. It misses the in-between.

Apart from wrestling with this question, I found it impossible not to become fascinated and intrigued by the place itself. Remarkable things do happen here, and not only on a running track. I was struck, as many people have been, by the comparison between Bolt and Marley as totemic figures but not one-offs. Rather they are the towering symbols of a much wider, deeper phenomenon. Between the mid-1950s and 2000, proportionally more recorded music came out of Jamaica than anywhere else: one new recording a year for every thousand people. About eight recognised genres have their roots in Jamaica, including rap, which came through reggae and dancehall. This must be the musical equivalent of placing first, third, fourth and fifth in a global athletics final, as Jamaica did in the men's 100 metres in Moscow in 2013.

I hadn't fully appreciated that the excellence on the track came first. 'You must understand,' P. J. Patterson told me, 'that our appearance on the world stage in sports preceded our appearance on the world stage in music.' He was talking about Herb McKenley, Arthur Wint; 1948 and 1952. But now Bolt, like Marley, has transcended his field. 'Bolt has become a new word in the dictionary,' Patterson said. 'It's a noun, it's a verb, it's an adjective.'

I mentioned the parallels between athletics and music to Yannis Pitsiladis. 'Exactly,' he said. 'But nobody talks about a music gene, do they?'

*

In August 2014, at the end of the quietest season of his career, Bolt made a cameo appearance at the Commonwealth Games in Glasgow, helping Jamaica to gold in the 4x100 metres. He competed for nine seconds, then took over an hour to do a lap of honour. Two weeks later, he called time on his season. It was, Ricky Simms says, a 'regeneration year for him, not beating his body up too badly'. On 8 October 2014, he began training for the 2015 season. During the Olympic Games in Rio, he will turn thirty. Can he win his third straight 100 metres title? 'Yes,' says Simms. 'He's just so much better than anybody else.'

He also has other priorities, admitting, with unusual candour, that he is looking for love. He had been in a brief relationship with a British athlete, Megan Edwards. They met at the Puma Jamaica kit launch in London, before the 2012 Games, and the twenty-two-year-old, an 800 metres runner and office worker from Dartford, subsequently went to Jamaica, spending time in Kingston and Trelawny. But a long-distance relationship wasn't for her and she broke it off. Bolt was said by Britain's tabloid newspapers to be 'devastated'. A couple of years later, he said he was keen to start a family. He was in Miami, at an event with his watch sponsor, Hublot, when he said, 'You do get a lot of offers for sure, it's one of the perks. You try to stay quiet, but I love women, and you try not to take advantage, but it's hard. I am trying to find a girlfriend now. I think I am getting to that age right now, twenty-eight, where I need to find somebody and I want to have a child . . . I'd like three or four kids maybe, it's always good to have brothers and sisters to look out for you.'

His father, Wellesley, told me that Bolt found his life 'too hectic sometimes. Everything he does, the camera finds him. He says it's hectic, he worries sometimes, because he cannot live a normal life. He just cannot live the way he wants to live.'

When I asked those who know Bolt what they thought he would do when he retires, most said he would leave Kingston and move to the countryside to live in a large house surrounded by friends (and his future family), passing his time playing dominoes. It seems entirely believable.

Yohan Blake was in Glasgow, but not at the Commonwealth Games. He competed in the Diamond League meeting at Hampden a couple of weeks earlier but didn't even last the full 100 metres, crumpling to the track clutching his hamstring. He left the arena in a wheelchair. His next stop: Munich, to see Dr Hans-Wilhelm Müller-Wohlfahrt. He would visit him again in November, and again in January 2015. 'It was really tough,' Blake told me. 'I'm not a patient guy. But you know, everything happens for a reason. I think it was my body saying: "Look, Yohan, you need a rest. You're going to have three hard years."

'That's nature,' he added.

Shelly-Ann Fraser-Pryce was below par too. Her best 100 metres was 11.01 in Monaco – the first time since 2007 she'd failed to break 11 seconds. Her coach, ever the ruthless taskmaster and dispenser of tough love, wondered aloud whether she would go on to win a third Olympic gold medal in Rio – something he thought her capable of, and which would surely confirm her as the greatest female sprinter of all time, irrespective of the 'impossible' world record. 'At the end of 2013 I would have said definitely she was going to get better,' Francis reflected.

Now he was not so sure. 'I am a realist, and understand that there's a reason why people don't keep going up, up, up, up. Sometimes your motivation falters, sometimes there are other areas of your life that take precedence. But what I will say is that if she is like she was in 2013 in terms of the hunger, and other things are not more important, then yeah, she will get better. But at her age it is hard to predict that is going to be the case. Because especially with women, many things start to go through your mind – is it time for this, is it time for that? What is my husband saying, blah blah blah blah blah. So you're realistic. It's all going to depend how she handles that kind of stuff.'

*

On my return to Jamaica, I wanted to try and identify the next superstar – a successor to Bolt. It meant catching up with three of the stars of Champs eight months on from that extraordinary gathering of people and talent: athletes who could be on the cusp of greatness, or not. These in-betweeners are on a knife edge: the margins between success and failure seem minuscule.

Since Champs, there had been the world junior championships in Eugene and the Youth Olympics in Nanjing. The 2014 Champs programme had proudly proclaimed that every global male 100 metres champion was Jamaican. By the end of the year, that was no longer the case. But something interesting seemed to be happening: a new phenomenon – or an old one, recycled – the return of the 400 metres specialists, reprising the previous golden generation almost seventy years after Helsinki and London.

But first, a 100 metres specialist. At the IAAF High Performance Training Centre I meet Zharnel Hughes, the nineteen-year-old from Anguilla. Glen Mills is the head coach here, but Leo Brown is in day-to-day charge. The nine athletes occupy the ground floor of a blue dormitory block on the edge of the University of the West Indies campus, close to the perimeter fence. It is a shabby building with peeling paint. Inside there is a kitchen, dining area, a list of rules for the athletes, and a living room with threadbare sofas and a small portable TV.

Bolt is a graduate of the centre and Hughes is in a similar mould. At six-three-and-a-half, he is tall, engaging and charming. Brown is convinced he has what it takes, whispering, 'This kid, I'm telling you, he can be the next Bolt.'

He is whispering because Hughes is in his room at the end of a small corridor, but he overhears, appearing and smiling: 'I *can* be the next Bolt.' Brown carries on regardless: 'I told his mother: "You must have done something. Because he is perfect: he doesn't curse, he doesn't do anything bad." Trust me, I have had lots of athletes. This one is special.'

Hughes grew up in the neighbouring island of Anguilla with his Jamaican mother, Zarnalyn (his name is an amalgamation of hers and his father Howell's: she is a housekeeper; he is a taxi driver). When I first met him after Champs, he spoke about his two passions, flying – he would like to be a pilot eventually – and athletics. He pulled out his phone, opened his YouTube favourites and showed me his 100 metres from Champs. It had been watched 40,000 times in a couple of weeks, with Hughes himself accounting for a fair few of the views. 'Look,' he said, as he pressed play and relived the race, 'I think I could have improved a little bit more on my start. It wasn't bad; I got out pretty good this time. But then I dipped a little too early. If I pause the video before the finish, I can see that I reached too soon. That cost me.' Yet his time, 10.11, was a full tenth of a second quicker than Yohan Blake's Champs record.

'Aaaarrrggghhhh!' was how Blake greeted Hughes at training a few days later. 'He yelled like a beast,' Hughes says, 'but then said: "Congrats, man. I'm proud of you. You're gonna run 19 and 9 this year."'

It didn't happen. Injuries interrupted his year. At the world junior championships, having reached the 200 final, he felt a twinge in his hamstring as he came off the bend and limped across the line. He didn't make it to the Commonwealth Games. 'I have to be patient,' he says. 'Coach Mills tell me that. He encourages me. "Zee, these things happen. Look at Yohan."

'I wanted to do well this year, but sometimes you shouldn't have your expectations too high. I have a long way ahead of me, I know these things happen. I do believe I can become something great.' He seems remarkably sanguine. But in an unguarded moment he adds: 'Man, I hope I'm not going to be one of them athletes who is always injured.'

Hughes started off thinking he would be a 200 and 400 metres specialist. Now he is a 100/200 sprinter. In the past, an athlete of his height wouldn't have been considered for the 100. But after Bolt, they are looking for tall sprinters: youngsters who are 'unusually coordinated'. Brown explains: 'All you need is for the tall one to get the same rhythm as the shorty and he's going to win by miles. If he can run with the same frequency, he'll kill these guys with the tiny steps.

'I told Zharnel,' he continues, ' "God made you, and a coach can help you develop that to the maximum, but this" ' – he points to his head – ' "is what determines it." '

At Wolmer's Boys' School, in the noisy, congested centre of Kingston, I meet Jaheel Hyde. Just seventeen, he's serious, self-contained, surly and shy, yet also sure of himself. At the start of the season he posted a picture on Instagram with the message: 'Look out, greatness is coming.'

He was right, as it happens. Yet in some ways he seems to be the anti-Bolt. In July, at the world junior championships in Eugene, he was introduced to the crowd before the 400 metres hurdles. He stood and scowled, his hands resting casually on his hips. The look on his face said that he really couldn't be bothered with the preliminaries; it said:

'Let's get on with it.' And when they did, he was in a class of his own. As at Champs, where he dominated the 400 and 110 metres hurdles, he was so smooth, so casual. As he moved into the lead on the final bend, he kept glancing to his right, to his left, but nobody was close. It looked easy. He barely celebrated.

At the Youth Olympics in Nanjing a month later, Hyde elected to do his other event, the 110 metres hurdles. The two are completely different: the 400 is all about pacing and rhythm, the 110 requires rhythm but also pure speed, power and explosivity. Nobody has ever been a global champion in both.

In Nanjing, Hyde burst out of the blocks, stealing a march on the others, then increased his lead as he appeared to glide, or float, over the hurdles. This was even more impressive than Eugene. All around him were the slumped and dejected bodies of his rivals, but he didn't stop to commiserate – didn't even seem aware of them – as he set off around the track for a lap of honour. His time, 12.96 seconds, was a world youth record by 0.16. That is Bolt-esque.

Hyde's father, Lenworth, is a Jamaican footballing legend, whose international career spanned thirteen years. 'Lenny' has five children: four boys and a girl. Predictably, Jaheel is the youngest. He began kicking a ball with his father when he was four. He was encouraged to play football, but he walked out on the national under-17 team to concentrate on athletics. 'It's my decision,' he tells me. Was his father happy? 'My parents on the whole will just have to support me whatever I do. My father knows I love track and field.'

How did he decide? 'You sit down, analyse which one you'll be best at.'

He is uncompromising. He wanted to go to Kingston College, but his brother Jamie, also a talented footballer, was already there. 'I said to myself, I didn't want to be living in his name. I wanted to make a name for myself.'

Stephen Francis would like Hyde to join MVP when he leaves Wolmer's, not least because he attends his old school. But it would have to be on Francis's terms. 'I've never spoken to him about coming here,' Francis told me. 'Whenever I speak to him, it's as one Wolmerian to another. I would hope he will come over here but I am not going to get into the war of recruiting him.'

Hyde loves hurdles, loves the technical side to it, the fact that 'you have to be very focused, you can't take your eye off no hurdle at any time'. He is a curious mix: a steely confidence runs through him, yet he is modest, almost bashful. He says he doesn't particularly enjoy the attention that comes with being a world champion – especially at school. 'People come up to you at school just to touch you, to spend five minutes with you. I tell them they can be themselves around me; talk about what they want, doesn't have to be track and field, could be life as a whole.'

I ask him what it's like to be surrounded by so many superstars in Jamaica. 'I must correct you there,' Hyde says. 'I'm not really in contact with the big athletes. I look up to Usain Bolt, the way he goes about things, but I haven't met him or spoken to him. He's a winner, just like myself. But I'm a very humble child, very quiet.'

Jaheel Hyde is the special one now, rivalled only, perhaps, by an even younger athlete, yet another 400 metres runner: Christopher Taylor of Calabar. In early 2015, he broke the age group world record in Kingston, running 45.69 seconds. He was fifteen: just like Bolt when he made his breakthrough. 'The quarter-milers are coming,' said Bert Cameron as he surveyed a burgeoning crop of 400 metres runners.

Twelve months earlier, the special one was another 400 metres runner and another Calabar boy: Javon 'Donkey Man' Francis. In July 2014, he signed as a professional with Puma. Pascal Rolling, the marketing executive who signed Bolt, was behind the deal. He saw similarities. 'The guy is also very charismatic and open, maybe not as much as Usain, and not as gifted as Usain was.' Like Bolt, he is raw and 'needs work'. Puma were arranging English lessons for Francis, as they once tried to do for Bolt. 'If he gets it together and if he progresses the way he has in the last two years, he can be a very good ambassador for Puma,' said Rolling.

I meet Francis at Calabar, the bond with his old school as strong as ever. He has decided to stick with what he knows, which meant remaining with his high school coach, Michael Clarke, training at Calabar's rough, bumpy old track, and living with his guardian, Andrea Hardware. Hardware says it was an easy decision, despite 'lots of very good offers'. Sitting on a bench inside the school grounds, overlooking the track, she explains that 'Calabar is a family and Michael Clarke and us have got him so far and we want to keep that structure around him. I did not want to break that up. Let's just see where his team can get him over the next two years.'

After Champs, Francis struggled to overcome the hamstring injury he suffered in the 200 metres: the race that everybody said he shouldn't have run. It was decided that he shouldn't compete in the Penn Relays a few weeks later. But he went anyway, to Franklin Field in Philadelphia, to support Calabar. 'I sit in the stand at the Penn Relays,' Francis tells me now, 'and watch my team lose. I started crying. I said to myself, If I was there, they would win.'

'He bawled,' Hardware confirms. 'He bawled in the stands when they lost the 4x400.'

Then he missed the IAAF world relays in the Bahamas in May. One night Hardware returned to find him crying in his room. She asked what was wrong. 'Mum, my picture's on the billboard in the Bahamas! It's my picture on the billboard and I'm not going to go!'

Francis kept trying to train and then having to stop and rest to give the injury more time to heal. It was a form of torture. And in the midst of all this he had to decide about his future. 'When the time come to leave Calabar, it was a sticky decision,' he says. 'Everywhere want me to come overseas, and I said to myself, Overseas, no. Jamaica, yes. I love Jamaica so much and if I go overseas I'm not going to see my mum, my dad, my relatives, my guardian. I'm going to stay here and work with my coach, Mr Michael Clarke. He do a lot for me, he's like a father to me.'

In the end, the only real bright spot in Francis's year, apart from his record at Champs, was signing with Puma. 'Yes, sir. Usain Bolt is a Puma lion, I'm a Puma lion too.' Bolt has encouraged him. 'Usain Bolt told me, "Track and field is an unfair game." He said, "Work hard, and make sure you have your education." He said, "Javon, you know that if you have education, no one can take that away from you. Track and field, God can take that away from you."'

A week later, I am back at Calabar talking to Michael Clarke, who is overseeing a training session involving twenty or so athletes. There is no sign of Francis. 'Javon is in Germany,' says Clarke. Germany? 'He's seeing a doctor. Something Puma has set up.'

The doctor . . . is it Dr Müller-Wohlfahrt? Clarke looks thoughtful. 'Dr Müller? That sound right, yes.'

It seems that Puma will have a big say in Francis's future. Rolling says they'll be watching carefully. Clarke is a proven coach at high school level. 'Any Jamaican coach thinks he can be as good as Mills and Frano [Stephen Francis],' Rolling says. 'Everyone thinks they can do it. It remains to be seen.'

Thinking about Javon Francis and how much is at stake for Clarke, for Calabar, but mostly for him, it can seem overwhelming. He is a man-child who dreams of greatness, of telling his grandchildren 'that when I was young I was the champion in high school, the greatest schoolboy in history, I can tell them that'. But he wants – needs – so much more. If he doesn't fulfil his great potential, he will become one of those athletes Raymond Stewart talked about who disappear, who remain only in people's memories as a candle that burned brightly but too briefly. Francis relates another conversation with Bolt, who told him that when he first went to a senior world championship, in Paris in 2003, he didn't even get to run, never mind win a medal, as Francis did in Moscow ten years later. 'But you come and get a medal at eighteen!' Bolt told him. 'Bwoy, the sky's the limit!'

'Yes, Usain, but the sky is not the limit – the sky doesn't have a limit. If you go to space, the sky goes on and on.'

'Well, Javon,' said Bolt, 'that's a good one.'

Hardware says she is confident Francis will be back: that we didn't see the best of him in Moscow, or at Champs. 'A couple of days ago I said, "Javon, how do you really feel?" "Mum, mi good, mi good. I'm popping the blocks, I'm getting out ahead of some of the sprinters in the club." He feels healed.'

After our conversation, Francis stands up, shakes my hand, says, 'Thank you, sir.' My eyes follow him as he jogs in the direction of the rutted track. Is he moving freely, without pain? It's hard to tell.

I am back in Dennis Johnson's house in the hills overlooking Kingston. On his porch, with DJ sitting in his usual seat, holding court in his shorts and flip-flops. He seems a little short of breath, a little older. But he is as combative and dogmatic as ever. And still questioning. 'Well, my friend? What do you think is the reason for this . . . this total dominance?' He emphasises the word to make sure I get it. Not success: *dom-in-ance*. Not that he gives me a chance to answer. 'Because this phenomenon is tantamount to a special disease, you understand?' he continues. 'A virus. Why does no one notice that?'

I have noticed. That's why I'm there. But I persist initially, arguing that it must be a combination of things. Surely there is no one single reason. Johnson isn't having it. 'Well,' I try, 'here's one interpretation: you came back to Jamaica in the 1960s, you brought Bud Winter's ideas about technique and relaxation, then you brought Bud Winter himself, and you began a culture of . . . teaching people how to sprint correctly, with form and technique, at a young age . . .'

'Now you're cooking on gas,' says Johnson.

'Because sprinting is a skill,' I say.

'Sprinting is a skill, yes. Very good. He's learnt something. So you've listened to Dennis Johnson. Why don't you write that?'

'I will.'

ACKNOWLEDGEMENTS

Several people in Jamaica provided a great deal of help, but two stand out. Renée Anne Shirley was a source of knowledge, encouragement and inspiration. She is now setting up projects in education and sport which, if they come off, should be of enormous benefit to Jamaica. I also owe special thanks to Michelle Neita, who runs Kingston's best guest house, Neita's Nest, on one of the hills overlooking the city. I loved it there. As well as being a wonderful host and a good friend, Michelle helped with introductions and interviews. Thanks also to Charmaine Smith for her sensational Jamaican cooking.

To Virginie, my wife, thank you. In the days after the London Olympics, when I was boring on about the contrast between the saccharine atmosphere of the Games and the quagmire of suspicion and innuendo that was the Tour de France, she suggested this book, possibly as a way of shutting me up, maybe also because she fancied a trip to the Caribbean. By good luck, another visit to Jamaica coincided with an assignment for my brother Robin, a brilliant photographer whose images feature on these pages – thank you, Robin (www.robindmoore.com).

I've known Matt Phillips, the editor at Yellow Jersey, for a few years, but this is the first time we have worked together. Matt's great enthusiasm and ideas helped make the book much better – as well as a far more enjoyable and rewarding process – than it would otherwise have been. Thanks too to Fiona Murphy, publicist extraordinaire, and to Mari Yamazaki and Kate Bland, who took up the publicity reins when Fiona was lured away. To Jack Skelton, thanks for help with transcribing interviews.

I am grateful as ever to my agent, David Luxton, for moral support and for never panicking. Or never appearing to panic. And heartfelt thanks to colleagues who helped in different and significant ways: Alan Pattullo, David Epstein, Mike Costello, John Leicester, Vikki Orvice, Rick Broadbent, Ian Chadband, Laura Williamson, Martha Kelner, Donald McRae, Shaun Assael, Sean Ingle, Simon Turnbull, Matt Slater, Lionel Birnie, Daniel Friebe and Susan Egelstaff. In Jamaica, thanks to Andre Lowe of the *Gleaner*, who always responded to my countless requests for phone numbers. Thank you Charlotte Elton for sneaking me in to Usain Bolt's party in Brussels. Thanks to Matt Rabin for helping me find out more about Dr Müller-Wohlfahrt. For his insights on Jamaica, and for writing a fascinating book, *The Dead Yard*, I am grateful to Ian Thomson. And big thanks to Ned Boulting, who provided invaluable feedback on a flabby first draft.

To the following I am especially grateful: Dennis Johnson, Stephen Francis, Glen Mills, Shelly-Ann Fraser-Pryce, Yohan Blake, Warren Weir, Paul Wright, Javon Francis and Zharnel Hughes. I am also indebted to Bruce James, Timothy Spencer and Omar Hawes for their help. Thanks to the other people I interviewed in the course of my research, most of whom appear in roughly the following order: Keith Barnier, Mark Ricketts, Michael Fennell, Donald Quarrie, Albert Corcho, Wellesley Bolt, Devere Nugent, Lorna Thorpe, Gloria Grant, the Most Honourable P. J. Patterson, Andrea Hardware, Noel Facey,

Michael Clarke, Gregory Daley, Vilma Charlton, Maurice Wilson, Edward Shakes, Pat Lightburn, Rachael Irving, Jermaine Gonzalez, Norman Peart, Ricky Simms, Steven Ming, Pascal Rolling, Simon Lewis, Mike Davison, Daniel Drepper, Stephen Roche, Mike Fish, Victor Conte, Dick Pound, Steve Mullings, Raymond Stewart, Jimson Lee, Errol Morrison, Yannis Pitsiladis, Jaheel Hyde, Bert Cameron, Carey Brown, Danny Williams, Leo Brown, Lascelve Graham, Orville Byfield, Martin Manley, Delano Williams, Daniel England and David Gillick. And thanks to Usain Bolt, who inspired the quest at the heart of this book (not to mention the title).

The following books were useful in helping me understand more about Jamaica and athletics, or Jamaican athletics:

Black Superman: A Cultural and Biological History of the People Who Became the World's Greatest Athletes, Patrick Cooper (Silent Partners, 2004)

The Dead Yard: A Story of Modern Jamaica, Ian Thomson (Faber & Faber, 2009)

Born Fi' Dead: A Journey Through the Yardie Underworld, Laurie Gunst (Canongate, 2003)

Drumblair: Memories of a Jamaican Childhood, Rachel Manley (A. A. Knopf Canada, 1996)

Slipstream: A Daughter Remembers, Rachel Manley (A. A. Knopf Canada, 2000)

The Longer Run: A Daughter's Story of Arthur Wint, Valerie Wint (Ian Randle Publishers, 2011)

The Voice of the Jamaican Ghetto: Incarcerated but not Silenced, Adidja Palmer (Vybz Kartel) (BookBaby, 2012)

Jamaican Athletics, A Model for 2012 and the World, Patrick Robinson (Black Amber, 2009)

The Making of a Sprinting Superpower: Jamaica on the Track, Arnold Bertram (2013)

Usain Bolt: Faster than Lightning, Usain Bolt with Matt Allen (HarperSport, 2013)

Champs 100: A Century of Jamaican High School Athletics, 1910–2010, Hubert Lawrence, ed. Michael A. Grant (Great House, 2010)

Jamaican Gold, eds. Rachael Irving and Vilma Charlton (University of the West Indies Press, 2010)

Jamaica Gold: Brilliance & Excellence, Mark Ricketts (2012)

The Gold Mine Effect: Crack the Secrets of High Performance, Rasmus Ankersen (Icon Books, 2012)

Sprinting Into History: Jamaica and the 2008 Olympic Games, Delano Franklyn (Wilson Franklyn Barnes, 2009)

Game of Shadows: Barry Bonds, Balco, and the Steroids Scandal That Rocked Professional Sports, Mark Fainaru-Wada and Lance Williams (Gotham Books, 2007)

The Sports Gene: Talent, Practice and the Truth about Success, David Epstein (Yellow Jersey, 2013)

Beyond a Boundary, C. L. R. James (Yellow Jersey, 2005)

Beyond C. L. R. James: Shifting Boundaries of Race and Ethnicity in Sports, eds. John Nauright, Alan Cobley and David Wiggins (University of Arkansas Press, 2014)

The Talent Code: Greatness Isn't Born. It's Grown, Daniel Coyle (Arrow, 2010)

Outliers: The Story of Success, Malcolm Gladwell (Penguin, 2009)

Pulphead: Notes from the Other Side of America, John Jeremiah Sullivan (Vintage, 2012)

Bass Culture: When Reggae Was King, Lloyd Bradley (Penguin, 2011)

Usain Bolt: Fast as Lightning, Mike Rowbottam (BlackAmber Inspirations, 2011)

Usain Bolt: The Story of the World's Fastest Man, Steven Downes (SportsBooks Ltd, 2011)

So You Want to Be a Sprinter, Bud Winter (Bud Winter Enterprises, 2010)

Friday Night Lights, H. G. Bissinger (Yellow Jersey, 2005)

20.0   19.9   19.8   19.7